THE ROUTLEDGE HANDBOOK OF MARITIME TRADE AROUND EUROPE 1300–1600

The Routledge Handbook of Maritime Trade around Europe 1300–1600 explores the links between maritime trading networks around Europe, from the Mediterranean and the Atlantic to the North and Baltic Seas. Maritime trade routes connected diverse geographical and cultural spheres, contributing to a more integrated Europe in both cultural and material terms. This volume explores networks' economic functions alongside their intercultural exchanges, contacts and practical arrangements in ports on the European coasts.

The collection takes as its central question how shippers and merchants were able to connect regional and interregional trade circuits around and beyond Europe in the late medieval period. It is divided into four parts, with chapters in Part I looking across broad themes such as ships and sailing routes, maritime law, financial linkages and linguistic exchanges. In the following parts – into the Mediterranean, the Baltic Sea, and the Atlantic and North Seas – contributors present case studies addressing themes including conflict resolution, relations between different types of main ports and their hinterland, the local institutional arrangements supporting maritime trade, and the advantages and challenges of locations around the continent. The volume concludes with a summary that points to the extraterritorial character of trading systems during this fascinating period of expansion.

Drawing together an international team of contributors, *The Routledge Handbook of Maritime Trade around Europe* is a vital contribution to the study of maritime history and the history of trade. It is essential reading for students and scholars in these fields.

Wim Blockmans is Professor Emeritus of Medieval History at the University of Leiden. His previous publications include *Introduction to Medieval Europe,* 2nd edition, with Peter Hoppenbrouwers (2014).

Mikhail Krom is Professor of Comparative Studies in History at the European University at St Petersburg.

Justyna Wubs-Mrozewicz is Assistant Professor in Medieval History at the University of Amsterdam.

THE ROUTLEDGE HISTORY HANDBOOKS

THE ROUTLEDGE HANDBOOK OF THE HISTORY OF THE MIDDLE EAST MANDATES
Edited by Cyrus Schayegh and Andrew Arsan

THE ROUTLEDGE HANDBOOK OF THE HISTORY OF RACE AND THE AMERICAN MILITARY
Edited by Geoffrey W. Jensen

THE ROUTLEDGE HANDBOOK OF THE HISTORY OF SETTLER COLONIALISM
Edited by Edward Cavanagh and Lorenzo Veracini

THE ROUTLEDGE HANDBOOK OF MATERIAL CULTURE IN EARLY MODERN EUROPE
Edited by Catherine Richardson, Tara Hamling and David Gaimster

THE ROUTLEDGE HISTORY HANDBOOK OF MEDIEVAL REVOLT
Edited by Justine Firnhaber-Baker with Dirk Schoenaers

THE ROUTLEDGE HANDBOOK OF MARITIME TRADE AROUND EUROPE 1300–600
Edited by Wim Blockmans, Mikhail Krom and Justyna Wubs-Mrozewicz

THE ROUTLEDGE HISTORY HANDBOOK OF GENDER AND THE URBAN EXPERIENCE
Edited by Deborah Simonton

THE ROUTLEDGE HANDBOOK OF MARITIME TRADE AROUND EUROPE 1300–1600

Edited by Wim Blockmans, Mikhail Krom and Justyna Wubs-Mrozewicz

Routledge
Taylor & Francis Group
LONDON AND NEW YORK

First published 2017
by Routledge

2 Park Square, Milton Park, Abingdon, Oxfodshire OX14 4RN
52 Vanderbilt Avenue, New York, NY 10017

Routledge is an imprint of the Taylor & Francis Group, an informa business

First issued in paperback 2019

British Library Cataloguing-in-Publication Data
A catalogue record for this book is available from the British Library

Library of Congress Cataloging-in-Publication Data
Names: Blockmans, Wim, 1945- editor. | Krom, M. M. (Mikhail Markovich), editor. | Wubs-Mrozewicz, Justyna, 1976- editor.
Title: The Routledge handbook of maritime trade around Europe 1300-1600 / edited by Wim Blockmans, Mikhail Krom and Justyna Wubs-Mrozewicz.
Other titles: Handbook of maritime trade around Europe 1300-1600
Description: New York, NY : Routledge, 2017. | Includes bibliographical references and index.
Identifiers: LCCN 2016032747| ISBN 9781315278575 (ebook) | ISBN 9781138899506 (hardback : alk. paper)
Subjects: LCSH: Europe—Commerce—History.
Classification: LCC HF3495 .R68 2017 | DDC 382.094—dc23
LC record available at https://lccn.loc.gov/2016032747

ISBN: 978-1-138-89950-6 (hbk)
ISBN: 978-0-367-87294-6 (pbk)

Typeset in Bembo Std
by Swales & Willis Ltd, Exeter, Devon, UK

CONTENTS

FIGURES

Cover illustration: *Allegory of Danzig Trade*, by Isaac van den Blocke. See further, Chapter 15 and Figure 15.2. Gdańsk History Museum, Main City Hall.

PREFACE

This project has come a long way before materializing in the present volume. Its genealogy can be traced back to the conference 'The Republican Tradition: From the Hanseatic League to the Era of the Enlightenment' held in December 2012 at the European University at St Petersburg (EUSP) under the auspices of the Res Publica Research Centre led by the EUSP Rector, Professor Oleg Kharkhordin. It was there that two of the three future editors met for the first time, and a number of the contributions to this collection originated from the 2012 conference papers.

In the course of further discussions, the project, which was initially titled Merchants' World, gradually took shape. It took on its present title in 2014; that same year, Justyna Wubs-Mrozewicz joined Wim Blockmans and Mikhail Krom and shared editorial responsibilities. We are happy that scholars from many European countries, the United States and Canada have accepted our invitations and invested their energy, expertise and friendly spirits in this collective enterprise.

In June 2015 we met at a workshop, again hosted by the European University at St Petersburg, to discuss the first drafts of chapters and to work out guidelines for their further elaboration. All the contributors, including those who were not able to attend the 2015 workshop, collaborated with great enthusiasm and willingly adapted their drafts to enhance the volume's coherence. The editors would like to express their special gratitude to Professor Richard W. Unger (University of British Columbia, Vancouver), the *éminence grise* of maritime history, who graciously advised them with regard to the Introduction and the concluding chapter.

We wish to thank the European University at St Petersburg for its hospitality and generous support. We willingly acknowledge the active involvement of the EUSP Research Centre Res Publica, which is currently supported by the Bank Otkrytie Financial Corporation, in the realization of our project from its very beginning till the end. We are also most grateful to institutions that made our meeting at the EUSP possible, including the Russian Federal State Company Goznak, the Netherlands Institute in St Petersburg and the Netherlands Organization for Scientific Research (NWO).

Katie Marshall (EUSP), our marvellous language editor, did her job with fantastic speed, efficiency and good humour.

Finally, at Routledge we enjoyed the competent and tactful guidance of Ms Catherine Aitken.

To all the aforementioned persons and institutions we express our sincere gratitude. None of them, however, is responsible for any errors that might be detected in the present volume.

Wim Blockmans, Mikhail Krom and Justyna Wubs-Mrozewicz

CONTRIBUTORS

Amélia Aguiar Andrade (amelia.andrade@fcsh.unl.pt) is Full Professor of Medieval History at the Nova University of Lisbon and Director of the Institute for Medieval Studies (IEM). She chaired the Scientific Committee of the European Association for Urban History between 2012 and 2014. Her research focuses predominantly on relations between space and power in the urban contexts of medieval Portugal. Her main publications include *La ville médiévale en débat* (co-ed.), 2013; *Ser mujer en la ciudad medieval europea* (co-ed., 2013); *Gentes de mar en la Ciudad atlántica medieval* (co-ed., 2012).

Wim Blockmans (wimblockmans7@gmail.com) is Professor Emeritus of Medieval History at Leiden University and former Rector of the Netherlands Institute for Advanced Study. He has published mainly on late medieval and early modern institutional and economic history of the Low Countries in a comparative perspective. His recent publications include *Metropolen aan de Noordzee: de geschiedenis van Nederland, 1100–1560* [Metropolises at the North Sea] (2010) and *Carlos V: La utopía del imperio* (2015).

Donatella Calabi (calabi@iuav.it) was chair of Urban History at the University IUAV of Venice until 2014. She has published and co-edited several books on the early modern European city: *Les Etrangers dans la ville*, (1999); *La città del primo Rinascimento* (2001); *Storia della città: Età moderna* (2001); *Cities and Cultural Exchanges 1400–1700* (2008); *Le ghetto de Venise: 500 ans* (2016) and *Venezia e il ghetto: 500 anni* (2016).

Georg Christ (georg.christ@manchester.ac.uk), PhD in Medieval History (University of Basel, 2006), has been a Senior Lecturer in Medieval and Early Modern History at the University of Manchester since 2012. Previously, he was a Research Group Leader at the University of Heidelberg. Recent publications include *Trading Conflicts: Venetian Merchants and Mamluk Officials in Late Medieval Alexandria* (2012), 'Did Greek wine become Port? Or why institutional interventions matter (*c.*1350–1780)', *Quaderni Storici* 143, no. 48/2 (2013). His current work focuses on maritime trade regimes in the Eastern Mediterranean and the Red Sea in the fourteenth century.

Albrecht Cordes (Cordes@jur.uni-frankfurt.de) holds the chair for Medieval and Early Modern Legal History and for Civil Law at the Goethe-Universität Frankfurt am Main. He has published on the communal constitution of villages and small towns in the Upper Rhine valley and in Northern Switzerland (1400–1800) (1992) and on Hanseatic company law in the late Middle Ages (1998). He is co-editor of the second edition of the *Handwörterbuch für Deutsche Rechtsgeschichte* (2004). His research is centred on the history of pre-modern commercial law and conflict resolution. He has co-edited and/or contributed to recent volumes on conflict resolution in commercial and maritime law (2012), *Conflict Resolution with Friendship or with Law* (2014), and *Dealing with Economic Failure* (2016).

Geir Atle Ersland (Geir.Atle.Ersland@uib.no) is Professor of Medieval History at the University of Bergen. His main fields are urban history, in particular medieval morphological and property history, Hanseatic history and the Hanseatic Archives with relevance to Norway. His third subject is medieval military history.

Edda Frankot (eddafrankot@yahoo.com) is Editorial Research Fellow and Project Manager on the Law in the Aberdeen Council Registers 1398–1511 project at the University of Aberdeen. She is the author of *Of Laws of Ships and Shipmen: Medieval Maritime Law and Its Practice in Urban Northern Europe* (2012) and has published on maritime law in Scotland, the Netherlands and the North Sea and Baltic regions.

Carsten Jahnke (jahnke@hum.ku.dk) is Associate Professor of Medieval History at the SAXO-Institute, University of Copenhagen. He is researching the history of the Hanseatic League, the history of the city of Lübeck and Scandinavian history. His main book is *Das Silber des Meeres: Fang und Vertrieb von Ostseehering zwischen Norwegen und Italien vom 12. bis zum 16. Jahrhundert* (2000). Recently he published a monograph *Die Hanse* (2014) and articles about the structure of the Hanse and the trade in the Baltic. At the moment he is preparing a volume on the history of Lübeck.

Stuart Jenks (stjenks65@gmail.com) was educated at Harvard College, Harvard Divinity School, Yale Graduate School and the Free University of Berlin. He is currently preparing a complete edition of the London customs accounts (1280–1560) and documents on the papal plenary indulgences (1300–1517) as well as continuing to publish the Enrolled Customs Accounts (English trade statistics).

Maryanne Kowaleski (kowaleski@fordham.edu) is Joseph Fitzpatrick SJ Distinguished Professor of History and Medieval Studies at Fordham University, New York. Her publications include: *Local Markets and Regional Trade in Medieval Exeter* (1995), *Medieval Towns: A Reader* (2006), two volumes of edited port customs accounts (1993, 2001), and four co-edited volumes of essays, three on medieval gender issues and the most recent, *Peasants and Lords in the Medieval English Economy: Essays in Honour of Bruce M. S. Campbell* (2015). She has also published articles on maritime history, marine fishing, port towns, demography, bioarchaeology, women and work, and family. Her current projects are an edition of maritime accounts and a monograph on maritime communities in medieval England.

Mikhail Krom (krom@eu.spb.ru) is Professor of Comparative Studies in History at the European University at St Petersburg. His research interests include medieval and early modern history of Russia and Eastern Europe, historical anthropology, history of concepts, historiography and comparative methodology. His recent books are: *Between Russia and Lithuania: Borderlands in the System of Russo-Lithuanian Relations at the End of the Fifteenth and in the First Third of the Sixteenth Centuries*, in Russian (2010); three chapters of the book are also available in English as a special issue of *Russian Studies in History*, 40/4, 2002; *A Widowed Tsardom: The Political Crisis in Russia in the 1530s and 1540s*, in Russian (2010); *Historical Anthropology: A Textbook*, in Russian (2010), and *An Introduction to Comparative History: A Textbook*, in Russian (2015).

Lovro Kunčević (lovro.kuncevic@gmail.com) is a research associate at CASA, Institute for historical sciences in Dubrovnik. He received his PhD in Medieval Studies at the Central European University, Budapest, in 2012. He has published on topics such as republican ideology, diplomatic rhetoric, image of the Other, and political institutions of pre-modern Ragusa. His main interest is the comparative history of medieval and early modern republics, especially their political cultures and ideologies, reasons for their political (in)stability, and modalities of decision-making. He has recently published a monograph about the discourses on collective identity in the Republic of Ragusa (fourteenth to seventeenth century).

Ivar Leimus (ivar.leimus@ajaloomuuseum.ee) is a researcher-curator and head of the numismatic collection at the Estonian History Museum. He obtained his PhD in 1989 from the Institute of History of the Estonian Academy of Sciences. Among his books are: *Das Münzwesen Livlands im 16. Jahrhundert (1515–1581/94)*, 1995, and *Sylloge of Coins of the British Isles 51. Estonian Collections. Anglo-Saxon, Anglo-Norman and later British Coins* (2001), with Arkadi Molvõgin. He has edited *Tallinna mündiraamatud 1416–1526 = Revaler Münzbücher* (1999). He is currently working on medieval and pre-modern prices, monetary and trade history as well as on Viking age coinages.

David Igual Luis (David.Igual@uclm.es; webpage: https://uclm.academia.edu/DavidIgualLuis) is Profesor Titular (Associate Professor) in Medieval History at the University of Castilla-La Mancha, Spain. His recent publications include: 'Social rise of the mercantile elite in cities of the medieval Kingdom of Valencia', in M. Asenjo-González (ed.), *Urban Elites and Aristocratic Behaviour in the Spanish Kingdoms at the End of the Middle Ages* (2013); 'Los grupos mercantiles y la expansión política de la Corona de Aragón: nuevas perspectivas', in L. Tanzini and S. Tognetti (eds), *Il governo delleconomia: Italia e Penisola Iberica nel basso Medioevo* (2014); 'La producción y el comercio del alumbre en los reinos hispánicos del siglo XV', in *Mélanges de lÉcole Française de Rome – Moyen Âge* (http://mefrm.revues.org/1567) 126/1 (2014).

Pavel V. Lukin (lukinpavel@yandex.ru) is Senior Researcher in the Centre of Old Rus Studies at the Institute of Russian History, Russian Academy of Sciences. He defended his dissertation habilitation, 'The Veche (assembly) in the social and political system of medieval Novgorod' in 2015. He has authored two monographs, *Popular Political Beliefs in the 17th Century Russia*, in Russian (2000) and *The Veche of Novgorod*, in Russian (2014), and many articles on various aspects of political culture in pre-Petrine Russia in Russian, English and French, including 'The Veche and the "Council of Lords" in medieval Novgorod: Hanseatic and Russian data', *Russian History* 41/4 (2014).

Anu Mänd (anu.mand@tlu.ee) is the head of the Institute of History, Archaeology and Art History at Tallinn University. She gained her PhD in medieval studies in 2000 from the Central European University in Budapest. She has published several monographs, including *Urban Carnival: Festive Culture in the Hanseatic Cities of the Eastern Baltic, 1350–1550* (2005), and edited *Images and Objects in Ritual Practices in Medieval and Early Modern Northern and Central Europe*, with Krista Kodres (2013), and *Art, Cult and Patronage: Die visuelle Kultur im Ostseeraum zur Zeit Bernt Notkes*, with Uwe Albrecht (2013). She is currently working on medieval merchants' networks, guilds and confraternities, gender and *memoria*.

Flávio Miranda (F.Miranda@fcsh.unl.pt.) is a FCT post-doctoral fellow in medieval economic history at the Instituto de Estudos Medievais (FCSH-Nova University of Lisbon) and at the Centro de Investigação Transdisciplinar Cultura, Espaço e Memória (University of Porto). His research interests include economic, maritime and urban history. His main publications are 'Network takers or network makers? The Portuguese traders in the medieval West', in A. Caracausi and C. Jeggle (eds), *Commercial Networks and European Cities, 1400–1800* (2014); and 'Before the empire: Portugal and the Atlantic trade in the late Middle Ages', *Journal of Medieval Iberian Studies* 5/1 (2013). He is currently coediting a special issue on merchants and conflict management in Europe (with J. Wubs-Mrozewicz) and writing a book on Portugal's commercial expansion.

Arno Neele (ArnoNeele@lkca.nl) received his PhD from the University of Utrecht. He works on the medieval and early modern history of the Dutch province of Zeeland with an emphasis on urban networks and the relationships between city and countryside. His publications include a book chapter in *Rise of Economic Societies in the Eighteenth Century* (2012) and several book chapters in the four-volume *Geschiedenis van Zeeland* (2012–14). Currently he works as a researcher at the Netherlands Centre of Expertise for Cultural Education and Amateur Arts (LKCA), Utrecht.

Agnete Nesse (Agnete.Nesse@hib.no) is Professor of Norwegian Linguistics at the University College of Bergen. Her research on historical linguistics includes the language contact between Low German and Norwegian during the Hanse era, where both text-oriented and sociolinguistic approaches are applied to the 400-year-long language contact period. One of her publications is *Four Languages, One Text Type: The Neighbours Books of Bryggen 1529–1936* (2012). Her research also includes work on more recent linguistic history, such as the Norwegian radio language of the twentieth century and the de-standardization process that followed the cultural changes of the 1960s and 1970s. Nesse is one of two main editors of the four-volume work on Norwegian language history: *Norsk språkhistorie* (to appear in 2016 and 2017).

Monique O'Connell (oconneme@wfu.edu) is Associate Professor of History at Wake Forest University. She studies the political and social history of Renaissance Venice. She is the author of *Men of Empire: Power and Negotiation in Venice's Maritime State* (2009), and, together with Eric R. Dursteler, *The Mediterranean World: From the Fall of Rome to the Rise of Napoleon* (2016). She also edits the *Rulers of Venice, 1332–1524* database and has written numerous articles on Venice and its Mediterranean colonies.

Thierry Pécout (thierry.pecout@univ-st-etienne.fr) is Professor of Medieval History at the University of Saint-Etienne. He published on royal and ecclesiastical institutions in the Angevin domains, especially in Provence, and directed the edition of ten volumes of a general survey ordered by the king of Sicily: *L'Enquête générale de Leopardo da Foligno en Provence (1331–1334)* (2008). His most recent publication is: Y. Codou and T. Pécout (eds), *Cathédrales de Provence* (2015). Among his works on Marseille are: 'Pourquoi Marseille ne fut-elle jamais capitale?', in É. Malamut and M. Ouerfelli (eds), *Villes méditerranéennes au Moyen Âge* (2014); 'Marseille au Moyen Âge', in R. Bertrand (ed.), *Histoire d'une ville: Marseille* (2012); T. Pécout (ed.), *Marseille au Moyen Âge, entre Provence et Méditerranée: Les horizons d'une ville portuaire* (2009).

Luisa Piccinno (piccinno@economia.unige.it) is Associate Professor in Economic History at the University of Genoa, where she teaches Economic History and Business History. Her major area of expertise is the economic history of the Republic of Genoa and of the Mediterranean and early modern period. Her research interests are focused on maritime history (private investments, sea trade, routes, risks), on the development of the port of Genoa (logistics, administration and labour), and on inland and sea transport: *Economia marittima e operatività portuale. Genova, secc. XVII–XIX* (2000); *Un'impresa fra terra e mare. Giacomo Filippo Durazzo e soci a Tabarca (1719–1729)* (2008);

'Genoa, 1340–1620: early development of marine insurance', in A. Leonard (ed.), *Marine Insurance: Origins and Institutions, 1300–1850* (2016).

Louis Sicking (l.h.j.sicking@hum.leidenuniv.nl) is Aemilius Papinianus Professor in the History of Public International Law at VU University Amsterdam and lectures on Medieval and Early Modern History at Leiden University. He has published primarily on maritime and overseas history, including *La naissance d'une thalassocratie: Les Pays-Bas et la mer à l'aube du Siècle d'Or* (2015). Among his (co-)edited volumes is *Diplomacia y comercio en la Europa atlántica medieval* (2015). He has contributed chapters to handbooks, including 'European naval warfare', in H. Scott (ed.), *The Oxford Handbook of Early Modern European History, 1350–1750*, vol. 2, *Cultures and Power* (2015). He is currently working on a project on maritime conflict management in pre-modern times.

Carlo Taviani (catavia@gmail.com) is currently Fritz Thyssen Fellow of the Deutsches Historisches Institut in Rome. He received his PhD at the University of Perugia. Among his recent publications are: 'An Ancient Scheme: The Mississippi Company, Machiavelli and the Casa di San Giorgio (1407–1720)', *Political Power and Social Theory* 29 (2015); 'La paga floreni: Utilisations politiques d'un impôt sur les dividendes à Gênes (fin du XVe siècle)', in K. Béguin (ed.) *Ressources publiques et construction étatique en Europe: XIIIe–XVIIIe siècle* (2015); 'Peace and revolt: oath-taking rituals to form unions between and against the factions in early sixteenth-century Italy', in S. Cohn Jr. *et al.* (eds), *Symbols and Rituals in Late Medieval and Early Modern Italy* (2013).

Mathias Tranchant (mathias.tranchant@univ-lr.fr) obtained his doctorate from the École Pratique des Hautes Études (IVe section) in Paris, and has taught at the University of La Rochelle since 1999. He has published extensively on the economy and society of La Rochelle and its region in the Middle Ages, and directed research programmes on the local and national level in the pluridisciplinary framework History and Sciences of the Sea, on maritime history and coastal activities. Since 2008, he has been Vice-President of the Board of Trustees of his university.

Richard W. Unger (richard.unger@ubc.ca) is Professor Emeritus in the history department of the University of British Columbia. He has published extensively on maritime history and the history of brewing in the Netherlands and throughout Europe in the Middle Ages and the Renaissance. His most recent publications include 'Commerce, communication and empire economy, technology and cultural encounters', *Speculum* 90 (2015); 'Trade, taxation and government policy in the High Middle Ages', *Viator* 46 (2015); 'The technology and teaching of shipbuilding 1300–1800', in M. Prak and J. L. v. Zanden (eds), *Technology, Skills and the Pre-Modern Economy in the East and the West* (2013); and, with John Thistle, *Energy Consumption in Canada in the 19th and 20th Centuries: A Statistical Outline* (2013).

Alexei Vovin (avovin@gmail.com), PhD (The Russian Academy of Science, 2015) is research fellow at the European University at St Petersburg. He has published a series of articles on the history of Pskov in the fourteenth and fifteenth centuries in comparative perspective.

Justyna Wubs-Mrozewicz (j.j.wubs-mrozewicz@uva.nl) is Assistant Professor in Medieval History at the University of Amsterdam. She has published on the institutional, social and cultural history of the Hanse and Scandinavia. Her recent publications include *The Hanse in Medieval and Early Modern Europe* (2013) (co-edited with Stuart Jenks) and 'Mercantile conflict resolution and the role of the language of trust: a Danzig case in the middle of the sixteenth century', *Historical Research* 88/241 (2015). Together with Flávio Miranda, she is co-editing a special issue of *Continuity and Change* on conflict management (2017).

Figure 1.1 Map of Europe by Gerard Mercator, 1569

1

MARITIME TRADE AROUND EUROPE 1300–1600

Commercial networks and urban autonomy

Wim Blockmans, Mikhail Krom and Justyna Wubs-Mrozewicz

The integration of European markets was brought about by both overland transport as well as of sea-borne connections. Around 1300, bulk cargoes of consumer goods became increasingly common, not only on the Mediterranean but also along the Atlantic, North Sea and Baltic coasts. The maritime connections around the continent became all-encompassing, more integrated and more relevant in terms of volume and variety. This book aims to get a better understanding of the ways in which obstacles to this extension and intensification of maritime commercial networks could be overcome. It does so by identifying the conditions under which maritime ports could effectively connect major trade routes. Thus, the position of each of them within the market hierarchy has to be related to the characteristics of their location, their hinterland, the dimensions of their connections, their institutional arrangements related to their commercial activities and the ways in which they tried to overcome cultural differences and resolve conflicts. One of the key questions to be raised will thus be the level of autonomy that port cities of a particular type needed to enjoy vis-à-vis other powers in their environment or network. Here, the approach chosen for this volume concentrating on maritime networks will complement the more conventional analysis of the relations between cities and states.[1]

For centuries, most historical research and teaching has primarily been framed in territorial units that were created in a top-down manner by aristocratic and monarchical dynasties. Their resources and powers were originally based on landed property, which the most successful contenders for power expanded and consolidated by superior means of physical violence. Matrimonial strategies and military conquest were the most common means of reaching the goal of greater, higher and, if possible, supreme power. The ensuing process of state formation deeply influenced the vision of history as states gradually increased their grasp on more aspects of daily life, tending towards the homogenization of the populations through religion, education and a variety of institutions.[2] In contrast to the stability of the imperial administration in China, no single power system has ever prevailed in European history: neither the Catholic Church, nor any empire or kingdom. The rivalry among the multiplicity of states continued to strengthen the inward-looking identification of populations and their rulers. On the other hand, economic systems developed along other paths, following different logics, defined by geographical conditions and locational advantages within wider contexts.[3]

Until the sixteenth century, apart from certain specific choke points such as straits, no single state had the means to permanently control sea routes. Instead, merchants' organizations – based on their own local communities and some inter-urban associations – created their own systems to regulate their risky businesses. They negotiated their privileged and protected status in foreign countries with the local authorities and intervened on behalf of their communities in cases of conflict among their fellow-countrymen and between themselves and local people.

In pre-industrial societies, mobility over land has always been slow. Nothing existed comparable to the system of nearly 100,000 kilometres of paved roads with relays in the Roman Empire. Around 1500, couriers bringing letters to Venice needed one week from Genoa and Munich, two weeks from Marseille and Paris, and three from Barcelona and Antwerp. Transportation of goods by carts and four-wheeled wagons drawn by six horses could carry up to 1,500 kg in one day over 30 to 40 kilometres.[4] Water-borne transport had always been considerably cheaper, safer, and in some cases even faster than overland transport. The growing demand for moving bulk cargoes such as grain, wine, salt, conserved fish and construction materials over ever-longer distances triggered the building of ships with greater capacity. Around 1300, such ships would link the Mediterranean with the Atlantic coasts, the North and Baltic Seas.[5]

These maritime routes connected different geographical and climatic zones, diverse economic systems, religious, linguistic, political and cultural spheres. The shippers needed to gain insight into the geographical and nautical conditions of the distant regions, while the travelling merchants needed to obtain information about the markets at greater distances and be able to negotiate with foreigners. Valuable products as well as common consumables from distant regions became available in greater quantities. The enterprising merchants negotiated and mediated, and used violence only reluctantly, mainly as a defensive device. Their dominant motivation was profit, even though they also ran high risks. They even created their own means of payment – bills of exchange – through which they avoided the risks of robbery, escaped ecclesiastical bans on paying interest on borrowed money and turned the monarchs' currency manipulations into speculative opportunities. Crossing all boundaries, maritime trade contributed to fostering a more integrated European market as well as a better understanding of otherness, in material as well as in cultural terms.

The term 'commercial networks' used in the subtitle of the present volume probably requires some explanation. For more than thirty years, urban researchers have reached some consensus on the use of the term 'network system' to describe trading links in which market hierarchies within a region can be combined with non-economic forms of interaction between towns unequal in size, the scope of their functions and the outreach of their connections. As Paul Hohenberg and Lynn Lees formulated it: 'A city in the Network System functions as a gateway for the towns in its regional *hinterland* and is linked to the larger network via its *foreland*.'[6] Locational advantages, links via roads, rivers, and especially seas, determined the role of gateways that linked regions with different social and economic regimes to each other and made exchanges a productive option. The larger the range of goods and services concentrated in a particular centre the more extended its commercial network could become, and the larger its need for support from a hinterland feeding it constantly with new citizens, food, raw materials and half-finished products to be reworked and marketed. Gateways, along with smaller towns in a descending cascade of markets, redistributed the scarce commodities and specialized services to their hinterland.

As Tom Scott has recently pointed out, the extensive discussions on the relation between European cities and their hinterlands have revolved around the extent of control, matters of jurisdiction, contrasts between the cities to the north and south of the Alps, and the manner of the acquisition of land by citizens.[7] In our volume, we move beyond the debates on the conceptual definitions and geographical boundaries of *contadi* in the south or north. From the maritime and mercantile point of view, the hinterland was a changeable category: it provided a city with the people and goods needed for subsistence, as well as raw materials and half-finished products for trade and manufacturing. It was also a market for its own merchandise. Dominance can take a political shape, but regulation of the markets for labour and goods can be imposed even without that. Superior concentration and accumulation of power – capital and the means of physical violence – ultimately determine this dependency.[8] We show, however, the economic and political interplay in the relationship between the city and its hinterland. From the maritime and mercantile point of view, the hinterland was a changeable category: it provided the goods needed for trade in a particular time, and for particular customers. Christopher Dyer formulated it nicely: 'For luxury and semi-luxury goods the whole of England formed London's hinterland [in the fifteenth and sixteenth centuries]. London also had its "*Umland*" in the sense that the debts reflect the capital's close connections with its immediately surrounding countryside from which the bulk of its food was carried.'[9]

The overly enthusiastic use of networks as a concept with positive connotations has been exposed, as being part of a network could have disastrous effects in the event of bankruptcy or when associates were untrustworthy or incapable.[10] But in spite of this (or perhaps due to the elasticity of the term), 'networks' have won ever-growing popularity with social scientists and historians alike. A recent volume published by Andrea Caracausi and Christof Jeggle specifically explores the applicability of the social network analysis to late medieval and early modern urban and commercial history. Apart from useful theoretical and historiographical overviews,[11] this collective work offers case studies of, for example, Italian, Castilian and Portuguese merchants' networks, and the Armenian diaspora in Venice. Angela Orlandi further developed this analysis mapping a sample of thousands of business letters exchanged with the Iberian associates of the Datini consortium during three years selected between 1396 and 1409. The correspondents were business contacts within as well as outside the enterprise. Nine graphs offer a visualization of the geographical distribution and the intensity of the contacts of the companies based in Barcelona, Mallorca and Valencia. To quote just one example, the most active of these companies was the Barcelonese, which in 1399 received 202 letters from Northern Europe (Bruges, Paris and London), 114 from other Iberian places, 446 from Southern France and 417 from Italy.[12]

The concept of commercial networks adopted in the present volume differs in several respects from that of Caracausi, Jeggle and their collaborators. First of all, while the latter focus exclusively on networks of merchants as individuals, the authors of this book, while analysing individual networks, pay greater attention to the connections between merchant guilds, towns, harbours, trade routes and to commercial and political alliances (e.g. the Hanse). The concept of networks is also indispensable in dealing with maritime empires that had an overarching political authority, such as those of the Italian and Aragonese cities. Secondly, Caracausi and Jeggle's volume privileges economic transactions, including a refreshing perspective on production networks. Here, we have chosen a more pluralistic approach, showing how connections on the level of cities were tightly interwoven with the institutional developments within them, and how this was translated into connections of maritime trade and mercantile exchange along the European coasts in terms of shipping, finance, information, law, language and architectural models.

This volume aims at a deeper understanding of the linkages between maritime trade networks around Europe, from the Black Sea to the Gulf of Finland. The central question is how shippers and merchants succeeded in the period from 1300 to 1600 at connecting regional and interregional trade circuits around Europe and beyond. The technical aspects of these contacts are better known than the institutional and cultural requirements that made the exchanges productive and lasting. In each of the regional systems, certain practices had emerged in shipbuilding, nautical knowledge, trading practices and maritime law, complementary exchanges and communication. The contributors intend to further develop insights about relations between coastal ports and their hinterlands, trading routes, market hierarchies and urban networks by connecting them on the basis of what Fernand Braudel called the 'circumnavigating economy'.[13] While Braudel saw the Mediterranean primarily as a physical and human unit, others have tried to apply his model to maritime trade networks in other times and regions, from the Mediterranean in the millennia before the classical age to the South and East Asian Seas in the present.[14] Our endeavour, however, is not limited to relatively closed maritime systems; it focuses instead on the linkages between various regional entities, which became increasingly connected in the period under scrutiny. In the course of the period 1300–1600, these regional systems gradually expanded and created a system encompassing the whole European continent, reaching out to the Black Sea and the North African coasts. The shift of the core of the European economic system from the Mediterranean to the North Sea and Atlantic coasts, combined with the decline of the German Hanse and the growing importance of intercontinental trade, marks the end of our period.

The question remains, indeed, to what extent particular geographical conditions help us to understand human mobility and exchanges. Without any leaning towards determinism, it is striking to observe that certain sections of the Mediterranean fostered the development of regional cultures through maritime connections long before the ancient and medieval periods. Around 2400 BCE, in modern north-west Syria, the city of Ebla came to prominence in its strategic location at less than 80 kilometres from the coast and on the crossroads of the route from the Euphrates and passages into Anatolia. It was the centre of a palace-based, highly differentiated economy, covering a surface of 55 hectares, and dominating a fertile hinterland of at least 10,000 square kilometres. Its archive room held 17,000 clay tablets with inscriptions in different languages related to the palatial economy, trade, politics and religion.[15] This type of expansive palace city spread over the Aegean islands, some of which, like Minoan Crete, influenced developments on some Cyclades islands, reaching the Peloponnese in the seventeenth and sixteenth centuries BCE. Maritime connections and trade relations gradually became the prevailing pattern of the most developed core areas of the Aegean, which were intensively affected by the outreach of the imperial states of Mesopotamia and Egypt via the Levant. Around 1650 BCE, the city of Avaris in the Nile Delta grew to a size estimated at 250 hectares. Coastal navigation closely linked the Delta to the whole Levantine coast, not the least to return with loads of cedar wood, captives and silver.[16]

The first empires in world history expanded thanks to great rivers that created fertile alluvial plains where agriculture provided high yields; moreover, these rivers facilitated transport of bulk cargoes far more conveniently than overland. Thanks to these links, construction materials were shipped to build grandiose palaces and cities, and surpluses could be concentrated to feed large urban populations. In their midst, specialized crafts arose, which applied scarce raw materials that were available thanks to further commercial outreach. The development of sophisticated cultures around the eastern Mediterranean was founded on the combination of highly productive agricultural areas with transport facilities on major rivers, along coasts and between islands and mainland. Geographical conditions such as the sea currents, prevailing winds and the density of the Aegean archipelago favoured connections that stimulated further development. Once this pattern was established, the advantages of a maritime trade network could be transferred to other locations in a different macro-economic context. In such a way, regions with a less extended fertile hinterland could become the heart of important expansions, such as those of the Peloponnese, Macedonia and central Italy. Those kinds of maritime connections, linked with productive hinterlands and sometimes with distant colonies or peripheries, can be envisaged as a model of the creative overseas interactions between different economic and cultural systems, to which the present volume is dedicated.

While it was not the first imperial states in Mesopotamia and Egypt that launched overseas expansion, the early development of several Aegean core areas followed from their outreach. The followers differed fundamentally from the initiators in their maritime orientation: it was the cosy connections along the coasts and keeping sight of land that linked Egyptian sailors with the Levant and Cyprus, from which others easily sailed further west to Crete, Rhodes and the Cyclades archipelago. On these islands, as on the Peloponnese, extended fertile plains were scarce and considerably smaller than in the Near East and Egypt, which may explain the lesser expansion of their territorial hegemony. If they were to expand, it would be overseas, as did the Athenian maritime empire in the fifth century BCE, and the Carthaginian Empire in the third.[17]

Extrapolation of the Mediterranean experience to a kind of ideal type doesn't really seem appropriate. As observed by Michael North, endeavours to apply Braudel's model of the Mediterranean to other maritime spaces led to the conclusion 'that it is not possible, nor meaningful to apply such paradigms to the Atlantic or the Pacific'.[18] Maritime connections are not necessarily related to a large, nearly closed-off sea. We will try to describe how, in the European case, a great variety of regional networks gradually became integrated into a new encompassing system linking the Mediterranean to the Atlantic, North Sea and Baltic coasts. The general concept may refer to different scales, conditions and forms. The relative intensity of routes can delineate such a space in a specific period, but not a given environment. It includes a variety of geographical units such as archipelagos, coastlines and open seas. Furthermore, the concept of 'maritime space' allows for differentiation in the analysis between different levels and sizes that may have an internal cohesion and a high intensity of exchanges, while also being linked to other and larger systems. We do not wish to suggest any geographical determinism. In our view, geographical conditions may offer opportunities as well as raise obstacles. The latter may trigger technical innovations if the expected gain is thought to compensate for the greater effort. On the other hand, favourable geographical settings are grasped as opportunities only if thriving forces are already active beyond the shores and tend to broaden horizons. Geographical conditions did not change that much over the centuries. It was the human interactions that could or could not make the best use of them within the specific constellation of economic, political, technical and cultural factors at any particular time. Connections, exchanges, economic and cultural transfers, and migrations are seen as the results of complex interactions between multiple human agencies. Human mobility constructed connections and networks by exploiting geographical bounties and facilities, but also overcoming natural obstacles.[19]

Some maritime spaces flourished several times in the course of the last four millennia. A fine example is the window of opportunity grasped around 2200 BCE by Adriatic seafarers from the region blessed with the highest rainfall in the Mediterranean near Split – where Emperor Diocletian would have his magnificent palace built around 305 CE. Two millennia earlier, the Cetina culture, with its core zone located in the ore-rich hinterland, expanded all around the Adriatic coasts, the Gulf of Corinth and the east coast of Sicily. It evaporated abruptly, probably in connection with climatic hazards, at the start of the second millennium BCE.[20] Its extension corresponded remarkably to the sphere of influence created by Ragusa in the fifteenth and sixteenth centuries.

Maritime connectivity developed mainly at the fringe of territorial states and empires that, until the eighteenth century, were unable to control the seas. The maritime networks typically crossed or bypassed all kinds of boundaries of a political, religious, cultural, ethnic, linguistic, legal and economic nature. What networks needed were safe havens where there was fresh water and other provisions for crews, repair facilities for the ships, protection against storms and pirates, and occasional profitable exchanges of merchandise. Crossing seas out of sight of land for several days, as was unavoidable between Crete and Alexandria, remained risky. Sailing in convoy was one of the ways to overcome this challenge, and such organization was set up on routes entailing the hope of high profit. As in pre-industrial societies, the transportation of bulky cargoes was always far more expensive overland than by ship, and massive supplies of locally unavailable or scarce commodities depended greatly on waterways and coastal navigation.

The Mediterranean had thus been connected by various thalassocracies – empires having a regional maritime outreach – before the Romans would label it as the *mare nostrum*.[21] The maritime empire of Carthage 'needed to be destroyed' to establish Rome's control over the massive grain exports from present-day Tunisia. The commercial networks in the eastern Mediterranean were integrated in the Roman system, which became entirely 'pacified' (or rather dominated) by Rome through the conquest of Egypt in 30 BCE. Although constructed around the sea and highly dependent on overseas supplies, the Roman Empire was truly conceived as a territorial unity. The massive maritime trade of grain, oil, wine, *garum* (concentrated fish soup) and luxury products was entirely in the hands of private merchants. The state created a massive demand in its centre but did not organize a merchant fleet. The navy, which was needed to suppress piracy, received far less attention than the army. Up to the seventh century there were regular shipments of grain from North Africa and Egypt to Rome and later Constantinople, organized by the Empire. The state-driven long-distance trade of bulk goods collapsed in the post-Roman period, leading to a common slow involution in demand and a localization and simplification of economic structures that lasted until the end of the eighth century.[22]

From the tenth century onwards, exchanges were intensified again, starting in the eastern Mediterranean. Relations between Amalfi, Constantinople and Alexandria were firmly developed, as is demonstrated by the establishment of substantial overseas settlements.[23] From the twelfth century onwards, Genoa, Pisa and Venice took the lead. Their activities in overseas port cities became consolidated in the form of *funduqs*, *fondachi,* and gradually also in that of outright colonies. *Funduqs* were aimed at protecting the persons and goods of foreigners in the Islamic cities, mostly limiting the radius of activity of those outsiders to a particular quarter of the city so that they would not disturb the order of the community. Within these limits, they were free to solve their internal conflicts and to have their religious cult and lifestyle. Trade with local merchants was regulated through local overseers.

Regular and intense maritime connections contributed to international integration across the seas. Interaction operated from the material, product-oriented level to the cultural level, with participants appreciating new taste preferences and recognizing otherness by dealing peacefully with multiple identities. Durable commercial interchange presupposed a shared understanding of the terms of exchange, including notions of value, valid currency and contractual obligations.[24] Specific institutionalized arrangements emerged to facilitate the interactions, mainly located in a particular port, and limited to a well-defined area. Local rulers guaranteed foreign merchants security for their persons and goods in exchange for stipulated returns in the form of tolls or taxes, adherence to regulations on the transactions, and their following of established procedures of conflict resolution. On a purely practical level, buyers and sellers needed to agree on common standards regarding the quality and value of the goods, their regularly available quantity, weights, measures and means of payment.

Over the centuries, these and similar networks emerged around the European continent, and their nodal points were cosmopolitan metropolises where regional networks connected.[25] This certainly did not mean that exchanges were made between equal partners. From the north–south perspective, Peter Spufford brilliantly attempted to make quantified estimations of the scale of commercial activity in the Mediterranean and the Baltic areas. Even when several caveats and source criticism are applied, 'it is clear that Mediterranean trade was many times greater in scale than that on the Baltic'.[26] But even when a smaller scale of comparison is applied, for instance in the North Sea and Baltic regions, there were significant differences between the cities as trading partners. These inequalities might well have been the main driving forces behind the traders' mobility. Major imbalances in the supply and demand compensated for the transportation cost and allowed for excessive profits. The price differences for grains led to massive long-distance transports during crisis years in the fourteenth and fifteenth centuries, and to a structural flow from the Baltic to the Low Countries from the sixteenth to the eighteenth.[27] In a similar way, specific regional products such as salt, herring, wine, beer, textiles, sugar, furs and the whole range of 'oriental' goods stimulated long-distance trade. The growing carrying capacity of the commercial fleets further increased opportunities to expand the range of products shipped around the continent. The nodal points of trade networks in the years from 1300 to 1600 can be differentiated depending on their status within the intercontinental economic system.

- Some maritime ports primarily functioned as the link between a region producing a limited range of scarce (and highly valued) commodities and the overseas consumers' markets; they connected a producing region with the intercontinental trading system. Examples are La Rochelle as an export centre of regional wines, the English ports exporting wool, Bergen exporting stock fish and timber, the ports in the eastern Baltic exporting furs and grain, and those in the Crimea exporting slaves, wine and grain.

- Some coastal cities primarily functioned as ports of call, as transit ports *en route* between the Mediterranean and the North Sea, between the Baltic and Lisbon, or between Italy and the Atlantic coasts, having regional products to sell as well as having a sizeable regional demand for imported products. Examples may be Palma de Mallorca, Valencia and La Rochelle.
- Some nodal cities connected major intercontinental trading networks with the European markets: the *funduqs* in Alexandria were the link with the Egyptian products as well as with the Arab trade in the Indian Ocean; the same applied to the *funduqs* in Tunis and the other ports that gave access to the products of the Maghreb as well as to those of the trans-Saharan caravans; Pera, the Genoese headquarters in Constantinople, controlled all the Genoese consulates in the Black Sea and Turkish area, with the sole exception of Caffa, thus connecting with the silk route.[28]
- Major cities functioning as centres of redistribution of major continental trading flows were the core of a large network, combining the supply of a highly valued regional production with an exclusive offering of exotic products for resale; the local and regional purchasing power is exceptionally high for a wide range of products imported from all the connected parts of the world. These were the cosmopolitan metropolises of Venice, Genoa, Barcelona, Lisbon, Bruges, Antwerp, London and Lübeck in the fifteenth, and Danzig in the second half of the sixteenth century.

The exchange of goods implied contacts between different cultures. This whole web of connections operated at the fringe of multiple state boundaries and beyond them, fairly independently of monarchical control. States had neither the competence nor the power to control maritime trading networks, and simply tried to tap from them as much in tolls, taxes or credit as they could. Massive state loans by Edward III to finance his military campaigns in France led the Florentine companies of the Bardi and Peruzzi to bankruptcy in 1342 and 1346, and the English fiscal policies of the following decades led to major shifts in the trading relations with their continental partners.[29] The networks' actors also needed to operate as cultural brokers, to be able to deal with the various partners. They generally insisted on the recognition of rights of extraterritoriality for their settlements. They then enjoyed their own jurisdiction, fiscal privileges, some measure of freedom of movement and trading and, where needed – such as by the Genovese in Pera and in Trebizond – fortification of their quarters. Conflicts and rivalries belonged to daily practice, even under the most extensive privileges.[30]

It is this volume's aim to explore the relations between the maritime networks' economic role, their handling of intercultural contacts, and their institutional arrangements in the ports. These included the aforementioned privileges, which often entailed the right to erect a *funduq,* or protected extraterritorial trading settlement for the often hundreds of merchants and shippers belonging to a particular 'nation'. For merchants to feel welcome in foreign port cities, they looked for hospitable and safe housing in the midst of their fellow-countrymen, reliable local officials applying known rules, the provision of regulations for mediation, expeditious and competent courts applying publicly known maritime law systems, provisions for trade and the potential for cultural exchange between different ethnicities, languages and religions, often through local interpreters, brokers or hostellers. The infrastructure of the port systems, their accessibility, the availability of storage space and trading halls all contributed to a harbour's role in long-distance routes. The larger a port city, the more facilities it could offer, such as banks and the possibility of paying with bills of exchange. These instruments were rather scarce north of Bruges, Antwerp and London, and east of the Rhine. Increasingly, the training of merchants became supported by practical manuals explaining the practices and providing details about the quality of typical products in the various places. Similar to these *Pratiche della mercatura*, more detailed nautical maps were disseminated, as were travel guides in different languages.[31]

In this volume, the case studies have been selected for their typological variety and the availability of recent research. Having no ambition to cover all the relevant cities, and taking into account the fact that the editors' wish list was not entirely attainable, the cases attempt to cover the main nodal points serving as linkages between regional systems as well as with some secondary ports. The selected cases represent various types: capital cities of colonial empires, single gateways with out-ports, main ports in a multipolar network and strategically located ports of call. Their relations will be scrutinized at the local level as well as at that of the linkages with their hinterland and trading routes belonging to other economic systems. The ties between the regional maritime networks that connected the Mediterranean with the Baltic area via the Atlantic and the North Sea coasts from Crimea to Novgorod are the main focus, but some explorations in the linkages to other continents are presented as well. This common line of questioning will lead to a comparative conclusion, pointing to the extraterritorial character of trading systems.

The subject was dealt with in major conference volumes published in 1974 from the viewpoint of comparative law on a broad comparative scale. Important regional studies are to be found in three heavy volumes.[32] Over the last four decades new approaches have been developed, leading to a better understanding of the many components of maritime connections such as the techniques of shipbuilding, navigation and cartography, economic institutions, as well as the prosopography of merchants and the analysis of their networks. Apart from Caracausi and Jeggle's volume on commercial networks discussed above, influential works of the last decade include Anver Greif's institutional analysis of medieval trade and the edited collection on cultural exchange in early modern European cities.[33] Another highly inspiring book deals with the position of merchant religious diasporas in the seventeenth century between Hamburg, Lisbon and the southern Low Countries. The author's prosopographical analysis demonstrates that different levels of integration among the local elites were related to their economic success rate.[34] One conference volume focused on the economic aspects of seafaring; another drew attention to the cultural exchanges around the North Sea; and yet another addressed the archaeological evidence of overseas exchanges with Riga.[35] There is also an ever-growing series of area studies highlighting different aspects of maritime trade in the Mediterranean, in the North Sea or in the Baltic region.[36] In general, these studies have focused on leading cities and ports in Europe. Some regions, especially Scandinavia and the Baltic in the late Middle Ages and early modern period, have been explored through a particular lens, in this case, the Hanse. Finally, it is striking that the more expansive comparative attempts have been made on the basis of early modern rather than medieval sources.

Drawing on a variety of new and older approaches, our project aims to offer an up-to-date, comprehensive and coherent vision covering the entire European maritime system. Strangely enough, present scholarship seems to be more divided into linguistically homogeneous circles than it was with previous generations. Looking at the exchanges between seafarers might offer a refreshing vision on Europe's integration from the seaside, which may well have been more effective and productive than the kinds of integration imposed by force by territorial states and empires. Having quite different backgrounds, the contributors to this volume saw it as their mission to imitate the merchants they are studying by crossing all kinds of boundaries that limit our insights – nowadays, strangely enough, even more so than in previous generations.

Chronologically, we focus on the thirteenth through sixteenth centuries, though that long period is not necessarily entirely covered in each of the case studies. In the first section, basic elements of the networks will be presented in general: what created unity in the multiple maritime networks? Was it sailing techniques, geographical units, legal or purely economic systems, or particular combinations of these factors? How did the merchants communicate practically? In the following sections, grouped into three maritime spaces, a selection of case studies addresses the following themes:

1. the state-of-the-art historiography and the available source materials;
2. location: advantages and challenges;
3. the hinterland: dimensions, opportunities for production and exchange;
4. connections: the character of overseas relations, their extension, frequency, direct and indirect linkages, content and balance of the trade;
5. local institutions fostering exchanges;
6. cultural idiosyncrasies and institutional arrangements for conflict resolution.

The diversity between the locations and the availability of sources lead to some variation in the analyses. Thus the themes are not a strict grid and the order and extent their discussions may vary. Yet this diversity is first and foremost an advantage for the reader. Specialized information, in many cases published only in media and languages with a limited dissemination, will be contextualized and made available to an international audience. Thus each chapter stands on its own, but by putting them together we hope to gain both in breadth and depth of the overall perspective.

Notes

1 C. Tilly and W. P. Blockmans (eds), *Cities and the Rise of States in Europe, A.D. 1000–1800*, Boulder, CO: Westview, 1994.

2 W. Blockmans and J. P. Genet (eds), *Visions sur le développement des états européens: Théories et historiographies de l'état moderne*, Rome: Ecole française, 1993; W. Blockmans, *A History of Power in Europe: Peoples, Markets, States*, Antwerp and New York: Mercator Fonds, 1997, pp. 203–65, 332–61.

3 W. Blockmans, 'Europe's history of integration and diversity', *European Review*, 14/2, 2006, pp. 241–56; idem, 'The growth of nations and states in Europe before 1800', *European Review*, 4/3, 1996, pp. 241–51.

4 F. Braudel, *Civilisation matérielle, économie et capitalisme,* vol. 1, *Les structures du quotidien: Le possible et l'impossible,* Paris: Armand Colin, 1979, pp. 365–77; trans. *Capitalism and Material Life 1400–1800,* London: Weidenfeld & Nicolson; Fontana 1974, pp. 309–21 (without graphs); P. Spufford, *Power and Profit: The Merchant in Medieval Europe,* London: Thames & Hudson, 2002, pp. 174–203.

5 Spufford, *Power and Profit*, pp. 395–408.

6 P. M. Hohenberg and L. H. Lees, *The Making of Urban Europe 1000–1950,* Cambridge, MA: Harvard University Press, 1985, pp. 47–73, esp. 59–66.

7 T. Scott, *The City-State in Europe, 1000–1600: Hinterland, Territory, Region*, Oxford: Oxford University Press, 2012.

8 C. Tilly, *Coercion, Capital, and European States, AD 990–1990,* Cambridge, MA: Basil Blackwell, 1990, pp. 16–20.

9 C. Dyer, 'Trade, urban hinterlands and market integration, 1300–1600: a summing up', in J. A. Galloway (ed.), *Trade, Urban Hinterlands and Market Integration c.1300–1600,* London: Centre for Metropolitan History, 2000, p. 106.

10 See the editors' introduction in A. Caracausi and C. Jeggle (eds), *Commercial Networks and European Cities, 1400–1800,* London: Pickering & Chatto, 2014, pp. 1–12; J. Poettering, *Handel, Nation und Religion: Kaufleute zwischen Hamburg und Portugal im 17. Jahrhundert*, Göttingen: Vandenhoeck & Ruprecht, 2013; J. Wubs-Mrozewicz, 'The medieval Hanse: groups and networks of traders. The case of the Bergen Kontor (Norway)', in J. A. Solórzano Telechea, M. Bochaca and A. Aguiar Andrade (eds), *Gentes de mar en la ciudad atlántica medieval*, Logrono: Instituto de Estudios Riojanos, 2012, pp. 213–33; David Hancock, 'The trouble with networks: managing the Scots' early modern Madeira trade', *Business History Review*, 79/3 (Autumn 2005), pp. 467–91, here 468–9, with a rich bibliography on network approaches in several disciplines. More recently, see Stuart Jenks' critical remarks with further references: Stuart Jenks, 'Conclusion', in J. Wubs-Mrozewicz and S. Jenks (eds), *The Hanse in Medieval and Early Modern Europe*, Leiden and Boston: Brill, 2013, pp. 255–81, here 255–61.

11 Caracausi and Jeggle, *Commercial Networks*, pp. 1–12, and pt. I, Approaches, with contributions by Mike Burkhardt and Christof Jeggle: ibid., pp. 13–64.

12 A. Orlandi, 'Le prestazioni di una holding tardo medievale rilette attraverso alcune teorie di management e la Social Network Analysis', in *Innovare nella storia economica: temi, metodi, fonti*, Prato: Fondazione Istituto di Storia Economica 'F. Datini', 2016, pp. 117–48, quote on 139.

13 F. Braudel, *The Mediterranean and the Mediterranean World in the Age of Philip II*, 2 vols, London and New York: Fontana/Collins, 1976.

14 F. Gipouloux, *Méditerrannée asiatique: villes portuaires et réseaux marchands en Chine, au Japon et en Asie du Sud-est, XVIe–XXIe siècles,* Paris: CNRS Éditions, 2009; F. Tabak, *The Waning of the Mediterranean 1550–1870: A Geohistorical Approach,* Baltimore, MD: Johns Hopkins University Press, 2007; C. Broodbank, *The Making of the Middle Sea: A History of the Mediterranean from the Beginning to the Emergence of the Classical World*, London: Thames & Hudson, 2013.

15 Broodbank, *Middle Sea*, pp. 294–304, 336–8.
16 Ibid., pp. 352–91.
17 Ibid., pp. 258–9, 446–7, 597–607.
18 M. North, *Zwischen Hafen und Horizont: Weltgeschichte der Meere,* Munich: C. H. Beck, 2016, p. 13. As this book was published at the time that our volume was in production, no other references could be inserted. Its focus on material and cultural exchanges, ports and networks is similar to ours.
19 J. Pryor, *Geography, Technology, and War: Studies in the Maritime History of the Mediterranean 649–1571,* Cambridge: Cambridge University Press, 1988, pp. 21–4; D. Abulafia, *The Great Sea: A Human History of the Mediterranean,* Oxford: Oxford University Press, 2011, pp. xxiii–xxxi; H. Küster, *Die Ostsee: Eine Natur- und Kulturgeschichte*, Munich: C. H. Beck, 2002.
20 Broodbank, *Middle Sea,* pp. 350–2, and the chapter by L. Kuncevic on Ragusa, in this volume.
21 Abulafia, *Great Sea*, pp. 166–211.
22 C. Wickham, *Framing the Early Middle Ages: Europe and the Mediterranean, 400–800,* Oxford: Oxford University Press, 2005, pp. 759–94, 820–4.
23 S. D. Goitein, *A Mediterranean Society: The Jewish Communities of the Arab World as Portrayed in the Documents of the Cairo Geniza,* 5 vols, Berkeley, CA: University of California University Press, 1967–93. Criticism by A. Greif, *Institutions and the Path to the Modern Economy: Lessons from Medieval Trade*, Cambridge: Cambridge University Press, 2006, was convincingly refuted by S. Ogilvie, *Institutions and European Trade: Merchant Guilds, 1000–1800,* Cambridge: Cambridge University Press, 2011, pp. 318–19.
24 F. Trivellato, L. Halevi and C. Antunes (eds), *Religion and Trade: Cross-Cultural Exchanges in World History, 1000–1900*, Oxford: Oxford University Press, 2014, pp. 5–23.
25 M. Bochaca and J.-L. Sarrazin (eds), *Ports et littoraux de l'Europe atlantique: Transformations naturelles et aménagements humains (XIVe–XVIe siècles),* Rennes: Presses Universitaires, 2007; A. Palmer, *Northern Shores: A History of the Baltic Sea and Its Peoples,* London: John Murray, 2005; M. North, *The Baltic: A History,* Cambridge, MA, and London: Harvard University Press, 2015; M. Pye, *The Edge of the World: How the North Sea Made Us Who We Are*, London: Viking, 2014; *The Sea in History*, vol. 2: M. Balard (ed.), *The Medieval World*; vol. 3: C. Buchet and G. Le Bouëdec (eds), *The Early Modern World*, Rochester, NY: Boydell and Brewer, 2017.
26 Spufford, *Power and Profit,* pp. 376–88, citation on p. 388; see comment in M. Burkhardt, 'Business as usual? A critical investigation on the Hanseatic pound toll registers', in Wubs-Mrozewicz and Jenks, *The Hanse*, pp. 215–37. Available sources are registers of taxes levied on the volume of the trade in particular periods and places. These sources are preserved only for some ports; they are surely incomplete, and in the Hanse the taxes were levied only in exceptional circumstances. In Lübeck, even within the decade from 1368 to 1379–84, the registered value of trade dropped by 57 per cent; this trend is confirmed by the shrinking to a half of the output of the Lübeck mint in these very years. All in all, however, the registers from 1379 to 1384 offer the only possibility of making a rough approximation of the volume of the trade in Lübeck and comparing it with figures for Genoa in the same period. The Mediterranean port handled five to six times as much trade as Lübeck, which in that period was the dominant city in the Baltic, while Genoa was rivalled, if not yet overshadowed, by Venice.
27 M. van Tielhof, *The 'Mother of All Trades': The Baltic Grain Trade in Amsterdam from the Late 16th to the Early 19th Century*, Leiden: Brill, 2002.
28 L. Balletto, 'Les magistratures génoises pour l'Orient', in M. Balard (ed.), *Etat et colonisation au Moyen Âge et à la Renaissance,* Lyon: La Manufacture, 1989, p. 103.
29 J. H. Munro, *Wool, Cloth and Gold: The Struggle for Bullion in Anglo-Burgundian Trade 1340–1478,* Brussels and Toronto: Editions de l'Université de Bruxelles, 1973; T. H. Lloyd, *England and the German Hanse, 1157–1611*, Cambridge: Cambridge University Press, 1991.

30 S. P. Karpov, 'Grecs et Latins à Trébizonde (XIIIe–XVe siècle', in Balard, *Etat et colonisation*, pp. 413–24.
31 F. B. Pegolotti, *La Pratica della Mercatura*, ed. A. Evans, Cambridge, MA: Medieval Academy of America, 1936; J. Gessler, *Le Livre des mestiers de Bruges et ses dérivés: Quatre anciens manuels de conversation*, 4 vols, Bruges, 1931.
32 *Les Grandes Escales*, Recueils de la Société Jean Bodin, 22–4, Brussels: Librairie Encyclopédique, 1974.
33 Anver Greif, *Institutions and the Path to Modern Economy: Lessons from Medieval Trade*, Cambridge: Cambridge University Press, 2006; Donatella Calabi and Stephen Turk Christensen (eds), *Cities and Cultural Exchange in Europe, 1400–1700*, Cambridge: Cambridge University Press, 2007 (Cultural Exchange in Early Modern Europe, ed. R. Muchembled *et al.*, vol. 2).
34 J. Poettering, *Handel, Nation und Religion: Kaufleute zwischen Hamburg und Portugal im 17. Jahrhundert*, Göttingen: Vandenhoeck & Ruprecht, 2013.
35 S. Cavaciocchi (ed.), *Richezza del mare, richezza dal mare, secc. XIII–XVIII*, Florence: Le Monnier, 2006, is a large collection of conference papers dealing with various highly relevant subjects; J. Roding and L. Heerma van Voss (eds), *The North Sea and Culture 1550–1800*, Hilversum: Verloren, 1996; A. Caune and I. Ose (eds), *The Hansa Town Riga as Mediator between East and West*, Riga: Institute of the History of Latvia, 2009.
36 H. Brand and L. Müller (eds), *The Dynamics of Economic Culture in the North Sea and Baltic Region in the Late Middle Ages and Early Modern Period*, Hilversum: Verloren, 2007; M. Fusaro, C. Heywood and M. S. Omri (eds), *Trade and Cultural Exchange in the Early Modern Mediterranean: Braudel's Maritime Legacy*, London: Tauris Academic Studies, 2010; J. Goldberg, *Trade and Institutions in the Medieval Mediterranean: The Geniza Merchants and Their Business World*, Cambridge: Cambridge University Press, 2012; D. Harreld (ed.), *A Companion to the Hanseatic League*, Leiden: Brill, 2015.

PART I

Thematic aspects

2
SHIPS AND SAILING ROUTES IN MARITIME TRADE AROUND EUROPE 1300–1600

Richard W. Unger

Ports existed because of trade. As often as possible ships carried the goods exchanged. Transport over water was superior because of the simple physical relation between the lower levels of friction between a solid and a liquid than between a solid and a solid. From the High Middle Ages to the early seventeenth century ships went through one of the greatest transformations in the history of their use by human beings. There were significant improvements in the vehicles of transportation over water. The changes were not just in the design of the ships but also in how they were manned, how captains and crews navigated and in the ways people shifted their cargoes in ports. The developments took place against a background of long-term swings in the volume of trade. While at the end of the thirteenth century traffic among ports had risen to the highest level of the Middle Ages there was a significant fall through the second half of the fourteenth century. Recovery was slow, though by the late sixteenth century it appears that commerce was at or beyond the levels of 1300. In 1600 the character of trade was considerably different with new commodities and new routes incorporated into maritime commerce.

A myriad of factors determined the routes ships followed. Many of those factors were cultural including religious and linguistic. Many of them were legal, including similarities of rules and the ability to gain redress for damages, physical or financial. Many were commercial, including simple economic considerations of whether or not there was profit to be made. As important as any of those was the environment which shaped the paths of ships, creating unmarked routes across the open seas which sailors had to follow to take advantage of prevailing winds and currents and to avoid dangers that lurked above and below the surface of the water.

The geography was largely immutable though natural forces could make changes. Human efforts to make adjustments in waterways could prove effective but were always on a small scale. The shape of land and sea created certain places where the choices of sailors were limited. Those choke points, places where ships had to pass, like the Strait of Otranto at the entrance to the Adriatic and the Sound at the entrance to the Baltic, were of strategic importance. They offered the potential for control over and taxation of shipping passing through them and for conflict over the right or power to impose burdens on trade.[1] Improvements in technology did increase the flexibility of shipping. The environment was subject to some minor changes. The combination of the winds and land masses that surrounded seas, along with the technology deployed to handle travel over water, shaped where ships went in going from haven to haven.

The dramatic improvements in the technology of maritime transportation from the High Middle Ages to the late Renaissance made possible more efficient shipment of goods, attracted investment in shipping and in the end opened the door to greater trade. Investment went into ships which became more sophisticated, increased in number and became more specialized in design and use. Investment went into infrastructure in ports, typically enhancing efficiency but with the potential to create fixed constraints. Better techniques for navigation and the dissemination of the knowledge of how to get from one place to another increased the opportunities to take advantage of better ships and better ports.

Geography and wind patterns

Europe is the peninsula jutting out at the far western end of a great land mass. To the north the North and Baltic Seas form one arm of the sea while to the south the Mediterranean and the seas that lie off of it such as the Adriatic, the Aegean and the Black Sea form the other arm. The two collections of seas almost encompass the continent. On the west is the open Atlantic Ocean with islands large and small off the coast. The stretches of open water on three sides give many places and parts of Europe direct access to the sea. If not on salt water the numerous rivers that penetrated into the interior of the continent offered indirect avenues to the open ocean. In the southern part of Europe mountains and the often hilly country meant that, with rare exceptions, rivers were short and difficult to use for transporting goods. In the north and east, on the other hand, the landscape was a more or less flat plain, penetrated by a series of rivers flowing northward and in the east and southeast flowing southward into the Black and Caspian Seas. Many of those streams were substantial, often with little change in elevation over long stretches. That made them candidates for avenues of waterborne commerce and interchange, ones exploited with varying levels of intensity.

Winds came from the west. Circulation came from off the Atlantic Ocean. Once those winds reached the European land mass they tended to split, turning southward off Iberia and turning northward around the British Isles. That flow drove the gyres, the ocean currents that dominated the eastern Atlantic, and established the forces sailors confronted. The so-called North Atlantic Oscillation serves to shape the flow of winds. There are two centres of atmospheric pressure in the ocean, one a low near Iceland and the other a high near the Azores. They vary in strength and move around during the year as well as over time. They influence the speed and direction of winds over the seas and so can change optimal sailing routes in both the short and long term. For any sailor at any time it was the specific weather of the moment that dictated decisions about when to travel and what direction to follow. Evidence, largely from the eighteenth century, suggests that while changes in wind patterns did generate small changes in time of travel they had little effect on the paths that ships followed across the seas.[2] The influence of the long-term evolution of climate was apparently minimal.

Above all, no matter the time of year or when in the period, the prevailing wind pattern meant that going in an easterly direction was easy and going west presented problems. Of course there were seasonal variations which could ease or compound the problem. Specific local or regional conditions, shaped by nearby land masses which dictated certain flows of wind, especially in the Mediterranean with its confined conditions and nearby mountain ranges, could force ships to follow certain routes. Navigators could find routes, perhaps lengthy ones, to get around the prevailing winds, whether a temporary aberration or a long-term established pattern. Even if there were long-term changes in the way the wind blew it was always the situation at the moment which mattered to the captain. Temperatures did, on average, fall in Europe from 1300 to 1600. Ice remained in harbours longer in the spring and narrows might be impassable for longer periods during the year. The Icelandic low may have been stronger or had more influence so that the flow of wind from the west was greater, especially across the North Sea. If that was the case, as with any adjustment in wind patterns, sailors understood that to be a problem to overcome and also as one which, in the short run, was unpredictable.

Navigation

Most voyages made for most of the Middle Ages were not over the open ocean. Sailors, as they had since prehistoric times, avoided leaving the sight of land. They used landmarks along the shore to guide them. Travelling along coastlines presented a serious danger, however. Contrary breezes could drive the vessel onto the shore. Fears of shipwreck made for caution and also for efforts, increasingly successful, to find ways to stand further out to sea. For short trips and along rivers and streams it was the surrounding lands that continued to offer guidance. Through the late Middle Ages sailors developed methods and tools of navigation which promoted longer, faster and safer voyages in the open seas and oceans.[3] The compass, which came into increasing use from the twelfth century, gave a sense of the direction travelled. There were devices that could generate measures of speed, even if their accuracy was suspect. Between those two it was possible to make a reasonable estimate of what a course from one place to another might look like and how long it would take to travel that course. Compilations of information on direction and distance in the form of small manuscript books listed ports and where they were relative to each other. Called portolans such guides were available in Southern Europe by the thirteenth century. They could be supplemented by sketch maps for sections of the coast. Already by the late twelfth century all that information about compass headings and distances could be brought together in portolan charts. They gained in sophistication so that by the late thirteenth century sailors could use them to estimate their position. To get a sense of location navigators could also use the lines which radiated out from the two standard compass roses to chart the course to follow from one port to another. Those rhumb lines showed compass headings for captains to follow, distances to be covered and the alternate courses if there was some obstacle along the way like an island or peninsula. The oldest surviving chart is from the late thirteenth century but presumably sailors used versions well before that date. The ones navigators used on board would have been much simpler than the copies that have found their way into museums and libraries. They also would not have lasted because of the conditions on board and their heavy use.[4]

Portolan charts improved over time and so did the books of directions, rutters. These books with detailed information about courses to follow, tides in Atlantic waters, the nature of coasts and the sea bottom as well as warnings about natural phenomena that might foretell trouble, came from Portugal. First developed in Southern Europe such handwritten books began to appear in the north by the end of the fourteenth century. By the mid-sixteenth books covering much of the European coast and even routes to the Far East were available.[5] Rutters could include or be part of a map which showed elevations of the coast, especially helpful in Northern Europe. Such graphic supplements appeared in books of sailing directions from the mid-sixteenth century and the visual descriptions of what the sailor would see as he went along the coast might even be added to relevant sections in books of portolan charts which appeared in the late sixteenth century.[6] Charts could be anything from grand works of art, presents fit for a king or pope, to simple, practical guides for use on board ship. Scholarly advances derived from classical precedent changed those portolan charts in the sixteenth century.

Sailors coming back to Lisbon from fishing or trading or exploring along the west coast of Africa found that to go northward they needed to stand out to sea, to overcome the prevailing winds. Far from land the pressing question was knowing when to turn east in order to make landfall in northern Portugal. While the masters of the ships may not have understood the concept they did need to measure what came to be known as latitude in order to get home. The practical need on that route and other long ones in the Atlantic coincided with an interest among humanists in the *Geographia* of Ptolemy of Alexandria. In the second century CE he described a method of locating sites using relative measures of latitude. Generalized, the method offered a way to map the world within a grid of perpendicular lines. Translated into Latin at Florence in 1406, Ptolemy's work drew considerable interest from scholars and from mapmakers. By the early sixteenth century depictions of the world, and especially of those including new lands beyond Europe, had scales of latitude. Looking at those depictions sailors would have had a notional way to locate their north–south position on the plane chart. First discussed by the Portuguese mathematician Pedro Nunes, Gerard Mercator as early as 1541 developed a map projection which created loxodromes, lines which intersect all meridians at the same angle. Those showed the true course of a ship so the navigator could chart a straight-line course on a spherical earth. The charts using his method made the task of selecting where to direct the ship considerably easier. The commercial instincts of Mercator made his maps using that projection widely available by the closing years of the sixteenth century.[7]

The impact of those significant advances in cartography had great potential but had limited immediate impact on the practices prevalent on board ships. The ability to visualize in general where shipping was going and to be able to present the information graphically might have legal and political implications.[8] On board ship masters still depended largely on traditional methods based on following celestial bodies, using soundings which brought information about sea depth and the character of the bottom and on the character of flora and fauna. They might well have compasses but that could easily be the total of their tools.[9] Using the new knowledge presented problems. Charts for use on board were not the masterful works created for kings and popes. Measuring latitude accurately was difficult. The astrolabe was effective as were more simple instruments like the backstaff, but they were hard to use on the deck of a ship in rolling seas. Gradually, better instruments made measurement more accurate.[10] The requirements of governments made the use of latitude measures more common. The Portuguese crown promoted the production of tables which gave seasonal relationships of the elevation of the sun and latitude. Those covered only a few years and were not easily available though they did get better over time. Governments in both Spain and Portugal in the early sixteenth century established offices responsible for mapping, in Seville and Lisbon respectively. The impetus was the development of new routes across the Atlantic and by sea to the Indies. The offices produced master charts, updating them using the latest information brought back by sailors who were required to report to their government's agency. By the early seventeenth century captains working for quasi-government companies were expected to record their position daily. Those sailors kept their log books perhaps haphazardly since often on long voyages position did not matter or could not be easily determined because of weather conditions. For short voyages around Europe, the captains of trading ships rarely if ever maintained records of where they were. Those men relied on experience. On shorter voyages travelling at night they could follow a specific star.[11] During the day they could use points of land. Church steeples were reliable points of reference and possibly even sited so that they were useful for navigators. Where there were no settlements other objects had to suffice, even old and big trees. Entering and leaving harbours presented the greatest danger since markers and lighthouses were still rare, especially in Northern Europe. A recurring problem was finding continuing institutions to take responsibility for maintaining the buoys that might indicate fairways. It is possible that surviving records insufficiently represent the guides set out in waterways for sailors, though the lack of evidence implies there was no certainty of consistency in the presence of signposts for them. In the Mediterranean harbour improvements of the fourteenth and fifteenth centuries did on occasion include towers which served as guides as to where to sail. Along the German North Sea coast and to a lesser extent in the Baltic often markers were of little value because of shifting sands and silting which altered fairways, changes coming even over very short periods of time.[12]

Improvements in navigation techniques, in establishing position and showing it graphically and in transferring information, did however yield direct benefits. It became possible to make longer voyages without stopping in ports. Already by the end of the twelfth century direct voyages from the western Mediterranean to the Levant were feasible.[13] By the late thirteenth century voyages out of the Mediterranean through the Pillars of Hercules and on to Northern Europe were feasible.[14] The identification of the most dangerous places gave warnings even to navigators new to stretches of water of the places to avoid. That information was helpful in cutting down on losses. Trade always involved a high level of risk and any way of reducing it was welcomed by merchants and even more by the men who handled the ships. Despite the improvements in navigational techniques and in mapmaking, for most sailors experience and information handed on by word of mouth remained critical for their success at sea. Similarly, it would also be wrong to underestimate the importance of a system of pilotage, both for negotiating passage in and out of ports and also on stretches of open sea. Those experts not only guided ships but also were probably the authors of the rutters which increased in number, quality and scope over time.

The ships

The rapid developments in nautical archaeology in the last half century have dramatically increased knowledge of ships from all periods. Though excavations, carried out underwater or in special enclosures protected from the waters around the site, yield little or no new information about rigging because masts and sails were destroyed over time, the remnants of hulls and equipment on board has revealed a great deal about the design and construction of vessels of all sizes and, as a result, about the evolution of ships. In the late Middle Ages shipbuilders improved the reliability, speed and carrying capacity of vessels. There was a period with a major breakthrough which was followed by gradual change, marked by exploration of the potential of that critical major development. In the latter phase people in ports and on the water found themselves working out of the implications for all phases of transport, seaborne and on land, and for organization in ports, of that technical improvement. The pace of advance was slow, as was typical of pre-modern economies, though the rate of change seems to have increased over time. Once technological changes moved from dramatic differences in the approach to building a ship to being advances on a smaller scale it was easier to introduce those improvements. The rise in the volume of commerce from the mid-fifteenth century meant the building of more ships and so there were more chances for shipbuilders to try new methods and variations on existing ones.

In 1300 European ship design was still, for the most part, divided into two traditions, each dominant in a large region of the continent. Mediterranean vessels were different from those sailing the northern seas. In the south shipyards continued to produce galleys, propelled by oars as well as sails. Changes in their design in the thirteenth century increased the number of oarsmen, making the vessels faster, but the larger crews and the need to carry food and water for them made those galleys almost exclusively warships and so of little commercial value.[15] In the drive to create an ever bigger and even more powerful warship the Venetian Arsenal, the state naval yard, produced a sailing ship with oars. That great galley proved in some of its forms to be moderately effective in battle. Moreover, it did have enough capacity to serve as a cargo ship. Though principally a sailing ship relying on wind for propulsion most of the time, the complement of oars allowed this type of vessel to move in and out of harbours almost at will and so keep it more or less to a schedule. Through the fifteenth and sixteenth centuries Venice, and for a short time Florence, operated regular sailings on fixed routes, with the practice dying out slowly during the sixteenth century. The vessels proved relatively safe with few recorded shipwrecks. Popular for high-value cargo such as pilgrims carried to the Holy Land, great galleys also made regular trips from Italy out into the Atlantic and north to England and the Low Countries, until they were replaced by more cost-effective sailing ships. It took some time before improvements in the newly developed carracks made them unquestionably superior to the great galleys even for the carriage of goods of high value.[16] The workhorses of Mediterranean commerce were sailing ships with one or two masts, each carrying a triangular or lateen sail. They came in a broad range of displacements and there seems to have been little variation in design. Hulls could be tubbier in larger versions to increase carrying capacity and sharper in smaller versions, say for fishing vessels, but in general all such vessels were built and handled in the same way. They were in use throughout the Mediterranean and to a limited degree in the Atlantic off Iberia and northwest Africa. Their rig apparently was not as well-suited as others to the open ocean. Sailing there was a task left to other types of vessel from the other shipbuilding region.

In Northern Europe, that is, on the North and Baltic Seas, by the fourteenth century the cog was the dominant carrier for bulk and many other types of goods. Along the Atlantic front vessels of older designs, derived from the Nordic tradition, continued to find a place. The evolution of the Scandinavian ocean-going cargo ship created a number of variants with a common root in Viking Age vessels. Relatively large cargo vessels operated throughout northern waters in the eleventh and twelfth centuries, and over time the use of the variants became more limited. By 1300 they survived in coastal waters and in certain parts of the Atlantic as ships of improved design replaced them in more and more trades. There is some question about the relationship of the word cog to the principal bulk carrier in the Baltic in the high and late Middle Ages. The term, like all names of ship types, was imprecise. It may have just referred to larger ships, at least as its use spread from the coast of Frisia to Scandinavia and into the Baltic after about 1150. By the late thirteenth century it had taken a leading role in carrying bulk goods in northern waters. Whatever the reliability of the written record the fact remains there was a kind of ship with common design features which turns up in illustrations and in excavations along the North Sea and Baltic shores. It had a flat or nearly flat bottom, a box-like cross-section and a single large square sail supplying motive power. The principal design features made it a highly efficient carrier.[17] There were variations from place to place and over time but there was some consistency in construction.[18] A relatively small crew could handle the single square sail and the sternpost rudder made control easier than with side oars, the previous practice both in the north and the south.[19] Cogs could be built of almost any size and they got considerably larger through the fourteenth and fifteenth centuries and possibly beyond, to the point that officials distinguished between large and small cogs.[20] They got big enough that by 1400 the type got the name hulk as well as cog. Scholars have often treated the hulk as a different type with a different pedigree which existed alongside the cog for centuries. Known for its excessively curved, almost banana-shaped hull and, in larger versions, a unique way of bringing planks together at the bow, it found use on rivers and in estuaries. The modifications to the cog in the late thirteenth century were attributed to a merger with the hulk. Efforts to identify a distinct hulk type have faltered. The term by the late fourteenth century could have just applied to variants of cog design with size being the most important characteristic.[21] More likely, though, the hulk type evolved so that it was hard to distinguish it, in larger versions, from the cog.

Northern Europe had extensive fisheries, most of them inshore, and those relied on small boats. By the end of the Middle Ages, however, scope had expanded with the development of a few deep water fisheries. Going after herring in the North Sea, for example, meant using sturdy and spacious vessels. The catch got preliminary treatment on board so the specialized busses in the fishery needed to have space to work and space for storage of the barrels to hold the treated fish. Work was seasonal so in the down time it was possible to use the vessels for cargo work, that is unless their designs were too specialized for the hunt for fish. The tendency towards a greater variety of ship types designed to deal with specific needs and tasks was a process promoted by the significant advances in deep-sea traders that started around 1300.

In the fourteenth and fifteenth centuries shipbuilders merged the different design traditions of south and north to dramatically increase the potential of sailing ships. It should be no surprise that the breakthrough came in or around Iberia. Along the Atlantic front both northern and southern building traditions were well known so the coasts of Portugal, Spain and southwestern France were a well-established area of information exchange. The rise in traffic along Europe's west coast, that is, after sailing out into the open ocean through the Strait of Gibraltar became feasible in the thirteenth century, exposed all builders to new options and to the temptation to borrow from the new types they saw. The first stage in the process of design integration came when cogs made their way into the Mediterranean. People there were, on the one hand, impressed with their capacity per unit of length and efficiency but, on the other hand, struck with their lack of manoeuvrability and heavy hull construction. The first stage was to convert the hull form from overlapping planking to planks that abutted. The integrity of the hull then depended not on the outer skin but on its internal ribbing, with caulking between the planks serving to keep the vessel watertight. It was a system developed in the early Middle Ages in the Mediterranean and one which would dominate large sailing ships from the fifteenth century on.[22]

At about the same time the vessel got a second mast near the stern with a triangular sail. That way it was possible to sail closer to the wind if needed, an advantage in narrow passages and in foul weather. This two-masted cocca or carrack found a place in Mediterranean commerce as well as in voyages between Northern and Southern Europe. The second and major advance came from the addition of a third mast near the bow with a square sail, balancing the sail on the mizzenmast near the stern. Iberian shipbuilders produced such full rigged ships with three masts and a combination of sails by the start of the fifteenth century. From there the new type, often usually just called a ship with no more specific designation, made its way to shipbuilding yards first in the Mediterranean, then to Northern Europe, into the Baltic and eventually around the world.

Shipbuilders continued to improve the full-rigged ship, making the type more versatile and more efficient. Most obvious were changes in the sail plan. Always complex, over time the arrangement of various sails became more divided, the giant mainsail on the mainmast becoming smaller relative to all the other canvas. Sails of reduced dimensions needed fewer men to deploy them. With more units hanging from the yards and closer in size to each other, a reduced crew could handle them one after the other. That trend made for better use of manpower on board. The hulls became less box-like in character, a process already begun with the earliest carracks in the Mediterranean. The form of hull construction and the three-masted sail plan made it possible to adjust the basic design more easily. It was possible to produce more specialized ships, ones intended for a specific trade or route or function.

The greatest sign of the specialization trend was the separation of warships from cargo ships. The addition of heavy gunpowder weaponry on ships from the fifteenth century allowed the sailing warship to emerge as a unique type. Even at the end of the sixteenth century cargo ships converted to use in battle were still part of naval forces. They were disappearing and rapidly, however, as governments in the north used their increasing command over resources through taxation to contract for the construction of heavily armed ships. Improvements in metal guns and their increasing numbers on board ships made warships more expensive, sharply decreased their ability to carry cargoes economically and made them more effective at attacking enemy targets on both sea and on land. In the Mediterranean specialist warships in the form of galleys had a long history. Full-rigged sailing warships joined them and gradually supplanted them in battle fleets.[23]

Cargo ships became more specialized too. The extreme case, coming in the late sixteenth century, was the Dutch fluyt. It carried an extremely simple rig. Much of the work of handling the sails, thanks to the arrangements of equipment, could be done from the deck. The hull had a square cross-section and the nearly flat bottom gave it a shallow draft, helpful in getting in and out of estuarine harbours like those in the Netherlands. The fluyt was relatively long which increased cargo capacity without significant harm to manoeuvrability. Typically fluyts carried few if any guns. The type was especially suited to handling bulk cargo effectively if slowly. First simply a relatively long cargo ship for use in the Baltic, Dutch shipbuilders over time would find ways to adapt the essential features of the fluyt to a wide variety of trades and routes.[24] That process of specialization began with full-rigged ships almost from their beginnings in the early fifteenth century and gathered momentum over time, fed by rising volumes of trade along fixed routes where the returns from purpose-built vessels could be gleaned and which had the potential to rise.

Fluyts were virtually defenceless but shippers used them typically in peaceful waters so the lack of armament and small crews did not present problems of safety. In wartime those specialist cargo ships could take advantage of the protection of specialist warships by travelling in convoy. Sailing in groups and hiring armed vessels for defence against predators began in Northern Europe with herring busses in Flanders in the fifteenth century.[25] Those fishing boats while hauling their long nets were easy prey for aggressors so owners would pay a levy, pooling their contributions to cover the cost of fighting ships to travel with the fishing boats which travelled in groups anyway in search of schools of herring. In the Mediterranean in the Middle Ages ships typically carried fighting men and defended themselves against attackers. There, as in the North though, the practice of moving in groups in the company of specialist fighting vessels became increasingly common over time. Convoys are only effective if a number of ships participate and if there is a way to finance the cost of protection. The increasing power of governments and their rising interest in seaborne commerce led to their organizing convoys and forcing shippers to only travel in the company of warships. That trend had begun by 1600, one promoted by another action of governments: the promotion of predation by independent entrepreneurs. The hiring of private individuals to deploy naval forces for the state was a well-established practice, for example in Genoa where it was the norm through the later Middle Ages.[26] The use of men interested in profit as proxies for government forces grew in the sixteenth century as Northern European governments gave recognition to attacks at sea, that is if those attacks were on ships from enemy states and if the proceeds from any success were shared with the state. Privateering thrived and by the seventeenth century became an integral part of naval warfare, a practice with late medieval roots and one which continued to the early nineteenth century when effective convoys and naval operations put an end to private warfare at sea.[27]

Different ships, different shipping patterns and differing port infrastructure

The increased capabilities of ships created by technological advances, major and minor, made possible changes in shipping patterns. Ships over time gained carrying capacity in part from being bigger and in part from having smaller crews per unit of cargo space. That enhanced capability could translate into larger cargoes or greater range or both. By having more space for provisions ships could make longer voyages without stops in ports to replenish food and water. That opened options to exploit new routes. The most obvious cases were those which Europeans first explored in the last decade of the fifteenth century to what was for them a New World and, exclusively by sea, to India. Over time access by sea to those sources of goods, many of them novel and almost universally of high value per unit volume, would funnel some expanding trades to certain ports on the Atlantic front. That shifted growth in trade and in population toward ports in the West with easy access to the open sea. Within Europe voyages from the eastern Baltic to Iberia and even into the Mediterranean grew in popularity and importance because full-rigged ships were well equipped to carry on the trade. Their manoeuvrability combined with the potential for loading on canvas where winds could be counted on for some consistency made them well-suited for standing out from the shore and for covering long stretches. Shippers had started using carracks to sail from the eastern Mediterranean to England from the early fifteenth century.[28] Voyages were in larger ships with smaller vessels apparently excluded.[29] Access in Lisbon to tropical goods, brought there by Portuguese ships coming back from Africa, attracted vessels from north German and Low Countries ports along with agents of German merchants.[30] In the sixteenth century it was full-rigged ships that made voyages from ports like Danzig in Poland to ports like Setubal in Portugal with grain to exchange for a back cargo of salt. By the end of the century those through trips were increasing and so was the length of the voyages, going at the least to Italy. Other types could make long-distance voyages. Caravels were lateen-rigged ships carrying one or two or possibly even three masts and so three sails. They were the workhorses of Portuguese exploration and for some trade along the coast of Africa. Fishing and whaling also found use for them.[31] Vessels of similar type served Genoese shippers for carrying goods from the Atlantic islands to the eastern Mediterranean.[32]

The Italian Jesuit Giovanni Botero in 1588 published a short book *On the causes of the greatness and magnificence of cities*. The issues he addressed prefigured the discussion of the economy for the next century and more. He said: 'to make a city great, the convenience of the site, the fertility of the land, and the ease of communication are all of great importance . . . I call a site convenient if it is so situated that many peoples need it for trade'.[33] For him it was commerce, the city functioning as a transit point, which distinguished the most important centres. His examples of great cities in his day were Lisbon, Antwerp, Genoa and Venice. Ease and convenience of transport, preferably by water, set apart those major cities.[34] He also knew how to rank cities: 'the greatness of a city does not consist in the extent of the site or the circumference of its walls, but in the number of its inhabitants and their strength'.[35] His choice of the measure was a logical one, given experience in his lifetime and the predominant pattern in the two centuries before he wrote. Population statistics indicate the impact of the rising volume of trade and its reorientation towards longer distance routes as well as how some cities were able to take advantage of the changing scale of commerce. From 1300 to 1500 the number of Antwerp residents doubled while that of Amsterdam rose fifteenfold.[36] The process of growth in ports continued, if anything becoming more marked over time. Those cities with access to the Atlantic in Iberia, the British Isles and the Low Countries showed the most impressive demographic performance.[37] Of the eighteen cities that doubled in population from 1500 to 1600, eleven were ports with direct access to open seas and oceans. The pattern continued through the following two centuries.[38] Between 1500 and 1700 more than half of the fifty-two major European ports doubled in size. Only 17 per cent stayed the same or declined. The ports that grew most were in Western Europe, which became the most urbanized part of the continent by a considerable margin, and which were centres of government. London and Lisbon were the most striking examples. The large increases in the number of residents suggests that the cities served as nodes of networks. The rise of the ports was because of the rise in trade and more specifically the increase in commerce along trunk routes.[39]

For some towns shipping was an essential part of their economy, especially those ports which were involved extensively in carrying goods for people from other cities. The extreme case in the sixteenth century may have been Ragusa. There the merchant marine reached a level of about one ton for every person in the town.[40] That ratio was dramatically higher than figures for other parts of Europe. Even Venice, another town deeply involved in the carrying trade, in the 1560s had a ratio of only about 0.18 tons per person. For all of England the figure was probably around 0.02, that is much lower, though the largest port, London, may well have boasted a ratio four times that. Even so the ratio was considerably less than for the Adriatic ports. The newly established Dutch Republic had a large merchant marine spread across many ports, big and small. There the tons per person was apparently about 0.17, virtually at the level of Venice. The figure close to that of an Italian maritime republic indicates the reliance of the Netherlands on shipping which was the cornerstone of the economic and political success of the new state. Estimates of ratios must be tentative and for most ports it is impossible to offer even the most vague of approximations. The rudimentary figures do indicate that the size of the merchant marine relative to the population was not as important to the success of the port as commercial connections and the ability to tap into the growth in overall trade.[41]

The longer distances vessels covered, more exotic commodities and larger ships combined with overall growth in the economy served to change shipping patterns. Shippers tended to exploit major long-distance routes more intensively. It proved prudent to carry larger quantities of goods along those routes and then deposit them in a port with facilities to accommodate the ships and to store goods easily. Those ports became distribution points, carrying the commodities to smaller markets or further into the interior of the continent along the arms of the sea or up the rivers and streams that fed those seas. While such a pattern had existed before over time, thanks to the rise of both extra-European as well as internal trades where the newer vessel types found work, commerce tended to concentrate in specific ports that served as foci of goods disbursal. The process proved self-reinforcing with the importance of certain ports attracting more trade and industries related to maritime commerce.

What emerged, not by plan but thanks to improvements in navigation and ship design along with a range of other factors, was much more of a hub-and-spoke system, with increasingly specialized vessels to handle the distribution of goods from those expanding ports. Certain harbours became nodes in networks, serving as points for distribution over a wider area, taking in cargoes in the bigger ships that serviced longer distance routes. It was a pattern and a body of practices which would become even more obvious as time went on. Smaller sea-going ships, in some cases idle fishing vessels, carrying three or more often two masts and at times with complex rigs, were to be found all over Europe. There were variations among regions, with Mediterranean vessels usually carrying lateen sails and northern vessels combinations of square sails with other types. Size varied but such carriers intended for short distance work were distinguishable from the ships designed for longer hauls.[42] Small boats with an una rig, that is a simple arrangement of two fore-and-aft sails with one behind and the other in front of the mast, and typically of shallow draft were already found in Northern Europe on rivers and in estuaries by the fifteenth century. Easily handled by one person, perhaps with some help from a crew member, they could make their way through narrow passages and reach almost any place on a waterway of any size. They made possible deep penetration of distribution networks.

River boats had a long history, some of them very simple. They continued to provide service down and, with proper rig, up major streams. While there was never any doubt about where the boat was thanks to landmarks on both banks, navigating along rivers was always difficult because of the shifting of currents, changes in the direction the stream took, narrow fairways and even occasional rapids or, more frequently, stretches where the water would run faster. Going downstream required little more than a raft with a tiller while going upstream meant using variable wind power in restricted spaces. As with sea-going vessels weather and wind direction could easily delay sailing. Canal construction to supplement natural rivers had started by the High Middle Ages and could offer a significant improvement in conditions for inland travel. The developing of man-made improvements in waterways was still in its infancy, rarely on any large scale and never of a long distance. Institutions were not yet adequate for any major enterprises. The work could be carried out by ports seeking to improve access to hinterland trade.[43] Though the gains were obvious the sizeable investment to build canals and the cost of maintaining them proved a strong deterrent. Advances in the rigs of small boats and the drive towards specialization made shipping along rivers and streams and lakes easier. By the end of the sixteenth century a broad range of types, some built for a certain type of trade or for a certain set of waterways, was emerging. The trend was most obvious in the Netherlands because of the varied topography and the combination of ocean, lakes, estuaries and rivers but the pattern was similar if less pronounced throughout Europe.

Ports more commonly invested in facilities to augment shipping in the cities themselves. In the Mediterranean there were quays left over from the Roman Empire that could be a starting point. By the twelfth century wharves and jetties specially built for cargo handling increased in number and quality.[44] In Northern Europe in the Middle Ages less sturdy but still serviceable docks were common. Wood was the typical construction material in the north, stone in the south. In the late Middle Ages northern ports got cranes on their quays, the number increasing as well as their size and complexity.[45] Cranes were absent apparently in the south, with cargo shifted by using ropes and pulleys fixed to the masts.[46] The rise in trade especially from the later fifteenth century led to increased building of quays and other facilities like systems to bring water to the docks. Connected to improvements in moorage was expanded storage for goods waiting to be moved on and the establishment of market places removed from but close to the sites where the ships stood.[47] Spaces for exchange had long existed in Mediterranean ports but there and even more prominently in Northern Europe those spaces increased in size and diversity towards the end of the Middle Ages. The districts of port towns where ships docked took on a more common appearance throughout Europe. Investment in harbour facilities sought to attract shipping and especially larger vessels with deeper draughts.[48] Greater government commitment, greater control and greater ability to finance not only construction but also continued maintenance such as dredging to overcome silting, improved the efficiency of cargo handling.[49] Also important was the improved organization of shifting cargo. There were already signs of better arrangements in some ports in the sixteenth century. While crews had doubled as stevedores through the Middle Ages larger ports like Antwerp moved to create guilds of workmen, that way guaranteeing that there would always be adequate personnel on hand to shift cargo. The longshoremen, armed with experience and equipment, could supplement or supplant crews in the jobs of loading and unloading. That being the case the manpower on board ship could be reduced. As the scale of traffic through ports rose, town governments saw the wisdom of organizing the transfer of cargoes from ship to shore and from quayside to warehouses or markets. Shippers, merchants and the trade of the ports benefited.[50] Harbours also saw the benefits of accommodating larger ships of new design. The harbours needed to change in response to the new technology. Those that could handle the full range of sea-going ships were those mostly likely to act as distribution nodes for the growing volume of trade.

Just as it is difficult to measure the pace of improvement in the efficiency of shipping after the major breakthrough in ship design around 1400 so it is difficult to measure the pace and degree of the evolution in the ways the movement of goods adjusted to the new potential. The system of distribution which took advantage of long-distance trade in larger ships and used certain ports as more important distribution centres emerged slowly and was far from uniform. The evolution and improvements in ship design and the increasing diversity of types, more suited for certain tasks, promoted the growth of some ports to the detriment of others. A hierarchy of harbours slowly grew, one indicated by population and the volume of trade.[51] The logic of a change to concentrating trade in a few bigger ports seems clear and the shift in practice is consistent with the direction taken by technological changes in shipping, navigation and shipbuilding. The rise of certain ports relative to others and the general success of port towns relative to other cities supports the supposition that routes changed. The rise in the total volume of trade from the late fifteenth century also supports the view that the people in charge in port towns figured out how to use changed ship design to their advantage.

Conclusion

Tramping, the practice of ships going from port to port, looking for cargoes and carrying them on to an appointed destination with the hope there would be more cargo at that next stop, did not by any means come to an end. That had long been the normal practice throughout Europe and ships, especially smaller ones and those confined to regional trading, still followed that tradition. The very nature of that kind of shipping meant that it was not well documented if documented at all. Records of taxes charged in ports would catch the cargoes offloaded but outside of ports with diligent collectors of fees there was little chance of any evidence of the short distance, coastal and intermittent trade showing up in surviving documents. Alongside tramping, though, long-distance shipping along trunk routes using the bigger, more reliable vessels that took to the seas from the fourteenth century emerged and became over time more common. Inspired by the technical potential and by the ability to consistently find certain cargoes at certain places, shippers increasingly exploited the economic possibilities of directing their ships to certain ports along certain routes. Those voyages were more likely to be recorded in detail, with documents surviving giving details of the trips. The process started even in the thirteenth century with cogs and then gained momentum with the development of carracks and finally of full-rigged ships. Improvements in navigational techniques and the spread of knowledge about using celestial bodies in combination with newly available charts and tables contributed to the shift in shipping practice. By the sixteenth century the use of certain routes on a regular basis had extended throughout Europe and beyond. Employing trunk routes funnelled more traffic through certain ports, ones well located with access to a hinterland through their own emerging distribution networks. Deeper anchorage and protection from foul weather was an advantage and one that could be and was increased through investment in facilities and effective organization of moving cargo. Ports closer to the open ocean had a clear advantage and one they could exploit effectively, making themselves into break-in-bulk points, with the proper policy choices and auspicious political, economic and environmental circumstances.

The longer the distances involved in trade, the more exotic the products traded, the wider was the geographic distribution of the goods. The geographical extension of trade routes to distant parts of Europe as well as to Asia and the Americas favoured sending goods to final consumers from a smaller number of sites. Longer distances also meant fewer sailings per year for any ship and made stopping at a number of ports impractical. The increased volume of trade, for example in grain, also promoted centralizing distribution, since for the long-distance trader time in port could be reduced while time at sea increased. Turnaround times, typically lengthy for medieval and early modern vessels, were a constant drag on shipping efficiency. It did not pay to have expensive capital assets, ships, literally tied up and not working. Longer distances travelled and greater volumes of commerce promoted the concentration of people and of services into some bigger ports and changed or rather limited the functions of lesser ports. It was not that those smaller ports did not benefit from the rising volume and value of goods carried by ship in Europe and beyond through the sixteenth century. Some ports became nodes of contact. All of them served as points of connection. Though functions may have changed, all of the ports found themselves integrated into local and regional as well as continental and global networks with connections, sometimes direct but often indirect, to all other ports.

Because of the character of developments in the technology and techniques of navigation, shipbuilding and shipping, some ports benefited more than others. Natural endowments, circumstances of geography, prevailing wind patterns, the actions of governments, the kinds of goods produced in the hinterland – all had significant impact on how well ports fared under the new conditions. Some ports certainly thrived and prospered. Some found they had new or adjusted roles. All found they had changing functions in the emerging ways of getting goods from producers to consumers.

Notes

1 F. Braudel, *The Mediterranean and the Mediterranean World in the Age of Philip II,* New York: Harper & Row, 1972, pp. 125–8; C. E. Hill, *The Danish Sound Dues and the Command of the Baltic: A Study of International Relations,* Durham, NC: Duke University Press, 1926, pp. 3–101.

2 D. Degroot, 'The frigid golden age: experiencing climate change in the Dutch Republic, 1560–1720', unpublished dissertation, York University, Toronto, ON, 2014, pp. 112–59; D. Wheeler and J. Suarez-Dominguez, 'Climatic reconstructions for the northeast Atlantic region AD 1685–1700: a new source of evidence from naval logbooks', *The Holocene* 16, 2006, pp. 39–49; C. Wilkinson, S. D. Woodruff, P. Brohan, S. Claesson, E. Freeman, F. Koek, S. J. Lubker, C. Marzin and D. Wheeler, 'Recovery of logbooks and international marine data: the RECLAIM project', *International Journal of Climatology* 31, 2011, pp. 968–79.

3 F. C. Lane, 'The economic meaning of the invention of the compass', in a Committee of Colleagues and Former Students (ed.), *Venice and History*, Baltimore, MD: Johns Hopkins Press, 1966, pp. 332–7.

4 R. W. Unger, *Ships on Maps: Pictures of Power in Renaissance Europe*, Houndsmills, Basingstoke, and New York: Palgrave Macmillan, 2010, pp. 38–44.

5 For example, João de Castro and A. Nunes de Carvalho, *Roteiro em que se contem a viagem que fizeram os Portuguezes no anno de 1541, partindo da nobre cidade de Goa atee Soez, que he no fim, e stremidade do mar Roxo. Com o sitio, e pintura de todo o syno Arabico*, Paris: Baudry etc., 1833 [*c.*1541]; A. Sauer and Handelskammer Hamburg. Commerzbibliothek, *Das 'Seebuch': Das ältesteerhaltene Seehandbuch und die spätmittelalterliche Navigation in Nordwesteuropa*, Hamburg: Kabel, 1996; R. Ward, *The World of the Medieval Shipmaster: Law, Business and the Sea c. 1350–c. 1450*, Woodbridge, UK, and Rochester, NY: Boydell Press, 2008, pp. 123–4, 152–6; also see Stuart Jenks later in this volume.

6 Unger, *Ships on Maps*, pp. 144, 147–50.

7 R. W. Unger, 'Dutch nautical sciences in the Golden Age: the Portuguese influence', *E-Journal of Portuguese History* 9, 2011, pp. 74–5.

8 For example, F. J. Dubiez, *Cornelis Anthoniszoon van Amsterdam; 1507–1553*, Amsterdam: H. D. Pfann, 1969, pp. 14–24; A. W. Lang, *Die 'Caerte van oostlant' des Cornelis Anthonisz. 1543: arte Nordeuropas und ihre Segelanweisung*, Hamburg: Kabel, 1986, pp. 22–6.

9 Ward, *Medieval Shipmaster*, pp. 128–52.

10 E. H. Ash, 'Navigation techniques and practice in the Renaissance', in D. Woodward (ed.), *The History of Cartography: Cartography in the Renaissance*, Chicago, IL: University of Chicago Press, 2007, pp. 514–19.

11 D. Ellmers, 'The cog as cargo carrier', in R. Gardiner and R.W. Unger (eds), *Cogs, Caravels and Galleons: The Sailing Ship, 1000–1650*, Conway's History of the Ship, London: Conway Maritime Press, 1994, p. 40.
12 Ward, *Medieval Shipmaster*, pp. 124–8.
13 J. H. Pryor, 'A medieval Mediterranean maritime revolution: crusading by sea ca. 1096–1204 (and the Normans)', Vancouver, BC, Public Lecture, 2010.
14 A. Lewis, 'Northern European sea power and the Straits of Gibraltar, 1031–1350 A.D.', in J. R. Strayer, W. C. Jordan, B. McNab and T. F. Ruiz (eds), *Order and Innovation in the Middle Ages: Essays in Honor of Joseph R. Strayer*, Princeton, NJ: Princeton University Press, 1976, pp. 139–64.
15 J. Dotson, 'Ship types and fleet composition at Genoa and Venice in the early thirteenth century', in J. H. Pryor (ed.), *Logistics of Warfare in the Age of the Crusades: Proceedings of a Workshop Held at the Centre for Medieval Studies, University of Sydney, 30 September to 4 October 2002*, Aldershot: Ashgate, 2006, pp. 65–6; F. F. Laures, 'The warships of the kings of Aragon and their fighting tactics during the 13th and 14th centuries AD', *International Journal of Nautical Archaeology and Underwater Exploration* 16, 1987, pp. 19–22.
16 S. Bellabarba, 'The sailing qualities of Venetian great galleys in the 15th century: evidence of their influence on the development of sailing ships in the Atlantic area during the following century', in C. Beltrame (ed.), *Boats, Ships and Shipyards: Proceedings of the Ninth International Symposium on Boat and Ship Archaeology, Venice 2000*, Oxford: Oxbow, 2003, pp. 201–5; F. C. Lane, *Navires et constructeurs à Venise pendant la Renaissance*, new edn, Paris: SEVPEN, 1965, pp. 12–22, 96–7.
17 D. Ellmers, 'Koggen Kontrovers', *Hansische Geschichtsblätter* 128, 2010, pp. 113–25; A. Englert, *Large Cargo Ships in Danish Waters 1000–1250: Evidence of Specialised Merchant Seafaring Prior to the Hanseatic Period,* Roskilde: Viking Ship Museum, 2014, pp. 117–24; C. Jahnke and A. Englert, 'Historical research on merchant seafaring in Danish waters and in the western Baltic Sea 1000–1250', in Englert. *Large Cargo Ships*, pp. 67–72; J. Flatman, *The Illuminated Ark: Interrogating Evidence from Manuscript Illuminations and Archaeological Remains for Medieval Vessels*, Oxford: John and Erica Hedges Ltd, 2007, pp. 25, 29–36.
18 O. Crumlin-Pedersen, 'Die Bremer Kogge – ein Schlüssel zur Geschichte des Schiffbaus im Mittelalter', in G. Hoffmann and U. Schnall (eds), *Die Kogge Sternstunde der deutschen Schiffsarchäologie*, Hamburg: Covent, 2003; R. Paulsen, 'Die Koggendiskussion in der Forschung Methodische Probleme und Ideologische Verzerrungen', *Hansische Geschichtsblätter* 128, 2010, pp. 41–7.
19 J. Lucassen and R. W. Unger, 'Shipping, productivity and economic growth', in R.W. Unger (ed.), *Shipping and Economic Growth 1350–1850*, Leiden: Brill, 2011, pp. 12–17.
20 C. Jahnke, 'Koggen und kein Ende Anmerkungen zu den Thesen von Reinhard Paulsen und Detlev Ellmers', *Zeitschrift für Lübeckische Geschichte* 91, 2011, pp. 309–12; Paulsen, 'Die Koggendiskussion', pp. 30–8.
21 J. Adams, *A Maritime Archaeology of Ships Innovation and Social Change in Medieval and Early Modern Europe*, Oxford: Oxbow Books, 2013, pp. 99–110.
22 Flatman, *Illuminated Ark*, pp. 17, 36–9; M. McCarthy, *Ships' Fastenings: From Sewn Boat to Steamship*, College Station, TX: Texas A&M University Press, 2005, pp. 44–9, 52–69, 79–81.
23 J. Glete, *Warfare at Sea, 1500–1650: Maritime Conflicts and the Transformation of Europe*, London: Routledge, 2000, pp. 1–39.
24 R. W. Unger, *Dutch Shipbuilding Before 1800: Ships and Guilds*, Assen: Van Gorcum, 1978, pp. 35–50; A. Wegener Sleeswyk, *De Gouden Eeuw van het fluitschip*, Franeker: Van Wijnen, 2003, pp. 17–89.
25 R. Degrijse, 'De konvooiering van de Vlamsche vissersvloot in de 15de and 16de eeuw', *Bijdragen voor de Geschiedenis der Nederlanden*, 2, 1948, pp. 137–58.

26 M. Balard, 'Genoese naval forces in the Mediterranean during the fifteenth and sixteenth centuries', in J. Hattendorf and R. W. Unger (eds), *War at Sea in the Middle Ages and the Renaissance*, Woodbridge, England: Boydell Press, 2003, pp. 137–45.
27 K. R. Andrews, *Elizabethan Privateering: English Privateering during the Spanish War, 1585–1603*, Cambridge: Cambridge University Press, 1964; D. J. Starkey, *British Privateering Enterprise in the Eighteenth Century*, Exeter: University of Exeter Press, 1990, pp. 253–71; D. J. Starkey, 'A restless spirit: British privateering enterprise, 1739–1815', in D. J. Starkey, J. de Moor and E. S. v. Eyck van Heslinga (eds), *Pirates and Privateers: New Perspectives on the War on Trade in the Eighteenth and Nineteenth Centuries*, Exeter: University of Exeter Press, 1997, pp. 137–9.
28 J. Heers, *Gênes au XVe siècle: activité économique et problèmes sociaux*, [Paris]: SEVPEN, 1961, pp. 271–8.
29 F. Melis and L. Frangioni, *I trasporti e le comunicazioni nel Medioevo*, Florence: Le Monnier, 1984, pp. 7–17.
30 H. Kellenbenz, 'Die fremde Kaufleute auf der Iberischen Halbinsel vom 15. Jahrhundert bis zum Ende des 16. Jahrhunderts', in H. Kellenbenz (ed.), *Fremde Kaufleute auf der Iberischen Halbinsel*, Cologne: Böhlau, 1970, pp. 267–8, 316–23; M. H. Kellenbenz, 'La participation des capitaux de l'Allemagne méridionale aux entrepreise portugaises d'outre-mer au tournant du XVe siècle', in M. Mollat and P. Adam (eds), *Les aspects internationaux de la découverte océanique aux XVe et XVIe siècles: Actes du cinquième colloque international d'histoire maritime (Lisbonne, 14–16 septembre 1960)*, Paris: SEVPEN, 1966, pp. 309–17.
31 H. Quirino da Fonseca, *A caravela protuguesa e a prioridade técnica das navegaçoes henriquinas*, 2nd edn, Lisbon: Ministério da Marinha, 1973.
32 J. Heers, 'L'expansion maritime portugaise à la fin du Moyen Âge: la Méditerranée', *Revista da Faculdade de Letras*, 2nd ser. 22, 1956; reprinted in *Société et économie à Gênes, XIVe–XVe siècles*, vol. 3, London: Variorum Reprints, 1979, pp. 20–4.
33 G. Botero, G. Symcox and ebrary eBooks, *On the Causes of the Greatness and Magnificence of Cities, 1588*, Toronto: University of Toronto Press, 2012, p. 17.
34 Ibid., pp. 17–21.
35 Ibid., p. 9.
36 The figure for Amsterdam is especially high because it was little more than a village in 1300, with city rights only just granted. P. Bairoch, J. Batou and P. Chèvre, *La population des villes européennes, 800–1850: Banque de données et analyse sommaire des résultats = The Population of European Cities, 800–1850: Data Bank and Short Summary of Results*, Geneva: Droz, 1988, pp. 11, 53.
37 D. Acemoglu, S. Johnson and J. Robinson, 'The rise of Europe: Atlantic trade, institutional change, and economic growth', *American Economic Review* 95, 2005, pp. 546–50.
38 J. De Vries, *European urbanization, 1500–1800*, Cambridge, MA: Harvard University Press, 1984, pp. 140–1.
39 P. Bairoch, *Cities and Economic Development: From the Dawn of History to the Present*, Chicago, IL: University of Chicago Press, 1988, pp. 177–88.
40 In the 1540s for every Ragusan there were about 0.46 tons of shipping. In the 1570s that proportion had risen to 0.95 tons per capita, while in the early 1600s it declined to the still impressive 0.56. See Lovro Kuncevic in this volume.
41 On the size of the merchant marines around 1600 see R. W. Unger, 'The tonnage of Europe's merchant fleets 1300–1800', *The American Neptune* 52, 1992, pp. 247–61.
42 The government of Tallinn (Reval) owned a boyer, one of the small types of vessels with a complex rig which kept down crew size and made the vessel a preferred one for coastal trades. See Ivar Leimus and Anu Mänd later in this volume.

43 R. W. Unger, 'Investment and risk: ships design and investment in port infrastructure, 1200–1800', in S. Cavaciocchi (ed.), *Ricchezza del mare ricchezza dal mare: secc. XIII–XVIII: Atti della trentasettesima Settimana di studi, 11–15 aprile 2005*, Florence: Le Monnier, 2006, pp. 330–1.

44 L. R. Martin, 'Horse and cargo handling on medieval Mediterranean ships', *International Journal of Nautical Archaeology* 31, 2002, p. 237.

45 D. Ellmers, 'Development and usage of harbour cranes', in C. Villain-Gandossi, S. Busuttil and P. Adam (eds), *Medieval Ships and the Birth of Technological Societies*, vol. 1, *Northern Europe*, Valletta: Malta: Foundation for International Studies, 1989, pp. 44–60.

46 Martin, 'Horse and cargo handling on medieval Mediterranean ships', p. 238; C. Tipping, 'Cargo handling and the medieval cog', *The Mariner's Mirror* 80, 1994, pp. 3–15; R. Ward, 'Cargo handling and the medieval cog', *The Mariner's Mirror* 80, 1994; T. Weski, 'Cargo handling and the medieval cog', *The Mariner's Mirror* 82, 1996.

47 G. Milne, 'Maritime topography and medieval London', in J. Bill and B. L. Clausen (eds), *Maritime Topography and the Medieval Town Papers from the 5th International Conference on Waterfront Archeology in Copenhagen, 14–16 May 1998*, Copenhagen: The National Museum, 1999, pp. 151–2; Unger, 'Investment and risk', pp. 324–5.

48 G. Milne, 'Medieval riverfront reclamation in London', in G. Milne and. B. Hobley (eds), *Waterfront Archeology in Britain and Northern Europe*, London: Council for British Archeology, 1981, pp. 34–6.

49 Unger, 'Investment and risk' pp. 326–8.

50 J. Lucassen, 'Work on the docks: sailors' labour productivity and the organization of loading and unloading', in Unger, *Shipping and Economic Growth*, pp. 271–5.

51 A. Polónia, 'Seaports as centres of economic growth: the Portuguese case, 1500–1800', in Unger, *Shipping and Economic Growth*, pp. 379–409.

3
CAPTURING OPPORTUNITY, FINANCING TRADE

Stuart Jenks

Long-distance trade always involved transferring assets over space. Maritime ports functioning as linking nodes on the circuits as well as gateways to extensive hinterlands had to offer financial facilities to fuel activities in transport, commerce and exchange. To capture the best opportunities for profitable exchanges, merchants were eager to get the latest news about supply and demand in the markets, as well as about conditions in general which might have an impact on their transactions. Seaports served as information hotspots in the late medieval and early modern periods, linking European commercial networks to one another. This chapter first discusses the context of the gathering of information, then deals with the various institutional forms of banks, and finally with the instruments of credit and exchange, most of which were typically developed in major maritime ports.

Harbours as centres of information

Harbours were superb places to pick up commercially useful information. There are three reasons why this should be so. The first is enforced idleness. English shipping contracts generally called for a turnaround time of twenty-one working days,[1] a bit more than a calendar month. The reason for this enforced idleness in port was, of course, the fact that harbours were logistical bottlenecks, where goods were transferred from one form of transport (sea-going) to another (river-based, land transport).[2] During this time, merchants and commercial agents accompanying the ship had plenty of time to scout out commercial intelligence. We are not limited to suspecting that this was so, we can demonstrate it. When the English crown directed that witnesses be heard to determine the question of whether Giuliano Gattilusio, the pirate who had attacked and captured the fleet provisioned and commanded by Robert Sturmy and John Heyton off Malta in 1458, was Genoese, a number of people came forward whose *obiter dicta* throw a good deal of light on how frequently information was exchanged in casual conversation in harbours, even between people of different nationalities. William Denys of Devonshire stated that he heard about the whereabouts of Sturmy's ship and Gattilusio's intentions in Rhodes, Candia (Herakleion on Crete), Corfu and Parenzo (Poreč on the Istrian peninsula in present-day Croatia) and picked up further common rumours in Venice.[3] William Crike not only claimed to know some 150 Genoese by sight who had served with Gattilusio, having seen them in port in Southampton and Sandwich, but had also talked to the inhabitants of Portofino near Genoa about the arming and victualling of Gattilusio's galley.[4] John Warde was able to report the substance of a conversation he had had in Bruges with Laurence Test, a servant of the London alderman Thomas Cock, about what Test had heard about Gattilusio while he was in Genoa.[5] Finally, a number of Venetians were able to confirm that Gattilusio was in fact Genoese, drawing on what had been 'commonly rumoured' and what they 'had been told by many people'.[6] Now, one might be inclined to dismiss this evidence as unrepresentative and therefore unpersuasive, were it not for the fact that even in the mid-seventeenth century Samuel Pepys went to the Royal Exchange every day and to taverns nearly as often to pick up gossip from foreign merchants on what was happening in Europe.[7] Commercial intelligence, in other words, was still being passed by word of mouth.[8]

The second major source of commercial information specifically available in harbours was the customs administration. From the moment in 1303 when Edward I agreed with foreign merchants to grant them a number of rights in exchange for certain new customs,[9] the customers were privy to price movements on a host of foreign markets, since all merchandise (saving wine and wax) imported by aliens was valued at purchase cost rather than at its market value in England[10] and had to be declared immediately upon entry into the kingdom. With the introduction in 1347 of the *ad valorem* poundage subsidy (normally 5 per cent) which applied to all denizen and alien imports and exports,[11] even fuller information became available, although poundage was only collected sporadically up to the 1390s. The result was that any customer worth his salt could, with very little effort, build up an exceedingly accurate picture of the ebb and flow of merchandise through his customs district.[12] Origins, type and amounts of merchandise entering the country as well as their prices at first purchase were at the customer's fingertips, as were the amounts and destinations of English merchandise being exported. This goes a long way to explaining the intense interest of urban mercantile elites, particularly in London, in having their members serve in the customs administration, although they received no salary:[13] being a customer was an excellent way of keeping tabs on the domestic and foreign competition by collecting information.[14] To be sure, England threw away this advantage when the crown introduced books of rates listing standardized prices for most, if not all products in the early sixteenth century and required the customers to use these prices when calculating the value of cargoes.[15] Although periodically updated, the books of rates clearly had only the loosest connection with current market prices overseas, so that the customs administration lost its value as a source of information to merchants.

But by that time this function had been superseded, as Englishmen trading with the country's principal export good (cloth) in its primary market (Antwerp) had formed a cartel (the Merchant Adventurers) – accepted by the crown in 1497 – to which all cloth exporters were required to belong.[16] This perfected the more ancient, but looser corporate organization of English merchants in the Low Countries[17] and established a permanent conduit for market information. In rapid succession, other English trading companies obtained royal charters granting them a monopoly on trade in a particular region, among others the Russia Company (1555), the Eastland Company (1579), the Levant Company (1581), the Morocco Company (1585) and the East India Company (1600).[18] But the formal constitution of a trading company by royal charter granting it a trading monopoly was only the last stage in a much longer process initiated by intense information gathering at home, the dispatch of one or more exploratory commercial expeditions and the establishment of permanent resident agents.[19] Information was flowing long before the companies were founded.

Finally, harbours functioned as funnels for information from their hinterlands into the wider world. It is simply a fact of geography that a good number of important European ports lie at the mouths of large, navigable rivers with a significant catchment area. Anyone can think of examples: Riga (Duna), Danzig (Vistula), Hamburg (Elbe), Rotterdam/Dordrecht (Rhine), London (Thames), Bristol (Severn), Nantes/Bourgneuf (Loire), Bordeaux (Garonne), Lisbon (Tejo), Marseille (Rhône) and so forth. While it is not to be denied that there are exceptions to this rule, it is nonetheless true that harbours located at these mouths had a particularly important role to play in the collection and diffusion of information. Bearing in mind that transporting goods by water cost less than a quarter as much as land transport, it stands to reason that harbours into which large, navigable rivers drained would tend to receive information from a much greater area than land-locked towns. Moreover, these ports benefited from linking leeward and seaward information, disbursing information from their own interior into the wider world and absorbing sea-borne information for use in their hinterlands, if for no other reason than the waiting time engendered by the transfer of merchandise from river-borne to sea-borne vessels and vice versa. By connecting the land with the sea, information was essential for the functioning of financial institutions and techniques traders made use of. It also fuelled their invention and development.

Banks and finance

Finance was of vital importance for trade, since it mediated between savers and investors by moving purchasing power around in time and space in order to direct savings to their highest value use, which in our period was usually long-distance trade. How much money was saved and invested – and at what price – was determined by supply and demand, as expressed by the prevailing interest rate. This makes the study of finance in Catholic Europe more difficult, since the Church capped its perennial condemnation of taking interest on loans[20] in 1311/12, when the Council of Vienne forbade both the licensing of 'manifest' usurers by urban authorities and the enforcement of their contracts.[21] This did not rid the world of interest-bearing loans, but it did drive them underground. A second difficulty is that businesses called 'banks' were not the not the only entities performing banking functions. Quite a lot of lending went on without the participation of any 'bank', and 'banks' played only a very minor role in facilitating international payments. That was the province of merchant-bankers, whom we designate as such to emphasize that they were first and foremost merchants and that facilitating international payments was merely an adjunct of their primary business.

'Banks' are very old. The earliest ones crop up in the very first surviving Genoese notaries' registers (1154). Originally, these Genoese 'bankers' were money-changers, whose name – *bancherius* – was derived from the bench (*bancum*) on which they sat while going about their business of exchanging foreign for domestic coin.[22] On the cusp of the thirteenth century the registers reveal that they had expanded their business horizons, accepting deposits on which they either paid interest[23] or credited a portion of the bank's profits.[24] They employed these deposits to grant loans at interest[25] and to invest in trade (as silent partners).[26] A suit before a Genoese court in 1200[27] reveals more:

1. A Genoese merchant generally had a bank account.
2. Payments, initiated by oral instructions, were customarily executed across bankers' books without use of ready money.
3. It was not unusual for a merchant to overdraw his account (with the permission of his banker).
4. Bankers had discovered the fractional reserve principle, whereby they only had to retain a certain portion of their deposits for day-to-day payments and could invest the remainder.
5. Payments from one merchant to another did not require that they be clients of the same banker, since all the bankers in town had accounts with one another and could clear debits and credits without resorting to cash payments.

Such deposit and transfer banks sprang up around the Mediterranean basin in the course of the thirteenth century – Florence 1211, Bologna 1245, Venice 1274, Barcelona and Valencia 1284, Palma de Majorca 1288, Montpellier 1293, Perpignan 1300, Lerida before 1301 – and shortly thereafter on the other side of the Alps (Lille 1294, Bruges 1300).[28] Note that most these cities were maritime ports, and all were connected to trade routes. At around the same time, 'exchange booths' (*Wechselstuben*) arose in Germany (Nuremberg and Nördlingen 1219, Cologne 1341, Speyer 1346, Basel and Strasbourg *c.*1350, Regensburg 1377), which fulfilled the same functions on the circuits along and to the east of the Rhine.[29] With two exceptions,[30] these deposit and transfer banks were strictly local in scope.

The dates and places given only mark the first unequivocal evidence that a bank was in operation, not the founding date of that institution, much less the date of origin of banking in that town. In some cases (Venice, Florence) indirect evidence points to the fact that banking was, indeed, much older.[31] However, we are entirely at the mercy of our sources, and consequently of the vagaries of survival of documents. It was far more common to engage the services of a notary to record a contract in Italy than it was north of the Alps, and notaries' registers have survived in greater numbers there, not least because the courts treated the entries in those registers as *prima-facie* evidence of transactions.[32] By sheer chance, a number of early notaries' registers survive in Genoa (and, to a lesser degree, in Lucca and Venice),[33] so that we are far better informed about early banking there than, say, in Florence, where the notarial record only begins around 1300, by which time entries in merchants' and bankers' ledgers had attained evidential value,[34] so that the surviving notaries' registers tell us very little about banking.

Informal banks

Formally constituted deposit and transfer banks were, however, only one part of a much larger picture. In fact, having a bank account was not as common as one might think. No more than one in thirty to thirty-five people had one in medieval Bruges[35] or Venice,[36] which works out to no more than one in seven to ten heads of households. However, many bank accounts in Bruges were temporary and existed only for a few days,[37] so that the frequency of bank account holding was in fact much lower. Moreover, whole groups opted out of the banking system, for instance the Hanseatic merchants who frequented Bruges in large numbers and were flush with money, but are only to be found in disappointingly small numbers in the account books of late fourteenth-century Bruges bankers.[38] Are we, then, forced to conclude with von Stromer that the Hanse, 'having no banking system', was primitive and backward?[39] In fact, informal banking was probably more significant – at least in terms of assets – than formal banking, even in the most highly developed European economies. Indisputably, the informal banking sector fulfilled bank functions – accepting deposits (with or without interest), extending credit and facilitating local payments – just as the formal sector did. In listing these financial services roughly in ascending order of importance, we must bear in mind that the evidence is so scattered that we cannot begin to estimate the volume of business done or to generalize confidently from the known examples. Finally, we must bear in mind that the categories are not watertight. After all, even formally constituted banks were anything but loath to loan funds on a pledge, thus functioning effectively as pawnshops, and quite generally people who provided financial services were opportunists, out to make a buck any way they could.

- Tradesmen extended *credit* to their customers in Bruges[40] and Florence[41] to enable them to make purchases. This is also likely to have been the case with John Thorpe, a York shopkeeper dealing in cloth, ironmongery, grocery and haberdashery, who died in 1435 with accounts receivable averaging 12s 3d (median 3s 2d), while his accounts payable were an order of magnitude greater (average £10; median 17s 4d).[42]

- Larger private *loans* were granted by bond in Bruges[43] and York[44] or by notarial contract in Florence.[45]
- In Florence, tradesmen allowed customers to *overdraw* their trade accounts and even granted them cash *loans*.[46]
- Again in Florence, customers with a credit balance with one tradesman used it to offset debts owed to another by *book transfer* without recourse to any bank. Fifteenth-century Hanseatic merchants in London transferred bonds to cover debts payable, although this was by no means as simple as it was in Florence.[47]
- In Bruges and Florence pawnbrokers were licensed, regulated and taxed by the urban authorities from 1350 onwards.[48] They were financially redoubtable, attracting considerable resources by accepting deposits at interest and selling shares in their pawnshops (Bruges only). Furthermore, they held current accounts with the bankers (Florence) or exchangers (Bruges), which suggests a complexity and volume of business not likely to have been characteristic of a petty lender. Finally, wherever we have their account books, they prove to have granted loans, secured by pledges, at a level 'far above the level of petty distress loans to the desperately poor',[49] counting noble rulers and substantial Hanseatic merchants among their clients. Even then, their bread-and-butter business seems to have been providing bridging loans for artisans short of liquidity who had to put food on the table every day and pay their workers' weekly wages but were only paid on completion of the job.

Formal and informal banking: Liaisons secrètes

It is clear that a number of institutions not formally constituted as banks were, in fact, fulfilling bank functions. Indeed, pawnbrokers seem to have been encroaching on the banks, offering financial services such as interest on deposits and current accounts. How did the banks manage to survive? Well, the answer is: in most cases, they didn't. In 1584, Doge Tomasso Contarini lamented that of the 103 banks founded since the twelfth century, 96 had failed, leaving only 7 survivors.[50] North of the Alps, exchanger bankers failed in large numbers between 1390 and 1400.[51] Banks may have failed, but banking went from strength to strength, as Robert Lopez, echoing Schumpeter, was fond of remarking. But that is only to push the problem onto another level: How did formally constituted banking survive? What was its edge in the market?

The crucial advantage of formally constituted deposit and transfer banks was their ability to offer clearing facilities, maintaining clearing accounts with one another which allowed book transfer of funds between two parties even if they were not clients of the same bank, since the banks would credit and debit their clearing accounts with one another accordingly.[52] Since Bruges pawnbrokers and hostellers (who provided financial services to their guests, especially to Hanseatic merchants)[53] had accounts with the major exchanger bankers, but not with one another, all payments in town ultimately had to run across the bankers' books (if one did not want to pay in cash). This created 'a seamless system of book transfers across both the hostel and the exchange'.[54] Just how crucial these clearing facilities were may be judged from the complete chaos which ensued when the Bruges magistrate forbade payment by book transfer and mandated cash payments for some (but not all) debts in 1399.[55] So in Bruges, the informal banks were hooked up to the financial system through the formally constituted deposit and transfer banks run by the exchangers. How characteristic this was of Europe as a whole in our period is difficult to say. Nonetheless, there are indications that formally constituted banks were the lynchpin of the financial system elsewhere. Pawnbrokers in Leuven and Antwerp seem to have been just as dependent upon formally constituted banks as were their counterparts in Bruges.[56] In Venice banks were central to the payments system: both Jewish and Christian pawnbrokers maintained accounts with the Rialto bankers and Venetian banks on the Terraferma cleared debits and credits among themselves via those banks, rather than doing so locally.[57] There is, however, one more indication that the deposit and transfer banks were, almost everywhere, the lynchpin of the financial system, namely that they handled the local payments associated with international transfers of money by merchant bankers from Italy, Barcelona and South Germany, and it is to them we must now turn.

Bills of exchange

The beginnings of cashless international payments can be traced to a specific problem Italian merchants faced in the twelfth century. Lucchese merchants traded silk cloth, woven in Lucca from silk imported via Genoa, for Flemish woollens at the fairs of Champagne, which they transported to Tuscany and sold there. At both ends of the line, merchants either had credit balances piling up which they wanted to remit or need of funds to borrow in order to invest in goods. Since transporting coins from one place to another was expensive, slow and dangerous, the Italians invented first the notarial instrument *ex causa cambii* in the twelfth century and then its successor, the bill of exchange,[58] on the cusp of the fourteenth century, in order to remit surplus funds from one place to another, that is to transfer purchasing power in space. This may look like a straight loan, since one party entrusted funds to a counterparty in exchange for a written promise of repayment. However, there were two crucial differences: the money was advanced in one currency but repaid in another, and the money was advanced in one place and repaid far away. For purposes of illustration, let us imagine a bill drawn in Bruges and payable in Barcelona (Figure 3.1).

A bill of exchange was an internal company document, in which a taker (whom we imagine here to have required ready cash in Bruges) acknowledged payment in Flemish écus in Bruges from a remitter (who wanted to transfer cash to Barcelona) and ordered a correspondent to pay the equivalent amount in Barcelonese currency in Barcelona. Money only changed hands locally, while the bill, having first been handed over to the remitter in Bruges, was physically transported between Bruges and Barcelona and delivered to the payee designated in the bill. There the payee

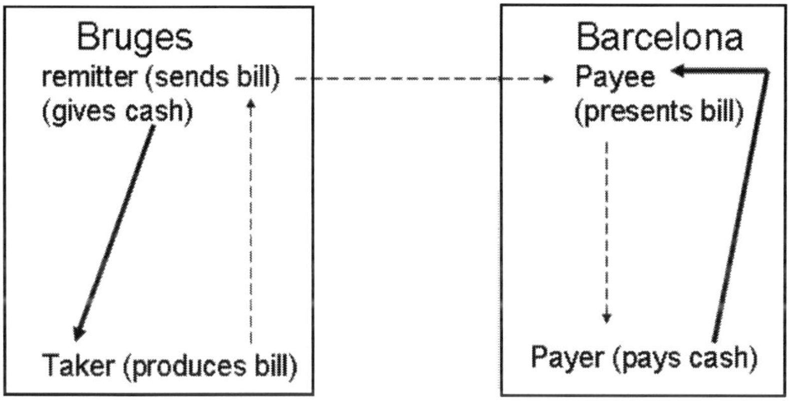

Figure 3.1 Bills of exchange

presented it to the payer. The bill itself was not payable until it reached maturity, at the end of the *usance*, which in the case of Barcelona was thirty days after sight. Bearing in mind that the correspondents in Bruges had cash in hand for two months before the Barcelona branch had to pay out a penny, interest was charged on what was essentially a loan. However, the bill itself gives no indication whatsoever that interest was paid, specifying only the amount of money received in Bruges and the exchange rate. This was by design, intended to allay ecclesiastical suspicions.

We only know that interest played a role because the correspondents of the Datini company quoted exchange rates in Bruges and Barcelona in their regular letters. Francesco di Marco Datini of Prato was an important, but not overarching, merchant based in Florence.[59] His business archives (1386–1410) with some 500 ledgers and accounting books, 150,000 business letters and countless other documents, cast a brilliant light on the dealings and the far-flung connections of his factors in Barcelona, Valencia, Palma de Majorca, London and Bruges, and numerous other partners in ports from Bristol to Tana. Bowing to universal convention, the rates were expressed in both cities as a variable number of shillings and pence Barcelonese for one Flemish écu. These rates were not equal, as they were comprised of two components, principal and interest. The Bruges rate was almost always higher, and this was typical of the fixed leg of every exchange rate quote in the Middle Ages. Of course, no businessman knew whether he had gained or lost until he repatriated his funds (Bruges → Barcelona → Bruges), even if the remitter usually had the advantage, garnering around 12–14 per cent p.a., irrespective of whether the transaction was initiated in Bruges or Barcelona. But there was a risk you might get burned, and it was just high enough to satisfy the requirements of the Church.

The spread between the Bruges and Barcelona rates widened and narrowed in a fairly regular manner, tending to be highest in the autumn and lowest in the early summer.[60] Italian merchant bankers knew precisely what caused these recurring phenomena, the low early summer interest rates, for instance, resulting from the arrival of cash-laden Hanseatic merchants.[61] Not only did the merchant bankers have a shrewd idea of what to expect on the money market, they also knew how to make money out of a fluid situation. The strategy was simple enough: always lend money when interest rates are high and borrow it when they are low, that is, be a remitter (buying bills) in the first instance and a taker (selling bills) in the second. However, you could get burned, because unpredictable events could upset all calculations: war (which required large withdrawals to pay soldiers' wages and outfit armies and navies), devaluations (which lowered the weight and fineness of one currency only) and even the advent of a papal collector (who only dealt in cash) all caused interest rates to skyrocket.[62] Nonetheless, a clever arbitrageur, who had a good sense of how the markets functioned and kept his eyes peeled and his ears open for news, could make money hand over fist by exploiting the differences between exchange rates. This was easiest in Venice, where the peaks and troughs of the interest rate were normally quite predictable, peaking from July to September when the state galleys departed for the Levant, since exporters were desperate to get their hands on cash and besieged anyone with money to lend, offering to sell bills payable in Alexandria, Beirut and other points east as well as in Bruges or London. The Florentines, who not only knew the score but also ran the show in Venetian banking, made sure to concentrate their assets in Venice when demand for ready cash was at its highest, causing exchange and interest rates to skyrocket.[63] The truly clever could take advantage of complete chaos to turn a quick profit. When the Bruges magistrate, doubtless at the behest of the Duke of Burgundy, ruled at the end of September 1399 that henceforth all bills of exchange were to be paid in hard coin, irrespective of whether they originated there or were drawn elsewhere on Bruges, interest rates rose dramatically and the markets were thrown into turmoil. Nonetheless, the Datini correspondents in Bruges came up with instructions to the Barcelona branch on how to deal with the situation by 17 October, and reported a month later that exchange arbitrage was so profitable that the Catalans had abandoned trade altogether.[64] If the town fathers had to mandate cash payments on all bills of exchange, then they must have been settled by another method before that. And indeed they were: in Bruges as well as elsewhere in the world of Italian business, book transfer across the ledgers of the deposit and transfer bankers was the universal method of settling claims arising from international payments by bill of exchange. Deposit and transfer banks were the indispensable link between the international and local finance markets.

Transfer of funds by bill of exchange was possible just about anywhere Italian merchants put down commercial roots in Europe. The map shows the more prominent centres of activity of these merchant bankers between the 1350 and 1450. However, the Muslim world was the end of the line. Bills of exchange could be directed to the Italian colonies in Constantinople and Tana, but beyond that Western finance could not reach, since Islamic law frustrated the development of an instrument corresponding to the bill of exchange despite the sophistication of Muslim bankers.[65] Beyond the confines of the *fondaco*, business was strictly on a cash or barter basis.[66]

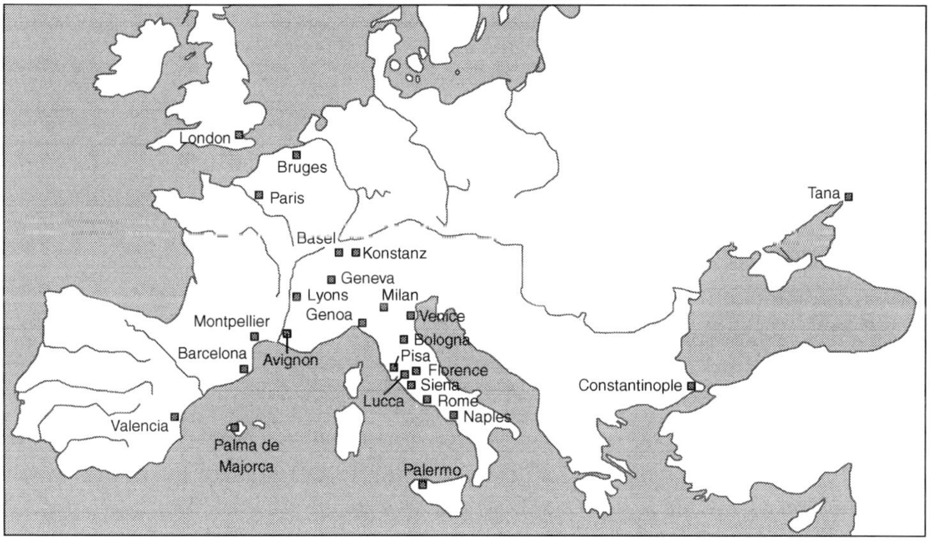

Figure 3.2 Some prominent centres of Italian bill trading (*c.*1350–*c.*1450)

Figure 3.2 does seem to show one huge gap east of the Rhine, but this is more apparent than real. The outermost points on the map mark only the borders of Italian bill trading.[67] South Germans, notably in Nuremberg and Augsburg, were certainly acquainted with Italian financial instruments by the fifteenth century and used them to great effect.[68] While Hanseatic merchants right around the Baltic and the North Sea were certainly conversant with bills of exchange from their inception, even if they called the transaction an *overkop*,[69] thinking of it in terms of buying and selling claims to payment rather than the exchange of one currency for another, they did not use them much in the Baltic area until the mid-sixteenth century, principally because bills were expensive and slow there and simple holograph bills were perfectly sufficient.[70] Even so, it was always possible to link into the Italian system in Bruges and Cologne, or in the sixteenth century in Nuremberg or Augsburg. Moreover, when the bill of exchange became more common as a financial instrument in the Hanseatic world, it was the ports – Cologne and Danzig in the late fifteenth century, followed by Hamburg in the sixteenth – which led the charge. However, even the Hansards reached their limits: Russians dealt only on a cash or barter basis.

Once the Italians had perfected the bill of exchange, there was no end of uses to which it could be put. A merchant was not limited to transferring surpluses from one place to another, he could draw a bill of exchange in one place (an international fair, for instance) on an expected surplus in another place, thus paying for goods with a bill, shipping those goods onward for sale and using the proceeds to pay off the bill when it matured. Johann Rosenkranz, a young merchant of Cologne, made use of this possibility in a straightforward manner in the 1430s, financing purchases of massive amounts of English cloth at the Antwerp fairs by drawing bills on his uncle (and principal) Gerhard von dem Viehof in Cologne, who in turn sold the cloth and paid off Johann's bills when they matured.[71] At the same time, Cologne merchants and London mercers built up a symbiotic relationship: Cologne merchants, requiring funds to buy English cloth for shipment to the Antwerp fairs, sold bills payable there to the mercers, who had excess funds which they wanted to remit to Antwerp in time for the fairs. The Cologners bought the cloth and shipped it to Antwerp, where they used the proceeds to settle the bills and remit any excess funds back to England, which they did by buying bills from the mercers, who used this ready money for purchases at the fairs, shipping their goods back to England, selling them and paying off the bills, whereupon the next cycle began.[72] As the Cely letters (1472–88) show, English staple merchants exporting wool to Calais and English merchants trading at the Antwerp fairs built up a similar cycle.[73]

Since a bill of exchange was, in substance, a loan, a merchant could borrow funds by selling bills. There were a number of methods of doing so, all designed to cloak the fact that loans were being granted at interest. The simplest one was *'dry' exchange*,[74] in which there was never any intention of paying out funds abroad. Either the payer abroad 'paid' (by prior agreement between the remitter and the taker) by drawing a second bill on the original taker, payable to the remitter and calculated at the then current local rate of exchange, or the payer simply refused to accept the outward bill, which threw it back on to the original taker. Fundamentally, the dry exchange was nothing more or less than a local loan, funds being advanced in one place in one currency and repaid in the same place and in the same currency. However, the rate of interest depended upon the current exchange rates abroad at the time the outward bill matured and upon the length of time both bills were under way. One popular form of dry exchange was the *cambium ad Venetias*,[75] the exchange on Venice. It took advantage of the fact that *usance* from Florence to Venice was five days after sight, assuming the bill took six days to arrive, but that *usance* from Venice to Florence was twenty days after date. So a dry exchange *ad Venetias* was a one month loan, the re-exchange rate being calculated at the rate current in Venice when the outward bill matured. There were corresponding dry exchanges between Venice and Bruges (a four-months loan) and Venice and London (six-months loan). Andrea Barbarigo, a Venetian merchant, raised cash in Venice for making purchases in the Levant by drawing bills on London, Bruges and Geneva on dry exchange.[76]

Public banks

From the beginning of our period to the end, bankers were suspected (not without some justice) of concealing assets before they fled from their creditors and depositors, which governments – beginning with Aragon 1300/01 – attempted to prevent by promulgating draconian measures designed to prohibit fraudulent accounting and ward off bankruptcy.[77]

The answer of the fifteenth and sixteenth centuries to the perceived dangers of private deposit and transfer banks was the public bank, which was forbidden to engage in any sector of business deemed to be risky and required to fulfil the useful bank functions at no cost to the public. Indeed, when the first public bank – the Taula de cambi of Barcelona – was founded in 1401, the authorities underscored the necessity of combating the bankers' 'greed'.[78] All subsequent public banks – Genoa (1407/8),[79] Venice (1587, 1619),[80] Amsterdam (1609)[81] and elsewhere – were placed firmly under civic or state supervision and strictly limited to low-risk business sectors. They were permitted to accept deposits and facilitate transfer payments across their books, in particular to settle claims arising from bills of exchange (in Venice and Amsterdam this was mandated above a certain level), but they were usually required to offer these services free of charge. Frequently, they were obliged to serve as a cashier for the supervising authority. Gradually, public banks began to act as a central clearing bank, at first for regional payments (in Barcelona and Genoa) and then for international payments (in Venice and Amsterdam). On the other hand, any business endeavour which looked risky – private loans, overdrawing accounts, discounting of bills of exchange and other credit instruments – was strictly prohibited. There was, to be sure, one fatal exception: the regulator himself, who gave himself permission to plunder the public banks' assets.

Since these manifold restrictions on their business activities left the public banks almost no room to earn profits, they only survived thanks to oppressive legal requirements, promulgated by their regulators, such as

1. the rule that certain assets had to be banked with them – in Barcelona, for instance, all assets of orphans had to be deposited with the Taula, in Genoa the Banca di San Giorgio was in charge of the exploitation of trading posts and colonies,[82]
2. that other transactions had to run across their books – in Venice, all bills of exchange had to be settled by book transfer in the Banco de Rialto from 1593 onwards, and from 1605 this rule was extended to all commercial payments over 100 ducats,
3. by dint of state restriction of the activities of their competitors, sometimes to the point of outright prohibition (Amsterdam 1609).

Given this tight corset of regulation, it is not surprising that financial innovation did not see the light of day in the public sector. Even the fabled Amsterdam Wisselbank ('exchange bank', founded 1609) succeeded not by innovating itself, but by bundling disparate innovations which the private sector had brought forth (e.g. the stable bank florin, multilateral international clearing).

Financial innovations of the fifteenth and sixteenth centuries

The fifteenth century improved on its predecessor by inventing a completely stable currency for international payments, by regularizing the rhythm of international payments to form a predictable quarterly system in place of the vagaries of *usance*, and by internationalizing clearing (which had hitherto been local). These innovations were hatched at the great international finance fairs of Geneva and Lyons.

Stable money of account, regularity of the financial year

Around 1400[83] the four yearly fairs of Geneva had established themselves as an important link between the Mediterranean and North European economies. Geneva's fairs quickly began to function as a clearing centre for international payments by bills of exchange between Italian merchant bankers. While Giovanni da Uzzanno's handbook for merchants (1425) makes no mention of Geneva as a banking centre and quotes no exchange rates on the écu, the Medici set up a branch there in the early 1420s, and by 1440 five further Florentine banking houses had established a permanent presence. From 1450, merchant handbooks leave no doubt as to the importance of Geneva in the banking world.[84] Indeed, it became so central that by 1460 Venice, which had been the financial link between the Mediterranean and Northern Europe, began to fade from the scene.[85] In their clockwork regularity, the finance fairs of Geneva continued and improved upon Venice's attraction for international payments. If Venice had recommended itself because of the predictability of the times of departure and return of its state galley fleets to the Levant (outbound July–September; return Christmas), Geneva went one better and offered almost precisely quarterly fairs (6 January, Easter, 1 August, 1 November). Increasingly, bills right across Europe no longer matured at *usance* (which could be almost any time), but at one of the four Geneva fairs, which made unpleasant surprises less likely.[86]

International clearing of bills of exchange

The exchange fairs of Geneva were supplanted around mid-fifteenth century by those of Lyons. The royal ordinance of 1463 showed just how far the monarch was prepared to go in wooing the bankers.[87] He agreed to forgo collecting customs and other tolls from visitors to the Lyons fairs. Abandoning the crown's bullionist policies, which aimed to retain precious metals within the kingdom, Louis XI dropped all exchange and currency controls, allowing merchants visiting the fairs freely to import and export any foreign or domestic coins (which were to circulate freely at the fairs at rates determined by the merchants themselves) and to remit money abroad without limit or restriction. Finally, he permitted those frequenting the fairs to loan money to one another from fair to fair at a maximum of 15 per cent p.a. interest, irrespective of what the Church might think. Essentially, Louis XI had created a financial free trade zone, in which any merchant could do anything he wanted as long as it was agreeable to all the others. That set the tone for Lyons: mercantile consensus was the foundation of its success. The Lyons model – founded on mercantile autonomy, transparency and consensus – proved to be eminently successful. Indeed, when the Genoese bankers were exposed to unwelcome pressure from the French crown and decamped to Besançon (1535) and thence to Piacenza (1579) to set up their own purely exchange fairs,[88] they refined and adapted the Lyons model to the vastly increased volume of business rather than striking out in a wholly new direction. In the end, Piacenza triumphed over Lyons, because the French crown's insatiable demands for credit – precisely the factor which had driven the Genoese out – overwhelmed the liquidity of the fairs.

Here, too, the Amsterdam Wisselbank may be regarded as the heir to Lyons.[89] International transactions, even if they originated outside of Amsterdam and without Dutch participation, increasingly were paid by bills of exchange drawn on accounts at the Wisselbank, which most large firms made sure to possess. More and more, the Wisselbank facilitated the international clearing of bills of exchange, while Piacenza went into decline from 1621 onwards.[90] With that, the Italian contribution to financial techniques in our period comes to an end. All further innovations were hatched in Antwerp and Amsterdam, which was much the same thing, since many members of Antwerp's mercantile community fled before marauding Spanish troops to Amsterdam in the late sixteenth century.[91]

Transferability

On the cusp of the sixteenth century, North European trade was financed predominantly by promissory notes, called bills (or letters) obligatory if they were informal holographs signed by the debtor and bonds if formally drawn up and sealed. These were of little use in a rapidly expanding economy unless they were negotiable, i.e. if they could pass from hand to hand, being given in payment of other debts. The essential element was the bearer clause at the end of the bill.

> Be it known to all men . . . that I, John Saxby, merchant of the staple at Calais, do owe unto Harry Grover, haberdasher of London, £68 6s 8d Flemish money, the which sum I promise to pay or cause to be paid to the afore named Harry or to the bringer of this my bill on 8 July next (dated 24 May 1542).[92]

Such informal bearer bills had been used to settle debts since the late Middle Ages. However, the legal claims of the bearer were uncertain, unless the original creditor formally transferred his claims on the debtor before a notary or a court of law. This was not a great problem if payments were scheduled from fair to fair, say in Antwerp or Frankfurt, since all parties could be called together without ado, but the difficulties increased as trade became more anonymous on the cusp of the sixteenth century. The solution to the problem was achieved by an Antwerp *turba* in 1507,[93] a *turba* being a sworn statement by honourable merchants before the Antwerp council that a certain practice had become customary and therefore had the force of law. In this case, the merchants stated that the bearer of a bill had an action at law against the original debtor even without a formal transfer of claims, since the bearer was in possession of all of the rights of the original creditor. This rule was adopted quickly by Bruges, Dordrecht and Utrecht and mandated for the Netherlands as a whole by imperial decree in 1537. As a result, bearer bills were given in payment repeatedly, especially those of particularly trustworthy debtors like the Fugger of Augsburg, and typically would circulate until given to the original debtor in payment.[94] However, the longer the chains became, the thornier the problem of liability proved to be: if A paid B with a bearer bill and B used the bill to cover a debt with C, who then presented the bill to A, who was on the hook if A refused to pay? The solution to the problem was provided in 1541 by an imperial decree that the (intermediate) assigner of a bearer bill was liable for the debt until the original debtor paid off the bill. Antwerp quickly worked out a practical method of dealing with the problem, simply pinning a slip of paper to the original bearer bill,[95] on which each successive assignee entered his name, but the original debtor remained liable until the bill was paid off.

Endorsement and discounting

Once bills of exchange became more important in Dutch trade, particularly with England and the Baltic, around 1550, and indeed had become the standard means of effecting international payments, the problem of how to settle them became acute. Successive prohibitions by the dukes of Burgundy had succeeded in destroying the exchanger-bankers' businesses by the end of the fifteenth century,[96] so that it was difficult to settle claims by bank transfer, even though so-called *kassiers* (cash-keepers) arose in Antwerp by the 1530s, accepting deposits from merchants and executing local payments for them. The Antwerp bourse, which had been erected in 1531 and flanked by its London counterpart in 1571, did a roaring trade in bills obligatory, particularly after the imperial decrees took effect,[97] but none of this applied to bills of exchange.

The first hurdle to be cleared was endorsement. From the late 1530s the bearer clause had been added to bills of exchange, clearly with the intention of applying the assignment principle to them, just as had been done with letters obligatory.[98] However, this raised the same problem of the protection of creditors (remitters). This was solved by an explicit authorization on the back of the bill of exchange, in which the remitter assigned a named third party to receive the money in his stead. The earliest known example of such an endorsement of a bill of exchange in Antwerp trade dates from 1571,[99] but the practice did not become common until the seventeenth century, by which time the centre of gravity of the financial world had shifted to Amsterdam. Even so, the authorization of a third party to receive payment of a bill of exchange was firmly rooted in the assignment system used with bills obligatory, which made legal responsibility absolutely clear if the payer made difficulties.

Discounting financial instruments is very simple in principle, but hard to demonstrate in practice. In principle, it involves nothing more than selling a financial instrument for cash for less than its face value to a third party before it matures. The evolution of discounting was, however, long drawn out. The first step – taken in

Italy as early as the thirteenth century and in the Netherlands a century later – was to ask the debtor to pay early, offering a discount on the face value of the instrument as an enticement. In Antwerp, the first known example of discounting to a third party (i.e. not the debtor) occurred in 1536 and involved a letter obligatory, not a bill of exchange. By the 1550s this sort of discounting had become fairly common on the Antwerp bourse. Its first known application to letters of exchange occurred in March 1560, when Antwerp *kassiers* bought up for cash and at a discount – bills of exchange due to mature in May and payable at the Lyons fair.[100] However, the practice did not become common until the seventeenth century, being restricted until then to times of acute stress in the markets, when money was tight and cash was at a premium.

Conclusion

'Unstinting credit was the great lubricant of the Commercial Revolution. It was altogether a novel phenomenon', since the Greeks and Romans of antiquity had known nothing of the sort.[101] In our period, merchants, led by the Italians but followed soon enough by the Germans, Netherlanders and English, devised an array of financial instruments to transfer purchasing power in time and space, achieving a reasonably fair balance of interests between creditors and debtors and even allowing the occasional change of mind to suit circumstances (discounting). However, even if there is nothing particularly maritime about finance, many fundamental innovations of financial techniques were invented in major maritime ports just because of the high concentration of information, opportunities and risks to be found there. It is simply the mirror of trade, which passed from land to sea and back.

Notes

1 Examples: TNA: PRO, KB27/788 m 31 (Bordeaux, 25 Apr. 1453), CP40/780 m 494 (Newcastle upon Tyne, 12 Jan. 1451). On charter-parties in general see R. Ward, *The World of the Medieval Shipmaster: Law, Business and the Sea, c. 1350–1450*, Woodbridge: Boydell, 2009, pp. 78–93.

2 D. Ellmers, 'Die Seehäfen der Hanse als Dienstleistungszentren eines weitgespannten Transportnetzes', *Hansische Geschichtsblätter* 123, 2005, pp. 109–28.

3 S. Jenks (ed.), *Robert Sturmy's Commercial Expedition to the Mediterranean (1457/8)*, Bristol: Bristol Record Society, 2006, pp. 71–2.

4 Ibid., p. 83.

5 Ibid., pp. 84–5.

6 Ibid., pp. 67–9.

7 J. H. Plumb, 'The commercialization of leisure', in N. McKendrick, J. Brewer and J. H. Plumb (eds), *The Birth of a Consumer Society: The Commercialization of Eighteenth-Century England*, London: Europa Publications 1982, p. 268.

8 The birth of a financial press worth the name was still a generation or so off: L. Neal, 'The rise of a financial press: London and Amsterdam, 1681–1810', *Business History* 30/2, 1988, pp. 163–79.

9 The *Carta mercatoria* (HUB II, no. 31, pp. 14–18) dates from 1 Feb. 1303, but was suspended at the instance of the Lords Ordainers from 1311 to 1322: N. S. B. Gras, *The Early English Customs System*, Cambridge, MA: Harvard University Press, 1918, p. 71.

10 S. Jenks, *England, die Hanse und Preußen*, Cologne: Böhlau, 1992, pp. 15–17.

11 W. M. Ormrod, 'The origins of tunnage and poundage: parliament and the estate of merchants in the 14th century', *Parliamentary History* 28/2, 2009, pp. 209–27, citing previous scholarship.

12 For a map of the sixteen customs districts see S. Jenks, 'Zollamt, Häfen und Außenhandel in England: ca. 1377–1470', *Vierteljahrschrift für Sozial- und Wirtschaftsgeschichte* 75/3, 1988, p. 308.

13 Ibid., pp. 316–28.

14 Farming the weighing stations in a port was another good way of keeping tabs on the competition. This was the reason the London Mercers studiously maintained the farm of the Small Beam in London (for all goods weighing less than 25 lb or 11.4 kg) and the Grocers the Great Beam (for heavier goods) in the fifteenth century: A. F. Sutton, *The Mercery of London: Trade, Goods and People, 1130–1578*, Aldershot: Ashgate, 2005, pp. 30–1, 352, 356, 360; P. Nightingale, *A Medieval Mercantile Community: The Grocers' Company and the Politics and Trade of London 1000–1485*, New Haven: Yale University Press, 1995, pp. 300–1, 496–7, 500.

15 Gras, *Early English Customs*, pp. 122–9; B. Dietz (ed.), *The Port and Trade of Early Elizabethan London: Documents*, London: London Record Society, 1972, p. ix. Gras, *Early English Customs*, pp. 694–706, published the book of rates dating *c.*1507 (noting that this was probably not the first such list), T. S. Willan (ed.), *Tudor Book of Rates*, Manchester: Manchester University Press, 1962, that of 1558. Using the values listed in the current book of rates was made obligatory in 1564 at the latest: TNA PRO, E159/350 Recorda Hilary m 319.

16 J. L. Bolton, *The Medieval English Economy 1150–1500*, London: Dent, 1980, p. 316; S. Jenks, 'England und die kontinentalen Messen im 15. Jahrhundert und die Entstehung der Merchant Adventurers', in P. Johanek and H. Stoob (eds), *Europäische Messen und Märktesysteme im Mittelalter und Neuzeit*, Cologne: Böhlau, 1996, p. 74. E. M. Carus-Wilson, *Medieval Merchant Venturers: Collected Studies*, London: Methuen, 1954, pp. 143–82.

17 Both the Danzig and the Low Countries' corporations of English merchants had been established and confirmed by royal charter on the cusp of the fifteenth century: S. Jenks, 'Die Ordnung für die englische Handelskolonie in Danzig (23. Mai 1405)', in B. Jähnig and P. Letkemann (eds), *Danzig in acht Jahrhunderten*, Münster: Copernicus, 1985, pp. 105–20; Bolton, *Medieval English Economy*, p. 315.

18 A number of companies were incorporated in the hope of commercial success which never materialized and thus died soon after birth. For an overview of the companies founded between 1575 and 1630 see T. K. Rabb, *Enterprise and Empire: Merchant and Gentry Investment in the Expansion of England, 1575–1630*, Cambridge, MA: Harvard University Press, 1967, pp. 147–64.

19 Jenks, *Robert Sturmy's Commercial Expedition*, pp. 32–45.

20 The classic work is J. T. Noonan, *The Scholastic Analysis of Usury*, Cambridge, MA: Harvard University Press, 1957. Useful summaries of the scholastic debates may be found in D. Wood, *Medieval Economic Thought*, Cambridge: Cambridge University Press, 2002, pp. 159–205, and J. W. Baldwin, *The Medieval Theories of the Just Price: Romanists, Canonists and Theologians in the Twelfth and Thirteenth Centuries*, Philadelphia: American Philosophical Society, 1959. On the individual opinions of scholastic authors see O. Langholm, *Economics in the Medieval Schools: Wealth, Exchange, Value, Money and Usury According to the Paris Theological Tradition, 1200–1500*, Leiden: Brill, 1992.

21 E. Friedberg (ed.), *Corpus juris canonici*, vol. 2, *Decretalium collectiones*, Leipzig, 1881, repr. Graz: Akademische Druck- und Verlagsanstalt, 1959, col. 1184.

22 In Florence and Barcelona, the bankers took their name from the table (*tavola*) behind which they sat: F. C. Lane and R. C. Mueller, *Money and Banking in Medieval and Renaissance Venice*, vol. 1, *Coins and Moneys of Account*, Baltimore, MD: Johns Hopkins University Press, 1985, p. 81; R. A. Goldthwaite, *The Economy of Renaissance Florence*, Baltimore, MD: Johns Hopkins University Press, 2009, p. 413; R. de Roover, *The Rise and Decline of the Medici Bank 1397–1494*, Cambridge, MA: Harvard University Press, 1963, repr. New York: W. W. Norton, 1966, p. 15.

23 For instance, one *Bernardus bancherius* accepted £11 on 9 Dec. 1190 from *Maria Sarda* in Genoa at 10 per cent p.a. repayable on eight days' advance notice: R. di Tucci, *Studi sull'economia genovese del secolo decimosecondo: La nave e i contratti marittimi. La banca privata*, Turin, 1933, no. 18, pp. 93–4.

24 Ibid., no. 11, p. 90 (11 Nov. 1190). When *Rubeus bancherius* accepted a deposit of £7 with a fifteen-day advance notice of withdrawal, he agreed, 'If God grants me a profit on this [the £7], then I will give you as much of the profit as seems reasonable'.

25 Ibid., no. 27, p. 101 (1 Mar. 1200). The interest rate was 20 per cent p.a.

26 Ibid., no. 39, p. 108 (11 Feb. 1190). The loan of £4 was granted for a commercial venture to Marseilles. One fourth of the profits was reserved for the creditor, *Enricus bancherius*.

27 R. L. Reynolds, 'A business affair in Genoa in the year 1200: banking, bookkeeping, a broker (?) and a lawsuit', in *Studi di storia e diritto in onore di Enrico Besta*, 4 vols, Milan, 1939, vol. 2, pp. 165–81.

28 P. Spufford, *Money and Its Use in Medieval Europe*, Cambridge: Cambridge University Press, 1988, pp. 257–8; idem, *How Rarely Did Medieval Merchants Use Coin?*, Utrecht: Stichting Nederlandse Penningkabinetten, 2008, p. 21; Lane and Mueller, *Money and Banking*, p. 85.

29 W. von Stromer, 'Funktion und Rechtsnatur der Wechselstuben als Banken', *Bankhistorisches Archiv: Zeitschrift zur Bankengeschichte* 1, 1979, pp. 9–11.

30 The Bruges exchanger-banker Collard de Marke (*c.*1370) was able to arrange book transfers beyond the boundaries of Bruges, to wit in Antwerp, Calais, Valenciennes and Ghent (all within a 100 km radius of Bruges): J. M. Murray, *Bruges, Cradle of Capitalism, 1280–1390*, Cambridge: Cambridge University Press, 2005, pp. 175, 237, 250–7. However, much of this seems to be an outgrowth of his obligation to deliver bullion to the mint at Ghent and supply coin to Bruges exchangers and hostellers, so that one cannot generalize confidently from this one example. Walter van Dijk, an exchanger-banker from Cologne, seems to have had a more than regional horizon (von Stromer, 'Funktion', p. 14), but von Stromer's attempt to elevate Wilhelm Scheuenpflug from Nuremberg into this league does not convince (von Stromer, 'Funktion', pp. 13–14; Wolfgang von Stromer, *Oberdeutsche Hochfinanz 1350–1450*, 3 vols, Wiesbaden: Steiner, 1970, vol. 2, pp. 342–5, 358–9). In Venice (R. C. Mueller, *Banks, Panics and the Public Debt, 1200–1500*, Baltimore, MD: Johns Hopkins, 1997, p. 84) and Florence (Goldthwaite, *Economy*, p. 413) deposit and transfer banks were firmly local in their operations.

31 Spufford, *How Rarely*, p. 21.

32 H. van der Wee, 'European banking in the Middle Ages and early modern times (476–1789)', in H. van der Wee and G. Kurgan-van Hentenryk (eds), *A History of European Banking*, Antwerp: Mercatorfonds, 2000, p. 83.

33 R. S. Lopez, 'The dawn of medieval banking', in *The Dawn of Modern Banking*, New Haven: Yale University Press, 1979, p. 10; Goldthwaite, *Economy*, pp. xv, 64. On Lucca and Venice see Goldthwaite, *Economy*, p. 64. All of the surviving Genoese registers from the twelfth century have been published: R. de Roover, 'New interpretations of the history of banking', *Journal of World History* 2, 1954, repr. in J. Kirshner (ed.), *Business, Banking and Economic Thought in Late Medieval and Early Modern Europe: Selected Studies of Raymond de Roover*, Chicago, IL: Chicago University Press, 1974, p. 200, n. 1.

34 This happened *c.*1200: van der Wee, *History*, p. 85; Lopez, 'Dawn', p. 11.

35 De Roover, *Money*, p. 254; Murray, *Bruges*, p. 169.

36 Mueller, *Banks*, p. 25.
37 Murray, *Bruges*, p. 170, agreeing with de Roover, *Money*, p. 253.
38 Murray, *Bruges*, pp. 97, 210–11.
39 Wolfgang von Stromer, 'Der innovatorische Rückstand der hansischen Wirtschaft', in K. Schulz (ed.), *Beiträge zur Wirtschafts- und Sozialgeschichte des Mittelalters*, Cologne: Böhlau, 1976, pp. 209–10. For the counter-argument, disputing Hanseatic backwardness, see Stuart Jenks, 'Small is beautiful', in J. Wubs-Mrozewicz and S. Jenks (eds), *The Hanse in Medieval and Early Modern Europe*, Leiden: Brill, 2013, pp. 191–214.
40 Murray, *Bruges*, p. 135.
41 Goldthwaite, *Economy*, p. 462.
42 TNA: PRO, CP 40/704 m 311d. The discrepancy between average and median is largely due to small sums owing to servants for wages and livery.
43 Murray, *Bruges*, pp. 134–5.
44 TNA: PRO, CP 40/704 m 311d. Debts of £8 and more were secured *per obligacionem*.
45 Goldthwaite, *Economy*, pp. 463–5.
46 Ibid., p. 462.
47 S. Jenks, 'Das Schreiberbuch des John Thorpe und der hansische Handel in London 1457/59', *Hansische Geschichtsblätter* 101, 1983, pp. 84–5.
48 Murray, *Bruges*, pp. 141–7; Goldthwaite, *Economy*, pp. 419–23.
49 Ibid., p. 420.
50 E. Lattes, *La libertà delle banche a Venezia dal secolo XII al XVII*, Milan, 1869, repr. Bologna: Forzi, 1977, doc. 124, p. 157, cited from Mueller, *Banks*, p. 122.
51 De Roover, *Money*, pp. 174–5; von Stromer, *Hochfinanz*, pp. 350–1; idem, 'Funktion', p. 18.
52 The clearest explanation of how this worked is provided by de Roover, *Money*, pp. 272–6.
53 On the financial services provided by hostellers in Bruges, see Murray, *Bruges*, pp. 210–15. On other services, ibid., pp. 196–205.
54 Ibid., p. 167.
55 R. de Roover, *The Bruges Money Market around 1400*, Brussels: Palais der Academiën, 1968, pp. 54–62.
56 R. van Uytven, *Stadsfinanciën en stadsekonomie te Leuven van de XII*[e] *tot het einde der XVI*[e] *eeuw*, Brussels: Paleis der Academiën, 1961, pp. 462–3, cited from Murray, *Bruges*, p. 147.
57 Mueller, *Banks*, pp. 20, 570, 89. However, we have only an imprecise notion of how the system functioned in Venice, since bankers' account books have not survived there: ibid., p. 81.
58 Good descriptions of the bill of exchange can be found in de Roover, *Bruges Money Market*, pp. 21–30; idem, *Money*, pp. 48–75; idem, *Medici Bank*, pp. 108–41; Spufford, *How Rarely*, pp. 16–20, 23–33; Mueller, *Banks*, pp. 288–355. The classic monograph is R. de Roover, *L'evolution de la lettre de change, XIVe–XVIIIe siècles*, Paris: Armand Colin, 1953.
59 G. Nigro (ed.), *Francesco di Marco Datini, the Man, the Merchant*, Florence: Firenze University Press, 2010.
60 De Roover, *Bruges Money Market*, pp. 111–15, 144–6. Italian merchants described these periods of high and low interest rates as *strettezza* and *larghezza* ('tightness' and 'looseness') respectively.
61 de Roover, *Bruges Money Market*, p. 49.
62 For more detail see ibid., pp. 49–50 (Bruges) and Mueller, *Banks*, pp. 303–14 (Venice).
63 Ibid., p. 306.
64 De Roover, *Bruges Money Market*, pp. 54–7.
65 E. Ashtor, 'Banking instruments between the Muslim East and the Christian West', *Journal of European Economic History* 1/3, 1972, pp. 553–73; A. L. Udovitch, 'Bankers without banks: commerce, banking and society in the Islamic world of the Middle Ages', in *Dawn*, pp. 255–73. In Venetian financial transactions with the Levant all parties were Venetian: Mueller, *Banks*, p. 314.

66 Ibid., p. 306.

67 Italians avoided the German market (by and large) by choice: de Roover, *Medici Bank*, p. 245.

68 Nuremberg: von Stromer, *Hochfinanz*, passim. Augsburg: P. Geffcken, 'Die Welser und ihr Handel 1246–1490', in M. Häberlein and J. Burkhardt (eds), *Die Welser: Neue Forschungen zur Geschichte und Kultur des oberdeutschen Handelshauses*, Berlin: Akademie Verlag, 2002, pp. 27–167.

69 M. North, 'Banking and credit in northern Germany in the fifteenth and sixteenth centuries', in *Banchi pubblici, banchi privati et monti di pietà nell'Europa preindustriale*, Genoa: Società Ligure di Storia Patria, 1991, pp. 816–24.

70 In my view, this is not to be interpreted as a sign of backwardness. Hanseatic firms, lacking a network of correspondents and branch offices, were not structured in such a way as to allow a merchant to draw on surpluses elsewhere, since this crucially depended on being able to debit the taker's account within the firm: Jenks, 'Small is beautiful'', pp. 192–3.

71 F. Irsigler, 'Kölner Kaufleute im 15. Jahrhundert. Die Akten des Prozesses Rosenkrantz/Viehof als Quelle für die kölnische Handelsgeschichte', *Rheinische Vierteljahrsblätter* 36, 1972, pp. 71–88.

72 S. Jenks, 'Kredit im Londoner Außenhandel um die Mitte des 15. Jahrhunderts', in M. North (ed.) *Kredit im spätmittelalterlichen und frühneuzeitlichen Europa*, Cologne: Böhlau, 1991, pp. 88–9; idem, 'Das Schreiberbuch des John Thorpe und der hansische Handel in London 1457/59', *Hansische Geschichtsblätter* 101, 1983, pp. 67–113.

73 Murray, *Bruges*, p. 240; A. Hanham (ed.) *The Cely Letters 1472–1488*, Oxford: Oxford University Press, 1975, pp. xviii–xx. For greater detail see idem, *The Celys and Their World*, Cambridge: Cambridge University Press, 1985.

74 The fundamental paper is R. de Roover, 'What is dry exchange? A contribution to the study of English mercantilism', *Journal of Political Economy* 52/3, 1944, pp. 250–66, repr. Kirshner, *Business*, pp. 183–99. Examples from the Medici papers are published in de Roover, *Medici Bank*, pp. 132–5.

75 The fundamental paper is R. de Roover, 'Cambium ad Venetias: contribution to the history of foreign exchange', in *Studi in onore di Armando Sapori*, pp. 631–48, repr. Kirshner, *Business*, pp. 239–59. See also Mueller, *Banks*, pp. 295–6, 318–20.

76 F. C. Lane, *Andrea Barbarigo, Merchant of Venice, 1418–1449*, Baltimore, MD: Johns Hopkins Press, 1944; Mueller, *Banks*, pp. 327–32.

77 M. Sánchez Sarto, 'Les banques publiques en Espagne jusqu'à 1815, in van Dillen, *History*, p. 3. On other public banks in today's Spain see Riu, 'Banking'. The Genoese authorities cited similar grounds when founding the bank of St George: G. Felloni and G. Laura, *Genova e la storia della finanza: una serie di primati?*, Genoa: Banco di San Giorgio, 2005, p. 37.

78 M. Sánchez Sarto, 'Les banques publiques en Espagne jusqu'à 1815', in van Dillen, *History*, p. 3.

79 H. Sieveking, 'Das Bankwesen in Genua und die Bank von S. Giorgio', in van Dillen, *History*, pp. 15–38; Felloni, *Genova*.

80 Luzzatto, 'Les banques publiques de Venise', in van Dillen, *History*, pp. 39–78.

81 J. G. van Dillen, 'The Bank of Amsterdam', in van Dillen, *History*, pp. 79–123.

82 See the chapter by Carlo Taviani in this volume.

83 The following is based on van der Wee, 'European banking', pp. 134–6.

84 De Roover, *Medici Bank*, pp. 280–3; Goldthwaite, *Economy*, p. 162.

85 Mueller, *Banks*, p. 304.

86 De Roover, *Medici Bank*, p. 280.

87 Ibid., p. 290.

88 Van der Wee, 'European banking', pp. 148–52.

89 Herman van der Wee, 'Monetary, credit and banking systems', in E. E. Rich and C. H. Wilson (eds), *The Cambridge Economic History of Europe,* vol. 5, *The Economic Organization of Early Modern Europe*, Cambridge: Cambridge University Press, 1977, pp. 290–392.

90 Van der Wee, 'European banking', p. 48

91 O. Gelderblom, *Cities of Commerce: The Institutional Foundations of International Trade in the Low Countries, 1250–1650*, Princeton, NJ: Princeton University Press, 2013, pp. 33–7; idem, 'Antwerp merchants in Amsterdam after the Revolt (1578–1630)', in P. Stabel *et al.* (eds), *International Trade in the Low Countries (14th–16th Centuries)*, Leuven: Garant, 2000, pp. 223–41.

92 O. de Smedt, *De Engelse Natie te Antwerpen in de 16e eeuw (1496–1582)*, vol. 2, Antwerp, 1954, p. 561.

93 H. van der Wee, *The Growth of the Antwerp Market and the European Economy*, vol. 2, The Hague: Nijhoff, 1963, pp. 343–4.

94 Van der Wee, 'Monetary, credit and banking systems', p. 326.

95 The assignees could not be entered on the back of the bill because that was used to record part payments.

96 De Roover, *Money*, pp. 339–41.

97 Van der Wee, 'Monetary, credit and banking systems', pp. 326, 331, 325.

98 The following is based on van der Wee, 'Monetary, credit and banking systems', pp. 322–32 and idem, *Growth*, vol. 2, pp. 348–52.

99 Van der Wee, *Growth*, vol. 2, p. 349. de Roover, *L'évolution*, p. 155 quotes *in extenso* an example from 1611.

100 Van der Wee, 'Monetary, credit and banking systems', p. 331.

101 R. S. Lopez, *The Commercial Revolution of the Middle Ages, 950–1350*, Englewood Cliffs, NJ: Prentice-Hall, 1971, p. 72.

4

TRADING SPACES IN EUROPEAN PORT CITIES

The architectural models of bourses, lonjas and exchanges

Donatella Calabi

The commercial cities of early modern Europe contained buildings that were used specifically by merchants engaged in international trade and finance. These sites often played key roles in gathering information, acquiring new forms of knowledge, learning languages and dealing in money, credit and expensive consumer goods; sometimes justice was administered there as well. They were focal points in their respective cities, and contributed to their identity and their political and social life.[1] These venues were thus more than buildings: they were institutions. What I would like to suggest here is that these institutions followed in the steps of the first public banks (from the fifteenth century onwards) and that they corresponded to the increasing importance of the cities and their political roles.[2]

During the sixteenth and seventeenth centuries, these buildings/institutions actually embodied processes of cultural exchange and served as models that were imitated in other countries. They had many different names and building types – *bourse* in France and the Low Countries, bourse and then 'exchange' in England, *lonja* in Spain and *loggia* or *portico del cambio* or *della mercanzia* in Italy – indicating to varying degrees, their origins, different functions and architectural forms.

A relationship between the sixteenth-century exchanges and the banking institutions that preceded them is often suggested, for example, in chronicles, Venetian travelogues or in engravings that allude to Piazza di San Giacomo di Rialto as a possible model of physical organization, even if it was considered less 'magnificent' than other examples.[3] From a functional point of view, even the collective management of the Piedmontese and Lombard banks in Northern Europe in the fourteenth and fifteenth centuries – with investment in large buildings in centrally located areas where a great deal of business was conducted in Bruges, Ghent, Antwerp and other cities – can be considered an important precedent to the exchanges, understood as real money-market creditors independent from the central government.[4]

In reality, the Venetian banks, which were precarious enterprises in a prevalently unstable economic environment, had for centuries retained a simple physical form similar to that of the modest moneychanger's table depicted by Carpaccio at San Giorgio degli Schiavoni (1501),[5] organized around a small porticoed square that was practically an interior court of a single building. The essence of this arrangement was the openness in which transactions were conducted, demonstrated by the presence of readily available money. These tables stood in the central square of the market island of Rialto and in 1587 were replaced on the same site by the public Banco-Giro with an open gallery at the ground level. Around 1600, when secular public banks began to be established in Rome, Milan, Genoa, Rotterdam, Amsterdam, Hamburg, Delft and Nuremberg, the siting of a Venetian bank within its square probably served as a significant model, underscoring a clear separation between large-scale financial transactions and the everyday business of the marketplace. This separation, however, had already been apparent in a less formal manner during the thirteenth and fourteenth centuries in cities such as Paris and London, where moneychangers occupied distinctive sites nearby but set apart from the crowded streets where commodities were sold. The architectural form, with an open gallery or loggia at ground level and rooms above that were sometimes used as courthouses, also had precedents in the market halls of the same period. Venice and Genoa were two of the most important republics on the Italian peninsula. To the extent that structures similar to those found in these two republics can undoubtedly be found in monarchical states, it is clear that these institutions dealt primarily with commercial regulations on the local level.

Some precedents are worth mentioning here. From the point of view of building typology, the fairs at which major international trade had been conducted for centuries – and which provided extraordinary opportunities for merchants to meet, negotiate contracts and exchange money – often relied on precarious structures, such as temporary wooden shops located on empty plots at the borders of settlements. Over time this would change. The merchant bankers whose representatives attended these fairs soon became the city's most dynamic economic class, and its most important affairs were concentrated in their hands. In the fourteenth and fifteenth centuries they founded various associations or companies, the most famous of which was the Medici Bank (1397–1494), though, in parallel, merchants in Florence, Genoa, Bologna, Lucca, Siena and other cities also organized themselves in a similar way. No longer satisfied with precarious shelters, they sought specific, recognizable points of reference.

This is also the context in which the exchanges developed in the fifteenth century within the Hanse, which profited from the circulation of merchandise between the northwestern countries and the Baltic Sea, brokering between the western and eastern regions. The commercial network was based on the harbours, on the role of the most important European cities and on the existence of buildings in London and Antwerp similar to those in Venice.

From the perspective of an institution dealing with agreements between foreign merchants and with the exchange of money that can be identified as a civic monument, it is worth mentioning the loggias in Barcelona (1352–7), Palma de Mallorca (1426–48) and Valencia (1482–1533). In all three cases these buildings had a large Sala de Contratación (contract or trading hall) that, architecturally speaking, was much more dignified than the square at Rialto but offered the same protection from the inclemency for comparable uses.

In Barcelona, there was initially a large, 14-metre high, enclosed space with three aisles and a wooden roof located right at the edge of the sea. To this were added a chapel in 1358 and in 1457–9 the Consolat de Mar (Consulate of the Sea), which gradually, and especially after the late eighteenth-century transformations, led to its use as a magistrate devoted to the commercial control, port inspections and maritime transport.

The Lonja de Palma de Mallorca was built between 1426 and 1448 after a plan designed by Guillem Segrera for the Colegio de la Mercaderia (the local merchants' company). Though its use was slightly different, it was similar from an architectural point of view: one large rectangular room was divided into three aisles separated by thin twisted columns supporting a cross vault. At the extremity of each of the four corners there was an octagonal tower, and on the facade and in the interior a gothic sculptural and decorative apparatus.

The decision to construct the Lonja in Valencia was made in 1469. After the difficulty of acquiring the area had been surmounted, three famous architects, Pedro Cote, Juan Yvarra and Johan Corbera, built it between 1482 and 1498. Here, too, the building had a large Sala de Contratación with three spans divided by five rows of magnificent twisted columns, a vaulted roof and a coloured marble floor. The impressive entrance was crowned by a statue of the Madonna of Rosary and the Aragon coat of arms. There was also a tower with a chapel on the ground floor and a spiral staircase that led to the upper floors, which were used as a debtors' prison. The loggia was connected to an adjacent, three-floor, late-gothic building with important interior decorations, the Consolat de Mar (1283) and finally a garden. Domingo de Urtuega completed the work in 1533. Originally intended primarily for trading oil, it eventually became a sort of maritime centre and finally a Llotja de la Seda (silk exchange).

What is certain is that the commercial cities of early modern Europe gradually constructed specific buildings intended for groups of foreign merchants active in international trade and finance. These were places where cities demonstrated their financial power. They were also trading halls and places where goods were displayed – not for sale, but as prototypes to be acquired through international agreements and sent to far-off destinations. In this respect they are also heirs to the Mediterranean loggias as important public buildings.[6]

These buildings signal, in reference to the form of sale mentioned above as well, a new phase in the evolution of finance that announced the institution of bills of exchange and credit notes as well as a specific, dedicated physical place: a building erected precisely for the purpose of finance and trade.

The name 'bourse' (*borsa, beurse*) has a well-known Flemish origin. Its derivation was recounted by Ludovico Guicciardini in his *Descrittione di tutti i Paesi Bassi*, a work that was first published in 1567 and did much to spread the fame of the Antwerp bourse.[7] In Bruges, the term, curiously enough, did not refer to a particular building, unless it was the hostel of the Van der Buerse family, where many foreign merchants resided and found logistic support for their business. The hostel was located between the *loggias* of the Genoese and the Florentine merchants, and close to those of the German Hanse and various other 'nations'. On the square in front of the hostel, near the crane where ships were unloaded, international merchants met every evening from the late fourteenth century to establish the exchange rates of foreign currencies mentioned in bills of exchange. For the purpose of the trade in goods, especially cloth, a first hall and a belfry had been built in the 1240s. This was extended in the 1280s at the south side of the market square, with an interior court, a large staircase and four big windows looking onto the market square. A new hall was built in 1285–95 at the east side in order to handle small boats loaded with precious goods under the roof of the 90-metre-long building with sixteen arcades and two floors. It was right at the corner of this building and the street facing toward the crane that four official 'banks' of moneychangers were installed since around 1300.[8] This pattern was transferred to buildings and squares with loggias and galleries in Antwerp, Rouen, Toulouse and London, built or designated as places where merchants could assemble out of the way of passing traffic and other impediments.

In Antwerp, the bourse, later the Oude Beurse, was created in 1515 behind the Great Market,[9] and resembled a general market rather than a loggia. It had four arcades (traces of which survive) around a central open court dominated by a tall clock tower with a bell. A chapel in the tower was accessible from the peristyle. An open corridor surrounded the patio where there was a garden (with oranges, fountains, and palms) in front of a tribunal and prisons. Every day the bell rang the hours for mercantile assemblies, even when the rest of the city seemed almost empty. In some respects this ensemble resembled the Rialto square in Venice.

In 1531, the city of Antwerp built a new, more elaborate bourse for the enormous sum of 300,000 golden crowns. The old bourse was not demolished, but this new one, though in *ipso fere civitatis umbelico*, was intended to provide a more sophisticated environment for business and incorporated Italian spatial principles and an architectural melding of Brabantine and Iberian Gothic styles.[10] The main language at the Antwerp bourse was now Italian, and its business was dominated by financial and credit transactions following Italian models.[11] The architect, Dominikus van Wagemakere, kept the old distributive scheme. A spacious square courtyard, to which four large gates gave access, was surrounded by four vaulted loggias with an arcade supported by thirty-six columns in dark stone. On the second floor, over the loggias, there were four galleries lit through dormer windows known as 'le Pant des peinctures' or painters' gallery. Here there were stalls selling rich merchandise and paintings that had, between 1555 and 1582, a far higher turnover than the older galleries in cloisters. Rent from the shops provided an income for maintaining the building. Two towers with clocks dominated the complex.[12]

Protected trading spaces of this type proliferated. In 1556, King Henry IV of France issued an edict, published in 1563, for the institution of a 'common square *(place)* in Rouen for all the merchants', stating that it was to be 'similar to the exchange of Lyon and to that of Toulouse, with the aim that there, as usual, merchants and their factors can meet twice a day and conduct their traffic, enterprises and commerce and bring there all the merchandise of foreign countries'. The merchants could hold their accustomed annual assembly in the gallery (as elsewhere) and elect members to give judgments, organize legal proceedings and register insurance and other contracts. The freedom of mercantile affairs was to be guaranteed by the prohibition on soldiers, sergeants and officials entering the space.

The Antwerp building, which was the site of the most dynamic market in Europe, had a widespread influence, most directly on London and then on Amsterdam.

In London the new bourse, funded by Thomas Gresham, the leading English merchant, financier, and the king's factor active in Antwerp, was a powerful 'modern' statement in the distinctive manner of Antwerp architecture.[13] In fact it had been designed on the model of the Antwerp bourse.[14]

With a spacious open courtyard surrounded by arcaded galleries where merchants could gather in bad weather, shops or stalls on the floor above the galleries, and a tower where a bell sounded the hours of trading, the overall design closely resembled that of Antwerp's New Bourse of 1531 – even the number of thirty-six great columns in the arcades was the same.[15] The architect of the London bourse was an Antwerp mason, Hendryck van Paesschen, who had been involved in the building of Antwerp's new Town Hall (largely completed by 1566) and perhaps in work on Gresham's private house in Antwerp. Stones for the building and slates for the roof were brought to London from Antwerp. The former included the *pierebize* (a dark stone probably resembling 'Tournai marble') used for the thirty-six columns, the 'jasper marble' used for columns at an upper level and for the most important columns at the two entries from the street, and the black-and-white marble slabs used for paving the galleries, all described admiringly by a French visitor in 1578.[16] The English identity of the building was proclaimed by arms and inscriptions and by a scheme for bronze statues of English kings, from William the Conqueror onwards, that would overlook the courtyard.[17] Otherwise, the building's most powerful message was that London belonged to the world of Antwerp, the market that more than any other united the commerce of Europe and provided links to Italy, Spain and new worlds across the Atlantic.[18] Another foreign allusion was soon applied to the name of the vaults beneath the galleries, where cloth was sold. This was 'New Venice', probably an allusion to the Venetian market square.

Grenade, the French visitor mentioned above, provides the fullest account of the first Royal Exchange in 1578. His description of trading practices there probably indicates habits that had been established long before on Lombard Street. He particularly noted the grouping of merchants by 'nations'. The English occupied about half the courtyard. The French had their own place, the Flemings and Walloons owned another one, and the same was true for Italians and Spaniards.

These groupings reflect communities of interest that were both linguistic and commercial. This feature of the geography of the trading area is even more apparent in an eighteenth-century plan of the Exchange identifying the 'walks', as the clusters of merchants were then known.[19] The French, Italians, Spaniards, Portuguese and Jews were close together, as were the Dutch, Armenians and jewellers. Shipbrokers stood in the centre. Merchants trading with the West Indies and with the North American colonies were close together, while dealers in cloth, cloth finishers and the Turkish merchants who supplied English cloth to the Levant formed a coherent line. A journalist of the time, with a rhetorical flourish also employed in describing other exchanges, noted how at the Royal Exchange a trader from India might make a bargain with one from Muscovy and how an Englishman might employ an Egyptian merchant to transmit money to Cairo. Likewise, representations of the traders at the Exchange during the seventeenth and eighteenth centuries include small numbers of individuals who are denoted by their dress as foreign. These include Dutchmen, Muscovites, Poles, Hungarians and Turks in turbans and robes. Some of these images, however, may have been purely symbolic, denoting the presence of trading connections in those territories but not necessarily that of merchants from those nations.[20]

The Exchange was an address at which one could receive mail (see the 'Finance and Information' chapter in this volume). The retail trade in the shops at and around the Royal Exchange came to reflect the specialized interests of those who did business there and, in particular, to meet their demands for new information and knowledge. The area became a focus for bookselling and publication, especially for works on navigation, commerce and travel, for maps, newspapers and for price bulletins.

The Royal Exchange was destroyed by the Great Fire of 1666 and rebuilt in the same area.[21]

There were, as mentioned, important *lonjas* in Spain. Some of them served different purposes, as they had for the most part been established in several cities from the late thirteenth century onwards to accommodate foreign merchants.[22] Here, as elsewhere, the term in due course came to denote a general facility for merchants, and it is sometimes difficult to distinguish its use for trade from that of finance. Seville's late sixteenth-century Casa Lonja de Mercaderes (or Lonja de Comercio) was exceptional for its scale (it covered at least three times the area of the next largest commercial loggias, at Palma and Zaragoza) and for its architectural character. Moreover, it represented the transfer of a Mediterranean institution to a new, Atlantic context, and at the same time seems to have drawn on the exchanges of the northern cities as functional models. Architecturally, however, the principal foreign influence was Italian, and included Palladio's cloister for the Carità in Venice.[23] The Casa Lonja was palatial in form, with basilican elements (used as audience halls and council chambers) arranged around a porticoed courtyard and a fine staircase leading to the upper floor.[24]

The story of its construction is well known. In response to the bishop of Seville's complaint against the merchants of the Consulado de Comercio who had taken over the steps of the cathedral as a site for their business, in 1572 King Philip II authorized the building of a house of commerce on a nearby site occupied by the Casa de Contratación de las Indias.[25] The budget for the project was set at 360,000 ducats, with more than 1,000 ducats allocated to pay the architect. The original scheme by Juan de Herrera, who was at that time engaged in the Escorial's construction, was possibly developed by his executant architects Juan de Minjares and Alonso de Vandelvira. It seems more likely, however, that de Herrera's design was followed and that it consciously reflected the king's interests in its allusion to Netherlandish style.[26] The building is a square of 56 metres, with its courtyard measuring 20 square. In style it is less severe than that of the Escorial, with motifs similar to those in the courtyard of the evangelists in the great convent, but with a less rigid architectural language that arises from the alternate use of stone and brick and the greater use of colour. The exterior walls have windows set between pilasters on two levels. One wall, on the side occupied by the great hall, lacks an entry, but each of the other three contains a principal doorway with two lesser doors beside it, making a total of nine entries leading into the courtyard and the galleries surrounding it.[27] This monumental, autonomous building stands isolated in the centre of the city, an effect increased by the steps and the pillars and chains that surround it. The steps and chains may have been intended to recall Las Gradas, where the merchants had earlier traded at the entrance of the cathedral.[28] To finance this project the consulate of commerce was authorized to impose a special tax on all merchandise entering and leaving Seville by land or sea, a source of revenue so prolific as to permit magnificence in construction, materials and workmanship of high quality. Stone came from carefully selected quarries in the region, but bricks were brought from Málaga, since those available in Seville were not good enough; for the doors and windows mahogany was shipped across the Atlantic from Havana. The constructors of the building were proud of the quality of the chosen material even if it was very expensive, being imported from afar. More than seventy skilled workers were continuously active on the site; the architects and surveyors had to dedicate their time exclusively to the project, and the use of slave labour was prohibited. Work began in 1584 and was officially completed in 1598, although as late as 1606 it was still proving difficult to persuade the merchants of Seville to transfer their business to the Lonja, away from accustomed places of trade.[29]

The Casa Lonja housed administrative and juridical as well as commercial functions. It became the seat of both the Consulado de Cargadores de las Indias and of the Casa de Contratación, bodies that governed all trade with the Americas, regulating contracts, shipping and migration, and exercising commercial jurisdiction. Much of the business at the Lonja concerned dealing in commodities. Brokers (*corredores*) had bases there and parts of the building were used for storing merchandise. Nevertheless, the core of its activity lay in commodity transactions, finance, commercial credit, money exchange and maritime insurance.[30] In 1717, with the transfer of the trade monopoly with the New World to Cadiz, the Casa Lonja lost its great commercial function, but the transformation of the building into the Archivo

General de Indias during the 1780s gave it a new role as a symbol of commercial exchange and of knowledge of distant worlds.[31]

In Amsterdam, which by 1600 was taking on many of the commercial functions of Antwerp as a consequence of the submission of the revolt in the southern Netherlands, this kind of activity became very important. In 1607 the Amsterdam authorities decided to establish a new building for mercantile transactions, to be placed on the southern side of the Dam.[32] They chose the simpler of the two schemes presented by the city architect Hendrik de Keyser. The new building accommodated its first assembly of merchants in August 1611 and was solemnly inaugurated in 1613, yet its monumental courtyard soon became too small to contain the multitude of curious visitors. The scheme followed that of the Antwerp exchange; the architect had also visited the recently completed exchange in London, which was based on the Antwerp model. The open rectangular courtyard was surrounded by a portico with twenty-three arcades supported by forty-five granite columns with Doric capitals. In the two long sides of the exterior were vaults to accommodate shops at ground level.[33] On the short sides, central arcades gave access to the court, with a bridge crossing over the water. Above one of them was a tower with a carillon clock to regulate trading activity. Each of the columns in the interior was associated with trade in a different commodity. More than 400 commodity prices were listed in the weekly price bulletins which Amsterdam had regularly sent to other places in Europe since 1585. The floor over the portico housed luxury shops and the markets dealing in money and stock. Rules governed the times of opening, prohibited access to beggars and those carrying arms, and forbade lamentation, outrages and children's games. From its origin the bourse was regarded as one of the city's most important monuments; it was mentioned by visitors and represented by painters and engravers. Gottfried Hegenitius described it in 1630. Francesco Belli noted it in 1632, as did the Venetian ambassador Antonio Donà in 1638.[34] William Brereton thought it less richly decorated with paintings and frames than the London Exchange.[35] John Evelyn maintained in 1641 that aspects of London's exchange were more splendid, but admitted that the ability of large boats to float alongside Amsterdam's building made the latter superior. Claude Joly in 1646 perceived it as similar to the *grande salle* of the Palais de Paris, while Filips van Zesen described it as 'a place of happiness, where you can hear sweet melodies'.[36] The Dutchman Jeremias de Decker stated that 'here, from the Amstel rises to the sky a living room which at mid-day is full of people of various kind, a public garden where Moors make commerce with Norwegians; a temple where Jews, Turks and Christians are one near to the other; where all languages are taught; a fair rich with every product; a bourse which spurs on the whole universe'.[37] The Comte de Montesquieu was overwhelmed and frightened by the multitude, which almost prevented him from walking. By 1668, the building was perceived as too small for its business and an extension was added.[38]

Exchanges in other cities (Rouen, Toulouse, Lille and Copenhagen) functioned in much the same way, and the rules and practices of their operation were often very similar. Architectural forms were also similar, and wherever exchanges were closely linked by trading connections, rivalry or aspiration – as with Antwerp, London and Amsterdam – the precise reproduction of built forms became an important episode of cultural transfer in itself. Recognizability, as an asset and a signal, became an element of a 'common' language. Collectively, the exchanges formed a place where the freedom of the mercantile affairs was to be guaranteed by the prohibition on 'soldiers, sergeants and officials' entering the space.[39] They were also home to a system of the communication of information, not unlike the nodes in a modern telecommunications network. To operate effectively that system had to be firmly rooted in place and in established patterns of trading and information flows, as the case of the London exchange demonstrates perhaps better than any other.

An incident from 1632 strikingly demonstrates those flows in action within the Roman Catholic world. The merchants of the Antwerp exchange tried to persuade their counterparts from the financial markets of Paris and Lyon to be suspicious of such a 'heretical usurper as the king of Sweden'. They were astonished by the fact that in such a pious and religious country as France no attention was being paid to the disorders occurring across Europe. In spite of the king of Sweden's declaration that in the cities he had seized from the emperor the free exercise of the Roman Catholic religion was permitted and clergy not to be harmed, facts spoke otherwise:

> We, who know the wisdom of the merchants, who have experience of the world . . . who speak our dialect and follow common sense and natural prudence . . . desire general peace for everybody, useful to your place as to our exchange; finally we desire what all the good Christians have to desire.
>
> For this reason, in the galleries of our Exchange a discourse has been read aloud, in a way that all the merchants and bankers who understand a little French could comment the content and the day after they came with some letters received from Cologne, Mainz, Trier, Worms and other German cities about recent events . . .
>
> Events which besides happened also in Copenhagen, when the governor had to retire in Wurzburg.[40]

It was a way to claim the existence of a kind of 'Republic of Merchants' that overlapped the usual system of government. And, even if not always consciously, it resembled the idea of 'Res Publica' – understood as public affairs – that Leonardo Bruni had proposed in the early fifteenth century (1403–4) in his *Laudatio Florentinae Urbis*.[41]

In conclusion, these buildings – destined primarily for the dealing in bills of exchange and other credit notes – played an important role in a network of relationships and the circulation of ideas among the different European countries in the early modern period. They facilitated the formal as well as informal transfer of knowledge on commerce, on everyday life, on the most exotic uses, on the consumption of luxury goods and on the most innovative architectural and artistic styles of the Renaissance. They shared a similar form, which in itself was an example of cultural exchange between cities that competed with each other and were characterized by a common ambition for a similar system of government: one largely independent from sovereign rule, as was the case in Antwerp, London and, particularly, in Amsterdam.

Notes

1 D. Calabi, *The Market and the City*, London: Ashgate, 2004, pp. 172–5.
2 V. Lampérez y Romea, *Arquitectura civil española de los siglos I al XVIII*, 2 vols, Madrid: Editorial 'Saturnino Collegja', 1922, vol. 2, pp. 206–8.
3 For example: L. Grenade, *Les singularitez de Londres: cité capitale du Royaume d'Angleterre*, Rome, Vatican Library, 1578, Reg. Lat. 672, f. 51–6 w; or John Evelyn who was in Venice in June 1645, quoted by A. Saunders, *The Royal Exchange*, London: Guardian Royal Exchange, 1991, pp. 14, 17; see also Auguste Christian Fleischmann's engraving showing the dealers at the exchanges in Venice, Nuremberg, Leipzig, Amsterdam and Hamburg, 1730.
4 F. Cannelloni, 'Casane e casenieri: attività e proprietà dei Lombardi nei Paesi Bassi (secoli XIV e XV)', *Reti Medievali* 15/1, 2014, pp. 3–35, and its rich, updated bibliography.
5 R. C. Mueller and F. C. Lane, *The Venetian Money Market: Banks, Panics and the Public Debt, 1200–1500*, Baltimore, MD: Johns Hopkins University Press, 1997, p. 426.
6 As described by the German traveller Paul Hantzner when he visited London in 1598 and by others who celebrated the Royal Exchange as one of the city's most important 'public ornaments': quoted in Saunders, *Royal Exchange*, p. 14.
7 L. Guicciardini, *Descrittione di tutti i Paesi Bassi, altrimenti detti Germania Inferiore*, Antwerp: Guglielmo Silvio, 1567, p. 67.
8 J. M. Murray, *Bruges, Cradle of Capitalism, 1280–1390,* Cambridge: Cambridge University Press, 2005, pp. 148–77, 186–215.
9 F. H. Mertens and K. L. Torfs, *Geschiedenis van Antwerpen*, 8 vols, Antwerp: J. P. van Dieren, 1846, vol. 3, p. 212; L. de Barsée, 'De bouwkunst te Antwerpen in de XVIe eeuw', in Genootschap voor Antwerpse Geschiedenis, *Antwerpen in de XVIe eeuw*, Antwerp: Mercurius, 1975, pp. 361–90, esp. pp. 369–72; I am grateful to Bruno Blondé for the information about this old Bourse.
10 L. Guicciardini, *Descrittione,* p. 67; about the *panden* or painters' galleries in Antwerp and the market for paintings: F. Vermeylen, *Painting in the Market: Commercialization of Art in Antwerp's Golden Age*, Turnhout: Brepols, 2003, pp. 51–8.
11 P. Subacchi, 'Italians in Antwerp in the second half of the sixteenth century', in H. Soly and A. K. L. Thijs (eds), *Minderheden in Westeuropese steden (16de–20ste eeuw)*, Brussels: Istituto Storico Belga di Roma, 1995, pp. 73–90.
12 Guicciardini, *Descrittione*, pp. 67, 117.
13 See the letter (before 1564) sent to Sir Thomas by Richard Cough, his factor in Antwerp: he claims that, in London, it is necessary to walk under the rain to have a discussion as normal pedestrians rather than as merchants, while in this country those who have to meet can do so in a place specific for this purpose, quoted in Saunders, *Royal Exchange*, p. 7.
14 It is the plan of the ground floor, which Gresham presumably sent to Lord Boughley, his protector, c/o the Queen (Hatfield House archive).
15 *Commentari di Ludovico Guicciardini delle cose più memorabilia seguite in Europa specialmente in questio Paesi Bassi dalla pace di Cambrai del MDXXIX insino a tutto l'anno MDLX*, Venice: Nicolò Bevilacqua, 1565, pp. 94–5.
16 L. Grenade, quoted in n. 3 of this chapter.
17 Saunders, *Royal Exchange*, pp. 9–10.

18 D. Keene, 'The setting of the Royal Exchange: continuity and change in the financial district of the city of London, 1300–1871', in A. Saunders (ed.), *The Royal Exchange*, London: London Topographical Society, 1997, pp. 253–71.
19 The exterior of the building and the interior courtyard were represented by F. Hogenberg in 1569 and republished by R. Wilkinson in 1810.
20 Saunders, *Royal Exchange*, pp. 48–9, 206–8; figs. 17, 72, 74.
21 Samuel Pepys mentions it several times on 16 March 1660 and again on 28 August 1665 and less than two weeks later on 7 September 1666, see Saunders, *Royal Exchange*, pp. 17–18; a very detailed analysis of the different designs and areas involved can be found in: D. Keene, 'The Royal Exchange', in D. Keene and I. W. Archer (eds), *The Singularities of London, 1578: Les Singularitez des Londres, noble, faeuse Cité, capital du Royaume d Angleterre: ses antiquitez et premiers fondateurs*, London: London Topographical Society, 2014, pp. 106–20.
22 O. R. Constable, *Housing the Stranger in the Mediterranean World: Lodging, Trade and Travel in the Late Antiquity and in the Middle Ages,* Cambridge: Cambridge University Press 2003, pp. 185-6.
23 P. González García (ed.), *Archivo General de Indias*, Madrid: Ministerio de Cultura, Dirección General del Libro, Archivos y Bibliotecas, 1995, which contains a historical account plus photographs, plans and other illustrations of the establishment; see pp. 53–71 for details of the construction.
24 V. Lampérez y Romea, *Arquitectura civil española de los siglos I al XVIII,* 2 vols, Madrid: Editorial 'Saturnino Calleja', 1922, vol. 2, pp. 234–7, and see pp. 208–28 for other *lonjas.*
25 J. Gestoso y Perez, *Sevilla monumental y artistica*, 3 vols, Seville: Excmo. Ayuntamiento de Sevilla, 1889–92, vol. 3, pp. 216–29; S. Izquierdo Alvarez, 'Felipe II y el urbanismo moderno', *Anales de Geografia de la Universidad Complutense* 13, 1993, pp. 81–109.
26 C. Wilkinson-Zerner, *Juan de Herrera: Architect to Philip II of Spain*, New Haven and London: Yale University Press, 1993, pp. 81–3 and n. 50. T. Falcón Márquez, *El Sagrario de la Catedral Sevilla*, Seville: Excma. Diputación Provincial, 1977, p. 42 and n. 26.
27 Lampérez y Romea, *Arquitectura*, vol. 2, pp. 234–7.
28 A. Morgado, *Historia de Sevilla, en la qual se contienen sus antiguidades, grandezas . . . hasta nuestros tiempos*, Seville: Andrea Pescioni & Juan de Leon, 1587, par. II.
29 D. Sánchez-Meza, 'El arte', in [A. Prieto (ed.),] *Historia de Andalucía*, vol. 5, *La cultura andaluza*, Madrid: Cuspa, 1981; Barcelona: Planeta, 1981, pp. 553–615, esp. pp. 585–6; L. Garcia Fuentes, 'Un ejemplo de la industria de la construccion en Sevilla en los s. 16 y 17: La Casa Lonja', in *Andalucía y America en el siglo XVII*, Seville : Escuela de estudios hispano-americano, 1985, vol. 1, pp. 271–324; V. Pérez Escolano, 'Ciudad y espacios de comercio en la España del siglo XVI: una aproximación al hilo de la Lonja de Mercaderes de Sevilla', and A. Marín Fidalgo, 'La Lonja de los Mercaderes: Intervención de las autoridades del Alcázar sevillano en la génesis de su construcción', both in M. Á. Aramburu-Zabala and J. Gómez Martínez (eds), *Juan de Herrera y su influencia: Actas del simposio, Camargo, 14–17 julio 1992*, Santander : Fundación Obra Pía Juan de Herrera, 1993, pp. 287–96 and 297–310, respectively; González García (ed.) *Archivo General de Indias*, pp. 56–8.
30 C. H. Haring, *Comercio y navegacion entre España y las Indias*, Mexico: Fondo de cultura economica, 1979, tr. from *Trade and Navigation between Spain and the Indies in the Time of the Hapsburgs*, Cambridge, MA: Harvard University Press, 1918.
31 A.-M. Bernal, *Credito y financiacion en la carrera de Indias 1492–1825*, Seville: Fundacion El monte, 1991.
32 H. Diederiks, 'Bankers, bank, and other financial institutions in the urban landscape of Amsterdam, late 16th–20th centuries', in H. Diederiks and D. Reeder (eds), *Cities of Finance*, Amsterdam: Royal Netherlands Academy of Arts and Sciences, 1991, pp. 251–64.
33 P. Scheltema, *De Beurs van Amsterdam,* Amsterdam: G. Portielje 1846.

34 G. Hegenitius, *Gottfried Hegenitii Itinerarium frisio-hollandicum et Abr. Ortellii Itinerarium gallo-brabanticum*, Leiden: Officina Elzeviriana 1630; F. Belli, *Osservazioni nel viaggio di D. Franc. Belli fatto col signor Luigi Giorgi ambasciatore di Venetia a gli stati di Olanda e di la Francia*, Venice: G. P. Pinelli, 1632; P. J. Blok (ed.), *Relazioni veneziane* (*Venetianske berichten over de Vereenigde Nederlanden van 1600–1795*), The Hague: M. Nijhoff, 1909, p. 111.

35 E. Hawkins (ed.), *Travels in Holland, the United Provinces, England, Scotland and Ireland, MDCXXXIV–MDCXXXV by Sir William Brereton, bart*, London: Chatham Society 1, 1844, p. 55; E. S. Beer (ed.), *The Diary of John Evelyn*, 6 vols, Oxford, Clarendon Press, 1955, vol. 2, pp. 46, 98, 433–4.

36 C. Joly, *Voyage ou description de toutes les villes de Munster en Westphalie, Hollande, Osnabruch, Cologne et autres lieux des Pais-Bas*, Paris: F. Clozier, J. De la Tourette & P. Aubouyn, 1672, pp. 106–7; L. J. Wagenaar, 'Les mécanismes de la prosperité', in H. Mechoulan (ed.), *Amsterdam XVII siècle. Marchands et philosophes: Les bénéfices de la tolérance*, Paris: Editions Autrement, 1993, p. 73.

37 Wagenaar, *Les mécanismes*, pp. 74–5.

38 C. L. de Secondat, Baron de Montesquieu, *Voyages de Montesquieu, publiés par le baron Albert de Montesquieu*, 2 vols, Bordeaux: Société des Bibliophiles de Guyenne 1894–6, vol. 1, p. 230.

39 BNF, Acte Royal 1557-03-00, *Edict du Roy sur la création et l'établissement en la ville de Rouen d'une place commune pour les marchands à la similitude et semblance du change de Lyon et bourse de Toulouse*, Rouen, 20 July 1563.

40 BNF, MP 1200, *Advis des Marchands de la Bourse d'Anvers à ceux de la place de Paris et du Change de Lyon*, 1632.

41 G. Kirner, *Della 'Laudatio Florentinae Urbis' di Leonardo Bruni: Notizie*, Livorno: Giusti, 1889, pp. 29–32; L. Bruni, *Laudatio fiorentinae urbis* (1403–1404), in *Dialogi ad Petrum Histrum (1370–1444)*, in E. Garin (ed.), *Prosatori Latini del Quattrocento*, Milan and Naples, 1952, p. 70.

5

LEX MARITIMA?

Local, regional and universal maritime law in the Middle Ages

Albrecht Cordes

Latin has lately seen a surprising comeback as a legal language, at least when it comes to christening new fields of international law. There is now talk of Lex Digitalis, Lex Petrolea, Lex Sportiva and the like, and, as mother of them all, a 'new' Lex Mercatoria[1] – new because supposedly there already existed a Lex Mercatoria in the sense of a universal, autonomous merchant law in the Middle Ages.[2] While the tags of the smaller of these new fields – Latin or not – do not seriously try to disguise their recent origin, the labelling of the 'Lex Mercatoria' does indeed serve to make those medieval roots more plausible. The same seems to be true for another of Lex Mercatoria's daughters, the so-called Lex Maritima.[3] This is the subject to be treated here.

This chapter will explain why I am just as sceptical about the concept of a universal medieval maritime law created by autonomous merchants and composed of their customary rules as I am about the same concept in regard to the broader legal field, the Lex Mercatoria. This is not a statement in regard to the value of concepts like Lex Mercatoria and Lex Maritima as part of the law of the ongoing globalization. But when it comes to history, it appears that in commercial law – in accordance with the evolution of trade techniques – local and regional legal concepts form the oldest layer, and generalization through reception, legal transfer, assimilation and harmonization was a secondary phenomenon.

The present study shall proceed in three steps. First it will explain the role maritime law plays in my general plan for exploring the history of trade law, define 'maritime law' and list its main sources, and will briefly present the state of research. In the second part a closer look will be taken at three prominent subdivisions of pre-modern maritime law, namely jettison and general average, bottomry and loan-financed sea trade, and finally shipwreck law and salvage. These three subjects are more than mere case studies because they have stood at the centre of attention ever since the establishment of commercial law and its subdivision 'maritime law' as an academic subject in the first half of the nineteenth century. The result is a complicated picture in which norms with various ranges of application become visible – some local, some regional and some so widespread that they might indeed be called universal in a medieval sense. In concluding, I will propose a general development model of geographic expansion, which can perhaps be described as 'from local to global'. Universal legal orders in the sense of Lex Mercatoria, Lex Maritima, etc. may or may not bear potential for future world law. But they cannot be traced back to the origins of trade law and its earliest sources.

Preconditions for exploring pre-modern maritime law

Lex Maritima as key witness for the Lex Mercatoria

A comparison of the company law in Hanseatic and northern Italian hubs of maritime trade[4] first led me to have serious doubts about the existence of a medieval 'Lex Mercatoria' in the sense that Harold Berman and others wanted to give it.[5] As it turns out, Lex Mercatoria is not derived from any 'national' legislator, nor is it a body of law in the sense of a coherent system of rules. Its most fundamental concepts and legal institutions do not originate in the High Middle Ages, but are of younger age.[6] There was no autonomous universal body of customary mercantile law, let alone one of written codes or statutes. No medieval collection of trade customs that were in general use has been preserved.

The two parts of the *ius commune,* canon law and imperial law, don't fill the gap. Canon law does claim to be universal because it rules the Catholic (*καθολικός*, all-embracing) Church. It does contain some rules concerning commercial law, namely against usury[7] and in favour of unchartered contracts (*pacta nuda*);[8] the popes as active legislators against shipwreck law will receive our attention shortly. Similarly, imperial law (which could substantially be Roman civil law or 'new' medieval rules set by the imperial court) was promulgated with universal intentions – at least theoretically.[9] But neither canon nor imperial law was created by autonomous merchants, and therefore neither was part of a Lex Mercatoria in the stated sense.

The absence of codes or other collections of universal, customary trade law seems to leave us with a stalemate in regard to the existence of such a set of norms. But it is possible to go one step beyond the *non liquet* that seems to impose itself due to the silence of the sources. The distinguishing traits of the character of non-learned medieval law (before and beyond the realms of the *ius commune* practised by university-trained jurists since the foundation of the Law Faculty at Bologna around 1100) make it virtually impossible that such a legal order could have existed at all. First, oral law is limited in space and time because it must rely on the range and the memory of the involved legal experts, be it lay judges, spokespersons or jurymen. A village, town or minor principality may be small enough to be governed by a set of rules that are only transferred orally, but nothing bigger.

Secondly, non-learned law is mainly procedural law. Substantive law is a secondary phenomenon, and some medievalists even doubt that there existed any substantive law before Bologna.[10] Procedural law, however, is always the law of one court or one court system. As soon as you cross a border into the jurisdiction of another court you will encounter another set of rules used by this court. Early medieval rulers, like Charlemagne in his Frankish kingdom or Henry II in England, worked hard and relatively successfully to impose similar rules for the courts within their realms. But a caravan of merchants from Venice to Frankfurt am Main or from Cologne to Novgorod would have crossed many borders on its way, and each different country would have meant a different set of rules for litigation. And even if there had been a body of trade law rules that all courts would have wanted to apply, legal history shows time and again that different courts employed identical rules differently. Therefore, the outcome would have been different from jurisdiction to jurisdiction anyway.

Finally, a universal Lex Mercatoria certainly did not exist under this name. Historical sources only provide a clear picture of a Lex Mercatoria in a narrower but more precise sense. Lex Mercatoria was the Latin name of the merchant law that was part of the English common law from the late thirteenth century onwards.[11]

Based on this historical evidence, I began to reconstruct medieval mercantile law without the constricting preconditions of a universal Lex Mercatoria. This research might be labelled with the motto 'diversity instead of unity', and attempts to map medieval commercial law from scratch.[12] This new map must take four parameters into account: space (active commercial towns or regions), time (periods of intensive economic activity), sources (statutes, privileges, contract charters, court records, etc.) and relevant legal matters (general average, bottomry or shipwreck law, to name just the three areas of maritime law that will be discussed here). These four parameters are necessary to distinguish what shall be called the 'hot spots' in the history of commercial law. Such hot spots were, to list a few obvious examples, Venice after the First Crusade around 1100, Bruges as turntable of European trade around 1250, Augsburg around 1500 when the Fugger family was at its apex or Antwerp before 1585 when the Spaniards drove the economic elite out of the city. Those 'hot spots' are the most likely places and moments of creativity in regard to new concepts of commercial law.

In order to draw this map 'beyond the Lex Mercatoria doctrine', one could describe the individual commercial spaces, as most other articles in this volume do; a comparison of the results should enable us to start painting thed map. Or one could take the legal matters as a guideline, focusing on one important issue at a time, and compare more than one city from this particular perspective, thus attempting to establish the local and regional similarities and differences. The latter method is the task undertaken in this study, which starts with maritime law as an especially likely candidate for universal rules. An investigation of other parts of the law of transportation, namely on rivers and on solid ground, must follow at a later stage.

Sources and topics of early maritime law

The most important laws and statutes of maritime law are well known, and new ones would come as a big surprise.[13] The oldest preserved text is book 14, chapter 2, of Emperor Justinian's *Digest* (529/534), containing the only preserved parts of the Rhodian Sea law whose age is under debate. Next came the more complete Byzantine sea laws of the eighth/ninth centuries. Simultaneously, Arab sea law started to leave important traces before the end of the first millennium. The main activity then moved to the west, to the Italian town laws – Amalfi and Pisa from the twelfth, Venice and Genoa from the thirteenth century – and then to the Catalan Llibre del Consolat de Mar, which was compiled around 1350 but contains older elements, and was the most important collection of medieval maritime law in the Mediterranean and on the Atlantic coast. The Scandinavian sources took hold in the thirteenth century or shortly before and contain remarkable cooperative elements. In Western and Central Europe the Rôles d'Oléron (the oldest preserved manuscript is from 1311) became an important model that travelled both west to northern Spain and north to England, Scotland, Scandinavia and then the Baltic Sea.

Court records and documents from daily trade routines, such as contract charters, notarial acts, town books, last wills, etc. play a crucial role for all research on maritime law, including the question of whether there existed a supra-regional trade routine for seafaring. Nevertheless, they are neglected here, not only in order to concentrate the focus by limiting the material, but for a methodological reason. By definition, such sources concentrate on a specific individual business transaction while the scope of this chapter is on similarities across borders. If the sea laws differ, it is not to be expected that the daily business routine would be similar. If it turns out that sea laws converge, a second step could be to examine if identical rules lead to similarities in business practice. This, however, would constitute a research project in its own right. The present chapter will be limited to the statutes.

The provisions in the statutes in question are not yet generalized and detached from individual cases in the way the articles of today's law codes are. They were penned in an era before the theory of modern general legislation was developed. Instead, they consist of collections of judgements and other decisions of single disputed questions. There was not yet a clear distinction between general laws and individual judgements. The most obvious evidence for this fact is the name the famous Rôles d'Oléron gave to themselves: *Jugements de la mer* – each of the twenty-four articles of the original text ends with the words 'Et cest le jugement en ceo cas'.[14] This observation is important because it is the reason we can't hope for a comprehensive answer to our question about the universality of maritime law. The best we can do is to follow these specific and casuistic rules on their journey through the medieval maritime codes.

Maritime law is understood here in a relatively narrow sense. This chapter will examine only questions of maritime trade law (*Seehandelsrecht*), and will omit public international law and law of war and peace in the Grotian sense (*De Iure Belli ac Pacis*, 1625). It will not deal with pirates or privateers, and will also place ship law, i.e. the set of rules governing life and conflicts on board as well as the labour law of the seamen, aside.[15] This is a not a recent distinction but was already made in the decisive Hanseatic codification of 1614: *Der ehrbaren Hanse-Städte Schiffs-Ordnung und See-Recht*. That doesn't mean that the same question asked here couldn't be examined with similar interest in ship law. But it is useful to follow the clear boundaries between the two related fields and not over-burden the current task.

The current state of research

The title of this chapter is borrowed from a juristic dissertation from Bremen (2012).[16] The author, Andreas Maurer, argues rather convincingly that there is a legal order of international maritime law in the process of emerging beyond national borders, an order he christens 'Lex Maritima'. This is a point that fits well into the influential school of Günther Teubner and its concept of post-state law. In a short introduction, Maurer uses medieval history in a more or less ornamental way in order to strengthen his argument.[17] Maurer does so without reference to the rich continental tradition of writings on maritime legal history. Are the writings of Levin Goldschmidt and his successors obsolete and forgotten? A short overview of the historiography of maritime law seems to be in order.

Until the middle of the nineteenth century, maritime law hardly existed as an academic subject. The publications were barely more than collections of the relevant sources mainly for practical reasons, written and compiled for active merchants.[18] This first period culminates with the comprehensive seven-volume collection by Pardessus (1828–45). Together with its younger British counterpart, *Twiss' Black Book of the Admiralty* (1871–6), this compilation remains unsurpassed today, though a number of the sources they include are now available in better editions.

The truly scientific treatment of maritime law begins with the doyen of the history of commercial law, Levin Goldschmidt. His monumental but unfinished *Universalgeschichte des Handelsrechts*[19] devoted an important chapter to the history of maritime law, and Goldschmidt's most important contribution to commercial law, comparatively as well as historically, was the *Zeitschrift für das gesammte Handelsrecht* (*ZHR*), which he founded in 1858, and which today is one of the oldest active juridical periodicals worldwide. He edited it for decades, and it was so closely connected with his name that it was simply known as 'Goldschmidts Zeitschrift'. The rich collection of articles on maritime law are listed and summarized in Landwehr's survey over the history of the *ZHR*.[20]

There have been few general approaches to the subject of medieval maritime law. The best ones are entries in a number of dictionaries;[21] one by Götz Landwehr stands out in particular, despite being twenty-five years old.[22] Apart from that, scholars have focused either on a limited nation, region or codification, typically praising this single subject above everything else. There is, in rough chronological order, a rich literature in regard to the Lex Rhodia de Iactu, the Islamic Sea Law, the maritime codes of the Italian cities, the Catalan Llibre del Consolat de Mar, the Rôles d'Oléron from western France, and the British, Nordic and Hanseatic sea law. But all of this is obviously not an approach by which comparative points can be made. Therefore these books and articles, as interesting as they are in their own right, can't attribute contribute much to the present argument. The abundant literature on the Rôles d'Oléron, for example, has sometimes presented its subject as proof of international mercantile law, although it regulated the wine and salt trade from the English province of Aquitaine to England, Scotland and Flanders, and should therefore be primarily regarded as English law. This does not exclude the possibility that some of the Oléron rules, e.g. the cutting of the table cloth as a symbol of the exclusion of one member of the ship crew from the community, were influenced by predecessors. But this observation is trivial; nearly all statutes and codifications profit from models and patterns from previous regulations enacted elsewhere. That does not make the new set of rules universal.[23] But a more detailed study of the Rôles d'Oléron as an example of the difficulties in distinguishing national and international law-setting (whether it should be called legislation remains to be seen) in the thirteenth and fourteenth centuries shall be published at a later occasion.

In other instances, scholars have focused on one of the great subjects of maritime law. There are the excellent monographs on sea insurance by Karin Nehlsen-von Stryk (1986) and on shipwreck law by Vilho Niitema (1955), and without doubt, the single-most discussed problem is the question of jettison, mainly because it received attention in the Corpus Iuris Civilis and in the Talmud as well.[24] While a number of these studies are of great quality and can serve as safe stepping-stones for the general research project, in and of themselves they are not sufficient to reach conclusions in regard to the general character of maritime law.

There have been some attempts to establish historical *Rechtskreise* of maritime law. *Rechtskreis* seems to be an originally German concept established by legal comparatists to group 'circles of law', 'families of law', with a common origin or other significant similarities, for example, all countries influenced by the French Code Civil.[25] While geography obviously suggests a two-way partition between the Mediterranean and Atlantic/northern sea law, Levin Goldschmidt (1888) proposed a three-way distinction between the South, the West, and the North. His label for the western sea law as 'frankish' did not stick, but the geographical divide between western and northern sea law is still very much in debate. It has recently been fuelled by Edda Frankot (2012),[26] who placed Scottish Aberdeen in a northwestern context, thus dividing it from the four other harbours she examined. These four were Hanse towns – the three Baltic harbours of Lübeck, Danzig and Reval, and Kampen on the mouth of the Ijssel river into the Zuiderzee. If one accepts this divide through the North Sea – it fits well with the geographic role of the Netherlands as hinge between East and West – and further assumes that there is a fundamental distinction between northern, i.e. Scandinavian, and Hanseatic maritime law, this would lead to a discrimination between northwestern sea law including France and Great Britain, northern sea law from Scandinavia and Hanseatic sea law.

But all of this is only of limited interest for the present argument. The mere fact that most historians and legal historians have made either this or a similar distinction shows that in their eyes the ships sailing the northern and western seas only look similar when seen from a distance. As soon as the vessels – as well as the norms ruling their voyages – are taken under closer scrutiny things become more complicated, and numerous differences strike the eye.

Central legal institutions of maritime law

It should be noted that I do not intend to treat any of the following institutions of maritime law in a comprehensive way. That would be close to impossible. For decades, in some cases centuries, countless scholars have been working on virtually every detail of these subjects. For example, the ten *leges* of the Lex Rhodia de iactu in book 14, chapter 2, of Emperor Justinian's *Digest* have been discussed since the foundation of the University of Bologna around the year 1100.[27] The Rôles d'Oléron from the thirteenth century have attracted only slightly less scholarly attention.[28] My focus is limited to the question of local/regional versus universal dissemination of these rules in space.

A first, telling case study has been presented on a previous occasion:[29] the question whether freight is due in the case of a voyage interrupted by *force majeure*. While there was and is consensus that no freight has to be paid for the merchandise lost in the accident, the quota due for the salvaged goods has been determined differently in different times and places. In 1759, the recently appointed Chief Justice of the King's Bench, Lord Mansfield, dealt with this question in the famous case of Luke v. Lyde. He ruled that the sum payable to the carrier should correspond to the part of the journey that had in fact been covered (*pro rata itineris*). Because the incident, a pirate attack, had occurred after seventeen of the twenty-one days the voyage should have taken, 17/21ths of the originally agreed freight parts were due. But Lord Mansfield's claim to have detected a universal principle was not correct. In medieval Hanseatic ship laws, and possibly already in Old Icelandic law, the distinctly different principle of half freight was applied: half of the freight was to be paid irrespective of the part of the journey covered.[30] And a third rule existed in Germany until 2013. According to §§ 630, 631 of the Handelsgesetzbuch (HGB, Commercial Code) from 1897, the sum the charterer had to pay was not only the fraction of the journey covered, but also the proportion of the costs and perils the carrier took upon himself. So for this admittedly somewhat narrow question we do not encounter one single answer, but rather at least three different ones – and no universal rule from some mysterious Lex Maritima.

Jettison and general average

The case of jettison is among the oldest of all legal sections of maritime law. The case of someone's merchandise being sacrificed in order to save the goods of the other owners and the ship herself stands at the centre of attention of the Roman maritime law, the Lex Rhodia de iactu. The principal rule is that the damage is divided by partly compensating the owner of the lost goods, followed by a rich and sophisticated discussion of possible controversies and complications typical for Roman jurisprudence. This is a striking example of continuity throughout most seafaring nations. Even today, the German HGB contains rules with great resemblance to the antique doctrine. The technical term however, which is more or less identical in all Western languages, does not come from Latin, but from the Arabic word عوار, (ʿawār) – damage: *avaria,* average, *avarie, haverei* and so on. This is a riddle that has not yet been solved: if the core of the substantive law derives from Roman (or as the name of the island of Rhodes may suggest, even Greek) antiquity, then why did the name and the thing not travel together? One would have to pursue the question by looking into Islamic maritime law.[31] But that remains to be done on another occasion.

The mere fact of this extremely widespread terminology seems to provide a valid example for the defenders of the concept of a universal Lex Maritima. If the argument stays vague enough and simply establishes the general principle of shared risk-bearing as a consequence of the dangerous joint voyage, then we do indeed seem to encounter a general principle that can be found in many, and possibly all, maritime laws. But is it only the challenge (fully loaded ships in dire straits) that is universal, or is the response universal as well? The principle is that a group bearing a joint risk compensates the group member for a sacrifice for the greater good of the whole group. But who belongs to this group?

As soon as the focus is sharpened, two different models become visible – the southern model, which includes the ship owner, and the northern one, which excludes him. Since antiquity, Mediterranean maritime enterprises included the owner of the ship and also the creditor of the freight (the carrier) in the community of risk-bearers, while the older northern principle was to exclude them, thus forming a group of only the merchants who owned and accompanied the cargo on board. Landwehr (1985) has described in detail how in the shaping of the Hamburg and Lübeck town laws in the second half of the thirteenth century the two principles collide; the southern one ultimately prevails.[32] A number of reasons for this change are discussed; the two most important are (a) that the outcome may be owed to the influence of the *ius commune* since Title 14.2 of the *Digest* became rather well known throughout Europe in the course of the twelfth and thirteenth centuries, and (b) that the new, more 'capitalistic' rule reflects the general tendency to neglect the cooperative character of older sea fare where all members of the expedition were on equal footing.

The difference is so plain that Landwehr divides the Hanseatic law in this question into two phases. The change did not take place at a given precise moment, nor was this a linear, irreversible development. Rather, the older principle in which equality played a bigger role stayed traceable for quite some time. One famous piece of evidence is the nickname *likedeeler* (equal-sharers) for the Victual brothers, the infamous pirates in the years around 1400.

Bottomry and loan-financed sea trade

The second case study deals with the financing of sea-related enterprises by third persons, and more precisely with contracts where the lender bears the marine peril

(German: *Seegefahr*), meaning that he loses his claim for refund and will not get his money back if the ship is lost.

All three sections of maritime law presented here deal – not surprisingly – with distress at sea. As a matter of fact, they could easily be chapters of one continuous story. One could, for example, imagine a ship travelling from Tyros home to Venice, or from Narva to Wismar. A heavy storm forces the captain to cut the mast and heave some barrels and boxes over board: as was previously mentioned, the rules for jettison may (in the Mediterranean and in phase two of the northern law) or may not (phase one of the northern law) apply. With her last bit of strength the ship reaches a safe midway harbour, such as Rhodes or Danzig (Gdańsk), and now the captain has to find a way to get the ship repaired. That is the subject of this section. The following, final section will examine the case that the thrown or lost merchandise is washed ashore.

Here it is the question of damaged ships that needed to be repaired in order to continue their voyage. If he couldn't pay upfront, the captain would have needed to borrow the repairing charges, and for that he would have needed securities. One security was conveniently at hand: the ship herself. That was no problem if the captain owned the ship. But should he also be allowed to use her as pawn if he was not the owner? The problem was so distinct that this type of contract received a proper name: bottomry, in German: *Bodmerei*. Here again, the legal terminology is telling. In this case we clearly deal with a word of Germanic origin: *Boden*, referring to the bottom of the ship, which serves as pawn. Only in this special situation of distress – in German: *Notbodmerei* – was bottomry permitted. Otherwise bottomry was forbidden, most likely because of its speculative character.[33] Apparently a loan secured by a pawn belonging to a third person was compared to gambling with other people's money. Similarly, and very typical for the Hanseatic mindset in general, every Hanse merchant who wanted to become a partner in a commercial company had to invest money. For a long time, work alone was not considered a sufficient contribution for a partnership.[34]

Some scholars want to construct a line of continuity from the *foenus nauticum* – the sea loan, which was frequently practised in the Mediterranean Sea from antiquity to the Latin Middle Ages – to the bottomry.[35] In the Mediterranean, contracts of this type were concluded since the times of Ancient Rome or even Greece. Its Latin name highlights the loan aspect of the contract. The *foenus nauticum* was extremely widespread in the South; it was one of the most popular instruments for financing sea trade. The contract contained a strong element of speculation, if not betting, on the safe return, and has been linked with early forms of sea insurance.[36]

There are indeed some similarities in the economic function and in the dogmatic construction, the most important being that the payback obligation was tied to the fate of the ship. The creditor was, of course, rewarded for taking over such a high risk with a high interest rate. So far, so similar. But (a) not all similarities indicate related legal thinking and (b) the differences outweigh the similarities by far.

(a) The similarity of one important trait of the contract, the fact that the lender bears the risk of *force majeure* accidents, can rather easily be explained without having to resort to the assumption of common legal concepts. It is a distinctive principle of northern, pre-*ius commune* property law that the pawn replaced the debt. So if the pawn was accepted the debtor was no longer obliged personally, and the creditor was limited to seeking satisfaction by keeping or selling the pawn.

(b) There are two main differences with regard to the frequency of the contract and its lawfulness. In Western and Northern Europe the attitude towards speculation was quite different. Here the rules were much stricter. The Rôles d'Oléron (*c.*1282 or earlier), which by the way did not label the contract at all, allowed it only in certain constellations. The Hanse diet even forbade it generally and made the said exception only for emergency bottomry (*Notbodmerei*). The economic function was different as well: it was a common and very popular instrument of general financing or sea travel and an investment popular since ancient times in the south, but in the north it only served as an emergency tool for the special case of arriving in a foreign harbour with a damaged ship.

And finally, unlike in the case of average, there was no common terminology that won recognition. This fact presents an important point for the general argument. Shall universality be measured in words or in facts? In German, one can oppose *Wortgeschichte*[37] to *Sachgeschichte*. Both can be valuable, and the overall research objective must dictate which approach fits better. The two are not independent from one another – they are interlocked. The movement of legal terms is an indicator for the parallel travel of the underlying legal concept. And the contrary, the absence of common terminology (apparent through loan words or translations), is evidence against influence. Similar words indicate relatedness, and different words indicate independent roots. Here, the two terms – one Latin, one Germanic – make independent origins more likely. That does not exclude mutual influence at later stages of the development. But – and with this turning to the *Sachgeschichte* perspective – such influence is not likely because there is no need for harmonization. This type of loan is a contract that typically would have been concluded between members of one and the same business community. As the financier's trust in the skipper would be crucial, they would know one another, and many types of bottomry would have been agreed upon before the ship set sail. This makes bottomry a part of something that can be designated as internal trade law, as opposed to the sale of goods, payment (including bills of change) and transportation, which would then be subdivisions of external trade law – with a much stronger necessity of harmonization.

Thus, this second case study leads to the conclusion that there was no common legal institution in the pre-modern maritime law regulating sea loans. Instead, there was a distinct difference between the Mediterranean and the northern maritime law.

Shipwreck law and salvage

The third case study regards shipwreck law and salvage – or more precisely, the fate of goods washed ashore (as opposed to merchandise still floating in the water;

the German word *Strandrecht* – law of the beach – is more accurate than the Latin *ius naufragii* or the English 'shipwreck law'), and the ensuing conflict of interest between the owners wanting to preserve their property rights, the finders and the owners of the ground upon which the goods were washed. The moment the goods touched the shore (or the river bank: river transport was governed by similar rules and goods transported on rivers were therefore exposed to the same danger of loss[38]) they could possibly be claimed either by a finder or by the owner of the ground they had landed upon. That was the issue, and as in the case of jettison, it was an issue affecting all transport over waterways. Should the question be regarded as one of maritime law? It certainly is a question of great practical relevance for maritime trade and is therefore included here, although typically the rules about shipwreck law do not appear in the same statutes and collections of customs. The sources that deal with shipwreck law touch mainly one or both of the following two questions: how can the property loss be prevented, and how can bystanders to the accident be motivated to help and not hinder the rescue? The second question is quickly answered: with the help of an important salvage fee – this was sometimes such a large percentage that it seems to border on ransom. The first question has a somewhat odd answer: since the oldest written evidence of shipwreck law, the legal consequence – loss of ownership – is denied!

The history of shipwreck law is practically identical to the endless repetition of its abolishment.[39] That is why the underlying legal claims that could result in the loss of the merchants' property are difficult to grasp. They are just barely visible behind the curtain of the century-long struggle to overcome them. One was based on the contact the lost or abandoned goods made with the ground when they reached shore. Not unlike King Midas turning things into gold with his touch, the contact between the goods and the ground would allow the owner of the ground to acquire the property of those goods as well. This was originally regarded as one of the royal prerogatives (*regalia*), documented, for example, when the Danish king granted the *appulsum* to newly created monasteries as part of the royal foundation privilege.[40] A competing concept was based on actual power as a basis for property rights. A person would lose ownership when he was no longer able or willing to execute power over his property and gave up the pursuit of lost goods, for example, stopped trying to fish them out of the water. In this case, the finder who kept the abandoned goods exerted his right of annexation.[41]

But regardless of justification and terminology, in any form and under any name, the 'beach-law' was a serious additional risk to the transport of all merchandise. Western authors usually date the beginning of the fight against it to the beginning of the twelfth century when, apparently thanks to Venetian lobbying after the First Crusade, the Lateran Council of 1110 abolished all shipwreck law within the realm of canon law. The Church was the driving force behind the harmonization and unification of the struggle against the numerous and varying regional attempts to abolish shipwreck law,[42] and a few decades later the new rule was introduced into imperial law as well.[43] But the struggle had already begun a century earlier, around the year 1000, within the Jewish communities in the upper and middle Rhine valley. A volume of expert opinions (*responsa)* by the famous Rabbinu Gershom ben Yehuda from Mainz also preserves a decision from legal experts who came together around or shortly after the year 1000 and decided that in the future – and in deliberate deviation from the Talmud, which states the opposite – Jewish merchants should no longer lose their property as consequence of a shipwreck.[44]

In the case of shipwreck law we thus encounter an impressive score of continuity – but not the continuity of a certain (customary or other) legal rule that would have solved the issue. Instead we see a continuity of the problem, of the conflict of interests. The Greco-Roman Lex Rhodia and the early Islamic laws hint at it, the Babylonian Talmud addresses the question, and both sea and river trade in the high and late Middle Ages are affected by the fact that accidents endanger travellers' lives and property both physically and legally. In the Hanseatic privileges the fight against shipwreck law is present like no other question of substantive law.[45] At least since the Fourth Lateran Council in 1215 the authorities did not tire of repeating that the shipwreck must not result in the loss of property rights, and rabbinic expertise (*responsae*) arrived at this result 200 years earlier. The third case study teaches us to make a clear distinction between conflicts of interest on the one hand, and legal solutions on the other. To encounter a great degree of continuity and uniformity on the side of the challenges must not be confused with the variety of responses tried out in the attempt to face that challenge. The bottom line remains the same: not a single example of a uniform legal response to a specific challenge of maritime trade law has ever been found.

Conclusion: universal maritime law?

To prove that something, e.g. a universal legal order, did not exist, has rightfully been called a *probatio diabolica.*[46] All that can be said is that, wherever one looks, at least two different, if not opposing, solutions can be found:

- The shipper whose goods were saved after a shipwreck but not transported all the way to the agreed destination could either be obliged to pay the carrier precisely one half of the agreed freight or a proportional part of the freight *pro rata itineris.*
- In the case of jettison, the shipper could either be included in or excluded from the common risk-bearing community.
- The rules could allow or forbid speculative loans that resembled bets on the safe return of ships.
- The lawmakers could either respect the old principle of winning property simply because it touched the grounds of the acquiring party, or they could protect the interests of the merchants transporting their merchandise.

While this empirical evidence from problems central to maritime law was collected, other factors came into view. There were cases like the word 'average' where technical terms migrated across borders,[47] and there were terms that stayed within their region. There were cases in which the challenge of solving a certain problem appeared more or less everywhere but the responses differed from town to town. Some questions were discussed since antiquity (e.g. jettison), some since the High Middle Ages (shipwreck law, since *c.*1000). Other institutions like sea insurance (fifteenth century) or stock companies (since 1600) are considerably younger. The regions were hard to distinguish from one another (Latin Greek–Muslim Mediterranean trade; Atlantic or northwestern – North Sea – Baltic – Hanseatic maritime law); within this context the concept of *Rechtskreise* ('legal circles' of 'families of law') was discussed but not pursued seriously.[48]

Was there universal maritime law in the sense of processes of assimilation, of learning from friends and foes? These were undoubtedly strong factors. But they did not amount to any cross-border conformity that would justify the labelling of the emerging rules as 'universal'. In the case of maritime law, one argument in favour of the international and possibly universal character is so obvious and so often repeated with great confidence that this in itself raises suspicion. The sheer fact that seafaring is international and includes permanent border crossing seems to suggest that the outcome has to be an international legal order. But is that really so obvious? Today's maritime law is composed of national and international legal orders, and it is not difficult to find out in which cases which set of rules applies. Even if the crew is 100 per cent Filipino, German labour law will apply if the ship sails under German flag. If, however, that same ship is damaged and therefore repaired in a dock in Bergen, Norwegian contract law will govern the repair contract. There is no denial that the international character of seafaring must have influenced maritime law to a great extent. But that is not the same thing as assuming the universal character of maritime law. Dutch skippers knew that their voyage would take place under the rules of the Vonnisse van Damme when they went West, but governed by the Ordinancie van de (Zuider)see when they set sail to the East. As these two sets of rules were not totally different, one might argue that at least the rules that are common to both are part of a universal Lex Maritima. But that is a theoretical and retrospective view. The merchants undertaking the respective trips knew which rules applied and which courts would hear their case should conflicts arise.

At least in the Latin part of the Mediterranean and in the northern seas, maritime law did not start out as a universal body of law that was then divided into smaller, regional sets of rules. Quite the contrary, the local legal orders, namely the town laws, are the older layer, and the tendency towards assimilation and towards rules with a larger area of application is a more recent phenomenon. The clearest example for this inverted sequence of events is the Hanseatic sea law. It starts in the late thirteenth century with town laws, namely from Hamburg, which were then also adopted by Lübeck. Then follow the provisions upon which the Hanseatic Diet agreed (early fifteenth century), together with serious efforts to collect all older norms; in legal history, such collective efforts typically precede codifications (Saxon law, canon law). And the last step, nearly at the end of the common Hanseatic era, was the all-Hanseatic codification from 1614, the 'Hanseatic ship and sea law', which is a few decades older than the first national codification of maritime law, the French 'Grande ordonnance de la marine' from 1681, when Louis XIV was at the apex of his power.

A recent study on the goals the Hanseatic merchants pursued in regard to court procedure showed that the objective was not uniformity but optimal results in each different county according to the local conditions and opportunities.[49] If the result from that paper is transferred to the present field of maritime law, it would seem that the main reason for the lack of universal rules was the lack of necessity for uniformity. Modern scholars, historians and jurists alike may search for similarities or even universal principles because these would make it easier to get an overview of the past, and from this perspective tend to assume that harmonization must have been a goal for medieval merchants as well. But a closer look reveals that there is neither much evidence nor much need for uniform rules. Merchants were able to switch from one legal regime to another just as well as they were able to switch from one language to another. The main reason for the apparent absence of universal rules in maritime law was that there was no necessity for full harmonization.

Notes

1 K. Günther and S. Kadelbach, 'Recht ohne Staat', in idem (eds), *Recht ohne Staat? Zur Normativität nichtstaatlicher Rechtsetzung*, Frankfurt: Campus, 2011, pp. 9–48.

2 H. J. Berman, *Law and Revolution: The Formation of the Western Legal Tradition*, Cambridge, MA: Harvard University Press, 1983.

3 A. Maurer, *Lex Maritima: Grundzüge eines transnationalen Seehandelsrechts*, Tübingen: Mohr Siebeck, 2012.

4 A. Cordes, 'Gewinnteilungsprinzipien im hansischen und oberitalienischen Gesellschaftshandel des Spätmittelalters', in G. Köbler and H. Nehlsen (eds), *Wirkungen europäischer Rechtskultur: Festschrift für Karl Kroeschell zum 70. Geburtstag*, Munich: C. H. Beck, 1997, pp. 135–50. The article dealt with a central question of company law, the partition of gains and losses between the partners. Already in that first case study nearly twenty years ago I discovered such distinct differences between Northern and Southern European contracts that it was impossible to establish 'the' commenda as a universally used type of maritime trade company.

5 Berman, *Law and Revolution*, p. 333, opening paragraph of ch. 11 on mercantile law: 'The crucial period of change were the late eleventh and twelfth centuries. It was then that the basic concepts and institutions of modern western mercantile law – Lex Mercatoria, "the law merchant" – were formed, and even more important, it was then that mercantile law in the west first came to be viewed as an integrated, developing system – a body of law'; similarly, but less sophisticated, L. E. Trakman, *The Law Merchant: The Evolution of Commercial Law*, South Hackensack, NJ: F. B. Rothman, 1983, p. 7.

6 A. Cordes, 'The search for a medieval lex mercatoria', *Oxford University Comparative Law Forum* 1 at http://ouclf.iuscomp.org/articles/cordes.shtml, 2003 (accessed 16 Feb. 2016). The paper started from Berman's general characterization (see previous note), dissected it into three parts, and then tried to falsify the three central elements of Berman's thesis. W. Decock, 'Capital confidence: updating Harold Berman's views on mercantile law and belief systems', *Rechtsgeschichte* 21, 2013, pp. 180–5, gives a well-balanced overview of the debate and partly defends Berman because he wrote in accordance with

what was more or less generally believed around 1980. That is probably a valid point although Berman could have taken Baker's more sceptical but also more precise view from 1979 into account.

7 H.-J. Gilomen, 'Wucher', in *Lexikon des Mittelalters,* vol. 9, Munich: LEXMA, 1998, cols 341–5.

8 P. Landau, 'Pacta sunt servanda: Zu den kanonistischen Grundlagen der Privatautonomie', in M. Ascheri et al. (eds), *'Ins Wasser geworfen und Ozeane durchquert': Festschrift für Knut Wolfgang Nörr,* Cologne: Böhlau, 2003, pp. 169–70.

9 A. Cordes, 'Acceptance and rejection of "foreign" legal doctrine by the Council of Lübeck around 1500', in S. Dauchy, H. Bryson and M. Mirow (eds), *Ratio decidendi: Guiding Principles of Juridical Decisions*, vol. 2, *'Foreign' Law*, Berlin: Duncker & Humblot, 2010, pp. 22–3.

10 K. Kroeschell, A. Cordes and K. Nehlsen-von Stryk, *Deutsche Rechtsgeschichte*, vol. 2, *1250–1650,* 9th edn, Cologne: Böhlau, 2008, p. 129: 'Das Urteil der mittelalterlichen Schöffen ist nämlich, wie W. Ebel (Geschichte der Gesetzgebung in Deutschland, 2. Aufl. 1958, 15) es formuliert hat, "die im Gericht gefundene Aussage über die Rechtslage, die Feststellung des in dieser Lage zu beachtenden Rechts. Mit anderen Worten: es hat prozessualen Charakter. [. . .] Das Recht, das die Schöffen in ihren Urteilen handhaben, ist also Verfahrensrecht! Gewiss ist dies der Grund, weshalb dem Versuch, den in dieser Hinsicht so schweigsamen Sprüchen Sätze des materiellen Rechts abzulauschen, etwas so Unwirkliches anhaftet."'

11 C. Donahue Jr., 'Medieval and early modern lex mercatoria: an attempt at the probatio diabolica', *Chicago Journal of International Law* 5, 2004, pp. 21–36.

12 A. Cordes, 'The future of the history of medieval trade law', *American Journal of Legal History* 56, 2016, pp. 12–20. The paragraph is a summary of the first part of that article.

13 The following is in accordance with G. Landwehr, 'Seerecht (Seehandelsrecht)', in *Handwörterbuch zur deutschen Rechtsgeschichte,* vol. 4, Berlin: Erich Schmidt, 1990, cols 1596–1614; A. Cordes, 'Seerecht' in *Lexikon des Mittelalters,* vol. 7, Munich: LEXMA, 1995, cols 1688–90.

14 K.-F. Krieger, *Ursprung und Wurzeln der Rôles d'Oléron*, Cologne: Böhlau, 1970, pp. 123–45.

15 For a comparison between the labour laws of the seamen according to the Rôles d'Oléron on the one hand and the Llibre del Consolat del mar on the other, see the dissertation of my student J. Schweitzer, *Schiffer und Schiffsmann in den Rôles d'Oléron und im Llibre del Consolat de Mar: Ein Vergleich zweier mittelalterlicher Seerechtsquellen*, Frankfurt a.M.: Peter Lang, 2007.

16 Maurer, *Lex Maritima.*

17 Ibid., pp. 7–11.

18 G. Landwehr, 'Die ZHR als Organ der Handelsrechtswissenschaft: Die wissenschaftlichen Abhandlungen Band 1–123 (1858–1960)', *Zeitschrift für das gesamte Handelsrecht und Wirtschaftsrecht (ZHR)* 150, 1986, p. 70.

19 L. Goldschmidt, *Universalgeschichte des Handelsrechts: Erste Lieferung,* Stuttgart: Ferdinand Enke, 3rd edn 1891 (ch. 7, pp. 335–54, on maritime law).

20 Landwehr, 'Die ZHR', nn. 224–37.

21 Among others: C. M. Moschetti, 'Nave, diritto intermedio', in *Enciclopedia del diritto*, Milan: Giuffrè, 1964, pp. 576–600; Cordes, 'Seerecht'; E. Harris and K. O. Scherner, 'Maritime law', in *The Oxford International Encyclopedia of Legal History,* vol. 4, Oxford: Oxford University Press, 2009, pp. 147–52.

22 Landwehr, 'Seerecht'.

23 C. Jahnke, 'Hansisches und anderes Seerecht', in A. Cordes, *Hansisches und hansestädtisches Recht,* Trier: Porta Alba, 2008, pp. 51–2, introduces the cited example, which indeed is important because of the symbolic value of the common meal. He interprets it as old-Nordic influence on the Rôles d'Oléron and takes this as proof that they should be

regarded as universal law. And while the former is an interesting piece of speculation that deserves further discussion, the latter goes too far. If it were true, any twentieth-century Civil Code would qualify as universal law because they all have incorporated rules from the French Code Civil (1804), the Austrian ABGB (1811) or the German BGB (1900).

24 E. Kleiman, 'Externalities and public goods in the Talmud', in A. Levine (ed.), *Oxford Handbook of Judaism and Economics*, Oxford: Oxford University Press, 2010, pp. 121–4.

25 The classic German textbook that perfected this concept is K. Zweigert and H. Kötz, *Einführung in die Rechtsvergleichung*, Tübingen: Mohr Siebeck, 3rd edn 1996.

26 E. Frankot, *'Of Laws of Ships and Shipmen': Medieval Maritime Law and Its Practice in Urban Northern Europe*, Edinburgh: Edinburgh University Press, 2012. Similarly, G. Landwehr, *Die Haverei in den mittelalterlichen deutschen Seerechtsquellen*, Göttingen: Vandenhoeck & Ruprecht, 1985, regularly (e.g. p. 44) makes a distinction between Western European and Northern European maritime law.

27 To cite just one recent example of the countless papers on the subject: C. Krampe, 'Römisches Recht auf hoher See: Die Kunst des Guten und Gerechten', in I. Fargnoli and S. Rebenich (eds), *Das Vermächtnis der Römer: Römisches Recht und Europa,* Berne: Haupt, 2012, pp. 111–50.

28 The excellent dissertation of K.-F. Krieger, *Ursprung und Wurzeln der Rôles d'Oléron*, Cologne: Böhlau, 1970, is still the best entry, although some details have since been studied in greater depth. See for example Schweitzer, *Schiffer und Schiffsmann.*

29 Cordes, 'The search'. The following paragraph sums up the results of that article.

30 G. Landwehr, 'Prinzipien der Risikotragung beim Seefrachtvertrag', in G. Köbler and H. Nehlsen (eds), *Wirkungen europäischer Rechtskultur in Wirkungen europäischer Rechtskultur: Festschrift für Karl Kroeschell zum 70. Geburtstag*, Munich: Beck, 1997, pp. 595–615.

31 That is a task made relatively easy with the help of two books by Hassan Khalilieh, *Islamic Maritime Law,* Leiden: Brill, 1998, and *Admiralty and Maritime Laws in the Mediterranean Sea (ca. 800–1050)*, Leiden: Brill, 2006.

32 Landwehr, *Haverei*, pp. 41 and 44; A. Cordes, 'Flandrischer Copiar Nr. 9. Juristischer Kommentar', in C. Jahnke and A. Graßmann (eds), *Flandrischer Copiar Nr. 9. See- und Schiffrechtsbestimmungen. Edition und Übersetzung*, Lübeck: Schmidt Römhild, 2003, pp. 130–1.

33 Cordes, 'Flandrischer Copiar', pp. 122–4.

34 A. Cordes, *Spätmittelalterlicher Gesellschaftshandel im Hanseraum*, Cologne: Böhlau, 1998, p. 319 and passim.

35 B. Matthiass, *Das Foenus Nauticum und die geschichtliche Entwicklung der Bodmerei*, Würzburg: Stuber, 1881. The dissertation, a very decent piece of work, and at 132 pages, thicker than the average pre-1914 JD thesis of its time, is an excellent example of the universal method of Levin Goldschmidt and his school. Matthiass starts his *tour d'horizon* in ancient India, continues to Mediterranean antiquity and ends in the northern seas, finding – quite like Lord Mansfield (n. 29) 130 years before and Harold Berman 100 years after him – *una et eadem lex,* one and the same law, wherever he looked.

36 K. Nehlsen-von Stryk, *Die venezianische Seeversicherung im 15. Jahrhundert*, Ebelsbach: Rolf Gremer, 1986, pp. 9–13.

37 *Wortgeschichte,* e.g. the history of words like *Bauer, Landwirt* (farmer or peasant), should not be confused with *Begriffsgeschichte*, which does not primarily regard terminology but the concepts standing behind words, e.g. the concept of a part of the population living through agriculture.

38 A. Cordes, 'Grundruhr', in *Handwörterbuch zur deutschen Rechtsgeschichte,* vol. 2, 2nd edn, Berlin: Erich Schmidt, 2012, cols 603–5.

39 A. Cordes, 'Strandrecht', in *Lexikon des Mittelalters,* vol. 8, Munich: LEXMA, 1996, cols 212–13.

40 V. Niitema, *Das Strandrecht in Nordeuropa im Mittelalter*, Helsinki: Suomalainen Tiedeakatemia, 1955, p. 62.

41 Niitema, *Strandrecht,* pp. 14–19.

42 Niitema, *Strandrecht*, pp. 91–118.

43 'Si quis vero miserabili personae fortuna naufragiorum aliquid abstulerit, poenae antiquae legum subiacet'; Art. 4 of Emperor Frederick I. Barbarossa's Constitutio Auximana from 4 Dec. 1177; *Monumenta Germaniae Historica, Leges* (*MGH LL*), vol. 2, ed. G. H. Pertz, Hanover: Hahn, 1837, p. 162.

44 M. Hoffmann, *Der Geldhandel der deutschen Juden während des Mittelalters bis zum Jahre 1350: Ein Beitrag zur deutschen Wirtschaftsgeschichte*, Leipzig: Duncker & Humblot, 1910, pp. 142–3; I. A. Agus, *Urban Civilization in Pre-Crusade Europe: A Study of Organized Town-Life in Northwestern Europe during the Tenth and Eleventh Centuries Based on the Responsa Literature,* Leiden: Brill, 1968, pp. 70–5.

45 A. Cordes, 'Die Erwartungen mittelalterlicher Kaufleute an Gerichtsverfahren: Hansische Privilegien als Indikator', in A. Cordes and S. Dauchy (eds), *Eine Grenze in Bewegung. Öfentliche und private Justiz im Handels- und Seerecht*, Munich: Oldenbourg, 2013, p. 60.

46 Donahue, 'Lex mercatoria'.

47 The Nordic, French and German words for 'sailor', *mǫtunautr/matelot/Matrose*, would be another example that Carsten Jahnke pointed out to the author.

48 The latest German handbook on comparative law, U. Kischel, *Rechtsvergleichung*, Munich: Beck, 2015, abandons this category and does not speak of *Rechtskreise* anymore. The problem with *Rechtskreisen,* 'legal circles', is that they suggest a static map with sharp borders. That leads to a tendency to label a rule as 'Hanseatic' or 'English' etc. without sufficient room for dynamics.

49 Cordes, 'Erwartungen'.

6

TRADE AND LANGUAGE

How did traders communicate across language borders?

Agnete Nesse

Introduction: historical sociolinguistics

When working with language change as a consequence of trade, the focus on the structure of the language should be accompanied by the question of why these structural changes happen in a certain place, at a certain time. Studying for example, the merger of the feminine and the masculine grammatical gender in the dialect of Bergen, Norway, we cannot ignore the fact that this change happened during the sixteenth century in the country's largest and most international trading city. Therefore, internal questions such as *How did the feminine and the masculine grammatical gender merge?* must be combined with external questions such as *How can we describe the speech community when this happened?* The combination of language-internal and language-external approaches means that historical sociolinguistics is an interdisciplinary way to work. Still, it is clear that the goal of our research is to learn more about language and language use as such, which means that historical sociolinguistics is a branch of linguistics.

Writing a chapter about linguistics in a book written by and most likely for historians, leads to a number of questions about the nature of interdisciplinary approaches. First of all, of course, there is the matter of making linguistic theories and data relevant for historians. They may be unfamiliar with looking at history with the eyes of a linguist. Hopefully, the linguist's view may enhance the historians' understanding of history and of historical texts, just as linguists draw on the findings of historians in *their* work.

The field of historical sociolinguistics emerged as a fusion between sociolinguistics and historical linguistics. Sociolinguistics, first introduced as an independent research discipline by William Labov and Peter Trudgill in the 1960s and 1970s, differs from structural linguistics in that even though language variation and change is *described* in the same way, the *explanation* of both variation and change is sought outside the linguistic system – in the speaker and her or his place in society. A natural hindrance in transforming the methods of sociolinguistics into historical sociolinguistics is that 'place in society' tends to be quite uniform in our old sources. The sources we rely on are most often texts written by men from the upper strata of society. Differences can be found in the written language of these – for example, between clerics and royals[1] – but nevertheless we are denied access to the language of the illiterate, and – with exceptions – the language of women.

Language use can indeed point to power and prestige relations in a society. A simple example of this is the topic of language death as opposed to language maintenance: if a language disappears, it is very likely that this language, and the people who spoke it, were not very prestigious. On the other hand, if a language is 'saved', or revitalized, it is likely that a norm of the society in question is that minority languages are valuable.

The study of language contact, which will be the foundation of this chapter, draws on language-external as well as language-internal insights. In order to use multilingualism to explain changes in one or more of the languages in contact, we must establish which languages were used in a certain communicative setting, and we must investigate the social relations between the speakers of the different languages. This method also applies to investigations of written sources of different periods through history. In principle, all texts can serve as valuable data – it merely depends on what questions you ask. An original document's value lies in the supposed close connection between the spoken and written form of a language. We take for granted that the written language in some way reflects the spoken variety of the writer. A later copy derives its value from the display of strategies that the copyist used when his 'modern' language met the 'old' language of the original. The linguist must then try to disentangle the different linguistic layers of the text in order to understand what is 'old' and what is 'new'.

A translation into another language can show the different translation strategies applied to different genres. There is a vast difference between the accuracy of legal translation and the free creativity of the translations of other genres.[2] If the languages of the translations are closely related, the closeness can be exaggerated in order to ensure the accuracy of the translation. For example, a group of documents concerning property were translated from Norwegian into Low German in the 1550s. At the time, both languages were undergoing some syntactic changes, and the word order pattern was relatively flexible in both languages. This flexibility was exploited during the process of translation so that the word order of the Low German translation deviates from the word order in the Norwegian original only in very few instances. These translations can also show the benefits of working with the same data across disciplines, and how modern interdisciplinary work can be carried out. As Geir Atle Ersland[3] has shown, these property documents were important for Hanseatic merchants in Bergen around the middle of the sixteenth century. The landowner wanted to raise the rent of the land considerably. During the conflict, it was not only the local Germans (who had a passive competence in Norwegian) who needed access to the documents. The leaders of the Hanseatic headquarters in Lübeck, who were not part of the Bergen bilingualism, might have been involved in the conflict, and therefore, translations into Low German were called for. In this case, the historian examines *why* the translations were made, while the linguist examines *how* the translations were carried out.

Trade and language

We will now step aside from the general issues of historical sociolinguistics and consider what specifically we must take into account when analysing trade and the consequences of trade for language use and language change. Do speakers and writers in a contact situation driven by trade treat language differently than those in a contact situation driven by war, colonialism, imperialism, etc.? The answer can be both yes and no; in this chapter we will concentrate on the 'yes', but, naturally, there is a need to consider the 'no' side of the story first. Since trade is a phenomenon that varies greatly, it can be difficult to distinguish, for example, between trade and colonialism and between trade and imperialism. In cases such as these, the distribution of power among the interlocutors will be extremely unbalanced, and the language of the colonizer or imperialist will dominate the results of the language contact that takes place.

When discussing the language of trade as such, however, we commonly refer to the communication between more or less equal trade partners – it's these communicational settings that will be discussed hereafter. Kurt Braunmüller, who has written several articles about the contact between German and Scandinavian traders, often uses as his starting point for discussing language contact between traders the notion that traders did not care about language, only about making money:

> Moreover, accommodation was the key technique in oral communication: speakers could adjust to their trading partners' or neighbours' variety and could immediately see which convergence strategy gave the best results. In addition, one will earn more money in trading contexts when one's accommodation strategy (here: the convergence towards the dialect of the addressee) is effective. The very positive effects of extrinsic (here: commercial) motivation and strategic accommodation can hardly be overestimated![4]

This makes clear that working with historical multilingualism differs from working with historical monolingualism, or at least with monolingual sources. Bi- or multilingualism enhances what we call *language awareness*: the speaker's awareness that language has form, and not just content. A simple explanation of this is that bilinguals know that a token, such as a ship, is named by different words in different languages. This opens up awareness of the variability of language and languages.

Trade and shipping have led the way to bilingualism throughout history. Ships are, according to David Trotter, 'by definition international in function'. Not only do ships sail from coast to coast, often in different countries; they also need to be maintained and repaired, often by people speaking another language than those sailing the ship.[5] But since there is very little information about the spoken language of traders, sailors and repairmen (and other occupations connected to trade), we rely on the written sources that they left behind, often accountancy books, shipping lists, etc. These may often be written in ways that make it difficult to sift out which passages are written in which language. Since names of the products bought and sold were frequently borrowed from one language to another, these words will often be the same in all the languages in question. In addition, the words describing the act of trade – *credit*, *debit*, *sell*, *buy*, etc. – would often be abbreviated in a way that could be interpreted as several languages. Trotter therefore argues that one should not try to disentangle the different languages of such documents.[6] When it comes to the ship terminology that emanated from the Mediterranean and spread to much of Europe, he claims that it is not multilingual, but rather *unlocalizable*.[7] The writing of shipping lists so that they were unlocalizable – by using abbreviations that would work in both languages, for example – can be found in the business writing that Laura Wright has studied in London. She writes about what she calls diamorphs:[8] abbreviations like *rec.*, that could be English, French or Latin. These diamorphs serve not only the standard function of abbreviation, i.e. saving place, paper, ink and effort, but they also serve to unify the different languages in question. In accountancy books from German merchants in Bergen, Norway, we see that even after the German speech community in the city had undergone a shift from written Low German to written High German,[9] the merchants used Low German spellings in some cases. Typically, these were the words that had been introduced into Norwegian in their Low German form. One typical example is the use of the Low German (and Norwegian) form *betalt* instead of the High German spelling *bezahlt*. This could, in Wright's term, be labelled a diamorph. There is, obviously, in this specific case, the possibility that the writer in question had the form *betalt* in his spoken variety, since the Germans in Bergen mostly came from the Low German-speaking areas. However, since they wrote dominantly in High German and only used Low German spelling in those instances where the Low German words had been taken into Norwegian, the diamorph theory is a likely explanation.

But not all business writing is like this, and Wright herself uses the diamorph theory only to explain those instances where there in fact is a possibility for joint spelling. Her London data are otherwise explained as a medieval mixed-language business system, where bilingualism emerged in the sense that writers mixed medieval Latin, Anglo-Norman, and Middle English in an orderly way. This code of writing was used 'whenever people needed to keep written track of money movement, such as accounts, inventories, bills and invoices'.[10]

What we see in the different studies of medieval European trade language is that a typical mix consists of Latin combined with the local vernaculars of the trading markets. However, there also seems to be a difference within Europe: even if Latin, at least during the early part of the Middle Ages, was also important in northern

Europe, the languages that were used together with Latin differed. In his article about the importance of language for creating commercial networks, Francesco Guidi-Bruscoli[11] emphasizes the importance of Italian as a trade language in the southern part of Europe, and Braunmüller and others have shown that Low German played this role in the north. A linguistic hierarchy may be drawn with Latin on the top, Italian and Low German as the second highest, and other vernaculars at the bottom. Among these was English, a language that nobody was expected to speak in the late Middle Ages if they were not English themselves.[12] As Wright has shown, English business writing was in fact bilingual, and Michael T. Clanchy[13] discusses the distinct functions performed by Latin, (Norman) French and English in written and oral communication in England. French was the oral speech used at court; Latin the language for formal, especially ecclesiastical and diplomatic use; and English the commonly spoken and written language. Many users were able to switch, depending on the context.

In addition to these languages, Italian became important, especially in the wool trade, since English wool was shipped to Italy. In Italy, the different Italian dialects could be mixed with both Latin and other languages. In his monograph on the use of the Venetian vernacular in the republic of Venice, Rembert Eufe has shown that trade in the Aegean in fact may have strengthened the use of Venetian at the expense of Latin.[14] During the thirteenth century Venetian was used, if not actually to write receipts and other mercantile texts, then at least to comment on the same texts, such as explanations on the backs of receipts. Eufe has also found a bilingual bank account from the fifteenth century where Latin was left out and the texts were written in Greek and Venetian. In Crete, one of the places where the Venetians had great interests and power, bilingualism seems to have been balanced during the Venetian reign – there were people of Greek ancestry who had Venetian as their first language, and people of Venetian ancestry who had Greek as their first language. What divided the groups was not language, but confession; only Catholics could be given land, no matter how they spoke.[15]

Religious differences were also important in Novgorod. According to Catherine Squires, who has researched the status and use of Low German in Russia, religion was one of the, if not *the* most, important extra-linguistic factors determining the contact between the Hanseatic merchants and the Russians. For the Russians, language became the symbol of these religious differences; therefore willingness to learn Low German might indicate willingness to adapt to Catholicism,[16] which was forbidden to them. Interestingly, it seems that the Hanseatic merchants did in fact adapt – at least linguistically – to the Russian religiously stamped literacy. In the Low German version of the contracts they signed with the Russians, the Hanseatic merchants used expressions like *kussede dat cruce* 'kissed the cross' instead of mention of the seal, such as *Schreuen vnder vnserm signete* 'written under our seal', to confirm an agreement.[17]

The question of religion was very different in Bergen, Norway, where both the Hanseatic and the Norwegian part of the population had the same confession:

Catholic before 1536/37, and Lutheran after that.[18] In Bergen, the division of the groups was tied to privileges rather than religion or other cultural traits. But even if the privileges were what constituted difference, language came to be an important identity-building factor in the city, as the one visible (or rather audible) feature that separated the groups. As we will return to shortly, there was not a widespread, active bilingualism in Bergen: the Germans spoke only German, and the Norwegians spoke only Norwegian. Still, accommodation took place, both in the sense that they borrowed words from one another (like *betalt*), and in that they overused common grammatical features (which led to the merger of grammatical gender in the local Norwegian dialect[19]).

During the late Middle Ages, the German merchants in Bergen wrote in Low German and used Norwegian loan words; these words were adjusted to the writing conventions of Low German. Based on the way they wrote these loan words we assume that they were also phonetically adjusted to spoken Low German. Many of these Norwegian loan words in the Bergen Low German are collected and grouped on the basis of semantics in an article by Olav Brattegard from 1934.[20] Brattegard divides the words into three groups:[21] words that describe trade, words that describe governing and law, and words that describe houses and living conditions, the harbour, and the town. The second group is the smallest, while the first and the third groups are similar. Brattegard lists approximately seventy words all in all, but the number may be larger if one also includes texts written after 1600.

(1) Words that describe trade. Most of these are names for fish, like Low German *roscher* or *rotscher* from Norwegian *ráskerðing*. This word also shows how a word that is not fully transparent tends to receive a new 'etymology' during the process of loaning. Norwegian *ráskerðing* meant a codfish that was split into two parts lengthwise so that only the tail fin of the fish was left together. The cod was then hung to dry. The split could take on a reddish colour, and this is supposedly why the Germans interpreted *rá*, 'rod' (to hang the fish on), as Low German *rot*, or 'red'.

(2) Words that describe governing and law. One of these words has also entered other languages; for example English, in the form *ombudsman*. The Old Norwegian form was *umboðsmaðr*, and the German sources from Bergen give examples like Low German *vnbadesman*, pl. *vnbadelude*. More curious is perhaps that the Low German *oltap* from Old Norwegian *ǫltappr* 'vending of beer' shows up in the German texts. One would suppose that the vending of beer was something that the Hanseatic merchants had their own word for. And so they did – *Bêrtappen*. But since the vending of beer was strongly regulated by the privileges and therefore a legal matter, the Norwegian word was used – at least in the texts concerning conflicts about the obeying of privileges.

(3) Words that describe houses and living conditions, the harbour and the town. A word that may have travelled from Novgorod and therefore must be regarded as primarily Hanseatic, rather than Norwegian or German, is the Old Norwegian *kannestol*, Low German *kandstuel*. The word described a certain kind of table

> (where the top could be opened, like a chest on legs). This has been connected to the Russian word *stolŭ*, which means 'table'. A word Old Norwegian and Low German had in common, but with slightly different meaning, was the Old Norwegian *garðr* 'farm, large building, garden' and the Low German *garde*, 'garden'. At Bryggen in Bergen, where the Hanseatic merchants lived, the word was used both for the houses and for the gardens. In the sixteenth century the houses had names like Middle Norwegian *systragardhe*[22] and Low German *sustergarden*[23] 'the houses of the sisters', and the gardens were called Old Norwegian *kálgarðr* and Low German *kôl garde* 'cabbage garden'.[24]

Trade, the privileges that regulated it, and the surroundings that traders lived in will be clear candidates for loan words in any trade situation. Most likely, the first loan words will come from the naming of products. Since, for example, Italian merchants from the late thirteenth century on traded English wool and delivered it to the Florentine wool industry, the English words for many qualities of cloth have Italian origins: from the mid-fifteenth century Italian loan words like *damaske*, *cremeson*, *satyn* and *tartaryn* show up in both Middle English and Anglo Norman texts, and in mixed texts.[25]

According to Marjorie Lorvik,[26] one should distinguish between the type of trade, as in the Italian/English example, where professional agents who spoke the required languages conducted the communication, and a type where the shippers themselves took care of the trade. Lorvik has examined the North Sea timber trade that involved the export of timber from the southwest of Norway to Scotland in 1550–1700. One important hallmark of this trade was that the shippers and farmers were connected by social ties, which might have led to a more intense language contact and more accommodation from both parties than would trade by multilingual merchants. The close ties that sometimes evolved between business partners is also commented on by Esther-Miriam Wagner in her studies of the Judaeo-Arabic used in Egypt during the Middle Ages. Of the situation in the eleventh century, she writes that

> Because of the general insecurity and the slowness of communications, international trade was largely dependent on personal relationships and mutual confidence. In some cases relationships between trading partners were maintained throughout a lifetime or even through generations of families, and were often secured by inter-marriages.[27]

Language contact

Accommodation has already been mentioned, and in this section we will take a closer look at different types of linguistic accommodation and how different kinds of trading patterns influence the kind of linguistic accommodation that takes place. Essentially, the act of linguistic accommodation takes place because human beings need each other. If we accommodate to our speaking partner, it is more likely that she or he will accept us, and it is more likely that we will achieve our goal with the conversation. There is, of course, also the possibility of diverging from the variety of our interlocutor if we want to make sure she or he does not miss the fact that there is an important difference between us, i.e. when it comes to status. When it comes to trade, however, such differences are often diminished in order to create a common base for the transaction in question.

Traders have often been in situations that require what we call 'short-term accommodation', which leads to specific kinds of linguistic change, especially simplification.[28] A typical example of short-term accommodation is the trader who comes to a town where a language is spoken that he does not have full command over. He conducts his buying and selling by making use of a core vocabulary consisting of product names, numbers and non-verbal gestures like pointing, nodding and shaking his head. Then he returns home. If such short-term accommodation is repeated often enough, it can result in a pidgin language (discussed below), for example, or, if the traders settle in the area where previously they had only visited, the nature of the accommodation will change into long-term accommodation. Long-term accommodation will affect the language of both groups in other ways than short-term accommodation. The difference has to do, for instance, with which parts of the language are being changed. During the process of short-term accommodation, the interlocutors, as mentioned, focus on core vocabulary related to the trade in question, and, naturally, on numbers and currency. In long-term accommodation, not only vocabulary, but phonology, morphology and syntax may change as well. In Bergen, for instance, many of the Low German loan words had already entered the local dialect in the fourteenth century when the Hanseatic merchants were new in town. But the important grammatical changes did not emerge until one or even two centuries later when the German settlement had become a stable factor. This implies that contact-induced changes in grammar generally tell us that contact between groups – in our case trading partners – was stable and long-lasting.

Whereas short-term accommodation, if we hold on to the picture of the trader who jumps ashore and trades his goods, will often be symmetrical, not favouring any one of the groups, long-term accommodation will more often than not be asymmetrical, and the dominant language will be the language of the most powerful speakers. In most cultures, people who do not speak the majority language as well as the majority speaks it suffer a loss of prestige. Moreover, in face-to face communication the one who has the best command of the language being used holds the strongest cards and may be more successful in their endeavour. In an article about the multilingual trading environment in Vyborg, Marika Tandefelt writes:

> Especially in a long-term perspective it is possible to see how changes in the power relations in a particular milieu have an effect on language users and thereby also for their language. Political power gives access to prestigious domains and the chance to assert language and cultural rights. Perhaps it is in reality only economic power, which can compete with political power, when it concerns the power and prestige of a language?[29]

This implies that the relationship between language use and power must be considered when one wants to investigate trade and its impact on language and linguistic practices. In my own investigations of the language contact between Norwegian and Low German in Bergen during the Hanseatic era, one of the most striking findings is the lack of evidence that the German-speaking part of the population spoke or wrote Norwegian, and also lack of evidence that the Norwegians spoke or wrote Low German. There are relatively few translations that are exceptions to this main pattern. Those that exist indicate that members of the speech community who were in fact bilingual belonged to the upper strata of the society.

Since the Hanse held on to its settlement in Bergen for approximately 400 years, and since a decline in Hanseatic immigration was balanced to some extent by immigration of independent German apprentices or traders, the language contact situation was very much a case of long-term accommodation. Four hundred years is a long time, and many features can change in a language during such a time span. The basis for the changes that developed in the dialect was the communication pattern, which involved passive (also called receptive) rather than active bilingualism. This kind of bilingualism involved learning to understand the language of the other group, but not speaking or writing it. In this way, a conversation between a German and a Norwegian was bilingual: the German spoke German and the Norwegian spoke Norwegian. A consequence of this was that none of the interlocutors lost 'face'. They both spoke (or wrote) the language they had full command over, and did not need to present themselves as the weaker party by speaking the language of the other group. This reflects the way the Bergen society presented itself as a whole during this period. Even if our sources show that the relationships between the Hanseatic merchants and the Norwegian inhabitants were dominated at times by conflict, the period was also distinguished by the balance between the two groups. It is therefore fruitful to consider the linguistic pattern as a symptom of the distribution of power in the city.

The emergence of the pattern of passive bilingualism in Bergen was also facilitated by the fact that the languages in question were closely related, and many words were similar and thus easy to understand for both groups. This must have helped the learning of the other group's language. In London and Bruges where the Hanse also established Kontore, the languages were similarly related to Middle Low German. However, there was one important difference: in Bergen, there was no use of French. The only non-Scandinavian language used in the city prior to the emergence of the Hanse was Latin, and that was a High language used for religious and royal purposes only. French was an important language, both in London and in Bruges, which meant that Low German not only came into contact with the local vernacular and Latin, but also with French. In Novgorod, the fourth city where a Hanseatic Kontor was established, the local vernacular was linguistically unrelated to Low German, and the linguistic challenges were quite different. In fact, the Hanseatic leaders in Novgorod considered Old Russian to be so difficult that people older than 20 years should not even try to learn it, and it was only taught to young men and boys: 'Nen lerekint boven twintich jar olt scal leren de sprake in deme Nougardeschen'.[30]

Hebertus Menke also comments on the link between power and linguistic competence when he writes about the Hanseatic settlement in Novgorod, or Naugard, as the city was called in Middle Low German.[31] In order to restrict the accessibility for other traders, the local branch of the Hanse monopolized translation: only the members of the Hanse were allowed to interpret between the German and Russian traders. Catherine Squires claims that the prohibition from 1423 to discourage Dutch, Zeelanders, Flemish or English people from learning Russian served to keep the ties between northern Russia and Western Europe under Hanseatic control.[32] Guidi-Bruscoli adds to this the assumption that interpreters who were appointed by local authorities might serve as spies for them, contrary to the merchants' own men, who most likely would be more loyal to the merchants.[33]

Through the contact with Low German, the Russian speakers imported Low German words connected to trade, shipping and organization. Examples are the Old Russian *borgomestr* 'mayor', *ratman* 'city councillor', *busman* 'boatman', *skiper* 'shipper'.[34] These words also entered the Scandinavian languages, and the modern Norwegian equivalents are *borgermester, rådmann, båtsmann, skipper.* On the other hand, the word for translation was borrowed from Russian and entered the Low German used in Novgorod.[35] The interpreter was called a *tolk* or a *tollik*, the act of interpretation was called *to tolken*, and the result was called *tolkinge* or *tolkie*. These words spread through Low German and into the Scandinavian languages; the modern Norwegian form is *tolk*, *å tolke* and *en tolkning*.

Trade pidgins

Another way to solve the linguistic challenges that trade leads to is to create a trade pidgin. A pidgin language is nobody's mother tongue, and is not a language in the ordinary sense of the word. The reason for this categorization is that a trade pidgin simply does not have the inventory needed for people to communicate all their needs in all of life's domains. In order to emphasize this, pidgin languages might as well have been called trade codes or, as they are often referred to, *jargons*.

The two most typical linguistic characteristics of a pidgin language or code are that the vocabulary is very small and that the grammar is simple, or almost nonexistent.[36] The most typical social characteristics are that it is made up of languages that are not closely related, and that most of the vocabulary comes from the language of the most powerful group.[37] Therefore, we often speak about English-based pidgins, Portuguese-based pidgins, etc.

The first attested trade pidgin is said to be the lingua franca, a trade language used in the southern part of Europe and the northern part of Africa in the Middle Ages. This language had vocabulary mainly from Italian, as well as from Spanish and French. Greek, Arabic and Turkish can also be mentioned as other sources for the vocabulary of lingua franca.[38] It is because of this trade pidgin, for example, that we call English a lingua franca today – it is the common language that we use across different language barriers in order to communicate with one another. However, there is reason to doubt whether lingua franca actually existed as a trade pidgin. Joanna Nolan gives a synopsis of the different views of what lingua franca actually was, from those who firmly believe it to have been a trade language, to those who, like the early Schuchardt (1883) and the modern Selbach (2008),[39] compare the lingua franca to a sea monster that everybody knows about but no one has ever seen. The fact is that it is *said* to have been a trade pidgin, but as Nolan claims:

> there are no trading documents in lingua franca, no accounts of trading conversations overheard in lingua franca, and nor does the later compilation of the pidgin's lexicon include trade terminology, with barely a mention of monetary terms, or merchandise.[40]

The data are mostly literary, where authors use this variety as a means to colour their descriptions of places and communication. Naturally, the lack of trade-related data does not necessarily mean that the language did not exist or that it was not used in trade. The methodological challenges connected to silent data are interesting and important, but we will leave the lingua franca and turn to a certain trade pidgin, which, even though its documentation is from a later period than the Middle Ages, can serve as an illustration of how speakers – traders – use the languages at hand in order to secure a minimum of useful communication.

In Norwegian, this variety is called *Russenorsk*, literally Russian-Norwegian (RN).[41] The trade in question was the Pomor trade, which involved Russian grain in exchange for Norwegian fish. The Pomor trade took place in the far north, and it was commonly Russian traders who came to Norway. There are sources of the use of RN from the mid-eighteenth to the early twentieth century, and it is assumed that RN was mainly used once a year. Unlike pidgins based on one language (as mentioned above, the language of the most powerful group), it seems that the quite small vocabulary of RN had about as many Norwegian as Russian words. In addition to this, there are parts of the lexicon that can be traced back to English, Low German, Sami and Finnish. Many of the Norwegians speaking RN were bi- or trilingual, since it was quite common in the northern part of the country to have some command of Sami, Finnish and Norwegian.

The vocabulary of RN typically included words needed to conduct trade, such as names for fish and grain; phrases like 'too much', 'not enough'; and words for the social activities connected to the trade, such as visiting the ship, drinking tea, inviting trade partners to the baptism of a child, etc. Typically, numbers were not simplified – all speakers knew how to count in both Norwegian and in Russian. It is said that Norwegian schoolchildren in the area where this trade took place even learned to count in Russian at school.

In addition to a small but relevant vocabulary, RN had very simple morphology. The words had only one form, and no declination or conjugation was used.

The only morphological feature was that most verbs ended in *–om*, and most nouns and adjectives ended in *–a*. In this way it was possible to distinguish between activity and object. One preposition known to both languages was used, written *på* in Norwegian and *po* in Russian, but pronounced in the same way.

Even if Russenorsk was younger than lingua franca and well attested for, there are also myths concerning RN. One is that the speakers were not aware that they spoke a pidgin, a simplified language. The Norwegians believed that they spoke Russian, and the Russians believed that they spoke Norwegian. This may be the case, and is reminiscent of stories of sailors who claimed to speak many languages but in fact only knew a few phrases in each. It also connects to the question of what it is to know a language – a question to which there is no firm answer.

The different ways of speaking with others that have been presented in this chapter all have to do with wanting to make oneself understood in order to conduct trade. And indeed, creative ways to overcome linguistic hindrances are the most important features of trade language as such. But for some groups, it has been necessary to conceal communication – in order to prevent the leak of trade secrets, for example. For Jewish traders, both Yiddish and Hebrew were potential languages that non-Jews did not understand, and could therefore serve as secret languages. Different groups of travellers, such as the Romani, had languages that were not intelligible to outsiders, and could serve the same purpose.[42] Due to the secret nature of these codes, however, they did not influence the language of the other groups in the society. Still, they represent the linguistic side of the historical fact that trade did not always happen in the open, for all to have insight into.

Concluding remarks

In this chapter, the emphasis has been on different types of linguistic results that can emerge from different trade situations, and examples from different language areas in Europe have been discussed. To sum up, we can consider the different dimensions that are important when it comes to linguistic output: (1) the languages in question, (2) the intensity and duration of the communication, (3) the linguistic features that are being changed.

(1) The languages in question: We have seen that the way the Hanse treated the linguistic challenge they met as international traders differed in the Kontore that they established in various European towns. In Novgorod, where the Slavic languages of the area had very little in common with the Low German of the Hansards, the business of interpretation became important, and controlling this business was a way to control trade. In Bergen, where a Germanic language closely related to Low German was spoken, the strategy was different, and a receptive bilingualism was developed. Whereas translation was the normal way to communicate in Novgorod, the only translations made in Bergen were those meant for readers outside Bergen. This means that it *does* matter which languages

are in contact with one another,[43] even if linguistic distance is not the only factor that governs the use of interpreters. Examples from more central parts of Europe show a willingness to make word lists or collections of phrases in several languages.[44] Such lists may indicate an awareness of multilingualism as a natural part of society.

(2) The intensity and duration of the communication: A pidgin language will be a likely result of trade that does not involve a settlement. This may explain why the settlement-based trade of the Hanse did not result in any pidgin languages, at least not that we know of. Traders who met seldom but repeatedly (once a year at a market, for example) might develop a pidgin consisting of a small core vocabulary and a minimum of grammar. In this case, the mother tongues of the speakers need not be changed. A trade situation that involves settlement, on the other hand, will lead to language contact and changes in the languages in question. The longer the duration and the more intense the contact, the larger the changes in the languages in question. The result can be a mixed language, if both languages are affected, or language death, where one language takes over in all domains in the society. As mentioned, power relations and politics also play a part here.

(3) The linguistic features that are being changed: The most important division is between vocabulary and grammar. Words, especially words for items or ideas that are important in a society, travel fast and change easily. We can follow the word *candy* from the Arabic *quandîj* (adj. 'of sugar') through Europe all the way to the languages of the north, demonstrating how the name of something popular spread along with the item itself. Second to vocabulary, it seems that expressions and word-forming affixes can be lent quite easily. These are linguistic tools speakers use to enrich the vocabulary by adding new nuances. The last thing to change is the phonology, meaning that words are most often pronounced in a way that fits the phonology of the receiving language.

In order to give a satisfactory explanation of the linguistic results of language contact, we must consider all three dimensions, which means that type of language, type of contact and the actual linguistic features must be looked at in an overarching way. In addition to religion and migration, trade is the most common source for language contact. The consequences of trade for the development of the languages can therefore not be overestimated.

Notes

1 E. Mørck, 'Sociolinguistic studies on the basis of medieval Norwegian charters', in E. H. Jahr (ed.), *Language Change: Advances in Historical Sociolinguistics*, Berlin and New York: Mouton de Gruyter, 1999, pp. 263–90.

2 A. Nesse, 'Bilingual texts from a bilingual city', in G. A. Ersland and M. Trebbi (eds), *Neue Studien zum Archiv und zur Sprache der Hanseaten,* Bergen: Museum Vest, 2008, pp. 47–64, and A. Nesse, 'Kong Kristoffers retterbot av 1444 slik den tolkes av forfattere mellom 1520 og 1648', in G. Alhaug, T. Bull and A.-K. Pedersen (eds), *Endre-boka: Postfestumskrift til Endre Mørck*. Oslo: Novus, 2014, pp. 95–118.

3 G. A. Ersland, *Kven eigde byen? Bygrunnlegging, grunneige og grunnleige i Bergen og eit utval nordeuropeiske byar,* Oslo: Dreyer, 2011, pp. 143–5.
4 K. Braunmüller, 'Semi-communication and beyond: some results of the Hamburg Hanseatic Project (1990–1995)', in L. Elmevik and E. H. Jahr (eds), *Contact between Low German and Scandinavian in the Late Middle Ages: Twenty-Five Years of Research,* Uppsala: Kungl. Gustav Adolfs Akademien för svensk folkkultur, 2012, p. 102.
5 D. Trotter, 'Oceano vox: You never know where a ship comes from: on multilingualism and language-mixing in medieval Britain', in K. Braunmüller and G. Ferraresi (eds), *Aspects of Multilingualism in European Language History,* Amsterdam and Philadelphia: John Benjamins, 2003, p. 15.
6 Ibid., p. 20.
7 Ibid., p. 22.
8 L. Wright, 'On the language of London merchants 1400–1900', in E.-M. Wagner and B. Beinhoff (eds), *Merchants of Innovation: The Language of Traders* (forthcoming): 'visual diamorphs', the written counterpart of synchronic codeswitching's 'homophonous diamorphs'.
9 M. B. Lange, 'The extrajudicial minutes of the Commerzdiputation Hamburg: a case study of minutes from the second half of the seventeenth century', in G. A. Ersland and M. Trebbi (eds), *Neue Studien zum Archiv und zur Sprache der Hanseaten,* Bergen: Museum Vest, 2008, pp. 101–16. Lange sets the change from Low to High German in Hamburg to the period 1530–1620. In Bergen, the development was somewhat delayed compared to this: 1580 was the starting point, when the newly appointed secretary of the Hanseatic Kontor changed the language of outgoing correspondence from Low to High German. But in protocols and similar texts meant for the Germans in Bergen, Low German was used until 1700.
10 L. Wright, 'On variation and change in London medieval mixed-language business documents', in M. Stenroos, M. Mäkinen and I. Særheim (eds), *Language Contact and Development around the North Sea,* Amsterdam and Philadelphia: John Benjamins, 2012, pp. 99–100.
11 F. Guidi-Bruscoli, 'Creating networks through languages: Italian merchants in late medieval and early modern Europe', in A. Caracausi and C. Jeggle (eds), *Commercial Networks and European Cities, 1400–1800,* London: Pickering & Chatto, 2014, pp. 65–79.
12 G. Mattingly, *Renaissance Diplomacy,* Baltimore, MD: Penguin, 1964, pp. 186, 205, here from Guidi-Bruscoli, 'Creating networks', p. 72.
13 M. T. Clanchy, *From Memory to Written Record: England 1966–1307,* Oxford: Blackwell, 1993, pp. 200–23.
14 R. Eufe, *Sta lengua ha un privilegio tanto grando. Status und Gebrauch des Venezianischen in der Republik Venedig,* Frankfurt: Peter Lang, 2006, p. 189.
15 Ibid., p. 197.
16 C. Squires, *Die Hanse in Novgorod: Sprachkontakte des Mittelniederdeutschen mit dem Russischen mit einer Vergleichsstudie über die Hanse in England,* Cologne: Böhlau Verlag, 2009, pp. 34–6.
17 Ibid., pp. 88–113. The example of mentioning of the seal is taken from *Diplomatarium Norwegicum,* vol. 23, no 337. The text was written in Hamburg in 1533.
18 Obviously, the transition did not happen overnight. The fact that a new confession was introduced top-down and that the common people needed several decades to get used to it was common for Norwegians and Germans.
19 A. Nesse, 'Written and spoken languages in Bergen in the Hansa era', in Braunmüller and Ferraresi, *Aspects of Multilingualism,* pp. 75–9.
20 O. Brattegard, 'Einige Norwegische Wörter in mittelniederdeutschen Hanseatischen Texten', *Norsk tidsskrift for sprogvidenskap,* 7, 1934, p. 284.
21 A division into five groups is offered by M. E. Soldani (here from Guidi-Bruscoli, 'Creating networks', p. 67): (1) units of measurement and quantities, (2) titles and qualification, (3) objects and merchandise, (4) technical, juridical and administrative terms, (5) time and space.

22 Oldest attested form, from 1419.
23 Oldest attested form, from 1562.
24 A. Nesse, 'Flerspråklige kilder fra Bergen', in H. L. Eklund, C. Wide, G. Harling-Kranck, S. Tiisala and M. Lamberg (eds), *Språket i historien – historien i språket*, Folkmålsstudier 47, Helsingfors: Föreningen för nordisk filologi, 2009, p. 123.
25 M. Tidderman, 'Early Anglo-Italian contact: new loanword evidence from two mercantile sources, 1440–1451', in E.-M. Wagner and B. Beinhoff (eds), *Merchants of Innovation: The Language of Traders,* forthcoming.
26 M. Lorvik, 'North Sea timber trade terminology in the early modern period: the cargo inventory for the *White Lamb* revisited', in M. Stenroos, M. Mäkinen and I. Særheim (eds), *Language Contact and Development around the North Sea*, Amsterdam: John Benjamins, 2012, p. 207.
27 E.-M. Wagner, *Linguistic Variety of Judaeo-Arabic in Letters from the Cairo Genizah*, Leiden: Brill, 2010, p. 15.
28 P. Trudgill, *Sociolinguistic Typology: Social Determinants of Linguistic Complexity*, Oxford: Oxford University Press, 2011, p. 40.
29 M. Tandefelt, 'Vyborg: free trade in four languages', in Braunmüller and Ferraresi, *Aspects of Multilingualism*, p. 85.
30 Squires, *Die Hanse in Novgorod*, p. 37.
31 H. Menke, 'Niederdeutsch als Geber-, Nehmer- und Mittlersprache', in H. H. Munske (ed.), *Deutsch im Kontakt mit germanischen Sprachen*, Tübingen: Max Niemeyer Verlag, 2003, p. 107.
32 Squires, *Die Hanse in Novgorod*, p. 38.
33 Guidi-Bruscoli, 'Creating networks', p. 73.
34 Examples from Menke, 'Niederdeutsch als Geber-, Nehmer- und Mittlersprache', p. 107.
35 Also Squires, *Die Hanse in Novgorod*, pp. 17–18 has *tolk* as a Russian loan word in Low German, even if this word enters Low German sources earlier than it does Russian sources: 1253 (LG) vs. 1418 (R).
36 Trudgill, *Sociolinguistic Typology*, p. 41.
37 J. Holm, 'Contact and change: pidgins and creoles', in R. Hickey (ed.), *Handbook of Language Contact,* Hoboken, NJ: John Wiley & Sons, 2012, p. 254.
38 I. Broch and E. H. Jahr, *Russenorsk – et pidginspråk i Norge*, Oslo: Novus, 1981, p. 12.
39 Here from J. Nolan, 'Lingua Franca – a not so simple pidgin', *SOAS Working Papers in Linguistics* 17, 2015, p. 99.
40 Ibid., p. 101.
41 The description of Russenorsk is based on Broch and Jahr, *Russenorsk – et pidginspråk i Norge.*
42 R. Iversen, *Secret Languages in Norway*, vols 1–3, Oslo: Dybwad, 1944.
43 Obviously, languages are only in contact with one another in the brains of bilingual people. What we discuss here is contact between speakers of different languages.
44 J. Gessler, *Le Livre des Mestiers de Bruges et ses dérivés: Quatre anciens manuels de conversation*, Bruges 1931.

PART II

The Mediterranean

7

VENICE

City of merchants or city for merchandise?

Monique O'Connell

Introduction

'What news on the Rialto?' This well-known phrase from Shakespeare's *Merchant of Venice* evokes both Venice's centrality as a marketplace of goods and information and the prominent role merchants played in the city's political and economic life. Medieval critics often pointed to Venetians' commercial interests when characterizing them as greedy, self-interested or untrustworthy; scholars in the twentieth century often saw Venetians as entrepreneurial protagonists of an emerging capitalist spirit. The merchant elite that dominated international commerce also claimed exclusive political power from the late thirteenth century. From the thirteenth to the sixteenth centuries, Venetian political and merchant networks were tightly intertwined. From the sixteenth century on, large-scale structural factors as well as local changes in politics and economic life loosened the connective tissue between Venetian politicians and merchants. There were not only new patterns of economic exchange, but the 'merchants of Venice' took on a much more diverse social profile. Recent scholarship has looked beyond patrician networks and focused on the brokers, agents, citizens and subjects who participated in Venetian trade networks. While there is no doubt Venetian participation in international maritime exchange was an important part of its economy, recent scholarship has emphasized the manufacturing and industrial dimensions of medieval Venetian economic life. This overview places Venice's well-known dominance of the luxury trade in spices and silks into the broader context of commerce in raw materials that fed Venetian manufacturing, and also suggests that medieval Venice gained institutional strength from the overlapping commercial and political interests of the patrician elite.

The sources available for the study of economic history in Venice are relatively limited compared to many other northern Italian city-states, and they certainly pale in comparison to the documentary riches of the Florentine archives. Historians of

Florence have benefited from the family memoirs (*ricordanze*) that offer rich insights into the overlapping networks of social, family and business relationships; there were more than 500 produced in Florence before 1500, while only one example for Venice survives.[1] Neither does Venice benefit from the notarial riches of the Genoese archives. The same imbalance exists when it comes to merchant account books and tax census data.[2] The archives of the state magistracies regulating commerce have suffered serious losses and the majority of the documentation dates to the sixteenth century and later.[3] The historiography of medieval merchants and commercial culture in Venice has thus focused on close analysis of a few examples rather than on serial or statistical analysis.

Location and hinterland: city, mainland and maritime realms

Situated on a chain of islands in a lagoon, Venice lacked both a traditional hinterland and a nobility dependent on landed estates for power. In environmental terms, the Venetian hinterland encompassed the lagoon, its estuaries and even the Brenta, Piave, Tagliamento and Isonzo river systems. Venice's aquatic location meant that the work of maintaining the city and managing the delicate lagoon environment was an ongoing concern. Crouzet Pavan has argued that the necessities of water management gave rise to public magistracies that intervened in urban development for the common good in a more continuous and thorough way than was the case in other medieval communes.[4] While medieval Venetians did exploit their marshy hinterland for fish and above all for salt, in comparative perspective Venice had far fewer local resources to draw on than did other cities. Thus, the organization of transportation systems emerged as a key Venetian contribution to the development of Mediterranean merchant networks (see Figure 7.1).

The territory that Venice conquered, colonized or ruled directly also had essential functions in the Venetian economic system. In the thirteenth century, Venetian power extended through the eastern Adriatic to the island of Crete and the Peloponnesian port cities of Coron and Modon. In the early fifteenth century, Venice began a programme of political and military expansion on both the mainland and in the maritime realms. The lagoon, Venice's mainland domains in north-central Italy and the maritime state were connected to one another by communicative channels and complex patterns of exchange. Venetian territorial dominion was further complicated by the fact that each subject city and town had its own immediate hinterland. But each region was tied to Venice by relations of production and exchange, often to the economic benefit of the capital city. The economic rhythms of the system were determined by the timing of fairs in Germany and elsewhere, but also by weather conditions: Alpine passes and sailing routes became virtually impassable in the winter. In the spring, Venetian galleys sailed out to the ports of the Levant, returning to the city in the summer and again in December in time to meet recently arrived transalpine merchants.[5]

Figure 7.1 Map of the eastern Mediterranean

In the lagoon itself, medieval Venetians relied on their aquatic *contado* for cultivation as well as for protection from foreign invasion.[6] Venetians hunted birds and fished in the lagoons, supplying the food markets of the growing city. Monasteries and other religious establishments claimed title to great aquatic domains, and in an early form of fish farming, weirs made of reeds and marsh grass controlled the seasonal migration of fish and created an abundant catch.[7] The lagoon also contained salt-flats; by the twelfth century Chioggia became one of the most active export centres of salt in the Mediterranean, and while competition and ecological change shifted salt production outside of the lagoon by the sixteenth century, the Venetians retained a monopoly on the production and sale of salt.[8]

Urban industries were dependent on far-flung networks for the provision of their raw materials as well as for markets for their end products, so it is not possible to entirely separate the commercial and manufacturing sectors of the Venetian economy.[9] The glass industry, relocated to Murano in the thirteenth century, relied on imported soda ash from the eastern Mediterranean. In the early fifteenth century, Venice became the world leader in glassmaking both because of its near-monopoly on high quality soda ash from Syria as well as technological innovations that allowed for the production of extraordinarily transparent crystal glass.[10] While Venice initially imported manufactured glass from the east, the city benefited from Levantine industrial decline in the fourteenth century, and the Venetians eventually reversed the pattern of trade, producing and exporting manufactured goods to the east.[11] Venetian glassworkers produced large quantities of glass, crystal, mirrors and beads for export to foreign markets. Some items, like mosque lamps, were designed specifically for Muslim markets in Egypt and Syria; by some estimates, over 20 per cent of Venetian glass was shipped to these markets.[12] Venice's predominance in the glass industry also allowed the city to specialize in the production of spectacles, which were exported from Venice all over Europe in the medieval period.[13]

As in the case of glass manufacture, the Venetian wool and silk textile industries relied on networks of commercial exchange to provide raw materials as well as for resale of finished products. Silk manufacture in the city, under way from the late thirteenth century, was encouraged by the immigration of about 300 silk artisans from Lucca in the early fourteenth century. Venetian merchants imported different types of raw silk from a variety of locations, including Persia, Syria and Palestine, Greece and the Balkans, southern Italy, and from the Italian mainland, and exported both finished and semi-finished products to European markets.[14] The wool industry of Venice was similarly supplied with raw wool and the 'industrial spices' needed for finishing and dyeing cloth such as alum and ash by merchants importing products from the Veneto, from southern Italy, from England and Flanders, and across the Mediterranean.[15] Some of the raw material was re-exported, but between 35 and 40 per cent was processed in Venice. Over the course of the fifteenth century, the number of woollen cloths produced in Venice grew, from 3,000–5,000 pieces annually in the first part of the century to 6,000 pieces per year by the end of the century.[16] By the fifteenth and sixteenth centuries, Italian textiles in general dominated Near Eastern markets, and Venetian silks and wools in particular had an ascendant position in the markets of the Levant.[17]

The maritime state, a string of port cities and towns down the Dalmatian coast and in the Aegean and including the Ionian islands as well as Crete and Cyprus, was important for the resources it provided as well as for its function as way stations for Venetian shipping. Frederick Lane famously called Venice's maritime domains an 'empire of naval bases', but in fact the commercial linkages in Venice's colonial network depended a great deal on the productive capacities as well as the human resources of its overseas territories.[18] Dalmatia produced salt for export to Venice; Crete produced wheat, oil, and cheese and wine for export to Venice as well as to the eastern Mediterranean, Anatolia and Alexandria; Cyprus produced sugar, cotton and salt for export as well.[19] Perhaps the most well-known element of Venetian maritime exchange was the trade in spices and luxury goods: Venetian merchants transported aloe, balm, camphor, madder-root, laudanum and mastic for medicines; sandalwood, cherrywood, porcelain, myrobalans, coral, lacquer, glass and ivory for decorative purposes; incense and musk for religious ceremonies; indigo, linen, silk and cotton for clothing; and cinnamon, cardamom, ginger, nutmeg, saffron and sugar for consumption. But the spice in which the Venetian merchants trafficked most heavily was pepper. Venetians brought about three times as much pepper back from Alexandria as they did any other spice, and spent more money on it than any other item.[20] By the beginning of the fifteenth century, Venetians had about three-quarters of the trade in spices imported into Europe; the rest was brought by merchants from Genoa, Catalonia, Marseille and Ragusa.[21]

Raffale de Caresini (1314–90), Grand Chancellor of the Republic and author of several accounts of Venetian history, asserted in his *Chronica* that 'It is Venice's concern to cultivate the sea, where honor and riches are abundant, and to leave the land alone, which repeatedly has brought her scandal and error.'[22] Some scholars have used this statement to imagine Venice as uninterested in the Veneto region until the fifteenth century conquest, but in fact the city was tied to the mainland by trade and by dependence on mainland resources, above all the timber resources and forests that supplied the city with building materials, firewood, charcoal and high-quality timber for the fleet.[23] Venetian patricians began to buy, develop and exploit mainland property from the thirteenth century, and much of this landownership clustered around Treviso.[24] After the Venetian conquest, the economy of mainland and metropole became even more tightly intertwined.[25]

The cities of the Italian mainland, including Padua, Verona, Vicenza, Treviso and Udine, were part of a highly urbanized socio-economic system of north central-Italy before the Venetian conquest, and each city maintained its own urban economic structures to varying degrees after the Venetian takeover. The silver mining industry around Vicenza reached its peak in the late fifteenth and early sixteenth century, and Brescia manufactured arms and armour that it was able to export widely because of the artisans' ability to produce armour adapted to a range of buyers' needs.[26] Despite some protectionist measures taken by Venice, the wool and silk industries of the mainland cities also manufactured both finished and semi-finished goods for markets in Venice and elsewhere in Italy.[27]

Venice's location created advantages as well as challenges. The Alpine passes that brought goods and merchants from the German trading hubs of Salzburg, Nuremburg, Ulm and Passau opened onto the Veneto floodplain, with multiple rivers providing transportation corridors to Venice. In Venice, the transalpine routes connected to the Mediterranean shipping lanes that touched the ports and harbours of the eastern Adriatic and then radiated out from the Ionian islands to the Black Sea, Egypt and Syria, and the western Mediterranean. Venice was thus at a nodal point where Northern European trade circuits intersected Mediterranean trade routes as well as a hub of transfer between the eastern and western halves of the sea.

Venetian trade policies emphasized this geographical advantage. In order to control the transportation networks that tied the cities, port towns and islands of its realm together, Venice claimed control over the communication and commercial networks that passed through its territory. In the Adriatic, which was referred to as the 'Gulf of Venice', no foreign armed ship was permitted to enter, and merchant ships had to have a passport, call at Venice and pay customs there.[28] The economic privileges of mainland cities varied, but there was a general trend towards making the Rialto markets and Venetian shipping the hub of mainland trade as well.[29] In neither case was Venice entirely successful at suppressing illegal trade that bypassed the capital and its customs house. While there remained a lively contraband trade, Venetian regulations were successful enough to make the city the premier point of exchange in the region, at least in the fourteenth and fifteenth centuries.

The copper trade provides a good example of the way Venice's role as a regional emporium intersected with its international commercial networks. In the later Middle Ages, Venice was the key market for the copper trade; it received some copper by sea from Bruges, but the majority of its supply came from mines in Slovakia.[30] Entrepreneurs from southern Germany had a hand in managing the mines themselves and also exported it to Venice, either by shipping it up the Danube to Vienna and then across the Alps or by transporting it across Hungary and Croatia and then across the Adriatic Sea. In Venice, the copper was sold at auction at the Fondaco dei Tedeschi, rerefined if necessary, and transported by Venetian merchants by ship to the Levant. From the fourteenth century, the single largest customer for Venetian copper was Mamluk Egypt, where it was used for coinage as well as for domestic and industrial containers, such as vats for sugar production. In Egypt, Venetian merchants would exchange the copper for spices and other goods that they would ship back to Venice and sell for transport beyond the Alps.

The densest network of Venetian commercial exchange was in the southeastern Mediterranean, focused on the cities of Damascus, Aleppo and Alexandria. Venetian merchants were trading in the ports of Egypt, Syria and Palestine before the Crusades, but the trading privileges and commercial quarters they received from the Crusader states in return for military and naval aid increased their access to eastern markets. Venetian diplomacy succeeded in preserving these privileges with the Mamluk state, as Christ's contribution to this volume details. Venice struggled with Genoa for commercial supremacy in the region through several wars in the thirteenth and fourteenth centuries, but after defeating the Genoese in the war of Chioggia (1378–81), Venetian trade networks predominated in the eastern Mediterranean.

Commerce and connections: state policy and patrician economic advantage

One of the foremost historians of the Venetian economy referred to the city's Senate as a 'board of directors', pointing to the unusually high degree of overlap and collaboration between politicians and merchants.[31] Tellingly, there was no separate guild for merchants in Venice. The right to participate in international trade was limited to patricians and some elite citizens; the state carried out policies and administer institutions designed to maximize mercantile profits. There were reciprocal benefits for individual Venetian merchants and the for the state in this arrangement, as merchants gained advantages over their competitors and the state financed itself in large part through taxing the revenues of the trade that flowed through the city. The key protections, privileges and incentives for international trade offered by the Venetian government were the state-run galley convoys, trade privileges and treaties negotiated with foreign rulers, a network of governors in directly ruled territories and consular representatives in trading ports, and the reduction of competition through protectionist legislation. At home, the government maintained a host of judicial and regulatory magistracies that offered reliable and trustworthy venues for exchange and functional methods for conflict resolution.

Starting in the fourteenth century, the Venetian government organized convoys (*mude*) with armed galleys that traveled along predetermined routes to the Black Sea, Cyprus, Alexandria, Beirut, Flanders, Southern France and North Africa.[32] The galleys were built in the state-run arsenal, but for each voyage individual galleys were auctioned to a group of investors who outfitted the ship and shared the profits of the voyage. Investment in the fleet played an important role in the formation of a merchant elite among the Venetian patriciate, and there was a core of galley patrons and captains who invested repeatedly in the same galley routes.[33] The defensive capabilities of these convoys lowered transaction costs and benefited Venetian merchants in several ways; for instance, Venetian insurance rates to Alexandria were much lower than for other merchants because they could rely on state convoys.[34] There was a wide range of merchandise permitted on the galleys, but merchants tended to transport high-value luxury goods such as spices and Levantine silks, while privately owned roundships or cogs transported commodities such as grain or oil. Recent scholarship has emphasized the importance of this private shipping in creating local networks of exchange, and has also highlighted the active role Venetians citizens and subjects played in this type of shipping.[35]

The peak of the galley system was in the mid-fifteenth century, the apogee of Venetian trade with the eastern Mediterranean.[36] In the 1430s and 1440s, Venice had 180 galleys sailing in convoy. The classic example of the patrician-merchant Andrea Barbarigo illustrates how service on the galleys could help a young patrician begin his career. Beginning with very little capital in 1417, Barbarigo sailed on the Venetian galleys as a 'bowman of the quarterdeck', a position that allowed him to load cargo without paying freight costs.[37] The state created these positions for young patricians as a sort of commercial and maritime apprenticeship; Andrea gradually built up his capital by working as an agent for other merchants abroad as well as for his relatives in Venetian Crete. As his wealth grew, Barbarigo stayed in Venice and entrusted his international affairs to others, leaving a comfortable fortune of 15,000 ducats. Barbarigo's success in business came in part from his close associations with other Venetian merchants, particularly the banker Francesco Balbi and the Capello brothers, who began their careers as patrons of the Flanders galleys and ended with prominent political positions. Barbarigo was typical in that he relied on a tight network of family members and partners who acted in collaboration.[38] The later history of Barbarigo's family illustrates the role agricultural estates on the mainland played in long-term patrician investment strategies.[39]

The survival of Giacomo Badoer's detailed account book from his four-year residence in Constantinople (1436–40) offers a window into the experience and business practices of a Venetian merchant abroad.[40] As was the case with many Venetian patrician families, Giacomo was in business while his brother Gerolamo occupied himself with politics. From Venice, Giacomo received wool and silk textiles as well as small quantities of other goods; in exchange he sent wax, pepper and other spices, Byzantine silk, and a wide variety of other textiles. Badoer also cultivated a wide network of correspondents and agents in other Mediterranean and Black Sea ports, including Kaffa, Tana, Trezibond, Crete, Beirut and Alexandria; relying on this network, he traded wine from Candia, linen from Alexandria, oil from Coron, Majorca and southern Italy, pork from Salonica, and ash from Syria for copper, lead, alum, slaves, silver and wheat from across the Mediterranean.

Badoer benefited from the multiple trade agreements the Venetian government negotiated with the Byzantine – and later the Ottoman – authorities in Constantinople.[41] These privileges – including reduced customs and tariffs and an autonomous merchant quarter – depended on Venetian diplomats who bargained for advantageous arrangements and defended the enforcement of the agreements. Ambassadors often were charged with resolving conflicts over commercial matters, asking for justice in cases where Venetian merchant goods had been impounded or tied up in litigation in foreign courts. In just one example, when royal officials in Valencia confiscated a cargo of silk and mercury from Malaga belonging to the citizen merchant Giovanni Marcanova, the Venetian Senate wrote to the Queen of Aragon and Sicily on Marcanova's behalf, demanding the restitution of the goods, and subsequently sent an ambassador to settle various commercial disputes.[42] In many cases, Venetian merchants were able to rely on the political and diplomatic support of the state to aid in conflict resolution; in other cases merchants preferred to settle disputes using local institutions or to use a combination of strategies to ensure the best outcome.

Venetian merchants also relied on the institutional and official aid provided by Venetian *fondacos* and Venetian consuls resident in the main international trading hubs. Consuls (or the Bailo in Constantinople/Istanbul) had both diplomatic and commercial responsibilities, ensuring that trade agreements and treaties were observed, arbitrating disagreements among Venetian merchants, and acting on behalf of merchants in commercial and banking matters.[43] Christ's detailed study of the activities of Biagio Dolfin, consul in Alexandria from 1418 to 1420, reveals the variety of conflicts in which consuls might be called upon to intervene: pilgrims' litigation over the sale of spices, arguments over the export of relics, disagreements over the timing of the convoy's departure, illicit confiscations at the customs house and merchants imprisoned for debt.[44] These state representatives were also able to build up reservoirs of local knowledge and expertise that benefited Venetian merchants at the beginning of their careers abroad. Giovanni Foscari, a young Venetian merchant trading between London, Bruges and Venice in the 1460s, did not yet have a wide network of correspondents and thus, as Montemezzo has demonstrated, relied heavily on Bartolomeo Zorzi, the Venetian consul in Bruges, as a guarantor and financial intermediary.[45]

Within territories directly ruled by Venice, governors, elected in the councils of the capital and sent to rule in Venice's name for terms of about two years, influenced the enforcement of Venetian economic policies. These governorships provided reciprocal benefits to patricians, the state and to merchants. Many of these governors moved from mainland to maritime governorships and then back to Venetian governing councils, meaning they had alternating roles in forming and enforcing policies of territorial governance.[46] Mueller's study of the Giustinian family demonstrates that at the same time as some family members ran a small commercial enterprise on Corfu, other Giustinian repeatedly served as castellan on the island, creating a network of family connections, property and influence that stretched from Corfu to Negroponte, Chios and Serifo.[47] Schmitt has documented the same mix of political and commercial influence for the Zorzi and Contarini families in Albania, and Arbel has shown the Corner family's intermeshed political and economic interests on Cyprus.[48]

Local institutions and conflict resolution: controlled competition and networks of trust

In the city of Venice itself, the government maintained a host of judicial and regulatory magistracies that offered reliable and trustworthy venues for exchange and functional methods for conflict resolution. The area around the Rialto bridge was Venice's main market, acting as a centre of information as well as housing many of the banking and financial services that facilitated trade and commercial exchange in the city. During the medieval period the market district developed specialized areas that reflected the increasing complexity of the intersecting governmental, financial and commercial sectors of the economy. The first private banks appeared near Rialto in the mid-twelfth century, and between 1250 and 1350 the district was reorganized, making the piazza near San Giacomo the centre of credit, marine insurance and other large-scale financial operations. The scale of the banking industry was large: in 1500, about one Venetian in thirty held a current account at Rialto, and bankers were estimated to hold about a million ducats in their accounts.[49] Clustered in the same area were the offices of the Consoli dei Mercanti, magistrates who had administrative and judicial competence to hear commercial disputes, including matters of overseas trade, bankruptcy, exchange rates, insurance contracts and brokerage fees.[50] The Giustizia Vecchia had a central role in the administration of the urban economy. The Giustizia Vecchia began by controlling the trade in foodstuffs and moved towards the regulation of the marketplace in general, overseeing craft guilds, weights and measures, price controls and enforcing the public laws of the market as well as small claims arising from transactions.[51] Merchants could also bring commercial disputes to the Giudici di Petizion, a court that heard lawsuits worth less than 50 ducats.[52] A special court, the Giudici del Forestier, heard civil cases regarding foreigners.[53] These magistracies and judicial organs were staffed by Venetian patricians elected for short, rotating terms in office, meaning that many of the officials responsible for overseeing trade within the city themselves had experience as merchants.

Economic historians continue to debate how trust in business transactions operates and institutions' role in creating that trust.[54] Venetian merchants, and in particular Venetian patrician merchants, operated in collaborative networks that demanded resident investors trust in their agents and representatives in far-flung ports. Shared access to institutional benefits such as the Rialto markets, galley convoys and trade privileges and representation abroad aided in the creation of trust as well as providing motivation for merchants to comply with the state's demands. Courier services delivering news and letters developed between the main European commercial centres in the thirteenth century, and by the late fourteenth and early fifteenth century commercial correspondence travelled relatively quickly throughout the Mediterranean. Melis and his students, using the surviving correspondence of the Datini group in Florence, demonstrated that letters between Venice and Florence took an average of five to seven days to deliver; letters between Venice and Constantinople took thirty-four to forty-six days.[55] Surviving collections of merchants' letters have allowed scholars to reconstruct, at least partially, the way that Venetian commercial networks developed and functioned across time and space.[56] One example is provided by Guglielmo Querini, a patrician merchant active in the mid-fifteenth century who never left Venice and who participated in a Mediterranean-wide business network solely through letters, relying on friends, relatives and agents to carry out his business for him.[57] These letters were sometimes instructions on business actions, but they also acted as a sort of circuit of information with economic repercussions, a huge asset to any medieval merchant.[58]

Getting such information before other merchants could offer a huge advantage, and therefore keeping news private was often as important as getting it first. Christ's analysis of a 1419 letter from Antonio Morosini to the Venetian consul in Alexandria,

Biagio Dolfin, shows that Morosini was providing a digest of political events in a very similar form to that found in his chronicle.[59] In a separate letter, Antonio's nephew Albano Morosini instructed Dolfin not to read the letter publicly, indicating that a part of the information's value was its exclusivity. The relevant question for understanding the degree of Venetian patrician group solidarity is the degree to which these commercial and correspondence networks extended beyond the patriciate. Using notarial records from fifteenth-century Alexandria, Apellàniz has shown that Venetians there transacted business with non-patricians, citizens by privilege, and Greek and Jewish subjects of Venice's empire, through an analysis of notarial records.[60] Similarly, Dursteler has found an extensive unofficial nation around the Venetian bailo's residence in Constantinople.[61] In Venice itself, patrician merchants relied on partnerships with citizens and recent immigrants: in the fifteenth-century banking industry, there were several partnerships between noble and non-noble bankers, and in the wool industry, there were multiple linkages between patrician merchants and artisan workers, both citizens and foreigners.[62]

While citizens of Venice had the same access to trading networks as patricians did, they were not able to hold political offices, limiting the kind of intersecting political and economic kinship networks some patrician families found so beneficial. The example of the citizen merchant Giovanni Marcanova is instructive in this case.[63] Giovanni was the son of a doctor from Verona who gained Venetian citizenship in 1381. Giovanni established himself in the London–Venice trade, living in London from 1417 to 1438, developing a wide range of connections with English merchants, and eventually marrying an Englishwoman. As many merchants did, Marcanova then returned to Venice for the second part of his career and invested in a variety of commercial ventures reaching to Egypt and Constantinople. Marcanova prospered during the 1420s and 1430s, when trade was booming, but his business took a sharp downward turn during the more turbulent 1440s and 1450s, ending in near-bankruptcy at his death in 1458. Both Barile and Clarke suggest that while citizens like Marcanova had kinship, business and social ties with patricians and also were able to build broad commercial networks, ultimately these networks were more fragile than those of patrician families, as citizens could not draw on the same resources, landed patrimonies or political connections to sustain their business ventures during difficult times.[64]

One Venetian institution designed to facilitate cross-cultural trade and to limit potential conflicts was brokerage. A broker (*sensali*) was required to complete any deal between merchants, and there were two groups of brokers operating in the medieval period: one in the Fondaco dei Tedeschi and the other on the Rialto. The communal revenue from the brokerage tax was substantial and provides a snapshot of the volume of trade conducted on the Rialto (the Germans and other foreign merchants were protected from increases in brokerage fees by treaty). In 1413, for instance, the brokerage tax was expected to yield 60,000 ducats a year, meaning an annual volume of trade totalling at least 6 million ducats.[65] In 1497, membership in the brokers' guild was limited to Venetian citizens alone, reflecting the

Venetian government's perspective that brokers were in the marketplace as impartial agents protecting state interests. In fact, as Rothman has demonstrated, brokers often forged personal ties of friendship and accommodation with their clients; furthermore, by the sixteenth century there were increasing numbers of Jewish, Armenian and Greek-Orthodox brokers, refugees from Venetian territories in the eastern Mediterranean, and converts and renegades.[66]

The Fondaco dei Tedeschi, a publicly administered enclave for the German merchant community modelled on *fondacos* for merchants found in the Muslim world, was in the medieval period a principal institution for regulating and controlling a foreign merchant community.[67] From the early thirteenth century, merchants from Germany, Poland, Bohemia and beyond were all compelled to lodge in the Fondaco and to store their goods there; Venetian authorities oversaw all business contracted there, appointed its officials and charged fees for lodging as well as levying taxes. Whenever a new merchant arrived, he was assigned to a broker, who mediated his commercial transactions and interactions with the city. State regulations not only compelled 'German' merchants to conduct their trade in the Fondaco, they limited Venetian merchants from travelling and trading with Germans in the mainland or in Germany. As a result, the exchange of wool, metals, fur, hides and leather from beyond the Alps for spices, cotton, sugar and silk from Levantine markets was funnelled entirely through the Fondaco, and by the late fifteenth century communal revenues from taxes and fees on this trade were 20,000 ducats per year or 100 ducats per day.[68]

Constable has argued that the Venetian adoption of this Muslim institution set it apart from the rest of Southern Europe, where similar institutions functioned more as a residence for traders doing business far from home, not a locus of state surveillance or control.[69] Other foreign merchants in medieval Venice did not have *fondacos*: traders from elsewhere in Italy as well as from Venice's maritime domains clustered in particular neighborhoods, but it was not until the sixteenth century that the Venetian state introduced other regulated residential enclaves, at a point when concerns about religious and confessional difference were increasingly of concern to the Venetian authorities. Only a few Jews were permitted to live permanently in Venice before the fifteenth century, although it seems that some evaded those regulations.[70] In 1516 the Venetian Senate established the Jewish Ghetto, an enclosed residential area under governmental control.[71] Throughout the sixteenth and seventeenth centuries, increasing numbers of foreign merchants, including Dutch, Armenians and Greeks, came to live and trade in the city; none had formal residential enclosures like the Fondaco dei Tedeschi or the Ghetto, although they did tend to cluster in particular neighborhoods.[72] Among these foreign merchants were Ottoman subjects, who included not only Muslims but Jews, Armenians and Greek residents of Ottoman lands. In 1621, the government established a Fondaco dei Turchi to house Levantine Ottoman merchants.[73]

Increased control over the city's Jewish residents was only one of a series of state initiatives in the early sixteenth century reacting to the sweeping economic and political changes in Venice and in the world around it. European penetration of the

Atlantic and Indian Ocean trading worlds did not end Venice's position as a transfer point between the Mediterranean and Northern Europe, but they did cause significant short-term fluctuations in the spice markets of Alexandria. At the same time, Venice faced a coalition of Italian and European powers during the war of Cambrai and a serious threat from the expanding Ottoman empire to the east; both conflicts highlighted the new fragility of Venice's international position in the sixteenth century. The Venetian state also added new institutions designed to control and direct international trade, establishing a Board of Trade (Cinque Savi alla Mercanzia) in 1507 to rationalize Venetian commercial policies, to attract foreign merchants to the city and to facilitate long-distance trade.[74]

By the later sixteenth century, two major changes transformed the maritime trading system of Venice, the first was the weakness and eventual end of the state-sponsored galley system. External factors such as repeated war with the Ottomans and the development of competing trade networks in the Atlantic world played a role in the system's difficulties, but changes in the political and organizational superstructure also had an impact. One of the main benefits of the convoy system was its regularity, which allowed foreign trading partners to rely on the arrival of Venetian goods and thus created robust local networks of common knowledge and expectations. Doumerc has documented the repeated late departures of the convoys and the way this lateness disrupted established trading patterns.[75] Furthermore, Judde de la Larivière has identified the increasing dominance of a small cadre of patricians over the galley auctions – meaning that access to the benefits of the system became the provenance of an increasingly exclusive elite.[76] The galley system eventually ended entirely in 1569 and Venetian trade became less predictable, as it was not tied to the centrally organized rhythms of the state convoys.[77]

The second major development was a change in the social composition of the merchants of Venice, both at home and abroad. The Levantine trade had been dominated by patricians, but from the sixteenth century on, patricians travelled abroad less often, relying on agents to do their work in faraway ports. But maritime trade was increasingly in the hands of non-patrician merchants from the Venetian mainland and maritime domains, including Jews from Venice, its colonies and the Ottoman realms.[78] These merchants faced increasing competition from English and Dutch merchants, many of whom worked in partnership with Greeks from Venice's colonies.[79] These shifts in shipping and trade patterns meant that the networks linking the mainland and maritime regions together passed less frequently through Venice and the markets of the Rialto: Ragusan, Greek and Armenian merchants came to the cities of the mainland to purchase wool fabrics produced there, as did merchants from Corfu, Cyprus and Crete.[80] Wool fabrics from Bergamo, Vicenza, Verona and Padua exported to southern Italy, Germany and the Balkans, but by the sixteenth century they were highly desired in Egypt and Syria.[81] Conversely, merchants from Bergamo as well as from Venice's Greek territories formed part of the Venetian merchant community in Constantinople in the sixteenth century.[82] By the end of the sixteenth century, the majority of Venetians present in England were Greek subjects.[83]

At the turn of the sixteenth century, Venice was not only among the four largest cities in Europe, it was the most prominent centre of Mediterranean trade, superseding other maritime ports in the reach of its hinterland, the size of its fleet and its control of the most extensive commercial network. It also demonstrated the greatest institutional specialization, particularly with regard to the administration of the state-owned galleys, and the most closely interwoven relationships between commerce and politics. Scholars interested in explaining Venice's changing position in the later sixteenth- and seventeenth-century Mediterranean have generally looked to external circumstances, including the rise of Atlantic trading networks and competition from foreign merchants for control of Mediterranean trade. In institutional terms, the end of the state galley system meant an end to the reduced transaction costs available to participants in the system, yet Venetian structures designed to protect property rights, resolve conflicts and facilitate access to information on market activities remained as strong as ever. Oscar Gelderblom has recently argued that institutional flexibility, particularly the ability to adapt legal institutions to merchants' needs, explains the shifting centrality of Bruges, Antwerp and Amsterdam to Northern European commerce between 1250 and 1650.[84] Seen through this interpretative lens, medieval Venice flourished because its institutions were flexible enough to accommodate networks of domestic and foreign merchants, yet strong enough to provide adequate stability, support and protection. This balancing act was facilitated by the overlapping commercial and political interests of the patrician elite.

Notes

1 J. Grubb, 'Memory and identity: why Venetians didn't keep ricordanze', *Renaissance Studies* 8/4, 1994, pp. 357–87; *Merchant Culture in Fourteenth Century Venice: The Zibaldone da Canal,* tr. J. E. Dotson, Binghamton, NY: MRTS, 1994.

2 F. Lane, *Andrea Barbarigo, Merchant of Venice, 1418–1449,* New York: Octagon Books, 1967, pp. 137–50; R. Mueller, *The Venetian Money Market: Banks, Panics and the Public Debt 1200–1500,* Baltimore, MD: Johns Hopkins University Press, 1997.

3 *Guida Generale degli Archivi di Stato, Venezia,* ed. M. F. Tiepolo, vol. 4, pp. 927–50, online http://www.maas.ccr.it/h3/h3.exe/aguida/findex_guida.

4 E. Crouzet-Pavan, *Venice Triumphant: The Horizons of a Myth,* tr. Lydia G. Cochrane, Baltimore, MD: Johns Hopkins University Press, 1992, pp. 1–45. An interesting potential comparison is the medieval trading centre of Novgorod, where the necessity to clear swampland gave rise to public works projects in paving.

5 F. Lane, 'Fleets and fairs: the function of the Venetian Muda', in *Studi in onore di Armando Sapori,* 2 vols, Milan: Cisalpino, 1957, vol. 1, pp. 649–63.

6 E. Crouzet Pavan, 'An ecological understanding of the myth of Venice', in J. Martin and D. Romano (eds), *Venice Reconsidered: The History and Civilization of an Italian City State, 1297–1797,* Baltimore, MD: Johns Hopkins University Press, 2000, pp. 39–64.

7 E. Crouzet Pavan, *La mort lente de Torcello: Histoire d'une cité disparue,* Paris: Fayard, 1995, pp. 176–96; H. Zug Tucci, 'Pesca e caccia in Laguna', in L. Cracco Ruggini, M. Pavan, G. Cracco and G. Ortalli (eds), *Storia di Venezia: Dalle origini alla caduta della serenissima,* vol. 1, *Origini–Età Ducale,* Rome: Enciclopedia Italiana, 1992.

8 J.-C. Hocquet, 'Le Saline', in Cracco Ruggini et al., *Storia di Venezia,* vol. 1; Hocquet, *Le sel et la fortune de Venise,* Villeneuve-d'Ascq: Publications de l'Université de Lille, 1978.

9 L. Pezzolo, 'The Venetian economy', in E. Dursteler (ed.), *A Companion to Venetian History, 1400–1797*, Leiden: Brill, 2013, p. 272.
10 D. Jacoby, 'Raw materials for the glass industries of Venice and the Terraferma, about 1370–about 1460', *Journal of Glass Studies* 35, 1993, pp. 65–90; P. McCray, *Glassmaking in Renaissance Venice: The Fragile Craft*, Brookfield, VT: Aldershot, 1999.
11 E. Ashtor, *Technology, Industry and Trade: The Levant versus Europe, 1250–1500*, London: Variorum Reprints, 1992.
12 R. Mack, *Bazaar to Piazza: Islamic Trade and Italian Art, 1300–1600*, Berkeley, CA: University of California Press, 2002, pp. 113–23; S. Carboni (ed.), *Venice and the Islamic World, 828–1797*, New York: Metropolitan Museum of Art, 2007, pp. 252–75.
13 P. Spufford, *Power and Profit: The Merchant in Medieval Europe*, New York: Thames & Hudson, 2002, p. 270.
14 L. Molà, *The Silk Industry of Renaissance Venice*, Baltimore, MD: Johns Hopkins University Press, 2000, pp. 55–88.
15 A. Mozzato, 'The production of woolens in Fifteenth and Sixteenth Century Venice', in P. Lanaro (ed.), *At the Centre of the Old World: Trade and Manufacturing in Venice and the Venetian Mainland, 1400–1800*, Toronto: Centre for Reformation and Renaissance Studies, 2006, pp. 75–80.
16 Ibid., pp. 80–3.
17 A. Caracausi, 'The wool trade, Venice and the Mediterranean cities', in A. Caracausi and C. Jeggle (eds), *Commercial Networks and European Cities, 1400–1800*, London: Pickering & Chatto, 2014, pp. 201–22.
18 F. Lane, *Venice, a Maritime Republic*, Baltimore, MD: Johns Hopkins University Press, 1973, p. 42.
19 For overviews of colonial production and further bibliography, see B. Arbel, 'Colonie d'oltremare', in A. Tenenti and U. Tucci (eds), *Storia di Venezia: Dalle origini alla caduta della serenissima*, vol. 5, *Il Rinascimento: Società ed economia*, Rome: Enciclopedia Italiana, 1996, pp. 976–9; idem, 'Venice's maritime empire in the early modern period', in Dursteler, *Companion to Venetian History*, pp. 220–35; D. Jacoby, 'The economy of Latin Greece', in N. I. Tsougarakis and P. Lock (eds), *A Companion to Latin Greece*, Leiden: Brill, 2014, pp. 185–216; F. Thiriet, *La romanie vénitienne au moyen âge: Le développement et l'exploitation du domaine colonial vénitien*, Paris: Bibliothéque des écoles françaises d'Athénes et de Rome, 1959.
20 E. Ashtor, 'The volume of Levantine trade in the later Middle Ages (1370–1498)', *Journal of European Economic History* 3, 1975, pp. 573–612.
21 Spufford, *Power and Profit*, p. 310.
22 R. Caresini, *Chronica 1343–1388*, ed. Ester Pastorello, in *Rerum Italicarum Scriptores*, vol. 12, pt 2, Bologna: Zanichelli, 1922, p. 58.
23 K. Appuhn, *A Forest on the Sea: Environmental Expertise in Renaissance Venice*, Baltimore, MD: Johns Hopkins University Press, 2009.
24 G. M. Varanini, 'Proprietà fondiaria e agricoltura', in Tenenti and Tucci (eds), *Storia di Venezia*, vol. 5, pp. 807–79.
25 P. Lanaro, 'At the Centre of the Old World. Reinterpreting Venetian Economic History', in Lanaro, *At the Centre of the Old World*, pp. 19–69.
26 E. Demo, 'Industry and production in the Venetian terraferma', in Dursteler, *Companion to Venetian History*, pp. 311–13; E. Ashtor, 'L'artiglieria veneziana e il commercio di Levante', in *Armi e cultura nel Bresciano, 1420–1870*, Brescia: Ateneo di Brescia, 1981, pp. 141–54.
27 Demo, 'Industry and production', p. 307.
28 Lane, *Venice*, pp. 57–65; but see O. Schmitt, 'Contrabannum – der adriatisch-balkanische Schmuggel im ausgehenden Mittelalter', *Südost-Forschungen* 67, 2008, pp. 1–26.
29 P. Lanaro, *I mercati nella Repubblica veneta: economie cittadine e stato territoriale (secoli XV–XVIII)*, Venice: Marsilio, 1999, pp. 53–77; idem, 'At the Centre', pp. 27–8.

30 Spufford, *Power and Profit*, pp. 325–6.
31 Lane, *Andrea Barbarigo*, p. 48.
32 F. Lane, 'Venetian merchant galleys, 1300–34: private and communal operation', *Speculum* 38/2, 1963, pp. 179–205; B. Doumerc, 'Le galere da mercato', in Tenenti and Tucci, *Storia di Venezia*, vol. 12, *Il Mare*, Rome: Enciclopedia Italiana, 1991, pp. 357–95.
33 D. Stöckly, *Le système de l'Incanto des galées du marché à Venise (fin XIIIe–milieu XVe siècle)*, Leiden: Brill, 1995.
34 Doumerc, 'Le galere', p. 374.
35 G. Christ, 'Quelques observations concernant la navigation vénitienne à Alexandrie à la fin du Moyen Âge', in S. G. Franchini, G. Toscano and G. Ortalli (eds), *Venise et la Méditerranée*, Venice: Istituto Veneto di Scienze, Lettere ed Arti, 2011, pp. 55–72; M. Fusaro, *Political Economies of Empire in the Early Modern Mediterranean: The Decline of Venice and the Rise of England, 1450–1700*, Cambridge: Cambridge University Press, 2015, p. 41.
36 E. Ashtor, 'The Venetian supremacy in Levantine trade: monopoly or pre-colonialism?', *Journal of European Economic History* 3, 1974, pp. 5–53.
37 Lane, *Andrea Barbarigo*.
38 F. Lane, 'Family partnerships and joint ventures in the Venetian Republic', *Journal of Economic History* 4, 1944, pp. 178–96.
39 P. Mometto, *L'Azienda Agricola Barbarigo a Carpi: Gestione Economica ed evoluzione sociale sulle terre di un villaggio della Bassa Pianura Veronese (1443–1539)*, Venice: Il Cardo, 1992.
40 T. Bertelè and U. Dorini (eds), *I libri dei conti di Giacomo Badoer (Constantinopoli 1436–1440)*, Rome: Istituto poligrafico dello Stato, Libreria dello Stato, 1956; G. Luzzato, *Storia economica di Venezia dall'XI al XVI secolo*. Venice: Centro internazionale delle Arti e del Costume, 1961, pp. 168–79.
41 E. Concina, *Fondaci: Architettura, arte, e mercatura tra Levante, Venezia, e Alemagna*, Venice: Marsilio, 1997, pp. 66–77; for Alexandria, G. Christ, *Trading Conflicts: Venetian Merchants and Mamluk Officials in Late Medieval Alexandria*, Leiden: Brill, 2012, pp. 49–54; more generally, M. P. Pedani, *Venezia porta d'Oriente*, Bologna: Il Mulino, 2010, pp. 43–60.
42 E. Barile, P. Clarke and G. Nordio, *Cittadini veneziani del Quattrocento: I due Giovanni Marcanova, il mercante e l'umanista*, Venice: Istituto veneto di scienze, lettere ed arti, 2006, pp. 316–17.
43 E. Dursteler, *Venetians in Constantinople: Nation, Identity, and Co-existence in the Early Modern Mediterranean*, Baltimore, MD: Johns Hopkins University Press, 2006, pp. 28–32; Christ, *Trading Conflicts*, pp. 55–96; Pedani, *Venezia*, pp. 77–100; Fusaro, *Political Economies of Empire*, pp. 159–73.
44 Christ, *Trading Conflicts*.
45 S. Montemezzo, 'Galley Routes and Merchant Networks between Venice and the North Sea in the Fifteenth Century', in A. Caracausi and C. Jeggle (eds), *Commercial Networks and European Cities, 1400–1800*, London: Pickering & Chatto, 2014, pp. 162–3.
46 M. O'Connell, *Men of Empire: Power and Negotiation in Venice's Maritime State*, Baltimore, MD: Johns Hopkins University Press, 2009, pp. 43–56.
47 R. Mueller, 'A Venetian commercial enterprise in Corfu, 1440–1442', in N. G. Moschonas (ed.), *Money and Markets in the Palaeologan Era*, Athens: National Hellenic Research Foundation, 2003, pp. 81–93; Mueller, 'Pubblico e privato nel dominio veneziano delle isole Greche a metà Quattrocento: Il caso dei Giustinian', in C. Maltezou and G. Ortalli (eds), *Venezia e le isole Ionie*, Venice: Istituto veneto di scienze, lettere ed arti, 2005, pp. 71–100.
48 O. Schmitt, *Das venezianische Albanien (1392–1479)*, Munich: R. Oldernburg Verlag, 2001, pp. 367–97; B. Arbel, 'The reign of Caterina Corner (1473–1489) as a family affair', *Studi Veneziani* 26, 1993, pp. 67–85.

49 Mueller, *Venetian Money Market*, p. 25.

50 The records of the Consoli dei Mercanti have been entirely lost, a significant obstacle to the study of economic practices in Venice.

51 J. Shaw, *The Justice of Venice: Authorities and Liberties in the Urban Economy, 1550–1700,* Oxford: Oxford University Press, 2006, pp. 22–9.

52 G. I. Cassandro, 'La Curia di Petizion e il diritto processuale di Venezia', *Archivio Veneto* 19, 1936, pp. 72–144, and 20, 1937, pp. 1–210.

53 M. Fusaro, 'Politics of justice/politics of trade: foreign merchants and the administration of justice from the records of Venice's Giudici del Forestier', *Mélanges de l'École française de Rome* 126/1, 2014, http://mefrim.revues.org/1665 (accessed Oct. 2016).

54 A. Grief, *Institutions and the Path to the Modern Economy: Lessons from Medieval Trade,* Cambridge: Cambridge University Press, 2006, pp. 170–8; Y. González de Lara, 'The secret of Venetian success: a public-order, reputation-based institution', *European Review of Economic History* 12, 2008, 247–85.

55 F. Melis, 'Intensità e regolarità nella diffusione dell'informazione economica generale nel Mediterranean e in Occidente dall fine del Medieoveo', in *Mélanges en l'honneur de Fernand Braudel: Histoire économique du monde méditerraneéen 1450–1650,* Toulouse: Privat, 1973, vol. 1, pp. 380–424.

56 B. Arbel (ed.), *Venetian Letters, 1354–1512: From the Archives of the Bank of Cyprus Cultural Foundation and Other Cypriot Collections,* Nicosia: Bank of Cyprus Cultural Foundation, 2007; Christ, *Trading Conflicts,* pp. 38–44; F. Thiriet, 'Les lettres commerciales des Bembo et le commerce vénetien dans l'empire ottoman à la fin du XVe siècle', in *Studi in onore di Armando Sapori,* Milan: Istituto Editoriale Cisalpino, 1957, vol 2, pp. 911–33; E. Vallet, *Marchands vénitiens en Syrie à la fin du XVe siècle: Pour l'honneur et le profit,* Paris: Association pour le développement de l'histoire économique, 1999.

57 Luzzato, *Storia economica*, pp. 168–79.

58 M. Infelise, 'From merchants' letters to handwritten political *avvisi*: notes on the origins of public information', in F. M. Bethencourt and F. Egmond (eds), *Cultural Exchange in Early Modern Europe,* vol. 3, *Correspondence and Cultural Exchange in Europe 1400–1700,* Cambridge: Cambridge University Press, 2007, pp. 33–52.

59 G. Christ, 'A newsletter in 1419? Antonio Morosini's chronicle in the light of commercial correspondence between Venice and Alexandria', *Mediterranean Historical Review* 20, 2005, pp. 35–66.

60 F. Apellániz, 'Venetian trading networks in the medieval Mediterranean', *Journal of Interdisciplinary History* 44, 2013, pp. 157–79.

61 Dursteler, *Venetians,* pp. 41–102.

62 Mueller, *Venetian Money Market*, pp. 82–3; Mozzato, 'Production of woolens', pp. 90–4.

63 Barile et al., *Cittadini veneziani.*

64 Ibid., pp. 174–5, 297, 371–3.

65 F. Lane and R. Mueller, *Money and Banking in Medieval and Renaissance Venice,* Baltimore, MD: Johns Hopkins University Press, 1985, pp. 188–9.

66 E. N. Rothman, *Brokering Empire: Trans-Imperial Subjects between Venice and Istanbul,* Ithaca, NY: Cornell University Press, 2012, pp. 29–84.

67 The fondaco is very well-documented; for an introduction and further bibliography see O. R. Constable, *Housing the Stranger in the Mediterranean World: Lodging, Trade, and Travel in Late Antiquity and the Middle Ages,* Cambridge: Cambridge University Press, 2003, pp. 315–27; Concina, *Fondaci*, pp. 125–217; K. Lupprian, *Il Fondaco dei Tedeschi e la sua funzione di controllo del commercio tedesco a Venezia,* Venice: Centro Tedesco di Studi Veneziani, 1978.

68 Constable, *Housing the Stranger,* p. 319.

69 Ibid., p. 314.

70 D. Jacoby, 'Les Juifs a Venise du XIVe au milieu di XVIe siècle', in H. G. Beck, M. Manoussacas and A. Pertusi (eds), *Venezia, centro di mediazione tra oriente e occidente, secoli XV–XVI: Aspetti e problemi,* Florence: Olschki, 1977, vol. 1, pp. 163–216; B. Ravid, 'The Venetian government and the Jews', in B. Ravid and R. Davis (eds), *The Jews of Early Modern Venice*, Baltimore, MD: Johns Hopkins University Press, 2001, pp. 3–19.

71 There is a substantial literature on the Ghetto: for an introduction and further bibliography, see Ravid, 'Venetian government'.

72 B. Arbel, *Trading Nations: Jews and Venetians in the Early Modern Eastern Mediterranean,* Leiden: Brill, 1995; M. Van Gelder, *Trading Places: The Netherlandish Merchants in Early Modern Venice,* Leiden: Brill, 2009; A. Zannini, *Venezia città aperta: Gli stranieri e la Serenissima, XIV–XVIII sec,* Venice: Marcianum Press, 2009, pp. 99–141.

73 Rothman, *Brokering Empire,* pp. 198–210; Pedani, *Venezia,* pp. 211–22; Concina, *Fondaci,* pp. 219–46.

74 Rothman, *Brokering Empire,* p. 38; Lanaro, *I mercati,* p. 86.

75 B. Doumerc, 'La crise structurelle de la marine vênitienne au XVe siècle: le problème du retard des *mude', Annales ESC* 40, 1985, pp. 605–23.

76 C. Judde de Larivière, *Naviguer, commercer, gouverner: économie maritime et pouvoirs à Venise (XVe–XVIe siècles),* Leiden: Brill, 2008; idem, 'The "public" and the "private" in sixteenth-century Venice: from medieval economy to early modern state', *Historical Social Research/ Historische Sozialforschung* 37, 2012, pp. 76–94.

77 Pezzolo, 'Venetian economy', p. 263.

78 Ibid., pp. 267–8.

79 Fusaro, *Political Economies of Empire,* pp. 57–63.

80 Demo, 'Industry and production', p. 299.

81 Ibid., p. 307.

82 Dursteler, *Venetians,* pp. 41–60.

83 Fusaro, *Political Economies of Empire,* p. 58.

84 O. Gelderblom, *Cities of Commerce: The Institutional Foundations of International Trade in the Low Countries, 1250–1650,* Princeton, NJ: Princeton University Press, 2013.

8

COLLAPSE AND CONTINUITY

Alexandria as a declining city with a thriving port (thirteenth to sixteenth centuries)

Georg Christ

In the late medieval and early modern period, Alexandria experienced a slow but steady urban decline. Nevertheless, it maintained its role as an important port. This decline-cum-continuity brought about the eventual relocation of the settled area from the old medieval walled city to the portal area. Such transformation of Alexandria was neither the sole result of the Crusades (most notably the Cypriot sack of the city in 1365) nor of the Portuguese opening a new maritime route to India, which bypassed Egypt. Rather, this transformation was the combined result of external shocks (climate change and subsequent waves of the plague and other epidemics) and of Alexandria losing its status as capital. It was eclipsed by the rise of Cairo – first as the new political, administrative, but also increasingly cultural, religious and economic centre of Egypt. By hanging onto its superior port, however, it could survive – as a port with a settlement.

The booming transit trade could not stop the decline of old Alexandria but did assure its continuous existence; it prevented collapse and facilitated the transformation to a new Alexandria. The city went through the following three stages between 1200 and 1600. It was first a central node in the Fatimid (later Ayyubid and Mamluk) and wider Islamic Mediterranean trade network and as such was an important port of call for Latin merchants as well during the Crusades. After the end of the *pax mongolica* and the easing of the papal bans on trade with the Mamluks in the 1340s, it gained a dominant position as the southern Mediterranean hub of the transcontinental trade route connecting India and the Far East with Europe. The Cypriot attack on Alexandria in 1365 underlined but did not challenge this position. Finally, in the sixteenth century, after the Ottoman conquest of Egypt in 1517 and the Portuguese reaching India, it lost its monopolistic position in the spice trade but was revived by an enhanced regional role within the wider Ottoman eastern Mediterranean. A city with a port – a former megalopolis and imperial capital – had by the end of the sixteenth century become a port with a settlement attached to it serving the city of Cairo.[1]

Many Arabic-Egyptian chronicles, though focused on Cairo, also covered events in Alexandria.[2] Nuwayrî al-Iskandarânî's multi-volume hybrid literary work, however, is entirely dedicated to Alexandria.[3] No archival material from Alexandria survived for the Mamluk period except for some awqâf (religious foundations) records.[4] Literary sources could provide more material but remain, thus far, underexplored.[5] The famous papers of the Cairo Geniza for the most part cover the period immediately preceding the period of investigation but can still shed some light on Alexandrian conditions at the time.[6] Archaeological sources include the fairly well-studied cisterns and ceramics, but most of medieval Alexandria fell victim to the rapid urban growth of nineteenth-century Alexandria.[7] Because it was a transcontinental hub, Alexandria can be studied not only through Egyptian-Arabic but also Western European (Venetian, for instance) sources.[8] The latter are particularly rich and aside from normative material also include rich judicial, notarial, private and business records.[9] A particularly dense documentation survives of the Venetian consul and merchant Biagio Dolfin's second term as consul in Alexandria (beginning of the fifteenth century).[10] Travelogues are another important type of source.[11]

Location: port and frontier city

Alexandria is located at the western fringe of the Nile Delta near the estuary of the Canopic branch of the river Nile. A former island (Pharos, the location of the mythic lighthouse) had been connected by a bridge to the mainland in antiquity.[12] This bridge had fostered the subsequent silting and the formation of a peninsula with a fan-shaped top, thus forming two harbours.[13] These harbours were a great advantage of the location. Yet they changed constantly due to silting and their entrances were relatively difficult to navigate, requiring the assistance of pilots who could not prevent the loss of ships to these conditions.[14] Yet the biggest challenge was posed by the considerable distance from the estuary of the Canopic Nile, which since antiquity had moved east and further away from the city. This often required goods to travel overland on their way to Cairo and thus to Upper Egypt/the Red Sea. There was a canal connecting Alexandria with the Canopic Nile. The canal facilitated transport to Alexandria and supplied water to top up the rainwater in the cisterns. Yet this canal was notoriously neglected and silted up. Consequently, from the second half of the fourteenth century onwards, it usually only carried water during the Nile flood.[15]

Alexandria was also a city at the border between *dâr al-Islam* and *dâr al-h'arb*, i.e. between the Islamic polity as well as the Egypt-based Islamic empires and the non-Islamic world (Figure 8.1). It therefore had the status of a frontier port: *thaghr*.[16] This meant that Alexandria was fortified against attacks from the sea. Walls (which were doubled for some stretches), towers and heavily fortified double gates surrounded

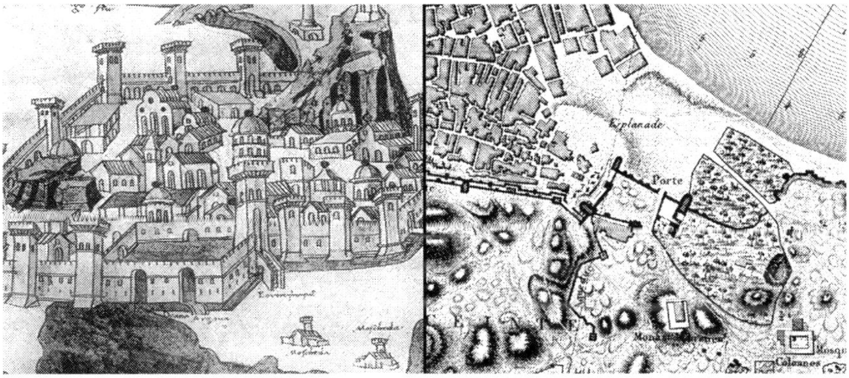

Figure 8.1 Alexandria: customs administration and zone of *fondachi* (see the List of Figures for full description)

the medieval city (which was built on but a small part of the surface of ancient Alexandria). The gates facing the harbour were part of an imposing fortress-like structure with four corner towers, thus alluding to the classical plan of a small coastal fortress (for the purposes of defensive jihad or *ribât'*).[17] More installations of this type were to be found on the peninsula north of the walled city, which probably served as nuclei for the settlement that would become the new, transformed Alexandria. These installations were, in the case of Alexandria, perhaps connected or identical to the houses of Sufi orders (Islamic mystics), which probably came to the city in the wake of trade travelling to Mecca or motivated by the possibility of engaging in *ribât'*, the pious work of defensive jihad (which would explain why *ribât'* gains additional meaning as a Sufi convent).[18] Be that as it may, the architectural and urban upgrading of the peninsula/harbour was driven by religious houses that were often built around the tomb of a saintly founder, and was further enhanced by the construction of the fort Qaitbay (which again might reflect *ribât'* architecture).[19]

A port losing its hinterland

A further challenge for Alexandria in the period of investigation was the gradual loss of its hinterland. This occurred in two senses: administrative power (e.g. taxation) over the delta had shifted from the former capital of Alexandria to Cairo, the new Islamic capital and principal urban centre, starting with the Islamic conquest of 639–41.[20] Yet Alexandria remained the capital of Coptic Egypt and the see of the patriarch who only gradually moved to Cairo in the Fatimid period.[21] It also possessed an excellent harbour and was home to a thriving textile industry.[22] Ceramic findings suggest that living standards peaked in the thirteenth century.[23] After 1327 Alexandria was stripped of its status as a provincial capital,[24] and the city's (and the port's) tax revenue was attributed to the sultan's treasury/private domains (*dîwân al khâs's'*).[25] The hinterland shrank as well. Neglect of the canal system precipitated the decline of the irrigation system and numerous villages were abandoned.

The land became either pasture for Bedouins or receded to desert in the wake of climate change and the demographic shocks starting with the mid-fourteenth-century outbreak of the plague.[26] Alexandria as a centre commanding the agricultural resources of its hinterland thus declined to the point of sheer irrelevance by the end of the fourteenth century. In the same period, after only a relatively short time, industrial production also declined sharply.[27] Wine production likewise had already declined back in the third century, thus requiring the import of wine from other parts of the delta. By the early fifteenth century at the latest, substantial amounts of wine were imported from Crete rather than the delta.[28]

Alexandria, hence, was reduced more and more to a theatrical staffage. It looked like a city to the traveller, who, upon entering the harbour, would first catch sight of the impressive frontispiece architecture of strong city walls and the customs complex. Yet what lay behind the skyline was, increasingly, rubble. True, the custom complex and the adjacent market streets where the Venetian, Genoese and other nations' *fondachi* were situated still bustled with life; this area teemed with merchants and many regional and exotic goods. But the further south one wandered the more one would see that parts of the city had collapsed.[29]

In the fifteenth century it retained chiefly one role – that of a transit port. Indeed, Alexandria's importance as a port had steadily increased in an inverse relationship to its urban decline.[30] The decline of old Alexandria led to a radical restructuration of the urban space. The city within the medieval city walls was slowly abandoned, fell to waste, and practically ceased to exist, while a new settlement grew in the portal area. It was as if Alexandria had moved out of its walls and resettled at the beach: on the peninsula, the portal area north of the old walled city.[31] Alexandria as a capital and metropolis had given way to Cairo, but it thrived in its function as a transit port.

Connections: Alexandria as a hub in the trade with India and regional trade

In Alexandria different trade routes and networks/systems were interlinked. Two principal trade routes crossed there: a north–south and an east–west route. After the dissolution of the Mongol empire in the mid-fourteenth century, for a short while the Mamluk empire enjoyed an almost monopolistic position as a hub in the intercontinental transit trade from India and the Far East through the Red Sea to Europe. Alexandria as the main port of Egypt would attract a great part of this trade, although Syrian ports, especially Beirut, were serious competitors.[32] On the Mediterranean section of the route galleys linked their Southern European home ports with Alexandria, catering to the grand commerce in bullion, copper[33] and (mainly cheaper) woollen and fustian cloth from Europe against Oriental spices (pepper, nutmeg, cloves).[34] The route continued from Alexandria through the Nile Valley or Sinai and Hijaz to the shores of the Red Sea and finally the Indian Ocean.[35] A variant of the route to the north led to Constantinople (later Istanbul) and the Black Sea. One important good travelling this route were slaves from the northern

Black Sea, including both male military slaves and slave girls. But slaves, some of which were exported to Venice, also hailed from the African branch of the southern route following the Nile into Nubia (Dongola) and from there to Central or West Africa.[36] Alexandria was a crucial junction and transhipment point on this route. It was the terminal of the route's Mediterranean leg dominated by Italians (first southern Italians, then Genoese, and, from the late fourteenth century onwards, increasingly the Venetians) and Catalans where the Egyptian leg of the route commenced.[37]

The east–west trade has been studied much less. Yet it was of crucial importance, as it linked not only Egypt to the North African part of the Islamic world but also the two principal realms of the Ayyubid and later Mamluk empires: Egypt and Syria. Goods exchanged along this route included agricultural products such as beans and grain[38] as well as (though perhaps increasingly less) raw materials for the Levantine industries (which were quantitatively declining in this period) and their finished products (textiles, soap, glass, metalwork).[39] Southern Europeans were also active on this route along the North African coast, including the Catalans and the Venetians (with their *galere del trafego* from 1460 to 1507).[40] This could be interpreted as a sign that indigenous North African – including Egyptian – navigation, which had been strong until the fourteenth century, had declined somewhat during this time but quickly recovered in the Ottoman period.[41]

Aside from the grand commerce (quantitatively more important) there was regional trade along the same routes,[42] such as the trade in wine or cheese between Crete and the Mamluk empire.[43] Other goods of the regional north–south trade included wine, nuts, honey, olive oil and grain from the eastern Mediterranean,[44] all of which were imported to Egypt (and some of it re-exported towards the Indian Ocean).[45] The regional trade cannot be classified neatly into the above-mentioned categories of north–south and east–west. Important hubs in the region and destinations for smaller craft leaving Alexandria included Tunis, Acre, Crete (and other Venetian colonies), Rhodes, Cyprus and Genoese Chios; and later Izmir and Salonika as well. Yet the vectors of regional trade active on different routes, such as Greek sailors from Venetian Crete, did not limit their trade to regional products such as foodstuffs.[46] The multipolar regional trade added a layer of flexibility to the tightly regulated grand commerce, which although usually overlooked, was crucial for the maintenance of trade links and the balance of payments. This was more than 'cabotage' or coastal navigation linking, for example, Hospitaller Rhodes to Alexandria and thus the Islamic integrated economic area of the Middle East and the Indian Ocean. In times of papal embargoes or other crises, for example, when Catalan corsairs attacked Mamluk ships, Rhodes became the terminal for Catalan merchantmen, which under these circumstances could not call on Alexandria. Aegean ship owners and sailors, sometimes financed by Venetian patrician merchants, (rather illegally) shipped spices from Alexandria to Rhodes and thus connected the Catalan and Mamluk legs of the spice trade.[47]

The quantitative dimensions of this trade are difficult to capture. If we assume that three to five galleys per year reached Alexandria, each with a capacity of 140–200 tons and up to eight cogs of about 300 tons (at the end of the fourteenth and beginning of the fifteenth centuries), and that they perhaps handled half of the entire Venetian (including Cretan) tonnage, we could then estimate a total Venetian trade volume of about 6,400 tons. If we estimate the total volume of other Latin nations being about the same as the Venetian (fourteen galleys and round ships and a number of smaller ships) and allow for about the same quantity of North African, Mamluk and Greek navigation, we could reach a very rough estimate of 20,000 tons.[48] Eliyahu Ashtor estimated the total value of Venetian trade to the Levant as being around half a million ducats (of which half to two-thirds would have been handled by Alexandria) and 160,000 for other Latin nations. This number is certainly far too low as it takes into consideration only the 'grand commerce', i.e. galleys and cogs, and accounts neither for contraband (which, as shown above, might have been a conspicuous share of the overall trade),[49] nor for smaller ships and their trade (which also included spices despite prohibition). One might thus estimate a value closer to a million ducats for the Venetian trade and about three million for all trade in Alexandria.[50]

Alexandria was thus a hub connecting different routes and networks of regional and inter-/meta-regional trade both horizontally (east–west, north–south) and vertically (local, regional and meta-regional), including the different mercantile networks operating them (such as Venetians, Genoese, Catalan, Egyptians, North Africans, Cretans and, until the late fourteenth century, also Kârimis[51]). Yet all the networks and trade systems meeting in Alexandria, while undoubtedly producing considerable revenues, did not stop the urban decline of the old city. Rather, they fostered the gradual reinvention of Alexandria as a port with a settlement. The transformation of the city seems surprisingly steady and similarly unaffected by the conjuncture (from about 1350) and decline of the Indian pepper trade (in the later sixteenth century). This is probably because the regional trade, which in any case accounted for the bulk of the trade, was expanding rather than declining in the Ottoman period.[52] The gains of the transit trade, however, would not remain in Alexandria, but mostly ended up being consumed and reinvested elsewhere – in Cairo or Southern European merchant cities.

Nor was Alexandria's position uncontested. Other port cities of the Nile delta, such as Rosetta or Damietta, challenged Alexandria's pre-eminence as the main hub and cross-road. To an extent this competition was mitigated by spatial and personal division of labour and specialization. Damietta had always been an important port but it was arguably mostly a node of the regional trade (again, both east–west and north–south). Alexandria, with its good harbour, attracted bigger vessels and hence the meta-regional trade. This reflected a division of labour between different yet intrinsically connected groups: Venetians and other Latin nations in Alexandria, Cretans and other local Aegean actors (Damietta), and Muslim merchants of many provenances in Egypt (Cairo). Rosetta had always played a role as a Mamluk (military) port, which Christian ships (officially) were not allowed to call on as the Canopic branch of the Nile might have allowed enemy ships to reach Cairo. Yet this direct waterway to Cairo, which was navigable all year long, was also Rosetta's competitive edge. When the canal to Alexandria was not navigable, Rosetta also unofficially handled bulky merchandise, such as wine, already in the Mamluk period.[53] As Alexandria's canal connection to the Nile increasingly deteriorated to the point that it was not even navigable during the Nile flood (seventeenth century), Rosetta boomed. Yet it never fully eclipsed Alexandria as a transit port because of the latter's superior harbour for bigger ships.[54]

Local institutions: consuls between community and metropolis

Alexandria did not develop strong urban institutions akin to Southern European merchant republics but was increasingly ruled by elites with only a transient presence. These elites were concerned primarily with political exigencies of domineering capitals: Cairo and the mother towns of the Southern European merchants.[55]

The Mamluk power centred in Cairo was represented by different institutions. There was the regular governor of the city, a Mamluk emir. More important for the transit trade, however, was the customs inspector and his administration. He directly responded to the *nâz'ir al-khâs's'*, the inspector of the sultan's private domains in Cairo. The customs was housed in the massive complex at the harbour gates. There were different entrances for people (and wine) and merchandise, a third gate for the use of the customs administration and the coastguard, and yet another gate between the customs complex and the city proper (hence its name in Italian: *fra do porte* = between the two gates). The customs administration was a complex entity both architecturally and functionally as it not only served its primary purpose of collecting customs dues, but also functioned as a bonded storage, a marketplace and a court for informal arbitration (Figure 8.2).[56]

The sultan's pepper was closely related to this institution. The Venetians were, in exchange for generous privileges, obliged to buy pepper from the sultan's stocks at an inflated price before they could purchase pepper on the open market. This can be interpreted as a peculiar form of a tributary system. The terms of these operations were negotiated between the Venetian consul on the one side and the customs inspector, the governor of Alexandria and the sultan's merchant conducting the spices to Alexandria on the other. As long as the consul could discipline his merchants (i.e. to prevent future trading-cum-credit deals that could predetermine the pepper price and thus limit the consul's room for manoeuvre) this meant that he could effectively act as quasi-monopolist and exploit the divide and rule set-up by striking a deal with either of the Mamluk interlocutors and thus negotiate favourable terms.[57]

Mamluk rule, however, was not only internally divided, but also contested. Traditionally the urban ulama and the offices it traditionally controlled such as the judge (*qâd'î*) and the market inspector (*muh'tasib*) would have formed a counterweight to the power of the Mamluk emir or governor and his staff. Yet this group,

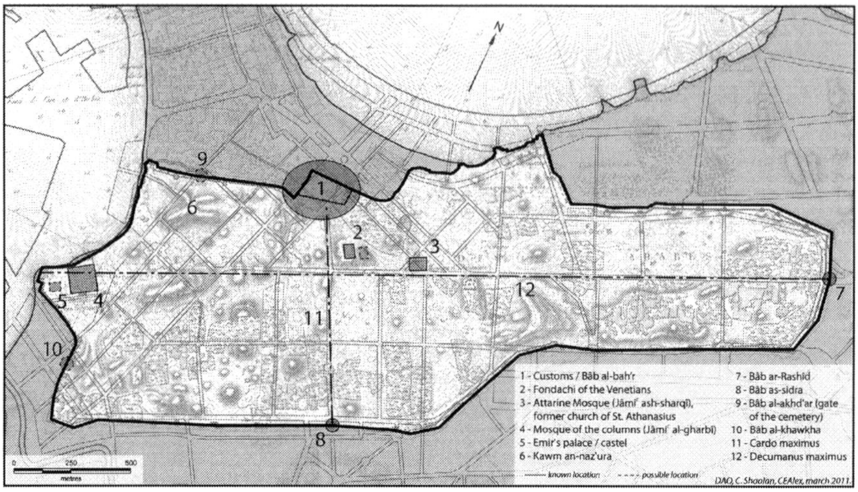

Figure 8.2 Map of medieval Alexandria at the beginning of the fifteenth century (see the List of Figures for full description)

which had also produced grand merchants, had increasingly lost its power to the Mamluk officials sent from Cairo.[58] Sufi groups and institutions in Alexandria remained powerful; because they formed various alliances with the common people, ulama, Mamluk officers or the sultan, they were a powerful group to reckon with.[59] Although they were not directly involved in trade, they might have served as catalysers of popular unrest and a voice for the sentiment that the industrial and urban decline of Alexandria in the period under investigation was causally linked to the privileged and presumably extractive foreign trade. Arguably, the old urban and newer Sufi elites (connected to North African immigrant communities) might have been more heavily involved in the east–west trade; yet even the latter, as shown above, was for a while at least partially in the hand of Venetians. In any case, urban discontent fermented in the late fourteenth and early fifteenth centuries and occasionally erupted. These eruptions, although not primarily directed against Latin merchants, still affected them when, for instance, popular rage led to the destruction of wine stocks, as happened in 1419.[60]

The Latin merchant communities were organized as widely autonomous nations. The Latin presence in Alexandria reflected the ups and downs of merchant cities in Italy: Merchants from Amalfi and Gaeta or later Pisa increasingly gave way to Genoese and Venetians (the latter installing a consul in 1172). The Genoese were particularly coveted (by the Mamluks) and notorious (in the West) as the Mamluks' main suppliers of military slaves from the northern Black Sea. They are chiefly targeted in the papal treatise 'De Alexandrinis'.[61] In the later fourteenth century they were increasingly eclipsed by the Venetians (in the pepper trade; the military slave trade had increasingly moved back to overland routes[62]), while still maintaining a substantial presence.[63] The Catalans were another important group, though it seems that they did not stay permanently in Alexandria but rather commuted from Rhodes.[64] Yet there were also merchants from a multitude of other places – some organized as nations with a consul (in 1419: from Venice, Genoa, Barcelona/Catalonia (with consul); southern France, Rhodes, Cyprus, Byzantium (possibly with consul), possibly also Ancona – and a few years later also Florence). The nations were organized in different ways but they all tried to reach 'most favoured nation' status, i.e. to obtain the same status that the most privileged foreign nation enjoyed.[65]

The Venetian nation can serve as an example. It featured bottom–up elements of self-governance, including a self-constituted council of twelve (made up of, if possible, Venetian patricians) and two *consiglieri* (councillors) as executives. Yet the community was also ruled top–down, as it was regulated by Venice and chartered and privileged by the Mamluks. It was headed by a consul, who *de iure* was a Venetian employee and colonial officer hailing from the lagoon armed with lengthy instructions to serve a two-year term in Alexandria. His main task was to watch over the Venetian community and to insist on the regular application of the Venetian privileges. He was loosely included in the Mamluk political taxonomy and was nominally entitled to receive a Mamluk (cash) salary (*jâmakiyya*).[66]

Venetian regulations tried to govern this community. The rules are recorded in the consul's instructions (which survived in three ever-growing versions). They mainly concerned internal jurisdiction and the finances of the Venetian community (in particular the consul's pay). They also repeated the Venetian endorsement of papal sanctions concerning the export of strategic goods to Muslim countries and some rules regarding Venetian navigation. The earliest surviving version of this consular instruction from 1284 provides no information on the actual institutions of trade, such as brokerage, customs, etc. It contains thirty-two paragraphs (*capitoli*), some of which are clearly additions to an older text (numerous specifications and even repetitions or rather restipulations in more detail) and the last two paragraphs cite (recent?) council decisions in maritime matters. It is likely that the original commission was no more than a slightly extended oath taken by the consul specifying his duty in adjudicating legal matters and a general clause to provide for the good of the Venetian community and state. Thus three distinct strands of additions can be identified: the ratification of papal prohibitions to export strategic military goods to the Mamluks (only weapons at first, then later extended to include wood and iron as well), the salary of the consul and the registration of gold imports. The commission of Girolamo Tiepolo of 1498 contains forty *capitoli*, while the post-1559 version stretches over 139 pages. By then it not only specified the rules applying to the governance of the Venetian nation and especially its public finance/communal funds more thoroughly, but also included a host of other regulations regarding navigation and elements of the Venetian privileges to which it now made explicit reference.[67]

This is not a priori surprising, as the Venetians clearly operated within the Mamluk realm and thus under Mamluk law, which is not exactly the same as Islamic law. Venetians were treated as protégés of the sultan under an *amân* (safe-conduct) regardless of the length of their stay. Islamic law would have declared them *dhimmîs* as soon as their stay in Islamic lands exceeded a year.[68] The Latin merchants thus enjoyed a favourable status inscribed in Mamluk decrees or privileges.[69] These documents were regularly renewed after the coronation of a new ruler, but at the same time they routinely invoked continuity. Indeed, the success of the Latin merchants' commercial insertion in the Mamluk empire relied on the long tradition and continuity of intercultural trade, as well as the personal endorsement of the tradition by the actual ruler who formally granted the privileges.[70] The privileges, motivated by the sultan's strong interest in the income from the spice trade, exempted the Venetians from certain taxes but eventually also established their responsibility to take over a substantial amount of the sultan's pepper at inflated prices.[71] In return the Venetian merchants enjoyed (in theory) perfect freedom of movement and of trade, being exempt from the seigneurial rights such as confiscation of intestate property of deceased merchants or stranded goods and communal collective responsibility (with the exception of piracy). They were, of course, obliged to duly pay their (partly reduced) canonical taxes and were urged to notarize their commercial transactions (in the regulated marketplace attached to customs).[72] They also enjoyed internal jurisdiction, direct access to the sultan's *maz'âlim* (disciplinary, 'secular') justice and the gratuitous use of their *fondaco* (caravanserai; from Arabic *funduq*, Greek *pandokeion*) where they could drink wine, and around which the communal life of the Latin nations centred.[73] It has been argued, therefore, that foreign merchants remained strongly isolated from the local communities. Although there is more than a grain of truth to this, there were also points of interaction. Credit relationships were established with local Arab merchants, and entertainers came to the *fondaco*. Local boys were taken as apprentices.[74] Prostitution and taking female slaves as second wives created another layer of interconnection, though perhaps less so with the local community as the slave girls seem to have come from the Balkans or the Caucasus rather than Egypt.[75] Prostitutes remain anonymous yet repeated prohibitions seem to indicate their continuous presence.[76]

Later Venetian regulations summarized in the consular instructions of the late fifteenth and sixteenth centuries limited this far-reaching freedom of trade granted by the sultans and banned speculative or otherwise risky practices: no forward purchases and no banking activity (notably the granting of credits closely connected to risky future speculation).[77] They also limited the granted freedom of movement by limiting the Venetian presence in Cairo.[78] These limitations therefore cannot be attributed to restrictions in the Mamluk provisions for foreign merchants, but rather reflect the Serenissima's concerns that unbridled liberties would result in costly bankruptcies and lawsuits.[79]

Attached to the consulate but in the service of the whole Venetian nation (and wider Latin and cosmopolitan merchant community) was a notary (doubling as the community's chaplain) and a medical doctor. This notary, puzzlingly, seemed to have been almost more popular with other nations than with Venetians. The tightly regulated system of official Veneto-Mamluk trade indeed would not seem to require much notarial corroboration (the *muda*: transports by Venetian state galleys, transactions through officially appointed brokers under supervision of Mamluk authorities and the consul).[80] More importantly, if they did not remain within the remits of the system (and a lot of merchants did not), they probably would have shrunk from going on (Venetian) record with shady deals (of which there were plenty: speculations in futures, credits to Mamluk merchants and officials, etc.).[81]

Conflict resolution

Local conflict resolution would seem difficult within this institutional framework, and one would expect cases to be brought to courts either in Cairo or Venice. Indeed, the Venetian metropolitan authorities tended to push for direct appeal to the sultan in Cairo. Yet this was a costly and protracted procedure. Hence conflicts were often solved on the spot – in Alexandria, for instance, by the Venetian consul and the emir or the customs inspector in direct negotiation without recourse to the respective central authorities and courts either in Cairo or Venice. These local settlements tended to produce solutions that were not fully in line with the Mamluk privileges and Venetian regulations and benefited officials and merchants present in Alexandria at the expense of both the sultan's and the Serenissima's treasuries.[82]

The Venetian *cottimo* or the Genoese *massaria* were communal funds financed by an extra tax paid by the nation. These funds were supposed to cover various communal costs either of a social nature (funerals, ransoms and support of prisoners) and, more importantly, the enforcement of the privileges. In practice this often meant some sort of bribing of Mamluk officials and paying for journeys to Cairo in order to appeal to the sultan (the costs of official Venetian or Genoese embassies from the mother cities were also partly covered by these funds).[83] They hence also played an import role in mediation and conflict resolution. The Venetian *cottimo* also covered the costs of gathering and distributing intelligence on the spice supply – for instance the deployment of an agent to Cairo who had to report on the pepper news of the Red Sea.[84] Yet in practice it increasingly served as a clearing fund and self-service credit institute for the Venetian merchants. They tapped into the *cottimo's* resources by declaring gifts they made to Mamluk officials as 'confiscations' which were deductible from the *cottimo* tax owed. These 'gifts' or 'confiscations' were an integral but sensitive part of transcultural trade characterized by strong state interventions and strong speculative elements. In order to anticipate quantities and arrival times of the spices and to secure good deals in advance (for instance through the above-mentioned future contract) close relations with Mamluk officials, including the sultan's merchants, were crucial. These officials were aware of this, and the establishment of such relations thus required an investment – a 'gift' or 'confiscation'. While mutually beneficial for both the Venetian merchant and the Mamluk official involved, the *cottimo* itself was taken advantage of and eventually depleted. The fund exhibited the classical features of a 'tragedy of the commons'.[85] Over the course of the fifteenth century it was so heavily overdrawn that it had to be reformed completely at the beginning of the sixteenth century. Although the losses incurred over time were considerable, this could be perceived as a positive trade-off, considering the generous privileges enjoyed by the Venetians.[86]

The normative backdrop for the fine-tuning of legal arrangements and conflict resolution in Alexandria at the intersection of Islamic and Byzantine/Latin Roman law is difficult to ascertain. The consul was instructed to judge according to custom and, if that was not known, according to conscience, i.e. common sense.[87] The privileges only emphasize that the Latin merchants were not subjected to the *qâd'î* courts but rather to the *maz'âlim* courts of appeal.[88] Perhaps the contrast between Islamic and Latin (as in Venetian, Genoese, Catalan) law was not as sharp as one might expect. A transcultural legal koiné of a faded but still potent (Roman) imperial heritage might have provided an additional layer to the common ground of long-established transcultural mercantile practice in Alexandria and the Levant – invoked in the Venetian instructions as 'custom'. Maritime law was very similar across the Mediterranean, as were essential features of business law – for instance, on the validity of contracts.[89] The locally used money of account was still the Byzantine gold Besant and Veneto. Cretans and other local sailors maintained connections across the former Byzantine imperial sphere. Mamluk sultans, on the other hand, tapped into Roman (and other) imperial heritage and thus somewhat overcame the commercially impractical Islamic division of the world in *dâr al h'arb* and *dâr al islâm*.[90] The sultans certainly understood that merchants and their goods had to be protected. The penultimate Mamluk sultan Qâns'ûh al-Ghûrî wrote in a letter to the doge in 1503: 'Merchants who come and go are like birds who do not sit down if not on water: if any mishap occurs they will never come back.'[91]

Urban transformation and urban transhumance

The population of foreign nations was not just composed of co-nationals, which is a problematic notion to start with. Venice, for instance, was a stratified society in which access to economic resources was differentiated by class. In Alexandria the class system was handled less rigorously. The consul had to be a patrician, as did his council of twelve. But other than that (and exceptions could be made even for the council of twelve)[92] underprivileged Venetians, such as *cittadini*, colonial subjects or Jews, could participate in the economic life of the Venetian community in Alexandria and even rise to prominence.[93] There is a case of a Florentine passing as a Venetian in the early fifteenth century who became one of the most influential long-term resident merchants in Alexandria but eventually had to leave in scandal and to relocate to Rhodes.[94] Venetian Jews, that is, primarily Jews from Venetian Crete, also played an important role in Venetian trade in Alexandria. There is no evidence of cooperation with local, i.e. Arabic-speaking Jewish communities in Alexandria. It seems that while the Venetian Jews gravitated towards Venice, the local Jews looked towards Cairo.[95]

The Venetian Cretans are representative of a wider group of (former) Byzantine, Greek-speaking, and probably mostly Orthodox merchants from the Aegean. These merchants seemed to have been a backbone of the regional trade and were arguably instrumental in continuously connecting the various parts of the eastern Mediterranean in the wake of the dissolution of the Byzantine empire. Although the Cretan consul (officially a Venetian vice-consul) resided in Damietta, a crucial hub of the regional trade, Cretans were also strongly involved in maritime trade in Alexandria, for instance as farmers of the Mamluk wine custom and wholesale wine traders.[96]

Mercantile presence in Alexandria was characterized by strong seasonal movements. The commercial high seasons were shaped by meteorological preconditions for navigation. While Alexandria could be easily reached for most of the year due to prevailing northerlies, the departure was much easier in spring and autumn when a more varied wind regime prevailed, which also (especially in spring) included strong southerlies. A short time before the Nile flood peaked, it allowed (as long as the canal remained navigable) riverine spice transports to reach Alexandria. Hence the commercial activity peaked in autumn (September and October) with the arrival of the Venetian galleys (and other ships), and in spring (March/April) when the Venetian cogs arrived. It was at this time that the merchant population of Alexandria was most substantial; it decreased during the lulls between the high seasons (although regional navigation never did fully come to a halt in terms of the operation of smaller craft able to cope with adverse winds and more locally experienced crews).[97] During these lulls merchants preferred to be elsewhere where better business could be made: in Cairo, Venice or Crete.

The focus on Christian foreign nations tends to overshadow other groups. Jews and Samaritans, although increasingly gravitating towards Cairo (and to a smaller extent, perhaps, Jerusalem), still formed important communities.[98] Sufis of various provenances came through Alexandria. Sufi leaders died and were buried in Alexandria. Sufi institutions sprang up around their tombs and attracted followers.[99] There was also North African immigration of sailors, among others, which sustained the growth of the settlement in the port area, thus giving the city's transformation a peculiar northward direction; the 'emigration' of Alexandria to the port and the peninsula.[100]

One might be tempted to invoke the beautiful image of a cosmopolitan Alexandria in the Middle Ages. Yet at this time, although characterized by the coexistence of different ethnic groups, Alexandria was very different from the cosmopolitan metropolis of antiquity, in the shadow and on the ruins of which medieval Alexandria flourished. And it was different from the other cosmopolitan Alexandria that emerged from those same ruins and programmatically borrowed from classical Alexandria in the nineteenth century. As the medieval city was in decline, the transformed and relocated settlement still was, it is true, of a cosmopolitan nature. It was, however, a different Alexandria all together. It was not a cosmopolitan diasporic community in the orbit of a thriving capital (antiquity) or an economic hub (nineteenth century). It was a city of diasporas without resident populations; diasporas in the shadows of ruins, in an empty city, dominated (economically and politically) by an absentee or rather transient elite. One did not have to live (permanently) in Alexandria in order to be commercially or politically active there. Temporary postings of Mamluk officials, the fading presence of the patriarch and the urban transhumance (i.e. seasonal presence) of the merchant elites hailing from Cairo are at the heart of Alexandria's decline-cum-survival in the late Middle Ages and the early modern period.

Notes

1 Good succinct surveys of the history of Alexandria in our period are given in the articles in the *Encyclopaedia of Islam* (*EI*): S.Y. Labîb, 'Iskandariyya', in P. J. Bearman *et al.* (eds), *EI*, 2nd edn, Leiden: Brill, 1960–2009 (also online), p. 132a; G. Leiser, 'Alexandria (early period)', in G. Krämer *et al.* (eds), *EI*, 3rd edn, Leiden: Brill, 2007 (online); in the longue durée J.-Y. Empereur and S. Compoint, *Alexandria Rediscovered*, London: British Museum, 1998; for the medieval period still essential also M. Müller-Wiener, *Eine Stadtgeschichte Alexandrias von 564/1169 bis in die Mitte des 9./15.Jahrhunderts Verwaltung und innerstädtische Organisationsformen*, Berlin: Klaus Schwarz, 1992. For the decline-cum-continuation problem, see C. Décobert and J. Y. Empereur, 'Alexandrie médiévale: l'économie florissante d'une ville endormie?', in C. Décobert *et al.* (eds), *Alexandrie médiévale 4*, Alexandria: CEAlex, 2011, pp. 9–14, here p. 9; M. J. Reimer, 'Ottoman Alexandria: the paradox of decline and the reconfiguration of power in eighteenth-century Arab provinces', *JESHO* 37/2, 1994, pp. 107–46; G. Christ, 'Eine Stadt wandert aus: Kollaps und Kontinuität im spätmittelalterlichen Alexandria', *Viator* 42, 2011, pp. 145–68.

2 These chronicles (Maqrîzî, al-'Aynî, Taghribirdî, Ibn Hajar, etc.) have informed M. Müller-Wiener, *Eine Stadtgeschichte von 564 1169 bis in die Mitte des 9. 15. Jahrhunderts Verwaltung und innerstädtische Organisationsformen*, Berlin: Klaus Schwarz, 1992.

3 Muh'ammad Ibn Qâsim Nuwayrî al-Iskandarânî, *Kitâb al-ilmâm bil-i'lâm fîmâ jarat bihî l-ah'kâm wal-umûr al-maqd'iyya fî waq'at al-Iskandariyya*, 7 vols, ed. Etienne Combe and Aziz Suryal Atiya, Hyderabad: Osmania Oriental Publications Bureau, 1968–76.

4 Cf. N. Christie, 'Reconstructing life in medieval Alexandria from an eighth/fourteenth century waqf document', *Mamlûk Studies Review* 8/2, 2004, pp. 163–90.

5 For a good discussion of Egyptian sources, see Labîb, 'Iskandariyya'.

6 Cf. S. D. Goitein, *A Mediterranean Society: The Jewish Communities of the Arab World as Portrayed in the Documents of the Cairo Geniza,* 6 vols, Berkeley, CA: University of California Press, 1999, in general and for studies of Alexandria specifically, M. Frenkel, 'Medieval Alexandria: life in a port city', *Al- Masaq* 26/1, 2014, pp. 5–35 and A. L. Udovitch, 'Alexandria in the 11th and 12th centuries: letters and documents of the Cairo Geniza merchants: an interim balance sheet', in C. Décobert (ed.), *Alexandrie médiévale 2,* Études alexandrines 8, Cairo: IFAO, 2002, pp. 99–112.

7 Y. Guyard, 'Les citernes médiévale d'Alexandrie: une première typologie', *Alexandrie médiévale 3*, Cairo: IFAO, 2008, pp. 279–312, cf. CEAlex project 'Historical and architectural study of El-Nabih cistern', http://www.cealex.org/sitecealex/navigation/FENETR_NAVetudes_E.htm, 19.10.2010); I. Hairy, 'Alexandrie médiévale: la question de l'eau', in Décobert, *Alexandrie médiévale 3*, pp. 263–77; V. François, *Céramiques médiévales à Alexandrie: Contribution à l'histoire économique de la ville,* Études alexandrines 2, Le Caire: IFAO, 1999; R.-P. Gayroud, 'Alexandrie médiévale et la Méditerranée: l'indice des importations céramiques', in C. Décobert and J.-Y. Empereur (eds), *Alexandrie médiévale 1*, Études alexandrines 3, Cairo: IFAO, 1998, pp. 65–9.

8 There is of course relevant (although less rich) material to be found in Genoa, Florence and other Italian archives. Worth special mention is the very rich Datini letter collection from the late fourteenth/beginning of the fifteenth century and the rich documentation

preserved in the archives of Barcelona. Eliyahu Ashtor was the first and the last trying to incorporate sources from all those places into his research culminating in his *Levant Trade in the Later Middle Ages*, Princeton, NJ: Princeton University Press, 1983.

9 Notarial material has been brought together in a database by F. Apellaniz, http://notaires-venitiens.com/notaries/users/login. For Apellaniz's research based on this data, see http://notaires-venitiens.com/notaries/intersticial.html. Published are: F. Rossi (ed.), *Servodio Peccator, Notaio in Venezia e Alessandria d'Egitto (1444–1449)*, Venice: Comitato per la pubblicazione delle fonti relative alla storia di Venezia, 1983, and C. Verlinden, 'Marchands chrétiens et juifs dans l'Etat mamelouk au début du XV siècle d'après un notaire vénitien', *Bulletin de l'Institut historique Belge de Rome* 51, 1981, pp. 19–86.

10 See G. Christ, *Trading Conflicts: Venetian Merchants and Mamluk Officials in Late Medieval Alexandria*, Leiden: Brill, 2012.

11 Wilhelm Heyd made excellent use of the material accessible to him without archival studies, notably of travelogues in his *Histoire du commerce du Levant au moyen-âge,* 2 vols, Leipzig: Otto Harrasowitz, 1885–6, reprint Amsterdam, 1959 (based on older German and Italian versions). For a more recent compilation of a wide range of travelogues relevant for the history of Alexandria, see O. Sennoune, *Alexandrie dans les récits de voyage VIe–XVIIIe siècles: Documents pour l'histoire ou sources historiques?* Paris: L'Harmattan, 2015, and her corpus available online on http://www.cealex.org/sitecealex/navigation/FENETR_NAVvoyageurs_F.htm. Not a travelogue, but worth mentioning: the crusading treatise by E. Piloti, *Traité d'Emmanuel Piloti sur le passage en Terre Sainte*, ed. P.-H. Dopp, Louvain: Éditions E. Nauwelaerts, 1958.

12 On the lighthouse, see H. Thiersch (ed.), *Pharos: Antike, Islam und Occident: Ein Beitrag zur Architekturgeschichte*, Leipzig: Teubner, 1909; on its destruction: M. Taher, 'Les séismes à Alexandrie et la destruction du phare', in Décobert and Empereur, *Alexandrie médiévale 1*, pp. 51–6.

13 B. Millet and J.-P. Goiran, 'Impacts of Alexandria's heptastadion on coastal hydro-sedimentary dynamics during the Hellenistic period: a numerical modelling approach', *Nautical Archaeology* 36/1, 2007, pp. 167–76.

14 Cf. for a ship run aground, Antonio Morosini, *Il Codice Morosini: Il mondo visto da Venezia (1094–1433)*, ed. A. Nanetti, Spoleto: Fondazione Centro Italiano di Studi sull'Alto Medioevo, 2010, pp. 755 seq., § 581.

15 H. Halm, *Aegypten nach den mamlukischen Lehensregistern,* vol. 2, Beihefte zum Tübinger Atlas des vorderen Orients B 38, Wiesbaden: Komm. Ludwig Reichert, 1979, p. 396; E. Combe, 'De la colonne Pompée au Phare d'Alexandrie', *Bulletin de la Société Royale Archéologique d'Alexandrie* 34, 1941, pp. 104–22, here p. 104.

16 Lit. Front-tooth, cf. C. E. Bosworth and J. D. Latham, 'al-Thughūr', *EI*^{2} online, accessed Nov. 2015, http://referenceworks.brillonline.com/entries/encyclopaedia-of-islam-2/al-thughur-COM_1214 (online 2012, print 1960–2007).

17 H. S. Khalilieh, 'The Ribât system and its role in coastal navigation', *JESHO* 42/2, 1999, pp. 212–25, here mainly p. 225; for the etymology of ribât', see J. Chabbi, and for the actual buildings, N. Rabbat, 'Ribāṭ', *EI*^{2}, accessed Nov. 2015. http://referenceworks.brillonline.com/entries/encyclopaedia-of-islam-2/ribat-COM_0919

18 É. Geoffroy, 'Les milieux des la mystique musulmane à Alexandrie aux XIIIe et XIVe siècles', in C. Décobert (ed.), *Alexandrie médiévale 2*, Cairo: IFAO, 2002, pp. 169–80, cf. G. Cecere, M. Loubet and S. Pagani (eds), *Les mystiques juives, chrétiennes et musulmanes dans l'Égypte médiévale (VIIe–XVIe siècles): Interculturalités et contextes historiques; actes du Colloque organisé à l'IFAO, 22–24 Novembre 2010,* Recherches d'archéologie, de philologie et d'histoire 35, Cairo: IFAO, 2013, n.v.

19 For the architectural history of the fortress, see K. Machinek, *Le fort Qaitbay Alexandrie,* Alexandrie: Harpocrates Publishing, 2009.

20 C. Foss, 'Egypt under Muʿāwiya Part II: Middle Egypt, Fusṭāṭ and Alexandria', *BSOAS* 72/2, 2009, pp. 259–78.

21 The consecration continued to take place in Alexandria until the beginning of the fifteenth century, cf. Christ, *Trading Conflicts*, p. 159.

22 A. Bahgat, 'Les manufactures d'étoffe en Égypte au moyen âge', *Bulletin de l'institut de l'Égypte,* 4th ser. 4, 1903, pp. 351–61; M. A. Marqûz, 'The T'irâz institution in medieval Egypt', in C. L. Geddes (ed.), *Mélanges en l'honneur du Pr K. A. C. Creswell*, Cairo: American University in Cairo Press, 1965, pp. 157–62.

23 V. François, 'Les céramiques médiévales d'Alexandrie: un témoignage archéologique d'importance', in Décobert and Empereur, *Alexandrie médiévale 1*, pp. 57–64.

24 Of the Buhayra province, C. Décobert, 'Alexandrie au XIIIe siècle: une nouvelle topographie', in Décobert and Empereur, *Alexandrie médiévale 1*, pp. 71–100, here p. 74.

25 Ibn al-Ji'ân, *Kitâb al-tuh'fa al-sanîya bi asmâ al-bilad al-mas'rîya* [Book of the yearly masterpieces by the names of the lands of Egypt], Cairo: Imprimerie Nationale, 1898, p. 138; cf. Halm, *Aegypten*, pp. 765–8.

26 Cf. S. J. Borsch, 'Environment and population: the collapse of large irrigation systems reconsidered', *Comparative Studies in Society and History* 46/3, 2004, pp. 451–68.

27 See note 29, below.

28 On wine production in the hinterland of Alexandria in late antiquity, see M. Rodziewicz, 'Wine production and trade in late Roman Alexandria', in C. Décobert *et al.* (eds), *Alexandrie médiévale 4*, Alexandria: CEAlex, 2011, pp. 39–53, here p. 53; on wine imports from Crete see Christ, *Trading Conflicts*, pp. 169–72; cf. Rodziewicz, 'Did Greek wine become port? Or why institutional interventions matter (c. 1350–1780)', *Quaderni Storici* 143/48(2), 2013, pp. 333–58.

29 Christ, 'Eine Stadt wandert aus'.

30 Alexandria was the only harbour in Egypt that could accommodate bigger round ships (cogs and later caravels, carracks and ships of northern design) employed from the thirteenth century onwards, cf. M. Gemignani, 'Mediterranean Sea', in J. B. Hattendorf (ed.), *The Oxford Encyclopaedia of Maritime History*, Oxford: Oxford University Press, 2007, p. 545.

31 Cf. Christ, 'Eine Stadt wandert aus'.

32 A. H. Lybyer, 'The Ottoman Turks and the routes of oriental trade', *English Historical Review* 1915, pp. 577–88, here pp. 579 seqq.; Ashtor, *Levant Trade*, pp. 103–6.

33 Cf. M. O'Connell's chapter on Venetian trade in this volume.

34 Heyd, *Histoire du commerce*; Ashtor, *Levant Trade.*

35 Cf. É. Vallet, *L'Arabie marchande: État et commerce sous les sultans Rasulides du Yémen (626–858/1229–1454)*, Paris: Publications de la Sorbonne, 2010; J. L. Meloy, *Imperial Power and Maritime Trade: Mecca and Cairo in the Later Middle Ages*, Chicago Studies on the Middle East, Chicago: Middle East Documentation Center, 2010.

36 G. Christ, 'Sliding legalities: Venetian slave trade in Alexandria and the Aegean', in C. Cluse and R. Amitai (eds), *Slavery and the Slave Trade in the Eastern Mediterranean (c. 1000–1500 CE)*, Turnhout: Brepols, in press, pp. 210–29.

37 For the connection of networks see also G. Christ, 'Beyond the network – connectors of networks: Venetian agents in Cairo and Venetian news management', in S. Conermann (ed.), *Everything Is on the Move: The Mamluk Empire as a Node in (Trans-)Regional Networks*, Göttingen: V&R unipress, Bonn University Press, 2014, pp. 27–59.

38 Cf. G. Christ, 'The Venetian consul and the cosmopolitan mercantile community of Alexandria at the beginning of the fifteenth century', *Al-Masaq* 26/1, 2014, pp. 62–77, here pp. 68, 76–7.

39 For the industrial decline see E. Ashtor, 'The economic decline of the Middle East during the Later Middle Ages – an outline', *Asian and African Studies: Journal of the Israel Oriental Society* 15, 1981, pp. 253–86; the textile industry in particular, M. Chapoutot-Remadi,

'Réflexions sur l'industrie textile dans le monde musulman au Moyen Âge: à propos d'un livre récent', *Annales. Économies Sociétés Civilisations* 35/3–4, 1980, pp. 504–11. The hypothesis is contested albeit not conclusively by M. Shatzmiller, 'A misconstrued link: Europe and the economic history of Islamic trade', in S. Cavaciocchi (ed.), *Relazioni economiche tra Europa e mondo islamico, secc. XIII–XVIII*, proceedings of the 'trentottesima settimana di studi', 1–5 May 2006, Florence: Le Monnier, 2007, pp. 237–415 for a more detailed discussion of the debate, see Christ, 'Eine Stadt wandert aus', pp. 147 seq. and passim on the entanglement of decline and continuity.

40 For the Venetian line: D. Stöckly, *Le système de l'incanto des galées du marché à Venise*, Leiden: Brill, 1995, pp. 2 seqq.; for Catalans transporting Muslim passengers, Müller-Wiener, *Eine Stadtgeschichte*, p. 76.

41 Ibid., p. 57; for the Ottoman east–west trade, M. J. Reimer, 'Ottoman Alexandria: the paradox of decline and the reconfiguration of power in eighteenth-century Arab provinces', *JESHO* 37/2, 1994, pp. 107–46, here p. 111.

42 D. Jacoby, 'Le consulat vénitien d'Alexandrie d'après un document inédit de 1284', in D. Coulon *et al.* (eds), *Chemins d'outre-mer: Études d'histoire sur la Méditerranée médiévale offertes à Michel Balard*, Paris: Publications de la Sorbonne, 2004, pp. 461–74.

43 See for instance D. Jacoby, 'Cretan cheese: a neglected aspect of Venetian medieval trade', in E. E. Kittell and T. F. Madden (eds), *Medieval and Renaissance Venice: Studies in Honour of Donald E. Queller*, Urbana, IL: University of Illinois Press, 1999, pp. 49–68.

44 S. Arenson, 'Food for a maritime empire: Venice and its bases in the Middle Ages', in K. Friedland (ed.) *Maritime Food Transport*, Cologne: Böhlau, 1994, pp. 177–85, here pp. 182 seqq.

45 S. Y. Labîb, *Handelsgeschichte Ägyptens im Spätmittelalter (1171–1517)*, Wiesbaden: Franz Steiner Verlag, 1965, p. 239.

46 Jacoby, 'Cretan Cheese', p. 60.

47 On private navigation and this episode: G. Christ, 'Quelques observations concernant la navigation vénitienne à Alexandrie à la fin du Moyen Âge', in S. G. Franchini, G. Toscano and G. Ortalli (eds) *Venise et la Méditerranée*, Venezia: Istituto Veneto di Scienze, Lettere ed Arti, 2011, pp. 55–72.

48 For the capacity of Venetian ships (galleys and cogs), see F. C. Lane, *Venetian Ships and Shipbuilders of the Renaissance*, Baltimore, MD: Johns Hopkins Press, 1934, pp. 15, 40; for estimates of the numbers of galleys and cogs calling on Alexandria see E. Ashtor, 'The volume of Levantine trade in the Later Middle Ages (1370–1498)', *JEEH* 4, 3, 1975, pp. 573–612. The number of smaller ships (two-masted lateeners, small cogs, *grippi*, etc.) is more difficult to assess: 40–50 ships of perhaps an average of 80 tons? Cf. Christ, 'Quelques observations', p. 57. My estimates are significantly higher than those of Heers and in his wake Wake, which did not take into account Ashtor's and more recent findings, J. Heers, 'Il commercio nel Mediterraneo alla fine del secolo XIV e nei primi anni del XV', *Archivio Storico Italiano* 1955, p. 113; C. H. H. Wake, 'The changing pattern of Europe's pepper and spice imports, ca. 1400–1700', *JEEH* 8/2, 1979, pp. 361–403, cf. his revised slightly higher numbers id., 'The volume of European spice trade at the beginning and the end of the fifteenth century', *JEEH* 15, 1986, pp. 621–35.

49 For contraband, see Christ, 'Trading conflicts' pp. 201–4.

50 Ashtor, 'Volume of Levantine Trade', cf. P. Spufford, *Power and Profit: The Merchant in Medieval Europe*, London: Thames & Hudson, 2002. Such estimates are of course problematic and to try to translate the ducat value into modern currencies would be even more problematic. I based my estimate on the assumption that although small ship private navigation would handle half of the volume of trade but not half of the total value as most of the merchandise was composed of bulkier agricultural goods (including wine) of lower value compared to spices.

51 Arabic traders mainly specialized in the trade between Yemen and Jidda, occasionally Egypt, cf. É. Vallet, *L'Arabie marchande*, pp. 505–16.
52 Reimer, 'Ottoman Alexandria', p. 108; M. Tuchscherer, and M. P. Pedani Fabris (eds) *Alexandrie ottomane 1,* Cairo: IFAO, 2011.
53 Christ, *Trading Conflicts*, p. 27.
54 Reimer, 'Ottoman Alexandria', pp. 112 seqq.
55 Whether this seems to reflect a wider tendency in the Islamic world that may or may not have an impact on the further development of the Islamic world cannot be considered here. Lapidus is certainly right to emphasise that the dichotomy between European communes vs. Oriental bureaucracies would be too simple. He emphasizes features of the Oriental city that remind us of our cities today: fewer specialized artisans but a relatively amorphous class of (academic) professionals, permeable and fluid social structures and hierarchies, I. M. Lapidus, *Muslim Cities in the Later Middle Ages,* Cambridge, MA: Harvard University Press, 1984, p. 185 seqq.
56 See the most comprehensive study by A. Sopracasa, *Venezia e l'Egitto alla fine del medioevo: Le tariffe di Alessandria,* Alexandria: CEAlex, 2013, particularly pp. 374 seqq.
57 Sopracasa, *Venezia*; Christ, *Trading Conflicts.*
58 Müller-Wiener, *Eine Stadtgeschichte*, pp. 278–80.
59 Ibid., pp. 271, 275 seq. where she is not explicitly linking Sufis to urban resistance, which I think is plausible, cf. Christ, *Trading Conflicts,* pp. 177–9, J. P. Berkey, *Popular Preaching and Religious Authority in the Medieval Islamic Near East,* Seattle: University of Washington Press, 2001, pp. 91, 95; see also Lapidus, *Muslim Cities*, pp. 105 seq., 109 seq., cf. p. 151; for Sufis in Alexandria see also note 8 above.
60 Cf. Christ, *Trading Conflicts*, pp. 167–84.
61 J. Trenchs Odena, 'Les "Alexandrini", ou la désobéissance aux embargos conciliaires ou pontificaux contre les Musulmans', in *Islam et chretiens du Midi (XIIe–XIVe),* Cahiers de Fanjeaux 18, Toulouse, 1983, pp. 169–93.
62 Marie Favereau, 'The Mamluk Sultanate and the Golden Horde: tension and interaction', in S. Conermann and R. Amitai (eds), *The Mamluk Sultanate and Its Neighbors: Economic, Social and Cultural Entanglements*, Göttingen: V&R unipress, Bonn University Press, forthcoming.
63 G. Petti Balbi, 'La massaria genovese di Alessandria d'Egitto nel Quattrocento', *Studi storici* 38/2, 1997, pp. 339–53, here p. 340.
64 For the Catalans and for Catalan trade see D. Coulon, *Barcelone et le grand commerce d'Orient au Moyen Âge: un siècle de relations avec l'Égypte et la Syrie-Palestine (ca. 1330 – ca. 1430),* Madrid: Casa de Velázquez, 2004, pp. 586–95.
65 Christ, *Trading Conflicts*, pp. 95–6; the Florentine embassy applied for a status akin to the Venetian, F. Brancacci, 'Diario di Felice Brancacci. Ambasciatore con Carlo Federighi al Cairo per il Comune di Firenze (1422)', *Archivio Storico Italiano* serie 4/8, 1881, pp. 157–88, cf. C. Caselli, 'Strategies for transcultural trade relations: Florentine attempts to reproduce the Venetian commercial system in the Mamluk Empire (first half of the fifteenth century)', in Georg Christ *et al.* (eds), *Union in Separation: Diasporic Groups and Identities in the Eastern Mediterranean (1100–1800),* Roma: Viella, 2015, pp. 267–84. See Petti Balbi, 'La massaria', pp. 349 seq. and p. 341 for the differences in the designs of the consular offices between local election and dispatch from the mother city.
66 G. Christ, 'The Venetian consul'.
67 M. P. Pedani Fabris, 'The oath of a Venetian consul in Egypt (1284)', *Quaderni di Studi Arabi* 14, 1996, pp. 215–22; Jacoby, 'Le consulat vénitien', pp. 461–74; Commissione ducale a Girolamo Tiepolo, console in Alessandria, 29 luglio 1498. 29.07.1498, BMC, ms. Classe III (olim Ms. Cicogna Commissioni nr. 70), 70; 'Il console dei Veneziani in Alessandria (XVI w.)', Biblioteka Jagiellońska, Cracow, Berol., Ms. Ital. Qu., 8 (Nr inw. 17640).

68 Cf. W. Heffening, *Das islamische Fremdenrecht bis zu den islamisch-fränkischen Staatsverträgen. Eine rechtshistorische Studie zum Fiqh*, Hannover: Orient-Buchhandlung Heinz Lafaire, 1925, pp. 28–34.

69 For a good general introduction, see J. E. Wansbrough, 'Venice and Florence in the Mamluk commercial privileges', *BSOAS*, 28, 1965, pp. 483–523, for the Venetian privileges see, G. M. Thomas (and R. Predelli pars II), (eds) *Diplomatarium veneto levantinum sive acta et diplomata res venetas graecas atque Levantis illustrantia a. 1300–1350 [pars I]; a. 1351–1454, [pars II]* Monumenti storici publicati dalla reale deputazione veneta di storia patria, Venice, 1880/1899; for Florence: M. Amari, *Diplomi arabi nel R. Archivio Fiorentino*, Florence: Le Monnier, 1863.

70 In the Ottoman period the distinction between the sultan's law (qânûn) and Islamic law (fiqh, including the sharia) became formalized even more, cf. C. Imber, *The Ottoman Empire, 1300–1650: The Structure of Power*, 2nd ed., New York: Palgrave Macmillan, 2009, pp. 230–4.

71 The practice started certainly much earlier than that reported in the privileges (e.g. M. P. Pedani, 'Gli ultimi accordi tra i sultani mamelucchi d'Egitto e la Repubblica di Venezia', *Quaderni di Studi Arabi* 12, 1994, pp. 49–64, here p. 64, most probably as early as with Barqûq in the late fourteenth century, cf. G. Christ, *King of the Two Seas: Mamluk Trade Policy as a Response to the Crisis of the 14th Century*? Ulrich Haarmann Memorial Lecture (Berlin: EB-Verlag, forthcoming). The privileges thus should be read carefully; they reflect Venetian wishes/grievances rather than conditions on the ground although of course the two are typically related.

72 Christ, *Trading Conflicts*, p. 53.

73 O. C. Constable, *Housing the Stranger in the Medieval World: Lodging, Trade, and Travel in Late Antiquity and the Middle Ages*, Cambridge: Cambridge University Press, 2003; in practice, the daily up-keep of the *fondaco* was often paid for by its inhabitants, i.e. the respective Latin communities, Christ, *Trading Conflicts*, p. 72 note 84; Petti Balbi, 'Massaria', p. 352; rather confusingly, the comparable institution in the Byzantine empire was called *mitaton*.

74 Christ, *Trading Conflicts*, pp. 135–9.

75 Ibid., p. 129 and id., 'Sliding Legalities'.

76 For the Fatimid period: S. D. Goitein, *A Mediterranean Society: The Jewish Communities of the Arab World as Portrayed in the Documents of the Cairo Geniza* vol. 1, Berkeley: University of California Press, 1999, p. 350; Jacoby, 'Le consulat', p. 26; cf. D. P. Little, 'Coptic conversion to Islam under the Bah'rî Mamlûks', *BSOAS, University of London*, 1976, vol. 39, pp. 552–69.

77 Christ, *Trading Conflicts*, pp. 229–49 and id., 'Filippo di Malerbi – un spécialiste du transfert clandestin en Égypte au début du 15ème siècle', in R. Abdellatif, D. König *et al.* (eds) *Acteurs des transferts culturels en Méditerranée médiévale*, München: Oldenbourg Verlag, 2012, pp. 100–10; cf. for this peculiar connection of forward purchase and credit in Rhodes, P. Bonneaud, 'The influential trade: community of western merchants on Hospitaller Rhodes (1421–1480)', in Christ *et al.* (eds) *Union in Separation*, op. cit., pp. 393–409, here p. 402. The explicit ban on banking is also reflected in a later consular instruction, Commissione Tiepolo cap. 40 (f. 9r/v): 'Venetian non possi [9v] tenir bancho in Alexandria in fontego over fuora.'

78 Deliberation (probably of the Senate), s.d. after 1376, in: 'Il console dei Veneziani', 11 r/v.

79 Cf. Christ, *Trading Conflicts*, passim.

80 F. J. Apellániz Ruiz de Galarreta, 'Collaboration des Réseaux Marchands à Alexandrie (XIVe-XVe Siècles)', in D. Ramada Curto (ed.) *From Florence to the Mediterranean and Beyond. Essays in Honour of Anthony Molho*, Florence: Leo S. Olschki, 2009, pp. 581–99, here pp. 595 seqq.

81 See note 78 for speculative practices; for Apellániz' discussion of the Venetian notary, see Christ 'Beyond the Network', pp. 31 seq.
82 Christ, *Trading Conflicts*, pp. 209–49.
83 Massaria: Petti-Balbi, 'Massaria'; cottimo: Christ, *Trading Conflicts*, pp. 77–81.
84 Christ, 'Beyond the Network', pp. 35 seqq. 45.
85 Christ, *Trading Conflicts*, pp. 81, 219–25.
86 For a description of the events in the late fifteenth and early sixteenth centuries, see F. J. Apellániz, *Pouvoir et finance en Méditerranée pré-moderne: Le deuxième état Mamelouk et le commerce des épices (1389–1517)*, Barcelona: CSIC, 2009, pp. 239–52.
87 Jacoby, 'Consulat vénitien' op. cit. p. 471: 'secundum usum, si usum sciero, et ubi usus michi defecerit dicam secundum conscienciam meam sine fraude.'
88 On the sultan's or state justice, see A. Fuess, 'Zulm by Mazālim? The political implications of the use of Mazālim jurisdiction by the Mamluk sultans', *Mamlûk Studies Review* 13, no. 1, 2009, pp. 121–47.
89 Rhodian sea law influenced both Islamic and Latin maritime legislation, see H. S. Khalilieh, *Islamic Maritime Law: An Introduction*, Studies in Islamic law and society 5, Leiden: Brill, 1998; *khiyâr/optio* ruled revoking of contracts and notices of defect similarly in both legal systems, J. Schacht, *An Introduction to Islamic Law*, Oxford: Clarendon Press, 1982, pp. 152 seq.
90 G. Christ, 'Masked cooperation with the infidel? The Venetian commercial privileges, political power, and legal culture in Mamlûk Egypt', in A. Cimdina and J. Osmond (eds) *Power and Culture: Hegemony, Interaction and Dissent*, Pisa: Edizioni Plus - Pisa University Press, 2006, pp. 33–51.
91 *Merchadanti che va et viene, son a condition de oxeli che non dismonta si non suxo l'acqua: si intravien alcun mal, non tornerà pùo in quello luogo*, letter of the Mamluk sultan al-Ashraf Qâns'ûh al-Ghûrî to the Doge of Venice, arrived December 1503, M. Sanuto (the Younger), *I diarii*, t. 5, Venezia: Visentini, 1881, p. 887.
92 Christ, *Trading Conflicts*, pp. 70 seq.
93 F. J. Apellániz Ruiz de Galarreta, 'Venetian trading networks in the medieval Mediterranean', *Journal of Interdisciplinary History*, vol. 44/2, 2013, pp. 157–79, here p. 170.
94 Chiaro Arcangeli, see Caselli, 'Strategies for transcultural trade relations', pp. 278 seq; Apellániz, 'Venetian trading networks', pp. 172 seq., 179.
95 G. Christ, 'Transients? Jews in Alexandria in the Late Middle Ages through Venetian eyes', in J. V. Tolan (ed.) *Expulsion and Diaspora Formation: Religious and Ethnic Identities in Flux from Antiquity to the Seventeenth Century*, Religion and Law in Medieval Christian and Muslim Societies, Turnhout: Brepols, 2015, pp. 195–216, here pp. 198, 215 seq.
96 Christ, *Trading Conflicts*, p. 27.
97 G. Christ, 'Quelques observations concernant la navigation vénitienne à Alexandrie à la fin du Moyen Âge', in S. G. Franchini, G. Toscano and G. Ortalli (eds) *Venise et la Méditerranée*, Venezia: Istituto Veneto di Scienze, Lettere ed Arti, 2011, pp. 55–72, here p. 61 seq.
98 Christ, 'Transients?', pp. 200 seq.
99 See note 18 above.
100 Müller-Wiener, *Eine Stadtgeschichte*, pp. 48, 56–7, 128; Fuess, 'Rotting Ships', pp. 65 seqq.

9

THE MARITIME TRADING NETWORK OF RAGUSA (DUBROVNIK) FROM THE FOURTEENTH TO THE SIXTEENTH CENTURY

Lovro Kunčević

Introduction

There, where your *argosies* with portly sail,
Like signors and rich burghers on the flood,
Or, as it were, the pageants of the sea,
Do overpeer the petty traffickers,
That curtsy to them, do them reverence,
As they fly by them with their woven wings

These verses from Shakespeare's *Merchant of Venice* have often been quoted in studies of Ragusan maritime history. Yet it seems fitting to abuse them once again, since they encapsulate so well the importance of Ragusan shipping during the Renaissance. Namely, the word 'argosy' which Shakespeare uses – and which in English designates a large merchant ship – is derived from the name Ragusa.[1] The fact that the Renaissance English developed such a strong associative link between a distant Mediterranean republic and maritime trade testifies to the importance of the Ragusan mercantile network.

Thus it might come as a surprise that, despite the otherwise vibrant historiography on Ragusa, its maritime history has been oddly neglected. Most of the fundamental research was done in 1940s, 1950s and 1960s, by authors such as J. Tadić, J. Luetić and S. Vekarić, and their works form the basis of this study. Although a number of ex-Yugoslav and Italian scholars have since worked on various economic themes, none of them focused specifically on maritime trade, and it remains a significant lacuna in contemporary research.[2]

Far from attempting to fill that lacuna, this study simply serves as a prolegomena regarding the history, nature and functioning of the Ragusan maritime network in the period between the fourteenth and sixteenth centuries. Its first section is dedicated to introducing the Ragusan Republic, especially those (geo)political factors that facilitated its rise to commercial importance. The second section provides an overview of Ragusan maritime trade in the late medieval and early modern period, sketching its development, main routes and trade commodities. The third section discusses the ways in which that network functioned, outlining its protagonists, organizational forms and institutions.

The protagonist: Ragusan Republic

The Republic of Ragusa (Dubrovnik) was a city-state on the eastern shore of the Adriatic whose territory consisted of a thin stretch of the coast and several adjacent islands. With a population around 50,000 and, at its maximum, around 90,000, it was one of the smallest independent states of Renaissance Europe. Constitutionally it was similar to its great competitor Venice – it was an aristocratic republic ruled by councils filled with members of the hereditary patriciate. Despite acknowledging the patronage and even nominal sovereignty of several great powers – most importantly, the Hungarian kingdom and the Ottoman empire – Ragusa survived as a *de facto* independent republic from the mid-fourteenth until the early nineteenth century, when it was conquered by Napoleon.[3]

What certainly helped Ragusa become a major trading power was its favourable location. It lay along the key naval route that followed the eastern Adriatic coast, connecting northern Italy and Central Europe with the Balkans and the Levant. Moreover, Ragusa enjoyed an important place on that route: it was situated at the end of the long chain of sheltering Dalmatian islands, just before the beginning of the South Adriatic, whose rocky, islandless and mountainous shore was unfavourable for navigation. Therefore, the city was either the last port for ships to refit before sailing to the open seas or the first major Adriatic port they encountered. Equally important, the western coast of the Adriatic was relatively close, and in good weather it could be reached in just one day. Last but not least, due to the somewhat milder geography of the Dinaric Mountains in its immediate hinterland, Ragusa had good access to the interior of the Balkan Peninsula. A vital thoroughfare – eventually even called 'the Ragusan road' and used as caravan route – connected the city with the Balkan towns and eventually led to major centres such as Thessaloniki, Sofia and Constantinople. Using this advantageous position, Ragusa developed a trading network that was strongly 'amphibious', that is, it combined land and maritime trade, thus enabling the city to adapt more easily to changing political and economic circumstances.[4]

However, Ragusa was situated at the crossroads not only in the geographical, but also cultural and political sense. Since the Ottoman conquest of the Balkans in the fifteenth century, Ragusa lay at a multiple frontier, a meeting point of three major religions, cultures, even civilizations: Catholicism to which it itself belonged, Orthodoxy and Islam, which dominated its hinterland. Geopolitically, Renaissance Ragusa was situated in the borderlands between the Ottoman empire, which controlled the Balkans; the Venetian Republic, which ruled the rest of Dalmatia; and the Aragonese/Spanish Habsburgs who ruled the opposite shore of the Adriatic. Albeit perilous, this frontier position also provided ample opportunities – and Ragusa made a career out of it. As this chapter will show, it became a mediator between the East and West, between the Ottoman empire and Christian Europe, thus turning into one of the major trading powers of the Renaissance Mediterranean.

Needless to say, such a position and function brought many perils. As a small merchant city without a colonial empire or significant military force, Ragusa was profoundly dependent on the goodwill of greater powers for its survival and the maintenance of its trading network. Therefore, the history of Ragusan foreign policy is largely one of balancing between the more powerful states which provided the city with protection and economic privileges. From the mid-fourteenth century Ragusa enjoyed the protection of its nominal but conveniently distant sovereign, the Hungarian-Croatian king.[5] In the mid-fifteenth century, it acquired an even more powerful patron – the Ottoman sultan, who came to rule the Balkan hinterland of the city. In return for an annual tribute and (mostly) symbolic signs of deference, Ragusa gained the protection of the Ottomans and broad privileges in the vast and unified market of the empire.[6] Close ties with the Ottomans, however, did not prevent the Republic from cherishing excellent relations with the major Christian powers as well, primarily the Spanish Habsburgs and the papacy.[7] Thus, Renaissance Ragusa managed to create an impressive web of international patronage, ensuring that its trading privileges and independence were guaranteed by several great powers, even those antagonistic to each other (e.g. Spain and the Ottoman empire). The city maintained such an international position through its traditionally humble diplomacy and obsessively professed neutrality, but also by playing a perilous double game. In order to appease its often antagonistic patrons, Ragusa spied for and distributed information to several Mediterranean powers, occasionally also providing them with other favours (e.g. sending skilled labourers, redeeming captives or providing transportation).[8]

Another fact which enabled the small state to attain such economic importance was that Ragusa was probably among the most intensely mercantile and maritime economies of Renaissance Europe. To begin with, the elite of the city was thoroughly mercantile itself: the Ragusan patriciate achieved its dominant position in the fourteenth century largely due to mercantile profits and remained intensely engaged in trade until the late sixteenth century. Secondly, in terms of GDP, trade was by far the most important segment of the Ragusan economy, never even approximated by industry or agriculture. The enormous importance of mercantile activities is illustrated by the fact that in the sixteenth century around 25 per cent of all adult male inhabitants, and probably more than that, were employed in maritime and, to a lesser extent, land trade.[9] Another suggestive indicator of the intensity of mercantile activities is the proportion between the number of inhabitants and the tonnage of the Ragusan fleet during its sixteenth-century peak. Thus, in the 1540s for every inhabitant of the Republic there was around 0.46 tons of ship space, in the 1570s that proportion grew to the remarkable 0.95 tons per capita, while in the early 1600s it declined to the still impressive 0.56.[10] Such strong investment of resources and manpower in maritime trade enabled the small republic to create a merchant fleet comparable to those of states with vastly superior resources and population sizes.

The network in time: Ragusan maritime trade from the fourteenth to the sixteenth century

Judging by the series of trade contracts that Ragusa made with Italian communes (e.g. Pisa, Ravenna, Ancona, Bari) and the privileges it obtained from Balkan princes, it seems that the city had a significant trading network already by the twelfth and early thirteenth centuries. Although mostly confined to the Adriatic, it reached as far as Pisa, Bulgaria and Byzantium, and, to a lesser extent, even the Levant and North Africa.[11] This first trading expansion of Ragusa was hindered by the momentous geopolitical change that marked the beginning of the thirteenth century. During the turbulent events of the Fourth Crusade, Ragusa was conquered by Venice and remained under its rule for the next century and a half. Venice ruled like a true maritime and mercantile power: it limited and intervened in Ragusan trade, adapting it to its own huge network. In short, the Venetian economic strategy vis-à-vis Ragusa, visible from several thirteenth-century treatises between the two cities, was the following: on the one hand, trying to limit Ragusan maritime trade only to the Adriatic, while, on the other, stimulating the city's land trade with the Balkan hinterland.[12] Despite such pressure, throughout the thirteenth and early fourteenth centuries Ragusans continued to trade in the broader Mediterranean area as well, but there is no doubt that a certain reorientation took place and that land trade became increasingly important. The relative importance of land and maritime trade in this period is still debated, but one fact is undeniable: it was then that Ragusa created the foundations of its later extensive trading network in the Balkans.[13]

This penetration into the hinterland proved immensely important in the long run. As Krekić has stressed, stimulating Ragusan trade with the Balkans – i.e. leaving that lucrative trade almost exclusively to Ragusans – proved to be a serious error of judgement for the Venetians in the long run.[14] Namely, in the thirteenth, but especially in the fourteenth and fifteenth, centuries the economic importance of Serbia and Bosnia grew significantly because of the exploitation of rich mines in these areas. Building on the positions created in the earlier period, by the mid-fourteenth century Ragusans managed almost to monopolize the export of precious mineral—primarily silver and lead, but also copper, iron, mercury and lapis lazuli—from the Balkans towards the Western Europe. In many of the Bosnian and Serbian mining centres – such as Srebrenica, Novo Brdo, Fojnica, Rudnik or Olovo – Ragusans formed their colonies, which enjoyed certain autonomy and were partially ruled from Dubrovnik itself. Due to a scarcity of sources, the estimates of production of Balkan mines vary widely, but in any case reveal it to be of European significance. Thus, the estimates of production of silver in the first half of the fifteenth century range from the most conservative of at least 12 tons annually to the maximalist of at least 30 tons. Despite the attempts of Serbian and Bosnian rulers to establish control over this profitable industry, the greater part of these precious metals ended in Dubrovnik to be traded further towards the west. It was only with the Ottoman conquest in the mid-fifteenth century that the Balkan mining industry started to decline.[15]

This economic boom of the Ragusan hinterland coincided with a major geopolitical shift. In 1358, after a military defeat, Venice was forced to cede Ragusa and the rest of its Dalmatian possessions to the Hungarian-Croatian king. Under the new and distant overlord, Ragusa managed to achieve factual independence. Thereby all the economic limitations disappeared and a strong expansion of the city's maritime trade began.[16] Fuelled by the profits from the Balkan trade and sponsored by state subsidies, Ragusan shipbuilding and its merchant fleet developed rapidly. Thus, between 1370 and 1396, the fleet already consisted of more than 120 ships of different types and employed some 2700 men.[17] Not only the number, but also the size of ships began to grow. In the early fifteenth century, most Ragusan ships were small vessels between 16 and 64 tons. The 1430s saw the emergence of those between 48 and 126 tons, while in the second half of the century most of them amounted to 112 to 144 tons, the largest reaching 370 tons.[18] In the first decades of the fifteenth century, two additional factors contributed to the strengthening of Ragusan maritime trade. The first was the destabilization and conquest of the Balkans by the Ottomans, which culminated in the fall of Serbia (1459) and Bosnia (1463). The second was the need of the rapidly growing Ragusan textile industry for raw materials. In sum, during this period Ragusa became an important maritime power – and thus also the main Adriatic competitor of its former ruler Venice, establishing an economic rivalry that was to last for centuries.

The crucial macroeconomic role that Ragusa acquired in the second half of the fourteenth and in the fifteenth centuries was that of mediator between the Balkans and Western Europe. Balkan goods reached Ragusa via land routes and were then loaded on ships and transported to the West, usually to Italian ports such as Ancona, Venice and the cities of South Italy and Sicily.[19] Besides this traditional combination of land and maritime trade, there were also purely maritime routes. Ragusan ships traded intensively in ports of Albania (Vlorë, Durrës), Greece (Thessaloniki, Zakynthos, Patras), and, to a somewhat lesser extent, Dalmatia (Zadar, Senj, Drijeva). Moreover, during this period Ragusan shipping encompassed the entire eastern Mediterranean (Istanbul, Alexandria, Cyprus, Rhodes), and even the Black Sea (Caffa).[20] The western Mediterranean was rarely visited: while some Ragusan merchants are mentioned in Catalonia and in England in the mid-fifteenth century, most Ragusan ships did not venture further than the western coast of Sicily.[21] Regarding the content of this trade, from the Balkans Ragusan merchants exported goods such as silver, lead, copper, wax, hides, skins, lapis lazuli, cattle, horses, honey and cheese (and, until the early fifteenth century, also slaves). On the other hand, Ragusans brought to the Balkans from Western Europe and their own city wares such as textiles, salt, saltpetre, glass, paper, weaponry, craftsman's products and various luxury goods.[22] Grain was a somewhat special case: there was intensive trade with the ports of Albania, Greece, southern Italy and Sicily, but it was strictly regulated by a government ever anxious to supply the needy city.[23] Although most of this trade went through Ragusa, there were already a number of ships in this period that traded between other ports and/or rented their services as carriers to foreign merchants and states.[24]

Ragusan maritime trade reached its greatest extent and value in the sixteenth century. Building on the already significant trading network in the eastern Mediterranean, Ragusan shipping now entered the western Mediterranean and the Atlantic, reaching as far as England and Flanders. Again, the main function that Ragusa performed was that of a mediator between the East and the West. However, in the changed geopolitical circumstances this meant mediating between the Ottoman empire and the Christian states, primarily the Habsburg imperial complex. Crucial for Ragusa's constant balancing between the great powers was the rigidly observed neutrality that enabled the small city-state not only to survive the wars of its many patrons, but even to use them to gain significant profits. Good illustrations of the effects of neutrality on trade are the sharp rises in the customs revenues of the Republic during the major conflicts between the Christian states and the Ottomans in the years 1537–40 and 1570–3.[25] In this same vein, the value of Ragusan trade tripled or quadrupled during the war years of 1538–40, while in 1570–3 it increased six to seven times.[26] These numbers reveal that during the major Mediterranean conflicts neutral Ragusans managed to seize a significant part of Christian trade with the Ottomans, primarily from Venice. Indeed, the small city-state was probably the most successful war profiteer of the Renaissance Mediterranean.[27]

The Ragusan trading network of the sixteenth century resembled that of the fifteenth, but it was far more extensive and somewhat differently structured. Importantly, Ragusan land trade in the Balkans recovered after the disruption of the Ottoman conquest and in the sixteenth century it again presented an invaluable complement to the city's shipping.[28] When it came to maritime trade, the most intensive communication was with the western shore of the Adriatic – Venice, Ancona and the ports of Apulia. To Venice and Ancona, Ragusans brought wares from the Balkans such as skins, wool, wax, cattle, salted fish, carpets, spices and flax. In return, they brought textiles, silk, various luxury items and fine Spanish wool back to Ragusa to be traded in the Ottoman empire. From Apulia, the Ragusan ships imported grain, wood and wine. Although these Adriatic lines employed the majority of ships, those were mostly smaller vessels; the greater amount of tonnage was employed in more profitable long-distance trade.[29] Within the broader Mediterranean area the most important regions were southern Italy and Sicily. Most of the tonnage and capital of the Ragusan fleet was invested in trade with this area, which was a communication nexus of the entire Mediterranean. As Braudel memorably put it, the Tyrrhenian Sea of this period would almost have become a 'Ragusan lake', were it not for the presence of Marseille and, later, Livorno.[30] Messina and other Sicilian ports served as places of reloading for ships bringing English and Flemish textiles, which were then transported further to the eastern Mediterranean, especially to Istanbul and Chios (a distribution centre for the Levant). Another important destination was Spain: Ragusan ships brought grain from Sicily and the Balkans and returned with fine wool, salt and colonial products. In the first half of the sixteenth century Ragusans also established intensive trade between England, Crete and the Ionian Islands, which involved the exchange of western textiles for wine and raisins.[31] As is apparent, most of this trade did not touch upon the Ragusan port, but connected the major centres of the Mediterranean and the Atlantic. Equally so, the wares with which Ragusans traded were mostly produced outside of the Republic. Both of these facts testify to the strongly mediating character of Ragusan maritime trade in the sixteenth century.[32]

This enormous trading network was maintained by an equally impressive fleet. In the sixteenth century, the size of Ragusan ships increased drastically. While in the fourteenth and fifteenth centuries Ragusans mostly built vessels whose carrying capacity remained below 200 tons, after 1500 much bigger ships were constructed. At the peak of this development in 1570–5, the Ragusan fleet included some forty ships between 320 and 640 tons, around thirty vessels above 640 tons and several huge ships over 1700 tons.[33] The number of Ragusan ships and the overall tonnage of the fleet increased throughout the century, culminating in the 1570s and 1580s. Thus, in 1540–4 the Ragusan fleet consisted of 132 ships that could carry 24,320 tons; in 1560–70 it had 180 ships with total capacity of 56,000 tons, while in 1570–85 it had 170 ships for 52,800 tons.[34] Although comparisons between the tonnage of Ragusan fleet with those of other states are highly unreliable, it does seem that during the sixteenth century Ragusa had one of the bigger fleets in the Mediterranean, which at its peak equalled that of Venice.[35] The investments and profits related to Ragusan shipping were correspondingly huge. The total value of the fleet amounted to some 200,000 ducats in 1540s and to around 700,000 ducats in the 1570s, while its annual income in the period from 1540 to 1600 oscillated between 180,000 and 260,000 ducats.[36]

However, there were signs of rapid decline in the Ragusan maritime trade already by the last decade of the sixteenth century. This is clearly visible from the sudden drop in numbers and capacity of the merchant fleet: in 1599 it consisted of 112 ships with around 37,925 tons, while in 1605 it numbered only 68 ships with 27,752 tons.[37] The reasons for this decline were multiple: the global change of maritime routes due to oceanic discoveries that finally began to affect Ragusan shipping; the penetration of the Mediterranean by the Dutch, English and French; the growing piracy in the Adriatic by Habsburg irregular troops, the Uskoks; and last but not least, the general economic weakening of the Ottoman empire which hitherto served as a prime market for Ragusan traders.[38] This decline continued throughout the seventeenth century – with short reversals during periods of Mediterranean warfare when Ragusa's neutral flag was profitable – and culminated after the great earthquake of 1667. Yet this decline was neither linear nor definite, since in the eighteenth century Ragusan maritime trade flourished again, but on somewhat different foundations.[39]

Institutions and *modus operandi* of the Ragusan maritime network

Ragusan merchants belonged to the very elite of the city. Historically, merchants actually *made* the elite: the patriciate – a group of families which formally monopolized power in the mid-fourteenth century – owed its rise largely to trade. This mercantile orientation persisted among the Ragusan patriciate until the end of the sixteenth century when, due to reduced profitability, it began investing elsewhere and turned into a rentier group.[40] Another social layer that played a significant role in trade was the secondary elite of the city, the citizens (*cittadini buoni/boni cives*), organized in two elite confraternities.[41] To a certain extent even the lower classes participated in maritime trade, since sailors had the right (the so-called *paraspodia*) to carry a small amount of wares on the ship and conduct business.[42] Interestingly, despite the enormous importance of trade – or precisely because of it – there was no merchant's guild in Ragusa. Its function was in fact performed by the state itself, which was the main promoter of the economic interests of both the patriciate and the citizen elite.[43]

It is plausible to assume that most Ragusan merchants were capable of at least rudimentary communication in more than one language. Their native Slavic was highly useful not only in the Balkans but also at the Ottoman court, where it was widespread, giving them a certain edge over their Italian and Western European competitors. The foreign language with which most Ragusan merchants were familiar was Italian, the lingua franca of the Mediterranean, but some of them could also use Latin (these two being the official languages of the Republic). The merchants trading and residing in the Ottoman empire sometimes learned Turkish, and were often used by the government as interpreters (dragomans) for the Republic's diplomats sent to the Ottoman authorities.[44]

Trade was usually a collective undertaking, since this enabled the concentration of capital and the minimization of risk. The cargo of ships was normally owned by many, and the same was true of the ships themselves. Traditionally, each ship was divided into 'karats' (*karati*), i.e. the shares of 1/24, which were bought and sold separately.[45] The ships were mostly owned by Ragusans themselves, and only in exceptional cases was a share owned by a foreigner – this practice was discouraged by the government, which legislated against it on several occasions. In most cases a ship had three to four owners, rarely more than six, and they were often connected through familial or personal ties.[46] During its sixteenth-century boom, shipping was exceptionally profitable. In the first decades of the 1500s the annual *netto* profits of

Ragusan ships amounted to almost the entire investment required for their construction. In the second half of the century this decreased to the still significant 50 to 60 per cent of the investment, but due to the raise of upkeep costs and salaries, it amounted *netto* to 25 to 30 per cent.[47]

Instrumental in the success of Ragusan traders was the highly developed consular service. The first Ragusan consuls emerged in the Balkans in the thirteenth century, while the earliest ones in the Mediterranean ports appeared in the late fourteenth century, in Messina and Syracuse. In the fifteenth century consulates were established in many Italian cities such as Ancona, Barletta, Otranto, Bari or Naples, but also in Marseille and Malta. Their numbers grew steadily, reflecting the expansion of Ragusan trade. In the late 1400s there were around twenty-two, while in the mid-sixteenth century there were some forty-four consulates in the western Mediterranean (among the new foundations were Palermo, Livorno, Pisa, Genoa, Sardinia, Corsica, Cadiz, Valencia and Mallorca).[48] In this period Ragusan consulates emerged in the Levant as well: the consul in Alexandria is first mentioned in 1490, and eight more consulates were created during the sixteenth century (e.g. Chios, Rhodes, Crete, Milos).[49] All in all, by the mid-sixteenth century, Ragusa had created a network of more than fifty consulates that spanned the entire Mediterranean.

The consuls were usually not Ragusans but rather members of the local elite. They were elected by the Ragusan senate for an indefinite period of time, so some of them held the office for decades, even turning it into a *de facto* hereditary position. They did not receive a salary, but rather specific dues (called *il consolato*) from Ragusan ships that entered the territory of their jurisdiction.[50] Their general task of promoting Ragusan trade included, on the one hand, lobbying with the local authorities, and, on the other, assisting Ragusan traders with their knowledge of local customs and regulations. Moreover, they performed tasks of an administrative nature: issuing various documents to Ragusan merchants such as sanitary confirmations, records of litigation, last wills and different contracts. Consuls also had important judiciary powers since the privileges of many European rulers granted them the right to adjudicate civil, and sometimes even criminal, cases between Ragusans. Additionally, consuls served as means of supervising the merchant network and enforcing the will of the central government across the entire Mediterranean. They had to monitor whether the merchants and captains obeyed the Republic's regulations and decrees, and they also sent detailed reports about their ventures, thus enabling the government to collect customs for goods which did not go through Ragusa. Last but not least, the consuls were an important part of the Ragusan information network, since they sent reports with news from their respective territories.[51]

Although a large portion of Ragusan maritime trade, especially in the sixteenth century, did not go through the city, Ragusa itself was a significant mercantile emporium. Throughout the fourteenth to sixteenth century there was a notable presence of foreign merchants in the city, among whom the most important were those from Italy and Catalonia. The Venetians were probably the most prominent, especially in the fourteenth century: besides exporting Balkan goods from the city, they also invested significant capital into Ragusan ventures in the hinterland mining industry. During the fourteenth century there was a significant Florentine presence as well, since the representatives of the great banking houses of Bardi, Peruzzi, Acciaiuoli and Buonaccorsi resided in the city. Another important group of Italians were merchants and craftsmen from Prato who played a key role in the organization and financing of the flourishing Ragusan textile industry in the early 1400s. Finally, the Catalan merchants traditionally exported slaves, captured in the Balkans, and imported the wool necessary for Ragusan textile industry.[52]

These foreigners did not have organized colonies or specific buildings at their disposal in the city. However, most of these merchants, some of whom resided for years and even acquired Ragusan citizenship, had their own consuls. The Venetian consul is mentioned already by 1368, and in the first half of the fifteenth century there were Catalan and Aragonese ones, as well as those of several Italian cities such as Genoa, Ancona and Messina. In 1449, however, the Ragusan government forbade its subjects to serve foreign rulers, which caused a momentary interruption in the functioning of consulates since many locals had to renounce their posts. Yet in most cases – with the notable exception of Venice – these consulates and many others (e.g. Florentine, French, Neapolitan) re-emerged during the fifteenth and sixteenth centuries, though they were, with some exceptions, held by foreigners. Besides promoting the trade of their countries, these consuls often managed the official correspondence of their rulers and, much to the dismay of Ragusan authorities, served as informers regarding the events in the Ottoman empire.[53]

Another important factor in the success of Ragusan trade was the well-organized public health service. The Ragusan government was among the first in Europe to establish a proper quarantine, decreeing in 1377 that all travellers arriving from places suspected of disease had to spend one month in strict isolation in predetermined places outside the city. In 1397 the unused buildings on the island of Mljet were turned into what was probably the first proper quarantine detention station or *lazaretto* in Europe. With time, the Ragusan *lazaretti* grew ever bigger and more developed. In the late fifteenth century they evolved into a self-contained complex with habitations, cistern, church and graveyard in the city's vicinity, while in the late sixteenth century the government began building a massive complex visible even today at the eastern end of the town. Along with the *lazaretti*, Ragusa also developed sophisticated sanitary regulations and magistracies. In the late fourteenth century the government appointed special officials to supervise the borders, certify the documents of those arriving and punish trespassers trying to enter without quarantine. In the fifteenth century these officials grew into important health magistrates, the so-called *officiales cazamortuorum* or *kačamorti*. Aside from supervising the enforcement of sanitary regulations and inspecting the new arrivals and their merchandise, they also had the broad authority to submit trespassers to torture and condemn them to physical punishment.[54]

Conclusion: trade, politics and autonomy in the Ragusan context

The Ragusan maritime network developed under conditions fairly different from those of most other cities analysed in this volume. On the one hand, Ragusa did not have the backing of a powerful supra-urban framework, be it a territorial monarchy (e.g. Lisbon, Danzig, London) or an organization like the Hanse (e.g. Lübeck). On the other hand, neither did Ragusa have a colonial empire like Venice or Genoa, an empire that ensured the trading network through territorial sovereignty over strategic sites. In sum, the small city-state was largely left to its own limited resources and minor diplomatic influence. Thus, the Ragusan trading network was acquired and maintained exclusively through diplomacy and economic competitiveness and *never* through armed force or a sovereign's will, as was often the case with other mercantile centers. In other words, the Ragusan trading network rested on an extensive patchwork of legal exemptions and concessions, the privileges which the city had to maintain and constantly renegotiate with more powerful foreign rulers upon whose goodwill it depended.

Importantly, this lack of the powerful external support or the colonial empire brought not only disadvantages, but advantages as well. Certainly, the absence of colonies made trade more vulnerable and dependent on the attitude of other states. However, the fact that the city did not have extensive possessions spared it from many trade-damaging wars, like the ones that Venice had to wage with the Ottomans. On a more subtle level, that lack of empire also enabled the Ragusan government to focus to a greater degree on promoting trading interests. Although it is impossible to clearly pinpoint this difference, it does seem that in conducting its economic policy Ragusa was not hindered by the need to appease various local elites under its rule or to ensure the defense of its extensive possessions. Since the Republic was not encumbered by the need to maintain an empire, in its foreign policy commercial interests could reign (almost) supreme. Indeed, as Ćirković put it, Ragusans administered their Republic with the same spirit with which they 'conducted the affairs of their trading companies'.[55]

Regarding the lack of a strong state as the promoter of the city's trade, the absence of such a patron certainly made it more difficult for the Ragusan elite to establish economic hegemony in the broader area.[56] On the other hand, it was precisely the blatant powerlessness of Ragusa that in some cases made it easier for the city to gain concessions from foreign rulers, even those antagonistic to each other. While they would certainly not have granted such privileges to the subjects of a powerful rival monarch, favouring a petty and neutral republic was much less problematic. Perhaps even more importantly, due to the lack of a strong sovereign, the patriciate did not have to defend its autonomy from royal encroachments, nor was it involved in the ruler's wars which would have damaged its trade.

In sum, when compared to imperial trading powers like Venice and state-sponsored centres like Lisbon, Ragusa clearly lacked political and military resources.

However, precisely by being marginal in the great power game, it gained enormously in diplomatic and economic versatility. It was able to exploit to a remarkable degree its position as a harmless neutral state, ideal for the role of a mediator between the great powers. This versatility was suggestively summarized by the sixteenth-century playwright Marin Držić. In a prologue to one of his plays, he stressed that Ragusan rulers are loved by the lords of both East and West, and finished with a wonderful metaphor: 'their ships sail on every wind'.[57]

Acknowledgements

This work has been fully supported by the Croatian Science Foundation, under the project number 5106.

Notes

1 For instance see: http://www.oxforddictionaries.com/definition/english/argosy; http://www.merriam-webster.com/dictionary/argosy (accessed June 2015). For the broader context see also J. Torbarina, 'Shakespeare and Dubrovnik', in R. Filipović and M. Partridge (eds), *Dubrovnik's Relation with England: A Symposium, April 1976,* Zagreb: University of Zagreb, 1977, pp. 237–40.

2 A good overview of Ragusan maritime historiography is: A. Di Vittorio, '*Tendenze ed orientamenti* della storiografia marittima ragusea', in A. Di Vittorio, *Tra mare e terra: Aspetti economici e finanziari della Repubblica di Ragusa in eta moderna,* Bari: Cacucci Editore, 2001, pp. 177–221. Regarding the documents relevant to the history of maritime trade, they are scattered though a number of series in the State Archives of Dubrovnik (Državni arhiv u Dubrovniku) and cover the period from the late Middle Ages until the nineteenth century. The laws and decrees of the government, many related to economic issues, are to be found in the minutes of the three councils of the Republic (*Acta consilii minoris, Acta consilii rogatorum* and *Acta maioris consilii*). Other important series are *Diversa cancellariae*, *Diversa notariae* and *Diversa de foris* which contain private documents such as contracts, liquidations of businesses, invoices, inventories, etc. For maritime history, highly relevant are also the series *Naula et securitates, Libri navigiorum, Privata, Debita notariae* and *Diplomata et acta.* A good overview of sources for Ragusan economic history is: J. Tadić, 'Les archives économiques de Raguse', *Annales. Économies, Sociétés, Civilisations* 16/6, 1961, pp. 1168–75.

3 A good recent synthesis of Ragusan history in English is: R. Harris, *Dubrovnik: A History,* London: Saqi, 2003. Older but still very useful is: B. Krekić, *Dubrovnik in the 14th and 15th Centuries: A City between the East and West,* Norman, OK: University of Oklahoma Press, 1972.

4 For the location of Ragusa, see: I. Rubić, 'Utjecaj pomorskih i kopnenih faktora na razvoj grada Dubrovnika' [The influence of maritime and land conditions on the development of Dubrovnik], in *Dubrovačko pomorstvo: U spomen sto godina Nautičke škole u Dubrovniku,* Dubrovnik: Odbor za proslavu sto godina Nautičke škole u Dubrovniku, 1952, pp. 309–22; A. Ničetić, *Povijest dubrovačke luke* [The history of the Ragusan port], Dubrovnik: Zavod za povijesne znanosti HAZU u Dubrovniku, 1996, pp. 30, 34–5, 40, 86, 93; B. Krekić, 'The contribution of foreigners to Dubrovnik's economic growth in the late Middle Ages', *Viator* 9, 1976, p. 375.

5 A standard overview is D. Dinić-Knežević, *Dubrovnik i Ugarska u srednjem veku* [Ragusa and the Hungarian Kingdom in the Middle Ages], Novi Sad: Filozofski fakultet u Novom Sadu, 1986. An English summary is: Harris, *Dubrovnik*, pp. 62–76.

6 Basic overviews of Ottoman-Ragusan relations are: I. Božić, *Dubrovnik i Turska u XIV i XV veku* [Ragusa and Turkey in the fourteenth and fifteenth centuries], Belgrade: SAN, 1952; T. Popović, *Turska i Dubrovnik u XVI veku* [Turkey and Ragusa in the sixteenth century], Belgrade: Srpska književna zadruga, 1973. For an English summary: Harris, *Dubrovnik*, pp. 77–100, 105–10.

7 The standard overviews are: *J. Tadić, Španija* i *Dubrovnik u XVI veku* [Spain and Ragusa in the sixteenth century], Belgrade: SKA, 1932; Đ. Körbler, 'Dubrovačka republika i zapadne evropske države: veze Dubrovnika s Napuljem, Sicilijom, Francuskom i Španolskom' [The Ragusan Republic and the states of Western Europe: the relations of Ragusa with Naples, Sicily, France and Spain], *Rad JAZU* 93, 1916, pp. 165–252. See also: Harris, *Dubrovnik*, pp. 101–5, 110–17.

8 S. Krasić, 'Dubrovačka Republika i umijeće čuvanja neutralnosti u međunarodnim sukobima' [The Ragusan Republic and the art of preserving neutrality in international conflicts], in M. Granić, I. Sanader, S. Berković and M. Andrlić (eds), *Diplomacija Dubrovačke Republike, Zbornik Diplomatske akademije br. 3,* Zagreb: Ministarstvo vanjskih poslova, Diplomatska akademija, 1998, pp. 69–97. For the economic consequences of neutrality: S. Anselmi, 'Motivazioni economiche della neutralita di Ragusa nell Cinquecento', in G. Benzoni (ed.), *Il Mediterraneo nella seconda metà del Cinqucento alla luce di Lepanto,* Florence: Leo S. Olschki Editore, 1974, pp. 33–70. On the rhetoric and methodology of Ragusan diplomacy: L. Kunčević, 'The rhetoric of the frontier of Christendom in the diplomacy of Renaissance Ragusa (Dubrovnik)', *Dubrovnik Annals* 17, 2013, pp. 37–68.

9 It has to be stressed that this cipher is somewhat misleading since many people had other professions besides trade. For this estimate see: L. Kunčević, 'O stabilnosti Dubrovačke Republike (14–16 stoljeće): geopolitički i ekonomski faktori' [On the stability of the Ragusan Republic (14th–16th century): geopolitical and economic factors], *Anali Zavoda za povijesne znanosti HAZU u Dubrovniku* 54/1, 2015, pp. 1–38.

10 This calculation was made by combining the data on the tonnage of the Ragusan fleet (discussed below) and the demographic data provided by N. Vekarić, 'The population of Dubrovnik Republic in the fifteenth, sixteenth and seventeenth centuries', *Dubrovnik Annals* 2, 1998, p. 26.

11 V. Foretić, 'Nekoliko pogleda na pomorsku trgovinu Dubrovnika u srednjem vijeku' [Several remarks regarding the Ragusan maritime trade in the Middle Ages], in *Dubrovačko pomorstvo*, pp. 117–26, 129–30; J. Lučić, 'O pomorskim vezama Dubrovnika sa Zadrom i ostalim gradovima Dalmacije u XIII. st.' [On the maritime relations of Dubrovnik with Zadar and other Dalmatian cities in the thirteenth century], in Lučić, *Dubrovačke teme*, Zagreb: Nakladni zavod Matice hrvatske, 1991, pp. 267–71; J. Lučić, 'Dubrovčani na jadranskom prostoru od VII st. do godine 1205' [Ragusans in the Adriatic space from the seventh century until 1205], ibid., pp. 48–9; J. Tadić, 'Istorija Dubrovnika do polovine XV veka' [The history of Ragusa until the mid-fifteenth century] *Istorijski časopis* 18, 1971, pp. 18–20.

12 This was achieved primarily by decreeing that Ragusan traders had to pay high customs for all wares from the Mediterranean but none for those from the Balkans; limiting the number of ships which could come to trade to Venice every year to four smaller vessels; and finally, forbidding the Ragusan ships to sail into certain areas. The treaties have been published in Š. Ljubić (ed.), *Listine o odnošajih izmedju južnoga slavenstva i Mletačke Republike I* [Charters concerning the relations of South Slavs and the Venetian Republic], Zagreb: JAZU, 1868, pp. 45, 55, 85. An excellent overview is B. Krekić, 'Dubrovnik and Venice in the thirteenth and fourteenth centuries: a short survey', in B. Krekić (ed.), *Unequal Rivals*, Zagreb-Dubrovnik: Zavod za povijesne znanosti HAZU u Dubrovniku, 2007, pp. 9–14. See also J. Lučić, 'Pomorsko-trgovačke veze Dubrovnika i Venecije u XIII. stoljeću' [Maritime and mercantile relations of Dubrovnik and Venice in the

thirteenth century] in Lučić, *Dubrovačke teme,* pp. 418–20, 422–3; Foretić, 'Nekoliko pogleda', pp. 119–20.

13 For several differing opinions on the relative importance of land and sea trade in this period: Lučić, 'O pomorskim vezama Dubrovnika sa Zadrom', pp. 272–3; Foretić, 'Nekoliko pogleda', pp. 125, 132; J. Luetić, 'Dubrovačka međunarodna pomorska djelatnost u XIV. stoljeću', *Rad Jugoslavenske akademije znanosti i umjetnosti: Razred za medicinske znanosti.* 16, 1980, pp. 78–9; J. Tadić, 'Privreda Dubrovnika i srpske zemlje u prvoj polovini XV. veka' [The economy of Dubrovnik and the Serbian lands in the first half of the 15th century], *Zbornik Filozofskog fakulteta u Beogradu* 10/1, 1968, pp. 519–20, 524–30.

14 B. Krekić, 'Developed autonomy: the patricians in Dubrovnik and Dalmatian cities', in B. Krekić (ed.), *Urban Society of Eastern Europe in Pre-Modern Times*, Berkeley-Los Angeles, CA, and London: University of California Press, 1987, pp. 187–8.

15 Basic works on the Balkan mining industry are: D. Kovačević, *Trgovina u srednjovjekovnoj Bosni* [Trade in medieval Bosnia], Sarajevo: Naučno društvo Bosne i Hercegovine, Djela, knj. 18, 1961; M. Dinić, *Za is toriju rudarstva u srednjovekovnoj Srbiji i Bosni* [On the history of mining in medieval Bosnia], vols 1 and 2, Beograd: Naučno delo, 1955, 1962; Tadić, 'Privreda Dubrovnika', pp. 519–35. Summaries in major languages are: S. Ćirković, 'The production of gold, silver and copper in the central parts of the Balkans from the 13th to the 16th century', in H. Kellenbez (ed.), *Precious Metals in the Age of Expansion,* Stuttgart: Klett-Cotta, 1981, pp. 41–69; S. Ćirković, 'Ragusa e il suo retroterra nel Medio Evo', in A. di Vittorio (ed.), *Ragusa e il Mediterraneo: Ruolo e funzioni di una Repubblica marinara tra Medioevo ed Età moderna,* Bari: Cacucci editore, 1990, pp. 15–26; Harris, *Dubrovnik*, pp. 155–7, 159–60; P. Pinelli, *Tra argento, grano e panni: Piero Pantella, un operatore italiano nella Ragusa del primo Quattrocento*, Florence: Firenze University Press, 2013, pp. 1–15.

16 Foretić, 'Nekoliko pogleda', p. 134; B. Krekić, 'Ragusa (Dubrovnik) e il mare: aspetti e problemi (XIV–XVI secolo)', in *Ragusa e il Mediterraneo*, p. 133. For the change in the political context in 1358: Z. Janeković-Römer, *Višegradski ugovor: Temelj Dubrovačke republike* [The Treaty of Višegrad: the foundation of the Ragusan Republic], Zagreb: Golden Marketing, 2003.

17 Luetić, 'Dubrovačka međunarodna', p. 77, for state subsidies p. 60; See also: S. Vekarić, 'Vrste i tipovi dubrovačkih brodova XIV stoljeća' [Kinds and types of Ragusan ships of the fourteenth century], *Anali Historijskog instituta JAZU u Dubrovniku* 10/11, 1966, pp. 40–1. For a different interpretation of this period, according to which maritime trade remained less important than the land trade and the fleet was more modest: Tadić, 'Privreda Dubrovnika', pp. 519–35.

18 J. Luetić, *Mornarica Dubrovačke republike* [The merchant fleet of the Republic of Dubrovnik], Dubrovnik: Dubrovački muzej, 1962, pp. 28–9; S. Vekarić, 'Naši jedrenjaci za dugu plovidbu kroz stoljeća' [Our long-distance sailing ships through the centuries] in Grga Novak and Vjekoslav Maštrović (eds), *Pomorski zbornik: Povodom 20-godišnjice Dana mornarice i pomorstva Jugoslavije, 1942–1962,* vol. 2, Zadar: Institut za historijske i ekonomske nauke 1963, pp. 150–1; J. Tadić, 'Organizacija dubrovačkog pomorstva u XVI veku' [The organization of Ragusan maritime trade in the sixteenth century], *Istorijski časopis* 1–2, 1948, p. 27. On shipbuilding see: S. Vekarić, 'O gradnji dubrovačkih brodova u XIV stoljeću' [On the building of Ragusan ships in the fourteenth century], in Grga Novak and Vjekoslav Maštrović (eds) *Pomorski zbornik,* vol. 1, Zadar: Institut za historijske i ekonomske nauke, 1963, pp. 465–76. The older historiography expressed ship tonnage in *carri,* a traditional South Italian measure also used in Dubrovnik, which amounted to roughly 1.6 of a ton or just under 20 hectolitres of grain (Harris, *Dubrovnik,* p. 163; *Di Vittorio, 'Tendenze ed orientamenti',* p. 113). In this text all the values expressed in *carri* have been converted to tons for the sake of clarity.

19 For an overview of Ragusan economic relations with various Italian states in this period: M. Spremić, 'Dubrovački brodovi i zapadno sredozemlje u XV. veku' [Ragusan ships

and the Western Mediterranean in the 15th century], *Istorijski časopis* 21, 1974, pp. 20–4; Foretić, 'Nekoliko pogleda', pp. 137–8, 141–4, 147–54.

20 Luetić, 'Dubrovačka međunarodna', pp. 69–70, 73–4; Foretić, 'Nekoliko pogleda', pp. 135, 154–63; Z. Janeković-Romer, 'Dubrovačko 15 stoljeće: vrijeme rada i bogaćenja' [The fifteenth century of Ragusa: an age of work and riches], in Filip de Diversis, *Opis slavnoga grada Dubrovnika*, ed. and tr. Z. Janeković-Römer Zagreb: Dom i svijet, 2004, pp. 23–4. A clear indication of the growing importance of Ragusan trade in the Levant is the privilege that allowed Ragusans to trade with the 'infidels' granted to the city in 1433 by the Synod of Basel (Foretić, 'Nekoliko pogleda', pp. 135–6; J. Lučić, '*Gospodarsko-društveni odnosi u* Dubrovniku u Stojkovićevo vrijeme' [Economic and social relations in Dubrovnik in Stojković's time], *Historijski zbornik* 38/1, 1985, p. 100).

21 Spremić, 'Dubrovački brodovi', pp. 25–6; Foretić, 'Nekoliko pogleda', pp. 145–6; V. Foretić, *Povijest Dubrovnika do 1808*, vol. 1 [The history of Dubrovnik until 1808], Zagreb: NZMH, 1980, pp. 259, 263.

22 Tadić, 'Istorija Dubrovnika', pp. 30–2, 36–7; Janeković-Römer, 'Dubrovačko 15. stoljeće', pp. 21–2; Lučić, 'Gospodarsko-društveni', pp. 101–2.

23 Basic works on the grain trade of medieval and early modern Ragusa are: D. Dinić-Knežević, 'Trgovina žitom u Dubrovniku u XIV veku' [Grain trade in Dubrovnik in the fourteenth century], *Godišnjak Filozofskog fakulteta u Novom Sadu* 10, 1967, pp. 79–131; Bogumil Hrabak, *Izvoz žitarica iz Osmanlijskog carstva u XIV, XV i XVI stoleću* [The export of cereals from the Ottoman Empire in the 14th, 15th and 16th centuries], Priština: Zajednica naučnih ustanova Kosova, 1971; S. d'Atri, 'Per conservare la citta tributtaria et divota: Ragusa (Dubrovnik) and the 1590–91 crisis', *Dubrovnik Annals* 14, 2010, pp. 71–98; S. d'Atri, 'Le navi e il mar, invece di campi e d'oliveti, tengono la città abbondante d'ogni bene: Il sistema annonario di Ragusa (Dubrovnik) in età moderna', *Storia urbana* 134, 2012, pp. 31–56; M. *Aymard, Venise Raguse et le commerce du blé pendant la seconde moitié du XVIe siècle*, Paris: SEVPEN, 1966.

24 For instance, Ragusan ships were prominent in that role in South Italy and Sicily (Spremić, 'Dubrovački brodovi', pp. 22–4).

25 While the customs income in 1535 amounted to roughly 14,000 ducats, in 1539 it rose sharply to 72,000 and in 1540 to over 62,000 ducats. Another great oscillation can be seen when one compares the income for 1579, which amounted to around 34,000, with the war years of 1570 and 1571 when it reached 68,000 and 140,000 ducats respectively. For these numbers: A. Di Vittorio, 'L'*impatto delle scoperte portoghesi* sull'economia di Ragusa nel secolo XVI', in A. *Di Vittorio* Antonio, S. Anselmi Sergio and P. Pierucci (eds), *Ragusa (Dubrovnik) una repubblica adriatica,* Bologna: Cisalpino, 1994, p. 22; O. Havrylyshyn and N. Srzentić, *Economy of Ragusa, 1300–1800: The Tiger of the Medieval Mediterranean,* Zagreb: Croatian National Bank, 2014, pp. 52–3, 58. Generally on the economic effects of neutrality see: Anselmi, 'Motivazioni economiche', pp. 33–70.

26 J. Tadić, 'Dubrovačka Republika do početka XVII. stoljeća' [The Ragusan Republic until the beginning of the seventeenth century], in *Historija naroda Jugoslavije II,* Zagreb: Školskaknjiga, 1959, p. 224.

27 Venice retaliated by trying to involve Ragusa in these wars or to at least damage its trade through diplomatic and military actions (Anselmi, 'Motivazioni economiche', pp. 28–34).

28 M. Moroni, *L'impero di San Biagio: Ragusa e i commerci balcanici dopo la conquista turca (1521–1620),* Bologna: Il Mulino, 2011.

29 Tadić, 'Organizacija', 39–40.

30 F. Braudel, *The Mediterranean and the Mediterranean World in the Age of Philip II,* vol. 1, tr. Sian Reynolds, London: Collins, 1972, pp. 121–2.

31 Tadić, 'Organizacija', p. 41.

32 B. Stulli, 'Dubrovačka Republika u XV. i XVI. stoljeću' [The Ragusan Republic in the 15th and 16th centuries], in B. Stulli, *Studije iz povijesti Dubrovnika*, Zagreb: Konzor, 2001, p. 22; J. Luetić, *Pomorci ijedrenjaci Republike Dubrovačke* [Sailing ships and mariners of the Ragusan Republic], Zagreb: NZMH, 1984, p. 25.

33 A good summary of various estimates, including other decades of the 1500s, is Vekarić, 'Naši jedrenjaci', p. 151. See also: Tadić, 'Organizacija', p. 27. The Italian Dominican Serafino Razzi describes in his travelogue the visit of an enormous Ragusan ship to the city of Vasto in 1577. Razzi states that this ship had 1200 carri (1920 tons) with a crew of 140 men, and was said to be 'the greatest [ship] which sails on the waves' (S. *Razzi, Viaggi in Abruzzo, (inedito del sec. XVI),* ed. B. *Carderi*, L'Aquila, L.V. Japadre, *1969*, pp. 240–3).

34 For these estimates see: Tadić, 'Organizacija', pp. 29–30; and a summary in: Krekić, 'Ragusa (Dubrovnik) e il mare', p. 151. While they are certainly representative, these ciphers should be taken with some caution. Tadić based his estimates on systematic research of the notarial records, recording every ship he found mentioned (Tadić, 'Organizacija', p. 28). Thus, on the one hand, there is a possibility of double counting, while on the other, it is likely that some of the ships were actually not mentioned in the scrutinized documents (according to Tadić as many as fifty to sixty such ships should be added to his estimates: Tadić, 'Organizacija', pp. 28, 30). Equally importantly, the estimates reached in this way are somewhat misleading since they represent the number of all the ships mentioned *in a longer time period,* sometimes over fifteen years, as in 1570–85. The problem is that some of the mentioned vessels doubtlessly went out of use at the very beginning of this period, while others were built only at its end – that is, not all of these ships were in use at the same time. However, Tadić's estimates do seem generally plausible, and they are also confirmed by the single surviving list of the fleet for *one year,* in 1599. The number and tonnage of the ships in this reliable document fit well with Tadić's numbers (taking into account the decline of the fleet): in 1599 Ragusa had 112 ships with some 38,000 tons (S. Vekarić, 'Dubrovačka trgovačka flota 1599 godine', *Anali Historijskog institute Jugoslavenske akademije znanosti i umjetnosti u Dubrovniku* 3, 1954, p. 427).

35 Harris, *Dubrovnik*, p. 164. For several estimates see: Tadić, 'Organizacija', p. 31; Luetić, *Pomorci i jedrenjaci*, pp. 23–4; V. Stipetić, 'Population and gross domestic product of Croatia (1500–1913) in the light of Angus Maddison's Book *The World Economy: A Millennial Perspective*', *Dubrovnik Annals* 8, 2004, p. 164.

36 Tadić, 'Organizacija', pp. 30–1, 42; Krekić, 'Ragusa (Dubrovnik) e il mare', pp. 149–50. Tadić made these estimates by calculating the average value of *carro* (basic unit for the carrying capacity of a ship) and then multiplying it by the total cargo capacity of the Ragusan fleet. Another important topic which can't be addressed here due to limited space is that of maritime insurance (see A. and B. Tenenti, *Il prezzo del rischio: L'assicurazione mediterranea vista da Ragusa (1563–1591)*, Rome: Jouvence, 1985).

37 Vekarić, 'Dubrovačka trgovačka flota', p. 427; Krekić, 'Ragusa (Dubrovnik) e il mare', p. 151.

38 Krekić, 'Ragusa (Dubrovnik) e il mare', p. 150.

39 For an overview of later developments of Ragusan maritime trade: Luetić, *Pomorci i jedrenjaci*, pp. 40–51.

40 D. Pavlović, 'O krizi vlasteoskog staleža u Dubrovniku XVII veka' [On the crisis of the Ragusan patriciate in the seventeenth century], *Zbornik radova SANU*, knj. 17, Institut za proučavanje književnosti 2, 1952, pp. 27–38; Tadić, 'Organizacija', p. 42.

41 An excellent recent monograph on this group is: Z. Pešorda-Vardić, *U predvorju vlasti: Dubrovački antunini u kasnom srednjem vijeku* [On the threshold of power: the *Antunini* of Dubrovnik in the late Middle Ages], Zagreb-Dubrovnik: Zavod za povijesne znanosti HAZU u Dubrovniku i Hrvatski institute za povijest, 2012. Regarding their role in maritime trade see: Z. Pešorda-Vardić, 'Od *barkuzija* do galijuna: Nekoliko crtica o ulozi

pomorstva u usponu dubrovačkoga građanstva u kasnome srednjem i ranome novom vijeku' [From the barcusium to the galleon: a few sketches on the role of seafaring in the rise of Dubrovnik's citizenry in the late Middle Ages and early modern era], *Povijesni prilozi* 47, 2014, pp. 143–83.

42 Tadić, 'Organizacija', p. 26; Harris, *Dubrovnik*, p. 163.

43 On the lack of merchant's guild in Dubrovnik: Pešorda-Vardiæ, *U predvorju vlasti*, p. 18. For a similar situation in Venice: F. C. Lane, *Venice: A Maritime Republic*, Baltimore, MD: Johns Hopkins University Press, 1973, pp. 104, 125; R. Mackenney, *Tradesmen and Traders: The World of the Guilds in Venice and Europe, c. 1250–c. 1650,* London: Croom Helm, 1987, pp. 3, 8.

44 V. Miović, 'Diplomatic relations between the Ottoman Empire and the Republic of Dubrovnik', in G. Kármán and L. Kunčević (eds), *The European Tributary States of the Ottoman Empire in the Sixteenth and Seventeenth Centuries,* Leiden: Brill, 2013, pp. 192–3.

45 J. Tadić, 'O pomorstvu Dubrovnika u XVI i XVII veku' [On the maritime trade of Ragusa in the sixteenth and seventeenth centuries], in *Dubrovačko pomorstvo*, p. 171; Tadić, 'Organizacija', p. 13.

46 Tadić, 'Organizacija', pp. 16–17.

47 Ibid., pp. 41–2.

48 I. Mitić, *Konzulati i konzularna služba starog Dubrovnika* [Consuls and the consular service of old Ragusa], Dubrovnik: Historijski institut JAZU, 1973, pp. 34–5, 37, 40.

49 Ibid., pp. 43–4: B. Hrabak, 'Konzularna služba Dubrovčana u Aleksandriji u XV i XVI stoljeću' [The Ragusan consular service in Alexandria in the fifteenth and sixteenth centuries], *Historijski zbornik* 31–2, 1978–9, p. 215.

50 Mitić, *Konzulati,* pp. 37, 44–5.

51 Ibid., pp. 35–6, 45–8.

52 Krekić, 'Contribution of foreigners', pp. 378–80, 393; R. Ćuk, 'I rapport economici fra Ragusa e Venezia nel Medio Evo', in A. di Vittorio (ed.), *Ragusa e il Mediterraneo: Ruolo e funzioni di una Repubblica marinara tra Medioevo ed Età moderna,* Bari: Cacucci editore, 1990, pp. 121–4; B. Krekić, 'Four Florentine commercial companies in Dubrovnik (Ragusa) in the first half of the fourteenth century', in B. Krekić, *Dubrovnik, Italy and the Balkans in the Late Middle Ages*, London: Variorum Reprints, 1980, vol. 1, pp. 25–41; F. Bettarini, *La comunità pratese di Ragusa (1414–1434): Crisi economica e migrazioni collettive nel Tardo Medioevo*, Florence: Leo S. Olschki editore, 2012; F. Bettarini, 'Mercanti fiorentini ed artigiani pratesi a Ragusa (Dubrovnik) nel Quattrocento', in L. Tanzini and S. Tognetti (eds), *'Mercatura è arte': Uomini d'affari toscani in Europa e nel Mediterraneo Medievale*, Rome: Viella, 2012, pp. 97–114; Pinelli, *Tra argento, grano e panni*; P. Pinelli, 'Le relazioni commerciali tra Firenze e Dubrovnik (XV–XVI secolo)', in P. Pinelli (ed.), *Firenze e Dubrovnik all'epoca di Marino Darsa (1508–1567),* Florence: Firenze University Press, 2010, pp. 48–50; N. Fejić, 'Ragusei e spagnoli nel medioevo: luci ed ombre di un rapporto commerciale', in A. di Vittorio (ed.), *Ragusa e il Mediterraneo: Ruolo e funzioni di una Repubblica marinara tra Medioevo ed Età moderna,* Bari: Cacucci editore, 1990, pp. 86–96.

53 I. Mitić, 'Predstavnici stranih država u Dubrovniku za vrijeme Republike' [The representatives of foreign powers in Dubrovnik during the Republic], *Pomorski zbornik* 4, 1966, pp. 381–401; Krekić, 'Contribution of foreigners', pp. 386–7, 389–90.

54 Basic overviews are: M. D. Grmek, 'Le concept d´infection dans l´Antiquité et au Moyen Âge, les anciennnes mesures sociales contre les maladies contagieuses et la fondation dela premiere quarantaine á Dubrovnik (1377)', *Rad Jugoslavenske akademije znanosti i umjetnosti: Razred za medicinske znanosti* 16, 1980, pp. 9–55, esp. pp. 47–54; V. Bazala, 'Pomorski lazareti u starom Dubrovniku' [Maritime *lazaretti* in old Dubrovnik], in *Dubrovačko pomorstvo*, pp. 293–307; Z. Blažina Tomić, *Kacamorti i kuga: Utemeljenje i razvoj zdravstvene službe u Dubrovniku* [Kacamorti and the plague: the establishment and development of the public

health service in Dubrovnik], Zagreb and Dubrovnik: HAZU, Zavod za povijesne znanosti u Dubrovniku, 2007. An English summary is: Harris, *Dubrovnik*, pp. 167–9.

55 S. Ćirković, 'Ragusa e il suo retroterra', p. 26. This is, of course, similar to the general point that Tilly makes about the prominence of commercial interest in all the states following the capital-intensive path; yet, for the aforementioned reasons, it seems to have been especially salient in Ragusa (C. Tilly, *Coercion, Capital and European States 990–1990*, Oxford and Cambridge, MA: Basil Blackwell, 1990, esp. pp. 150–1).

56 Although the two most important patrons of the Republic – the Hungarian king and the Ottoman sultan certainly helped its economic development through privileges and occasional diplomatic lobbying, their support was far from the strong royal patronage enjoyed by, for instance, Lisbon or London.

57 M. Držić, *Djela* [Works], ed. M. Rešetar, Zagreb: Tisak nadbiskupske tiskare, 1930, p. 70.

10

GENOA

A city with a port or a port city?

Luisa Piccinno

In the late Middle Ages and the early modern period, wide areas of Western Europe underwent deep economic, civil and cultural changes, mainly spurred by capital and its mercantile functions. The population began to grow, albeit still slowly, and progressively moved to the cities. Port cities in particular soon began to attract people with their dynamic businesses. This process was supported by a dense network of economic and social relations, which developed in spite of natural obstacles and political borders. The urban layout of port cities would follow these changes, at times with an apparently disorganized and irrational building pattern coupled with a revived movement of people, goods and cultures.[1] For all these reasons, planning needs and decision-making by local authorities in port cities became rather complex. So much so that an urban planning culture proper was developed, far ahead of any such policies by other hinterland cities. Increased storage requirements following the commercial revolution in the thirteenth century, the building and extension of port facilities, and increasing traffic volumes would all push any activities that did not need to be close to the docks and piers – such as warehouses for public commodities, craftsmen's shops, and even more complex manufacturing plants – back into the city. At times, the port area would somehow grow independently of the rest of the city. As pointed out by the urban planning historian Ennio Poleggi, when explaining the distinction between a 'city with a port' and a 'port city', the growth of a port does not always lead to a port city; namely, it does not necessarily bring about deep transformations to the urban landscape.[2] As a matter of fact, an extensive network of ports – of cities with a port, but few port cities, including, most prominently, Venice, Genoa, Barcelona, Naples and Palermo – would dot the Mediterranean coasts in medieval times.[3]

From this point of view, Genoa is quite peculiar: its urban layout, which had been developing since the late Middle Ages, was strongly affected not only by its port, but also by all port-related trading activities. The harbour, with its spoke-like arrangement of piers and quays, is circled by a long line of palaces called Ripa. With its bowed alignment, the Ripa follows the coast contour acting like an 'interface between two ever distinct worlds',[4] and like a hinge between the city and the port area. Both zones are trade centres, one for local trade and the other for the entire Mediterranean and beyond.[5] This is what Edoardo Grendi wrote in 1987 on the matter:

> Genoa, a port city: a seamless centuries-old urban development. So much so that the notion that the port is just a variable in the unpredictable fate of a city, rather than a guarantee of its everlasting role, is lost in contemporary conscience.[6]

Therefore, a port city is indeed characterized by a strictly port-related process of urbanization and economic growth. Port cities are not necessarily big, nor does their port have to play any leading role in European economy, nor are port cities only to be found on Mediterranean shores. We could take the city of Bergen, also examined in this book, as an example: apparently so different from Genoa in terms of importance, size and traffic volumes, and yet so similar in its strong economic dependence on its port due to the lack of major inland communication roads.

The historiography of Genoa and its port and traffic between the late Middle Ages and the early modern era, though quite extensive, is mostly somewhat outdated, and only a very small part is available in English. Actually, five or six studies were published every year since the Second World War on Genoa's maritime history in the modern era. Most of these works focus on well-defined periods – with a generally clear distinction between the Middle Ages and the modern era – and on specific topics, such as the institutional and legal framework, routes and trading flows, port development, movement of capital, etc.[7] Conversely, few comprehensive and comparative studies have so far been published, in which the Genoese case is examined taking a longer period view beyond the late Middle Ages/early modern dividing line, or looking not only at economic issues, but also at geographic, urban planning, political and social aspects. Thus, the path of leading scholars like Roberto Sabatino Lopez and Edoardo Grendi, referred to when outlining the evolution of Genoa port traffic, will not be followed in this work.[8] Rather, a different approach will be taken, centred on the port city, its construction, fast development and evolving processes under the impact of changing mercantile practices. The purpose of this chapter is to identify a model of homogeneous development for all major port cities within the European economy during the period under examination, starting from the case of Genoa. Genoa's specific geographic features and, in particular, its political and social organization over the centuries will be described and, wherever possible, compared with the other case studies examined in this book.

Localization and hinterland: the sea as source of supply

Genoa was the capital city of one of the oldest regional states in the Ancien Régime. Initially established as an independent commune between the end of the eleventh and the beginning of the twelfth centuries, it went through troubled political times, mostly caused by rivalries among the city's wealthy noble families, which rivalries lasted until 1528 with the establishment of an aristocratic Republic promoted by Andrea Doria. The age of the Doge's life tenure began in 1339 with the election of Simone Boccanegra and ended in 1528 due to reforms that envisaged the election of a Doge for only a two-year term. Meanwhile, internecine power struggles did not subside, thus weakening the Republic, which first fell under French rule (1396–1409), then under the long domain of the Visconti and the Duchy of Milan, and finally under French rule again.[9] The administrative and political organization of this period was strongly affected by the Casa di San Giorgio, an institution unanimously considered a real 'state within the state'. Initially set up in 1407 as a consortium of public creditors, it began banking activities in 1408, becoming the only body entitled to grant loans to the commune. In return for loans granted to replenish a cash-poor state treasury, and as both pledge and interest payment on loans, the Casa di San Giorgio would gain authority to levy public taxes, collect state revenues and even be assigned whole swaths of land, ranging from overseas colonies to Corsica, and some areas in the mainland.[10] The Casa di San Giorgio was therefore a very complex and quite unique institution in the whole of Europe, strictly linked with the public administration, and with very special connections to the city and its economy that need to be duly considered.

Despite its political and military weakness, the internecine struggles and scarce resources, Genoa succeeded in becoming the leading marine republic that ruled over a vast colonial empire stretching between the eastern Mediterranean and the Black Sea, and, when the empire had already been lost, later became a financial power. As stated by Giuseppe Felloni, not least among the reasons for this success was 'the amount of resources that both the public and private sectors were able to pool under emergency needs, with few other examples in history as to imagination, ingenuity and originality'.[11]

Genoa lies at the centre of the Ligurian Gulf overlooking the north Tyrrhenian Sea, and stretches along a natural arch bordered by two non-navigable rivers, the Bisagno and Polcevera. At its back, it is surrounded by the Apennine chain separating it from the rich Po Valley in Piedmont and Lombardy, which are in turn bordered by the Alps. Owing to this location, Genoa has always been a 'Gate to Italy': it was in fact the shortest route for goods on their way to the North of Europe, as well as the nearest Tyrrhenian port for exports to Mediterranean markets.

This geographically favourable position was (and still is) hindered by the difficult crossing of the Apennines, which constitute a natural obstacle. In the past, goods could only be carried across the Apennines along devious trails stacked on the backs of animals and under extremely difficult conditions, especially during the winter season. Most of the region is covered with mountains reaching to the coast, and crossed by valleys where streams flow. The coastal flat area is about 260 km long (120 km to the east and 140 km to the west of Genoa), but never more than 30 km wide. Agricultural plains are practically non-existent. As is well known, the subsistence area for a city was strictly connected to its size and number of inhabitants. For Genoa, such an area would comprise the whole of the Republic's territory, namely the whole region of Liguria. However, two main factors should be considered: all trade between the two Rivieras and the capital city was carried out only by sea. Local resources were in any case insufficient. Genoa was thus forced to rely on faraway lands for its own survival: the sea was thus complementary to the land, providing a privileged channel for the import of food and other raw materials for local manufacturers, the trade of goods and products, and for export.

As early as in the late Middle Ages, Genoa was a leading population magnet: taking into account population fluctuations due to recurrent plague epidemics, in the fifteenth century Genoa had 40,000–45,000 inhabitants, reaching 60,000 inhabitants by the end of the following century. During the same period, the overall population in the entire Republic amounted to about 270,000–290,000 people.[12] In order to feed the whole region, 500,000 *mine* of wheat (corresponding to 45,000 tons) were required every year. Considering the very low local yield, this meant that 350,000 *mine* had to be imported, mostly to meet the needs of the capital city. For this reason as well as for tax purposes, the Republic's government enforced very strict controls on sea imports, over which the port of Genoa held a monopoly.[13] Actually, all major merchant cities in those times would have had the same policies: to meet the needs of population inflows they were attracting, they would often have to rely on food imports. This is the reason why city authorities would prefer to strictly control these flows of traffic by concentrating them in one single port.[14]

Food supplies had always been a major, if not the overriding, concern that pushed Genoese merchants, ship owners and businessmen to shipping. However, such huge volumes of trade would raise other issues: the right goods for trading had to be looked for, the production and trade of high added-value products had to be controlled, and monopolies were to be established. From a quantitative point of view, grain imports were the leading type of goods unloaded in the port of Genoa. The main supplies came from the Black Sea and, when this area fell under Turkish rule, they would mostly be imported from the Kingdom of Naples and Provence. These markets were also important bases for major businesses that the merchant fleet of the Republic of Genoa carried out on behalf of third parties. Only around the end of the sixteenth century – as illustrated below – would ships loaded with grain from Northern Europe call at the port of Genoa in huge numbers in order to overcome the severe famine that hit the Mediterranean in those years. This fact thoroughly changed traffic routes to and from Genoa. The area around Genoa was also poor in raw materials, hence manufacturing would be totally dependent on imports: the expensive production of silk, velvet and damask used raw silk imported from Sicily,

Spain and the Far East; wrought iron manufacturing, which had developed in the valleys of the Ligurian Apennines since the fourteenth century, used iron from the island of Elba. The situation was quite similar for paper production as well, which began to develop in the seventeenth century. To feed the local paper mills, textile rags were brought in from the whole of the Italian peninsula, as well as from abroad. All these activities, which had high raw material costs in common, required huge capital investments and targeted mainly international, not only European, outlet markets. Some of these products, such as paper for example, were even exported to the New World.[15]

Commercial networks and port evolution

During the first centuries of the new millennium, the three marine republics of Genoa, Pisa and Venice had gradually risen to dominate the seas from an economic point of view. The latter in particular had taken on the leadership of European trade and beyond. Genoa did not simply stand by but, starting in the second half of the twelfth century, it also acquired a leading commercial role. Following the conquest and development of a wide network of colonies and commercial bases (including Chios, Pera, Famagusta and Caffa) and intense piracy actions, by the end of the thirteenth century the Genoese acquired full control over sea traffic in the Black Sea, the Azov and Aegean Sea. On this east–west route, mainly alum – used to fix textile dyes – was carried, as well as wine, sugar and, to a lesser extent, spices – the latter trade being mainly in the hands of Venetian merchants. All these goods were then distributed not only throughout the Mediterranean ports, but also along inland routes, to Central and Northern Europe. In 1277, the first regular maritime connection between Genoa and the North Sea was established, following a specific strategic decision whereby Genoa's interests would soon be redirected to the West.[16] While the same route would later be followed by Majorcan, Catalan and Venetian ships as well, until the mid-fourteenth century it was still dominated by Genoese galleys. It was during this period that products from the East began to reach North European ports following thousands of kilometres-long sea routes. In the opposite direction, mainly textile products were shipped.[17] All this led to a significant growth in maritime traffic, so much so that some authors have referred to it as the 'medieval invention of globalization'.[18]

In order to respond to these changes, at the end of the thirteenth century the infrastructures of the port of Genoa were already designed to meet the needs of businessmen, carriers and the types of cargo they were handling. There were six mooring piers, each specializing in the handling of a different type of goods. At the head of each of them were the tax collectors' buildings in charge of levying customs duties, and a bit further down, there were the so-called *rebe* and *clape*, namely public warehouses for food commodities (mostly used for pulses, grains, oil and fish). Around 1283–5, a small dock was also built (*Darsena*) to meet the needs for more calm water areas.[19] It was divided into two discreet compartments: one for short sea shipping merchant vessels, the other for galleys. In addition to these facilities, there was also an arsenal for the construction, repair and fitting of ships. However, unlike other ports such as Venice, it was not particularly important from a military point of view. The Republic generally resorted to the fleets provided ad hoc by powerful private ship owners, and shipbuilding was mainly carried out in small temporary shipyards along the coast.[20]

The strong economic expansion led by Genoa and enjoyed throughout the Mediterranean area died out in the fourteenth century. The age of easy and huge gains from trade with the East was over. As estimated by John Day, traffic volumes for Genoa even in the best years of this century were hardly half those recorded at the end of the previous century.[21] According to some authors, the Republic went through some sort of adjustment crisis during the fourteenth century: on the one hand it was looking for new markets and trying to move its trading interests to the western Mediterranean, on the other it was trying to strengthen its own colonial monopoly in the Near East. Genoa's difficult economic situation was further worsened by the economic crisis that had hit the whole of Europe, particularly after the arrival of the Black Death. Genoa reacted to this dramatic decrease in traffic, which continued until the first decades of the following century, by further moving its commercial interests to the West, which was further prompted by the loss of its colonies after the fall of Constantinople in 1453. However, the move from expensive oriental products to the transport and sale of less valuable and bulkier goods led in turn to the use of much bigger ships.[22]

During this period of relative commercial slump, some new dynamic elements had emerged from the Genoese economic landscape: Genoa became the most active insurance market centre, a sector in which merchant and financial interests would merge. The first insurance policy, drafted in 1343, was allegedly issued in Genoa. The early use of double entry accounting, for both private and public accounts (around the beginning of the fourteenth century) and the introduction of innovative financial tools such as the bill of exchange (*cambium per litteris*), already common in Genoa in mid-thirteenth century, are other notable achievements for which Genoa can take credit.[23]

In the course of the fifteenth century and in the first decades of the following century, the port layout, with its spoke-like arrangement of piers built off the Ripa, remained practically unchanged. With its defeat by Venice in 1380 and the end of its primacy over the seas, Genoa, though still among the wealthiest cities in Europe, had lost its leadership. Indeed, only the improvement of already existing facilities, which were revamped, upgraded and strengthened, plus some additional dredging to allow access to larger vessels, was carried out in this period. Maintaining or recovering a proper draught in the harbour was a constant concern for city authorities, and constantly required considerable financial resources. The huge amount of silt and debris brought to the sea by the rivers flowing through the city was the main cause of recurrent silting within the harbour.[24]

As is well known, Genoa came to the fore again in the mid-sixteenth century, thanks to multi-sectoral economic activities balancing shipping, trade, manufacturing and finance. It was thanks to the skills of Genoa's inhabitants as bankers that this century was called the 'Age of the Genoese'. Genoa was a leading naval power already by the beginning of the century. Indeed, if we look at its fleet and port traffic volumes, the still strong link between the city's economy and the sea is quite evident. Excluding small short sea shipping vessels, the Genoese fleet in 1509 amounted to 15,000 tons, very close to Venice's and still bigger than that of Dubrovnik, which began to boom around 1520.[25] Excluding galleys, Genoa is estimated to account for 30 per cent of the entire Christian tonnage in the Mediterranean.[26] In the 1530s, three-quarters of port traffic in Genoa was accounted for by Genoese vessels, but the proportion of foreign ships began to grow. By 1564, they would even exceed the number of Genoese vessels calling at the port of Genoa. During the 1556–8 period, Genoa's total fleet tonnage reached a peak of 29,000 tons. Over the following decades, it gradually decreased back to the overall tonnage recorded at the beginning of the century.[27] Regarding the type of goods traded, there were significant differences from previous centuries. During the sixteenth century, the majority of goods handled and unloaded in the port of Genoa were timber, foodstuffs and raw materials (Table 10.1).

The last decade of the sixteenth century was characterized by a major change in the composition of vessels calling at Genoa: namely, the sudden arrival of vessels from Northern Europe, which would quickly increase their share from 2–3 per cent up to one quarter of total port traffic. This new trend, which would continue throughout the following century, was triggered by one of the greatest crises ever to hit the Republic of Genoa: in 1590, following poor harvests all over the Mediterranean, the Genoese Government and the Casa di San Giorgio reached an agreement in order to ensure the necessary commodity supplies to the local population. For only one year, all vessels calling at any port in Liguria with at least two-thirds of their cargo in grain would be exempted from customs duties.[28] Such a

Table 10.1 Main goods unloaded in the port of Genoa in the sixteenth century

Type of goods	*Average amount (in tons)*
Firewood and timber for other uses	23,500
Wheat	14,000
Salt	9,500
Wine	6,000
Olive oil	1,000
Wool	1,500
Silk	110
Iron ore	350
Marble	260

Source: G. Doria, 'La gestione del porto di Genova dal 1550 al 1797', in G. Doria and P. Massa Piergiovanni (eds), *Il sistema portuale della Repubblica di Genova: Profili organizzativi e politica gestionale (secc. XII–XVIII)*, Genoa: Società Ligure di Storia Patria, 1987, pp. 140–1.

measure was renewed a year later, but with a major change: duty exemption was to be granted only to vessels calling at the port of Genoa. The city rulers believed that concentrating all deliveries in a single port would not only facilitate the distribution of commodities among the population, but also the export of any surplus goods to other Mediterranean ports. At the same time, local authorities committed to looking for supplies from Northern European countries. Here, with the support of Genoese merchants based in Antwerp and with help from Northern European traders living in Venice, commissions were paid out in all different markets for the purchase of grain. Between the end of 1591 and the beginning of 1592, Northern European vessels full of grain continued to come in great numbers to the port of Genoa. However, vessels from other areas as well would be enticed to call at the port of Genoa in order to benefit from higher gains derived from free trade conditions, as well as a much larger market area. Within few months, about 200 vessels landed in Genoa, carrying cargo totalling almost 36,000 tons of grains.[29] In the following years new measures were enforced, aimed at limiting the free trade regime, which would be confined to the port of Genoa and exclusively to vessels with a minimum carrying capacity of 300 *mine* (around 27 tons) coming from the West, and from beyond Gibraltar in particular. At the same time, the minimum share of grain cargo was brought down to half the vessel's total cargo.[30]

Starting at the beginning of the seventeenth century, there was another turnaround, since the free trade area regime began to be employed by local authorities not only to tackle food supply emergencies, but also as a tool to boost the economy and help the port of Genoa acquire a privileged role in Mediterranean shipping routes. To this end, new free trade regulations were enforced in 1609: with a renewable ten-year duration, they applied to all goods unloaded in the port of Genoa except for those coming from other ports under the *Dominio* rule, namely politically controlled by the Republic of Genoa.[31] Finally, in 1623, more organic regulations were adopted with the abolition of the majority of previous limitations and the implementation of a 'general, very general Free Trade Area' ('Portofranco libero, generale e generalissimo'), applicable to 'every single vessel irrespective of its tonnage, coming from any part of the world beyond Antibes to the West, and beyond Viareggio to the East, as well as from the South, and calling at the port of Genoa, with any type of cargo'.[32] Following these recently enforced regulations, the port of Genoa began to play a new role: namely, not only as an importer of supplies necessary for the city itself, but also as a major centre from which a wide range of different products would be exported again. However, in order to win over competitors like the port of Leghorn and Marseille, Genoa had to provide sufficient mooring and storage places. Hence, the flow of money from the Casa di San Giorgio – which was in charge of the management of the Free Trade Zone – proved to be crucial to fund the works needed to extend and upgrade the existing facilities. The link between San Giorgio and the port had very ancient origins. The Casa di San Giorgio was in charge of levying the majority of state taxes, including the *carati maris*, a tax raised on all goods loaded and unloaded both in the port of Genoa and in all the other Ligurian ports. This was most likely the original reason for the joint fate of the Casa di San Giorgio and the port of Genoa, a link that, over the centuries, became stronger and even more complex.[33]

Between 1550 and 1650, the authorities managing the port – which will be discussed later – carried out expansion works to increase the length of mooring piers available to vessels within the area between the outmost tip of the breakwater dam (Molo Vecchio) and the arsenal, up to about 3,000 metres. The extent of port facilities was in those times considered to be sufficient and to provide a major competitive edge to Genoa over the other two leading ports in the Tyrrhenian Sea. As a matter of fact, Leghorn had only 2,000 metres of quays available, while Marseille had only 1,700 metres. However, there were still problems related to shallow port waters, which were further worsened by the increasing carrying capacity (and hence draught) of the vessels recorded in this period. Despite huge excavation works carried out over and over again, at the beginning of the seventeenth century the situation was still critical. Near some quays, the draught was still less than 5 metres.[34] Works to build a new breakwater dam (Molo Nuovo) designed to protect the port from southwesterly winds began in August 1638. This technically demanding work had international resonance and was completed in 1643 (Figure 10.1). The new 375-metre-long dam had cost 2.3 million liras, and was jointly funded by the Republic, Casa di San Giorgio and some private sponsors.[35]

Figure 10.1 The port of Genoa in the seventeenth century: overcrowded mooring piers specialized in the handling of different types of goods

During the same period, port storage areas were significantly increased as well, with the building of new warehouses, funded in this case by the food administration authority (the so-called Magistrato dell'Abbondanza) and the Casa di San Giorgio. The latter institution, which held a monopoly over the salt trade, oversaw the enlargement of salt warehouses: from about 26,000 cubic metres available before 1550, up to 45,000 cubic metres in 1642, making a total of thirty-three warehouses, which would also include eight new buildings.[36] Extension works for grain storage carried out by the Magistrato dell'Abbondanza were equally important: between 1564 and 1568, eight new warehouses were built for grain, but, already by the end of the century, they were no longer sufficient. The situation improved slightly in 1606 when four new warehouses were built, each with its own landing pontoon. In the meantime, new storage places were also built for wine as well as oil, by enlarging the medieval facility and building new tanks inside the Palazzo Ducale, which was the government building of the Republic and where the Doge lived. When, in 1609, the free trade regime was extended to all types of goods, different needs arose not only in terms of quantities, but also for different warehouses designed for 'general cargo' (also including many itemized goods, with a very high unit price), which began to be handled in the port of Genoa in huge quantities. From mere transit areas for goods waiting for customs clearance, these warehouses would thus become proper storage places, where the goods could be stored for longer periods before being shipped again. Therefore, new and bigger warehouses were needed. Once again, the Casa di San Giorgio took up responsibility for this job and, in less than a century, was able to increase storage areas from 1,700 square metres to around 6,000 square metres.[37]

A cosmopolitan city: foreign merchants, Genoese aristocracy and dockers

A port and its traffic trends have a triple impact on a city's economy and, more generally, on its entire region: on entrepreneurs, by attracting capital and generating wealth; on the labour force, by promoting migration during times of favourable economic conditions; and on public finance, by ensuring a proper balance between tax revenues and infrastructural management costs.

Valuable information on the composition of the Genoa-based merchant class can be obtained from a recent work by Van Doosselaere, who has examined and classified 20,000 notarial deeds for the period from 1150 to 1435.[38] Some interesting elements emerge from his work: first of all, during the commune period, Genoa was a very open city ready to welcome outsiders – namely people coming from outside its municipal borders. It did so through permissive regulations, which would grant a whole set of rights and privileges to anyone who came and lived in Genoa for at least three months a year. These people would not be granted citizenship rights, but rather the status of *habitatores*, whereby they would be allowed to own real estate and take part in export partnerships, provided they paid their taxes. While mostly

Flemish and French – mainly from Provence – these outsiders would also come from neighbouring cities like Asti, Lucca, Siena and Piacenza. There were also people coming from the countryside and other places along the Ligurian coast. The latter group, however, did not play any significant role in the thirteenth-century expansion of Genoese commerce. The number of outsiders, both from Liguria and from other places, reached its peak in the twelfth century, when it would account for 54 per cent of all established merchant networks, while gradually dwindling in the following centuries to only 15 per cent between 1340 and 1355. This drop was caused by the Genoese noble class entering the fray of long-range commerce, especially beginning in the second half of the thirteenth century.[39]

The successful leading role played by the local aristocracy and the ever more evident combination of merchant and financial transactions had been driven by the new organization of Genoese commerce since the fourteenth century. Starting in this period, all the most important Genoese families played key roles in international commerce enterprises. While seldom carried out on an exclusive basis, commerce would most often be coupled with banking and other investment businesses. They would consolidate their business relations through private partnerships – duly recognized by the government – which led to the creation of clans, or clusters, called *alberghi*. While their number fluctuated throughout the Middle Ages – there were seventy-four of them in the fifteenth century – these *alberghi* reached their final structure only with the reform carried out by Andrea Doria in 1528, when twenty-eight of them were recognized and formalized. They were finally abolished in 1576. Based on the principle of territorial aggregation rather than on common family origins, these *alberghi* became city centres of power and key players in long-range commerce and financial businesses. Based on an analysis of tax documents, Gourdin has calculated that in 1445 80 per cent of the ninety-two merchants who were living in port cities along Genoese commerce routes actually belonged to the main *alberghi* (including the Doria, Grimaldi, Giustiniani and Adorno families).[40]

Therefore, the brilliant results achieved in trade and finance between the end of the Middle Ages and the modern era were the product of a limited number of entrepreneurs from the most important Genoese noble families. From their headquarters in Genoa they would run their businesses through worldwide branches. Each foreign branch was an important link in a system of well-integrated enterprises whose mutual relations were based on corporate connections, family ties and social status. One of the most popular forms of long-distance trading partnerships was the *commenda*. It was based on a contract which, first introduced by Italian merchants in the Middle Ages, had spread all over Europe. It envisaged a partnership between a sedentary partner and a travelling one who was in charge of accompanying shipments and finalizing their sale. Further, in order to share navigation risks among more parties, ship ownership was carved up into shares (*carati*).[41]

Genoa was a cosmopolitan city with a significant number of Jewish, French, Catalan and Flemish merchants, and equally important relations with traders from

Lombardy and Tuscany and their cities of origin. Already by the end of the twelfth century, Genoa acted as a bridge between the West and the East, and as a sort of forced stopover for traders and businessmen carrying on their businesses between the Champagne fairs and the other Mediterranean ports. For this reason, the city's leading class was also culturally and socially open to foreigners. Genoa, for example, never enforced any anti-Jewish regulations.[42] Further, as pointed out by Naser Eslami, commerce was – and for that matter still is – a powerful means to 'carry culture across geographic borders, into uncharted, not yet penetrated land'.[43] It was indeed through overseas trade that oriental culture penetrated Genoa, leaving important traces in its architecture, language, cuisine, as well as in the organization of its urban spaces, which are still present today.[44]

This Genoese openness towards foreigners not only influenced trade and urban architecture, but also the labour market. In the Middle Ages, apothecaries were only from outside Genoa, while masons were all from Lombardy and Switzerland. Conversely, mostly natives from the valleys in the province of Bergamo, Domodossola and Switzerland were working in the port. They were mainly working in the Dogana (Customs) and in the free trade zone, with significant privileges over local dockers. In the long run, this situation would lead to disputes between the two categories of workers.[45] The first certain data on the labour market in the port date back to the sixteenth century, when guilds became an important system in the organization of crafts and trades. Approximately 1,000–1,300 workers have been calculated as working within the port in those times, accounting for 2 per cent of Genoa's population, then amounting to about 55,000 inhabitants. Of these workers 80 per cent were dockers in charge of cargo handling. They had different skills by type of goods handled at the various quays and played a key role in port operations. They would work also outside the port area since unloaded goods had to be manually carried to the warehouses, shops and *stationes,* from where they would be carried across the mountains on pack animals. Owing to Genoa's urban layout, wheeled transport could only be used in some larger thoroughfares. At the end of the sixteenth century, in addition to dockers' guilds, there were other corporations of skilled workers inside the port, including those for boatmen, pilots, rescue workers, interpreters, coopers, etc., for a total of twenty different guilds. Their number would further increase in the following centuries.[46]

Managing the port and public finance

In order to understand the impact of port traffic on public finance, we must first of all outline the features and responsibilities of institutions that were managing the port. All Italian ports were often governed by very old regulations that dated back to Roman times and had developed over the centuries. Different administrative models were applied. For example, in southern Italy, a centralized system would prevail, whereby a guardian called the *portulano* was in charge of the port. The *portulano,* in turn, had to report to the *Maestro portulano* on a regional level. Tax collection and controls of ships and cargoes were among his tasks. Conversely, any legal issues and disputes were handled by maritime courts, the so-called *Consolati*. In other cities, however, including Genoa and Venice, ports were governed by *Magistrature*. These were complex institutions employing people with proven expertise and experience. Over the centuries, they gradually increased their responsibilities and scope of action along with the increasing importance acquired by the port they were managing within the city's economy.[47]

The port and maritime traffic in Genoa were under the control of different bodies, each having specific responsibilities. The main *magistratura* in charge of port management was the Padri del Comune. Although formally established by Doge Simone Boccanegra in 1340, it was already operating a full century earlier under the name of *Sabarbarii portus et moduli*. The legislation of the Genoese Republic would focus a lot on commerce, which was governed by a rich body of regulations, much more than any other civil sector, (for example) to ensure fair trade practices and fight fraud. The Uffici di Mercanzia and Robarìa were in charge of controlling and protecting trade, while the Ufficio di Gazaria was responsible for anything related to navigation and shipping. Responsibility for marine insurance was entrusted to the Ufficio di Mercanzia, which was replaced by the Rota Civile in 1529 as part of the reforms enforced by Andrea Doria. The latter body was a sort of court made up of three highly experienced foreign lawyers who would ensure a quick handling of commercial disputes, issuing decisions that were mostly based on merchant practices rather than on applicable regulations, which would often be overridden. The court was in charge of all civil cases exceeding 100 liras, even if it was specialized in the mercantile field.[48] The conflict resolution procedure seems to be quite similar to the one of the Consulate of the Sea in Valencia (illustrated in this volume) and Barcelona, but at present there isn't any in-depth comparative study available on this subject.[49]

Therefore, the port *magistratura* was granted responsibilities and powers that were initially confined to the management of the port. It also had jurisdiction over anything happening within the port boundaries. Its power increased with time and extended over the whole city, although only in some specific sectors which, more or less directly, could affect the operations of the 'port system'. For example, it was responsible for cleaning the streets to avoid having accumulated waste materials end up in the port area. It was in charge of sewage maintenance to ensure proper sanitary conditions, and had to check the quality of building materials and make sure that the houses near the port were properly constructed. It would also manage the municipal aqueduct, which reached the port and was used to supply water to the ships.[50] With the reform enforced by Andrea Doria in 1528 and the establishment of the oligarchic Republic, new regulations regarding the Padri del Comune further increased their responsibilities outside the port, especially concerning urban planning. For this reason, in 1588 the office was divided in two sections, each responsible for port and non-port activities, respectively: the first section was called 'Padri del Comune Conservatori del Porto e del Molo', the second one 'Padri del Comune Conservatori del Patrimonio'. Administrative and financial control over the port was the core of the work carried out by the Padri del Comune, as well as a centre of power for those who held politically relevant positions in the Republic's government. They were in charge of collecting most taxes and duties, either directly or through contractors, from all carriers transiting through the port of Genoa. They would then use the relevant revenues to meet the high construction and maintenance costs of port infrastructures. According to the results of a study by Paola Massa on the accounting books of the *magistratura* for the period 1340–1548, the highest port investments coincided with periods of particularly flourishing port traffic. From 1340 to 1440, the annual costs incurred, including seabed excavations, upgrading of piers and quays, signalling light operations and workers' wages, amounted to 2,550 Genoese liras on average. During the same period, revenues from tax duties levied on carriers would range from the oldest levy – the so-called 'gabella dei fanali', namely a tax on signalling lights in the port – to entry and mooring duties, as well as duties on specific types of goods. These taxes, however, were rather low and, although increasing over the years, they would never be enough to cover all port operation and maintenance expenses. Hence, the port balance sheets were most often reporting losses, albeit with significant yearly fluctuations. For example, in the 1406–7 financial year, reported losses amounted to 12 per cent, while in 1371–2 a 63 per cent loss was reported, which three years later went up to 66 per cent – mainly driven by work on the breakwater dam. Also the huge 75 per cent losses reported in 1380–1 were due to major works on the docks.[51] Financial problems linked to low tax revenues were partially relieved by a whole set of other non-port-related revenues by which the Padri del Comune were able to keep the port alive and, at the same time, strengthen its connection with the city. These other revenues were not related to port traffic, but, for example, they would derive from guilds – i.e. membership fees or fines and penalties – rentals of property owned by the *magistrature*, as well as from shares (*luoghi*) of San Giorgio.[52] However, as already mentioned, the Casa di San Giorgio would often help port authorities carry out some extraordinary works on port facilities by funding them with more or less grant-in-aid.

While all civil matters were in the hands of the Padri del Comune, the *Conservatori delle Navi,* established in 1490 and later (since 1546) called *Conservatori del Mare*, was in charge of managing justice, with regard to all matters and disputes involving ship owners and ship crews. Finally, health and sanitary surveillance in the port of Genoa (as well as throughout the territories under the Dominio) was under the responsibility of the *Conservatori di Sanità*, an institution set up in the fifteenth century. Its main functions were to check the health conditions of crew members and of incoming goods, as well as to issue health certificates to departing vessels. In order to properly carry out their job, these authorities had to keep constantly abreast of health conditions both in the city and outside, recording any reports of suspect areas they would receive from officers located in different, also faraway places, and collecting news from crews of ships calling at the port.[53]

Conclusions

As already mentioned at the beginning of this chapter, from a strictly urban planning point of view, there is a difference between a port city and a mere city with a port. This difference depends on the more or less synergistic growth trajectory followed by the two components: namely, the city on one hand, and the port and its infrastructures, on the other. Following this approach, I agree with Jacques Heers when he states that there were quite few actual port cities in the western Mediterranean in the Middle Ages. In many instances, the emergence of major traffic routes connected to a specific port of call or even the development of shipbuilding activities had only limited effects on cities which, following their own independent growth, would remain detached or in any case marginalized from port-related processes.[54] From several points of view, the development paths followed by port cities since the late Middle Ages had some traits in common. Rather than tied to their geographic location, they were linked to the morphology of their respective hinterlands or to whether there were any communication routes other than by sea. As I have tried to prove in this chapter, as early as in the Middle Ages, Genoa can be considered to be a port city in all respects, despite the arcade of the Ripa acting as a 'separation' between the port facilities and the city. Most likely, the port of Genoa needed the city more than other ports: it had neither a military base nor shipbuilding, nor was it a stopover port for ships sailing on long-range Mediterranean routes. Hence, the port drew significant financial resources for its management and operations from the city. At the same time, it would supply the city with all the essential commodities that the immediate region failed to offer. Port activities would affect the city in many ways: from a population point of view, by attracting a labour force and promoting the settlement of foreign merchant colonies; from an urban planning point of view, by fostering its growth and pushing all businesses that were not strictly related to port traffic and navigation back into the city; and last but not least, from an economic point of view, by diversifying its activities and driving growth in port-related sectors. From 1300 to 1600, the port of Genoa was thus the engine of the city's growth. Despite the changes in the Republic's economy during the sixteenth century, when local businessmen were beginning to focus their interests on financial activities, the port was still the place where public administration and private capital plans and objectives would meet and be shared.

Notes

1 A. Grohman, 'Introduzione', in A. Grohman (ed.), *Spazio urbano e organizzazione economica nell'Europa medievale*, Naples: Esi, 1995, pp. 7–38.

2 E. Poleggi, 'La costruzione della città portuale, un nuovo tema di storia', in E. Poleggi (ed.), *Le città portuali del Mediterraneo: Storia e archeologia*, Atti del Convegno Internazionale di Genova 1985, Genoa: Sagep, 1989, pp. 7–9.

3 P. F. Simbula, *I porti del Mediterraneo in età medievale*, Milan: Bruno Mondadori, 2009, p. 13.

4 Poleggi, 'La costruzione della città portuale', p. 9.

5 P. Massa Piergiovanni, *Lineamenti di organizzazione economica in uno stato preindustriale: La Repubblica di Genova,* Genoa: Ecig, 1995, p. 44.

6 E. Grendi, *La repubblica aristocratica dei genovesi: politica, carità e commercio fra Cinque e Seicento,* Bologna: Il Mulino, 1987, p. 309.
7 G. Felloni, 'La storiografia marittima su Genova in Età Moderna', in A. Di Vittorio (ed.), *Tendenze e orientamenti nella storiografia marittima contemporanea: gli stati italiani e la repubblica di Ragusa (secoli XIV–XIX),* Naples: L. Pironti, 1986, pp. 29–46. On the Middle Ages, see G. Pistarino, 'La storiografia marittima su Genova medievale', ibid., pp. 3–28.
8 R. S. Lopez, *Su e giù per la storia di Genova,* Genoa: Università di Genova, Istituto di paleografia e storia medievale, 1975, pp. 43–80; Grendi, *La repubblica aristocratica,* pp. 309–64.
9 On political changes during the age of the Republic of Genoa and on the consequences on its maritime policy, see T. A. Kirk, *Genoa and the Sea: Policy and Power in an Early Modern Maritime Republic, 1559–1684,* Baltimore, MD: Johns Hopkins University Press, 2005, pp. 14–28.
10 See Carlo Taviani's chapter in this book (pp. 177–91) on how Genoese colonies were run. On the Casa di San Giorgio, see the extensive bibliography by Giuseppe Felloni (and recently G. Felloni and G. Laura, *Genova e la storia della finanza: dodici primati? Genoa and the History of Finance: Twelve Firsts?,* Genoa: System Graphic srl, 2014, pp. 39–42), who is to be credited with the organization and filing of the wealth of documents preserved at the State Archives of Genoa (http://www.lacasadisangiorgio.it, accessed July 2015).
11 Felloni and Laura, *Genova e la storia della finanza,* p. 12.
12 Grendi, *La repubblica aristocratica,* p. 177; G. Felloni, 'Per la storia della popolazione di Genova nei secoli XVI e XVII', in Felloni., *Scritti di storia economica,* vol. 2, Genoa: Società Ligure di Storia Patria, 1999, pp. 1177–8.
13 Only vessels with a carrying capacity of over 400 *mine* – then from 1526 decreased to 200 *mine* – were required to unload their grain cargos in the port of Genoa (Grendi, *La repubblica aristocratica,* pp. 178–9).
14 See for example in this book (pp. 333–42) also the regulations enforced in the Middle Ages in favour of the port of Lisbon.
15 J. Heers, *Genova nel Quattrocento: Civiltà mediterranea, grande capitalismo e capitalismo popolare,* Milan: Jaca book, 1984, pp. 201–2; Massa Piergiovanni, *Lineamenti,* pp. 43–69.
16 The first evidence dates back to 17 Apr. 1277, when two sailors stated before a Notary Public that they were signing on a galley owned by Nicolosio Dugo Spinola which was sailing to Flanders (A. Nicolini, 'Commercio marittimo genovese in Inghilterra nel Medioevo 1280–1495'), *Atti della Società Ligure di Storia Patria,* NS 47/1, 2007, p. 220). This document was first published by R. Doehaerd, 'Les galères génoises dans la Manche et la Mer du Nord à la fin du XIIIe et au début du XIVe siècle', *Bulletin de l'Institut historique belge de Rome* 19, 1938, pp. 1–76.
17 Heers, *Genova nel Quattrocento,* pp. 260–1; Kirk, *Genoa and the Sea,* pp. 10–12.
18 N. Walton, *Genoa, 'La Superba': The Rise and Fall of a Merchant Pirate Superpower,* London: Hurst & Co., 2015, p. 56.
19 This was constructed employing probably local workforce. In Genoa there was a guild of Lombard 'magistri antelami' (bricklayers). There is hardly any information on this subject until the mid-fourteenth century.
20 F. Podestà, *Il porto di Genova dalle origini fino alla caduta della Repubblica Genovese (1797),* Genoa: E. Spiotti, 1913, pp. 101–34; E. Poleggi, 'L'Arsenale della Repubblica di Genova. 1594–1797', in E. Concina (ed.), *Arsenali e città nell'Occidente europeo,* Rome: NIS, 1987, pp. 83–96.
21 J. Day, *Les douanes de Gênes, 1376–1377,* Paris: SEVPEN, 1963, pp. xxiii–xxiv.
22 R. S. Lopez, 'Market expansion: the case of Genoa', *Journal of Economic History* 24, 1964, pp. 445–64; G. Pistarino, 'Genova medievale tra Oriente e Occidente', *Rivista Storica Italiana* 81/1, 1969, pp. 45–73.

23 Felloni and Laura, *Genova e la storia della finanza*, pp. 11–109. On the Genoese insurance market, see L. Piccinno, 'Genoa, 1340–1620: early development of marine insurance', in A. Leonard (ed.), *Marine Insurance: Origins and Institutions, 1300–1850*, Basingstoke: Palgrave Macmillan, 2016, pp. 25–45.
24 E. Poleggi, 'Forme ed attrezzature del porto di Genova sino al 1903', in *1128–2000: Il porto di Genova*, Genoa: Sagep, 1971, pp. 28ff.
25 See in this volume the chapters on Venice (pp. 103–20) and Dubrovnik (Ragusa) (pp. 141–58).
26 C. Costantini, 'La Repubblica di Genova nell'età moderna', in G. Galasso (ed.), *Storia d'Italia*, vol. 9, Turin: UTET, 1978, p. 164.
27 Ibid., pp. 165–8. Grendi, *La repubblica aristocratica*, p. 336.
28 G. Giacchero, *Origini e sviluppo del portofranco genovese*, Genoa: Sagep, 1972, pp. 51–9.
29 Ibid., pp. 29, 33, 45, 62–9; Costantini, 'La Repubblica di Genova in età moderna', pp. 168–9. On the Northerners' arrival in the Mediterranean and on its economic consequences on Italian maritime trade see M. Fusaro, 'The invasion of northern litigants: English and Dutch seamen in Mediterranean courts of law', in M. Fusaro, B. Allaire, R. J. Blakemore and T. Vanneste (eds), *Law, Labour and Empire: Comparative Perspectives on Seafarers, c. 1500–1800*, Basingstoke: Palgrave Macmillan, 2015, pp. 23–7.
30 A. Brusa, 'Dal Portofranco della Repubblica genovese al deposito franco dei giorni nostri', in *Il porto di Genova nella mostra di Palazzo San Giorgio*, Milan: Alfieri, 1953, pp. 134–5.
31 V. Tigrino, 'Il dibattito storico-politico sul Dominio della Repubblica di Genova in età moderna: feudi, ex-feudi, città e quasi-città', in M. Schnettger and C. Taviani (eds), *Libertà e dominio: Il sistema politico genovese: le relazioni esterne e il controllo del territorio*, Rome: Viella, 2011, pp. 323–9.
32 Giacchero, *Origini e sviluppo del portofranco*, p. 119.
33 G. Giacchero, 'San Giorgio e il porto', in *Il porto di Genova nella mostra*, pp. 121ff. On taxes on Genoese trade, see G. Felloni, 'La fiscalità nel dominio genovese tra Quattro e Cinquecento', *Atti e Memorie della Società Savonese di Storia Patria*, NS 25, 1989, pp. 91–110. On the link between the Casa di San Giorgio and the sea port see L. Piccinno, *Economia marittima e operatività portuale. Genova, secc. XVII–XIX*, Genoa: Società Ligure di Storia Patria, 2000, pp. 99–100.
34 Doria, 'La gestione del porto di Genova', pp. 145–51.
35 G. Costamagna, 'La costruzione del Molo Nuovo ed il suo finanziamento', in *Il porto di Genova nella mostra*, pp. 128–31; G. Giacchero, *Il Seicento e le Compere di San Giorgio*, Genoa: Sagep, 1979, pp. 336–40, 359.
36 Podestà, *Il porto di Genova*, pp. 62, 149; G. Costamagna, 'I magazzini del Magistrato del sale e del Magistrato dell'abbondanza', in *Il porto di Genova nella mostra*, pp. 164–5; Doria, 'La gestione del porto di Genova', p. 154.
37 Ibid., pp. 154–7; Brusa, 'Dal Portofranco della Repubblica genovese', p. 145.
38 Q. Van Doosselaere, *Commercial Agreements and Social Dynamics in Medieval Genoa*, New York: Cambridge University Press, 2009, pp. 1–231.
39 Ibid., pp. 150–5.
40 P. Gourdin, 'Présence Génoise en Méditerranée et en Europe du nord au milieu du XVème siècle: l'implantation des hommes d'affaires d'après un registre douanier de 1455', in M. Balard and A. Ducelier (eds), *Coloniser au Moyen Âge*, Paris: A. Colin, 1995. See also Van Doosselaere, *Commercial Agreements*, pp. 50–82, 180–6.
41 J. H. Pryor, 'The origins of the *Commenda* contract', *Speculum* 52/1, 1977, pp. 5–37. On the *commenda*'s network in Genoa from 1154 to 1315, see Van Doosselaere, *Commercial Agreements*, pp. 100–17.
42 On the presence of Jews and their economic role in port cities in the Modern and Contemporary ages, see D. Cesarani, 'Introduction', in D. Cesarani and G. Romain (eds),

Jews and Port Cities: 1590–1990: Commerce, Community and Cosmopolitanism, London and Portland, OR:Valentine Mitchell, 2006, pp. 1–13.

43 A. N. Eslami, *Genova e il Mediterraneo: I riflessi d'oltremare sulla cultura artistica e l'architettura dello spazio urbano XII–XVII secolo,* Genoa: De Ferrari Editore, 2000, p. 20.

44 M. Cerasi, 'Prefazione', ibid, pp. 10–12.

45 Massa Piergiovanni, *Lineamenti*, p. 312. On conflicts between local and foreign dockers, see Piccinno, *Economia marittima e operatività portuale*, pp. 243–6.

46 Piccinno, *Economia marittima*, pp. 113–94; L. Piccinno, 'Una "impresa portuale": organizzazione interna e servizi offerti dalla manodopera operante nello scalo genovese in Età Moderna', in S. Zaninelli and M. Taccolini (eds), *Il lavoro come fattore produttivo e come risorsa nella storia economica italiana*, Milan:Vita e Pensiero, 2002, pp. 507–22.

47 V. Piergiovanni, 'Dottrina e prassi nella formazione del diritto portuale: il modello genovese', in Doria and Massa, *Il sistema portuale della Repubblica di Genova*, pp. 17–18.

48 At present, the only available study on conflict resolution between merchants is V. Piergiovanni, 'Una raccolta di sentenze della Rota Civile di Genova nel XVI secolo', in Piergiovanni, *Norme, scienza e pratica giuridica tra Genova e l'Occidente medievale e moderno*, Genoa: Società Ligure di Storia Patria, 2012, pp. 239–50. This is based on a manuscript preserved in the State Archive of Genoa (*Decisiones Magnficae Rotae Civilis Genuae*) collecting the judgments of the Rota Civile from 1563 to 1590.

49 On this subject see V. Piergiovanni (ed.), *The Courts and the Development of Commercial Law*, Berlin: Dunker & Humblot, 1987.

50 Piergiovanni, 'Dottrina e prassi', pp. 24–5.

51 P. Massa Piergiovanni, 'Fattori tecnici ed economici dello sviluppo del porto di Genova tra medioevo ed età moderna (1340–1548)', in Doria and Massa, *Il sistema portuale della Repubblica di Genova*, pp. 79–86.

52 On port revenues from 1340 to 1548, ibid., p. 130.

53 G. Felloni, 'Organizzazione portuale, navigazione e traffici a Genova: un sondaggio tra le fonti per l'età moderna', in D. Puncuh (ed.), *Studi in memoria di Giorgio Costamagna,* Genoa: Società Ligure di Storia Patria, 2003, pp. 337–64.

54 J. Heers, 'Paysage urbains et societé dans les différents types de "villes portuaires" en Mediterranée occidentale au Moyen Âge', in Poleggi, *Città portuali del Mediterraneo*, p. 11.

11

THE GENOESE CASA DI SAN GIORGIO AS A MICRO-ECONOMIC AND TERRITORIAL NODAL SYSTEM

Carlo Taviani

The Casa or Bank of San Giorgio (or San Giorgio for short) managed the public debt of the commune of Genoa from 1407 to 1805. It incorporated the credits of all the Genoese commune's creditors. Unlike other public debt, such as the debt managed by the city-states of Florence and Venice, or even public debt nowadays, the Genoese commune did not manage its own debts. Creditors federated themselves;[1] they had a palace where they met and administered their powers and rights. The credits were guaranteed by taxation. Gradually San Giorgio acquired the right to collect taxes in all lands under the Genoese dominion, a territory that extended from Capo Corvo (northern Tuscany) to the Principality of Monaco. Taxes provided the money to repay the interest (*paghe*) due to the persons who held San Giorgio's shares (*luoghi*). Along with this power San Giorgio developed prerogatives and powers typical of other institutions. It was also a deposit bank from 1408 to 1444 and from 1530 to 1805. Genoese artisans, merchants and even big private bankers put their money into the bank; some of them obtained credits from San Giorgio. The ledgers of the bank permitted them to manage transactions without using coins. It has been argued that it was the scarcity of gold in Genoa that led to the formation of the bank.[2] San Giorgio also had a monopoly on the salt trade and taxation, and played an important role in the construction of the port and in ruling the Portofranco (the free trade area).[3]

Along with the public debt, banking and taxation rights, San Giorgio also acquired territorial power. From 1446 to 1562 it acquired and ruled lands that had previously been under the administration of the commune of Genoa. It ruled and governed them with the *ius gladii* and the *plena iurisdictio*, the fullest extent of sovereign power at the time – the same powers held by the commune of Genoa over other lands in Liguria. These included the whole island of Corsica, the city of Famagusta in Cyprus, the towns of Pieve di Teco, Ventimiglia and Levanto in Liguria, the regions of Lunigiana in northern Tuscany, and various trade posts and dominions in the Crimea and along the coasts of the Black Sea.

Given that the elite that ruled Genoa was a homogeneous group of merchants, scholars in past decades have attempted to view the commune of Genoa and San Giorgio as an integrated system without any divisions.[4] My argument, however, is that after a few decades, an institutional separation occurred between the commune and San Giorgio that in the long term led to a fracturing of sovereign power in Genoa. San Giorgio gradually developed powers and characteristics that were autonomous from the commune of Genoa. The aim of this chapter goes even further. To what extent is it possible to see these two institutions as separate? How deep did the separation involve their actual functions? If a separation did exist between the two institutions, was the circulation of people and objects within the Genoese lands and dominions affected by it?

This chapter first focuses on the central power of San Giorgio. An introductory paragraph answers the question whether San Giorgio may be defined as an autonomous political power while the commune continued to exist in Genoa. It then focuses on sources, dominions (location) and administrative power of San Giorgio (institutions), a central organization that progressively acquired multiple offices and resources. It presents findings related to the possibility of studying the nodal system of San Giorgio through the internal circulation of merchants, material culture and offices (connections and conflict resolution). It concludes with an analysis of the characteristics of the nodal system of San Giorgio as a financial and territorial framework.

A double power in Genoa

Some scholars in past decades have denied the existence of two well-differentiated institutions and powers in Renaissance Genoa, the commune and San Giorgio.[5] The main argument for this view was that various members of the same Genoese families held offices both in San Giorgio and in the commune. If the families were the same why should there have been two powers? This view arose in opposition to a traditional view developed by Niccolò Machiavelli. In the early sixteenth century Machiavelli wrote a memorable passage in his *Istorie fiorentine* in which he discussed the Casa di San Giorgio. He explained that San Giorgio was founded because the commune of Genoa needed money and did not know how it would pay its creditors. Those who had lent money to the commune joined together and formed San Giorgio, which in the space of a few years acquired control over Genoa's customs revenues and, subsequently, several territories that the commune had pledged as security. Machiavelli considered this acquisition of territory as the high point in

San Giorgio's power. He maintained that San Giorgio had gained control over most of Genoa's lands and subject cities, that it defended them and ruled over them, sending out its own rectors every year so that the city didn't have to bother about them. This situation led to a shift in the citizens' affections away from the commune of Genoa itself to San Giorgio 'on account of the tyranny of the former, and the excellent regulations adopted by the latter'.[6] Machiavelli also added that this brought with it changes to the government, which often found itself under the control of a particular faction such as the Adorno or the Fregoso, or foreign domination by the Milanese or the French. It wasn't San Giorgio that kept changing its government, but the commune.

> An example truly rare, never found by the philosophers in all the republics they have imagined and seen; to see within the same circle, among the same citizens, liberty and tyranny, civil life and corrupt life, justice and license.[7]

The positive terms (liberty, civil life and justice) pertained to San Giorgio, the negative terms (tyranny, corruption and license) to the commune. Machiavelli closes the passage by expressing the hope that San Giorgio would one day conquer all of Genoa, at which point the city would surpass even Venice.

The reaction to Machiavelli's view of San Giorgio focused in particular on sixteenth-century Genoa, a period that saw the stabilization of the Republic. However, Machiavelli's view of the opposition between San Giorgio and the commune of Genoa was developed in the early sixteenth century and drew on events from the fifteenth century. During this period, an opposition between San Giorgio and the commune of Genoa did exist. We can see this in various areas of finance and politics. When the commune of Genoa wanted to confiscate the shares of public debt held by Genoa's enemies, San Giorgio protested. It defended the autonomy of finance and the importance of maintaining the investors' trust in the Casa. Even enemies had the right to see their investments protected. More importantly, San Giorgio gradually acquired financial powers weakening the communal financial offices. During the fifteenth century, the commune of Genoa controlled a system of direct taxation, the *avaria*. From 1490 onwards, San Giorgio managed to abolish this and took possession of all the revenues from taxation. Indirect taxation substituted for direct taxation. San Giorgio promised to pay for the expenses once covered by direct taxation and in return asked for all the profits from indirect levies. The commune of Genoa, and its financial office, the Ufficio di Moneta, lost its financial and fiscal power.

Inside San Giorgio's administration, a close group of people – a faction – gradually became very powerful. A secret report written for the duke of Milan around 1465 referred to a faction within San Giorgio, the *boteschi*.[8] Like the wooden staves of a wine barrel, the *boteschi* were bound together. One member of this faction, Battista de Goano, was an influential politician, a doctor of law, who persuaded Genoa's assembly to hand over various lands to San Giorgio. He was present at the assembly during the acquisition of Pietrasanta, Corsica, Famagusta and Caffa. Another *botesco*, Bendinelli Sauli, speculated in the shares of San Giorgio. Later he confessed his financial sin to the famous preacher Angelo da Chivasso who came to Genoa to audit his ledgers. With the money provided by the Sauli family, the great church of Carignano was built in Genoa. The *boteschi* were a factional group within San Giorgio and they helped the company to become the power that faced off against the commune, at least during the fifteenth and the sixteenth centuries.

To summarize schematically the process that led San Giorgio to increase its power, it first took possession of all the parts of the public debt (the *compere*) and financial rights, later it acquired lands.

San Giorgio's authority was also recognized abroad by various foreign powers. In 1455, Pope Callixtus III recognized that the *dominium* of Caffa pertained to San Giorgio.[9] During the war against Florence for the control of Sarzana in 1485, San Giorgio's ambassadors as well as the ambassadors of the commune arrived and stayed a long time in Rome under Pope Innocent VIII. The Florentine ambassadors became aware that they were dealing with two Genoese powers. They described the arrival at the papal court of both the Doge's and San Giorgio's ambassadors, each group with its own symbol. In the end, it was not the commune's ambassadors, but those of San Giorgio who dealt with them.[10] While this awareness may be seen in many documents (reports of Florentine and Milanese ambassadors, letters of princes, accounts on Genoa, etc.) it only became completely clear and evident in Machiavelli's passage at the beginning of the sixteenth century.

Sources and studies on San Giorgio

San Giorgio's archives contain a huge number of sources. Thousands of registers of financial transactions and hundreds of registers and folders related to land administration. However, a dichotomy exists for the period we are dealing with. San Giorgio ruled lands from 1446 to 1562. For the second half of the fifteenth century many chancellery registers have survived. These record the central decisions taken by San Giorgio, the debates over the acquisition of lands, such as Corsica, Caffa, Famagusta, etc. This kind of documentation is very similar to the commune of Genoa's registers and it mirrors the city's humanistic tradition. Some of the chancellors, such as Bartolomeo Senarega (communal chancellor) or Antonio Gallo (San Giorgio's chancellor) were historians who wrote chronicles and histories of the city or of the Genoese.[11] The registers are well organized and preserved. However, from the early sixteenth century, there is a shift in the sources: the centre of San Giorgio becomes less visible while the periphery is very well documented. Chancellors of San Giorgio kept track of information in various folders (*filze*) containing hundreds of separate pieces of paper. These were not written down in a register. Moreover, this documentation refers mainly to the local administration of land, not to the centre. We do not find the discussions among members of San Giorgio. Hundreds of folders document the local administration of Corsica, while no debates were recorded for the year when all the lands came back to the Republic of Genoa in 1562. Thus, the 'head' of San Giorgio – the centre – is visible for the period 1446–*c.*1510, while one can study mostly the 'members' – local administrations of the dominions – for the period *c.*1520–62.

During the early modern and modern periods, San Giorgio's model held an extensive fascination for contemporary institutions, thinkers and businessmen. In the nineteenth and twentieth centuries it was envisaged to be the exemplary prototype of a business corporation (or joint stock company). Legal historians, such as Levin Goldschmidt, Karl Lehmann and pre-eminently Heinrich Sieveking – who studied San Giorgio for his PhD dissertation under the supervision of Max Weber – considered San Giorgio as an institution very similar to the Dutch and the British East India Companies, the Bank of England and the Mississippi Company.[12] Their view was often anachronistic, but Sieveking's study remains nowadays one of the most informed. In the same period, Genoese scholars and archivists devoted various studies to San Giorgio.[13] During the twentieth century, authors such as Jacques Heers and, more recently, Giuseppe Felloni studied San Giorgio. The information on San Giorgio in Heers' book devoted to fifteenth-century Genoa is dispersed but it remains useful.[14] As for Felloni, he completed a web-project that merges his comprehensive inventory of San Giorgio's archives with an explanation of San Giorgio's financial and political structure and mechanisms.[15] This is an interactive platform that provides scholars with a very useful tool that makes possible the pursuit of new research projects. As for the lands of San Giorgio, unfortunately, there are no comprehensive studies on its dominions, but only various specific studies on certain land holdings.[16]

San Giorgio's lands and seas

Some of San Giorgio's dominions were very far from Genoa, like Caffa in Crimea; others very near, like Pieve di Teco or Levanto. The geographical environment as well as the variety of population differed greatly from one land to another. Some territories were small towns within Liguria in the northern Mediterranean (*Mar Ligure*), while other possessions were whole islands or extensive lands, such as those in the Crimea or on other coasts of the Black Sea. Famagusta in Cyprus was at the centre of Mediterranean commerce and was home to a variety of peoples such as Genoese, Greeks, Syrians, Jews. Cyprus – like Corsica – had in previous centuries been a *Mahona*, a Genoese territorial institution guaranteed by a portion of public debt (*compera*). The main difference from San Giorgio's dominion was that the *Mahona* did not have the *ius gladii* and the *plena iurisdictio*, the sovereign powers over lands. In this period only the commune possessed those rights (thirteenth to fourteenth centuries). Together with the geographical element, the temporal framework also matters in considering the history of San Giorgio's dominions. San Giorgio's territorial power over the lands in Lunigiana, Corsica and the towns of the Liguria lasted for many years, in some case also for almost a century (Ameglia in Lunigiana, Corsica), while the dominions in the Black Sea lasted only twenty-five years.

The Black Sea, or Mare Maius, was a large area. Here San Giorgio had both territorial holdings with sovereign powers and trading posts (Figure 11.1). The territorial holdings were Caffa (Feodosia), Soldaia (Sudak), Cembalo (Balaklava, neighbouring Sevastopol) and Samastri (Amasra). The main trading posts were Gozia, Vosporo (Kerch), Copa (Slavjansk na Kubani in Russia), Savastopoli (Sukhumi, Abkhazia/Georgia), Trebisonda (Trabzon, in Turkey), Sinope (Sinop, in Turkey) and Tana (Azov, in the Sea of Azov). Other minor trading posts also existed in this area (see Figure 11.2). Along with the rule of the lands, the control of the sea was also important. The large networks of trade posts and territorial holdings made it possible for San Giorgio to have intense power over the Black Sea. In the Crimea there were Russians, Genoese, Armenians, Ruthenians, Bulgarians, Wallachians, Bosnians, Greeks and Georgians. The Crimea and Caffa were traditional hubs for merchants coming from Russia or from even further east. Caffa had been a central node for the 'Mongol silk road', but at the time of San Giorgio's dominion (1453–75) it was important mainly for the slave trade.[17] Here the relationship between the Genoese and the Tatar Khanate of Hacı Giray was quite complex. Initially the Genoese had conflicts with the Khan, but after the arrival of the Ottomans, things improved. Even if San Giorgio did not encourage the coinage of local coins in its lands, in Crimea a strange coin (the *follaro*) was minted. One side of the coin represented St George and the dragon, the symbol of San Giorgio, the other side depicted the Tatar Thamga of Hacı Giray.[18] The coin symbolizes the porous sovereignty over this land. Even later in 1481, when San Giorgio had lost its lands in this region, the relationship with the Khanate persisted. At that time ambassadors were sent from Genoa to the Khan to plan a war against the Ottomans to reconquer San Giorgio's Crimea. The Genoese dominions in the Black Sea are a good observation point from which to ask a series of questions about the importance of territorial dominion. How extensive were the Genoese outposts along the coast and into the hinterland? Did land matter in the control of the sea and of the routes and terrestrial roads?

In the areas of the Black Sea, in places such as Soldaia and Caffa, bases defending the roads running eastward were useful to extend Genoese control into the hinterland. Other centres, such as Samastri and Trebizond, were important to keep the route or to stop for a certain period and were used only as trading posts. Especially when the threat of Mehmet the Conqueror loomed, the latter became places where some of the San Giorgio's officers refused to go; it was difficult to find a replacement for them. The Black Sea and its coasts were an area rich in classical Roman heritage. In Samastri relics of the ancient Roman colony, reused by the Byzantines, remained. The Genoese in turn reused roads, bridges and ancient buildings. Together with the physical elements, the knowledge of the past also covered other aspects, such as the use of trade routes. Trebizond had been in Roman times an important landmark for venturing in the Black Sea and so it was also for the Genoese who occupied and preserved it more as a place to orient their routes than as a trading post.

Corsica was – along with the Black Sea lands – a large territory compared with other Genoese dominions (Figure 11.1). The population was quite homogeneous unlike possessions in the Black Sea and in Famagusta. People in Corsica had a tradition of rebelling against the Genoese. The transition to rule by San Giorgio was not easy. Some places preferred to stay under the commune of Genoa.[19] Less threatened by external enemies than Famagusta or the Black Sea, Corsica nonetheless experienced a series of political tensions and revolts during the century of San Giorgio's dominion. From the second decade of the sixteenth century pirates ravaged the island's coasts.

San Giorgio's dominions in the Lunigiana (northern Tuscany, Figure 11.1) were close to Liguria and Genoa. Here San Giorgio acquired Pietrasanta – the first of its dominions – in 1446 and held it until 1484, and also Sarzana (which San Giorgio held between 1484 and 1487 and from 1496 to 1562). All the other dominions of this same area were held without interruption by San Giorgio until 1562. Ameglia was acquired in 1446, Lerici in 1479, the towns of Sarzana and Sarzanello in 1496, the castle of Falcinello in 1500, those of Bolano and Godano in 1510, the town of Santo Stefano Magra in 1499, and Castelnuovo, Ortonovo and Nicola in 1494. Some towns of the Lunigiana had previously been dominions of the Fregoso family (Sarzana), but others were also in the hands of Lucca and Florence (Pietrasanta).

San Giorgio's dominions in Liguria (Figure 11.1) were much more peaceful, and here the population was homogeneous and similar to the population in Genoa and in the rest of the Riviera. In the eastern Riviera San Giorgio acquired Pieve di Teco and the Valle Arroscia (previously a dominion of the family Spinola) in 1512 and the town of Ventimiglia in 1514; in the western Riviera the port of Levanto in 1514. Both Ventimiglia and Levanto were places at the boundaries of the Genoese dominions. The hinterland of Lunigiana and Liguria wasn't wide. The Genoese Riviera was a thin strip of land that stretched along the sea. San Giorgio's dominions, if we except the Valle Arroscia, never penetrated to the hills and the mountains beyond the coast, an area where another, and even more private power, that of the Genoese feudal families (Fieschi, Fregoso, Spinola), exercised strong control.

The territory of Corsica was much wider than those of the Riviera and the Lunigiana. San Giorgio was unable to strictly control this area. Here rebels and bandits took refuge against the invasive power of San Giorgio, and here the wild landscape became a label for their activities: in the words of San Giorgio's officers these persons were said to be 'a la selva' (literally, in the woods).[20] But Corsica was also a fruitful land. San Giorgio had established plantations in the region in 1539, planned the kind of crops to be grown and populated the colony with peasants from Liguria. It dispatched officers to examine the situation in Corsica and developed an immigration plan.[21] As in many other situations, San Giorgio did not directly pay all the expenses itself, but relied on traders. It issued concessions in various areas (Ajaccio, Portovecchio, Aleria) and sold concessions to Genoese noble families (de Marini,

Salvago, Passano-De Ferrari, etc).[22] San Giorgio had established similar ways of dealing with local resources in Pietrasanta many years before. In 1455 it had issued a concession to extract iron in the area around Pietrasanta in northern Tuscany (concession for Martino de Grimaldi and Francesco Scalia, in 1455).[23]

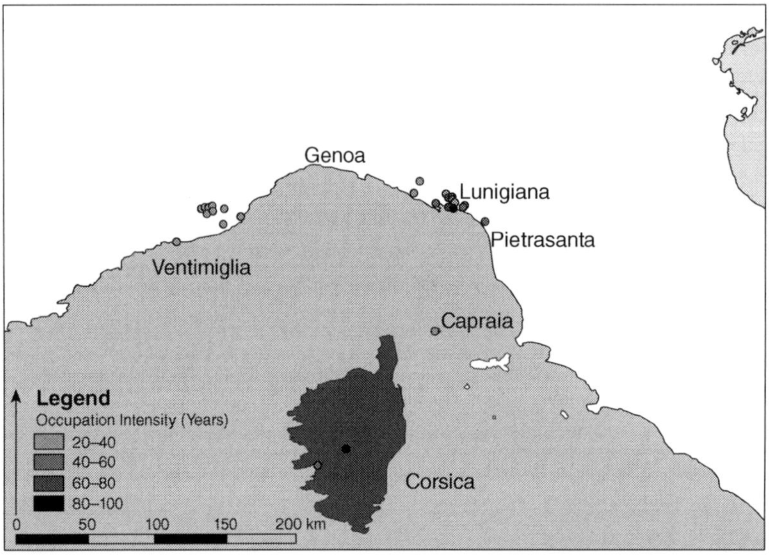

Figure 11.1 San Giorgio's western dominions

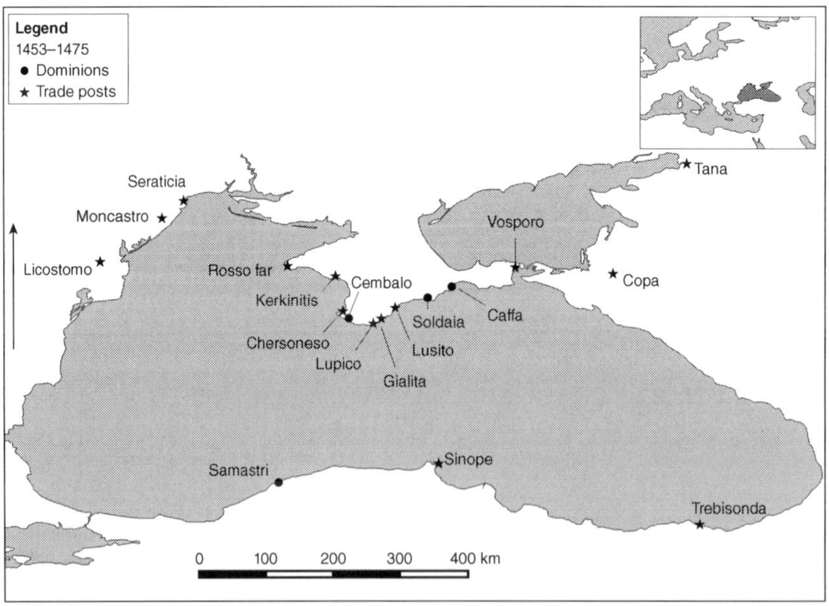

Figure 11.2 San Giorgio's dominions and trade posts in the Black Sea

Homogeneous characteristics of San Giorgio's administration

Is it possible to study San Giorgio's dominions from a comprehensive perspective? The historiography of the past centuries and decades has referred to the dominions of San Giorgio in the Black Sea and in Cyprus as colonies, while the towns and lands in the region of Liguria and northern Tuscany were called 'terra ferma'.[24] However, while the words 'terra ferma' exist in the sources, the word 'colony' does not. Moreover, the use of the concept of colony becomes increasingly pointless as we get closer to Genoa itself. Pietrasanta in northern Tuscany was certainly not a colony, but what can we say about Corsica? Scholars of Genoese history do not use the word 'colony' for Corsica, but why was Corsica different from Caffa in the Crimea or from Famagusta in Cyprus? Even if the word colony could be useful to describe lands such as Famagusta in Cyprus and the Crimea, far from Genoa, in this chapter I will not use the term since my aim is to build connections rather than make a distinction that I was not able to find in Genoese sources.

From the middle of the fifteenth century all the lands of Genoa far from Liguria (the so-called colonies) were taken over by San Giorgio. Only the *mahona* of Chios controlled by the Giustiniani family was not in the Casa's hands. The main reason for the commune of Genoa giving away its lands to San Giorgio was that it could not afford to govern and administer them. These lands have in common that the cost of maintaining them was too high. The reason why San Giorgio acquired these lands was that it probably wanted to protect its fiscal gains. Among the most important revenues there were those on commerce and on salt.

Over time San Giorgio developed similar ways of dealing with the acquisition and the administration of its lands. San Giorgio and the commune of Genoa did not sign any contract to regulate the Casa's first territorial acquisition of Pietrasanta in 1446, but in the following years they signed a contract to regulate the acquisition of all the other lands. All these other contracts follow the same pattern. A preamble explained the reason why San Giorgio was taking possession of lands. Usually the reason given was the difficulty the commune was facing with the Ottomans in the eastern Mediterranean who wanted to take possession of the Crimea and Famagusta, or the Aragonese who threatened Corsica. For each contract the commune sold the land with the *plena iurisdictio* and the *ius gladii*. The geographical features were described with similar words. The contract mentioned the inhabited areas, *civitates*, *urbes*, *terra*, *oppida*, *castella* and *fortilia* and the land resources, forests, ports, rivers, lakes and the areas for fishing and hunting. The richest of San Giorgio's lands in terms of resources and habitat was the Crimea, but all the contracts contain a geographical description.

San Giorgio account books were highly detailed. It is possible to find a correlation between the method of bookkeeping San Giorgio adopted to keep track of its bank and the public debt and the way it recorded the budgets of its lands. San Giorgio's chancellors and scribes entered hundreds of thousands, perhaps even millions, of financial transactions[25] in thousands of ledgers and *giornali* (the register written up on a daily basis). Shares of public debt, as well as their interest, the *paghe*, were exchanged in Genoa by merchants, artisans and various kinds of investors every day. The same happened with bank transactions. Every client had his transactions recorded under his name. This well-established accounting practice used the double entry method of bookkeeping, typical of San Giorgio. When San Giorgio acquired lands after 1446, the same practice was used to record the expenses. Hundreds of books (*Massarie* volumes) had his transactions recorded under every client's name. The total of these expenditures ended up in San Giorgio's central ledgers, the series of *introitus et exitus*.[26] These last volumes contain information about the acquisition of lands. We find accounts named *expenses Sarzanae*, as well as *Dominium nostrum Caffae*, or *inceptum Corsicae,* etc. Here even small items appear, such as the flag of San Giorgio brought to Caffa in 1453.[27] Not many territorial states during the Renaissance in Italy and Europe had the same number of ledgers as San Giorgio. None of them, neither Florence, nor Venice, seems to have developed such a fine practice of territorial accounting.

The judicial as well the military and political administration of the dominions was carried out from above. The central office of San Giorgio (the eight *protettori*) named a governor, one captain and various officers. San Giorgio issued similar statutes in Caffa and Famagusta. Here it gradually included local elites in the government. The so-called 'white Genoese', mainly Syrians, were permitted to acquire a certain strategic position within the government of Cyprus.[28]

When it was faced with significant threats San Giorgio raised an army. This happened in Corsica to put down a rebellion and in the Crimea to defend its lands from the Ottomans. In both cases, San Giorgio enlisted Genoese inhabitants of Liguria, the area around Genoa.

San Giorgio's symbols were constantly present in the lands under its control. Bas-reliefs showing St George and the dragon were carved on marble city gates in various places. Today they still exist in Ventimiglia, Levanto and in the island of Capraia (close to Elba). San Giorgio built up a strong system of fortresses and walls. These are still visible in Soldaia (Sudak) in the Crimea, in Corsica and in the small island of Capraia. These military structures defended San Giorgio's dominions from external enemies and controlled the subject populations.

The nodal system

Within the nodal system of San Giorgio many people moved from one place to another. It would be possible to find references to some specific figures that operated only within San Giorgio's lands. Thus, when Ottomans threatened the city of Caffa in 1455, the Corsican bishop Deodato Bochone helped San Giorgio to obtain a papal privilege. He moved from his usual field, Corsica, and focused on another one of San Giorgio's areas, the Crimea. Another example would be the artists who worked for San Giorgio, such as the marble carvers who worked in Pietrasanta and various other areas of the Lunigiana. Chancellors or even soldiers moved from one land to another within San Giorgio's dominions. That was the case with the ancestors of Napoleon Bonaparte, Francesco Bonaparte – a soldier of San Giorgio – and Caterina da Castelletto – daughter of a chancellor of San Giorgio, Guido – who came from San Giorgio's dominions in Lunigiana.

However, more common were cases like that of Martino Cigala, who in 1455 brought 114 slaves from Caffa (San Giorgio's dominion) to Chios (the Mahona of Giustiniani).[29] To better understand the role of San Giorgio, rather than viewing these lands as an impermeable space, one can think of them as very porous. San Giorgio did not develop commercial power, only financial. Some of San Giorgio's lands had already had a portion of public debt (a *compera*) attached to them in the past. This was the case with Corsica (Mahona Corsicae) and with Famagusta (Mahona Cyprii). San Giorgio gradually acquired these *compere*. The shares of the credit of these lands became part of San Giorgio's credit. The pieces of debt became pieces of land. San Giorgio collected taxes on these and on all the other lands. With these revenues it repaid the shareholders. The dominions of Famagusta and Crimea were particularly important, since they controlled the trade in luxury goods and slaves. In the Mediterranean closer to Genoa, the islands of Corsica and Capraia on the one hand and the lands in northern Tuscany (Lunigiana) on the other, were nodal points for controlling the trade that converged directly on Genoa from southern Italy and North Africa.

The commune of Genoa handed over Famagusta and the Black Sea lands to San Giorgio in the hope the Casa would effectively deal with these external areas of commerce. San Giorgio resisted until 1475. Until this date San Giorgio's dominions and trade posts spread over a vast area (up to the Black Sea and Cyprus in the southern Mediterranean), but they were later reduced into a smaller area (between Corsica, northern Tuscany and the Liguria). The merchants who moved in both these areas remain mostly unstudied and unknown. What also remains unknown is their relationship with San Giorgio. Here I present two case studies.

1. Borbone Centurione was a wealthy and powerful merchant-banker. He carried out his business in both San Giorgio's dominions and in the area of the commune. The fact that he worked in one area or in the other did not affect his business and made no difference to him. In 1437, he provided wheat to the community of Pietrasanta. Later, in 1447 he founded in partnership with Geronimo Lercari a private bank and financed the silk production in Genoa. In 1454, he financed another loan with Giovanni Tommaso de Negro, receiving in return the revenues of commercial taxation (*drictus*) from Tunis.[30] By 1453, however, he had become so connected to San Giorgio as to plan one of the most difficult-to-imagine political operations in Genoa of the time. He offered Genoa's Doge Pietro Campofregoso around 30,000–40,000 ducats in exchange for the commune's entire sovereign power.[31] He did not want that power for himself; he was dealing on behalf of San Giorgio and wanted San Giorgio to become the only power of Genoa. This remained only a proposal since the two men did not reach

any agreement. However, the utopian idea expressed in Machiavelli's sixteenth-century passage had already emerged sixty years before as a real political proposal in Borbone Centurione's plan, itself a real political proposal.

2. Manuele de Oliva was a merchant with intense business activity between Genoa and Cyprus during the 1440s. In 1446, the commune of Genoa issued him the right to receive money from the taxation of commerce in Cyprus in exchange for a loan (*drictus Famagustae*).[32] Manuel de Oliva acquired the *drictus* and provided the commune with the loan. He was among the same persons who a few months earlier had decided on the acquisition of Pietrasanta. One year later San Giorgio took possession of Famagusta. At that time the *drictus* was revoked and San Giorgio acquired the revenues in exchange for the loan.

Manuel de Oliva and Borbone Centurione operated throughout the territories of the commune and San Giorgio. However, both these merchant-bankers were very well connected with San Giorgio and influenced its policies. What one might infer from these two case studies is that, even if there were specific groups of people or even of goods and objects moving inside the nodal system of San Giorgio, it does not make sense to split the flows of trade and traders into two separate economic circuits. It would be misleading to claim that two different commercial geographies existed. Instead, San Giorgio provided the financial framework that embraced, as much as possible, the whole of Genoese society.

San Giorgio's principal aim was to provide two kinds of structures: financial and territorial/maritime. Within this framework economic activity was able to spread. We already saw how the territorial/maritime structure worked. How did the financial infrastructure work? Among the many financial tasks of San Giorgio, it can be useful to consider its relationships with external powers. The process illustrates also the relationship between San Giorgio and the Genoese society. In various periods of time from the mid-fifteenth century to the mid-sixteenth century, San Giorgio gave loans to various princes, such as Francesco Sforza, duke of Milan, or Pope Sixtus IV. The process went through five phases.

1. San Giorgio received a huge amount of money from various Genoese merchants.
2. San Giorgio gave loans to the prince and in return received some security (the right to exploit the salt taxes, etc.).
3. San Giorgio issued many small shares to many Genoese citizens. These were exchanged in the secondary market among Genoese. At this point the big merchant bankers who gave the initial sum of money to San Giorgio made a profit by selling their shares on the secondary market.
4. The secondary market created by San Giorgio lasted for different periods (from six to ten years) and San Giorgio started to acquire income from the prince (salt taxation, etc.).
5. Small investors received interest on their shares. The longer the secondary market lasted, the longer San Giorgio was able to make profits.

One last example shows how San Giorgio's financial activities were connected with the control of the land. During the acquisition of Caffa in 1455 San Giorgio came up with a complex financial scheme to acquire funds. A set of interests was sold on the market without the existence of the corresponding shares of public debt. Thus the circulation of these *paghe* was seen as usury.[33] Pope Callixtus III, after some weeks of debate, issued a special deliberation *(Bulla)* for San Giorgio. He recognized San Giorgio's right to issue these particular shares, because the Bank ruled and defended the city of Caffa. Both the *defensionem* and the *regiminem*, the papal document stated, pertained to San Giorgio. It was its territorial dominion, in the end, that gave San Giorgio the authority to speculate in finance.

In governing lands and ruling people, San Giorgio dealt with various kinds of factional, jurisdictional and economic conflict. Within the towns of Lunigiana and in Liguria San Giorgio elaborated a political discourse that constantly made use of the concept of the *bonum commune* (common good) against the local factions. According to this notion, San Giorgio was the only good prince on these lands and had the right to fight the factions that attempted to disrupt its sovereign power. In Liguria, San Giorgio entered the conflicts between the factions of the Adorno and the Fregoso (mainly in Levanto and Ventimiglia), in Lunigiana San Giorgio fought the Fregoso faction, which wanted to reconquer its former possession. In Corsica a similar kind of political discourse was elaborated, but here the population perceived it as more rhetorical than effective.[34] Here San Giorgio repressed the revolts of Giovan Paolo de Leca (1487–9) and Rinuccio della Rocca (1502), members of powerful factions, with military force.

The jurisdiction of San Giorgio often overlapped with that of the bishops. Both the case of Corsica and that of the Black Sea's dominions show how San Giorgio interacted with bishops. The bishop of Mariana Agostino Giustiniani, a fine scholar and historian, wrote a work with the purpose of attacking San Giorgio's government and to denounce the corruption of its officers in Corsica.[35] In Caffa San Giorgio had problems both with the Catholic bishop and with the Dominican friars. In order to weaken their power, it empowered the Franciscan friars, who were less traditionalist.[36]

A final case is offered by the subject of conflict resolution related to economic quarrels within San Giorgio's dominions. Unfortunately, the latter is probably the least studied among the various kinds of conflicts. Further research needs to be undertaken on this subject. At the moment, it is possible to say that if the local population applied to San Giorgio's officers to solve the conflicts, the Genoese could instead apply to Genoese magistrates directly in Genoa.

Conclusion

San Giorgio's nodal system was not a commercial one. San Giorgio did not have any interest directly in commerce. It did, however, collect taxes on commerce. The system was quite open to the merchants, and merchants were among the most important persons in San Giorgio; they wanted and supervised the acquisitions of lands.

San Giorgio provided both the financial and territorial framework for ruling lands and let the merchants make money. Walls, cities, fortresses, plantations, garrisons, armies and governors controlled lands and seas. Merchants and goods circulated throughout these lands and seas and among them. San Giorgio received money and issued financial shares that were sold to the same merchants, to many artisans and merchants in Genoa and even to non-Genoese investors. San Giorgio's dominions as well as the areas under the commune's control constituted the physical space of commercial transactions, but San Giorgio's financial space was larger and without borders.

Notes

1 A. Molho, 'Le città-stato e i loro debiti pubblici: quesiti e ipotesi sulla storia di Firenze, Genova e Venezia. Italia 1350–1450', in *Tra crisi, trasformazione, sviluppo (XIII Convegno di studi: Pistoia, 10–13 maggio 1991)*, Pistoia: Centro Italiano di studi di Storia e d'Arte, 1993, pp. 185–215, 210.
2 E. Aerts, 'The Casa di San Giorgio and the "monetary famine" of the Late Middle Ages', in G. Felloni (ed.), *La Casa di San Giorgio: Il potere del credito*, Genoa: Società Ligure di Storia Patria, 2006, pp. 27–62.
3 On the role of San Giorgio in the construction of the port of Genoa and on the Portofranco, see here the chapter by Luisa Piccinno.
4 C. Bitossi, 'Il governo della Repubblica e della Casa di San Giorgio: i ceti dirigenti dopo la riforma costituzionale del 1576', in Felloni, *La Casa di San Giorgio*, pp. 91–107.
5 C. Bitossi, 'Il governo della Repubblica e della Casa di San Giorgio', pp. 91–107.
6 N. Machiavelli, *Opere storiche*, ed. A. Montevecchi and C. Varotti, Rome: Salerno, 2011, 2 vols.
7 Niccolò Machiavelli, *Florentine Histories,* tr. E. Brenner and H. C. Mansfield, Jr, Princeton, NJ: Princeton University Press, 1988, p. 352.
8 C. Taviani, 'Hanno levato l'amore dal comune e postolo a San Giorgio', in M. Schnettger and C. Taviani (eds), *Libertà e dominio: Il sistema politico genovese: Le relazioni esterne e il controllo del territorio*, Rome: DHI, 2011, pp. 267–80.
9 J. Kirshner, 'The moral problem of discounting Genoese Paghe, 1450–1550', *Archivum. Fratrum Praedicatorum* 47, 1977, pp. 109–67.
10 C. Taviani, 'Hanno levato l'amore'.
11 B. Senarega, *De rebus Genuensibus commentaria: Ab anno 1488 usque ad annum 1514*, ed. E. Pandiani, in *Rerum Italicarum scriptores*, ed. L. A. Muratori, Bologna: N. Zanichelli, 1929–32, 24.8, and A. Gallo, *Commentarii de rebus Genuensium et de navigatione Columbi,* ed. E. Pandiani, Città di Castello: S. Lapi, 1910–1911.
12 See H. Sieveking, *Genueser Finanzwesen mit besonderer Berücksichtigung der Casa di S. Giorgio*, vol. 1, *Genueser Finanzwesen vom 12. bis 14. Jahrhundert;* vol. 2, *Die Casa di S. Giorgio,* Freiburg: Verlag von J. C. B. Mohr, 2 vols, 1898–9. On the model of San Giorgio and its fascination, C. Taviani, 'An ancient scheme: the Mississippi Company, Machiavelli, and the Casa di San Giorgio (1407–1720)', in E. Erikson and V. Assenova (eds), 'Chartering capitalism: organizing markets, states, and publics', *Political Power and Social Theory*, 29, 2015, pp. 239–56.
13 A. Lobero, *Memorie storiche della Banca di S. Giorgio compilate dall'archivista*, Genoa: tip. Ponthenier e f., 1832. C. Cuneo, *Memorie sopra l'antico debito pubblico, mutui, compere e banca di San Giorgio in Genova*, Genoa: stamperia dei Sordi Muti, s.a. (1842).
14 J. Heers, *Gênes au XVe siècle: Activité èconomique et problèmes sociaux*, Paris: SEVPEN, 1961, pp. 97–190.

15 G. Felloni <www.lacasadisangiorgio.it>.
16 On the colonies in the eastern Mediterranean, see M. Balard, 'Il Banco di San Giorgio e le colonie d'Oltremare', in Felloni, *La Casa di San Giorgio*, pp. 63–73. On the territorial power of San Giorgio in Corsica, see A. M. Graziani, 'Ruptures et continuites dans la politique de Saint-Georges en Corse (1453–1562)', in Felloni, *La Casa di San Giorgio*, pp. 75–90. A. M. Graziani, 'Saint Georges et la Corse: un "bon gouvernement"?', in M. Schnettger and C. Taviani (eds), *Il sistema politico genovese: Le relazioni esterne e il controllo del territorio*, Rome: Viella, 2011, pp. 267–80. See also V. Marchi Van Cauwelaert, *La Corse génoise, Saint Georges, vainqueur des 'tyrans' (milieu XVe-début XVIe siècle)*, Paris: Classiques Garnier, 2011. On San Giorgio in Lunigiana, see A. Bernardini, 'Ai confini della Repubblica. Il dominio di San Giorgio in Lunigiana (1476–1500)', unpublished thesis, Università degli Studi di Pisa, 2009.
17 Heers, *Gênes au XVe siècle*.
18 G. Pistarino, *I signori del Mare,* Genoa: Civico Istituto Colombiano, 1992.
19 Taviani, 'Hanno levato l'amore'.
20 Marchi Van Cauwelaert, *La Corse génoise*, pp. 162–8.
21 L. Russo, 'La politica agraria dell'Officio di San Giorgio in Corsica (1490–1553)', *Rivista Storica Italiana* 1934/4, pp. 422–68, and 1935/1, pp. 1–48.
22 Ibid.
23 G. Pipino, 'Il Banco di San Giorgio e le miniere di Pietrasanta (1446–1484)', *L'industria mineraria: miniere e cave, geologia applicata, metallurgia, fonti di energia: rivista di tecnica, economia e diritto* (Faenza: Giuseppe Pipino Editore), 28, July–Aug. 1977, pp. 244–51.
24 Balard, 'Il Banco di San Giorgio', pp. 63–73. On the terraferma, see G. Felloni, online inventory: www.lacasadisangiorgio.it.
25 G. Felloni <www.lacasadisangiorgio.it>.
26 Ibid.
27 Archivio di Stato di Genova, Archivio del Banco di San Giorgio (new number: 185,02049), *Introitus et exitus* of 1453, c. 336v, 7 lire and 4 soldi. See also Archivio di Stato di Genova, Archivio del Banco di San Giorgio, *Introitus et exitus* del 1484, c. 61v.
28 L. Balletto, 'Genovesi e Piemontesi nella Cipro dei Lusignano nel tardo medioevo', *Rivista di storia arte archeologia per le province di Alessandria e Asti* 103, 1994, pp. 83–137.
29 Ibid.
30 See Archivio di Stato di Genova, Archivio Segreto, 547, c. 191r, J. Heers, *Gênes au XVe siècle: Activité èconomique et problèmes sociaux*, Paris: SEVPEN, 1961, pp. 93 and 250. See also M. Marengo, 'Genova e Tunisi, 1388–1515', Atti della Società Ligure di Storia Patria, 32, 1901, p. 78. On *drictus* in general, see M. Buongiorno, *Amministrazione genovese nella 'Romania': Legislazione, magistrature, fisco,* Genoa: F.lli Bozzi, 1977.
31 C. Shaw, 'Principles and practice in the civic government of fifteenth-century Genoa', *Renaissance Quarterly* 58/1, 2005, p. 62.
32 N. Banescu, *Le Déclin de Famaguste: Fin du royaume de Chypre*, Bucharest: Institut Roumain d'Études Byzantines, 1946, pp. 87–96.
33 Kirshner, 'Moral problem – ', pp. 109–67. Kirshner, however, did not focus on the sovereign power of San Giorgio. He did not notice that the papal document mentioned it.
34 Marchi Van Cauwelaert, *La Corse génoise*.
35 A. Giustiniani, *Description de la Corse; préface, notes et traduction de Dialogo nominato Corsica de Antoine-Marie Graziani*, Ajaccio: Éditions Alain Piazzola, 1993.
36 M. Małowist, *Kaffa – kolonia genueńska na Krymie i problem wschodni w latach 1453–1475* [Caffa – Genoese colony in Crimea and the oriental question during the years 1453–1475], Warsaw: Towarzystwo Miłośników Historii, 1947, pp. xxvi–xxvii.

12
MARSEILLE
A supporting role

Thierry Pécout

Marseille has rich archives and yet, paradoxically, they have inspired only a small number of studies of its commercial activities and its outreach in the Middle Ages and early modern period.[1] A first synthesis dealt with these themes in the late 1940s, but it was based on old and fragmentary source publications, a biased body of judiciary sources, and focused on case studies. Moreover, it interpreted economic evolution as having had a close relationship with political events.[2] The works available in those days dealt with commercial techniques.[3] Since then, remarkable new interpretations have been proposed of Marseille's commercial structure since the thirteenth century, especially with regard to its position in the Levant,[4] and comparative studies have been started with the great ports of the western Mediterranean, especially with Genoa and Pisa.[5] New insights have been gained on the social groups involved in the exchanges, and on navigation techniques.[6] The main bulk of source material, however, has consisting of the notarial archives of the fourteenth to sixteenth centuries, has not yet been analysed systematically.[7] On the other hand, archaeological research has brought notable testimonies about the port infrastructure to the fore,[8] and the typological study of imported artefacts has provided indications about the city's exchanges and the technical models – in particular, ceramics originating from the production areas near Valencia, in Catalonia, and North Africa.[9]

The city and its political context

Provence has been open to exchanges since ancient times, and between 1300 and 1600 Marseille continued to be one of the main outlets for the trade on the Rhône going to or from the Mediterranean.[10] The city, however, never reached a central position, nor was it able to support its commercial development with a concomitant political outreach.[11] From 1265 onwards, Marseille, along with the counties of

Provence and Forcalquier, suffered political vicissitudes through their integration in the kingdom of Naples, and from 1481 onwards in the kingdom of France. It had been the count of Provence who gradually imposed the city's administrative unification, slowly progressing between 1252 and 1343. Several seigniorial domains divided the urban area: the lower parts consisted of a section originally ruled by viscounts whose rights had been bought off by the commune; the higher parts, under the rule of the bishop and the chapter; the Benedictine abbey of Saint Victor held the lordship of a suburban area. The lower city had achieved communal autonomy starting in the late twelfth century, first under consuls, then under a *podestà*, but it was submitted by Charles of Anjou (d. 1285), the count of Provence, between 1252 and 1262.

The social and economic elites succeeded in striking an alliance with the Angevin dynasty. Especially under Joan I (d. 1382), Queen of Sicily, they gained numerous judicial and commercial privileges in return for fiscal concessions and for resources from the maritime trade. A civil war at the end of the fourteenth century brought an urban oligarchy to power over the city, under the protection of Queen Marie de Blois of Sicily and her son Louis II (d. 1417). Until the beginnings of the early modern period, families prominent in commerce, finance, public offices and rural lordship ruled the city. As the royal court and the administration of the county of Provence were located in Aix, Marseille lacked the functions of a capital city and royal residence. Similarly, the papal court's residence in Avignon from 1309 till 1403 provided a commercial boost for Marseille that attracted Lombard and Tuscan banks, but nevertheless dispersed central functions in the region.[12]

Marseille was the great embarkation port for pilgrims and Crusaders in the years 1187–90, 1212, 1239 and 1248, and the nodal point for religious orders oriented towards the high sea: Templars, Hospitallers and then Trinitarians.[13] It became the war port under Count Charles II (d. 1309), and Robert of Anjou (d. 1343) around 1300, but the city was unable to grasp the full profit of its political links with Italy. Instead, it had to contribute financially in arms, shipbuilding and crews for the maritime operations against the crown of Aragon. And it had to pay a heavy price for the Angevin defeats in Sicily and the western Mediterranean.[14] Under these circumstances in the fourteenth century, Marseille's long-distance trade fell into a recession, contracting to the Angevin continental space, especially Naples, where Tuscans were active competitors. A new upward movement appeared towards the end of the century, which became a real boost only in the second half of the fifteenth and the early sixteenth.

A contrasting environment

The city, which was home to a little fewer than 20,000 inhabitants in the first half of the fourteenth century, went through a deep demographic recession.[15] The sixteenth century was marked by steep growth, which rose to around 40,000 people by 1600. The location offered evident advantages that had been exploited since its foundation, such as proximity to the delta on the east side of the Rhône valley, where a rocky section of the coast with deep waters was free from the streams causing silting further to the west (Figure 12.1). The port, on the low north bank of a creek, had storage and shops just opposite the landing stages, which facilitated transshipment. Marseille is situated in the middle of the west Mediterranean coastline, stretching from Catalonia along Liguria, and from Tuscany southwards to Sicily, including the islands. From that position on the margins of the spaces under the hegemonic power of Genovese, Catalans, royal France and Savoy, the city could control the coastal trade as well as the access to Alpine Provence through the Durance river and attract transshipment from the Rhône valley – in particular the grain trade from Arles, which was regulated by commercial agreements. All those assets might be combined favourably, but this potential did not turn out to be a decisive advantage vis-à-vis neighbouring ports, especially Montpellier.[16]

On the land side, Marseille was situated in coastal lowlands that were isolated by mountains from a part of the Provençal hinterland. It did have access to the central parts of the Provence through overland roads, which connected to the Durance valley leading to the highlands, to the Rhône valley, and to the land roads to Italy, either along the coast or through the Durance valley and the Alpine passes. The communal territory was defined in 1789 as measuring 23,000 hectares, which was only a fraction of the medieval *viguerie* (Latin *vicaria*), the local circumscription constituted since 1257. The urban judicial district was delimited between 1275 and 1294 with regard to commercial and fiscal disputes related to the ban on the import of foreign wines.[17] Marseille's hinterland produced a limited quantity of grain but was abundant in wines, which could be commercialized in the coastal trade and doubtless also in its overseas *fonduks*.[18] Marseille did not really control a *contado* because it did not develop into a largely autonomous commune, and the territory under its administration since the thirteenth century shrank considerably over the centuries.

Marseille's development was hampered by the presence of several competing commercial centres in the region. In the time of the commune, it held a truly seigniorial lordship over some small ports on the way eastward towards Liguria such as Toulon, Hyères and Nice, and thereafter remained well established there. Nothing similar occurred in the western direction. Arles was never more than a secondary *portus* on the Rhône; its elites remained bound to landed property. It did not become a maritime actor due to the difficult access through its relative terrestrial isolation, with the only bridge being in Avignon and Tarascon competing as the salt warehouse. The greatest impact, however, was that the Rhône was a political border. In Languedoc, under the French Capetian dynasty, Narbonne and later on Aigues Mortes profited from royal protection. They were situated at the outlet of production areas of textile and salt-making, and fertile grain-growing regions. The natural conditions were not really favourable in these two locations, due to silting-up of the access to the sea through coastal marshes, and the stern streams. Notwithstanding a relative decline during the fourteenth century, these two ports

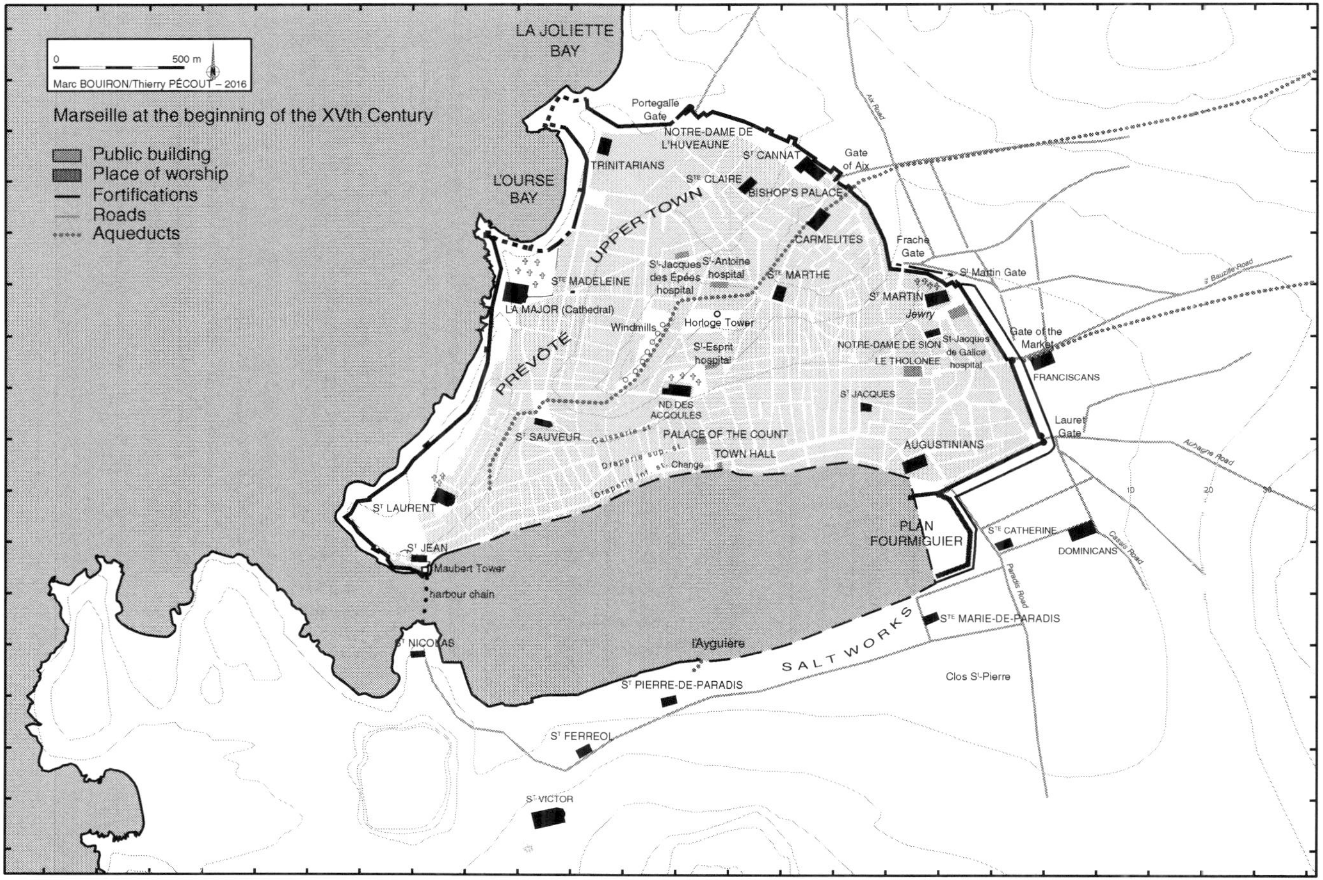

Figure 12.1 Map of the city and port of Marseille

profited from the presence of the papal court in Avignon and continued to attract Genoese and Tuscan merchants.

Most of all, Montpellier pursued circuits similar to those of Marseille: it was an outlet for the Champagne fairs in the thirteenth century, had settlements in the Levant, was a contact point for merchants from Pisa, Liguria and an out-port for papal Avignon.[19] Her access to the sea was anything but easy, via the out-port Lattes, the river Lez and the lake of Pérols. In contrast to Marseille, however, Montpellier's outreach was supported by a protecting and expanding political environment, such as the Catalan and Mallorcan rulers until 1349, and then the new overlords of the Capetian dynasty. Marseille was unable to impose itself in this fragmented political space. The papal settlement in Avignon stimulated various out-ports; among which Marseille just was the principal one, along with Montpellier, Saint-Chamas on the lake of Berre, and Bouc at its mouth to the sea. This dispersal was significant: Marseille was not a structuring core in the Low Rhône area; it was just an element caught in a highly competitive environment.

A hinterland?

No synthetic analysis has yet been made of the city's and its port's outreach into the continent. The seigniorial influence of the cathedral in the area would constitute a first indication. The domains of the abbey of St Victor extended far beyond the diocese since the eighth century, up to the Provençal highlands (the region of Digne); in the eleventh century they reached Catalonia up to Llobregat, the highlands of Languedoc, Gévaudan (the high valleys of the Lot and Tarn rivers), Sardinia (Cagliari) and Liguria (Genoa).[20] At the end of the eleventh century, the viscount's family reached its greatest expansion at the city's eastern side towards Toulon; and in the west, in the lower central Provence, bits and pieces as far as Arles.[21] Until 1252 the area in which the commune of Marseille could extend its political dominance as the heir of those rights consisted of only a small part, with essentially the coastal locales of Bouc, Hyères and Brégançon and *castra* securing access to the plains.[22] Only the abbey of St Victor was able to maintain its old seigniorial rights, while the city and its lords saw them significantly reduced before 1300 without establishing a lasting political dominance.

A substantial number of peasants lived in the city, in its immediate suburbs or in its territory. The great ecclesiastical institutions, however – the cathedral and the bishop, the abbey of St Victor, the military orders, and hospitals – held firmly onto important landed properties in the periphery, from which they received rents. They contributed significantly to capital-intensive investments in the surrounding countryside, fostering the intensification of production through the construction of irrigation systems, terrace cultivation, vineyards, orchards, mills, tools and, most of all, land clearance and parcelling.[23]

The city of Marseille's economic influence, however, was merely an imperfect substitute for its lack of political control. In the first place, urban merchants, including Jews, developed trades of ordinary textiles and agricultural products in the neighbouring villages to be sold to relatively well-to-do peasants and lords.[24] Jewish moneylenders provided small consumer credit in the region; they were linked by an intricate system of associations to wealthy Christian families in the city, who invested their capital through them.[25] This area extended to the west as far as until Salon and to Toulon in the east, within a radius of around 40 kilometres. This was probably the area of regular economic levying and redistribution of local or imported ordinary artisanal production.

Beyond that area of immediate influence, Marseille attracted specialized trades linked to the axes of the Rhône and Durance, consisting mainly of foodstuffs, the products of stockbreeding and textiles. It is possible that ceramics, produced or imported in Marseille, also belonged to this traffic. Its area extended primarily to the western high Provence (especially the Lubéron region), the high Dauphiné, the Rhône valley upstream to Valence, the Diois and part of Savoy. The butchers and furriers from Marseille found their raw materials there; external merchants came to Marseille to buy fish and cloth. Although these trades have not yet been studied in depth, especially not for the fourteenth century, it appears that small retail traders and moneylenders operated in this area, representing people who were not themselves involved in maritime trade.[26] Spruce-fir, beech and oak timber required for shipbuilding and other construction works were harvested in the high valley of the Durance.[27] Merchants from Marseille, however, were rarely present in the exchanges of salt and livestock that were essential to the inland Provence economy. The continuous circulation did not lead to close relations with the Provençal area. Marseilles traders did not establish long-lasting networks in the high Provence. They rarely took the most profitable royal taxes on lease, while people from Florence, Lucca and Siena were very active in this domain from the last decades of the thirteenth century.

In that same period, the city undeniably attracted people from the whole region. Two-thirds of the immigrants came from Provence and further away, in relatively equal numbers, from royal Languedoc, other regions of France and northern Italy. Most of them came to work in crafts related to maritime trade, fishery, coastal navigation and in domestic services.[28] Some pioneers were able to make a fortune and attain high social status. In the thirteenth century the Manduel family, originating from the region, rose to the status of navigation entrepreneurs and notables of the lower city in three generations. The Favas came from the Quercy and specialized in drapery and its long-distance trade in the fourteenth century. The Forbin family, from Bourgogne, started a shop and attained high offices by the end of the fifteenth century. The Palermo family came from Naples, and more modest people came from the kingdom of France.[29] The family names Temple and Jérusalem may refer to origins in the Holy Land. Apart from Italians, few immigrants came from other Mediterranean coasts, other than slaves bought on markets in Iberia, North Africa or Sicily, who were employed mostly in domestic services.

This immigration pattern reflects a form of dominance. Although great numbers of credit operations have been observed among merchants and artisans in Marseille, especially in the sector of consumption of goods, nothing like a Marseille bank existed.[30] Since the late thirteenth century, whenever the Angevin court needed massive money transfers, especially in the time that pontifical dimes had been ceded to them, it was the Spini and the Bardi who were mobilized to operate them.[31] The early presence of merchants from Piacenza, Asti and later on from Tuscany did not trigger the necessity of organizing local financial institutions.[32] The immigration of qualified entrepreneurs, factors and brokers demonstrates the attraction of the port and its activities, just as it reveals the lacunae in their financial structures. From the twelfth century more specialists arrived from the Iberian peninsula, especially Jews such as the Tibbonides from Granada. These were learned men who stimulated the intellectual activity of the Jewish community in Marseille and helped to consolidate the links with the maritime space from Bejaïa (Bougie) to Valencia.[33] In the fifteenth century, the withdrawal of the Anjou dynasty from Naples under the pressure of the Durazzo and then of the Aragonese, led numerous families based in the kingdom of Naples to pass through Marseille. This was typical for the city's hinterland, both from a commercial and a demographic viewpoint: discontinuity, weak structures and the overbearing nature of close relations that coexisted with specific migration streams.

Long-distance trade and economic activity

Inhabitants of Marseille never occupied a dominant position, not even in long-distance trade, which could therefore not outweigh its other structural weaknesses. There were surely favourable conditions, such as the creation of a minting workshop in 1185, which was confirmed in the treaty with Charles of Anjou in 1257 and allowed for the strike of local *gros* and *menu* coins, the royal *coronat*, and even *millares*, which were in fact imitations of Arab *dirhams*.[34] This mint remained in constant activity until 1551, even if its role faded away through the competition of other coins struck in Provence on behalf of the count, and later on behalf of the king.[35] After Charles of Anjou's conquest of the city, the juridical basis formulated in the statutes of 1253 and the peace articles of 1257 have been interpreted as fiscal and commercial privileges.[36] The reign of René of Anjou was particularly advantageous for Marseille's commerce: in 1455, the king renovated the treaty with Genoa, in 1447 he created two fairs in Marseille, and in 1472 he confirmed its commercial franchises and safe-conducts, including those for Muslims. In 1466 he created a commercial tribunal. Two judges would deal with litigation between merchants, first under the authority of the royal *viguier* (officer), and from 1475 onwards under that of the city itself.[37]

People from Marseille were interested in the Levant in a very early stage, as shown in Raymond of Saint-Gilles' 1103 grant of a section of Djebaïl to the monks of St Victor, even if it remained without consequence. From the early thirteenth century, Marseille was the redistribution centre for continental merchandise over long distances, primarily textiles from Flanders and Artois,[38] the fairs of Provins, Lendit and Chalons, Languedoc and Roussillon (Narbonne and Elne). Their redistribution trade was diversified, not specialized. Imports included products related to the textile industry (alum, scarlet, indigo, kermès), the fell-trade (leather from Cordoba, various fells), and spices (pepper, ginger, muscat, clove, saffron and sugar). Grain, fish and wax were bought, as were raw materials such as coral, timber and metals, slaves, and manufactured products, including cloth of various qualities, linen and, more rarely, silk and precious tissues, and processed coral.

Merchants from Marseille provisioned a continental region extending from the fairs of Beaucaire to the region of Albi,[39] the fairs of Champagne and those of Lendit in Saint-Denis. Some of these merchants appeared in English sources in the 1240s, but this space was not structured into a set of Marseillais networks, as most of the travellers were strangers to the city. They went there to trade and even to invest in parts of cargoes or ships, but they did not build a truly integrated hinterland. Similarly, merchants or shippers from Marseille did not directly sail into the Atlantic or North Sea spaces. In this respect, Marseille was not a central place: it participated in circuits but didn't dominate them, as it didn't control the circulation of capital and information. This was exemplified by the long predominance of the *comanda* as a commercial and financing technique, the late emergence and narrow scope of associations, the scarcity of practices such as maritime loan, the reinvestment of commercial surpluses in land and lordships, and the weak credit capacities as compared to the Lombard and Tuscan competitors.

Therefore, there is a need to reassess the predominance in the urban economy of commercial activities linked to the open sea.[40] The agricultural production of Marseille's territory and doubtless also the stockbreeding certainly remained below the city's nutritional needs. Therefore, grain provisions had to be sought in the space from Sardinia to Sicily, along the coasts of Languedoc and Catalonia, in Arles, and, in the fourteenth century, even in Apulia.[41] The urban economy also leaned heavily on the very active artisanal sector, which was included in communal life from a very early stage onwards and was unique in Provence. Craftsmen had access to credit and some of their products were exported over long distances.[42] This was particularly the case for coral processed both by Christians and Jews. Fishermen from Marseille collected it near Sardinia and brought it to the continent, Provence and maritime trading posts; after processing it was sold from there to Morocco and, in the fifteenth century, to Alexandria.[43] Coral workers from Marseille were active in Naples in the fourteenth century. A specialized company, to be active in Annaba (on the coast of present-day Algeria), was founded in 1552 with the participation of the most prominent families. On a more modest level, some of the leather skins imported to the city, the *cordouans*, were processed on the spot. Small enterprises coexisted and flourished with larger ones, though without a true integration occurring.[44] The dynamism of the Jewish community, which was fully integrated in urban society and largely linked to the *aljamas* in the Iberian lands and North Africa, may be characteristic for the manifold agencies of their Christian homologues as well. They focused on artisanal production, moneylending and investments as mediators for Christian capital owners, but also on landed property.[45] It was the variety of activities that helped the city to overcome the deep and lasting depressions of the long-distance trade in the fourteenth century.

The commercial techniques applied by the merchants of Marseille have attracted historians' attention from an early stage onwards and were considered as typical features of technical advancement. This concerned the capacity to form a juridical framework stimulating the mobilization of capital, and to split benefits and risks in ways favouring the owner at the expense of the navigating merchant. Further themes were the creation of trust and networks that facilitated the circulation of information, and the methods to transfer funds. The focus fell on the familiarity with emblematic instruments of financial transactions such as the bill of exchange.[46] The merchants of Marseille remained attached to fragile practices for a long time, and their financial constructions were modest. The *comanda* was dominant during most of the thirteenth century.[47] This did not so much reflect a delayed development as it did the adaptation of local capitalistic methods to operations, most of which were moderate in size. For larger affairs, the Angevin dynasty and the Avignonese papacy attracted and perpetuated the intervention of exterior expertise in Provence.

The maritime network

The activity of the port of Marseille can be observed only from the very end of the twelfth century. Frequent relations were developed with Sicily (Messina) under Frederick II's protection, with Ifriqiya (Bejaïa and Ceuta in particular) starting in the Almohad period, and with the Balearic islands after their conquest by Christians. There is mention of a consul in Bejaïa starting in 1220, and of another one in Ceuta starting in 1228. This reflected the core of Marseille's maritime activity. A place of pride was further held by coastal navigation between the ports of the Rhône delta such as Arles and Avignon, the Beaucaire fairs, and the coast of Provence from Bouc to Nice, passing by Toulon, Hyères and Cannes.[48] This activity is connected with navigation on longer distances focused on the western Mediterranean. Hyères and Toulon were important ports for salt trade, and Nice was a contact zone with the Genoese. Merchants from the north were met in the locations on the Rhône, and the papal court at Avignon boosted the trade in luxury products such as silk, pigments, precious metals and paper (Figure 12.2).

Among the more distant maritime destinations, the most frequent contacts were with the coasts of Languedoc and Catalonia, the Baleares, Sardinia, Sicily and the kingdom of Naples, and North Africa with Bejaïa and Annaba.[49] In 1230, King James I of Aragon (d. 1276) granted the commune a settlement with extended land on Mallorca that became the basis of Marseille's expansion to the coasts of Morocco and Ifriqiya. A *fonduk* of Marseille, under Almohad and Hafsid rule,[50] is mentioned in Bejaïa starting in 1220; those in Ceuta, Wahrân and Tunis followed in 1228.

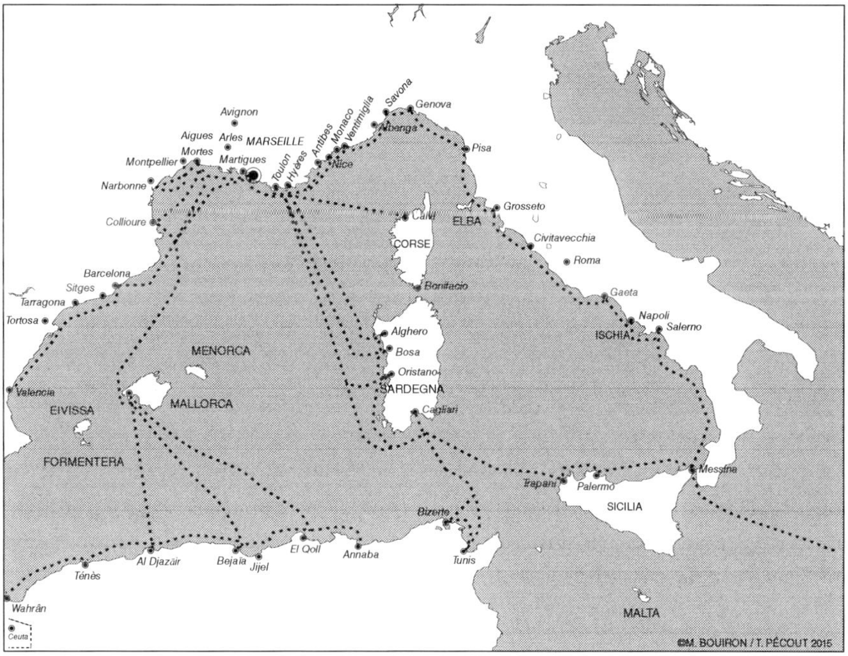

Figure 12.2 Marseille's main connections in the western Mediterranean

The one in Bejaïa, whose consul was appointed by the commune, and later by the Angevin prince and his *viguier* in Marseille, included an office of scribes, storage and abodes, artisan's shops, a tavern, and a St Peter's chapel.[51] Local Jews in Bejaïa and Tunis who were in contact with their co-religionists in Provence participated in the local trade with the Marseillais. The latter were also intensively active in Ceuta, where the routes along the Atlantic coasts ended at Nifé.[52] These must have been the most profitable routes, as we can see from the great quantities of ceramics imported from Valencia, Málaga, the Catalan coast, and Bejaïa that were found in the suburbs of Marseille.[53] In turn, local artisans were inspired by their design models and baking techniques. While the Baleares functioned as a bridge-head towards North Africa, Sardinia had very different roles. Until the 1360s, the Marseillais fishermen and merchants were regularly there to harvest coral and to buy various foodstuffs – mainly cereals, salt, wine, and oil. They were nearly entirely absent from Corsica and the Adriatic was closed for them, but they were present along the peninsula's entire west coast, from Savona to Messina. It appears as if the Marseillais elites saw their close alliance with the Angevin princes as a source of considerable profit. One can have doubts, however, about the long-term effects of their relations with the kingdom of Naples. They were surely beneficial for the provisioning of cereals and profitable for the export of wine, but in the fourteenth century the Marseillais elites remained far behind their Genoese and Tuscan competitors in that region.

Marseille's maritime ambitions were concentrated in their projects to create commercial settlements in the oriental Mediterranean. In the 1180s these were developed in Tyre, then in Acre and, in the beginning of the thirteenth century, even in Alexandria, along with many merchants from Languedoc and Italy. They were in Limassol and Famagusta on Cyprus, the essential crossroads and stopping-place. Provençal commanderies of the military orders were established there from the 1230s. Later on, Rhodes would attract these emanations of the crusading spirit and the appetite for profit.[54] In the years 1247–50 the commune went as far as forging charters to underpin their claims to the exploitation of trading settlements and *fonduks* in Acre, Tyre and Jerusalem.[55] From the 1230s onwards, leading families such as Gasqui, Jerusalem and Temple grasped the opportunities of the Levantine trade towards Acre, Tyre and Cyprus, but their expansion was limited by the competition of Italians and people from Montpellier.[56] Bankers from Asti and Piacenza provided the financing for this first Levantine boost. Saffron was shipped along with coral and cloth. After the evacuation of Acre, connections continued in the north of the Levant at Ayas (Yumurtalik) and were then reinstated by the end of the fourteenth century with the *fonduk* in Alexandria.

In the fifteenth century, Marseille strengthened its links with the kingdom of France, as it appears from the activities of King Charles VII's grand treasurer Jacques Coeur and his factor in Marseille, Jean de Village, who also enjoyed the protection of King René of Anjou, count of Provence. From 1440 to 1451, Jacques Coeur chose Marseille as the basis of his Mediterranean operations, keeping four ships there for the export of Flemish cloth, baskets, linen from Lyon, and the direct import of spices and perfumes, thus bypassing the Italian intermediaries. He also invested in the lease of municipal and royal taxes and in real estate.[57] In the next century, from at least 1569 onwards, the trading posts erected in the Levant, Beyrouth, Tripoli and Alexandria confirmed the continuity of these links thanks to the excellent relations between France and the Ottoman empire.

Marseille was confronted with insuperable obstacles that kept it in a supporting role. There had always been regional competition and the city was unable to impose itself as the unique contact point for the merchants from Genoa and Pisa or the Tuscan bankers.[58] The Genoese hampered Marseille's consolidation in Sicily, notwithstanding the privileges granted by Frederick II that allowed their people to settle in Syracuse and Messina. Finally, the Aragonese chased them from there. The Genoese were present in Provence with their currency and traders at Marseille's gates – in Nice, Hyères and Toulon. The Catalans waged war with the Angevins, which made life difficult for all Provençals in the fourteenth and fifteenth centuries.[59] The routes to Sardinia were no longer sure and coral fishing became dangerous. Francesco Balducci Pegolotti noted around 1340 that Marseillais were settled in the suburbs of Pera, in Constantinople, in Acre, Famagusta, in Sicily and Apulia, Florence, Pisa and Genoa.[60] At that time, however, Marseille's population probably was far inferior to that of Montpellier, which, like its Catalan overlords (until 1349), had diversified its connections from Cilicia, to the Levant and

Morocco. The decline of the Champagne fairs deeply affected the trade on the Rhône from the middle of the fourteenth century onwards, which severely perturbed the Marseillais trade with Flanders and the Parisian region. In all likelihood, the requests for exemption from circulation taxes, granted by Queen Joan in 1366 and Queen Marie de Blois in 1386 and 1387, were signs of a partial withdrawal of activities to the Provençal area nearby.[61]

The Marseillais trade couldn't generate sufficient surplus and their commercial techniques remained for a long time far inferior in comparison to those of the Genoese, Pisans, Sienese and others. Its port was one of fishermen, maritime entrepreneurs, merchants and Christian moneylenders linked to the local Jewish elites by complex credit circuits. They looked for profitable investments in shipping-trade and long-distance exchanges, but did not create banks or launch large financial transactions. That business remained the domain of men from Piacenza, Siena, Lucca and Pistoia who played that role for the Angevin monarchy, the papacy and for the Marseillais themselves from the thirteenth century. The fairs of Lyon stimulated new economic growth in the fifteenth century, and from 1481 the role of military port was oriented towards Italy or served as the gate to the Ottoman empire. However, none of these opportunities proved sufficient to elevate the merchants of Marseille above their traditional secondary position vis-à-vis the Venetians and Genoese for whom they continued to serve as brokers in the spice trade in the sixteenth century.[62] This relative retreat also revealed a capacity to integrate into the networks of the great commercial actors. This aptitude for connectivity doubtless constituted the predominant asset of the Marseillais merchants.

Notes

1 R.-H. Bautier and J. Sornay, *Les sources de l'histoire économique et sociale du Moyen Âge, vol. 1, Provence, Comtat Venaissin, Dauphiné, États de la maison de Savoie, vol. 2, Archives ecclésiastiques, communales et notariales. Archives des marchands et des particuliers,* Paris: CNRS Éd., 1971, pp. 983–9, 1213–32, 1392–5.

2 For the thirteenth century, pride of place was given to the fund of the Manduel family, issued from a judiciary proceeding, and to the first notary's register of 1248. R. Busquet and R. Pernoud, *Histoire du commerce de Marseille*, vol. 1, *L'Antiquité, le Moyen Âge jusqu'en 1291*, Paris: Plon, 1949; É. Baratier and F. Reynaud, *Histoire du commerce de Marseille*, vol. 2, *De 1291 à 1481*, Paris: Plon, 1951; J. Billioud, *Histoire du commerce de Marseille*, vol. 3, Paris: Plon, 1951, pp. 169–563; the introduction to the first volume presents a brief historiographical overview to be completed by G. Lesage, *Marseille angevine: Recherches sur son évolution administrative, économique et urbaine, de la victoire de Charles d'Anjou à l'arrivée de Jeanne Ire (1264–1348)*, Paris: E. de Boccard, 1950; L. Blancard, *Documents inédits sur le commerce de Marseille au Moyen Âge: Contrats commerciaux du XIIIe siècle*, Marseille: Barlatier-Feissat, 1884–5.

3 L. Blancard, 'Note sur la lettre de change à Marseille au XIIIe siècle', *Bibliothèque de l'École des chartes* 39, 1878, pp. 110–28; A.-E. Sayous, 'L'activité de deux capitalistes commerçants marseillais du XIIIe siècle: Bernard de Manduel (1227–1237) et Jean de Manduel (1233–1263)', *Revue d'histoire économique et sociale* 17, 1929, pp. 137–55; 'Le commerce de Marseille avec la Syrie au milieu du XIIIe siècle', *Revue des études historiques* 95/4, 1929,

pp. 391–408; 'Le commerce terrestre de Marseille au XIIIe siècle', *Revue historique* 1930, pp. 27–50; 'Les opérations du capitaliste et commerçant marseillais Étienne de Manduel entre 1200 et 1230', *Revue des questions historiques* 16, 1930, pp. 5-29; 'Les transferts de risques, les associations commerciales et la lettre de change à Marseille pendant le XIVe siècle', *Revue historique de droit français et étranger* 1935, pp. 469–94.

4 D. Abulafia, 'Marseilles, Acre and the Mediterranean, 1200–1291', in P. W. Edburry and D. M. Metcalf (eds), *Coinage in the Latin East*, Oxford: Oxford University Press, 1980, pp. 19–39.

5 G. Jehel, *Les Génois en Méditerranée occidentale (fin XIe–début XIVe siècle): Ébauche d'une stratégie pour un empire*, Amiens: Centre d'histoire des sociétés, Université de Picardie, 1993; E. Salvatori, *Boni amici et vicini: Le relazioni tra Pisa e le città della Francia meridionale dall'xi alla fine del XIII secolo*, Pisa: ETS, 2002; G. Airaldi, 'Genoa and Barcelona: two hypotheses for a "global" world', in R. Gertwagen and E. M. Jeffreys (eds), *Shipping, Trade and Crusade in the Medieval Mediterranean: Studies in Honour of John Pryor*, Farnham and Burlington, VT: Ashgate, 2012, pp. 223–9.

6 H. Villard, 'Jean Casse, armateur et marchand marseillais du XIVe siècle: Sa maison, son comptoir, sa bastide', *Annales de la Société d'Études provençales* 4, 1907, pp. 73–117; H. Villard, 'Un médecin du roi Robert de Naples, négociant à Marseille au XIVe siècle', *Bulletin officiel du Musée du Vieux Marseille* 1934, pp. 82–90; D. Hauck, *Das Kaufmannsbuch des Johann Blasi (1329–1337)*, doctoral thesis, Saarbrücken, 1965; C. Maurel, 'Structures familiales et solidarités lignagères à Marseille au XVe siècle: autour de l'ascension sociale des Forbin', *Annales ESC* 41–3, 1986, pp. 657–81; C. Barnel, 'Les boutiques des frères Favas, drapiers et draperie à Marseille au XIVe siècle, *Provence historique* 49, 1999, pp. 61–78; 'Les Favas, une famille de drapiers de la Marseille angevine, 1302–1473', *Provence historique* 39, 1989, pp. 367–83; D. Carraz, 'Les Lengres à Marseille au XIVe siècle: les activités militaires d'une famille d'armateurs dans un port de croisade', *Revue historique* 2009/4, pp. 755–77; R. K. Berlow, 'The sailing of the "Saint Esprit"', *Journal of Economic History* 39/2, 1979, pp. 345–62; J.-V. Murat, 'Les routes et les périodes de navigation au XIVe siècle à travers les sources marseillaises', *Neptunia* 229, 2003, pp. 40–5.

7 The judiciary sources connected to the notarial archives have been studied recently from the viewpoint of social relations, the relation to space and conflict regulation; information about commerce is scattered in these works: D. L. Smail, 'Common violence: vengeance and inquisition in fourteenth-century Marseille', *Past and Present* 151, 1996, pp. 28–59; Smail, 'Démanteler le patrimoine: les femmes et les biens dans la Marseille médiévale', *Annales: Histoire, sciences sociales* 52, 1997, pp. 343–68; Smail, 'Notaries, courts and the legal culture of late medieval Marseille', in K. Reyerson and J. Drendel (eds), *Urban and Rural Communities in Medieval France, Provence and Languedoc, 1000–1500*, Leiden: Brill, 1998, pp. 23–50; Smail, *Imaginary Cartographies: Possession and Identity in Late Medieval Marseille*, Ithaca, NY: Cornell University Press, 2000; Smail, *The Consumption of Justice: Emotions, Publicity and Legal Culture in Marseille, 1264–1423*, London: Rodopi, 2003. S. A. McDonough, *Witnesses, Neighbors, and Community in Late Medieval Marseille*, New York: Palgrave Macmillan, 2013. This attraction for representations and social history, inspired by the approach of historical anthropology, is characteristic of an entire generation of intellectuals; as a consequence, economic and commercial history became less popular.

8 R. Pernoud, 'Essai sur l'histoire du port de Marseille, des origines à la fin du XIIIe siècle', PhD thesis at the Université de Paris, Marseille, 1935; X. Corré, 'L'activité du port de Marseille dans l'Antiquité. Modélisation à partir de l'analyse des sources antiques, médiévales et modernes', PhD thesis in archaeology, Université d'Aix-Marseille, 2009 (manuscript).

9 On the still partial results of many years of excavations: M. Bouiron (ed.), *L'Alcazar, 26 siècles d'occupation suburbaine à Marseille,* Document final de synthèse, Marseille, 2001; M. Bouiron (ed.), *Marseille, du Lacydon au faubourg Sainte-Catherine (Ve s. av. J.-C.–XVIIIe s.): Les*

fouilles de la place Général-de-Gaulle, Paris: Éd. de la Maison des sciences de l'homme, 2001; M. Bouiron and H. Tréziny (eds), *Marseille, trames et paysages urbains de Gyptis au roi René: Actes du colloque international d'archéologie, Marseille, 3–5 novembre 1999,* Études massaliètes, 7, Aix-en-Provence: Édisud, 2001, pp. 13–20; C. Barra, M. Guillaume, O. Maufras, B. Vasselin and C. Voyez, *Les fouilles archéologiques du tunnel de la Major à Marseille (Bouches-du-Rhône)*, Document final de synthèse, fouille d'archéologie préventive, INRAP, 2004; M. Bouiron, F. Paone, B. Sillano, C. Castrucci and N. Scherrer (eds), *Fouilles à Marseille: Approche de la ville médiévale et moderne*, Paris: Éd. Errance, 2011.

10 H. Bresc, 'La Provence médiévale: L'horizon d'un Orient romanesque', *La pensée de midi* 1, 2000, pp. 12–19.

11 Th. Pécout, 'Évêques et identités urbaines dans les cités des comtés de Provence et Forcalquier (XIIe–fin XIIIe siècle)', in P. Gilli and E. Salvatori (eds), *Les identités urbaines au Moyen Âge: Regards sur les villes du Midi français,* Turnhout: Brepols, 2014, pp. 129–46.

12 V.-L. Bourrilly, *Essai sur l'histoire politique de la commune de Marseille, des origines à la victoire de Charles d'Anjou (1264)*, Aix-en-Provence: A. Dragon, 1925; C. Maurel, 'Fractures et renouveau d'un organisme urbain médiéval: la société marseillaise à l'épreuve du sac des Aragonais (1423)', in C. Dolan (ed.), *Événement, identité, histoire*, Québec: Sillery & Septentrion, 1991, pp. 39–63; Maurel, 'Pouvoir royal et pouvoir municipal (XIVe–XVe siècle)', in T. Pécout (ed.), *Marseille au Moyen Âge: Les horizons d'une ville portuaire*, Méolans: Éd. Désiris, 2009, pp. 225–31; T. Pécout, 'Pourquoi Marseille ne fut-elle jamais capitale?', in É. Malamut and M. Ouerfelli (eds), *Villes méditerranéennes au Moyen Âge*, Aix-en-Provence: Presses Universitaires de Provence, 2014, pp. 101–20.

13 D. Carraz, 'Les commanderies dans l'espace urbain: Templiers et Hospitaliers dans les villes de l'Occident méditerranéen (XIIe–XIIIe siècle)', in C. Caby (ed.), 'Espaces monastiques et espaces urbains de l'Antiquité tardive à la fin du Moyen Âge', *Mélanges de l'École française de Rome – Moyen Âge* 124/1, 2012, pp. 119–36; Carraz, *L'ordre du Temple dans la basse vallée du Rhône (1124–1312) : Ordres militaires, croisades et sociétés méridionales*, Lyon: Presses Universitaires de Lyon, 2005; G. Cipollone, *La casa de la santa Trinità di Marsiglia (1202–1547): Prima fondazione sul mare dell'ordine trinitario*, Vatican City: Typis Polyglottis Vaticanis, 1981.

14 Malta, Naples, Nicotera and the Formigues Islands before the Catalan coast: H. Bresc, 'Marseille dans la guerre des Vêpres siciliennes', in I. Bonnot (ed.), *Marseille et ses rois de Naples: La diagonale angevine, 1265–1382*, Aix-en-Provence: Presses Universitaires de Provence, 1988, pp. 43–9.

15 No information at all is available about the impact of the plague of 1347 in Marseille; more is known about the 1361 outbreak in the Provence.

16 K. Reyerson, *Business, Banking and Finance in Medieval Montpellier,* Toronto: Pontifical Institute of Mediaeval Studies, 1985, demonstrates the intermediary role played by the Montpellier financial market from the late thirteenth to the first decades of the fourteenth century.

17 T. Pécout, 'Marseille: une ville et son territoire, XIe–XIVe siècle', in É. Malamut and M. Ouerfelli (eds), *Villes en Méditerranée au Moyen Âge et à l'époque moderne, 24–27 septembre 2014, colloque international de Marseille et Aix-en-Provence, MUCEM et Université d'Aix-Marseille*, Aix-en-Provence: Presses Universitaires de Provence, 2016 (forthcoming).

18 J. Billioud, 'Le *vignoble marseillais*, du XIIIe siècle à l'adduction des eaux de la Durance (1847)', *Provence historique* 6, 1956, pp. 166–185; É. Baratier, 'Production et exportation du vin du terroir de Marseille du XIIIe au XVIe siècle', *Bulletin philologique et historique du Comité des travaux historiques et scientifiques,* 1959 (Paris, 1960), pp. 239–49.

19 The Languedoc ports were discussed in several contributions to F. Fabre, D. Le Blévec and D. Menjot (eds), *Les ports et la navigation en Méditerranée au Moyen Âge: Colloque de Lattes 2004,* Lattes: Éd. Le Manuscrit, 2009.

20 É. Baratier, 'La fondation et l'étendue du temporel de l'abbaye de Saint-Victor de Marseille', *Provence historique*, 1966, pp. 395–441; 'Les prieurés sardes de Saint-Victor de Marseille',

in F. Artizzu *et al.* (eds), *Studi sui Vittorini in Sardegna*, Padua: CEDAM, 1967, pp. 13–22; M. Lauwers, 'Réforme, romanisation, colonisation? Les moines de Saint-Victor de Marseille en Sardaigne (seconde moitié du XIe s.–première moitié XIIe siècle)', in *Cahiers de Fanjeaux* 48, *La réforme 'grégorienne' dans le Midi (milieu XIe–début XIIIe siècle)*, Toulouse: Privat, 2013, pp. 257–310; J. Belmon, 'Les débuts d'un prieuré victorin en Gévaudan: Le Monastier-Chirac (XIe–XIIe siècles)', *Bibliothèque de l'École des chartes*, 152, 1994, pp. 5–90.

21 F. Mazel, 'Les vicomtes de Marseille', in Pécout, *Marseille au Moyen Âge,* pp. 145–66.

22 Saint-Marcel, Allauch, Aubagne: Bourrilly, *Essai sur l'histoire politique*, pp. 118–21.

23 Pécout, 'Marseille: une ville et son territoire'.

24 Aubagne, Ceyreste, Gémenos, Roquevaire, Gardanne, La Ciotat, Le Castellet, La Cadière, Le Beausset, Auriol, Cassis, Trets.

25 J. Shatzmiller, *Shylock Reconsidered: Jews, Moneylending and Medieval Society*, Berkeley, CA: University of California Press, 1989; J. Sibon, 'Le crédit et l'entreprise des juifs à Marseille après la Peste noire (1348)', *Entreprises et histoire* 52, 2008, pp. 27–35; Sibon, *Les Juifs de Marseille au XIVe siècle*, Paris: Les Editions du Cerf, 2011, pp. 60–86; Sibon, 'Bondavin revisité. Le prêteur juif de Marseille Bondavin de Draguignan (*ca.* 1285–1361), suite et fin', *Le Moyen Âge* 118, 2013, pp. 641–59.

26 Jean Blaise (d. 1337) seems to represent this type: Hauck, *Das Kaufmannsbuch des Johann Blasi;* N. Coulet, 'Le livre de raison d'un marchand: Jean Blaise, c. 1329–1337', Pécout, *Marseille au Moyen Âge,* pp. 275–7.

27 J. V. Murat, 'Charpentiers et travailleurs du bois: les artisans de la construction navale', Pécout, *Marseille au Moyen Âge,* pp. 267–70.

28 F. Michaud, 'Travail et mouvements migratoires avant et après la peste noire à Marseille', *Provence historique* 49, 1999, *De Provence et d'ailleurs: Mélanges offerts à Noël Coulet*, pp. 367–83; 'From apprentices to wage-earners: child labour before and after the Black Death', in J. Rosenthal (ed.), *Essays on Medieval Childhood: Responses to Recent Debates*, Donington, Lincs.: Shaun Tyas, 2007, pp. 75–92.

29 É. Baratier, 'Les avitailleurs de nefs immigrés français à Marseille au XIIIe siècle', in *France du Nord et France du Midi: Contacts et influences réciproques. Actes du 96e Congrès des sociétés savantes (Toulouse, 1971). Section philologie et histoire*, 1, Paris: Comité des Travaux historiques et scientifiques, 1978, pp. 429–54.

30 Sibon, *Les Juifs de Marseille*, pp. 60–86.

31 K. Toomaspoeg, *Decimae: Il sostegno economico dei sovrani alla Chiesa del Mezzogiorno nel XIII secolo. Dai lasciti di Eduard Sthamer e Norbert Kamp*, Rome: Viella, 2009, pp. 71–83; Toomaspoeg, 'L'Église et la fiscalité au royaume de Sicile (XIe–XIVe siècles)', in D. Menjot and M. Sànches Martìnez (eds), *El dinero de Dios. Iglesia y fiscalidad en el Occidente medieval (siglos XIII–XV)*, Madrid: Instituto de Estudios Fiscales, 2011, pp. 91–100; A. Leroux, 'Mise en place des collecteurs et des collectories dans le royaume de France et en Provence (1316–1378)', in *Lusitana sacra, O papado de Avinhão nos reinos do Ocidente* 22, 2010, pp. 45–62; 'Des collecteurs spécialisés aux collecteurs généralistes, l'établissement du système collectoral en Provence (1249–1514)', in J. Morello Baget (ed.), *Financiar el reino terrenal. La contribución de la Iglesia a finales de la Edad Media (s. XIII–XVI),* Barcelona: Consejo Superior de Investigaciones Científicas, 2013, pp. 107–29.

32 P. Racine, 'A Marseille en 1248: l'activité des hommes d'affaire de Plaisance', *Annales du Midi*, 1966, pp. 221–33; J. Hayez, 'Pratiques et discours de marchands migrants : Les Toscans d'Avignon aux XIVe et XVe siècles', in C. Quertier, R. Chilà and N. Pluchot (eds), *Arriver en ville: Les migrants en milieu urbain au Moyen Âge*, Paris: Publications de la Sorbonne, 2013, pp. 225–41.

33 C. Denjean and J. Sibon, 'Pratiques des hommes d'affaires juifs en Méditerranée occidentale au XIVe siècle', *Archives juives* 47, 2014, pp. 10–28.

34 L. Blancard, *Le Millarès, étude sur une monnaie imitée de l'arabe par les chrétiens pour les besoins de leur commerce en pays maure*, Marseille: Barlatier-Feissat, 1876.
35 L. Blancard, *Essai sur les monnaies de Charles Ier comte de Provence*, Paris, 1868, pp. 166–7; H. Rolland, *Les monnaies des comtes de Provence. XIIe–XVe siècles: Histoire monétaire, économique et corporative. Description raisonnée*, Paris: Libr. de J. B. Dumoulin, 1956.
36 R. Pernoud, *Les statuts municipaux de Marseille,* Monaco and Paris: Archives du palais, 1949; Bourrilly, *Essai sur l'histoire politique*; P. Chastang and F. Otchakovsky-Laurens, 'Les statuts urbains de Marseille: acteurs, rhétorique et mise par écrit de la norme', in D. Lett (ed.), *La confection des statuts: Les acteurs de la norme dans les sociétés de la Méditerranée occidentale à la fin du Moyen Âge (XIIe–XVe siècle), colloque de Rome, 26–27 juin 2014*, Paris: École française de Rome, forthcoming.
37 M. Zarb, *Les privilèges de la ville de Marseille du Xe siècle à la Révolution*, Paris: A. et J. Picard & Cie, 1961.
38 From Ypres, Bruges, Saint-Quentin, Arras, Douai and Cambrai.
39 C. de Gourcy, *La foire de Beaucaire*, Montpellier: Firmin et Montane, 1911; M. Contestin, *La foire de Beaucaire, un grand marché européen*, Montpellier: Les Presses du Languedoc, 1995.
40 Abulafia, 'Marseilles, Acre and the Mediterranean'.
41 G. Lesage, 'Les difficultés du ravitaillement de Marseille en blé au XIVe siècle', *Bulletin officiel du musée du vieux Marseille* 56, 1938–1941, pp. 3–6; L. Stouff, *Ravitaillement et alimentation en Provence aux XIVe et XVe siècles*, Paris: Mouton, 1970; 'Nourrir la ville, XIIIe–XVe siècle', in Pécout, *Marseille au Moyen Âge,* pp. 239–46; L. Stouff, 'Arles et Marseille dans les derniers siècles du Moyen Âge', *Marseille* 117, 1979, pp. 82–9.
42 J. Billioud, 'De la confrérie à la corporation: les classes industrielles en Provence aux XIVe, XVe et XVIe siècles', *Mémoires de l'Institut historique de Provence*, 6, 1929, pp. 235–71; 7, 1930, pp. 5–35; E. Brin, 'Le corps et communauté des patrons pêcheurs de Marseille, des origines à la Révolution', Thesis of the l'École nationale des chartes, 1942 (manuscript); M. Dupanloup, 'La corporation des cuiratiers à Marseille dans la première moitié du XIVe siècle', *Provence historique* 29, 1969, pp. 189–213; F. Michaud, *Un signe des temps: Accroissement des crises familiales autour du patrimoine à Marseille à la fin du XIIIe siècle*, Toronto: Pontifical Institute of Mediaeval Studies, 1994; D. L. Smail, 'La topographie socio-professionnelle de Marseille au XIVe siècle', in Bouiron and Tréziny, *Marseille, trames et paysages urbains*, pp. 307–16.
43 H. Bresc, 'Pêche et commerce du corail en Méditerranée de l'Antiquité au Moyen Âge', *Scienze e materiali del patrimonio culturale* 5, Bari, 2000, pp. 41–53; Sibon, *Les Juifs de Marseille*, pp. 100–67; 'Les corailleurs juifs', in Pécout, *Marseille au Moyen Âge,* pp. 279–87.
44 The families in the coral company were the Forbin, Riquetti, Leche, Cabre and Albertas: C. Maurel, 'Grands marchands et "petites et moyennes industries" à Marseille au bas Moyen Âge (1350–1480)', in *Le Marchand au Moyen Âge, 19e Congrès de la Société des Historiens médiévistes de l'Enseignement supérieur public*, Paris: Saint-Herblain, 1991, pp. 105–12.
45 I. Loeb, 'Les négociants juifs à Marseille au milieu du xiiie siècle', *Revue des études juives* 16, 1888, pp. 73–83; M. Schwab, 'Livre des comptes de Mardoché Joseph (manuscrit hébréo-provençal)', *Notices et extraits de manuscrits de la Bibliothèque Nationale et autres bibliothèques* 39, Paris, 1913, pp. 1–38; A. Crémieux, 'Les Juifs de Marseille au Moyen âge', *Revue des Études juives* 46, 1903, pp. 1–47, 246–68; 47, 1903, 62–82, 243–61; Sibon, *Les Juifs de Marseille*, pp. 33–223.
46 L. Blancard, 'Note sur la lettre de change à Marseille au XIIIe siècle', *Bibliothèque de l'École des chartes* 39, 1878, pp. 110–28.
47 J. H. Pryor, 'Commenda: the operation of the contract in long distance commerce at Marseilles during the thirteenth century', *Journal of Economic European History* 13, 1984, pp. 397–440; Pryor, 'Mediterranean commerce in the Middle Ages: a voyage under contract of *commenda*', *Viator* 14, 1983, pp. 133–94; *Business Contracts of Medieval Provence: Selected*

Notulae from the Cartulary of Giraud Amalric of Marseilles 1248, Toronto: Pontifical Institute of Mediaeval Studies, 1981; Pryor, *Commerce, Shipping and Naval Warfare in the Medieval Mediterranean*, London: Variorum Reprints, 1987; Pryor, 'The commenda in Mediterranean maritime commerce during the thirteenth century: a study based on Marseilles', PhD dissertation, Toronto, 1974.

48 J.-V. Murat, 'Pratiques et succès du cabotage en Méditerranée nord-occidentale au xive siècle', *Rives nord-méditerranéennes* 13, 2003, *Cabotage et réseaux portuaires (xve–xixe siècle)*, pp. 23–32; Murat, 'Le *conservagium* en Méditerranée', in *Stations navales et navigations organisées en Méditerranée, Actes du Colloque de Toulon des 12, 13 et 14 septembre 2002, Société Française d'Histoire Maritime*, Marseille: Éditions de la Nerthe, 2004, pp. 123–33. On the port of Nice, see A. Venturini, 'Nice et Villefranche: ville et plage, *castrum* et port (fin X^{e}–fin XIVe siècle)', in J.-A. Cancellieri and V. Marchi Van Cauwelaert (eds), *Villes portuaires de Méditerranée occidentale au Moyen Âge: Iles et continents, XIIe–XVe siècles*, Palermo: Quaderni di Mediterranea: Richerche storiche, 2015, pp. 43–55.

49 D. Valérian, *Bougie: Port maghrébin, 1067–1510*, Rome: École française de Rome, 2006.

50 Archives Municipales Marseille, HH 334, Nov. 1220.

51 L. de Mas-Latrie, 'Chartes inédites relatives aux États de Bougie et de Bone (1268–1295–1480)', *Bibliothèque de l'École des chartes*, 2, 1841, pp. 388–97; Valérian, *Bougie*; Valérian, 'L'essor de l'activité commerciale de la façade maritime du Maghreb aux XIIIe et XIVe siècles', in Fabre *et al.*, *Les ports et la navigation en Méditerranée*, pp. 225–32.

52 J. Caille, 'Les Marseillais à Ceuta', in *Mélanges d'histoire et d'archéologie de l'Occident musulman, hommage à Georges Marçais*, vol. 2, Alger: Revue des études byzantines, 1957, pp. 20–30.

53 Namely in Bourg des Olliers and Bourg Sainte-Catherine: H. Marchesi, J. Thiriot, L. Vallauri and M. Leenhardt (eds) *Marseille, les ateliers de potiers du XIIIe et le quartier Sainte-Barbe (V^{e}–XVIIe s.)*, Paris: Editions de la Maison des sciences de l'homme, 1997; J. Thiriot and L. Vallauri, 'Le bourg des Olliers à Marseille: conception d'un espace artisanal périurbain au xiiie siècle', in Bouiron and Tréziny, *Marseille, trames et paysages urbains*, pp. 369–74; Bouiron, *Marseille: Les fouilles de la place Général-de-Gaulle.*

54 N. Coureas, 'Provençal trade with Cyprus in the thirteenth and fourteenth centuries', *ΕΠΕΤΗΡΙΔΑ* 22, 1996, pp. 69–92.

55 H. E. Mayer, *Marseilles Levantehandel und ein akkonensisches Fälscheratelier des XIII. Jahrhunderts*, Tübingen, 1972, whose arguments are based on his predecessors' work quoted in Busquet and Pernoud, *Histoire du commerce de Marseille*, vol. 1, pp. 138–9.

56 C. Carrère, 'Marseille, Aigues Mortes, Barcelone et la compétition en Méditerranée occidentale au XIIIe siècle', *Anuario des Estudios Medievales* 10, 1980, pp. 161–72; K. Reyerson, 'Le rôle de Montpellier dans le commerce international des draps de laine avant 1350', *Annales du Midi* 1982, pp. 17–40; J. Combes, 'Saint-Gilles et le trafic de l'Europe occidentale au XIIe siècle', in *Les zones palustres et le littoral méditerranéen de Marseille aux Pyrénées*, Montpellier: Fédération historique du Languedoc méditerranéen et du Roussillon, 1983, pp. 51–71.

57 M. Mollat (ed.), *Les affaires de Jacques Cœur, journal du procureur Dauvet: Procès-verbaux de séquestre et d'adjudication*, Paris: Colin, 1952–3, pp. 200–10; K. Reyerson, 'Le procès de Jacques Cœur', in Y.-M. Bercé (ed.), *Les procès politiques (XIVe–XVIIe siècle)*, Rome: École française de Rome, 2007, pp. 123–44; C. Maurel, 'Marseille en 1474, à la veille de son union à la France: entre le port de commerce et le foyer de pèlerinage', *Provence historique* 41, 1991, pp. 543–66.

58 Carrère, 'Marseille, Aigues Mortes, Barcelone'.

59 Maurel, 'Fractures et renouveau d'un organisme urbain médiéval'.

60 Francesco Balducci Pegolotti, *La Pratica della mercatura,* ed. A. Evans, Cambridge, MA: Medieval Academy of America, 1936.
61 E. Baratier, 'La franchise des Marseillais en matière de droits de péage', *Provence historique* 1, 1950, pp. 45–51.
62 B. Doumerc, 'La lente agonie des ports du Midi: Narbonne, Montpellier et Marseille confrontés à l'évolution des circuits d'échange (fin XVe s.–début XVIe s.)', *Annales du Midi* 1994, pp. 317–31.

13
VALENCIA
Opportunities of a secondary node

David Igual Luis

Introduction

The city of Valencia, halfway down the east coast of the Iberian peninsula, passed from Muslim to Christian control in the thirteenth century. From that time onwards it began to play a fairly important maritime and mercantile role in the western Mediterranean. The process culminated in the fifteenth century, when Valencia achieved the rank of a centre of middling importance for European coastal transport and communication routes. The city developed along these lines as the capital of the kingdom of Valencia and as part of the crown of Aragon. The latter was the state-level structure that in different phases eventually comprised, along with the Valencia area, the Catalan counties and the kingdoms of Aragon and Majorca in the Iberian sphere, and Sicily, Sardinia and Naples in what is now Italy. Thus, Valencia was incorporated in a political unit to which other outstanding commercial centres also belonged, such as Barcelona, Majorca, Palermo and Naples.

The nature of the position achieved by Valencia in this context has been written about by historians for many years, thanks to the great quantity and variety of sources that have come down to us on the topic. However, the historical analysis has been reinforced in the last thirty years by massive research of certain types of local documentation (from notarial, judicial, fiscal or municipal origins, for example), and on the development of new approaches, such as the prosopography of merchants and the analysis of their networks. In fact, the recent studies have highlighted how, for the period between the end of the Middle Ages and the beginning of the early modern period, the history of Valencia would be inconceivable without the Mediterranean and mercantile frame of reference.[1]

With these foundations, the purpose of my contribution is to synthesize the conclusions of the historiography on Valencia around the themes proposed by the volume editors. In the text I have thus focused on the opportunities afforded to

Valencia by its territorial location; the contacts that the city established with its hinterland and with the urban and semi-urban network to which it was linked, especially within the kingdom of Valencia; the density of the trading connections that it developed; and the role played by institutional and socio-cultural factors. I have also devoted a particular section to the lengthy timeframe in which I will move throughout the chapter, from the mid-thirteenth to the mid-sixteenth century, because it is an important aspect in understanding Valencia's position in the hierarchy of maritime ports.

Location advantages and the foundations of a regional economy

Geostrategic questions were influential in the Valencian expansion. The eastern frontier of the kingdom was over 500 km of coastline. Land routes ended there that occasionally began in inland Aragon and neighbouring Castile. Moreover, the long coastline of Valencia enjoyed a favourable location, as it was the point of intersection for numerous Mediterranean routes that in turn linked up with the Atlantic. The positive effects of these circumstances were gradually seen, above all, from 1300 onwards, when the development of the structure of international trade and the contemporary dynamic of the westernization of European business turned out to be advantageous for Valencia. In short, as Braudel would put it, the territory and its capital city benefited from the changes in the great 'trading games' of the period.[2]

Nevertheless, apart from these factors, the mercantile development of Valencia and its orientation towards the sea were the consequence of a complex historical process in which numerous political, social, economic and cultural factors played a part, both internal and external. In the end, they all combined to create a regionally based reality, defined at the outset by two aspects that were also consolidated gradually: the first was the way the city of Valencia interrelated with its kingdom and how links were forged between the city and the countryside; the second, the leadership of the whole assumed by the city, located as it was in the physical centre of the coastline.[3] Economically speaking, this city combined the boom in certain artisanal, mercantile and naval trades with the control of an agricultural area rich in exportable produce, although it lacked other staples that had to be obtained through trade. The local supply needs, the strength of exports and the options chosen by the dominant urban groups made Mediterranean circulation very important. Such an orientation was followed to a greater or lesser extent by the rest of the kingdom, either because of its own momentum, or as the mere transmission of what was happening in the capital.[4]

The gradual structuring of Valencian trade led to an integration of markets on sectoral and territorial levels. In this integration, during the fifteenth century especially, the role of the city of Valencia has been judged to be that of a simple 'Mediterranean port',[5] a 'mercantile centre',[6] an 'emporium',[7] and a centre of 'convergence of economic opportunities'.[8] These are different formulas, but they serve to stress what Valencia came to mean as a trading and consumer city, even though it was simultaneously the scene of important industrial and financial activities as well. In the fifteenth century, however, the multipolar nature of Valencia's role was only fundamental for a few nearby circuits in the western Mediterranean, as it generally remained more subordinate in longer distance initiatives and in the pecking order with other major European seafaring centres (Venice, Genoa, Barcelona or Bruges, for example). The expansion of Valencia describes the model of the slow emergence of an economy that was a minor player on a global level to begin with and which eventually achieved a solid mercantile identity, within a framework of relations that ranged from the local to the international.[9]

The development of maritime trade in Valencia

As was suggested at the beginning of the chapter, the construction of this framework of relations began after the Christian conquest of the territory, from the middle of the thirteenth century onwards.[10] The precedents of mercantile development during the Muslim period did not prevent this construction from being based on new foundations. The circulation in several directions of agricultural crops and textile products demonstrates the prominence that trade soon achieved in Valencia. It made use of the network of weekly markets, annual fairs and seaports that was quickly established in the kingdom, usually stimulated by the monarchy. This is how the internal variables of trade were organized that also began to connect with the external routes, above all the traditional ones in the crown of Aragon and especially with Catalonia and its merchants. Indeed, within this crown, before the end of the thirteenth century Valencia seems to have consolidated itself through the importation of manufactured goods, the exportation of agrarian resources and intermediation with Castile.[11]

In the fourteenth century the upward trajectory of trade was confirmed. In Valencia at the beginning of the period we can detect the presence of groups consisting of native and foreign operators, who were well versed in commercial dealings. These groups spread their business all over the kingdom, but they also made it possible for the territory to be connected, now on a regular basis, with many seafaring regions: Granada and North Africa, Majorca, Sicily and Sardinia, Catalonia and what is now the south of France, and even with the Atlantic coast of Andalusia. On the contrary, sailing on other, longer routes from Valencia (to Flanders, peninsular Italy or the Levant) seems to have been very sporadic at that time.[12] This would tie in with the peripheral position that, despite everything, Valencia and its kingdom continued to occupy in the Mediterranean as late as the mid-fourteenth century. Nevertheless, the population of 30,000 inhabitants that the city neared in that period had already made it a not inconsiderable centre of production and consumption.[13]

Around 1350, and in 1380 especially, a certain leap forward in the aspirations of Valencia began to be self-evident. There were three key reasons for this: the reorganization of the countryside and its specialization in produce such as sugar, silk, raisins, rice, kermes, saffron, almonds and wool; the improvement of local textile manufacturing, based essentially in the city; and the increase in the westward direction of Mediterranean shipping, heading for the Atlantic through the Straits of Gibraltar, which contributed to the success of the Iberian ports of call between Valencia and Seville or Lisbon. The development of ports on the south coast of the Iberian peninsula was based too on the westernization of international shipping and on rural and internal growth. In these conditions, the ports of the kingdom of Valencia were in a position to supply and receive interesting articles with which to supply Europe's food markets, households and industries, or those of the territory of Valencia itself.[14]

Based on all this, the late fourteenth century was a period of particular economic effervescence in Valencia. In terms of commercial and maritime relations, the greatest effect was the establishment of more permanent links with Flanders, on one hand, and with the cities and regions of northern Italy, on the other. It is therefore not surprising that from then on Italian merchants – Ligurians and Tuscans mainly, although Venetians and Lombards too – should have frequented the shores and the markets of Valencia, at times in large numbers.[15] These new developments and the maintenance of the classic western Mediterranean routes led, around 1400, to Valencia's full insertion in the international maritime economy and trade. This was aided by the combination, which was starting to be fundamental, of the functions performed by local commercial agents and those of Italian businessmen.

The situation remained the same for most of the fifteenth century, which meant that the merchants of Valencia were able to consolidate the prestige of their profession precisely by way of seafaring ventures. Additionally, three more dynamics strengthened the position of Valencia in the global context in the fifteenth century: the city's consolidation as a monetary and financial centre; the opportunities implied by the Aragonese conquest of Naples (1442) and by the election in Rome of two Valencian popes (Callistus III in 1455–8 and Alexander VI in 1492–1503); and the first consequences after 1450 in the south of the Iberian peninsula, above all on the axis Valencia–Andalusia–Portugal, of the European geographical 'discoveries'.[16]

All this set the scene for an outstanding period for Valencian trade, which was reflected in other equally brilliant areas of urban society and especially in the size of the population: by 1490, the city of Valencia was one of the largest in the Hispanic kingdoms, if not the largest. Some estimates give a population ranging from about 40,000 at the lowest end to 70,000 at the highest.[17] This combination of brilliant factors has led to the fifteenth century being called the true Valencian 'golden age' on many occasions. And yet, at least as far as the economy is concerned, the prosperity must have been ephemeral.

In actuality, the mercantile progress of Valencia had materialized with various structural imbalances. The most important ones were the weakness of the Valencian merchants' influence abroad and the groups of local entrepreneurs' lack of capital accumulation. The most negative aspect of these circumstances was revealed when, in the years around 1500, different political, social and economic events set the city on a critical path. Then, the promotion of business was blocked in some strategic areas of Valencian trade such as Granada and North Africa, local traders sometimes preferred to adopt the strategy of the rentier in order to make their fortunes and the city of Valencia even began to find itself partially replaced in its maritime activities by nearby shores such as those of Alicante (still in the kingdom of Valencia) or Cartagena, in the kingdom of Murcia.[18]

Of course Valencia was still a very dynamic and attractive territory for all shipping routes in the late fifteenth century. But elements were being generated that in the future would bring about a significant loss of trade. From the first half of the sixteenth century onwards, the capital's port became less interesting for ships sailing on the major European routes, although it kept its role for those that were putting in from nearby shores. At the same time, the city depended more on the Castilian economy and ceased to spin in the orbit of Italian cities, although Italian companies still worked in the city. The definitive shift of the world's economic centre to the Atlantic and increasing domestic problems slowed down Valencia's contact with international nerve centres. This resulted in a regionalization of trade with regard to the coast of the kingdom, apparently culminating around 1550.[19]

The interrelationship of the city with its kingdom

The development I have just described made it possible for the city's connection with the sea to take shape, from the material point of view, subject to an organizational model that has been defined as bipolar: the vertices of mercantile and maritime decision-making remained in the city in institutional and human terms, while its coastline attracted the operational activities of naval trade.[20] This shoreline was about 3 km from the city and, from the thirteenth century, Vilanova del grau de la mar, a neighbourhood linked to the city of Valencia and wholly devoted to seafaring activities, grew on it. Vilanova was north of the Turia river mouth. This was Valencia's river, which allowed the communication and the transport of commodities with very small boats between the coast and the city, along with a parallel road on the left bank of the river. On the coastline, the bay and its beach were the spaces used as a port. In fact, during the entire period under consideration, Valencia lacked a port as such with stable commercial docking infrastructures, although we know that there were several initiatives to improve them. Obviously, the larger vessels could not dock on the beach. In these cases, it was necessary to use the services of light boats to facilitate the tasks of loading and unloading. It seems that this mechanism was sufficient to maintain the maritime position of Valencia.[21]

Immigration contributed to the increase in the number of inhabitants of Vilanova del grau de la mar, as was also the case in the city proper. These migrants came mostly from the rest of the kingdom of Valencia. This is a first factor demonstrating the interrelationship that arose between this kingdom and what was its main urban centre. In fact, the population drift towards the capital was one of the reasons for the pronounced top-heaviness that the territory experienced: the population of the city always greatly exceeded the next level of localities, and in the second half of the fifteenth century it absorbed nearly a quarter of the region's inhabitants.[22]

In spite of this, the kingdom was notable for the density of its urban fabric, inherited in part from the Muslim period. After the capital, the next category of small or medium-sized towns fluctuated, more or less permanently during the fourteenth and fifteenth centuries, in a range of between 5,000 and 15,000 inhabitants. These would be towns such as Morella, Castellón, Alcira, Játiva and Orihuela. However, below this series of towns, there extended another even denser network of smaller places, with about 1,000 or 2,000 inhabitants, also from the fourteenth century onwards. Such places (San Mateo, Onda or Sueca, for example) were at least semi-urban in appearance, as they provided the peasants in nearby hamlets with services and manufactured goods, and a significant percentage of their population did not work in farming. It is important to stress that all the localities mentioned, each at its own level, performed economic and politico-administrative functions in the kingdom and controlled from an economic perspective the surrounding countryside, which acted as a place of production and trade.[23]

With regard to rural production, the specialization of agrarian economies and the effects of the processes of commercialization led to a fragmentation of the territory into various zones, especially after 1380: the livestock-farming and wool-producing north, based on Morella and San Mateo; the central areas, including the farming land of Castellón, Valencia, Játiva and Gandía; the inland region around the southern mountains, from Onteniente to Cocentaina and Alcoy, producing almonds and other dried fruit and nuts, cumin, aniseed and kermes, but which was also an important manufacturing area; the southern coast between Denia and Alicante, where raisins, figs and good-quality wines were produced; and the fields of Elche and Orihuela, the kingdom's main cereal granary and a cattle farming centre basically supplying meat.[24] Through this division, which can already be partially observed around 1400 in the sources that Italian commerce in Valencia has left us, it was possible to implement intensive production and to combine mercantile capital and peasant labour.[25]

Concerning the trade that emerged from the countryside and which was related to Valencia's urban and semi-urban network, one of the arenas where it materialized were the markets and fairs that were scattered around the kingdom. From the thirteenth to the fifteenth century we have evidence of forty-four royal privileges for the creation of markets and another thirty-seven for the establishment of fairs, granted to Valencian places of differing sizes.[26] However, the impact of both institutions on economic development was greater for the medium-sized and smaller places, which in this way managed to become incorporated in the network of circuits that connected the needs and the resources of the villages, towns and cities of Valencia.[27]

The ports that sprang up on the coast of Valencia also contributed to the development of the above-mentioned trade. Between approximately 1250 and 1520, over forty sites on the shoreline were used for loading and unloading merchandise (see Figure 13.1 at the end of the chapter). Most of them were small anchorages that also represented the gateway to the outside world for rural areas. They were therefore frequently used to make the local agrarian produce circulate beyond the frontiers of the kingdom or to facilitate its internal redistribution, especially towards the capital city itself. As is demonstrated for the second half of the fifteenth century, the city of Valencia received innumerable shipments from the rest of the ports in the kingdom of Valencia. These shipments redistributed consignments of food and raw materials using light sailing vessels.[28]

In actual fact, within the kingdom's network of ports the concentration of initiatives on the capital did not happen by chance. Complex and variable socioeconomic and political dynamics led Valencia to impose itself on the rest, introduce a hierarchical division of naval and mercantile labour and even rely materially on the functions performed by other ports, such as Denia and Cullera. At the same time, the city acquired the capability to try to force the territory's loading bays to observe exportation guidelines in keeping with the city's own interests. This was clearly seen in the case of the cereal trade during the fourteenth century, given that the city authorities tried to extend their power to prevent the exportation of grain by sea over the entire region whenever the capital's supply was not assured.[29]

Indeed, the supplies of all kinds that a city like Valencia demanded and the ambitions of its oligarchy favoured the adoption of a position of dominance in relation to the kingdom's territory, particularly from the commercial point of view. It is true that the political and economic control that the capital exercised over the kingdom was not complete: for example, the rights assumed by the feudal nobility in the lordships that remained well established in the kingdom and the presence of other relatively strong oligarchies, above all in the southern part of the territory, limited the dominion of the capital. Therefore, the overall model in Valencia of relations between the city and its territory cannot be compared exactly to that of Italian city-states. Nevertheless, in the long run it was possible to extend the tentacles of urban power over the kingdom using different mechanisms: the logic of mercantile demand, the purchasing of agrarian properties, the investment in the credit market and the management of revenue from rents and taxes. This not only made it possible for the kingdom's resources to be channelled towards the capital, but also for the kingdom to become a sort of primary marketplace for the city of Valencia.[30]

The routes that converged on the shores of Valencia

Outside the kingdom of Valencia, the rest of the crown of Aragon also constituted a commercial sphere to which preferential attention was given. The contacts with Catalonia and Majorca were always essential. Indeed, the triangle between Valencia, Barcelona and Majorca acted as the axis of an extensive system of economic relations in which a certain division of functions could be seen. At least for the period between the late fourteenth and the early fifteenth centuries, the sources, Italian once again, suggest that Barcelona was a centre of economic dominance, insurance and finance, while Majorca and Valencia were operational markets and destinations for trade routes.[31] This outline has merited some qualifications by historians, who have pointed out not just the appropriateness of incorporating into the design the role assumed by the areas of the crown in the interior of the Iberian peninsula, but also the changes that subsequent development in the fifteenth century introduced to the above-mentioned division of functions. In particular, the rise of Valencia in the Mediterranean regions created a context that was already clear by 1450, characterized by the lesser superiority of Barcelona and the greater complexity of the connections between the different markets of the crown. Nevertheless, especially with respect to the position achieved by Barcelona and Valencia during the fifteenth century, two elements must be recognized: first, the economic relationship between the two cities was frequently marked by complementarity and rivalry; secondly, Valencia's development did not allow the city to arrive at the same point of commercial success that Barcelona reached at its moment of maximum economic growth. Then, on the Iberian east coast Barcelona generally remained the primary node in the international economy. The primary role of Barcelona was challenged by Valencia in certain moments of the second half of the century, such as during the Catalan civil war between 1462 and 1472 and some years after.[32]

In maritime terms, it cannot be denied that the integration of Valencia with Catalonia and Majorca made the constant development of multiple routes possible, criss-crossed by countless small ships. However, besides this traffic, the habitual analyses of the routes in which Valencia was involved point out that, during the phases of its commercial heyday in the fifteenth century, four more areas determined the territory's seafaring prominence:

- The Muslim coasts of Granada and North Africa, to which Valencian woollen cloth was exported, and from where gold, leather, silk, kermes, spices and slaves were imported;
- Sardinia, Sicily and Naples, the eastern markets of the crown of Aragon, where Valencian woollen cloth was also traded for agricultural produce from Naples and the islands (Sicilian grain above all);
- Sailing to the Levant, including the chartering of galleys promoted by the Valencian municipal authorities, trying to help Valencian merchants get a foothold there in the trade in western fabrics and eastern silk and spices;
- The long coastline between northern Italy and Flanders, which could be sailed by ships that together connected the Mediterranean with the Atlantic, or which were split into shorter routes that only linked Valencia with Italy, or with the Atlantic coast of Andalusia, Portugal or Flanders.[33]

If, from the capital of the kingdom, we observe the above pattern of relations, the local merchants' success was associated with the opportunities found in three of the areas mentioned, which had already been functioning since the fourteenth century and at times since the thirteenth: Catalonia-Majorca, Granada and North Africa and, especially, Sardinia, Sicily and Naples. In those areas, the actions of the Valencians tied in closely with the general structure of trade in the crown of Aragon and therefore they were frequently associated with those of the Catalans and Majorcans. Although it was also integrated with the Catalan impetus, the Valencian presence in eastern trade was always weak. Besides that, the various ways of organizing the route between northern Italy and Flanders were also the subject, from the late fourteenth century onwards, of the activities in Valencia of Catalan, Majorcan and Valencian operators. However, on the routes corresponding to this sector between Italy and Flanders, other groups of seamen and merchants intervened: Castilians (Basques, Galicians and Andalusians), Portuguese and, of course, Italians.

The participation of these other groups in the Italy-Flanders sector could imply the functioning of Valencia as a port of call on longer routes that escaped its control. The best example of this was the inclusion of the port of Valencia in the round trips of the Venetian and Florentine *galere da mercato*. Remember that these galleys moved around the Mediterranean in groups, under the protection of their respective states, and they eventually extended their voyages to the Atlantic.[34] Testimonies of the convoys in Valencia date from 1391 to 1534, but they are more regular from the 1420s onwards. At that time the stopover in the capital of two Venetian routes was consolidated, with Valencia as the final unloading destination on the outward voyage, and the initial loading port on the return voyage. The two routes were that of Aigues Mortes, which covered the northern coast of the western Mediterranean (Venice–Sicily–Aigues Mortes–Valencia), and that of the Barbary Coast, which did the same on the southern shore (Venice–Sicily–the Barbary Coast–Valencia). Aside from these fleets there was another Florentine Barbary route, which also put in to Valencia from 1447 onwards, and above all those that were bound for Flanders and also visited the port of Valencia: sporadically in the late fourteenth century in the Venetian case, and more regularly after 1425 in the Florentine one.[35]

The convergence in the kingdom of the entire series of routes, which used it as an intermediate stop or as the initial or final port of call, has produced some important figures. From February 1395 to March 1398, the Datini correspondence between Valencia and Majorca has information on 300 ships that put in to and set sail from the bay of Valencia.[36] Moreover, the records of just one urban notary (Jaume Salvador) bear witness, between 1474 and 1513, to the drafting in Valencia of 740 maritime chartering contracts, which very often stipulated what was being exported from the kingdom. Meanwhile, the taxation of the maritime importation business certifies 559 stopovers of ships in the port of Valencia in 1488 and 420 in 1494.[37] With this same source, just the voyages to Valencia from the anchorages in the northern part of the kingdom amounted to about 300 movements in 1488, 1491 and 1494 together, 135 of them in the first of those years.[38]

Obviously, not all the movements included in these figures were equally important. For example, domestic shipping in Valencia or that linked to Catalonia and Majorca generally entailed the movement of a large number of repeated voyages. In the main this entailed the movement of modest goods, usually small in volume and cheap, whose owners differed little in profession and operations. Such images contrast with those emerging from international trade, such as the ones that have been deduced in the second half of the fifteenth century from the examination of Valencia's contact with central and northern Italy (Rome and Latium, Tuscany, Liguria and Venice): less habitual voyages, but with larger vessels (*naus*, galleys or caravels); the intervention of experts in mercantile shipping and business, often not from Valencia; and the most varied kinds of goods traded, in large quantities, although with the intense presence of cargoes (wool, cloth and dyes) that were highly prized in Mediterranean markets. Moreover, the revenue from tariffs that these products left in Valencia was substantial.[39]

The political and institutional context of trade

Taxation was in fact one of the key factors in the organization of Valencian markets, as it was everywhere. It is also a window through which we can observe the main problem of the relations between politics and the economy, between institutions and commerce. From the thirteenth to the sixteenth centuries, any approach to the subject in Valencia must take into account the superimposition of different levels of authority, apart from those deriving from the feudal lords and the nobility. There was local power based on the municipal councils, organs of expression of the ruling groups in each town in the territory; that power developed in the kingdom of Valencia, based on the *corts,* or parliament, and the *Generalitat*, a body that from 1418 acted as a sort of representative of the kingdom; and then there was the sovereign authority of the king of the crown of Aragon, the sole and joint ruler of the different countries in this composite state.[40] In this context, the fate of the city of Valencia was invariably linked to the three jurisdictions (municipality–kingdom–monarch). It is true that the city's power often made it the self-proclaimed spokesman of the interests of the entire kingdom. It is also true that, in matters of economic policy, the capital enjoyed great decision-making capability, at least until the end of the fifteenth century. However, it was never in a position to dispense with the sources of power above the municipality, especially that of the Aragonese king. This was very much the case in the sphere of maritime activities and of foreign trade. These matters largely fell within the sphere of competence of the king and his delegates in Valencia, above all the *Batlle General*.[41]

When applying political measures to the economy, the conditions I have just mentioned made institutional differences almost inevitable. But, far from any total autonomy of the city of Valencia or any possibility of absolute royal intervention, negotiations between the different authorities and the attempt to balance between the authorities and the affected social groups were the order of the day as one of the cornerstones of the region's economic reality, especially during the fifteenth century. On the whole, despite everything, the institutional constraints on Valencian trade were normally weak at that time. The methods of intervention used by the monarchy or the capital's municipal council were usually limited to consolidating the development of trade in markets, fairs and ports, establishing the fiscal regulations of traffic, reinforcing the food supply and, in short, ensuring the regular movement of transactions through privilege and favourable treatment.[42]

These last circumstances should come as no surprise. From the closing stages of the fourteenth century, for the rulers of the city of Valencia commercial activity became the prime example of urban wealth and the sector that had to be given the greatest possible stimulus. But this activity referred above all to the sea as the basis for financial gain and social fame.[43] Besides, in relation particularly to the trading by foreigners in Valencia, chiefly the Italians, the institutions' strategy was also directed towards granting exemptions and facilities of passage, opening up spaces and reducing costs. With respect to these foreigners then, Valencia seems to have situated itself as a market with a tendency to be open thanks to the functions that the international operators performed in the territory. Nevertheless, up until 1500 this could not prevent the existence of disputes with local businessmen or situations of protectionist closure.[44]

This whole political and institutional framework developed thanks to the general laws and the general governmental bodies in Valencia. For example, with regard to the laws there are numerous chapters on mercantile and seafaring life contained in the 'Laws of Valencia' (the *Furs*). These constituted the overall legal organization of the kingdom and were enacted by the king in about 1238–40, although they were expanded with the addition of new regulations, as happened in 1261 and 1271.[45] As for the governing bodies, the royal court itself, the delegation of the *Batlle General* or the city's municipal council were the scene of repeated actions and regulatory decisions on the subject of trade. In the case of the city council, from the moment when the members of the political elite started to come mainly from families emerging from the ranks of the merchant class, this oligarchy logically legislated massively on a subject that was close to its heart. Hence, between 1300 and 1500, the urban authorities expressed some fairly constant concerns: favouring the economy and consumption, guaranteeing the security of purchases or ensuring the supply of families and units of labour.[46]

In that period in Valencia, however, there was one institution that eventually became specifically mercantile and which was shared with other parts of the crown of Aragon: the Consulate of the Sea. After a few thirteenth-century Catalan precedents, the Consulate proper was created in Valencia by a grant of the king in 1283. From there it expanded, suitably adapting to the local situation, in Majorca (1343–5), Barcelona (1348), Tortosa (1363), Gerona (1385), Perpignan (1388) and, still inside Catalonia, San Feliu de Guíxols (1443). It was a tribunal that ruled on maritime and commercial matters, although it also assumed the defence of the interests of sailors and merchants as a sort of corporate body. But this characterization was the result of a change. Up until about 1360, the Consulate in Valencia was chiefly a legal and maritime institution. After that date it extended its competence to mercantile actions, coinciding with the growing presence in the body of merchants and with the importance that commerce was acquiring in Valencia.[47]

The Consulate involved the expression of autonomous jurisdiction. As a tribunal it was made up of two consuls and one appeals judge, elected each year from among the citizens that enjoyed prestige and had knowledge of the ways and customs of the sea and, from the middle of the fourteenth century, commerce. They had to ensure that disputes between parties were settled, using a particular law that could be expressed simply and quickly, and be materialized virtually without a trial. The application of customary criteria in procedures did not prevent the customs on which the consuls based their sentences from being compiled in a book, the *Llibre del Consolat del Mar,* which includes a formulation of the mercantile and maritime regulations that were used in the territories of the crown of Aragon. The copy that is now preserved in Valencia dates from 1409 and was commissioned by the city's municipal authorities.[48]

From conflict resolution to the social status of merchants

In Valencia in the fourteenth and fifteenth centuries, the appeal to the merchants' traditional customs or to the development of lawsuits through mercantile channels also appears in other courts that were used to settle differences between traders, for example, before the city's *justícies* (magistrates) or the urban notaries. The *justícies* dealt with civil and criminal cases and the urban notaries could legally formalize arbitration between private agents. Thus, there were several authorities to which economic operators resorted to settle disputes between them. The different channels were not necessarily mutually exclusive, and they could even complement one another.[49] Despite these data, it has to be admitted that the subject has been studied very little in Valencia. But the information that we have suggests conclusions similar to those noted for contemporary Barcelona,[50] especially as far as two elements are concerned.

First, there was the need felt by traders in the kingdom of Valencia to find judicial mechanisms that, by comparison with common law, would be quicker, less solemn and complicated, and better adapted to the merchants' socio-professional status. To achieve this, as a second element, the Consulate of the Sea and private arbitration offered good alternatives. Referring specifically to arbitration, this seems to have spread in the city of Valencia at the same rate as the mercantile economy had done since 1300. The majority of the referees appointed by the merchants of the capital in the disputes were, strictly speaking, arbitrators – that is, people not trained as lawyers, but whose decisions were guided by good faith and experience. Generally speaking, they were people considered experts in commerce, with a good reputation and who were authorized to issue verdicts based on their technical and professional expertise. Arbitration therefore implied prompt and inexpensive justice, which was settled by factual means emanating from practice.[51]

In fact, the use of practical procedures pervaded much of the merchant's life and was the basis that led to knowledge of his trade. Far more so in a case like Valencia, where there were no corporate rules to limit admission to the profession. With just the above-mentioned practice and social recognition, it was easy for anyone, regardless of his origins or wealth, to call himself a merchant. This was the reason for the group's high permeability and even its size. For the period 1400–50 it has been calculated that there were about 1,000 men working as merchants in the city of Valencia. They included men from the kingdom who were hoping to succeed in the capital, craftsmen and shopkeepers from the city who were taking a professional step up, traders originally from other Hispanic and European regions and Jews converted to Christianity. However, alongside these external channels of growth of the urban merchant class, endogamous pathways of reproduction also appeared, either coming directly from local merchant families, or emerging from social classes similar to that of the merchants (such as notaries, jurists and moneychangers).[52]

In their economic strategies up until the early decades of the sixteenth century, the merchants from the city of Valencia allowed themselves as a rule to be governed by prudence and the search for contexts of confidence and security. This conduct was aimed at reducing the risks of a trading profession subject to enormous contingencies. In keeping with this was the frequency with which small sums of capital were invested and efforts were made to pursue the diversification of routes, products and business. This series of characteristics was clearly expressed within the units of commerce that became very habitual in Valencia: societies and companies, commonly family-based and short-lived although renewed periodically.[53]

This definition must not hide the fact that, deep down, among local merchants there was a great diversity of conduct due to the different social levels and activity that is possible to identify in the group. In the capital, obviously, there were big differences between merchants who operated in the maritime routes and those who barely got beyond being small-scale city traders. In the kingdom as a whole, the traders from other urban or semi-urban localities were on average more limited in their means than their colleagues in the city. Moreover, the cosmopolitan nature of Valencian markets contributed to the variety of local environments: the inroads made by foreigners in the territory created a host of socio-cultural contrasts that, observed in the long timeframe of the fourteenth and the fifteenth centuries, led to a number of situations of ambivalence between integration and competition with the people born in the kingdom.[54] Finally, from the point of view of diversity, in those two centuries the actions of the Jewish and Muslim merchants of Valencia were also important; they had solid foundations in the trade with Granada and North Africa and collaborated with the other groups of merchants.[55]

It is obvious that the convergence of all these subjects in the markets gave rise to a motley mixture of people. This explains why, at the end of the fourteenth century, the ecclesiastic Francesc Eiximenis recommended to merchants that they ought to master grammar in order to be able to talk to the foreigners inside their country or elsewhere.[56] Eiximenis was a Catalan Franciscan who lived in Valencia in the years 1383–1408 and left an important written legacy. Part of its content enables us to describe the author as a true ideologue of both the city's municipal council and of its ruling elite, among other things, for the way in which Eiximenis constantly defends trade as the sector that contributed the greatest wealth to the city.[57] His concern for the merchants' knowledge of grammar is therefore not coincidental. It has to be placed in a context in which, above all from about 1380 onwards, the city's commercial and material progress was matched by a theoretical formulation that appreciated the figure of the merchant.

Of course, in the closing stages of the Middle Ages, the merchant's prestige was not something exclusive to Valencia. However, it did achieve particular importance there, due not only to the work of Eiximenis but also to the discourse developed by the city council, in which throughout the fifteenth century, it insisted on the benefits of trade for society[58] – benefits that the local authorities attempted to make visible. Between 1482 and 1548, in order to replace an earlier building that had existed since the fourteenth century, the Llotja (exchange building) was built, and still stands today. The new building was promoted by the municipal council to provide a place where merchants could meet. The headquarters of the Consulate of the Sea was also included in it. The building was so magnificent that, apart from meriting the admiration of contemporaries, it has become a representative example of European civil gothic architecture. The very design of the Llotja and its iconography and decoration make it an authentic temple of commerce, perhaps the clearest expression of what this really meant for the rulers of Valencia.[59]

Final considerations

It would be a good idea to end by remembering two of the questions that have been discussed in this chapter. The first is that the main period of all kinds of trade in Valencia, but primarily maritime, was relatively short. It lasted around 100 years, between the end of the fourteenth and the end of the fifteenth centuries. In that period, Valencia's growth potential as an outstanding element of mercantile traffic may be considered as one of the most evident new developments in the western Mediterranean.[60] Secondly, that the case of Valencia, analysed from a global perspective, was then an example of a type of intermediate European area that, while not being part of the principal vertices of the international economic networks, was very suitable for commercial circulation due to its advantageous geographical location and the fortunate combination that arose within it between the economy and politics.[61]

The city of Valencia was a port, strategically situated, whose functions were consolidated through numerous and varied stimuli that, in short, allowed the conversion of the capital into a cosmopolitan trading centre. Nevertheless, in strictly economic terms, the important thing is that it was the convergence of internal and external variables that helped Valencia to gather momentum and ensured that it would eventually be included as an integral part in local, regional and international circuits. These took into account the political frontiers (beginning with those of the kingdom of Valencia), although they also went beyond them.

Those circuits were straddled and superimposed so that the changes in the intensity and the nature of some influenced the organization of the others.[62] This is

Figure 13.1 Ports in the kingdom of Valencia

particularly noticeable in Valencia in the correlation between small- and large-scale, and local and international commerce. The strength and the frequency of the former were doubtlessly enlivened by the importance of the latter and, in turn, they were able to compensate for the fluctuations in contacts with other countries, far more so if we consider the fact that, in the closing stages of the Middle Ages, Europe and the Mediterranean experienced an increase in short- and medium-distance trade.[63] Such an integrative structure must have been maintained until at least around the year 1500, when difficulties began looming on the horizon of Valencian trade. Still at that time, however, some sources point to what the foundations of the city and its kingdom's economic boom had been. While the German traveller Hieronymus Münzer defined the capital in 1494 as 'in the forefront of trade today' in comparison with Barcelona, in 1519 an anonymous Milanese merchant was still stressing that Valencia was a 'beautiful and mercantile city', and that in his opinion it had a population of about 100,000 souls.[64] In these circumstances, and despite the problems that could already be glimpsed, it is no surprise that in 1503 the urban rulers of Valencia considered it to be the 'greatest city in Spain'.[65]

Acknowledgements

This study is supported by the Spanish government (Ministry of the Economy and Competitiveness), project no. HAR2011-28861, and by the University of Castilla-La Mancha (Spain), research group SEHISP.

Notes

1 P. Iradiel, 'El siglo de oro del comercio valenciano', in I. Aguilar Civera (ed.), *El comercio y el Mediterráneo. Valencia y la cultura del mar*, Valencia: Generalitat Valenciana, 2006, pp. 111–29; P. Iradiel, G. Navarro Espinach and D. Igual Luis, 'Ricerche valenzane sul mondo urbano dell'Europa mediterranea (secoli XIV–XVI)', *Medioevo. Saggi e rassegne* 25, 2002, pp. 111–41.

2 P. Iradiel, 'El comercio en el Mediterráneo catalano-aragonés: espacios y redes', in H. Casado Alonso and A. García-Baquero (eds), *Comercio y hombres de negocios en Castilla y Europa en tiempos de Isabel la Católica*, Madrid: Sociedad Estatal de Conmemoraciones Culturales, 2007, pp. 143–4, 149.

3 D. Abulafia, 'Mercati e mercanti nella Corona d'Aragona: il ruolo degli imprenditori stranieri', in R. Narbona Vizcaíno (ed.), *XVIII Congrés Internacional d'Història de la Corona d'Aragó*, vol. 1, Valencia: Universidad de Valencia, 2005, p. 810; E. Cruselles Gómez, 'El puerto de Valencia en el Mediterráneo medieval (siglos XIII–XV)', in J. Hermosilla Pla (ed.), *Historia del puerto de Valencia*, Valencia: Universidad de Valencia, 2007, pp. 68, 105.

4 Iradiel, 'El siglo', pp. 111–12; D. Igual Luis, '*Non ha portto alcuno, ma sola spiaggia,* La actividad marítima valenciana en el siglo XV', *Aragón en la Edad Media* 25, 2014, pp. 114–18.

5 J. Guiral-Hadziiossif, *Valencia, puerto mediterráneo en el siglo XV (1410–1525)*, Valencia: Alfons el Magnànim, 1989.

6 J. Hinojosa Montalvo, 'Valencia, centro mercantil mediterráneo: Siglos XIII al XV', in S. Cavaciocchi (ed.), *Fiere e mercati nella integrazione delle economie europee. Secc. XIII–XVIII*, Florence: Le Monnier, 2001, pp. 597–607.

7 R. Narbona Vizcaíno, 'Valencia, emporio mediterráneo (ss. XIV–XV)', in *Reino y ciudad, Valencia en su historia. Actas del simposio*, Madrid: Fundación Caja de Madrid, 2008, pp. 83–119.

8 P. Mainoni, 'Mercanti italiani a Barcellona e a Valenza nel tardo Medioevo', in M. Del Treppo (ed.), *Sistema di rapporti ed élites economiche in Europa (secoli XII–XVII)*, Naples: Liguori, 1994, p. 206.

9 E. Cruselles Gómez, 'Los mercados aseguradores del Mediterráneo catalano-aragonés', in S. Cavaciocchi (ed.), *Ricchezza del mare, ricchezza dal mare. Secc. XIII–XVIII*, Florence: Le Monnier, 2006, p. 611; D. Igual Luis, 'La difusión de productos en el Mediterráneo y en Europa occidental en el tránsito de la Edad Media a la Moderna', in Cavaciocchi, *Fiere*, pp. 477–8.

10 The city of Valencia was conquered by the Christians in 1238. By 1245 the major military campaigns in the area had ended, and thus the original kingdom of Valencia was established. After this initial configuration, the kingdom was extended southwards in 1304–5

with the definitive annexation of Alicante and other border regions. In the thirteenth century these southern areas were part of the dominion of Castile.

11 D. Igual Luis, 'L'economia comercial i marítima de València durant el regnat de Jaume I', in M.T. Ferrer i Mallol (ed.), *Jaume I. Commemoració del VIII centenari del naixement de Jaume I*, vol. 2, Barcelona: Institut d'Estudis Catalans, 2013, pp. 719–46.

12 J. L. Soler Milla, 'El comercio en el reino de Valencia durante la primera mitad del siglo XIV: instituciones, rutas y grupos mercantiles', unpublished thesis, 2 vols, University of Alicante, 2015.

13 A. Furió and A. J. Mira Jódar, 'La ciudad y el campo', in J. Hermosilla Pla (ed.), *Historia, geografía y arte de la ciudad de Valencia*, vol. 1, Valencia: Universidad de Valencia, 2009, p. 229.

14 D. Igual Luis and G. Navarro Espinach, 'Relazioni economiche tra Valenza e l'Italia nel Basso Medioevo', *Medioevo. Saggi e rassegne* 20, 1995, pp. 79–80. In the case of Lisbon, its development from the fourteenth century has several similarities with Valencia, as can be seen in the chapter by A. A. Andrade and F. Miranda.

15 J. Hinojosa Montalvo, *De Valencia a Flandes: La nave della frutta,* Valencia: Generalitat Valenciana, 2007; D. Igual Luis, *Valencia e Italia en el siglo XV: Rutas, mercados y hombres de negocios en el espacio económico del Mediterráneo occidental,* Valencia: Comité Económico y Social de la Comunidad Valenciana, 1998.

16 E. Cruselles Gómez, *Los mercaderes de Valencia en la edad media (1380–1450)*, Lérida: Milenio, 2001; Iradiel, 'El siglo', pp. 112–22. The two popes were members of the outstanding aristocratic family Borja of Valencia. Their election intensified the presence and activities in Italy of Valencian people (noblemen, merchants, ecclesiastics) and, inversely, the presence in Valencia of Italian merchants that operated in the papal court.

17 G. Navarro Espinach, D. Igual Luis and J. Aparici Martí, 'Los inmigrantes y sus formas de inserción social en el sistema urbano del reino de Valencia (siglos XIV–XVI)', *Revista d'Història Medieval* 10, 1999, pp. 172–3.

18 P. Iradiel, 'El comercio en el Mediterráneo entre 1490 y 1530', in E. Belenguer Cebrià (ed.), *De la unión de coronas al Imperio de Carlos V*, vol. 1, Madrid: Sociedad Estatal para la Conmemoración de los Centenarios de Felipe II y Carlos V, 2001, p. 105; D. Igual Luis, 'Social rise of the mercantile elite in cities of the medieval Kingdom of Valencia', in M. Asenjo-González (ed.), *Urban Elites and Aristocratic Behaviour in the Spanish Kingdoms at the End of the Middle Ages*, Turnhout: Brepols, 2013, pp. 166–7.

19 Igual Luis, *Valencia*, p. 76.

20 Cruselles Gómez, 'El puerto', p. 113.

21 Ibid., pp. 114–25; Guiral-Hadziiossif, *Valencia*, pp. 71–96.

22 P. Iradiel, 'Ciudades, comercio y economía artesana', in *La historia medieval en España: Un balance historiográfico (1968–1998)*, Pamplona: Gobierno de Navarra, 1999, pp. 619, 634; A. Furió and F. Garcia-Oliver, 'The horizons of the city: Rural mobility in a frontier land (the Valencian country, 1250–1350)', in S. Carocci (ed.), *La mobilità sociale nel Medioevo*, Rome: École française de Rome, 2010, pp. 509–54.

23 A. Furió, 'Producción agraria, comercialización y mercados rurales en la Corona de Aragón', in J. Á. Sesma Muñoz (ed.), *La Corona de Aragón en el centro de su historia, 1208–1458: Aspectos económicos y sociales*, Zaragoza: Grupo CEMA, 2010, pp. 368–9; Furió and Mira Jódar, 'La ciudad', p. 227.

24 Furió, 'Producción', pp. 399–400.

25 Igual Luis, 'La difusión', pp. 473–4.

26 Furió, 'Producción', pp. 419–22.

27 Igual Luis, 'L'economia', pp. 727–9.

28 D. Igual Luis, 'Great and small trade in the crown of Aragon: the example of Valencia in the late Middle Ages', *Imago Temporis: Medium Aevum* 3, 2009, pp. 237–42. The map in Figure 13.1 is based on M.T. Ferrer i Mallol, 'Navegació, ports i comerç a la Mediterrània

de la Baixa Edat Mitjana', in J. Pérez Ballester and G. Pascual Ballester (eds), *Comercio, redistribución y fondeaderos: La navegación a vela en el Mediterráneo*, Valencia: Universidad de Valencia, 2007, pp. 136–45, and Igual Luis, '*Non ha portto*', pp. 101–34. The author thanks Juan Antonio García González (University of Castilla-La Mancha) for the cartographic design of the map. The spots marked in bold letters are the main Valencian ports according to their economic and institutional functions.

29 Igual Luis, 'Great and small', pp. 237–8; Igual Luis, 'Política y economía durante la Baja Edad Media: el papel de la monarquía en el comercio exterior valenciano', in J. A. Barrio Barrio (ed.), *Los cimientos del Estado en la Edad Media : Cancillerías, notariado y privilegios reales en la construcción del Estado en la Edad Media*, Alcoy: Marfil, 2004, pp. 256–7.

30 Furió and Mira Jódar, 'La ciudad', pp. 229, 243; Cruselles Gómez, 'El puerto', pp. 105–8.

31 F. Melis, 'L'area catalano-aragonese nel sistema economico del Mediterraneo occidentale', in L. Frangioni (ed.), *F. Melis. I mercanti italiani nell'Europa medievale e rinascimentale*, Florence: Le Monnier, 1990, pp. 215–31.

32 D. Igual Luis, 'Los grupos mercantiles y la expansión política de la Corona de Aragón: nuevas perspectivas', in L. Tanzini and S. Tognetti (eds), *Il governo dell'economia. Italia e Penisola Iberica nel basso Medioevo*, Rome: Viella, 2014, pp. 14–17, 22–5.

33 Cruselles Gómez, 'El puerto', pp. 72–6; Iradiel, 'El siglo', pp. 112–22.

34 See the chapters by M. O'Connell on Venice and G. Christ on Alexandria.

35 D. Igual Luis, 'Las galeras mercantiles venecianas y el puerto de Valencia (1391–1534)', *Anuario de Estudios Medievales* 24, 1994, pp. 179–200; Igual Luis, *Valencia*, pp. 375–8, 389–99.

36 A. Orlandi, 'Estudi introductori', in Orlandi (ed.), *Mercaderies i diners: La correspondència datiniana entre València i Mallorca (1395–1398)*, Valencia: Universidad de Valencia, 2008, pp. 102–20.

37 Guiral-Hadziiossif, *Valencia*, pp. 35, 256–7.

38 Igual Luis, 'Great and small', p. 241.

39 Ibid., pp. 241–6.

40 It must be remembered that, from the 1470s onwards, the marriage of the Catholic Kings (Ferdinand of Aragon and Isabella of Castile) made the dynastic union of the crowns of Aragon and Castile possible and their confluence in a single Hispanic monarchy. However, the institutions of both the kingdom of Valencia and the crown of Aragon remained the same until the beginning of the eighteenth century.

41 J.V. García Marsilla, 'Las bases económicas de la ciudad medieval. Las políticas económicas del *consell* municipal', in Hermosilla Pla, *Historia, Geografía*, p. 205; Igual Luis, 'Política', pp. 253–4.

42 Iradiel, 'El siglo', p. 126.

43 Cruselles Gómez, 'Los mercados', pp. 611–12; Igual Luis, 'Política', pp. 251–2.

44 Iradiel, 'El comercio en el Mediterráneo catalano-aragonés', pp. 145–6; D. Igual Luis, '¿Los mercaderes son *egualadors del món*? Autóctonos y extranjeros en el comercio bajomedieval de Valencia', *Anales de la Universidad de Alicante: Historia Medieval* 18, 2012, pp. 121–53.

45 Igual Luis, 'L'economia', pp. 726–33.

46 A. Furió and F. Garcia-Oliver, 'Estudi introductori', in Furió and Garcia-Oliver (eds), *Llibre d'establiments i ordenacions de la ciutat de València. I (1296–1345)*, Valencia: Universidad de Valencia, 2007, pp. 31–6.

47 D. Duran i Duelt, 'El context institucional particular de mercaders i homes de mar', in Duran i Duelt (ed.), *Un mar de lleis. De Jaume I a Lepant*, Barcelona: Institut Europeu de la Mediterrània, 2008, pp. 195–202; Iradiel, 'El siglo', p. 126.

48 Narbona Vizcaíno, 'Valencia', pp. 104–9; D. Igual Luis, 'Merchants in conflict in the Crown of Aragon (13th–15th centuries): between public justice and arbitration', paper presented at seminar 'Merchants and commercial conflict in Europe, 1250–1600', Lisbon, Oct. 2013. Compare the responsibilities and the ways of procedure of the Consulate of the Sea with

the similar ones of the Ufficio di Mercanzia in Genoa, as shown by L. Piccinno in her chapter.

49 Igual Luis, 'Merchants'.

50 M. E. Soldani, *Uomini d'affari e mercanti toscani nella Barcellona del Quattrocento,* Barcelona: CSIC, 2010, pp. 207–26.

51 Igual Luis, 'Merchants'.

52 Cruselles Gómez, *Los mercaderes*, pp. 57–99, 292–356.

53 E. Cruselles Gómez, 'Pràctiques i cultura mercantils en la Corona d'Aragó durant la Baixa Edat Mitjana', in Duran i Duelt, *Un mar*, pp. 133–44.

54 Igual Luis, '¿Los mercaderes', pp. 121–53; Igual Luis, 'Social rise', pp. 162–5.

55 Orlandi, 'Estudi', pp. 40–1; J. Hinojosa Montalvo, *En el nombre de Yahveh: La judería de Valencia en la Edad Media,* Valencia: Ajuntament de València, 2007, pp. 514–37. In the case of the Jews, the action mentioned took place until 1391. That year, the attack on and the destruction of the Jewish quarter of Valencia reduced the number of Jews in the city and gave rise to their conversion en masse to Christianity.

56 Eiximenis addresses his recommendation to the 'middle and higher ranks' of society. But he explains that the 'middle ranks' include powerful merchants and drapers. See X. Renedo (ed.), *Francesc Eiximenis. Dotzè llibre del Crestià*, vol. 1/1, Gerona: Universitat de Girona and Diputació de Girona, 2005, pp. 29, 250.

57 Cruselles Gómez, *Los mercaderes*, p. 117.

58 A. Rubio Vela, 'Estudi introductori', in Rubio Vela (ed.), *Epistolari de la València medieval (II),* Valencia and Barcelona: Institut Interuniversitari de Filologia Valenciana and Abadia de Montserrat, 1998, pp. 42–9.

59 S. Aldana Fernández, *La lonja,* Valencia: Generalitat Valenciana, 1994; Hinojosa Montalvo, 'Valencia', pp. 606–7. Compare the meaning of the Llotja in Valencia with other European exchange buildings analysed by D. Calabi in her chapter.

60 Iradiel, 'El comercio en el Mediterráneo catalano-aragonés', p. 143.

61 G. Rossetti, 'Incontro GISEM 1986. Relazione introduttiva', *GISEM 1984–1989: Bollettino* 1, 1989, p. 26.

62 Iradiel, 'El comercio en el Mediterráneo catalano-aragonés', p. 149.

63 Abulafia, 'Mercati', pp. 810–11. At the end of the Middle Ages, the importance of the small trade is corroborated by other chapters in this volume, such as the ones by M. Kowaleski on London and G. Christ on Alexandria.

64 J. Münzer, *Viaje por España y Portugal (1494–1495),* Madrid: Polifemo, 1991, p. 43; L. Monga (ed.), *Un mercante di Milano in Europa. Diario di viaggio del primo Cinquecento,* Milan: Jaca Book, 1985, pp. 142–3.

65 E. Belenguer Cebriá, *Fernando el Católico y la ciudad de Valencia,* Valencia: Universidad de Valencia, 2012, p. 12.

PART III

The Baltic

14
LÜBECK AND THE HANSE
A queen without its body

Carsten Jahnke

The aim of this chapter is to describe the development and institutions of a port city, Lübeck. In doing this, the development of another institution – the Hanse – must come into focus as well, because both Lübeck and the Hanse were often, albeit wrongly, seen as one. In older German research especially, the urban development of Lübeck and the development of the Hanse were parallelized and the history shaped after the idea of the late absolutistic monarchy – a more than inadequate approach, as we know today. It is therefore the aim of this chapter to look at Lübeck more in its geographical and economic situation than in the context of an idealized German domination of the Baltic Sea area. By doing this the early development of the Hanse can be described in a new way – from a Lübeck perspective, but not as a Lübeck unity.

Some remarks on the historiography and the sources for Lübeck and the Hanse

In the context of German historical research, the position of Lübeck and especially the position of the Hanse are problematic. Many works have been dedicated to the history of that city since the chronicles of the High Middle Ages; most of them are highly patriotic and regional. Since the eighteenth century an increasing number of historians were instrumental in the research of Lübeck's history since the scientific revolution.[1] But the longer the research on the Hanse went on, the more Lübeck was connected with an overgrowing 'Hanseatic' impetus.

This impetus was deeply connected to the historiography of the Hanse. Interestingly, the first historian of the Hanse, at the beginning of the nineteenth century, called it a 'harmless and nearly forgotten antique' (*harmlose halbvergessene Antiquität*),[2] and declared it non-political enough to be dealt with in the commotions of the Napoleonic era.

Only forty years later, however, historians had attached a highly political importance to this organization. From the 1840s onwards, the Hanse was reinterpreted in the context of actual political developments. The Hanse was first synonymous with civil liberty, as it soon became a symbol of German sea power. This concept was, in the 1860s/1870s, first mixed up with rampant hyper-nationalism, and from the 1920s connected to the concept of racism and nationalism. Thus most interpretations of this organization exactly mirror political developments in Europe since the middle of the nineteenth century.

In this conceptual climate the history of Lübeck was inextricably linked to the history of the Hanse. Lübeck was not only seen as its driving force (which was also nearly exclusively interpreted as a sea-going organization) but as the founder, the spirit and the queen of the Hanse – Lübeck and the Hanse became synonymous. Some Lübeck-Hanseatic historians of that time such as Dietrich Schäfer (1845–1929) and especially Fritz Rörig (1882–1952) were influential promoters of this concept. Lübeck was seen as the proud symbol of the German Hanse, German economic power and power at sea. Consequently, Lübeck became an excellent target for the Allied war-offensives: the city was disastrously destroyed by the very first Allied air raid on Palm Sunday in 1942.

The destruction of the historic centre of Lübeck in 1942 paved the way for ongoing and extensive archeological research of the town. Since the 1950s/1960s more and more details have become known, correcting older opinions. But it was not before the 1990s that old opinions about the history of Lübeck and the Hanse were changed. Aside from a new, younger set of scholars entering the field, this was based mainly on the return of the Lübeck historical records. Shortly before the start of the Allied air raids, 1,003 boxes with records from the Lübeck archives were taken to a mine in Bernburg. Here they became the booty of Soviet troops and were brought partly to East Berlin and partly to different Soviet Republics where, nearly inaccessible, they were preserved until they were returned to Lübeck in the early 1990s. So very few historical records were accessible from 1942 up to 1992, and these were already interpreted and placed within the framework of the older research.

Today, the sources for Lübeck and the Hanse are manifold and rich. For Lübeck we have, aside from the rich city archives that include an uninterrupted house-register, some customs lists from the fourteenth and fifteenth centuries, eleven volumes of urban documents from the twelfth century up to 1470, printed in the *Codex Diplomaticus Lubecenis* as a couple of chronicles – among others inter alia the *Lübeckischen Chroniken in niederdeutscher Sprache* – and an extensive edition of the Lübeckchronicles in the *Chroniken der deutschen Städte vom 14. bis ins 16. Jahrhundert.*[3]

For the Hanse some documents, such as the *Hanserecesse* and the *Hansisches Urkundenbuch,* had been printed in two series since the late nineteenth century. The former was meant to publish the most important documents. But, as recent research has shown, the edition of these documents, arranged and sorted out by the editors, presented not the historical development of the Hanse, but rather created an artificial image of a sea-going power as created by late nineteenth-century ideas.[4]

Because of this, the history of the Hanse has to be reinterpreted by using more regional sources from different areas.

Location advantage and challenges

Location advantage and challenges of the city of Lübeck

Lübeck, situated on a peninsula between the rivers Trave and Wakenitz, 27 km upstream on the river Trave from the Baltic Sea, was known as a port even in the Slavic times, i.e. the eleventh century at the latest, and was mentioned around 1100 in a runic inscription on the island of Gotland.[5] Lübeck was a local high-medieval port at the Baltic Sea, typically situated upstream to be secured from attacks from the sea, with a Slavic castle controlling the only admission point on the land side.

Lübeck got its local importance in the time of the Christianization of northern Germany when the demand for Lenten food rose. The city of Lüneburg is situated 116 km south of Lübeck, with the most important, best and productive saline in northern Germany. The salt produced in this saline was very suitable in conserving the Baltic herring demanded by abbeys, clerics and laymen who had to eat Lenten food at least 160 days per year. Heading north from Lüneburg one comes to Bardowick, a German-Slavic border station since the time of Charlemagne. From there the nearest way to the coast was by the Trave in Lübeck. Because of this Slavic Lübeck was the natural harbour of the Eastern Saxonian and Westfalian merchants who traded salt to the north and herring to the south.[6]

This situation can clearly be seen in Lübeck's development from a Slavic to a German town. In the beginning of the twelfth century the duke of Saxony and the count of Holstein conquered the Slavic areas around Lübeck. In 1143 Count Adolf of Holstein founded the 'German' city of Lübeck, because he saw how suitable the harbour of Lübeck was.[7] And indeed, the harbour was so well situated that the merchants of Bardowick moved permanently to the river Trave, thus stripping the duke of Saxony of his income and customs. So Duke Henry the Lion forced the city from his vassal and in 1159 'founded' the city of Lübeck for the third time, to secure the income for himself.[8] But because of conflicts between the duke and the emperor, the city was besieged by emperor Friedrich I Barbarossa in 1188, given back to the count of Holstein, and later, in 1201, forced to open its gates to the king of Denmark. Between 1201 and 1227 the city of Lübeck was part of the Danish empire and was experiencing its first economic upswing.[9] In 1227, the city made a civil commotion against the king of Denmark and, by bribing the emperor and distorting privileges, received the imperial immediacy. From 1226/7 up to the year 1937 Lübeck was an independent state of the German empire, and up until the beginning of the sixteenth century was the most important port in the Baltic Sea area before Danzig.

As can be shown from the town's layout and its first privileges, Lübeck was oriented from the beginning to the north–south traffic, from the Baltic Sea to Saxony and Westphalia.[10] As an international port town Lübeck was, at the beginning, of less importance compared with the city of Schleswig, for example.[11] But a long period of peace between 1201 and 1227, secured by the powerful Danish central power, opened up new ways into the town. On the one hand Lübeck became the main port for Crusaders fighting in Livonia, and on the other, Lübeck itself tried to establish a channel of trade to Hamburg.[12] Hamburg, a river port on the Elbe, was the nearest harbour en route to the North Sea (more correctly the Western Sea, *mare occidentale*), but was situated 70 km away from Lübeck. Lübeck therefore had to make sure that the merchants could pass between the cities without humiliation by the local nobility or bandits and had to make this route more economically lucrative than the older 18 km connection between the Western and Baltic Sea at the city of Schleswig. The road to Hamburg, the *platea hamburgensis*, was first finished in 1241 and was secured together with a new bridge and city gate in Lübeck, the very famous Holstentor (the gate of Holsatia, rebuilt in the late fifteenth century). From 1241 onwards Lübeck's commerce flowed in two directions: the older trade from eastern Westphalia and Saxony to the north, and the transit between the Western and the Baltic Sea.

Connecting the Western and the Baltic Sea by land was of particular importance because the seaway around the Skaw (the Cape of Skagen) was, until the twentieth century, one of the most dangerous sea routes in Europe. So even if there was regular traffic around the Skaw, the so-called *Ummelandfahrt*, merchants from the twelfth to the fifteenth century preferred the land route as a secure alternative for their precious goods.

The possibility of sailing around the Skaw was also the greatest challenge to the fate of the city of Lübeck. Until the end of the fourteenth century the city's situation was very positive. Precious goods went through Lübeck, even if the city since the fourteenth century had been too far inland and ships had to be lightened on the roadstead upstream of the Trave. In the year 1368, for example, 680 ships of unknown tonnage came to Lübeck, making 1775 trips in all;[13] between 1492 and 1496 an average of only 760 trips can be counted, rising up to 2,000 in 1580.[14] Bulk goods, however, went mostly around the Skaw. In between the Scanian markets at the Sound (in Denmark, presently in Sweden) was an international connection between the economical spheres of the Western and the Baltic Sea.

But after a war between the federation of Baltic cities and the Danish king in 1368-70, the Wendish cities (the cities of the former Slavic countries) assumed power over the Scanian markets and forced their competitors from England and Flanders out of the market. As a result, these merchants started a direct sailing connection to the eastern Baltic, followed shortly after by the Hollanders and Zealanders. From the late fifteenth century onwards Lübeck got more and more on the lee side of international transit trade, which now took the route via Elsinore at the Sound. However, no precise figures of the development from the fourteenth to the sixteenth centuries can be given. What can be shown are only two rough numbers of the Lübeck fleet: in 1380 120 shippers lived in Lübeck, and in 1595 253 ships were registered in the town.[15]

Lübeck certainly tried to stop the negative development. On the one hand, two channels were built. One, the Stecknitzkanal, built in 1392–8 and in use up to 1900,[16] was between the city and the river Elbe, mostly improving the salt trade from the south. The other was the Alster-Beste channel, connecting Lübeck and Hamburg directly. It was constructed from 1448 to 1529 and closed again due to technical problems in 1550.[17] The city also tried to exclude its rivals from the Baltic Sea in long and bitter fights against Hollanders and Zealanders.[18] But in the end the direct trade between the Western (North) and the Baltic Sea was unstoppable, and so the merchants of the city arranged themselves in accordance with the new situation.

Transit and the regional trade is just one explanation of the glory of Lübeck. The other is the city's international importance in terms of trade. Lübeck was a very young city compared with the old trading centres like Cologne or London. On the other hand, however, Lübeck was the oldest of the 'new' German cities on the Baltic Sea, at least half a decennium older than Riga and seventy years older than Danzig, and thus the ideal and archetype. The Lübeckians had no natural or historical trading area in the international trade, and thus had to look for opportunities where they could find them. This is the reason why Lübeck merchants were present at many markets, from England, Flanders and over to Norway and up to Novgorod – and they certainly held their influence in the new towns on the Baltic, such as Reval, or even founded some, such as Elbing, in Prussia. It is clear that Lübeck's involvement in many conflicts in many markets can be seen as one driving force in the foundation of the Hanse.

Location: advantage and challenge of the Hanse

The Hanse has been, since the middle of the nineteenth century, depicted as a unified German organization and a state within the state. This perspective, born in the age of hyper-nationalism, has no foundation in source material and it is at the moment the subject of intensive debates. Nowadays it seems obvious that the Hanse was only a loosely integrated institution and organization, in which different regions with interests in trade and commerce could approximate their fellow fields of interest and could seek help for problems in their trade.[19] Or as it was stated in 1449 by delegates of the Hanse itself: the Hanse was no society (*societas*) and no fixed structure (*universitas*) because the Hanse could neither be described by terms of secular or canon law nor had the Hanse common interests (*res communes*), a common treasury, a common seal, a common syndic, common employees or common negotiating positions. But the Hanse described itself as a firm *confoederatio* made by commercial cities (*civitates*), towns (*oppida*) and other institutions (*communitates*), which had interests in the sea and land traffic to stave off pirates, bandits and other dangers so that merchants could trade in peace.[20]

The Hanse was a product of the fourteenth century, as can recently be shown.[21] Even if older German research tried to track or to construct the existence of the

Hanse as early as the twelfth century, this has no foundation in the source material. What can be seen is a more regional form of organization in the different regions of northern Germany. If we direct the focus to Lübeck, this regional organization becomes obvious. The imperial power in the Holy Roman Empire weakened in the beginning of the thirteenth century, and the more the emperor was entangled in Italy, the more his possibility to control and to secure the northern territories loosened. Regional powers took over, fighting with and against each other. In this situation the merchants forced their city magistrates to conclude alliances with other cities in order to secure roads, shipping, trade and commerce.[22] Aside from this, the city of Lübeck consolidated its position in the former Slavonian region – the so-called Wendish region – by using its power as a juridical high court, the Oberhof, to unify this area as one with corresponding economic interests.[23]

Lübeck's role as an 'Oberhof' was not only juridical or political but also economic. The regular contact between the cities, which gave birth to the idea that the cities had common interests in trade at foreign markets and that internal standardizations would reduce transaction costs, occurred in 1354 and derived its name from the idea of the *mercatores in hensa Theutonicorum existentibus*.[24] Since then, meetings between the different regions became more regular and were institutionalized in 1379 as the meetings of the common Hanseatic cities.[25]

The Hanse in the fourteenth und fifteenth century was needed because of the weakness of the imperial power. Contrary to England, Scotland or parts of France, there was no powerful lord who was able to protect 'his' merchants or to support their interests abroad. Au contraire, regional lords in small German territories tried to strip merchants as far as possible, and when abroad the single merchant was not strong enough to gain a sufficient negotiating position. The idea of a common action was used by Lübeck together with the Wendish cities, because the merchants of these cities were represented at many trading-routes and places and were thus involved in many conflicts. Lübeck could therefore also easily use the idea of the Hanse in order to protect the interests of its own politics and the city at the Trave, and therefore declared many of its regional conflicts as Hanseatic.

The Hanse united the interests of merchants of the Northern German landscapes, mostly Lower German-speaking. This covered an area reaching from Reval in the northeast of the Baltic via Prussia and Pomerania to Saxony and the northern Dutch areas in the north to a line from Cologne via Magdeburg and Thuringia to Prussia and Cracow in the south. In this area approximately 200 cities were more or less integrated in the Hanseatic networks.[26]

The area covered by the Hanseatic network lay between the huge production and consumption centres of Europe. In the east the large areas of Russia, Lithuania and Poland produced wax, honey and furs. In the south the mountain region of Slovacia/Hungary exported copper and salt via the Hanseatic areas, and Poland exported wood and later grain. The Hanseatic area was also connected via the Wistula to the Central Asian trading ways via Lviv, the southern areas were connected to the Mediterranean via the Frankfurt market (which was not part of the Hanse) and the south German wine areas. In the north fish and iron were produced and in the west luxury goods and cloth were available, such as woollens from Flanders and England, and spices and exotic fruits or other high-quality products from the Bruges markets. The Hanse merchants were filling the gap between the producers and consumers by bridging the distance between Novgorod and London or Bergen and Naples.

Starting in the late thirteenth century and onwards, the Hanseatic merchants developed a special and closed network system to bridge these long distances. It allowed them to handle trading goods at all stations at the same time, without leaving their home town. This system, which reduced the transaction costs significantly, gave them an enormous commercial advantage that could hold their competitors out of the system until the end of the fifteenth century.

However, starting at the end of the fifteenth century the Hanse was challenged by three developments. First, the internal differences between the regions prevailed over the common consensus. For instance, Lübeck's policy, which opened up direct sea traffic between Prussia and England, brought forth very different economic ambitions as it caused a political break with the city of Cologne in the late fifteenth century. Secondly, the significance of the Northern German/Baltic trading area changed at the beginning of the sixteenth century. The discovery and conquest of the American colonies reduced the importance of the old economic areas. The trade of the Hanseatic area, though not unimportant, was minor compared to the Atlantic trade; and new trading methods emerged. As a result the Hanseatic network came under dissolution, opening the area to new competitors and trading partners. Thirdly, the independent state of most of the merchant cities came to an end. In the thirteenth and fourteenth centuries, the wealthy merchants in these cities were able to buy their lords out of the urban regiment. In the fifteenth century and onwards, however, these lords gained more military and economical power, and urban politics were once more subordinated to their will. The time of independent merchants making decisions was over when trading routes, such as from Russia westwards, were also changed by princely will, as appeared in the case of Novgorod.[27]

Finally, the loosely integrated institution of the Hanse no longer fit the new circumstances in the sixteenth century. Some members of the Hanse, like Lübeck, tried to keep the organization alive (mostly to secure their own interests), but its economic value was lost. In the end, the Hanse disappeared silently because it was economically unimportant. In summation, it can be stated that Lübeck and the Hanse had very different location advantages and challenges.

The Lübeck hinterland: dimensions, opportunities for production and exchange

As in the case of most medieval European cities, the Lübeck hinterland was composed of different levels. The *marchia civitatis* of Lübeck, surrounding the city, was relatively small when compared to the high medieval size of the city. When the city of Lübeck was founded as a 'German' city in 1159 the situation was complicated. The land west and south of the city had been part of the Saxonian district of Holsatia and Stormia since time immemorial. The areas in the southeast and the east of the city, on the contrary, were areas newly conquered by the same Duke Henry. This duke founded not only Lübeck, but also the city and bishopric of Ratzeburg, 24 km to the southeast, and Schwerin, 68 km to the southeast. The city of Wismar, 62 km to the east, was founded by a local count in approximately 1226. Thus, the possibilities for Lübeck to get its own *contado* were minimized from the beginning.[28]

To compensate for the minor *marchia civitatis,* the Lübeck council and the Lübeck elites developed different strategies to secure the city's supply. On one hand the city brought all channels of supply – via land and rivers – under its control. Already at the beginning of the thirteenth century the city tried to secure the access routes in all directions,[29] even if the way to Hamburg, *die Hamburgische Straße*, was first developed at the beginning of the thirteenth century and secured in 1241.[30] In the course of the next centuries, the council of Lübeck gained control over the most important land routes into the city. In the case of the Hamburgische Straße, Hamburg and Lübeck together acquired most areas along this road in the following centuries, making the main road between these cities a domestic highway until 1937.[31] The city had also, up to the end of the thirteenth century, brought all waterways around the city under its control.[32] On the other hand, the city tried to extend its hinterland by indirect control via private acquisitions of urban councilors and merchants or via acquisitions of the urban abbeys and institutions controlled by an urban reeve and the urban elite.[33]

The third way of building an urban hinterland was accomplished by Lübeck's role as juridical centre of the Wendish area. Around fifty years after its foundation it became clear that Lübeck would become the most successful city in the area. At the same time, from the beginning of the thirteenth century onwards, a new wave of 'German' colonization took place in the areas east of Lübeck, when many 'new' cities were founded in Holstein, Lauenburg, Mecklenburg and further east in Pomerania. At least thirty-five cities there got Lübeck law.[34] Under the act of foundation, the choosing of a by-law was a considered and active choice of the founding fathers. By giving this law to a city it was automatically integrated into the Lübeck trading network, because all merchants under this law received the right to trade freely and under the same conditions in all other towns with the same law and especially in Lübeck itself.[35] Thus Lübeck developed as the main centre of regional trade in an area of about 100 km around the city, mostly in the east. In the hierarchy of towns between the river Trave and the river Oder the city of Lübeck became the most important, first for juridical and economic reasons, and later on because of its role in the Hanse as well.

This area was sufficient to cover the urban demand for grain, vegetables and firewood. It also delivered a minor part of the hops used at the Lübeck breweries – one of the most important industries in the town.[36] But this hinterland was not huge enough to supply the city with grain for its breweries. We are missing concrete numbers for Lübeck, but it was estimated that the slightly smaller city of Hamburg with *c.*18,000 inhabitants was in the need of *c.*2,000 tons grain p.a. for bread and *c.*7,000 tons of grain (150,000 quintals) for brewing.[37] Conservative estimates show that Hamburg needed 2,160 square kilometres of hinterland for food and fuel, and *c.*1,200 square km for brewing – meaning a radius of *c.*50 km around the city.[38] We can assume nearly the same annual amount for Lübeck too. This means that Lübeck stood in very hard competition with the other large-scale brewer cities in this area: Hamburg, Rostock and Wismar.

To secure the supply of grain the city conducted a very active privilege policy in an area of *c.*250 km around the city, from Stendal i.A. in the south up to the Danish islands of Lolland and Falster in the north.[39] This area can be seen as the wider hinterland of the town. In addition, Lübeck was closely connected to the two seaports of Aalborg in Denmark[40] and Bergen in Norway,[41] where the Lübeck merchants got a prominent (and in Bergen a dominant) position. From Aalborg, the city was supplied with grain and herring, and from Bergen with stockfish.

Connections and balance of the trade

At first, Lübeck merchants as such had no connections. The merchants coming to the Trave were inlanders from Westphalia and Saxony, looking for a harbour to go to Scania or to Russia. Thus not only was the number of Lübeck merchants small, but the number of Lübeck ships was minimal as well.[42] For instance, in 1201 the Danish king was able to capture the whole Lübeck fleet when visiting the Scania herring fisheries in the autumn.[43]

Visiting the Danish herring fisheries was also one of the main purposes of the Lübeck trade. As mentioned before, the city was the transit harbour between the Lüneburg salt and the Danish herring. Simultaneously, Duke Henry invited the nations of the Baltic Sea to come to his new town, thus building up a competition to the old city of Schleswig.[44] The Lübeck chronicle reported: 'The duke sent out ambassadors to the cities and northern kingdoms of Denmark, Sweden, Norway and Russia, offering them peace and free trade in his new city of Lübeck.'[45]

This marks the starting point of the Lübeck trade, as can also be seen shortly after 1200 in the first urban customs list: 'No burgher of Schwerin has to pay customs in Lübeck, no Russian, no Norwegian, no Swedish, no men from the island of Öland, no men from the island of Gotland, no men from Livonia or from any other nordic folk.'[46] Lübeck was a transit harbour in the north–south traffic, depending on a constant inward flow of foreign merchants and ships.

A phase of consolidation arose, however, with the occupation of the city by the Danish king in 1201. Lübeck became not only a transit harbour for Livonian troops and merchants, but started to play a more important role by itself. From the start of the thirteenth century onwards, we can see Lübeck merchants in sea-bound markets all over Europe: in Portugal, France, England,[47] in Flanders,[48] in Norway, Denmark and Sweden, as well as in Livonia (where the city of Reval and Lübeck were called the two arms of the crucifix) or in Russia,[49] as well as in the inland markets in Northern Europe down to the Frankfurt fairs[50] and later on to Venice. Up to the fifteenth century, the direct Lübeck–Bergen–Boston–Flanders trade was an important branch of the Lübeck economy,[51] as was the trade to Lisbon,[52] to the Brouage, Bruges, the Scheldt estuary,[53] the Scanian markets and Denmark,[54] Novgorod and the Baltic Sea area.

But Lübeck was not only important for its own direct trade or the export of Lübeck brewed beer. The city on the Trave was more important because of its geographical central position in the North European trade network. From the middle of the thirteenth century onwards, 'German' merchants used Lübeck as a transit station in their trade from the Western Sea to the Baltic,[55] and when the commercial revolution took place and the merchants stayed home, Lübeck became the main information centre for the whole North European trade. Because of its geographical situation and because the merchants avoided the tour around the Skaw until the fifteenth century, most of the precious goods passed the city on the way to or from the east. Because of this, many goods were just passing by on their way from Novgorod to London,[56] Bruges and Amsterdam. They could be sold in the city because of the huge supply of goods, but normally Lübeck was not the main market. But with goods information followed as well, and because Lübeck merchants were involved in many markets and goods from many directions were passing by, Lübeck was *the* focal point for information.[57] This predestined the city for a leading role in the Hanse – and as result, the leading role in the organization intensified the informational advantage.

Lübeck was the main centre of trade up to the sixteenth century, even if Lübeck merchants traded on routes outside the Lübeck harbour and markets, and even in light of the fact that the city at the Trave was in an offside position when the direct trade between the Western and the Baltic Sea was strengthened.

Lübeck contributed to the regional and international trade with its beer[58] and a kind of woollen known as the Lübeck cloth.[59] The importance of these goods for this city's balance of trade has not been examined until now, but it seems that the city was not a centre of important production. Finding numbers for the transit-trade, however, is nearly impossible. The condition of sources is such that we just have customs lists for the in- and outgoing sea-trade, and even these are not entirely complete.[60]

The numbers that come closest to an overall view of the Lübeck trade are from 1368, from a time of crisis and war. In this particular year at least 2,500 merchants were enrolled in the customs lists.[61] The imports were estimated at *c*.296,000 mark lüb. and the exports at 158,089 mark lüb.[62] That is by no means a sign of problems in the balance of trade, but just a result of the customs modalities. Every good, once declared, did not have to pay duties again upon leaving Lübeck. The same applies for all other goods coming from towns of the Hanse, if the custom was paid there. Thus the given number for the year 1368 is just the absolute minimum, not considering the land traffic into and out of the town.

Also dependent on these modalities was the distribution of the different means of trade. In the 1368 declarations 24 per cent of all goods came from Gotland and Sweden, 20 per cent from Denmark and Livonia, 15 per cent from Finland but only 8 per cent from the west,[63] as these goods were already declared in Hamburg or other western towns. A different picture can be drawn for the values of the different goods. The far most valuable goods declared were woollens from Flanders with 157,243½ mark lüb, followed by herring, salt, skins and wax,[64] indicating the two typical routes of the Lübeck trade: the salt–herring trade between Luneburg and the Scanian fairs, and the east–west trade with woollens and wax.

Local institutions fostering the exchange and conflict resolution

The city of Lübeck is not particularly famous as a host for foreign merchants, at least not after the middle of the thirteenth century. Lübeck was more geared towards the outside: it was deeply embedded into the Hanseatic network and its function was, as mentioned, a transmission centre inside this network rather than an entrepôt for incoming goods. Nevertheless, there were foreigners coming to Lübeck. Many of them, like the Florentine merchant and banker Gherardo Bueri,[65] or the Nurembergian Johan Lange[66] or Mathias Mulich,[67] became burghers of Lübeck and part of the urban elite. But others stayed in the town for a short time only, like the father of Mathias Mulich, Kunz Mulich.[68] It is an unresolved question of how many foreigners went to the Trave. Scholars in the past wrote about a strong influence,[69] but this seems to be partly wrong.[70] It is clear that the Lübeck merchants went abroad, for example, to Frankfurt, but it seems that the Frankfurt merchants in return did not come to the Trave.[71]

One group coming to Lübeck regularly were Nuremberg merchants,[72] who also had special privileges.[73] But they were not very popular and the city of Lübeck tried to restrict their trade in town and in the whole Baltic Sea area at least from the end of the fifteenth century.[74] Aside from them, we can also find a small group of Florentine bankers.[75] To assess the importance of these and other groups of foreign merchants such as Scandinavians, Flemings or others, research is still needed. Evidence evaluated until now suggests that merchants from other sea-going nations like France, England or Scotland did not venture to Lübeck in great numbers. If we look into the ordinances (*Burspraken*), it appears that there were foreign merchants coming with flax from the eastern Baltic[76] and with hops, mostly imported from Mecklenburg, Thuringia and the Mark Brandenburg.[77] No other products, with the exception of herring, are mentioned directly, something that seems characteristic for the Lübeck trade with foreigners.

The foreign merchants coming to Lübeck were seen more as competition to the burghers than as enrichment.[78] They had to stay at hostellers and could only sell their goods in the cellars of their hosts.[79] The goods of the foreigners had to be available for burghers only, at first for three days, but after some complaints by merchants this changed to eight days.[80] Foreigners, with the exception of merchants from Nuremberg, were not allowed to hold open selling places (cellar), and burghers were not allowed to work together in trade with the foreigners.[81] The only situation when Lübeck attracted 'foreign' merchants was at the diets of the Hanse, the *Hansetage*. These diets were non-regular assemblies of Hanseatic city-councillors – most of them took place in Lübeck. But the city profited from these days only from the collecting of (mostly written) knowledge. Most of the assemblies were only visited by a few councillors.[82] How much they traded – aside from their political work – is unknown. But the tradition of Lübeck as the permanent secretary of the Hanse and scene of the diet fixed the position of this town in northern Germany until the middle of the seventeenth century.

As for local institutions for foreign trade in Lübeck only two should briefly be mentioned. First, the town council farmed the office of the local brokers out to the grocer company. But these brokers at the harbour had to deal with herring and grain only.[83] Other brokers were free to deal over the whole city, but they had to observe the restrictions for guests. Second, there were two public town scales, at the harbour and at the market, also rented out to some burghers.[84]

Even the harbour of Lübeck was not equipped for huge foreign traffic. The situation of the earliest Lübeck harbour is not known, but up to the mid-thirteenth century it was located on a very narrow strip at the northeastern part of the city.[85] In the middle of the thirteenth century the harbour was extended and split into an inner harbour, south of the Holstenbrücke at the end of the later Stecknitz channel, and the sea harbour, now extending to the north corner of the city. Up to the nineteenth century the harbour structures were relatively simple: only a wooden quay that was one metre above river level existed, which was extended with swimming prams that could accommodate two larger ships and one small ship each. It is doubtful whether larger sea-going ships could reach the harbour at all, because of the depth of the Trave, which was 2.3 metres in the seventeenth century, and the first dredger used to deepen the river is known already in 1461. Most of the ships could only come to the roadsteads in the Breitling, halfway between the sea to the city, where they were lightened into prams. No cranes existed in the harbour itself, only some yards that were used as arms, mostly to lighten small ships and prams.[86] In the long run Lübeck harbour was too far inland, too narrow and ultimately not equipped well enough to compete with other harbours on the Baltic sea such as Danzig. It is therefore remarkable that Lübeck did not develop its possession at the estuary of the Trave, Travemünde, into a harbour before the nineteenth century, something that could have changed the situation.

One institution often mentioned in the old historiography is the Lübeck or the Hanseatic sea law. But, as newer research has shown, neither Lübeck nor the Hanse had a strong influence as such – indeed, quite the contrary. Up to the fifteenth century, Lübeck had no sea law of its own,[87] and the Hanseatic renewals of the fifteenth century were improvements in the law of the loads and a criminalization of the onboard hierarchy.[88] The Lübeck and Hanse merchants were not interested in ships, but rather in safe transport and liability laws – and according to this, they set new standards.

Conflict resolution is obviously a topic that ties in with international trade. Inside the Hanseatic network of trade, merchants tried to solve conflicts inside their own groups or with the help of friends, as Justyna Wubs-Mrozewicz recently has shown.[89] If this was not possible, the Lübeck merchants were bound by rules, given by themselves as the common merchants at the river Trave,[90] and by the Lübeck law, which was especially created for use by merchants. Foreign merchants coming to Lübeck had, like in all other north German cities, their own court, the Gastgericht.[91] Foreigners not only were able to deal with their problems there, but could also accuse Lübeck burghers before this court.[92] However, this topic has been little researched and still needs to be addressed systematically.

Conclusions

The city of Lübeck was undoubtedly one of the most important cities in the Baltic Sea area of the Middle Ages. The city was also a relatively important harbour of that region, but the more that the economic development of the fifteenth and sixteenth centuries went on the more the city at the Trave lost its status in international shipping. Lübeck was the typical North European harbour of the High Middle Ages, nearly 30 km away from the sea, upstream a river. For the twelfth and thirteenth centuries the city was, as the main connecting point between the inland area and the sea, between the Western and the Baltic Sea, well placed. But with the ongoing development of international shipbuilding and ships becoming ever bigger, the harbour of Lübeck became insufficient. Lübeck could only hold its position in the international economy because of its geographical position at the centre of the Hanseatic trading network. As a result Lübeck became more the capital of information transfer than the capital of sea transport.

It is thus an irony that the German historians of the nineteenth century placed Lübeck at the centre of a historical myth: the German Hanse as a sea-going power. Certainly Hanseatic merchants used sea transport, but the majority of Hanseatic towns lay inland and had no interest in the sea at all.[93] The Hanse was first and foremost a trading network and Lübeck was one of the main knots. As it has been shown in this chapter, the position of Lübeck and the Hanse in international history must be revised.

Notes

1 Ferdinand Heinrich Grautoff (1789–1832), Ernst Deecke (1805–62), Wilhelm Mantels (1816–79) or Carl Friedrich Wehrmann (1809–98).

2 G. F. Satorius, *Geschichte des Hansischen Bundes*, part I, Göttingen: Heinrich Dieterich, 1802, p. vi.

3 K. Wriedt, 'Geschichtsschreibung in den wendischen Hansestädten', in H. Patze (ed.), *Geschichtsschreibung und Geschichtsbewußtsein im späten Mittelalter,* Sigmaringen: Thorbeke, 1987, pp. 401–26, esp. pp. 403–8.

4 A. Huang and U. Kypta, 'Ein neues Haus auf altem Fundament: Neue Trends in der Hanseforschung und die Nutzbarkeit der Rezessedition', *Hansische Geschichtsblätter* 129,

2011, pp. 1–30. C. Jahnke, 'Die Hanse: Überlegungen zur Entwicklung des Hansebegriffes und der Hanse als Institution resp. Organisation', *Hansische Geschichtsblätter* 131, 2013, pp. 1–32.

5 D. Kattinger, *Die gotländische Genossenschaft: Der frühhansisch-gotländische Handel in Nord- und Westeuropa*, Cologne: Böhlau, 1999, pp. 25–6.

6 C. Jahnke, 'The city of Lübeck and the internationality of early medieval trade', in J. Wubs-Mrozewicz and S. Jenks (eds), *The Hanse in Medieval and Early Modern Europe*, Leiden: Brill, 2013, pp. 37–58, here pp. 42–6.

7 *Helmoldi Presbyter Bozoviensis Chronica Slavorum*, MGH SS rer. Germ, vol. 32, ed. B. Schmeidler, Hanover^2: Hahn, 1937, cap. 48, s. 95, cap. 57, pp. 111ff.

8 C. Jahnke, 'Handelsstrukturen im Ostseeraum im 12. und beginnenden 13. Jahrhundert: Ansätze einer Neubewertung', *Hansische Geschichtsblätter* 126, 2008, pp. 145–85, here pp. 153–6.

9 Ibid.

10 Ibid., pp. 156ff.

11 C. Jahnke, '"... und er verwandelte die blühende Handelsstadt in ein unbedeutendes Dorf": Die Rolle Schleswigs im internationalen Handel des 13. Jahrhunderts', in G. Fouquet *et al.* (eds), *Von Menschen, Ländern Meeren: Festschrift für Thomas Riis zum 65. Geburtstag*, Tönning: Der Andere Verlag, 2006, pp. 251–68.

12 Jahnke, 'Handelsstrukturen', pp. 166–71.

13 G. Lechner, *Die hanischen Pfundzollisten des Jahres 1368*, Lübeck: Hansischer Geschichtsverein, 1935, p. 65.

14 R. Hammel-Kiesow, 'Lübecker Hafen von den Anfängen bis heute', in R. Hammel-Kiesow (ed.), *Seefahrt, Schiff und Schifferbrüder: 600 Jahre Schiffergesellschaft zu Lübeck, 1401–2001*, Lübeck: St. Annen-Museum, 2001, pp. 75–82, here p. 77.

15 R. Hammel-Kiesow, 'Vom Koggen zum RoRo-Verkehr: Die Lübecker Handelsflotte vom Mittelalter bis zum Ende des 20. Jahrhunderts', in Hammel-Kiesow, *Seefahrt*, pp. 83–90, here pp. 83–4.

16 G. Stolz, *Kleine Kanalgeschichte: Vom Stecknitzkanal zum Nord-Ostsee-Kanal*, Heide: Boyens, 1995.

17 K. Mahrt, 'Der Alster-Beste-Kanal – seine Überreste in heutiger Sicht' *Mitteilungen des Canal-Vereins* 16/17, 1996, pp. 97–109.

18 D. Seifert, *Kompagnons und Konkurrenten: Holland und die Hanse im späten Mittelalter*, Cologne: Böhlau, 1997.

19 A. Pichierri, *Die Hanse – Staat der Städte: Ein ökonomisches und politisches Modell der Städtevernetzung*, Opladen: Leske & Budrich, 2000.

20 Hansisches Urkundenbuch (HUB), vol. 9, no. 584, § 2, pp. 463–4.

21 C. Jahnke, 'Die Hanse. Überlegungen zur Entwicklung des Hansebegriffes und der Hanse als Institution resp. Organisation', *Hansische Geschichtsblätter,* 131, 2013, pp. 1–32.

22 Ibid., pp. 7ff.

23 C. Jahnke, 'Der Aufstieg Lübecks und die Neuordnung des südlichen Ostseeraumes im 13. Jahrhundert', in R. Czaja and C. Jahnke (eds), *Städtelandschaften im Ostseeraum im Mittelalter und in der Frühen Neuzeit*, Toruń: Towarzystwo Naukowe w Toruniu, 2009, pp. 29–72, here pp. 37ff. Jahnke, 'Institution resp. Organisation', pp. 9–15.

24 HUB vol. 3, no. 17, p. 10. Jahnke, 'Institution resp. Organisation', pp. 11–25.

25 Jahnke, 'Institution resp. Organisation', pp. 26–30.

26 C. Jahnke, 'Die Hanse am Beginn des 15. Jahrhunderts: Versuch einer Beschreibung', in M. Hundt and J. Lokers (eds), *Hanse und Stadt: Akteure, Strukturen und Entwicklungen im regionalen und europäischen Raum. Festschrift für Rolf Hammel-Kiesow zum 65. Geburtstag*, Lübeck: Schmidt Römhild, 2014, pp. 15–27.

27 See Pavel Lukin's chapter in this volume.

28 See C. Jahnke, *The Early Economic Development and the Urban Hinterland*, forthcoming.

29 A. Graßmann, 'Die Urkunde', in O. Ahlers and A. Graßmann (eds), *Lübeck 1226: Reichsfreiheit und frühe Stadt*, Lübeck: Hansisches Verlagskontor H. Scheffler, 1976, pp. 9–19, here p. 18.
30 Jahnke, 'Handelsstrukturen', pp. 167ff.
31 E. Schulze, *Das Herzogtum Sachsen-Lauenburg und die lübische Territorialpolitik*, Neumünster: Wacholtz, 1957, pp. 74–94 and passim.
32 Jahnke, 'Aufstieg Lübecks', pp. 40–1; 'Lübecks Hoheitsrecht über die Trave, die Pönitzer Wyk und den Dassower See', *Zeitschrift des Vereins für Lübeckische Geschichte und Alterthumskunde* 6, 1892, pp. 243–326. Jahnke, *Urban Hinterland*, forthcoming. G. Fink, 'Lübecks Stadtgebiet, Geschichte und Rechtsverhältnisse im Überblick', in A. von Brandt and W. Koppe (eds), *Städtewesen und Bürgertum als geschichtliche Kräfte, Gedächtnisschrift für Fritz Rörig*, Lübeck: Schmidt-Römhild, 1953, pp. 243–96, here pp. 257–64.
33 A. Düker, *Lübecks Territorialpolitik im Mittelalter*, unpublished dissertation, Hamburg, 1932, pp. 39ff. K. Fritze, 'Probleme der Stadt-Land-Beziehungen im Bereich der wendischen Hansestädte nach 1370', *Hansische Geschichtsblätter* 85, 1967, pp. 38–58, here pp. 44–5. See in general Jahnke, *Urban Hinterland*.
34 Jahnke, 'Aufstieg Lübecks', pp. 58–69.
35 Ibid., pp. 65ff.
36 W. Frontzek, *Das städtische Braugewerbe und seine Bauten vom Mittelalter bis zur frühen Neuzeit*, Neumünster: Wacholtz, 2005.
37 Frontzek, *Braugewerbe*, pp. 18ff.
38 Numbers courtesy of Richard Unger. See also his article 'Thresholds for market integration in the Low Countries and England in the fifteenth century', in L. Armstrong *et al.* (eds), *Money, Markets and Trade in Late Medieval Europe: Essays in Honour of John H. A. Munro*, Leiden: Brill, 2007, pp. 349–80. Frontzek, *Braugewerbe*, pp. 19–20, has much higher numbers.
39 Jahnke, 'Aufstieg Lübecks', pp. 53–8.
40 See in general B. Poulsen, 'Fra middelalder til renæssance: Vækst og strukturændringer i søfarten på Aalborg 1518–1583', in *Søfart, Politik, Identitet: Festschrift für Ole Feldbæk*, Kronborg: Museet for Søfart, 1996, pp. 43–64.
41 M. Burkhardt, *Der hansische Bergenhandel im Spätmittelalter: Handel – Kaufleute – Netzwerke*, Cologne: Böhlau, 2009; A. Nedkvitne, *The German Hansa and Bergen, 1100–1600*, Cologne: Böhlau, 2014.
42 Jahnke, 'Handelsstrukturen', pp. 160ff.
43 Arnold von Lübeck, *Chronica Slavorum*, MGH SS rer. Germ. in usum scholarum, 14, ed. Johann Martin Lappenberg, Hanover: Hahn, 1868, cap. VI.13, p. 234.
44 Jahnke, 'Handelsstrukturen', pp. 160–1.
45 Helmold, *Chronica*, cap. 86, pp. 168–9.
46 HUB, vol. 1, no. 223, pp. 69–70. B. am Ende, *Studien zur Verfassungsgeschichte Lübecks im 12. und 13. Jahrhundert*, Lübeck: Schmidt-Römhild, 1975, pp. 46–7.
47 C. Jahnke, '"Homines imperii" und "osterlinge": Selbst- und Fremdbezeichnungen hansischer Kaufleute im Ausland am Beispiel Englands, Flanderns und des Ostseeraumes im 12. und 13. Jahrhundert', *Hansische Geschichtsblätter* 129, 2011, pp. 1–57, here pp. 18–24.
48 Ibid., pp. 24–9.
49 Ibid., pp. 48–53.
50 W. Koppe and G. Koppe, *Die Lübecker Frankfurt-Händler des 14. Jahrhunderts*, Lübeck: Schmidt-Römhild, 2006.
51 M. Buckhardt, 'One hundred years of thriving commerce at a major English sea port: the Hanseatic trade at Boston between 1370 and 1470', in H. Brand and L. Müller (eds), *The Dynamics of Economic Culture in the North Sea- and Baltic Region in the Late Middle Ages and Early Modern Period*, Hilversum: Verloren, 2007, pp. 65–85.
52 See Amelia Andrade and Flávio Miranda's chapter in this volume.

53 See Louis Sicking's article in this chapter.
54 C. Jahnke, *'Das Silber des Meeres': Fang und Vertrieb von Ostseehering zwischen Norwegen und Italien vom 12. bis zum 16. Jahrhundert*, Cologne: Böhlau, 2000.
55 Jahnke, 'Handelsstrukturen', pp. 156–75.
56 On the development of London see Maryanne Kowaleski in this volume.
57 See Stuart Jenks's chapter in this volume.
58 Frontzek, *Braugewerbe*.
59 A. L. Huang, *Die Textilien des Hanseraums*, Produktion und Distribution einer spätmittelalterlichen Fernhandelsware, Cologne: Böhlau, 2015, pp. 215–17.
60 C. Jahnke, 'Pfundzollrechnungen im Ostseeraum – Bestand und Fragen der Auswertung', in H. Nowak and J. Tandecki (eds), *Die preußischen Hansestädte und ihre Stellung im Nord- und Ostseeraum des Mittelalters*, Torun: Uniwersytet Mikołaja Kopernika, 1998, pp. 151–68.
61 G. Lechner, *Die hansischen Pfundzollisten des Jahres 1368: 18. März 1368 bis 10. März 1369*, Lübeck: Verlag des hansischen Geschichtsvereins, 1935, p. 46.
62 Lechner, *Pfundzollisten*, p. 53.
63 Ibid., p. 51.
64 Ibid., p. 53.
65 G. Fouquet, 'Ein Italiener in Lübeck: der Florentiner Gherardo Bueri (gest. 1449)', *Zeitschrift des Vereins für Lübeckische Geschichte und Altertumskunde* 78, 1998, pp. 187–220. C. Jahnke, 'Lübeck, der Bankenplatz des Nordens? Lübecker Banken des 15. Jahrhunderts als Indikatoren eines neuen Kommunikationsmodells und eines sich ausweitenden Handelsraumes', *Scripta Mercaturae* 40, 2006, 149–68.
66 F. Rörig, 'Großhandel und Großhändler in Lübeck', in Fritz Rörig, *Wirtschaftskräfte im Mittelalter*, ed. Paul Kaegbein, Weimar: Hermann Böhlaus Nachfolger, 1959, pp. 216–46, here p. 240, note 33a.
67 G. Fouquet, 'Geschäft und Politik, Ehe und Verwandtschaft – Briefe an den Nürnberg-Lübecker Kaufmann Matthias Mulich vom Winter 1522/23', in H. Bräuer and E. Schlenkrich (eds), *Die Stadt als Kommunikationsraum: Beiträge zur Stadtgeschichte vom Mittelalter bis ins 20. Jahrhundert. Festschrift für Karl Czok zum 75. Geburtstag*, Leipzig: Leipziger Universitätsverlag, 2001, pp. 311–46. F. Rörig, 'Das Einkaufsbüchlein der Nürnberg-Lübecker Mulichs auf der Frankfurter Fastenmesse des Jahres 1495', in F. Rörig, *Wirtschaftskräfte im Mittelalter*, ed. Paul Kaegbein, Weimar: Hermann Böhlaus Nachfolger, 1959, pp. 288–350, here p. 297.
68 Rörig, 'Einkaufsbüchlein', p. 297.
69 G. Fink, 'Die Lübecker Leonhardsbrüderschaft in Handel und Wirtschaft bis zur Reformation', in *Lübische Forschungen, Jahrhundertgabe des Vereins für Lübeckische Geschichte und Altertumskunde*, Lübeck: H. G. Rathgens, 1921, pp. 325–70.
70 C. Jahnke, *'Gott gebe ihnen ewige Seligkeit': Die Mitgliederverzeichnisse der Lübecker St. Antonius-, St. Leonhards- und Heilig-Leichnams-Bruderschaft zur Burg*, Veröffentlichungen zur Geschichte der Hansestadt Lübeck, Reihe B, Lübeck, in print.
71 Koppe and Koppe, *Lübecker Frankfurt-Händler*, pp. 263–72.
72 C. Nordmann, *Nürnberger Großhändler im spätmittelalterlichen Lübeck*, Nürnberg: Verlag der Hochschulbuchhandlung Krische, 1933.
73 *Urkundenbuch der Stadt Lübeck* (*UBStL*), Lübeck: Aschenfeldt, 1843–1905, vol. 3, no. 117.
74 E. Birkner, 'Die Behandlung der Nürnberger im Ostseegebiet', *Zeitschrift des Westpreußischen Geschichtsvereins* 69, 1929, pp. 1–54, esp. pp. 18–25. Nordmann, *Großhändler*, pp. 144–6. G. Fouquet, 'Lübeck als Reichsstadt – die Zeit Friedrichs III ', in Fouquet *et al.*, *Von Menschen*, pp. 277–305.
75 K. Weissen, 'Briefe in Lübeck lebender Florentiner Kaufleute an die Medici (1424–1491)', *Zeitsschrift des Vereins für Lübeckische Geschichte und Altertumskunde* 83, 2003, pp. 53–81.
76 *UBStL*, vol. 6, no. 783, here p. 764.

77 Wilhelm Ebel, *Lübisches Recht*, vol. 1, Lübeck: Schmidt-Römhild 1971, pp. 389–90.
78 See in general Schultze, 'Über Gästerecht und Gastgericht in den deutschen Städten des Mittelalters', *Historische Zeitschrift* 101/3, 1908, pp. 473–528, here pp. 498–525.
79 *UBStL*, vol. 6, no. 783, here p. 764.
80 Ibid., here pp. 764ff. Ebel, *Lübisches Recht*, p. 389. *UBStL*, vol. 3, no. 189.
81 *UBStL*, vol. 6, no. 783, here pp. 762ff.
82 See for example D. W. Poeck, *Die Herren der Hanse: Delegierte und Netzwerke*, Frankfurt a. M.: Peter Lang, 2010.
83 *UBStL*, vol. 6, no. 783, here p. 763.
84 Ibid., no. 783, here p. 764.
85 Hammel-Kiesow, 'Lübecker Hafen', p. 75.
86 Ibid., pp. 75ff.
87 C. Jahnke, 'Hansisches und anderes Seerecht', in A. Cordes (ed.), *Hansisches und hansestädtisches Recht*, Trier: Porta Alba, 2008. pp. 41–67.
88 G. Landwehr, 'Die hanseatischen Seerechte des 16. und 17. Jahrhunderts', in *1667 års sjölag i ett 300-årigt perspektiv*, Lund: Institutet för Rättshistorisk Forskning, 1984, pp. 75–127. G. Landwehr, 'Das Seerecht im Ostseeraum vom Mittelalter bis zum Ausgang des 18. Jahrhunderts', in J. Eckert and K. Å. Modéer (eds), *Geschichte und Perspektiven des Rechts im Ostseeraum*, Frankfurt a.M.: Peter Lang, 2002, pp. 275–303. G. Landwehr, *Das Seerecht der Hanse (1365–1614): Vom Schiffordnungsrecht zum Seehandelsrecht,* Hamburg: Joachim Jungius-Gesellschaft, 2003.
89 J. Wubs-Mrozewicz, 'The late medieval and early modern Hanse as an institution of conflict management', *Continuity and Change* 32/1, 2017 (accepted, forthcoming).
90 L. von Winterfeld, 'Versuch über die Entstehung des Marktes und den Ursprung der Ratsverfassung in Lübeck', *Zeitschrift des Vereins für Lübeckische Geschichte und Alterthumskunde* 25, 1929, pp. 365–488, here pp. 461–5 and 473–7.
91 H. Rudorff, *Zur Rechtsstellung der Gäste im mittelalterlichen städtischen Prozess*, Breslau: Marcus, 1907, pp. 1–27, 37–86 and 147–94.
92 Ibid., pp. 59ff. and 158–9.
93 Jahnke, 'Die Hanse am Beginn des 15. Jahrhunderts', pp. 15–27.

15

DANZIG (GDAŃSK)

Seeking stability and autonomy

Justyna Wubs-Mrozewicz

In 1608, the painter Isaac van den Blocke, a Danziger with Netherlandish roots, completed a challenging assignment. The Danzig municipal council had commissioned a painting that was to be an all-out portrayal of its power, autonomy and connections. The extensive checklist for the painter included: an impressive panorama of the city with the hand of God holding firmly on to the municipal hall; the main festive building of the city (the *Artushof*), which was the gathering spot both for denizens and foreigners zealously engaged in business; the Vistula river as the main artery of the grain trade and the connection with the Polish capital in Cracow; and a central view onto the sea that conveyed the notion of appealing distance. The artist used a symbolic, mannerist depiction to meet all the demands, and joined the elements with a classicist triumphant arch supporting the successful city, and the arch of a rainbow. The latter was a reference to God and the ultimate justice of the Last Judgment when all good deeds (of the municipal council) were recognized, but in this painting it also explicitly told the onlookers that 'We are all connected by the celestial arch' (*Coelesti iungimur arcu*). The painting, and cover image of this volume, came to be known as the *Apotheosis of Danzig*, or the *Allegory of Danzig Trade*. It still adorns the ceiling of the municipal council chamber in the huge medieval city hall in modern-day Gdańsk.[1]

This self-representation of the Danzig municipal council, commissioned at the very height of the city's prosperity as one of the main European centres of exchange of western and eastern goods (Figure 15.1), touches upon all the topics that are central in this volume. The painting shows that it was one of the many important cities located at the mouth of a river and at the seaside, with a vast hinterland and multiple connections by waterways and land routes, attracting specialized ships and entrepreneurs from various corners of Europe, and that it had developed institutions that had made their mark on the townscape. In addition to universality and connectedness, the painting displays some local details, like the gesture of a Polish nobleman shaking

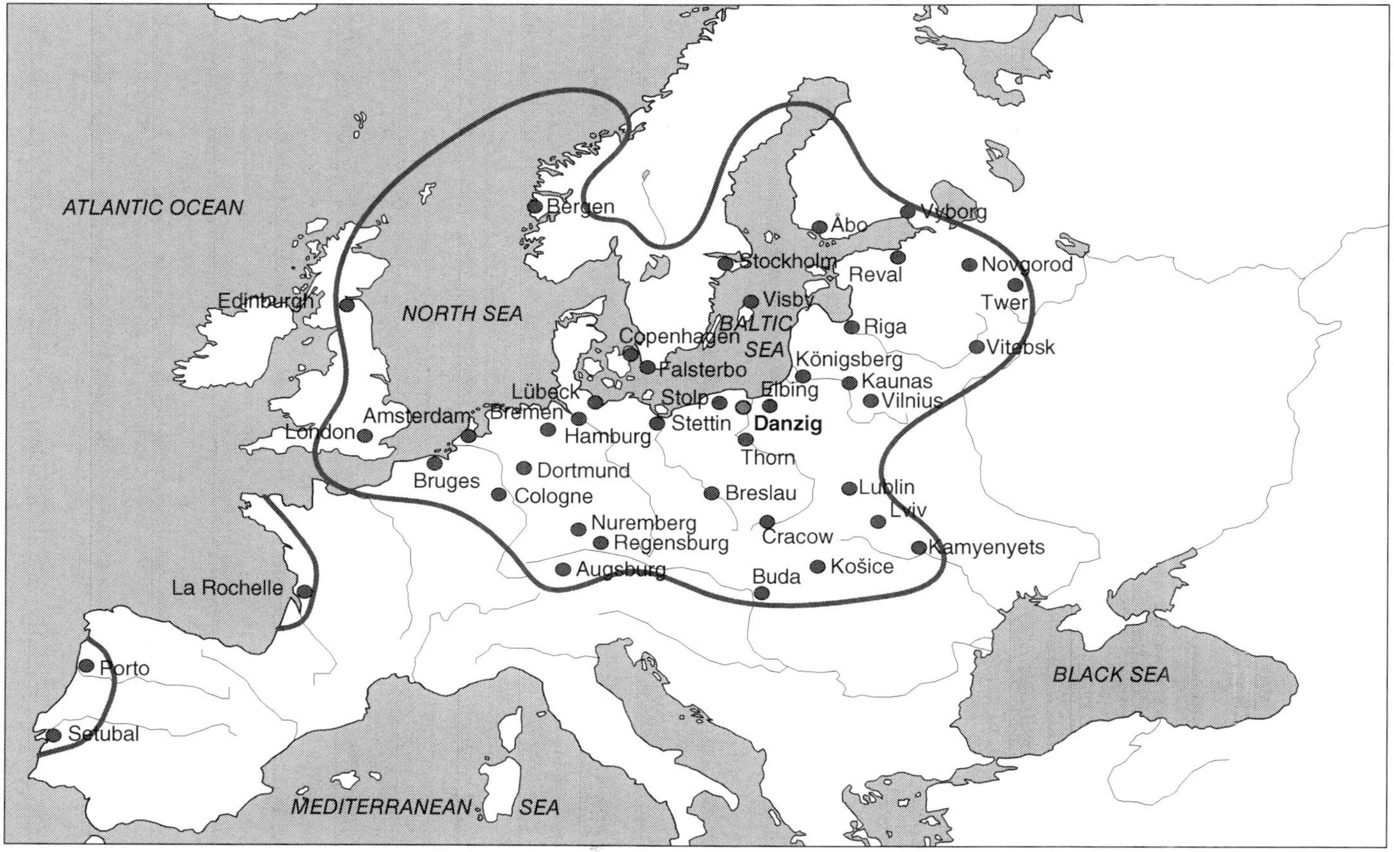

Figure 15.1 The connections of Danzig in the late Middle Ages.

hands with a Danzig trader after a concluded business deal or the competing high towers of the city hall and St Mary's. Above all, the perpetually renewed autonomy of the city, indicated by the architectural style of the *arc de triomphe*, is the centrepiece of this idea of Danzig.

Most scholars who have dealt with late medieval and early modern Danzig have acknowledged the fundamental role of autonomy in the development of the city's mercantile power. Yet their argumentation has usually placed this question of autonomy in relation to one of the political powers that could influence the position of Danzig. For the period discussed in this volume, these powers included the Teutonic Knights (from 1308 until the mid-fifteenth century) and thereafter the Polish king as the city's sovereign; the German emperor who laid fiscal and juridical claims on the city at the turn of and during the sixteenth century, despite the fact that Danzig was not a part of the empire; and the Hanse (especially Lübeck). The focus has been on what threatened the autonomy of the city. What is striking, although understandable when set against the modern history of Danzig/Gdańsk, is the diversity of the interpretations of this threat. In nineteenth-, twentieth- and even twenty-first-century German and Polish historical works on the medieval history of Danzig, the portrayal swung between documenting, respectively, the German and Polish roots and loyalties of the city.[2] This was especially politically charged in the *interbellum* (the period when the city had the status of a free city) during and after the Second World War, when the question of whose hands the city should be in and how to deal with its loss was a current matter. The issue of the medieval roots and loyalties of Danzig was therefore often the central argument in historical works; otherwise it was referred to in passing statements. Even the resolute choice of the double toponym Danzig/Gdańsk (for the medieval and early modern period) in some English-speaking publications, which was meant to signal the wish for a neutral approach, has to be seen as a reaction to this discourse, and thus not entirely free of it.[3]

In this chapter, the main argument will be Isaac van den Blocke's, and thus indirectly the municipal council's. Reappearing threats to their autonomy may be something they discussed in their letters, minutes of meetings, and instructions for envoys and also what springs to the eye of a historian, but the autonomy itself had an internal logic in the eyes of the burgomasters, councillors, judges and officials dealing with various matters of the city. This logic was hierarchically harmonious, well placed in the natural order of landscape and economic exchange with areas far and near, and blessed by the highest power. My point is that this rationale was the blueprint for the choices the municipal council made in political, economic, organizational and social terms. And in Danzig's case the municipal council was to a large extent not only synonymous with the political and commercial elite, but from the early sixteenth century on, also with the larger pool of economically active groups that held opinions on the balance between connections and autonomy (*Dritte Ordnung*, which comprised lesser merchants and craftsmen).[4] Departing from the purely economic discourse on merchants, guilds, cities and states, which revolves around the factors of and choices for economic growth, I will argue that, in Danzig, the primary concern was stability within the city itself, and in relation to the multiple parties it dealt with. The unprecedented economic boom of the sixteenth and early seventeenth centuries was certainly welcome and conspicuously flaunted, but it was perceived as a result of the care invested in erecting and renewing the autonomous foundations of the city's functioning.

This chapter is based on a very broad survey of extant primary sources for the chosen period.[5] First of all, the State Archives in Gdańsk are a treasure trove of municipal records, including correspondence, various types of minutes of the municipal council and the bench of aldermen, accounts and juridical sources. Even though a part of the evidence was lost as a result of the Second World War, it is still one of the richest Polish and Hanseatic municipal archives, with sources that are unique in Northern Europe. The sources from the 1530s onward have hardly been published, or even used by researchers. For the preceding period, source publications will also be used here.[6]

Location

The geographical location of Danzig was certainly advantageous for urban growth, and one of the prerequisites for its rise as a late medieval and early modern centre of commercial power. It allowed the Danzig merchants to combine riverine and sea trade: on the one hand, there was the protected harbour at the mouth of Vistula, a long river that connected several towns and agricultural regions. Bulk goods, most prominently grain and timber, could be easily transported to the city. And on the other hand, its very central position at the southern shore of the Baltic Sea was convenient for developing trading connections with Livonia, Russia, Finland and Sweden, including Finland, Denmark and the Hanseatic towns at the Baltic Sea. Through the Sound Straits, the outreach toward the North Sea was a logical prolongation of these connections.

The convenience of this location was recognized early. Ancient Roman sources (Pliny the Elder) recounted settlements on the southwestern shores of the Baltic, and archaeological finds confirm the existence of varied communities in the seventh and eighth centuries. In the second half of the tenth century a fortified settlement in what is now the centre of Gdańsk became the leading hub in the region. At the end of the century written sources document the existence of 'Gyddanyzc'. It was these early beginnings that have been a matter of historiographical discussion, namely the origin of the name (Germanic, Gothic, Latvian or Slavic; the current consensus being the latter), and who these early inhabitants were: Germanic peoples or Slavs. Several German scholars in the nineteenth and twentieth centuries put a German stamp on these origins to legitimize seeing modern Danzig as German. In turn, Polish excavations after the Second World War were focused on this 'either–or' question, and have produced extensive evidence of an early Slavic settlement. More recent research points to an influx of Slavic tribes from the seventh century and ongoing mixing with the local population, which was in part Germanic. When Danzig received official city rights in the first part of the thirteenth century for the first time (under a Pomeranian prince), it had Lübeck law. It is clear that many German settlers flowed in, especially Lübeckers. Beginning in the 1340s, Kulm law was introduced.[7]

Yet a geographically convenient position did not always guarantee straightforward prosperity for the city. Its potential in creating income through trade and customs was also noticed by various rulers, and accordingly Danzig was, several times, either a bone of contention or the main prize in wars. Early Danzig was under the rule of Pomeranian princes who, to varying degrees, recognized Polish supremacy over the region and the city, causing repeated struggle in the eleventh and twelfth centuries. In the thirteenth century the princes ruled independently, but it was still a disorderly period. The city came under the siege of the Teutonic Knights three times (in 1230 the military order, which was rapidly expanding its influence in the region, was brought in to subdue and convert the pagan Prussians). In 1271, Danzig was conquered by Brandenburgers, and thereafter various territorial princes assumed power over the city. In 1308, the Teutonic Knights were this time called in for help during a Brandenburgian siege, on the condition they would leave afterwards. Instead, after the victory, a massacre of Danzig's inhabitants followed, and as archaeological evidence shows, the city was partly burnt down: an act which forever earned the Knights the labels of 'treacherous' and 'brutal' in Polish historiography and popular imagery. For almost 150 years, Danzig would remain under the rule of the Teutonic Order.[8]

A major shift took place in the mid-fifteenth century. In 1454, the council turned to the Polish king to dispose of the Knights and put the city under his rule. Among other things, this was due to the fact that the Knights took the income from the pound toll (*Pfundzoll*), which was originally a Hanseatic tax collected when needed for war purposes. Trade interests were also put forward as a motivation in the correspondence with the Hanse.[9] The king agreed and after the city underpinned the request with military and financial contributions, he granted in 1457 a privilege that would be the foundation of the city's autonomy for centuries. The three settlements that had been administratively separate (Old, Young and Main Danzig) were merged into one;[10] almost 1,000 square kilometres of land properties were given to the city (decreased later, in part). In addition to the right of mint, the council was entitled to decide on the appointments of almost all ecclesiastical and secular offices in the city, no royal castles were to be built within 30–40 km of the city, and the city largely gained control of the Baltic coast from Stolp to Elbing (which were connected in interests with Danzig as Hanseatic towns, but had their own urban and mercantile identities). Furthermore, almost no staple rights of other towns and cities in the Crown were to obstruct Danzig's free trade, and the councillors could themselves decide on admitting foreigners to its commerce. The transition to the Polish Crown was not automatic or peaceful: the so-called Thirteen Years War against the Teutonic Order ensued, and only with the victory of Poland and Danzig could the privilege come into force.[11]

Danzig was not the only harbour in Prussia: its direct competitors in foreign trade were Thorn and Elbing, the latter being close to the site of the trading emporium Truso.[12] This legacy made it possible for its thirteenth-century rulers, the Teutonic Knights, to use it as a counterweight to the developing Danzig. Yet the changing shape of the mouth of the Vistula decreased Elbing's importance. In the late Middle Ages Elbing did not participate in the large-scale export of grain. It was mainly an importer of English cloth and could partly cover the needs of an export harbour, something that was incidentally (in the 1570s) used by the Polish king to put Danzig under pressure, but had no lasting effect on the grain trade.[13] The riverine harbour and town of Thorn was founded by the Teutonic Knights in the 1230s. In the second half of the fourteenth century they gave it staple rights for goods transported on the Vistula to the sea and thus created a commercial centre, which in the fourteenth century was a leading one in Prussia. Yet with the development of Danzig's harbour and the withdrawal of the Teutonic Order from Royal Prussia after 1466, when even its stronghold, the Marienburg castle (Malbork), came into Polish hands, Thorn's staple right was less observed and grain goods were mostly sold in Danzig.[14]

Moreover, there was also at least a twofold basis for cooperation between these towns: first of all, from 1440 onward, they were part of the Prussian Confederation, which was meant to safeguard the economic and political rights of the Prussian Estates (nobility and major towns and cities), and which played an important role both in the war with the Teutonic Knights in the mid-fifteenth century, and in keeping the autonomy of the region under the Polish Crown.[15] Second, all three trading centres were members of the Hanse, an organization of traders and towns that, whenever needed, pooled resources to secure shared trading privileges and protect their commerce. Cooperation between the Prussian towns in the Polish Crown thus outweighed competition.[16]

Changes in the geological, political and trade-organizational context clearly boosted Danzig's position in the region. When examining Danzig's locational advantages in the fifteenth and sixteenth centuries, what's striking is that the councillors, traders and city dwellers had made the most of it, and had thus superseded any port in the Baltic. The council controlled the entry to the harbour (as well as the exit) through the Vistula mouth fortress and lighthouse, an extensive waterfront infrastructure had been erected (including the huge treadwheel crane loading goods on ships, which as Krantor/Żuraw had become the symbol of Danzig), and there were shipyards and dozens of granaries that kept cereals conveniently stored and ready for shipment on the Isle of Granaries. Since the 1330s, there was also the Great Mill, which made it possible to export not only grain, but also meal (flour) on a large scale.[17] Like in other cases discussed in this volume, the developing infrastructure of the port was a crucial element in the growth of the city.

Bearing in mind that a convenient location would yield the most profit in a politically stable situation, the Danzig council was cautious when engaging in wars that would have an impact on its territory or have an adverse effect on the economy. In the sixteenth century, it repeatedly sought neutrality, trying to communicate that it functioned as an autonomous city within the Crown, and thus was not politically identical to the large state with its bellicose ambitions. It must be noted that, even though the legal concept was still to be developed in the seventeenth century, pragmatic neutrality was being negotiated earlier in Europe, as the case of Ragusa described in this volume also shows. The example of the conduct of Danzig's councillors, both as judges and envoys to the Polish and Danish kings during the Northern Seven Years' War (1563–70), demonstrates that it was the city's geographical position between the political powers in the Baltic, next to economic interests, that prompted the city officials to proceed with care. Such pursuit of the neutrality of Danzig's position was one of the ways to uphold its autonomy.[18]

This was connected to a particular challenge posed by the location of the city. Especially in the fifteenth and sixteenth centuries, Danzig's municipal council and its traders faced the problem of piracy and privateering. The attacks on Danzig ships could – and did – happen anywhere in the North and Baltic seas and were bitterly deplored in letters by injured citizens and by the city council, though the city itself was also often an actor in this play. On the one hand, privateers were based in Danzig and sent out as part of the city's policy or the joint policy of the Hanseatic towns. All towns engaged in sea trade were active users of privateers, while at the same time persecutors of pirates (even though they were often the same persons). On the other hand, in the sixteenth century the Polish king had also decided to make use of this main harbour of the Polish Crown (and the neighbouring town Putzig with its dependent port, which Danzig pawned from him), for his own privateers. This resulted several times in a conflict of interests for Danzig's councillors and traders, namely when ships of their sovereign attacked their business partners and the city was made liable for the losses. The geography of a commercial centre, however wide the boundaries of its autonomy were, was inextricably connected to politics and economy.[19]

Hinterland and connections

This also becomes apparent when we step outside the city itself and its immediate vicinity, and turn to its hinterland. What should we see as Danzig's hinterland?

In many respects, Danzig's hinterland is archetypical for a significant trading centre: it covered a huge area and provided a flagship product, which turned out to be in high demand in other parts of Europe. Specifically, the hinterland covered large parts of what is now Poland, western Ukraine, and parts of Lithuania and Russia (see Figure 15.2). This area had connections, through both waterways and land transport, to the Vistula and thus could ship large quantities of its produce downstream. Isaac van den Blocke's painting illustrates the whole infrastructure of this transport: various types of ships and barges (some of which were dismantled once they arrived in

Danzig), peasants who were boatmen and their lodgings in Danzig. The main goods they transported were cereals: rye, and to some extent wheat and barley. A secretary of the emperor remarked in 1534 that, thanks to this supply of grain, 'la ville de Danzwick, laquelle ne souloit estre que ung village, est a ceste heure plus puissante et plus riche ville de toute la mer d'Oostlande' (the city of Danzig, which was not much more than a village, is right now the most powerful and wealthy city in the Baltic Sea area).[20] The grain was then in part turned in Danzig into beer and meal (and in the latter form exported to the countries that had few mills or could not compete with milling prices, like Norway), and in part stored in Danzig's many granaries and then shipped further. Researchers have mostly pointed to the second half of the fourteenth century as a starting point for an increase of scale, which in the sixteenth century was to become explosive, and Danzig would be known as 'the granary of Europe'.[21]

A recent analysis rejects this view, claiming that the fifteenth-century Prussian grain trade has been overestimated quantitatively, which means that, in the sixteenth century, it was all the more explosive.[22] This conclusion may lead to interesting additions or modifications of what until now have been considered the reasons for the gradual surge: the pastoralization, urbanization and industrialization of the

Figure 15.2 Mercury and merchants, *Allegory of Danzig Trade*, by Isaac van den Blocke (fragment). Detail from cover illustration

Low Countries combined with poor harvests in Western Europe, which resulted in increased demand for grain there (especially after Amsterdam started to re-export the grain); demand for grain in Scandinavia; weakened English agriculture that couldn't cover the demand in other countries; the increase of ties and involvement of the Polish nobility in the production and export of grain after 1466; the urbanization of Prussia itself (at the end of the sixteenth century around 35 per cent of the inhabitants of Royal Prussia lived in towns); the rise of shipping in Holland and Zeeland; and finally the availability of cheap French and Portuguese salt that could be brought on the way to Danzig as cargo. The numbers on the surge are telling: at the end of the fifteenth century, Prussia exported *c.*10,000 lasts of grain per year (22,000 tons), in the second half of the sixteenth century *c.*40,000 lasts (88,000 tons) and in 1618–19 even 100,000 lasts (220,000 tons) per year. Of this export 80 per cent went through Danzig, which illustrates well the position of the city in the Baltic region.[23]

Yet grain was not the only merchandise that this hinterland channelled to and through Danzig: another important product was timber, needed for the construction of ships in Danzig's shipyards, but also for orders from shipbuilders in the Low Countries, England and Portugal. Tar and hemp were also in demand for this industry, while ash was needed for the textile industry and the making of glass; wax from eastern beehives lit churches and houses in Western Europe, furs provided warmth and splendour, and Baltic amber adorned necks and fingers.[24]

Next to the direct hinterland, there were connections through riverine trade and relatively close sea routes that made Danzig an important crossroads in trade. Hungary provided copper (needed, for instance, for cooking vessels), southern Poland sent lead (i.e. for roofing or fastening stained glass), and southern Germany sent mining products for metallurgical industries. Scania, at that time under Denmark, and the Sound were the main places where herring was fished and sent off to Danzig, catering to the consumption needs during the many fast days. Finland, then part of Sweden, also provided wood products: on a more modest scale, but in a continuous flow.[25] Sweden was a major provider of metal, and in the sixteenth century Danzig was second after Lübeck in importing and re-exporting Swedish copper and iron ore, which were exchanged for western goods and grain. In a source from the 1560s, the city councillors stated that thousands of people in Danzig (numbering then 60,000–80,000 inhabitants) depended on the trade with Sweden and cutting it off would leave them beggars. This utterance was, quite typically, made when the Polish king forbade this trade during the Northern Seven Years' War.[26] The anxieties the Danzig municipal council repeatedly voiced on the changes of and hindrances posed to the supply of goods from this diversified hinterland are documented in their internal discussions and writing to their king and other rulers. Their ideal situation is portrayed in the *Allegory of Danzig Trade*: the solid arch supporting the city has its foundations in a well outlined, controllable and peaceful hinterland and trading connections close by.

The stability of the relations with the hinterland also depended on the supply of goods from afar that Danzig had to guarantee: the typical Polish nobleman had an almost proverbially huge appetite for fine wines, exotic fruits, spices, and fabulous woollens and silks, which he (or more often, his Jewish business representative) received in exchange for grain and other hinterland goods. But townsmen, peasants and clergy also wanted Flemish, Brabantine, and Hollandish and English woollens of qualities and prices that matched moneybags of various sizes, and cheap salt to season and preserve their food. Books and (church) art from the West were also in high demand: the culture that Danzig traders and students encountered during their travels and studies was readily accepted in the city.[27] This supply went hand in hand with a marked foreign presence in Danzig: in a 1536 source, the municipal council stated that their city was 'als corpus auss manicherley nation zusamen gesetzt' (as a body consists of many 'nations', i.e. groups with various backgrounds).[28] This is also easily visible in van den Blocke's painting, where the variety of traders depicted is placed at the forefront. But the connections went beyond the city itself. There were ties to be entertained with foreign towns, states and organizations of traders who were not burghers in Danzig. This diversity meant that various interests had to be balanced: connectedness brought both possible gains, and also challenges. Three main areas of connections of supply and demand, which branched off further, can be discussed here: Hansards, Hollanders and Zeelanders, who ceased to be perceived as Hansards in the first half of the fifteenth century, and non-Hansards.

The prime network of connections for Danzig was the Hanse. Traders from the main city of Danzig, primarily German settlers, established contacts with Lübeck in the thirteenth century and were among the Hanse members who witnessed and perpetrated the organic growth of the organization. From 1361 on, they attended Hanse Diets, and in the first half of the fifteenth century when the contours of the Hanse became clearer, Danzig was prominently within its boundaries. Joining this organization of towns and networks was an efficient way to gain access to collective rights and privileges from various foreign rulers, enjoy the protection of settlements abroad, and particularly in the four main Kontore (in Bruges followed by Antwerp in the sixteenth century, London, Bergen and Novgorod). Through trading partnerships that combined distant markets in Europe, Danzig could be admitted to a large pool of information exchange, operate with the very solid currency of trust and reputation, and was able to muster collective resources to protect shipping and ward off (or even launch) military attacks against its own and foreign rulers.[29] (One more feature, conflict resolution, is discussed separately, in the last section.) In other words, it was an attractive network for Danzig traders and municipal councillors to be part of. What probably also played a major role was that several towns in the relative vicinity (in Prussia, Pomerania, Brandenburg and Livonia) were also members of the Hanse – Danzig being the most prominent one and thus having extra clout in the Baltic region.[30] Fellow Hanse traders cooperated with Danzigers in bringing in the goods desired in the city and its hinterland, and shipped off the grain: they were the main players until the middle of the fifteenth century, when Hollanders and Zeelanders gradually took over. In the sixteenth century, the Low Countries (and Amsterdam in particular) and Danzig were communicating vessels in terms of grain trade.[31]

For Danzig the drawback of membership in this network was that in the sixteenth century appeals to its resources were made several times to support the military endeavours of other Hanse towns, most notably Lübeck. The sources show that the Danzig municipal council had ideas and interests quite the opposite of Lübeck, especially if they concerned Hollanders. In order to avoid or limit its involvement, the Danzig municipal council had to deploy diplomatic skills or be prepared to face harsh criticism.[32] Another downside was the obligation to observe some of the shared rules of the Hanse, for instance keeping the wine and cloth staple in Bruges, when Danzig gradually preferred to venture to its Brabantine competitor, Antwerp.[33] Finally, in the second half of the fifteenth century, a recurring issue was the question of the shared Hanseatic liability: the rulers of England and the Netherlands wanted to treat the Hanse as one body, where the deeds of the traders or privateers from one town made burghers of other Hanseatic towns juridically and politically responsible. In the view of Danzig's councillors, this erroneous idea of the Hanse was a serious threat to the city.[34]

The links with the Hanse traders and towns had to be balanced with the increasing trading interest that joined Danzig with Hollanders, Zeelanders and, in the sixteenth century, merchants of Antwerp. Until the early fifteenth century, this did not constitute a major problem. Hollanders and Zeelanders were part of the Hanse in economic, political and organizational terms.[35] Moreover, the scale of Danzig's foreign trade was then still relatively modest. With the definition of Hollanders and Zeelanders as non-Hansards, and the influx of shippers from these countries who offered competitive freight prices for the shipment of grain, the situation became more complex for Danzigers. Recognizing the opportunities brought by direct contact with the cloth-producing and grain-demanding Netherlands, which also happened to be able to ship large quantities of Portuguese and French salt, the Danzig municipal council chose to tread a cautious middle road. It stayed in the Hanse, but let trade contact with the Netherlands increase steadily. While according to the extant sources there were eleven ships coming per year in 1460 and five towns were mainly involved, in 1498 this rose to 402 ships and thirty-one registered place names in the Netherlands, and in 1583 reached 1,070 ships and fifty-seven places in the various provinces of the Netherlands.[36] Even though the active trade of Danzigers with the Netherlands (i.e. their own travelling there) gradually decreased in this period, sources show they were present in the places where the economic boom was happening in the sixteenth century, namely Antwerp and Amsterdam. The Dutch Revolt did not weaken the importance of these contacts: quite the contrary, demand for the grain only increased and, as a Spanish diplomat once stated, without the Danzig grain the war would soon starve away.[37] Moreover, the economic contacts were strengthened by intellectual exchange: from the end of the sixteenth century, Danzigers studied in Leiden, Franeker, Groningen and from the seventeenth century on, in Utrecht and Amsterdam. Among them was Philipp Cluver (Cluverius), a Leiden professor and the father of historical geography: yet another example of the approach of Danzigers to their connections in Europe.[38]

The English constituted an important non-Hanseatic pool of connections. The contacts were early and, at first, stimulated by the English demand for Baltic furs and hides. From the thirteenth century on, ties between Danzig and England were established through Lübeck and later primarily through the Kontor in London. Next to the Bruges settlement, this Kontor was the one most frequented by Danzigers.[39] The portrait of such a trader, Georg Gisze (Giese), painted in the sixteenth century by Hans Holbein, is often put forth as the emblematic image of a Hanseatic trader holding in his hands the prime tool of his trade: namely business letters, which allowed his connections to span as far as ships and the imagination would go. Yet the contacts with the English were complex: politically, the Danzig council was often more opposed to them than other Hanseatic councils, especially in the period 1467–74 when Danziger ships were attacked, and the Anglo-Hanseatic War ensued. There were tensions in both London and Danzig. The English were clearly less welcome than Hollanders. At the same time, trade – which, beginning in the fifteenth century included the import of English cloth – was highly profitable.[40] During the reign of the Tudors, economic relations improved, on the one hand, probably because of the high demand for wood and other shipbuilding materials. Yet on the other hand, English protectionism and difficulties posed to the Hanseatic Kontor in London, triggered many times by clashes and lawsuits within Danzig, contributed to keeping this connection knotty. The creation of the Eastland Company in 1579, and, in the 1570s, the settlement of the English in the fellow-yet-competing Elbing, did not reverse this trend.[41]

Finally, there were other groups of non-Hansards in contact with Danzig. Scotsmen came as petty merchants and often settled permanently in the city itself, its suburbs or in Prussia. The connection with Norway was based on an exchange of codfish for grain, but Danzigers were never prominent in the Bergen Kontor.[42] Furthermore, there were links to the Atlantic coast, most importantly through the import of French salt. Most of this salt was brought to Danzig by other Hansards and Hollanders, but Danzigers also ventured west. The salt business was supplied by imports of wine, fruits and spices from southern France. In the fifteenth and early sixteenth centuries Danzigers went to Portugal as well to fetch the same types of products and exchange them for wood and products needed for shipbuilding, linen and grain. Last but not least, Italians met with Danzigers in the whole period analysed here in Bruges and Antwerp, and Florentine ships occasionally ventured to the Baltic. In the end of the sixteenth century, the demand for Baltic grain connected Venice with Danzig through sea and land routes.[43] This is yet another dimension of the adage in Isaac van den Blocke's painting: 'We are all connected'.

Institutions: keys to stability and autonomy

In a recent publication on the reasons for the demise of Lübeck and Danzig in the seventeenth century, Erik Lindberg put forward the thesis that municipal institutions should be seen as one of the factors that hampered the integration of foreigners and openness of trade. In other words, these municipal institutions held back economic growth.[44] His argument to a large extent squares with Oscar Gelderblom's findings that the proactive policy of municipal councils, in this case Antwerp and Amsterdam, played an important role in securing a dominant position on the European mercantile stage.[45] What would Isaac van den Blocke, an offspring of an artistic family from Mechelen and a second-generation Danziger, have thought of the constraints and opportunities created by local institutions, when he painted his *Allegory of Danzig Trade*? His work received an honorary exhibition spot in the meeting chamber of the municipal council, so perhaps he was more than inclined to render the official version of this main urban institution. The painting shows that there was room for people from various backgrounds in Danzig. That is, as long as they brought prosperity to the city and conducted their business under the overarching supervision of the municipal council. It was all part of an established order: at the top of the painting was God, in the middle the municipal council and at the bottom the god Mercury danced around Danzigers and foreigners (see Figure 15.2).

In the middle of the fifteenth century, when Danzig became part of the Polish Crown, there was a marked shift in institutional terms for the city. The impact and autonomy of the council increased significantly. As mentioned earlier, the three cities of Danzig (Old, Young and Main, only the latter being part of the Hanse) became one, which meant that the position of the council gathering in the Main City hall, largely composed of influential merchants conducting international trade, was strengthened. The council combined administrative, political and judicial roles in the persons of the four (rotating) burgomasters and fourteen councillors (with the addition of five from the Old City, now a city quarter). Both the burgomasters and councillors were charged with specific tasks within the whole city. Outside of it, they functioned as envoys to the Polish king, other rulers and to Hanse meetings. There was also an extended form of the council, which comprised the bench of twelve aldermen and its president (*Schöppengericht*), and from 1526 on, the *Dritte Ordnung*, which gathered the representatives of lesser traders and craftsmen.[46]

There were also other institutions with direct links to the council. From the second half of the fifteenth century, there was the *Burggraf*, a representative of the king but chosen among the councillors, and the judicial body called the *Wette* (which further developed and gained importance in the fifteenth and sixteenth centuries) for trade and criminal matters, as well as registering new burghers. In judicial matters specifically concerning the Old City, the five Old City councillors functioned as a separate council. All these bodies overlapped as jurisdictions, or were instances of appeal to each other (for instance, the narrowly defined municipal council for the bench of aldermen and the Old City council), and also doubled as institutions where commercial deals, contracts, debts, inheritances or the outcomes of arbitration were registered: a role fulfilled elsewhere by notaries. The latter only started to make an appearance in the city in the second half of the sixteenth century.[47]

Since 1341, an important economic institution connected to the municipal council and the city hall, was the *Pfahlkammer*. It was led by two councillors who supervised the collection of mooring fees from incoming ships and their use in the development of the harbour, as well as the prevention of illegal ballast disposal in the harbour. This way the increase of trade facilitated a positive spiral of improved infrastructure, and in turn more trade. Right next to the city hall in van den Blocke's painting was the ornamental building of the Artushof, with a nod to the legend of the noble brotherhood of knights of King Arthur. Since the mid-fourteenth century, and especially in the sixteenth and seventeenth centuries, it was a pivotal socio-religious and economic institution of the city, housing several confraternities. It gathered prominent burghers, mainly traders and councillors, and welcomed foreign traders as well. Here, with a beaker of strong Danzig beer in hand, future business deals and outlines of the city's inner and outer policies took shape. The integration of this institution into an overall idea of stable municipal government appears from the location of the bench of aldermen right next to it, and the arrangement that two councillors were charged with supervising it. The municipal council and the related institutions controlled most aspects of life in Danzig.[48]

The fact that the municipal council firmly held on to the institutional autonomy gained in the mid-fifteenth century is visible mainly in three aspects, namely the question of courts and appeal, substantive law, and citizenship versus guest law. First of all, the municipal council was wary of external jurisdictions intermingling in its affairs: ecclesiastical courts were defined this way, as were courts of foreign rulers and towns, with the exception of courts of other Hanseatic towns (see the section on 'Conflict resolution').[49] The municipal council also vehemently opposed the introduction of new royal institutions that would curb its own judicial competences: this appears from a conflict with the king that erupted in 1568/70 after he had established the Maritime Committee (the Court of the Admiralty, operating as a royal institution until 1572), which was to deal with matters of piracy and unruly privateering.[50] As is stated in one of the sources, the city *had* sea law (as a result of the 1457 privilege), meaning not only that substantive law on these matters was formulated, but also that the council had the (exclusive) right to adjudicate these cases.[51] The issue of appeal from the verdicts of the municipal council was hotly debated and only in some matters accepted from the Prussian Council (which was a gathering of the Estates, i.e. nobility, and representatives of the Prussian towns) and the Polish king. In 1526, the king agreed with the city on the level of appeal, namely that all civil cases concerning property or sums lower than 500 Polish gulden (złoty) were to be resolved in Danzig and no appeal to him was possible. This meant that, in theory, only large and complex matters were liable to be adjudicated further outside of Danzig.[52]

Second, the agreements from the mid-fifteenth century also gave significant autonomy to the formulation of laws and regulations in Danzig. This substantive law was an essential institution from the mercantile point of view.[53] Initially, Danzig was governed by the Lübeck law, a set of rules based on Saxon law, which made a substantial mark on the Baltic Sea area. In the 1340s, the Teutonic Order, then overlord of Danzig, changed it to the Kulm law, a variant of the Magdeburg law, another influential Saxon law code. It gave less autonomy to the cities and towns.[54] From the mid-fifteenth century on, at the latest, the Danzig municipal council formulated its rules (*Wilkore*), adapted and read aloud many times every year. These rules dealt with the specificities of Danzig, to a large extent trade, foreigners and sea matters, in issues not covered by the Kulm law.[55] As subsidiary law in criminal matters, the council used Constitutio Criminalis Carolina (1532), promulgated by Emperor Charles V, and in questions of violence on country roads, a constant matter of concern for traders, it also followed the decisions on the breach of the imperial *Landfriede* (1495, promulgated in Mainz).[56] Yet as with the use of the Kulm/Magdeburg law, this was kept strictly apart from the political allegiance of the city. In the course of the late fifteenth and the sixteenth century, the city several times rejected fiscal and juridical claims of the emperor, most notably contributions to the war against Turks and litigation before the imperial highest court (*Reichskammergericht*).[57] Finally, a source for the formulation of city rules and regulations, especially in sea matters, were the decisions (*Recesse*) taken at the Hanse Diets (*Hansetage*). Whenever these decisions were considered beneficial for a city they were incorporated in the *Wilkore* – and only then were seen as valid for this city in the Hanse context, another example of how Danzig's autonomy was safeguarded in an institutional context. These decisions concerned practical matters like freight, obedience to the shipmaster or procedures in case of shipwreck and jettison, and were explicitly evoked whenever it was seen as beneficial.[58] When the sea matter was politicized, such as when the municipal council had to adjudicate whether a ship seizure was an act of piracy or privateering, they turned to the law applying to land, and thus the municipal itself.[59]

An important institution in the life of any town or city was citizenship. The sources on the *Dritte Ordnung* show that rules regarding burghership were established after lengthy discussions within the council, and if there were concerns about the impact of newcomers, they came from the representatives of lesser traders and craftsmen. But even they welcomed 'Redtliche auffrichtige vnd vermagene leutt die mitt keiner falschen opinion befleckett' (reasonable, honest and wealthy people of good reputation).[60] This complied with the general rule on being approved as a new burgher in Europe. A prime concern connected to new burghers also surfaces in the context of religious unrest. Lutheranism came in two waves (in the 1520s and 1550s, when it was officially allowed after 1555), but since it was largely accepted by the city councillors, as was mainstream Calvinism, it was not an issue undermining the stability of this institution. Control was the key word here as well: it is no coincidence that the tower of the city hall is just one metre shorter than the tower of St Mary's, and after all, the council decided on the appointments to the ecclesiastical offices. Lutheranism became a way to mark distinctiveness and autonomy towards the rest of the Polish Crown, which was largely Catholic.[61] Religious movements defined as sects and heretics, on the other hand, were a different matter, the example of Anabaptists in Münster (1534) being a nightmare for both Danzig and other Hanseatic towns. Therefore disruptive movements were forbidden.[62] But foreigners, who were not given this access, could still settle in one of the suburbs, and in such a way they were still part of the economic life of the city itself, through craftsmanship and local trade. This concerned people from some Protestant movements, like Mennonites, who were not tolerated within the city proper. These places also accepted Jews or petty merchants like Scotsmen. This shows that religious tolerance, to the extent that it did not interfere with the safety of the city, was at work.[63]

Because the sources on acquiring citizenship are patchy for our period, since (last) names in Northern Europe do not provide hard evidence, and since once someone became a burgher his background was hardly ever mentioned in the sources if it was not relevant to the matter, it is difficult to establish the extent of immigration and settlement. Still, qualitative sources suggest that there was substantial influx of new burghers and inhabitants from the Low Countries, the Hanseatic towns, England, Scotland and Scandinavia. These were not only merchants and seamen, but also craftsmen – in particular, specialists in shipbuilding, infrastructure (harbour and fortifications), brewing, textile weaving, architecture and art. Apart from the material mark still visible in the Danzig townscape, place names and landscape in the vicinity, sources on religious matters show that the foreign element, which stayed permanently in and close to Danzig, was considerable.[64]

Finally, connected to the institution of citizenship was the institution of guest law. It can, on the one hand, be seen as substantive law, namely rules concerning non-permanent stay. The prime rule was that guests were not allowed to trade with each other, resell goods or conduct retail trade of cloth and spices (*Wilkore* of 1455).[65] Moreover, the 1457 privilege allowed the municipal council to decide for itself and per group on which terms foreign guests were allowed to stay, that is, to formulate substantive guest law and regulations.[66] On the other hand, and perhaps more importantly, it was procedural law, pronouncing that commercial and sea-related matters were to be adjudicated swiftly. In this respect, it can be seen as part of the all-European idea that trade conflicts had to be dealt with efficiently if trade was to function properly – in other words, what was understood as Lex Mercatoria.[67] It must be underlined that this institution was present prominently in Danzig: an analysis of concrete cases shows that it was asked for, applied and communicated to the external world, i.e. to rulers and other towns. If the municipal council or one of the other jurisdictions failed to comply with it and a case dragged on, they were rebuked by the authorities whose burghers were involved in the case.[68] At times, the Polish king wrote to the Danzig council on behalf of a foreigner who had to wait too long for justice.[69] What is striking is that the council did not see the institution of guest law and the possibility to be called to task as an encroachment on their autonomy. This was perhaps because it was a general rule in commercial centres, and they understood that it was vital for their economic stability. Institutions in late medieval and early modern times, whether as organizational bodies or more abstractly as rules of the game, existed to provide stability.

Conflict resolution

The example of conflict resolution illustrates how this stability was pursued, and which means were employed to find a balance between economic and political, and internal and external interests. The large-scale conflicts have already been addressed in part in the section on location: military clout was used carefully in the period discussed here, and almost always in cooperation with other parties like the Polish king or Lübeck. The 1576–7 war against the Polish elected king, Stefan Batory, was an exceptional situation. It was seen as an ultimate step to safeguard the autonomy of the city.[70] The councillors preferred diplomacy, and accordingly they invested a lot of money, time and effort in it. A telling illustration is that when the Danzig representatives were invited to the coronation of the Danish king in 1537, rather than spending their time feasting and watching old-fashioned jousting, they preferred drafting a diplomatic list of demands concerning commercial damages resulting from the recent war, and lobbying important people in Copenhagen for it.[71] Gift-giving was also a persuasive tactic in relations with Polish noblemen to smooth out conflicts and buy autonomy (a tactic Polish magnates also used).[72] On a larger scale, the aforementioned pursuit of neutrality was also a conflict resolution strategy.[73]

Here, I would like to turn primarily to conflict resolution that was a result of individual or group commercial conflicts. The existence of the institution of guest law in Danzig, and its application in mercantile cases, points to the general attitude that mercantile needs had to be catered to. This also appears from how problems resulting from the mobility of traders were approached, most notably the question of complicated inheritances having to be retrieved from many places. Merchant widows and orphans especially could count on the listening ear of the city jurisdictions.[74] Furthermore, there were councillors specifically charged with problems of shippers and crews, shipments of goods, and the throwing of ballast in the harbour, a recurring nuisance for the city as ships usually arrived with lighter goods and departed with heavier grain. (The repeated bans might have resulted in the long run in the increased import of salt from France and Portugal to even out this imbalance.) Altogether, the further development of institutions in the sixteenth century would indicate that the Danzig municipal council was well aware of the competitive advantage of properly functioning and specialized institutions of conflict resolution.[75]

In a very brief overview of a complex matter and vast material, what appears from a systematic analysis of conflict resolution cases of foreign traders and shippers, conducted across several types of sources related to the municipal council in the period 1450–1580?[76] First of all, it turns out that the cases concerned every thinkable aspect of mercantile life, including criminal matters, as was the case elsewhere. Apparently, the Danzig courts were considered competent to adjudicate these matters, or at least this was hardly questioned, while foreign complaints on the speed of the procedure did occur.[77] Second, it is striking that individual cases involving foreigners very often had a political underpinning. This transpires from the fact that foreign towns and rulers were involved in the background from an early stage, either by providing letters of support, testimonials or exerting pressure through various channels, including the Polish king.[78] Even small issues could potentially turn into a large-scale conflict, so the municipal council was clearly preparing for this event by documenting the proceedings in writing, and if necessary, providing copies of it. Following the general development in the functioning of European administration, courts and diplomacy, the late fifteenth and sixteenth centuries witnessed a veritable communicative explosion in terms of the paper trail produced: among other things, in connection with the availability of cheap paper. The whole of the legal procedure changed with the increased use of procedural Roman law in the courts, for instance by introducing extensive witness hearings, which all became registered in writing. This also entailed a surge in the correspondence on all matters, including mercantile conflicts, with powers like the regent of the Netherlands, the queen of England, the Prussian duke, or towns and cities in the Netherlands and the Hanse. Individual mercantile matters, even when dealt with in a court, were thus always set within a larger political and economic context.[79] Third, this politicization led to the formulation, and consistent use, of the concept of reciprocity in mercantile conflict resolution matters, both in relations with Hansards and non-Hansards. When looking specifically at legal proceedings it remained mostly implicit, but the correspondence about it was very explicit: rulers and municipal councils asked for fair treatment, 'as you would like us to treat your merchants'. Failure to do so, in either a legal or political forum in Danzig (the latter, for instance, when the municipal council declined to pay restitutions for privateering) could and often did result in collective reprisals.[80]

Two general remarks refer to the conflict resolution of the two largest groups of foreigners, namely traders and shippers coming from the Netherlands, and the English. While the latter appeared frequently before the courts and in correspondence, the former were surprisingly infrequent given the intensity of the contacts. It could mean that many conflicts were resolved by arbitration and thus were not registered by the institutions and in the written sources. Another possibility is that the provenance of a defendant or plaintiff from Holland, Zeeland or Brabant was not always registered, especially if he was (about to) become a burgher. Second, it is striking that the correspondence on conflict resolution within Danzig, or concerning Danzigers abroad, was conducted with the English rulers (king and council), while in relation to the Netherlands, the contact persons were both the rulers (regents) and the municipal councils of the individual towns and cities involved in the case. For instance, there is ample correspondence on such matters with Amsterdam, Dordrecht, Middelburg and Antwerp. In this respect, the communication on *individual* cases of conflict resolution resembled the workings within the Hanse.

This brings us to an important institution of conflict resolution for Danzig, namely the Hanse. Elsewhere, I argue in more detail that next to being an organization of cities, towns and traders, the Hanse functioned for its members as an efficient institution of conflict resolution.[81] This was probably one of the main aspects of the added value that membership in the Hanse provided. Specifically, three things stand out as quite different from conflict resolution with non-Hansards: the fact that Hanse traders and municipal councils treated each other's courts as their own legal forums (which appears from their definitions of foreign courts, and of the legal practice), that the Hanse Diet could also function as a forum for non-judicial conflict resolution, and that the pragmatically oriented merchant-councillors developed conflict resolution strategies for conflicts *within* the Hanse. This entailed almost automatic and repeated mediation by neighbouring municipal councils, and a clear effort to avoid the use of collective reprisals. There was evidently awareness that this measure often turned into a vicious circle of violence and endless litigation. Other aspects of Hanseatic conflict resolution were not different from conflict resolution with traders and municipal councils outside of the Hanse in the mechanisms themselves, only in their degree and sometimes subtle (although significant) variations. For instance, Hansards provided more extensive information on the legal proceedings to each other and accepted each other's written proofs and testimonials more readily. There was also – even stronger than outside of the Hanse – an expectation of reciprocity in the fair treatment of each other's burghers. However, it was usually not formulated as a veiled threat, but as an assurance of long-lasting, friendly relations.[82]

The Hanse was also present as an institution of conflict resolution in issues with neighbouring Hanseatic towns in Royal and Ducal Prussia. A case in point was the prolonged conflict of Danzig with Königsberg. This was political in the background, as the two cities vied for precedence as Prussian towns, being after the mid-fifteenth century the main centres of Royal and Ducal Prussia, respectively. Politically, it was irresolvable, but the shared membership in the Hanse and mediation of other towns made it possible to continue economic relations.[83] The fact that Danzig remained a member of the Hanse even in the period when the organization was gradually losing its political and economic power – while Danzig's own standing skyrocketed – might be ascribed at least in part to the fact that Hanseatic conflict resolution provided clear benefits. And as such, it also increased the stability of Danzig as a commercial centre in the Baltic region.

Conclusions

The case of Danzig shows that in a relatively autonomous mercantile centre, its councillors and tradesmen were well aware of the advantages and challenges of its location, of the opportunities offered by its hinterland, and of the need to balance its economic and political connections. They acted upon this, and adapted the city's institutions accordingly. Early Danzig faced a political lack of stability, which the city's traders, who were most often also its city councillors, sought to compensate through participation in mercantile networks like the Hanse. Once a political and to a large extent also legal and economic autonomy was established under the Polish Crown from the mid-fifteenth century onward, a major goal was to safeguard this position and keep the political and economic connections stable. This manifested in the pursuit of neutrality whenever possible, and resulted in an economic boom from the sixteenth century on, which made Danzig the main grain trade centre in the Baltic and an important player in Europe's vast mercantile network. Through connections in the Low Countries, Baltic grain became a staple in far-flung places in Europe, and at the same time it financed the market of luxury goods in Danzig and its vast hinterland. Making sure that both the infrastructure and institutions of conflict resolution were up to date and attractive to those foreigners that the city wanted to welcome was also part of the pursuit of stability of economic connections. This was the daily task of the councillors and other city officials. The *Allegory of Danzig Trade* contained thus not only a checklist for the painter, but also – and perhaps primarily – one for the city council and the institutions it controlled.

Acknowledgements

The research for this chapter was funded by The Netherlands Organization for Scientific Research (NWO).

Notes

1 On the cover of the volume, Gdańsk History Museum, Main City Hall, Red Chamber.

2 P. Simson, *Geschichte der Stadt Danzig*, 3 vols, Danzig: Scientia Verlag, 1913–17; E. Keyser, *Danzigs Geschichte*, Danzig: Rafemann, 1921; E. Cieślak (ed.), *Historia Gdańska* [The History of Gdańsk], vols 1 and 2, Gdańsk: Wydawnictwo Morskie, 1978, 1982; G. Labuda, *Historia Pomorza* [The History of Pomerania], vols 1 and 2, Poznan: PTPN, 1972, 1976; T. Maćkowski, 'Gdańsk caught between Lübeck and the Polish kingdom', in H. Brand (ed.), *The German Hanse in Past & Present Europe: A Medieval League as a Model for Modern Interregional Cooperation?* Groningen: Hanse Passage/Castel International Publishers, 2007; M. Biskup, 'Prusy Królewskie w II połowie XV i w XVI stuleciu' [Royal Prussia in the second half of the fifteenth and in the sixteenth century], in J. Axer (ed.), *Panorama lojalności: Prusy Królewskie i Prusy Książęce w XVI wieku* [A panorama of loyalty: Royal and Ducal Prussia in the sixteenth century], Warsaw: OBTA 2001; P. O. Loew, *Danzig: Biographie einer Stadt*, Munich: C. H. Beck, 2011. See also the contributions in E. Kizik (ed.), *Prusy Królewskie: Społeczeństwo, kultura, gospodarka 1454–1772* [Royal Prussia: society, culture, economy 1454–1772], Gdańsk: Muzeum Narodowe w Gdańsku, 2012, as well as B. Dybaś and D. Makilla, *Prusy i Inflanty między średniowieczem a nowożytnością. Państwo – społeczeństwo – kultura* [Prussia and Livonia between the Middle Ages and the early modern period: state, society, culture], Toruń: WUMK, 2003.

3 Maria Bogucka, *Baltic Commerce and Urban Society, 1500–1700: Gdańsk/Danzig and Its Polish Context*, Aldershot: Ashgate Variorum, 2003.

4 C. Biernat, *Recesy gdańskich ordynków 1545–1814* [The recesses of the Third Order 1545–1814], Gdańsk: Gdańskie Towarzystwo Naukowe, 1958.

5 State Archives in Gdańsk (henceforth APG): 300 D Correspondence and documents until 1525; 300,1 Burgomaster; 300,3 Burggraf; 300,5 Vice-Burgomaster; 300,6 Judge; 300,10 Recesses of the orders; 300,12 Kämmerei; 300,17 Fiscal matters; 300,27 Missiva; 300,28 Hanse; 300,41 Altstadt; 300,43 Schöffengericht (Aldermen's Bench); 300,44 Ordinances; 300,53 Correspondence after 1525; 300,58 Wette; 300,59 Libri Memorandorum; 300,60 Burghership books; 300,93 Edicts; 300 R Bibliotheca Archivi; 359 Brotherhoods.

6 *Hanserecesse/Hanserezesse*, Leipzig, 1870–1970, four series and a total of 26 vols (henceforth HR); *Hansisches Urkundenbuch*, Halle, 1876–1939), 11 vols (henceforth HUB); *Bronnen tot*

de geschiedenis van den Oostzeehandel 1122–1499, ed. H.A. Poelman (henceforth BGO). For the sixteenth century, *Niederländische Akten und Urkunden zur Geschichte der Hanse und zur deutschen Seegeschichte*, ed. R. Häpke, Munich, 1913–23), 2 vols (henceforth NAU) complement the sources from the archive in Gdańsk. To close some of the gaps caused by the Second World War, P. Simson (ed.), *Danziger Inventar*, Danzig, 1913 (henceforth *DI*) is used as some of the lost sources have been described in extensive regests there.

7 F. Biermann, 'Schmerke i Mittenwalde – nowe dane do absolutnej chronologii wczesnosłowiańskiego osadnictwa na obszarze północno-wschodnich Niemiec', in M. Dulinicz (ed.), *Słowianie i ich sąsiedzi we wczesnym średniowieczu* [Slavs and their neighbours in the early Middle Ages], Lublin: Wydawn. Uniwersytetu Marii Curie-Skłodowskiej, 2003, pp. 101–8; K. Jażdżewski, *Gdańsk wczesnośredniowieczny w świetle wykopalisk* [Early medieval Gdańsk in the light of excavations], Gdańsk: Polskie Towarzystwo Archeologiczne, 1961.

8 Maćkowski, 'Gdańsk caught between Lübeck and the Polish kingdom'.

9 M. Biskup, *Trzynastoletnia wojna z Zakonem Krzyżackim 1454–1466* [The thirteen years war with the Teutonic Order 1454–1466], Warsaw: Wydawnictwo Obrony Narodowej, 1967; APG 300,27/5 fol. 235v; HR 2:4 nos. 325, 377, 603; HR 2:5 nos. 24, 29

10 As the name suggests, the Old City was the oldest settlement (from the tenth/eleventh century). The Main City (in the sources from the thirteenth century on) was a member of the Hanse. The Young City was founded by the Teutonic Knights, and existed in the period 1380–1455. After 1457, the hall of the Main City became *the* city hall of Danzig. It must be noted that in the Old City there was a concentration of sailors, foreign merchants and craftsmen. J. Zdrenka, *Główne, Stare i Młode Miasto Gdańsk w latach 1342–1525*, Toruń: Wydawnictwo Marszałek, 1992; B. Możejko, 'The rent as subject of communications between King Kazimierz Jagiellończyk, the Polish nobility and Gdańsk', in Martin Čapský (ed.), *Komunikace ve středověkých městech*, Opava: European Social Fund, 2014, pp. 81–94. Since the 1454 privilege, Danzig paid yearly 2,000 florins to the King (until the partitions in the eighteenth century), see B. Możejko, 'Financial obligations of the City of Gdańsk to King Casimir IV Jagiellon and his successors in the light of the 1468–1516 ledger book', in Roman Zaoral (ed.), *Money and Finance in Central Europe during the Later Middle Ages*, New York: Palgrave Macmillan, 2015, pp. 181–91.

11 J. Wijaczka, 'Prusy Królewskie: Dzieje polityczne do 1660' [Royal Prussia: political history until 1660], in Kizik, *Prusy Królewskie*, pp. 34–42.

12 S. Gierszewski and A. Groth (eds) *Historia Elbląga* [The history of Elbląg], vols 1 and 2, Gdańsk: Wydawnictwo Marpress, 1993–6.

13 APG 300,27/38 fol. 244v–245; H. Zins, *England and the Baltic in the Elizabethan Era*, Manchester: Manchester University Press, 1972.

14 M. Biskup (ed.), *Historia Torunia* [The history of Toruń], vols 1 and 2, Toruń: TNT, 1992–9.

15 Biskup, 'Prusy', pp. 9–12; M. Biskup, 'Die Stände im Preußen Königlichen Anteils 1466–1526', in H. Boockmann (ed.), *Die Anfänge der ständischen Vertretungen in Preußen und seinen Nachbarländern*, Munich, 1992; K. Górski, M. Biskup and I. Janosz-Biskupowa (eds), *Akta stanów Prus Królewskich,* vols 1–8 (1479–1526) [The Acts of the Estates of Royal Prussia], Toruń and Warsaw: Państwowe Wydawnictwo Naukowe, 1955–93.

16 H. Samsonowicz, 'Die Hanse im Ostsseeraum', in Z. H. Nowak and J. Tandecki (eds), *Die preussischen Hansestädte und ihre Stellung im Nord- und Ostseeraum des Mittelalters*, Toruń: Państwowe Wydawnictwo Naukowe, 1998, pp. 7–14.

17 APG 300,17/1 fols. 379–90; J. Litwin, 'Medieval Gdańsk – centre of shipbuilding and maritime trade on the Baltic', in W. Ossowski (ed.), *The Copper Ship: A Medieval Shipwreck and Its Cargo*, Gdańsk: Narodowe Muzeum Morskie, 2014, pp. 15–56.

18 J. Wubs-Mrozewicz, 'Neutrality before Grotius. The 1564–67 salt ships' case between conflict and conflict resolution in the Baltic and North Sea areas' (under review). Also in the 1540s in relations with France, see APG 300,27/17 fols. 363v–364v; APG 300,27/28: fol. 154.

R. I. Frost, *The Northern Wars 1558–1721*, Harlow: Longman, 2000, pp. 23–44, 74–81; Wijaczka, 'Prusy Królewskie' [Royal Prussia], pp. 131–202; P. G. Schwarz, 'Die Haltung Danzigs im nordischen Kriege 1563–1570 mit besonderer Berücksichtigung der Beziehungen zu Schweden', *Zeitschrift des westpreussischen Geschichtsvereins* 49, 1907, pp. 1–100.

19 APG 300,27/34 fols. 27v–39, 185v; APG 300,27/27 fol. 16; APG 300,27/30 fols. 106–9, 149–52v; S. Bodniak, *Polska a Bałtyk za ostatniego Jagiellona* [Poland and the Baltic at the age of the last Jagiellonian king], Kórnik: Fundacja Zakłady, 1946; K. Friedland, 'Maritime law and piracy: advantages and inconveniences of shipping in the Baltic', in A. MacInnes, F. Pedersen and T. Riis (eds), *Ships, Guns, and Bibles in the North Sea and Baltic States, c. 1350–c. 1700*, East Linton: Tuckwell Press, 2000, pp. 30–8.

20 NAU 1 no. 178 § 28; APG 300,3/6 fol. 111.

21 Bogucka, *Baltic Commerce*; B. Możejko, 'Shipping and maritime trade in Gdańsk at the turn of the 14th century: the maritime and commercial background of the sinking of the copper ship in 1408', in Ossowski, *Copper Ship*, pp. 57–74; R. C. Allen and R. W. Unger, 'The depth and breadth of the market for Polish grain 1500–1800', in J. Ph. S. Lemmink and J. S. A. M. Koningsbrugge (eds), *Baltic Affairs: Relations between the Netherlands and North-Eastern Europe 1500–1800*, Nijmegen: Instituut voor Noord- en Oosteuropese Studies, 1990, pp. 1–19; A. Mączak, *Miedzy Gdańskiem a Sundem: Studia nad handlem bałtyckim od połowy XVI do połowy XVII w.* [Between Gdańsk and the Sound. Studies in the Baltic trade from the 1550s until the 1650s], Warsaw: Państwowe Wydawnictwo Naukowe, 1972; H. Samsonowicz, 'Dynamiczny ośrodek handlowy' [A dynamic commercial hub], in E. Cieślak (ed.), *Historia Gdańska*, vol. 2, Gdańsk: Wydawnictwo Morskie, 1982; A. Attman, *The Struggle for Baltic Markets*, Göteborg: Vetenskaps- o. vitterhets-samhälle, 1979; M. Małowist, 'The economic and social development of the Baltic countries from the fifteenth to the seventeenth centuries', *Economic History Review* 12/2, 1959, pp. 177–89. See also the contributions in Lemmink and Koningsbrugge, *Baltic Affairs*; M.-L. Pelus-Kaplan, 'Gdańsk dans les échanges commerciaux et culturels de la Pologne avec l'Europe occidentale aux XVIe et XVIIe siècles', in M.-L. Pelus-Kaplan and Daniel Tollet (eds), *La Pologne et l'Europe occidentale du Moyen-Age à nos jours*, Poznań: Uniwersytet Adama Mickiewicza, 2004, pp. 49–62.

22 C. Link, *Der preußische Getreidehandel im 15. Jahrhundert: Eine Studie zur nordeuropäischen Wirtschaftsgeschichte*, Cologne: Böhlau, 2013.

23 Wijaczka, 'Gospodarka Prus Królewskich', in Kizik, *Prusy*, pp. 131–202, esp. 151.

24 H. Samsonowicz, 'Miejsce Gdańska w gospodarce europejskiej w XV w' [The position of Gdańsk in the European economy in the fifteenth century], in Cieślak, *Historia Gdańska*, vol. 2, pp. 77–92, and H. Samsonowicz, 'Dynamiczny ośrodek handlowy', ibid., pp. 93–175.

25 Samsonowicz, 'Dynamiczny ośrodek', pp. 97–102, 128–35, 155–60.

26 HR 3:8 nos. 58 and 62; 300,28/123 fols. 21-33v; see also 300,27/29 fols. 59–61v.

27 NAU 1 no. 178 § 28; APG 300,3/3 fols. 62–5, 107.

28 HR 4:2 no. 495.

29 R. Hammel-Kiesow, *Die Hanse*, 5th edn, Munich: Beck, 2014; S. Selzer, *Die mittelalterliche Hanse*, Darmstadt: WBG, 2010; J. Wubs-Mrozewicz, 'The Hanse in medieval Europe: an Introduction', in J. Wubs-Mrozewicz and S. Jenks (eds), *The Hanse and Late Medieval Europe*, Leiden: Brill, 2013, pp. 1–35.

30 APG 300,27/14 fols. 89–92; APG 300,27/23 fols. 304v–305v; HR 3:5 no. 116.

31 APG 300,59/9 fol. 465; APG 300,27/17 fols. 77v–78v; APG 300,10/1 fol. 316v § 19, fol. 325 § 58; 300,27/24 fols. 16–17; APG 300,53/796 fols. 187–9; APG 300,93/55a fol. 100; W. Blockmans, 'Der holländische Durchbruch in der Ostsee', in S. Jenks and M. North (eds), *Der hansische Sonderweg? Beiträge zur Sozial- und Wirtschaftsgeschichte der Hanse*, Cologne: Böhlau, 1993, pp. 49–58; A. Christensen, *Dutch Trade to the Baltic about 1600: Studies in the Sound Toll Register and Dutch Shipping Records*, Copenhagen: E. Munksgaard, 1941; M. van

Tielhof, *'De Hollandse graanhandel, 1470–1570: Koren op de Amsterdamse molen* [Hollandish grain trade 1470], The Hague: Stichting Hollandse Historische Reeks, 1995.

32 HR 3:5 no. 85; HR 3:5 no. 92; HR 3:5 no. 105 § 17, 247, 314; HR 3:9 no. 72; HR 3:9 no. 98; HR 4:1 no. 168; HR 3:8 no. 452; NAU 1 no. 44; H. Brand, 'Habsburg and Hanseatic diplomacy during the Sound controversy of 1532', in H. Brand, P. Holm and L. Müller (eds), *The Dynamics of Economic Culture in the North Sea and Baltic Region (c. 1250–1700),* Hilversum: Verloren, 2007, pp. 102–21.

33 HR 3:6 nos. 16, 67–85, 630 § 4, 700 § 12; HR 3:7 no. 39 § 60; HR 4:2 no. 202; HR 3:6 no. 630.

34 HR 3:3 no. 175; HR 3:3 no. 181; HR 3:3 no. 188; HR 3:3 no. 552; HR 3:3 no. 678; HR 3:4 no. 157; HR 3:4 no. 158; HR 3:4 no. 189; HR 3:6 no. 188 §§ 120, 129.

35 D. Seifert, *Kompagnons und Konkurrenten: Holland und die Hanse im späten Mittelalter,* Cologne: Böhlau, 1997; J. Weststrate, 'Abgrenzung durch Aufnahme. Zur Eingliederung der süderseeischen Städte in die Hanse, ca. 1360–1450', *Hansische Geschichtsblätter* 121, 2003, pp. 13–40; J. Wubs-Mrozewicz, 'The close "other": medieval and modern perspectives on Hollanders and the Hanse', *German History* 31/4, 2013, pp. 453–72.

36 Samsonowicz, 'Dynamiczny ośrodek', pp. 135–9.

37 M. Bogucka, 'The Baltic and Amsterdam in the first half of the 17th century', in *The Interactions of Amsterdam and Antwerp with the Baltic Region 1400–1800. De Nederlanden en het Oostzeegebied, 1400–1800,* Leiden: Springer, 1983, p. 51; APG 300,93/55a fols. 110, 118.

38 E. Kizik, 'Oświata, literatura, nauka i kolekcjonerstwo w Prusach Królewskich' [Education, literature, science and collectors in Royal Prussia], in Kizik, *Prusy*, pp. 276–7; W. Troszyński, 'Filip Clüver (Cluverius) (1580–1622), twórca geografii historycznej' [Cluverius, the creator of historical geography], in *Zasłużeni ludzie Pomorza Nadwiślańskiego XVII wieku: szkice biograficzne* [Esteemed Pomeranians in the seventeenth century: biographical sketches], Wrocław: Zakład Narodowy im. Ossolińskich, 1982, pp. 43–7.

39 N. Jörn, *'With money and bloode': Der Londoner Stalhof im Spannungsfeld der englisch-hansischen Beziehungen im 15. und 16. Jahrhundert,* Cologne: Böhlau, 2000; S. Jenks, *England, die Hanse und Preußen,* Cologne: Böhlau, 1992.

40 APG 300 D/31, fol. 863 19.08.1542; 300,27/10 fols. 106–106v 15.09.1545; APG 300,27/20 fols. 121–3, 1547; APG 300,27/21 fol. 272; APG 300,53–746 fols. 51, 53, 55.

41 APG 300,27/35 fols. 26–30.

42 J. Wubs-Mrozewicz, *Traders, Ties and Tensions: The Interaction of Lübeckers, Overijsslers and Hollanders in Late Medieval Bergen,* Hilversum: Verloren, 2008; M. Burkhardt, *Die Geschichte des Bergenhandels im Spätmittelalter – Handel. Kaufleute. Netzwerke,* Cologne: Bohlau, 2009; A. Nedkvitne, *Utenrikshandelen fra det vestafjelske Norge 1100–1600,* PhD, University of Bergen, 1983; the 2014 edition is virtually the same.

43 Samsonowicz, 'Dynamiczny ośrodek handlowy', pp. 144–60.

44 E. Lindberg, 'Club goods and inefficient institutions: why Danzig and Lübeck failed in the early modern period', *Economic History Review* 62/3, 2009, pp. 604–28.

45 O. Gelderblom, *Cities of Commerce: The Institutional Foundations of International Trade in the Netherlands, 1250–1650,* Princeton, NJ: Princeton University Press, 2013.

46 H. Samsonowicz, 'Wer traf die Entscheidungen in den selbstverwalteten Städten des mittelalterlichen Polen?', in E. Mühle (ed.), *Rechtsstadtgründungen im mittelalterlichen Polen,* Cologne: Böhlau, 2011, p. 383; R. Czaja, *Grupy rządzące w miastach nadbałtyckich w średniowieczu* [The governing groups in the Baltic towns in the Middle Ages], Toruń: TNT, 2008; J. Tandecki, 'Aufbau der Verwaltung und der Gerichtsbarkeit in den preussischen Grosstädten im Mittelalter', in U. Arnold, M. Glauert, and J. Sarnowsky (eds), *Preussische Landesgeschichte: Festschrift für Bernhart Jähnig zum 60. Geburtstag,* Marburg: Elwert, 2001, pp. 247–52.

47 APG 300,3/6 fol. 111; APG 300,5/2 fol. 1; APG 300,41/15 fol. 360; APG 300,43/8 fols. 78v–79; APG 300,43/4b fol. 7; APG 300,43/5b fol. 157; APG 300,43/16 fol. 321v; APG 300,59/7 fol. 11; APG 300,59/8 fols. 121v–123; APG 300,59/10 fols. 142–3, 429–31, 522; APG 300,5/223; K. Kamińska, *Sądownictwo miasta Torunia do połowy XVII wieku na tle ustroju sądów niektórych miast Niemiec i Polski* [Courts and adjudication in Toruń until the middle of the seventeen century in comparison to chosen towns in Germany and Poland], Toruń: Państwowe Wydawn, Naukowe, 1980, p. 75; P. Simson, *Geschichte der Danziger Willkür*, Danzig: L. Saunier, 1904.

48 APG 300,3/6 fol. 111; APG 300,59/9 fol. 407; APG 300 R Bb 28 XVI.

49 J. Wubs-Mrozewicz, 'The late medieval and early modern Hanse: as an institution of conflict management', *Continuity and Change* 32/1, 2017; APG 300,93/25 fol. 9; APG 300,58/8 fols. 170v–171; APG 300,27/8 fols. 76–7; APG 300 D/82 fols. 227–67.

50 Bodniak, *Polska a Bałtyk*.

51 APG 300,27/34 fols. 185–185v 19.02.1574; APG 300,10/1 fols. 351–356v; APG 300,10/3 fol. 93.

52 APG 300, 10/1 fol. 352v; APG 300,17/1 fols. 77–9; APG 300,27/35 fol. 28; APG 300,43/4b; 300,43/5b; APG 300,93/25 fols. 254–8; APG 300,R V,20 XVI; Z. Rymaszewski, *Sprawy gdańskie przed sądami zadwornymi oraz ingerencja królów w gdański wymiar sprawiedliwości XVI-XVIII w* [Danzig cases before royal courts and the intervention of kings in Danzig's legal proceedings in the sixteenth-eighteenth centuries], Warsaw: Zakład Narodowy im. Ossolińskich, 1985.

53 Biskup, *Trzynastoletnia wojna*.

54 E. Kizik, 'Prawo w Prusach Królewskich' [Law in Royal Prussia], in Kizik, *Prusy*, pp. 96–109; A. Cordes, 'Hansisches Recht: Begriff und Probleme', in idem, *Hansisches und Hansestädtisches Recht*, Trier: Porta Alba, 2008, pp. 205–13; F. Ebel, 'Magdeburger Recht', in A. Fijal and H.-J. Leuchte (eds), *Unseren fruntlichen grus zuvor: Deutsches Recht im Mittelalter im mittel- und osteuropäischen Raum*, Cologne: Böhlau, 2004, pp. 217–36; J. Ziekow, *Recht und Rechtsgang: Studien zu den Problemen mittelalterlichen Rechts anhand von Magdeburger Schöppensprüchen des 15. Jahrhunderts*, Pfaffenweiler: Centaurus, 1986; W. Ebel, *Lübisches Recht*, Göttingen, 1971.

55 Simson, *Geschichte der Danziger Willkür*; K. C. Leman, *Das alte kulmische Recht*, Berlin: F. Dümmler, 1838; D. Janicka, *Prawo karne w trzech rewizjach prawa chełmińskiego z XVI wieku* [Criminal law in three revisions of the Kulm law of the sixteenth century], Toruń: TNT, 1992.

56 W. Meincke, *Das Strafrecht der Stadt Danzig bis zur Carolina*, Marburg: Philipps-Universität zu Marburg, 1932, pp. 4–12; Simson, *Geschichte der Stadt Danzig*, vol. 2, p. 346; G. Radbruch, *Die peinliche Gerichtsordnung Kaiser Karls V. von 1532 (Carolina)*, Berlin, 1926; D. Kaczor, *Przestępczość kryminalna i wymiar sprawiedliwości w Gdańsku w XVI–XVIII wieku* [Criminality and justice in Gdańsk in the sixteenth to eighteenth centuries], Gdańsk: Wydawnictwo Uniwersytetu Gdańskiego, 2005.

57 HR 3:7 no. 39 § 231; HR 3:8 no. 110 § 75a; APG 300,28/103 (1522); APG 300D 20/362–4; HR 3:4 no. 76; 79 § 259; 81 § 26; no. 138; no. 170; HR 3:7 no. 113 § 113; H. Samsonowicz, 'Rola Gdańska w życiu stanowym Prus Królewskich' [The role of Gdańsk in Royal Prussia], in *Historia Gdańska*, vol. 2, p. 278; P. Oestmann, *Rechtsvielfalt vor Gericht Rechtsanwendung und Partikularrecht im Alten Reich*, Frankfurt/M: Klostermann, 2002.

58 APG 300,27/13 fol. 375; APG 300,59/9 fols. 214–15; APG 300,95/56 fol. 51; APG 300,93/56 fols. 59–60; APG 300,93/56 fols. 65–8.

59 APG 300,28/102.

60 APG 300,10/4 1571–3 fol. 13 § 2; APG 300,27/23 fols. 47v–51v; APG 300,58/120 fols. 7–10; APG 300,10/7 1578–9 fol. 47.

61 APG 300,27/23 fols. 47v–55v.

62 R. Postel, 'Der Niedergang der Hanse', in J. Bracker *et al.* (eds), *Die Hanse: Lebenswirklichkeit und Mythos*, Lübeck: Schmidt-Römhild, 1999 (1989), pp. 174–6.
63 S. Kościelak, 'Dzieje wyznaniowe Prus Królewskich w XVI–XVIII w' [The history of religion in Royal Prussia in the sixteenth-eighteenth centuries], in Kizik, *Prusy*, pp. 204–24.
64 E. Kizik, 'Niederländische Einflüsse in Danzig, Polen und Litauen vom 16. bis zum 18. Jahrhundert', in M. Krieger and M. North (eds), *Land und Meer: Kultureller Austausch zwischen Westeuropa und dem Ostseeraum in der Frühen Neuzeit,* Cologne: Böhlau, 2004, pp. 51–76.
65 Simson, *Willkür.*
66 S. Jenks, 'Zum hansischen Gästerecht', *Hansische Geschichtsblätter* 114, 1996, pp. 3–59; H. Rudorff, *Zur Rechtsstellung der Gäste im mittelalterlichen städtischen Prozess vorzugsweise nach norddeutschen Quellen*, Breslau: M. & H. Marcus, 1907.
67 A. Cordes, 'The search for a medieval *lex mercatoria*', in V. Piergiovanni (ed.), *From Lex Mercatoria to Commercial Law*, Berlin: Duncker & Humblot, 2005, pp. 53–68; HR 3:6 p. 115, note 1; HR 3:9 no. 743; APG 300 D 20/306; APG 300 D 20/342; APG 300,43/195 fols. 83–6.
68 APG 300,27/35 fols. 136–137v.
69 APG 300,53/4, 1534; 300,53/9, 1544; 300,53/22, 1549–71.
70 APG 300,53/30; M. Bogucka, 'Zatarg z Batorym – stosunek Gdańska do planów bałtyckich Zygmunta III' [The conflict with Batory; the attitude of Gdańsk towards the Baltic policy of Sigismund III], in *Historia Gdańska*, vol. 2, pp. 579–85.
71 HR 4:2 no. 577, 625; HR 4:2 no. 611 § 29.
72 Wijaczka, 'Polityka' [Politics], in Kizik, *Prusy*, p. 46.
73 Wubs-Mrozewicz, 'Neutrality'.
74 APG 300 D 20/452,453, 457, 457c; 300,R/T,37 fols. 35–7.
75 J. Wubs-Mrozewicz, 'Mercantile conflict resolution and the role of the language of trust: a Danzig case in the middle of the sixteenth century', *Historical Research* 88/241, 2015, pp. 417–40.
76 NWO VENI project 2011–15.
77 APG 300,53/30; NAU 2 no. 243.
78 APG 300,53/794 fol. 193; APG 300,53/795 fols. 117, 131–3.
79 APG 300,27/35 fols. 26–30, 84–89v, 135–8, 302–302v; J. Wubs-Mrozewicz, 'Mercantile conflict resolution in practice: connecting diplomatic and legal sources from Danzig c. 1460–1580', in Heikki Pihlajamäki (ed.), *Historiography and Sources of Commercial Law*, Leiden: Brill, 2016 (forthcoming).
80 APG 300,28/102; 300 D 20/338; 300 D 20/359; APG 300, 53/795 fols. 115–17; NAU 1 no. 58; U. Andermann, 'Spätmittelalterlicher Seeraub als Kriminaldelikt und seine Bestrafung', in W. Ehbrecht (ed.) *Störtebeker – 600 Jahre nach seinem Tod*, Trier: Porta Alba, 2005, pp. 23–36; W. Ehbrecht, 'Ruten, roven, dat en is gheyn schande, dat doynt de besten van dem lande. Bemerkungen zu adligem Land- und Seeraub', ibid., pp. 253–71.
81 Wubs-Mrozewicz, 'Institution of conflict management'.
82 APG 300,27/34 fol. 303; APG 300 D/21, 168; APG 300 D/24 F, 146; APG 300,27/8 fols. 76–7. H. Wernicke, 'Hansetag, Recht und städtischer Alltag', in S. Urbanski, C. Lamschaus and J. Ellermayer (eds), *Recht und Alltag im Hanseraum: Festschrift für Gerhard Theuerkauf*, Lüneburg: Deutsches Salzmuseum, 1993, pp. 429–38.
83 HR 3:7 no. 39 § 136; HR 3:7 no. 195; HR 3:7 no. 197 § 5; HR 3:7 no. 198; HR 3:7 nos. 213–15; APG 300,27/7 fols. 297–297v, 1507; APG 300,27/8 fols. 5v–7, 28v–29, 1509; APG 300,27/17 fols. 326–30, 1542.

16

REVAL (TALLINN)

A city emerging from maritime trade

Ivar Leimus and Anu Mänd

The three largest cities in medieval Livonia (corresponding approximately to the territory of present-day Estonia and Latvia) were Riga, Reval (Tallinn) and Dorpat (Tartu), which also became members of the Hanse.[1] Reval, situated at the southern shore of the Finnish bay, emerged in the first half of the thirteenth century after the conquest of Danish King Valdemar II in 1219. The city council (*Rat*) was first mentioned in 1248, when Reval was granted the Lübeck law. The city's overlord changed in 1346 when the king of Denmark sold northern Estonia to the Teutonic Order. In 1561 Reval fell under Swedish rule. Due to its geopolitical position with its well-located port, Reval developed into a medium-size maritime trade city. It benefited, on the one hand, from the emerging Hanse network, and on the other, from its vicinity to the Russian resources and markets. Reval became the second biggest city in Livonia after Riga: its population in the fourteenth century was *c.*5,000, growing to 7,000–8,000 by the middle of the sixteenth century. The city's social and ethnic composition was relatively varied: while the upper class consisted mostly of Germans and the lower class predominantly of local Estonians, there were also residents of Scandinavian and Finnish origin among the middle class, especially Swedes. The merchants who dealt with long-distance trade were almost all Germans.[2]

The aim of this chapter is to study how the city of Reval was integrated into the Hanse network, what kind of role it played in the trade relations between the East and the West, who its main trade partners were, and how the social and business connections benefited from the membership in guilds.

Sources and historiography

Written sources on medieval Reval, including its trade and merchants, are abundant: the archives of the city are some of the best-preserved medieval archives in Europe. The majority of the sources available for the study of the maritime trade are kept in the Tallinn

City Archives and can roughly be divided into two groups: first, the customs records of the port, which cover the years 1373, 1378–84 and 1426–96 (excluding the years 1472–8 and 1495) and contain information on incoming ships, goods and so on.[3] These materials have been thoroughly analysed by several scholars, such as Wilhelm Stieda, Wilhelm Koppe, Karl Heinz Sass and Thomas Wolf.[4] Unfortunately, the customs records from the sixteenth century have been preserved in rather poor condition and they have hardly been studied so far. The second major group of sources includes the account books of the Reval merchants (e.g. Hans Selhorst, Helmich Ficke, Jasper Kappenberg, Tönnis Smidt), mainly from the sixteenth century, which allow us to get a diverse and detailed picture of their daily activities, trade partners, exported and imported goods, bookkeeping practices and so on.[5] These account books have been analysed, among others, by Gunnar Mickwitz, Vilho Niitemaa, Jorma Ahvenainen and, in recent decades, by Carsten Jahnke.[6] In addition to the aforementioned sources, the numismatic ones must also be mentioned. These have been investigated primarily by Arkadi Molvõgin and Ivar Leimus.[7]

The social and business connections of the Reval merchants can also be studied on the basis of guild records. The two merchants' organizations in the city – the Great Guild and the Brotherhood of the Black Heads – kept various (account) books, in which they wrote down the new members, participants in their annual festivals and the names of the deceased commemorated in the guild.[8] A closer look at these records has revealed that merchants from other Hanse cities around the Baltic Sea, most notably Lübeck, were frequently admitted to the guilds in Reval and that they remained members until their death, in spite of living and running business in their home towns.[9] The extent of such simultaneous guild membership in several cities and its impact on (personal) trade networks is undoubtedly a topic that deserves to be studied in greater detail.

A subject that has thus far merited almost no attention is the role of women in maritime trade. As is widely known, long-distance trade was predominantly a male domain. However, there were also women involved in overseas trade. At least one such example is documented in early sixteenth-century Reval – Gertrud, the daughter of the local burgomaster Johan van Grest, first married to Hans Surenpe from Turku (Åbo), and then to Reval city councillor Victor van der Lippe. Gertrud's business letters to the Turku cathedral provost Pawel Scheel, to whom she sold salt, iron, butter and Rhine wine, are kept in the National Library of Finland in Helsinki.[10] Although based on the current state of research it appears that Gertrud's career was rather exceptional, future studies on women's involvement in the Baltic Sea trade would not only broaden our knowledge of the history of commerce in the region but also contribute to gender studies.

Reval, the Hanse and the Novgorod Kontor: becoming part of a network

The early history of Reval merchants is rather unclear. A citation of Pope Gregory IX of 1234 indicates that sometime around 1230 the Brethren of the Sword invited

200 merchants from Gotland, believed to be Germans, to grab land *in Revaliam,* giving them fiefs in Jerwen (Järva) County. It is unclear whether the name Revalia was used to refer to the city of Reval or Rävala County back then, whether these men ever got there or whether they stayed in Jerwen County instead. However, the fact that there were merchants in Reval in early times is also proven by a clause in the same document that accused the Brethren of the Sword of robbing the property of many merchants in addition to occupying the stronghold of Reval and many other terrible sins.[11]

Due to its favourable location, especially on eastern trade routes, Reval soon had to join the trade network that operated on the Baltic Sea before the Hanse (*universitas mercatorum*), which was also called the Gotland Society after its central hub. Unlike the later Hanse, the society was a rather loosely connected association of merchants of different origin. The first announcement of the commercial interests of Reval dates back to the 1250s. Namely, the Lübeckians informed the Revalians about the injustice suffered by German merchants in Novgorod. In response, the vice-regent of the Danish king in Reval and the Reval city council sent a joint letter to Lübeck, where they confirmed their friendship and support for the benefit of the market.[12] This indicates that Reval was already involved in the Novgorod trade in the mid-thirteenth century.

More consistent messages about the presence of *universitas mercatorum* in Reval date back to the 1270s. And they do not just illustrate friendly relations between the merchants of Reval and pre-Hanseatic ones. The old local right of salvage played a part in this, as it did not go with the rapidly developing trade environment. In 1277, a row broke out between the vice-regent of the Danish king in Reval, Eilard von Oberch, and the council of Lübeck about the goods robbed from the merchants of Lübeck, Soest, Dortmund, and Münster after a shipwreck. It seems that as a result of this row King Erik Klipping in 1278 gave the Lübeckians all the rights in Reval that he and his ancestors had admitted for them in Denmark, and these probably included trading privileges as well. In 1280, he took German, Gotlandic and other merchants who came to Estonia under his protection. The commercial activity of foreigners must have caused dissatisfaction among local merchants. In any case, the Danish authorities prohibited foreigners from Germany and Gotland from retailing certain goods, such as linen and woollen fabric, wadmal, herring and salt, without the permission of the Reval city council in 1279 and 1282. This indicates that the central authority was initially the one that had to worry about the security of trading. Elsewhere in Estonia, trading was also largely supported by landlords in the thirteenth century.[13] The cities and towns were still too weak to pursue an independent trade policy.

Trade centres elsewhere on the Baltic Sea were developing and strengthening at the same time. In 1280, the two leading agents – Lübeck and the Visby German community – entered into a contract for the protection of trade on the Baltic Sea and at its ports. Riga joined the contract in 1282.[14] For the first time, the three cities had taken over the main function of the Gotland Society – that is, the protection of merchants.

The north German trade cities that had signed the Rostock Peace Treaty – the so-called Wendish cities – established a federation in 1283, where Lübeck once again started to play the leading role.[15] The backbone of the Hanse began to form, and it soon demonstrated its strength. Norwegian King Eric II Magnusson (1280–99) had started restricting the privileges of trade cities in his state to which they responded with a successful trade blockade. On 13 March 1285 the king promised to compensate German merchants for the injustice caused to them in his state and confirmed their old privileges. Reval was now mentioned for the first time alongside the other trade cities: Lübeck, Hamburg, Wismar, Rostock, Stralsund, Greifswald, Stettin, Demmin, Anklam, Gotland (i.e. Visby), Elbing and Riga.[16] This places Reval among the core of the further Hanse as early as in the 1280s.

However, this developing position of Reval was shaken by the events of 1287. Namely, another ship from Lübeck ran aground in Wierland (Virumaa) in north Estonia and fell victim to Estonian robbers, as the old tradition went back then. The loot went to local vassals and, according to some accounts, even to the Cistercian monks of Falkena (Kärkna). Some of the stolen items, however, were also sold in Reval with the help of the townspeople, which the council was well aware of. The Lübeckians did everything they could to get their goods back, but even the intervention of the Danish crown did not make the vassals change their minds. Finally, on 24 June 1287, the Gotland Society adopted a resolution that prohibited the sale of items from shipwrecks and established punishments for offenders. It gave Reval, which was opposed to the resolution, time to think it over until the next Midsummer Day. After that, Reval was to face expulsion from the society (which now had to be interpreted as a confederation of cities).[17] Reval was obviously already treated as a fully fledged, if obstinate, member of the society at the time. It appears that the fear of finding themselves in isolation forced Revalians to change their minds. Exactly a year later, on Midsummer 1288, the king of Denmark and the duke of Estonia, Eric Menved, took the local burghers and their property under their protection, and confirmed all of their rights and privileges.[18] Any differences of opinion had obviously been resolved by then. Word for word, the king guaranteed German trade cities protection against the right of salvage in 1294, and also gave them permission to freely conduct their business in his Estonian domain and to travel on to Novgorod from there.[19]

The regulation of the Novgorod marketplace of 1346 became a certain precondition to the rise of Reval among Hanseatic cities. The representatives of Livonian and overseas cities agreed to restrict the ports that merchants returning from Russia in spring could use to three urban centres: Riga, Reval and New Pernau (Uus-Pärnu). Travelling by land via Prussia, Courland and Sweden (i.e. Finland) and sailing through the ice to the island of Ösel (Saaremaa), Courland or elsewhere was also prohibited.[20] However, this does not yet provide grounds to speak about the staple right of Livonian cities in the Russian trade, because the Hanse simply had no other suitable ports with regulated and guarded living and business arrangements for sailing back from Russia. It was more a struggle against competing (corner) ports and (side) roads in and next to Livonia; politics that can be observed throughout the Middle Ages.

The next push that increased the importance of Livonian cities in the trade with Russia was given by Valdemar IV of Denmark, who in 1361 conquered Visby and thereby unleashed a war with the Hanse. Although Visby remained a Hanse town, its heyday was over for good. The Hanse Diet of 1366 decided that the decisions made by the merchants of Novgorod Peterhof would enter into force not only with the consent of the former hegemons of Lübeck and Visby, but also of Riga, Dorpat and Reval.[21] This marked the end of the autonomy of the Kontor.

From the end of the fourteenth century, the issues of the Novgorod Kontor and Russian trade in general were resolved with ever-increasing frequency by Livonian cities. In 1402, Reval rented the Gutagard trading post of the Gutes in Novgorod on behalf of the entire Hanse and was still paying the Russians for it in 1560. The Stralsund Hanseatic Diet of 1442 finally legalized the right of Riga, Reval and Dorpat to manage the Kontor, control the Novgorod trade and make peace.[22] The importance of the Novgorod Kontor actually started decreasing at this time. Ivan III conquered Novgorod in 1478 and deliberately began to change the old organization of trade. The local merchants were deported on the order of the Grand Prince and replaced by new people from Moscow and elsewhere from eastern Russia. Trading was repeatedly discontinued and the old privileges of the Hanseatic merchants in weighing wax, counting hides, keeping pubs, etc. were gradually abolished.[23]

City councillor Gottschalk Remlinkrode from Reval and Thomas Schrowe from Dorpat were sent to Moscow in 1494 as representatives of the Hanse to sort things out. The negotiations, however, were unsuccessful. At the same time, the merchants of Peterhof were presented with a claim for 900 Novgorod grivnas as compensation for the injustice caused to the Russians. This meant almost two quintals of silver, which the Hanse obviously refused to pay. The Grand Prince responded by having forty-nine merchants arrested and 96,000 marks worth of goods and jewelry confiscated from them, including the property of the Kontor and St Peter's church. The marketplace was closed and the Russians justified this as a response to the injustice they had suffered in Livonia and the execution of two Russians in Reval in 1493 and 1494. One of them had distributed counterfeit money; the other had been caught having intercourse with a mare. The ambassador of Reval Remlinkrode was also thrown in jail as a punishment. He was held there for three years and died soon after his release.[24]

The Kontor was finally reopened in 1514 with the Novgorod peace treaty. However, it was no longer attractive to overseas Hanse towns – it was easier for them to trade with the Russians in Livonia. Protectionist sentiments started spreading there. In 1510, the Reval city council prohibited the Dutch from buying grain from anyone other than burghers of Reval, threatening them with loss of life and property. The Livonian Diet of 1513 and the Diet of Towns of 1516 decided that visitors would not be permitted to trade with each other in Livonian towns. However, the first serious clash between the Livonians and the other members of the Hanse about trading with the Russians occurred as late as 1540, and was probably caused by the decision made by the Livonian Diet of 1539 in Riga, which repeated the prohibition on foreigners trading with one another. As the repeated regulations of Livonian towns and the numerous protests of Hanse towns show, protectionism in the region started to deepen in the 1540s and 1550s.[25] Even compatriots fell victim to exclusion. The Teutonic Order was not permitted to trade at the port of Reval in 1509, and in 1541 the city council closed it completely to the Order. Estate owners were not permitted to trade at ports in 1542–3. In 1530, Reval also started restricting the trading activities of Dorpat merchants at its ports and later extended the prohibition it imposed on estate owners to these merchants as well. Burghers of Narva could only send their goods to Reval, and the Revalians then passed them on. However, none of these attempts succeeded for long and the old situation was soon restored. The outbreak of the Livonian War in 1558 finally ended the squabbling.[26]

The functioning of the network

Large-scale trade was also long-distance trade. This set its own requirements for the organization of trading activities. First, merchants had to be able to buy and sell their goods abroad. Second, they had to be familiar with market conditions. And third, they had to have capital. Merchants themselves travelled with their goods to the target markets only at the beginning of Hanseatic trade. This was the most labour-intensive and risky as well as the most unreasonable way of conducting one's business, as merchants had no information about the market conditions at all, or if they did, it was outdated. The two Reval ships that were seized by Greifswald's men on 1 May 1312 could be examples of such trade voyages. The Danish king Erik Menved was in conflict with German seaside towns at the time and, as we know, Revalians were his subjects. However, when it became evident that the vessels belonged to friends (or more likely business partners) of the Greifswalders, the ships were returned to the owners. The latter had to swear that they would not hold a grudge about the events. In total fourteen men (including two captains of the ships) headed by Reval city councillor Sifrid van Hanek signed the text of the oath.[27] This suggests that the men were Reval merchants on a business trip, and that they also owned the ship.

Trading via commissioners was more efficient. A companion located abroad sold the goods sent to him and arranged all settlements, and in return sent the requested and purchased goods or his own goods and money. No fee was charged for this, and mutual favours were counted instead. The fact that goods could be sold and bought abroad was not the only advantage of this system. The commissioner also kept the merchant informed about the conditions on the faraway market. However, this system only met the first two requirements for long-distance trade – it did not increase capital. Joining trade associations, where several merchants put their money together, was the only solution to this issue. Partnerships between merchants from different places were the most practical – business was good, information was moving, capital was growing and risks were borne jointly. A merchant could belong to several partnerships at the same time and also conduct his personal business on the side. Merchants who established trade associations entered into contracts with one another.

Capital could be formed in many ways: either the members made different contributions to the company and shared any income according to their investments; or (as was usually the case) they all invested a small and often fairly equal amount in the business. In Reval, even the most affluent merchants worked mainly with their own capital, which they had obtained as inheritance from previous generations and via marriage. But partnerships with other partners also brought in extra money. One form of association, known as *widderlegginge*, was particularly helpful when starting a business. Wealthier merchants gave capital to their apprentices or to less affluent merchants on the condition that if they added an equal amount of their own money, they could then use the total amount. Any income was divided between the two parties. Goods were often bought on credit, which made them more expensive.[28] Such business associations were common in Reval by the first half of the fifteenth century at the latest, and probably even earlier. One of the most famous merchants, who in 1406 established a trade association with his Reval and Dorpat partners, was a man of international calibre, Hildebrand Veckinchusen, along with his brother Sivert.[29] Almost all the important merchants who operated in Reval in the sixteenth century also belonged to trade associations.

A less known but illustrative example is the case of Hans Selhorst, who originated from Hamm in Westphalia. As a young man, he headed to Lübeck and established a business relationship with his brother Peter, Bernd Pal from Münster, Hans Buck from Lüneburg and in particular with Jürgen Vilhering, a Reval merchant who in turn used Selhorst as a mediator in communication with Hans Bissenbeke from Hamburg. After Vilhering's death in 1505, Selhorst travelled to Reval to take care of some business, got married, joined the Great Guild, became a burgher and was elected a city councillor. With Bissenbeke and the Lübeck burgher Hans von Scherffen, he established a trade association that had companions in London, Bruges and Amsterdam. Selhorst also established several partnerships: with Lutke Opperheim, Anders Opperheim and Hans Castorp I and II from Lübeck; Hans Opperheim from Hamburg; and Laurens Molsen from Danzig. In Livonia, Selhorst had trade contacts with Frederik Korff from Narva and Hans Muster, probably from Riga. Later on he established a new trade association with Herman Wiggering from Danzig and another with Reymer Sandow from Lübeck. In Stockholm, he had two partners: Michel Hardenberch and Wilm Schotten. His Livonian contacts were Jacob Burssel, Reinolt Krus and Jacob Krabbe in Dorpat. Selhorst also had correspondents in Pernau and Riga. Whilst his business was rather modest when he was a young man, he left behind over 13,000 Riga marks in cash and impressive real estate after he died in 1536.[30]

The example of Selhorst indicates that mutual relationships between merchants are not the only things to consider about the medieval trade network – the trade associations of trade partners were also important. Other trade relationships, which covered other regions or goods, concentrated around their main structure. This led to the formation of a network that covered a large part of Europe in which goods, money, information and ideas moved.[31]

Trade partners of Reval and goods exchanged

Reval (and Livonia as a whole) was important to Western Europe because of its geographical location en route to the Russian market and goods. Being part of the Hanseatic trading network made it possible to play a pivotal role in the exchange between western and eastern goods and contact between traders.

Turning towards the East, the only trade partners of Reval were the Russians, especially the merchants of Novgorod.[32] Trade with Russia took place in two ways: in the Novgorod Kontor, the Peterhof, which lost its importance in 1494; and in Reval. The Russians had a church there, which was used for Greek Catholic services and also as temporary accommodation and a place of storage. The church had no stoves, however, so at least in winter Russian merchants had to live as tenants in private houses, usually those of their business partners, and also use their cellars to store goods. The issue of stoves was therefore one of the main bones of contention in the relationship between the Revalians and the Russians.[33] 1554 seems to be the last year that a large number of Russians still visited Reval.[34] For a couple of years, eastern trade took place via Narva and Dorpat. In 1557, however, Tsar Ivan IV called his merchants back from Livonia for good and cut off all trade.[35]

The majority of the goods that Reval exported to the West came from Russia – mainly furs and wax. Furs came in many varieties.[36] In 1368, Reval exported at least 75,000–80,000 thousand pelts and 18.5 tons of wax, despite the blockade imposed by the Livonian Master of the Teutonic Order against the Russians due to the war between them that had begun in 1367. As restrictions of that kind were against the merchants' interests, they were often violated. The demand for wax to illuminate churches rose. Sources from the end of the fourteenth century show that a ship heading from Reval to Flanders carried 15,000 mark-pounds (*c.*6 tons) of wax on board. By the end of the fifteenth century, annual exports of wax had increased to *c.*130 tons in good years, and at the time wax may have comprised approximately three-quarters of the total value of exports from Reval.[37] But other products, such as melted fat (also used for lighting), blubber (needed for broadcloth production), leather, flax and hemp (for shipbuilding), hides and leather gloves, were also exported. In return, the majority of goods from the West were sent east from Reval – salt, fabric, herring, malt, spices, luxury goods, silver bullion and coins, and other metals. The copper and tin that were essential for making bronze were strategically important, so the Teutonic Order tried to control and restrict the export of non-ferrous metals to Russia. The same applied to weapons and horses, but the fact that exporting these had to be repeatedly prohibited suggests that the businessmen's thirst for money was stronger than the regulations of the Order. Grains, mainly rye, were a product of Livonia itself that were exported to Russia, especially to Novgorod, which suffered from frequent famines.[38]

The northern and western partners of Reval varied somewhat over time. The mention of Reval in the document of the king of Norway in 1285 (see above) could be an indication of the city's interests in Scandinavia. The activity of Revalians in the trade centres of Finland in the mid-fourteenth century has been proven – they acquired privileges for marketing fabric, salt, wine, grains, hops, wax and fur.[39] However, the listed assortment of goods also suggests that the products brought to Reval from both the East and the West were the same that were brought in throughout the Middle Ages. This shows that either direct or indirect ties with the countries that supplied the relevant goods already existed at the time, and probably earlier as well. Some grains were also transported to the southern coast of the Baltic Sea at the time. There are few data about this, however, as one might expect – the economic structure there was the same as in Livonia.[40]

One can get a better glimpse of the trade relations of Reval in the final decades of the fourteenth century, as relatively thorough customs records from this period have been preserved. Flemish ships that carried salt from the Bay of Bourgneuf mainly visited the port of Reval at the time. This salt import, from western France, and to a lesser extent from Lisbon and Lüneburg as well, has been estimated at *c.*2,000–3,000 lasts (at *c.*2 tons) per year. Lübeck's share in the maritime trade of Reval may have been around one-fifth or one-sixth of the total volume at the time.[41] The customs records show no communication with other Livonian centres or with close neighbours Finland and Sweden, but an old treaty was confirmed in 1375 between King Albert of Sweden and the Livonian Master of the Teutonic Order, which gave both parties permission to trade in grains in each other's countries.[42] Livonia was probably the party that exported grains. What the customs records do confirm is frequent visits by Gotland merchants in the 1370s and 1380s – judging by the names, at least eighty burghers of Visby traded with Reval at the time.[43]

The next customs records survive from the period 1426–35 and provide a somewhat different picture. One-third of the ships that arrived in Reval still carried French salt, which was now mainly transported by the Dutch. However, almost as many ships came from Lübeck, and over a quarter of the ships came from Danzig. The war between the Wendish towns and Denmark that broke out in 1426, and which made the Danish straits unsafe, is seen as the reason for such a radical change in trade partners. The pre-war situation in the transport of salt was restored a couple of years later, but broadcloth trade from England and the Low Countries remained in the hands of Lübeck merchants. They also supplied other goods, such as honey, hops and herring.[44]

As for the second half of the fifteenth century, the Dutch maintained the leading role in the shipment of salt. However, the share of ships and goods from Lübeck, Danzig and other ports along the Baltic Sea was not much smaller than that of the Dutch.[45] The Hanse as well as local merchants in Livonia tried to curb the business activities of the Dutch as much as possible. The norm that took hold in the first half of the fifteenth century was that the Dutch were allowed to sell imported goods *en gros* and to purchase goods only for export, not for resale. Similar to other foreigners, retailing was off-limits to them. Nor were the Dutch permitted to have business connections with the Russians. By the middle of the fifteenth century, their stays were limited to three months and they were not allowed to spend the winter here. Those who were forced by circumstances to stay for the winter were not allowed to trade at the time. Non-Hanseatic merchants were not allowed to learn the language, travel to small towns and rural areas, or send their apprentices there. However, in reality, it was difficult to check whether these requirements were met.[46]

Getting a detailed overview of maritime trade of the sixteenth century is, due to the condition of sources, not possible. The Dutch were still engaged in salt imports. In terms of exports, their vessels were loaded with flax, hemp, and leather, but their main interest was grains. In general, it seems that a breakthrough occurred in the first few decades of the sixteenth century when it comes to the export of grain. Increased demand in Western Europe raised the price and made the grain business profitable. In the mid-sixteenth century, an estimated 4,000–5,000 lasts of grains per year were shipped out of Reval, but in the best years exports reached approximately 10,000 lasts.[47]

Reval's connections with Lübeck and Danzig remained the strongest. The city's merchants would have been unable to trade with the Low Countries without Lübeck acting as a mediator. Western goods like broadcloth (in the 1420s and 1430s on average 12,000 sheets), herring (from Scania and Aalborg), and metals (tin, lead and copper) moved to Reval to a large extent via Lübeck. Lübeck was also the transit centre for the wax, fur, blubber, flax, hemp, leather, iron, etc. exported from Reval. Danzig was more of a mediator in its relationship with Reval. Salt, broadcloth balls, gold and other western goods, as well as metals and Prussian hops (in the period 1426–35 on average 264 sacks of hops per year), were partly shipped on to Reval. Exports to Danzig consisted partly of goods that were shipped on to the Low Countries, partly of food such as dried fish and butter, and partly of limestone slabs.[48] The latter were used for grave slabs, altar stones and floor tiles, sometimes made according to the customer's samples. The Danes brought herring to Reval and took flax back with them.[49] There was also trade in food: the fifteenth- and sixteenth-century sources mention dried cod, rice, beer, Braunschweig *mumme* (thick, strong beer), French, Spanish and Rhine wine, fruit, raisins and so on. Other imports included glass, pearls, paper from the Low Countries, and pepper, ginger, and other spices as well. All these goods were partly sent on to Russia.[50]

Communication with Finland and Sweden remained active: salt, broadcloth and spices from the West; Russian wax, hemp and leather; and Livonian grains were taken there. Iron, copper, silver, butter, fish and sometimes leather were received from Sweden in return, while Finland provided leather and other animal products, fish and a little hemp and butter. At least one merchant in sixteenth-century Reval, Helmich Ficke, specialized in trade with Finland and Sweden, and he had dozens of clients in the northern neighbour states.[51]

Hinterland and the balance of trade

Being primarily a transit port, Reval's international trade hardly depended on the hinterland during the thirteenth–fifteenth centuries. However, its significance increased in the sixteenth century in accordance with the growing demand for grain and, to a lesser extent, wood and fibres in the West. The most important suppliers of grain were landowners, the noblemen in the countryside, who mainly sold it on credit but also for salt or other imported commodities. Reval's hinterland was rather extensive and comprised approximately a half of today's Estonian territory around the city. Grain was also provided by other Livonian merchants, in particular from Dorpat and Narva. The role of peasants here was much smaller but not irrelevant. A special, mutually beneficial relationship between a merchant and a peasant was called friend-trade. Friends (Low-Ger. *söbber* > Est. *sõber*) were the merchant's local agents, mainly wealthier peasants, who took care of his business and logistics in the countryside.[52]

In terms of the trade volume of Reval, it can (taking into account the continuous depreciation of money) only be compared to other more or less similar centres. Unfortunately, as research stands at the moment, such a comparison can only be done for the end of the fourteenth century. Back then, the annual trade volumes of Reval ranged from 100,000 to 200,000 Lübeck marks on average. This was about two times less than Lübeck and Hamburg, almost the same as Stralsund, and considerably more than Rostock.[53]

As a rule, the trade balance of Reval seemed to be in surplus with the West – with Lübeck the ratio was 2:1 at the end of the fifteenth century, which is natural in the case of a wealthier consumer and poorer supplier. However, such a big difference in imports and exports is deceptive. Wealthier trading partners compensated for this with precious metals, primarily with silver in the Hanseatic space. In 1530–40 silver comprised over 40 per cent of the value of the shipments of goods from Lübeck to Reval, and more and more of it had already been minted into thalers.[54] The proportion of gold, which was mostly transported in the form of coins, bars and wire, decreased here over time. The Reval mint and goldsmiths needed precious metals, but most of the silver moved on to Russia.[55] The conclusion from this should be that more goods were sent to Reval from Russia than Russia received in return.

In terms of the turnover of individual merchants, data exist only for the sixteenth century. They indicate that even the wealthiest Reval merchants, many of them city councillors, did not achieve annual turnovers higher than around 20,000 Riga marks. This was a lot less than the turnovers of their Danzig colleagues. The profit margin of the most successful Reval merchants may have reached 20 per cent at times (on average, it could be around 11–12 per cent), which was considerably more than that of south German merchants. However, modest turnovers meant that the wealth of even the most affluent Revalians did not even come close to that of the richest westerners. The same has to be said about the entire volume of Reval's trade in the sixteenth century.[56]

Maritime transport

As a rule, western goods arrived in Reval by sea. At the end of the fourteenth century, most ships had the capacity to carry cargo weighing 40–120 tons; only a few could carry more than 200 tons. The rise in the volume of commerce from the mid-fifteenth century resulted in the building of more and larger ships;[57] for example, salt vessels coming from further away could carry up to 700 tons of goods. However, their capacity mostly remained between 230 and 380 tons. The cargo-carrying capacity of ships increased further in the sixteenth century, but the difference between traffic on the North Sea and the Baltic Sea remained. The captains were usually Dutch, but there were also some Germans among them. There is evidence from the early fourteenth century that Revalians had their own ships, but there is no mention of them later. Local merchants, like Hans Selhorst, had shares in ships, but never majority holdings. However, the Reval city council had its own small two-mast sailing vessel (*bojer*) in the mid-sixteenth century. Transporting goods was rather profitable – Reval's little vessel could have earned *c.*1,000 Riga marks per year.[58]

Ships usually visited Reval just once or twice a year. The voyage itself did not even take that long – one could sail from Lübeck to Reval in a couple of weeks or even in eight days if the wind was good. However, loading and unloading goods in Lübeck took about a month. This meant that a return trip between Lübeck and Reval took two months on average. When the time spent at the port of Reval is accounted for, then it becomes clear that it was impossible to make more than two trips during the navigation period that lasted from April to October.[59] Salt vessels from further away didn't manage even that.

Trading on the North Sea and the Baltic Sea also differed in terms of chartering. Dutch captains bought salt from France or elsewhere, exchanged it for rye in Livonia, and sold it in Amsterdam or gave it to ship owners to sell. On Baltic Sea ships, the goods usually belonged to the merchants. Chartering was organized by a special charterer, who entered into contracts with captains about the division of the cargo. It was up to the merchant to decide which goods he would fill his share of the cargo with.[60]

The course of loading was precisely determined. As the goods were taken on board, the ship clerk first made a list, which was then used to prepare the necessary documentation. This included the names of the owner and recipient of the goods, and the quantity and marking of goods. The merchant sent a letter (a way-bill in today's terms) with the cargo, which contained exact data about the goods, such as grade, quantity, price and the various costs incurred. The letter was sealed and given to the captain, who delivered it to the addressee. The latter could then check the goods against the letter when they were received. Any inconsistencies were resolved by agreement between the sender and the captain.

Payment for transport was always made at the port of destination. The price of the service varied a great deal. Transport of more expensive goods (broadcloth, fur and other items that had to be transported dry under the deck) cost considerably more than cheaper goods (e.g. iron, salt, herring and honey). The fee for transport also depended on the market conditions. It was higher in autumn than in summer, and was higher during war than in peacetime. In the sixteenth century, the transport of one last of mass goods from Lübeck to Reval cost 3–4 Riga marks on average, while the cost of transport in the opposite direction was 3–4 Lübeck marks.[61] If someone wanted to travel with their goods, they did not have to pay for it. However, they had to bring their own food or pay the captain to provide it. Food was rather cheap: a passenger spent only *c.*1–2 Riga marks on it during the voyage.[62]

Merchants' organizations: the Great Guild and the Black Heads

Guilds and brotherhoods were established in order to offer social security to merchants, protect their professional interests and promote social life and religious rituals. However, the first guilds in Reval – those of St Canute and St Olaf – were not formed on the basis of profession, as they had members representing various social layers and professions, including merchants and craftsmen. In about the mid-fourteenth century an organization was finally established just for merchants as a result of the strengthening of the social hierarchy and the drawing of clearer lines between different social layers and ethnic groups. At first it was called Kindergilde, but from the late fifteenth century it became known as the Great Guild. It was the city's elite guild, consisting mostly of merchants engaged in large- and medium-scale long-distance trade. The high status of the organization is also proven by the fact that city councillors were only selected from among its members.[63]

Another merchant organization appears in sources from 1400: the Brotherhood of the Black Heads, which was probably named after the black St Maurice. While the members of the Great Guild were predominantly married and burghers of the city, the Brotherhood of the Black Heads united young unmarried merchants and journeymen. Seamen and foreign merchants temporarily staying in the city were also admitted. When a Black Head married and became a fully fledged merchant and burgher, he joined the Great Guild. The relatively high mobility of journeyman merchants meant that membership of the Brotherhood of the Black Heads was considerably less stable than that of the Great Guild: on average, a member remained in the brotherhood for five years. The emergence of the Black Heads fell in the period when brotherhoods of journeymen were being actively established in German towns. The Brotherhood was probably founded at a time when it became necessary to draw a clearer line between merchants and journeymen, and burghers and foreign merchants. Marital status was also an important criterion: with a few exceptions, merchants who did not marry (e.g. Berndt Pal from Lübeck) remained members of the Black Heads.[64]

Although the members of the Great Guild were mainly the city's own merchants, some, including councillors, were merchants from other Livonian cities and small towns (e.g. Dorpat, New Pernau and Narva). A number of foreign merchants, especially from Lübeck but also from Danzig, Visby, Bremen and Kampen, also belonged to the Guild. At the same time, they were also members of merchants' guilds in their hometowns, e.g. the Zirkel-Gesellschaft in Lübeck. In addition to commercial interests, there were additional reasons for being guild members in several cities: it guaranteed the numerous intercessory prayers so necessary for a merchant's soul, and the liturgical and secular commemoration of the deceased. It also reassured the merchant that, if he were to die abroad, his guild brothers would make sure that he received a proper Christian funeral befitting a man of his social stature. For example, Lübeck burgomaster Johan Luneborch, who died in Reval in 1374, was buried in the chancel of St Olaf's church, and at least ten city councillors from Lübeck were commemorated in the Great Guild in the fifteenth century (see Table 16.1).[65]

The guilds and brotherhoods offered, above all, a platform for social communication, which strengthened the existing partnerships and offered an opportunity to establish new connections. These organizations also solved small-scale conflicts among the guild members, such as quarrels and misbehaviour that emerged during the festival atmosphere.[66] They were not, however, the institutions that solved conflicts related to maritime trade – this was done on the level of the city council, landlord, regional diet of the cities, or diets of the Hanse.[67]

Table 16.1 City councillors of Lübeck as members of the Great Guild in Reval

Name	*Member of Great Guild*	*Member of Zirkel-Gesellschaft in Lübeck*	*City councillor in Lübeck*	*Death*	*Commemorated in Great Guild*
Bere, Ludeke	1435	1443	1460	1488	1490
Bere, Johan	1435/36	1447	1455	1457	1458
Bramstede, Jacob	1409	1429	1426	1455	1455
Brutzkow, Hans	1416	1429	1439	1449	1450
Castorp, Hinrick	unknown	1452	1452	1488	1489
Luneborch, Johan	1435	1443	1467	1474	1475
Rentelen, Bertram van	1443	1452	1477	1488	1490
Segeberch, Johan	1441/42	1429	1426	1464	1465
Stiten, Hinrick van	1425	1447	1447	1484	1485
Westphale, Johan	1421	1429	1447	1474	1476

Sources: Tallinn City Archives, coll. 191, inv. 2, no. 1; S. Dünnebeil, *Die Lübecker Zirkel-Gesellschaft: Formen der Selbstdarsellung einer städtischen Oberschicht*, Lübeck: Archiv der Hansestadt Lübeck, 1996, pp. 208–9, 238; E. F. Fehling, *Lübeckische Ratslinie von den Anfängen der Stadt bis auf die Gegenwart*, Lübeck: Schmidt-Römhild, 1925.

Conclusion

Reval, which grew into a city in the first half of the thirteenth century, quickly became a part of the Baltic Sea trade network due to its favourable position between Western Europe and Russia. The fall of Visby under the power of Denmark in 1361 turned out to be particularly advantageous for Reval and other Livonian urban centres. The control of the Hanse Kontor in Novgorod gradually passed to Livonian cities. After Ivan III closed the Novgorod Kontor in 1494, trade with the Russians moved to

Figure 16.1 Detail of the high altarpiece of St Nicholas Church in Reval. St Nicholas is saving a Hanse cog, decorated with the banners depicting the coats of arms of the Great Guild and the Brotherhood of the Black Heads. The arms not only commemorate the donors but also convey a message to the community: the saint protects the merchants of *our city*. Workshop of Hermen Rode, Lübeck, 1478–81

Livonian cities where protectionist tendencies began to spread. The Russian-Livonian War, which started in 1558, ended the conflicts with other Hanseatic cities created by these tendencies, and it has also been traditionally regarded by scholars as marking the end of the Middle Ages (including medieval trade) in the region.

Reval's trade was based on transit, but the city also exported some of its own goods, such as agricultural and forest products. The communication in the western and northern directions took place predominantly by sea, and people mainly used waterways to travel to Novgorod as well. The origin of goods covered an even broader geographic scope, as it reached from Lisbon and western France (salt) to Russia (wax and fur).

In order to facilitate commerce, the merchants of Reval – who often originated from Germany – established trade associations with their companions. As their relatives and business partners were also connected to other merchants in the Hanse region, this resulted in the emergence of a pan-European network in which goods, money, information and ideas moved. Among the preconditions for the functioning of such a network were the development of seafaring and the cargo-carrying capacity of ships, as well as a fairly advanced level of accounting. The business and social networks were also promoted by guilds and brotherhoods, which admitted not only local merchants but also those from other Hanseatic cities. The close interweaving of the city council and the city's elite guild – the Great Guild of merchants – guaranteed the protection and the representation of the merchants' commercial and political interests, both on the local as well as on the international level (Figure 16.1). Thus, it can be concluded that Reval owed its development during the Middle Ages largely to the maritime trade made possible by the city's geopolitical location, and to the integration in the Hanseatic networks.

Notes

1 Throughout the chapter, historical German place-names are used, since they predominate in historiography and are close to the usage found in medieval sources. The modern Estonian equivalent is given in brackets. The article was written under the auspices of the research project no. IUT18-8, financed by the Estonian Research Council.

2 For medieval Reval, see P. Johansen and H. von zur Mühlen, *Deutsch und Undeutsch im mittelalterlichen und frühneuzeitlichen Reval*, Cologne: Böhlau, 1973.

3 Tallinn City Archives, collection (coll.) 230, inv. 1, no. Ad 6, no. Ag 1–4.

4 W. Stieda (ed.), *Revaler Zollbücher und -quittungen des 14. Jahrhunderts*, Halle: Buchhandlung des Waisenhauses, 1887; W. Koppe, 'Revals Schiffsverkehr und Seehandel in den Jahren 1378/84', *Hansische Geschichtsblätter* 64, 1940, pp. 111–52; K. H. Sass, *Hansischer Einfuhrhandel in Reval um 1430*, Marburg am Lahn: Herder Institut, 1955; T. Wolf, *Tragfähigkeiten, Ladungen und Masse im Schiffsverkehr der Hanse, vornehmlich im Spiegel Revaler Quellen*, Cologne: Böhlau, 1986, pp. 110–12.

5 Tallinn City Archives, coll. 230, inv. 1, nos. Af 21, 23–4, 32–9, 40–4.

6 G. Mickwitz, *Aus Revaler Handelsbüchern: Zur Technik des Ostseehandels in der ersten Hälfte des 16. Jahrhunderts*, Helsingfors: Akad. Buchh., 1938; V. Niitemaa, *Der Binnenhandel in der Politik der livländischen Städte im Mittelalter*, Helsinki: Suomalainen Tiedeakatemia, 1952; J. Ahvenainen, *Der Getreidehandel Livlands im Mittelalter*, Helsinki: Soc. Scientiarum Fennica,

1963; C. Jahnke, *Netzwerke in Handel und Kommunikation an der Wende vom 15. zum 16. Jahrhundert am Beispiel zweier Revaler Kaufleute*, unpublished habilitation thesis, Kiel, 2003.

7 For example, A. Molvygin, 'Über die Münz- und Geldgeschichte Estlands vom Beginn der einheimischen Münzprägung bis zum II. Viertel des 15. Jahrhunderts', *Nordisk Numismatisk Årsskrift* 1969 [1970], pp. 37–42; I. Leimus, *Das Münzwesen Livlands im 16. Jahrhundert (1515–1581/94)*, Stockholm: Stockholm Numismatic Institute, 1995; I. Leimus (ed.), *Tallinna mündiraamatud 1416–1526/Revaler Münzbücher 1416–1526*, Tallinn: Tallinna Linnaarhiiv, 1999.

8 Tallinn City Archives, coll. 87, inv. 1, nos. 20–1; coll. 191, inv. 2, nos. 1, 15.

9 See T. Derrik, *Das Bruderbuch der Revaler Tafelgilde (1364–1549)*, Marburg: Tectum, 2000, pp. 34–8; A. Mänd, 'Social relations of Hanseatic merchants as mirrored at festivals: the example of medieval Reval and Riga', in I. Misans and H. Wernicke (eds), *Riga und der Ostseeraum: Von der Gründung 1201 bis in die Frühe Neuzeit*, Marburg: Verlag Herder-Institut, 2005, pp. 227–32; A. Mänd, 'Suurgildi ajalugu kuni Liivi sõjani' [History of the Great Guild until the Livonian War], in T. Liibek (ed.), *Tallinna Suurgild ja gildimaja*, Tallinn: Eesti Ajaloomuuseum, 2011, pp. 35–7, 42–3; A. Mänd, 'Membership and social career in Tallinn merchants' guilds', in L. Bisgaard, L. B. Mortensen and T. Pettitt (eds), *Guilds, Towns and Cultural Transmission in the North, 1300–1500*, Odense: University Press of Southern Denmark, 2013, pp. 244–5.

10 National Library in Helsinki, the collection of Paul Scheel, A.I.47. For Gertrud, see A. Mänd, 'Kaupmeheproua Gertrud ja tema hauaplaat Risti kirikus' [Merchant's wife Gertrud and her tombstone in Risti Church], *Tuna: Ajalookultuuri Ajakiri* 4, 2013, pp. 26–35.

11 T. Kala, 'Tallinna tekkeloo peegeldumine kirjalikes allikates' [The founding of Tallinn as reflected in the written sources], in V. Lang (ed.), *Keskus – tagamaa – ääreala: uurimusi asustushierarhia ja võimukeskuste kujunemisest Eestis*, Tallinn: Teaduste Akadeemia Kirjastus, 2002, pp. 391–408.

12 F. G. von Bunge, *Das Herzogthum Estland unter den Königen von Dänemark*, Gotha: Perthes, 1877, p. 222; *Liv-, Esth- und Curländisches Urkundenbuch nebst Regesten* (hereafter *LECUB*), vol. 1, ed. F. G. von Bunge, Reval: Kluge & Ströhm, 1853, no. 215; D. Kattinger, *Die Gotländische Genossenschaft: Der frühhansisch-gotländische Handel in Nord- und Westeuropa*, Cologne: Böhlau, 1999, pp. 362–3.

13 *LECUB*, vol. 1, nos. 451, 459, 463, 465, 478; I. Leimus, 'Kaubandus ja rahandus' [Trade and finances], in A. Selart (ed.), *Eesti ajalugu* [History of Estonia], vol. 2, Tartu: Tartu Ülikooli ajaloo ja arheoloogia instituut, 2012, p. 207.

14 Kattinger, *Die Gotländische Genossenschaft*, pp. 394–6.

15 Ibid., pp. 416–17.

16 *LECUB*, vol. 1, no. 495; Bunge, *Das Herzogthum Estland*, pp. 222–4.

17 *LECUB*, vol. 1, nos. 511–13, 517–19, 521, 523.

18 Ibid., no. 523.

19 Ibid., no. 555.

20 W. Schlüter (ed.), *Die Nowgoroder Schra in sieben Fassungen vom XIII. bis XVII. Jahrhundert*, Dorpat: Mattiesen, 1911, p. 123, no. 4; E. Tiberg, *Moscow, Livonia and the Hanse 1487–1550*, Stockholm: Almqvist & Wiksell, 1995, pp. 20–6.

21 E. Groth, *Das Verhältnis der livländischen Städte zum Novgoroder Hansekontor im 14. Jahrhundert*, Hamburg: Baltische Ges., 1999, pp. 27–38.

22 P. Osten-Sacken, 'Der Kampf der livländischen Städte um die Vorherrschaft im Hansekontor zu Novgorod bis 1442', *Beiträge zur Kunde Liv-, Est- und Kurlands*, vol. 7, Reval: Kluge, 1912, pp. 318, 368–71; Leimus, 'Kaubandus ja rahandus', p. 208.

23 N. A. Kazakova, *Russko–livonskie i russko-ganzeiskie otnosheniya: Konec XIV–nachalo XVI v.* [Russian–Livonian and Russian–Hanseatic relations: late 14th to early 16th century], Leningrad: Nauka, 1975, pp. 129–200; Tiberg, *Moscow*, pp. 38–44; Leimus, 'Kaubandus ja rahandus', p. 209.

24 L. K. Goetz, *Deutsch–Russische Handelsgeschichte des Mittelalters*, Lübeck: Waelde, 1922, pp. 178–87; Kazakova, *Russko–livonskie*, pp. 261–337; Tiberg, *Moscow*, pp. 44–72; I. Masko, 'Die Polozker Falschmünzer Ende des XV. Jh.', *Eesti Kollektsionäär* 2/3, 1992, pp. 21–3; A. Selart, 'Zur Geschichte der Russen in Livland um die Wende der 15. zum 16. Jahrhundert: Der Vorwand zur Schließung der St. Peterhofs in Novgorod im Jahre 1494', in N. Angermann (ed.), *Städtisches Leben im Baltikum zur Zeit der Hanse*, Lüneburg: Carl Schirren Gesellschaft, 2003, pp. 177–210. See also the chapter by Pavel V. Lukin in this volume.
25 Tiberg, *Moscow*, pp. 197–208; Leimus, 'Kaubandus ja rahandus', pp. 209–10.
26 Niitemaa, *Der Binnenhandel*, pp. 153–65; Ahvenainen, *Der Getreidehandel Livlands*, p. 181.
27 *LECUB*, vol. 1, no. 640.
28 Mickwitz, *Aus Revaler Handelsbüchern*, pp. 115–43; Sass, *Hansischer Einfuhrhandel*, p. 125.
29 W. Stieda (ed.), *Hildebrand Veckinchusen: Briefwechsel eines deutschen Kaufmanns im 15. Jahrhundert*, Leipzig: Hirzel, 1921, p. xliii.
30 Mickwitz, *Aus Revaler Handelsbüchern*, pp. 11–16; Jahnke, *Netzwerke in Handel und Kommunikation*, pp. 173–327; C. Jahnke, 'Zum Nutzen der guten Stadt Reval. Hans Selhorst, ein Kaufmann und Ratsherr zu Beginn des 16. Jahrhunderts', *Vana Tallinn* 16/20, 2005, pp. 88–107.
31 C. Jahnke, 'Handelsnetze im Ostseeraum', in G. Fouquet and H.-J. Gilomen (eds), *Netzwerke im europäischen Handel des Mittelalters*, Ostfildern: Thorbecke, 2010, pp. 189–212.
32 The most comprehensive studies on the topic are: Goetz, *Deutsch–Russische Handelsgeschichte*, and A. L. Khoroshkevich, *Torgovlya Velikogo Novgoroda s Pribaltikoi i Zapadnoi Evropoi v XIV–XV vekah* [Trade of Novgorod the Great with the Baltic countries and Western Europe in the 14–15th centuries], Moscow: Akademia nauk, 1963.
33 The first Russian church there was located at Sulevimägi Hill, but was moved to Vene Street around 1410. The Orthodox St Nicholas Church still stands there today, although in its nineteenth-century appearance. I. Kleinenberg, 'Tallinna vene kaubahoovi ajaloost XV–XVI sajandil' [On the history of the Russian merchants' yard in Tallinn in the 15th–16th centuries], *Eesti NSV Teaduste Akadeemia Toimetised* 3, 1962, pp. 248–9.
34 Mickwitz, *Aus Revaler Handelsbüchern*, p. 231.
35 Tiberg, *Moscow*, p. 250.
36 Squirrel pelts were the most common export article, and they were divided into four grades by quality. They were also distinguished on the basis of colour and skinning technology. Marten, stoat, mink, ermine and beaver pelts, tanned sheepskin, and lower-grade pelts that consisted of several pieces that had been stitched together, were also traded. Fox and otter pelts were sometimes brought from Sweden.
37 Goetz, *Deutsch–Russische Handelsgeschichte*, pp. 80–1; Khoroshkevich, *Torgovlya*, pp. 75–87, 109–15, 145–52; W. Stieda, *Über die Quellen der Handelsstatistik im Mittelalter*, Berlin: Königl. Akademie der Wissenschaften, 1903, pp. 46–52. Mickwitz, *Aus Revaler Handelsbüchern*, pp. 80–2.
38 Goetz, *Deutsch–Russische Handelsgeschichte*, pp. 248–335; Mickwitz, *Aus Revaler Handelsbüchern*, pp. 33, 46–82; Ahvenainen, *Der Getreidehandel Livlands*, pp. 45–56; Tiberg, *Moscow*, pp. 228–40.
39 *LECUB*, vol. 1, no. 777, 901; Bunge, *Das Herzogthum Estland*, pp. 223–4.
40 Ahvenainen, *Der Getreidehandel Livlands*, pp. 56–63.
41 Stieda (ed.), *Revaler Zollbücher*, pp. lviii–lix; Koppe, 'Revals Schiffsverkehr und Seehandel', pp. 111–52; Wolf, *Tragfähigkeiten*, pp. 110–12.
42 Ahvenainen, *Der Getreidehandel Livlands*, pp. 38–9.
43 D. Wase and T. Svensson, *Medeltidsgotland: Invånarna i meddeltidens Visby*, http://www.medeltidsgotland.se/page6.html (accessed June 2015).
44 Sass, *Hansischer Einfuhrhandel*, pp. 28–49; Wolf, *Tragfähigkeiten*, pp. 113–16.
45 Wolf, *Tragfähigkeiten*, pp. 116–19.

46 Niitemaa, *Der Binnenhandel*, pp. 308–12; Ahvenainen, *Der Getreidehandel Livlands*, pp. 75–85.
47 Niitemaa, *Der Binnenhandel*, pp. 346–7; Ahvenainen, *Der Getreidehandel Livlands*, pp. 160–2; J. Schildhauer, 'Zum See- und Handelsverkehr Revals im 16. Jahrhundert auf der Grundlage Revaler Hafenzollregister', *Tartu Riikliku Ülikooli Toimetised* 258, 1970, pp. 33–42; cf. Mickwitz, *Aus Revaler Handelsbüchern*, pp. 69–70.
48 Mickwitz, *Aus Revaler Handelsbüchern*, pp. 79–80.
49 Ibid., pp. 38–43, 46–82; Sass, *Hansischer Einfuhrhandel*, pp. 80–8.
50 Mickwitz, *Aus Revaler Handelsbüchern*, pp. 64–5.
51 Ibid., pp. 32–3; G. Kerkkonen, *Borgare och bondeseglare: Handelssjöfart på Reval genom och i SV-Finlands skärgård under tidigt 1500-tal*, Helsingfors: SHS, 1977.
52 Niitemaa, *Der Binnenhandel*, pp. 238–48; Ahvenainen, *Der Getreidehandel Livlands*, pp. 120–35; J. Kivimäe, 'Põllumajanduse turusidemed' [Agricultural market relations], in *Eesti talurahva ajalugu* [History of Estonian peasantry], Tallinn: Olion, 1992, pp. 244–5.
53 Stieda, *Revaler Zollbücher*, pp. lvii–lix; Koppe, 'Revals Schiffsverkehr und Seehandel', p. 114.
54 M. North, *Geldumlauf und Wirtschaftskonjunktur im südlichen Ostseeraum an der Wende zur Neuzeit (1440–1570)*, Sigmaringen: Thorbecke, 1990, pp. 142–50; Mickwitz, *Aus Revaler Handelsbüchern*, p. 89.
55 Khoroshkevich, *Torgovlya*, pp. 263–91.
56 Mickwitz, *Aus Revaler Handelsbüchern*, pp. 217–38; cf. Jahnke, *Netzwerke in Handel und Kommunikation*, pp. 446, 453, 459, 465, 469.
57 For the main types ships and for the development of shipbuilding, see the chapter by Richard W. Unger in this volume.
58 Mickwitz, *Aus Revaler Handelsbüchern*, pp. 165–7; Sass, *Hansischer Einfuhrhandel*, pp. 58–65; Ahvenainen, *Der Getreidehandel Livlands*, p. 182; Wolf, *Tragfähigkeiten*, pp. 120–88.
59 Mickwitz, *Aus Revaler Handelsbüchern*, pp. 155–7.
60 Ibid., pp. 158–9.
61 A Lübeck mark corresponded to approximately 1.5 Riga mark, ibid., p. 85.
62 Ibid., pp. 159–65.
63 The guild was first mentioned in 1363. For the Great Guild in Reval and other major Livonian cities, see Mänd, 'Membership and social career', pp. 229–32; A. Mänd, *Urban Carnival: Festive Culture in the Hanseatic Cities of the Eastern Baltic, 1350–1550*, Turnhout: Brepols, 2005, pp. 29–38.
64 Mänd, 'Membership and social career', pp. 232–40.
65 Ibid., pp. 244–6; Mänd, 'Suurgildi ajalugu', p. 43, table 5. For Luneborch, see *LECUB*, vol. 7, no. 344.
66 Mänd, *Urban Carnival*, pp. 248–56.
67 See, for example, the chapters by J. Wubs-Mrozewicz, C. Jahnke and P.V. Lukin in this volume.

17

NOVGOROD

Trade, politics and mentalities in the time of independence

Pavel V. Lukin

Introduction: sources and historiography

It has already been pointed out that one of the main challenges of the studies of medieval Novgorod is absence of its official archive.[1] It obviously did once exist, but disappeared at some point. Most likely it was not taken to Moscow (the inventory of the Tsar's archive does not mention any document which might have come from the Novgorod archive), and its fate is unknown. It could have perished in the sixteenth century after Novgorod lost its independence and its documents were no longer of great importance to the new authorities).[2] On the other hand, students of Novgorod may be relatively happy, as no other Russian medieval polity (perhaps except for Kiev and later on Moscow) has left such a wide range of sources.

Several Novgorod chronicles from the independence era have survived. The most important of them is the *Novgorod First Chronicle*.[3] Its earliest extant copy (Sinodal'nyj manuscript) dates back to the mid-thirteenth century. The earliest copies of its Younger Recension, continuing into the fifteenth century, are from the 1440s.[4] Also important are the chronicles deriving from the hypothetical 'Novgorod-Sophia Compilation' (first half of the fifteenth century): *The Novgorod Fourth Chronicle*, *The First Sophia Chronicle*, *The Novgorod Karamzin Chronicle*, *The Avraamka Chronicle*.[5] Either the authors of the *Novgorod First Chronicle* or the author of the *Novgorod-Sophia Compilation* borrowed material from the 'Novgorod Archbishop Compilation', which is considered by students of the Novgorod annalistic tradition to have been written from the 1130s on by the scribes of Novgorod archbishops. This makes the chronicles sources of paramount significance. They contain a relatively large amount of information on Novgorod politics and political ideology, international relations, warfare, etc. However, their data on the social and economic aspects of Novgorod's history are rather scarce and fortuitous. In addition, the chroniclers' religious and cultural background, their status as officials of the Novgorod bishopric and, last but not least, specific traits of their narrative structures deeply affect their contents. One can no longer see chronicles (as nineteenth-century historians would) as a kind of a 'reservoir' for pure historical facts. Their accounts should be juxtaposed with information provided by more reliable sources.

Of these non-narrative and much less 'ideological' sources, the most important classes are charters, birch-bark letters and Hanseatic documents written (sometimes in Latin but usually in Middle Low German) by German merchants in Novgorod. The purposes of the birch-bark letters or Hanseatic documents usually had nothing to do with a political agenda, and they tell us much more about the everyday life of Novgorod than chronicles do.[6] Hanseatic documents and birch-bark letters to some extent can be seen as a substitute of Novgorod's lost archive. One also should not underestimate another type of source – material objects. In the course of the unprecedented archaeological excavations in Novgorod that have been carried out since the 1930s, an abundance of evidence for Novgorod's social and economic life and its international contacts with its Baltic neighbours has been unearthed.[7]

Since the nineteenth century Novgorod has been a focus of unceasing discussions in Russian and Soviet historiography (and sometimes even abroad). The main point of the discussions has always been the highly controversial issue of a 'democratic' or 'republican' alternative in Russian history, for which Novgorod would have served as a classical and paramount model. For different reasons, conservative, Marxist and, more recently, postmodernist scholars have usually tended to disprove or 'deconstruct' the liberal model of Novgorod as an incarnation of Old Russian primordial democracy.

Presently, the paradigm of Novgorod studies is shaped by numerous works by the head of the Novgorod archaeological expedition, Valentin L. Yanin, who is the severest critic of the 'democratic' model. Despite criticisms (sometimes quite harsh) of some of his theories, Yanin's interpretations remain a kind of a reference point for all students of medieval Novgorod. As for Novgorod trade and Novgorod's contacts with its western neighbours, classical monographs by Leopold Karl Goetz are still topical.[8] Newer data (also from the excavations and birch-bark documents) are represented in the works by Elena A. Rybina and Norbert Angermann.[9] Of great importance is Catherine R. Squires' pioneering research of language contacts between Novgorod and the Hanse.[10] Social and political implications of close contacts between medieval Novgorod and the West have been studied since recently on the basis of Hanseatic sources,[11] but there is still a lot to be done.

In recent years a heated discussion has arisen about the internal social and political system of Novgorod, concerning first of all the applicability of the terms 'republic' and 'commune' to it. This debate is also relevant to the topic of this chapter as Novgorod's contacts with its western neighbours have been traditionally seen as a major factor in the development of 'republican' polities in the northwest of Rus'.[12] So the general problem can be posed in the following way: was the history of Novgorod the Great a kind of a 'Sonderweg' (which is implied by many students), or should aspects of its economic, social and political system be seen rather in the context of the evolution of other European maritime trade centres? More specifically, this chapter is aimed at concrete examples of the impact made by Novgorod's maritime trade with its western partners on the functioning of Novgorod's 'republican' political institutions as well as the influence exerted by Novgorod-Western contacts on the attitudes in the West towards Novgorod and its political system in the West.

Location and hinterland

Novgorod arose in the Ilmen lowland area, on the elevated territories along the Volkhov river not far from its source on Lake Ilmen.[13] To date, archaeologists have not found any evidence of Novgorod's existence prior to the tenth century, and the first clear evidence for urban life dates to the middle of that century.[14]

The natural and geographical conditions of the Novgorod Land are notable for their ambiguity.[15] On the one hand, although the so-called *Poozerye* (Lakeland) that was immediately adjacent to the source of the Volkhov was known to be favourable for agriculture, the soil in Novgorod Land, in general, was not particularly fertile. Over all, the huge, sparsely populated territory with its forests, swamps and very small number of cities made Novgorod socially and economically very different from the principal centres of southern Russia and, above all, Kiev. Thus, when the Mongols invaded Russian lands in 1237, there were only fourteen cities in the Novgorod Land (including minor strongholds), while the smaller Kievan Land had seventy-eight cities, i.e. five times more, the Novgorod Land being greater in area than any other Russian land.[16] To what extent this fact can be evidence of the *level* of economic progress is a complex issue, but in any case it illustrates the *type* of Novgorod economy, based on the exploitation of the vast and sparsely populated periphery by the centre.

On the other hand, Novgorod was located at a strategic point on the system of rivers within the Ilmen Basin, which connected it to the Western Dvina (and across it, with the Dnieper and southern Rus'), the Upper Volga and Lake Peipus (Chudskoe). Thanks to its geographical position Novgorod could control the main trade routes following the waterways in the north of Eastern Europe. Though Novgorod was not a maritime centre in a proper sense, Novgorod had access to both the Baltic Sea, to which it was linked via the Volkhov, Lake Ladoga and the Neva, and to the fur-rich territories of the Russian north. Novgorod's location and the climatic conditions in which its own economy developed contributed to its very early involvement in the trade system and international relations in the north of Europe. Subsequently, a vast peripheral territory, extending from the upper reaches of the Volga in the south to the White Sea in the north, and from the shores of the Baltic Sea in the west to the Ural Mountains in the east, was subject to Novgorod. Solely the area of the future Novgorod *piatiny* ('fifths', the districts into which the Novgorod Land was divided, apparently even after its submission to Moscow) – that is, the most developed part of the Novgorod domain – covered, by the end of the fifteenth century, almost 300,000 square kilometres.[17] Contemporaries were convinced of the huge size of Novgorod's domain: indeed, Venetian diplomat Giosafat Barbaro characterized it as *terra grandissima* in the late 1480s to early 1490s.[18]

It was the Novgorodians who pioneered the settlement of the northern expanses of what is now Russia (Figure 17.1). The peripheral areas subordinate to Novgorod were the main source of its wealth, and it was primarily these areas that supplied the goods that Novgorod exported. Usually the subjugation of peripheral territories began with imposing tributes, and this type of exploitation often remained the primary one in relations between Novgorod and dependent Finno-Ugric and other non-Slavic ethnic groups. Novgorod chronicles abound in accounts of Novgorodians' campaigns against their potential or rebellious tributaries. There is an account of the expedition from Novgorod against the Finno-Ugric Chud Land in 1212 telling how the levying of tribute could have been organized. The tribute was shared: one-third was given to the prince's retinue and two-thirds to the Novgorodians.[19] Large incomes enabled Novgorod's elite to build strongholds in the periphery where Novgorod's administration and garrisons were located. For instance, in the territory adjacent to the Gulf of Finland this role was filled, since the mid-thirteenth century, by the fortress of Koporye.[20] Later on some more detailed evidence of exploitation of the rural population of the Novgorod Land (and not necessarily only its non-Slavic part)

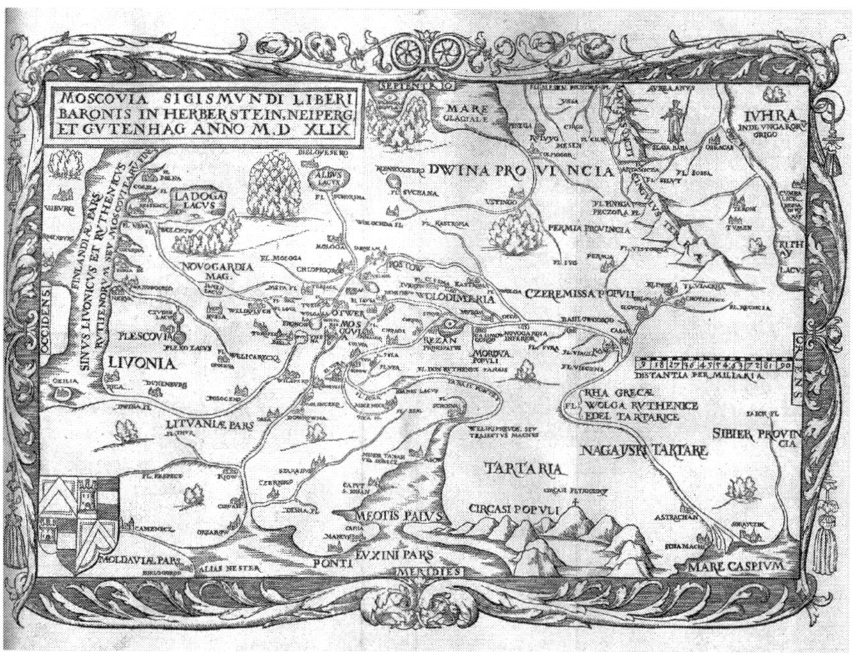

Figure 17.1 A map of Muscovy and neighbouring countries etched by the German artist and cartographer Augustin Hirschvogel for the first edition of Sigismund von Herberstein's *Rerum Moscoviticarum Commentarii* (Vienna, 1549). The cities of Novgorod and Pskov are indicated in the north-western part of the map as 'Novogardia Mag[na]' and 'Plescovia'.

by the commune of Novgorod can be traced. A chronicle account written after the fall of Novgorod's independence tells about wall-building in Novgorod ordered by the Moscow officials in 1534. And the chronicler sorrowfully remarks that walls had previously been built only by the population of the Novgorod *volosti* (i.e. periphery) and townspeople had been the customers (now things had changed and these duties were imposed on all Novgorodians).[21]

The policy of Novgorod towards its periphery may be labelled as a 'carrot-and-stick' approach. It apparently went beyond military campaigns, annexations and imposing tributes. There is some evidence of incorporation of members of local elites into the Novgorod boyar aristocracy. For instance, a certain Ivan Valit is mentioned in the fourteenth century as a person who was in charge of building a fortress in Porkhov, not far from the Grand Duchy of Lithuania.[22] The name Valit is most likely a Karelian one, Karelians being ethnic groups of Finnish descent, some of which were subject to Novgorod.[23]

Despite its size, however, this periphery was populated sparsely. From the accounts by Muscovite officials soon after the annexation of Novgorod, it is inferred that Novgorod's total population at the time could have reached 520,000 people.[24] This calculation, however, is very approximate and possibly imprecise. Other estimates, for example, suggest that there were 400,000 people in the second half of the fifteenth century.[25] At earlier times, the population of the Novgorod Land was, obviously, much smaller (and the above figures may have been exaggerated).

As has been already mentioned, the Novgorod Land was very little urbanized. Among all its cities, Novgorod itself clearly stood out. Excavations in Novgorod revealed large tracts of construction. This allows us (with a degree of reservation indeed, but more reliably than is usually the case with old Russian cities) to estimate the size of its population in various periods of its history. Thus, in the mid-twelfth century, Novgorod's population was apparently about 15,000 people, and in the first half of the fourteenth century it was no greater than 25,000.[26] These are rather large numbers. According to estimates by the most authoritative researchers, in the eleventh to early twelfth centuries the populations of the largest trading centres on the Baltic, such as Szczecin and Wolin, were about 5,000 to 10,000 people.[27] Thus, Novgorod was the largest settlement in the eastern Baltic as early as the twelfth century.

Later, Novgorod, whose population may have grown to about 25,000 people, was comparable to Europe's major urban centres.

In 1517, Polish writer Maciej Miechowita stated that 'by size, Novgorod is a little larger than Rome' (!), its circumference being 35 Italian miles (about 65 km) and Rome's only 32.[28] Neither Maciej Miechowita nor the aforementioned Barbaro had ever been to Novgorod, but their testimony clearly reflects the fairly realistic perception of its power and scope that prevailed in other European countries.

On the other hand, taking into account the likely very low population density of the Novgorod Land and the enormous gap in size and rank between its metropolis and subordinate towns, Novgorod's urban system, even on the eve of its annexation by Moscow, should be considered as much more 'immature' than the most 'immature' West European urban systems.[29]

One can see an exception in Pskov. Situated at a beeline distance of about 200 km from Novgorod, its influence was comparable to Novgorod in northwest Rus' in the fifteenth to early sixteenth centuries,[30] though by this time it had already been the centre of an autonomous land (for details see the chapter by Vovin and Krom). The nature of relations between Novgorod and Pskov at different historical stages remains a contentious issue in historiography. It seems that at first, at the very least until the 1130s, Pskov was actually a *prigorod* (literally 'suburb', which meant a town dependent on another one) of Novgorod, though it subsequently got away from the control of its powerful neighbour.[31] Nevertheless, assumptions about Novgorod's seniority in relation to Pskov lingered until much later. Novgorod chronicles give indications that Pskov belonged to Novgorod's *volost'* (i.e. was in Novgorod's possession).[32] Novgorodians even had the notion of Pskovites as their 'younger brothers' and tried to exploit this idea for political purposes. As Hanseatic sources have shown, this terminology was not purely rhetorical, but was actually used in political and legal practice. It was known perfectly well abroad. Thus, on 30 May 1436, during a negotiation with Novgorod authorities, Hanseatic merchants complained of the injustices done to them by Pskovites. They wrote that in the previous winter some German traders had been captured by 'the Pskovites, their [the Novgorodians'] younger brothers (*ore jungesten brodere*) . . ., and they kept them cruelly imprisoned with their goods'. On 23 June of the same year, during the next round of negotiations, the Germans (with some irony perhaps), referred to the Novgorod 'kindred' designation of the Pskovites:

> Furthermore, we have said of the Pskovites, whom they consider as their younger brothers . . . that they [the Novgorodians] ordered them [the Pskovites] to release the Germans, whom they have kept in custody with their goods against God's will and the kissing of the cross, since as their fathers do not detain them, sons and younger brothers should not detain them either.[33]

There were other towns lesser in both size and significance. Ladoga, which had an advantageous position at the crossroads of trade routes in the lower reaches of the Volkhov, arose as early as in the mid-eighth century.[34] The foundation and early history of another important urban centre of the Novgorod land – Rusa (now Staraya Russa) – are still not clear enough.[35] In the fifteenth century, Rusa became an important industrial centre for production of salt. It is only from the beginning of the sixteenth century, however, that the earliest data on the export of salt produced in Rusa are recorded.[36] Torzhok (Novyi Torg) arose in the middle part of the stream of the Tvertsa river no later than the first half of the eleventh century, taking control over the trading routes for grain that stretched to Russian territories in the further south and were vitally important to Novgorod.[37]

Novgorod and its main trade partners: from Scandinavia to the Hanse

The history of the diverse relations between Novgorod and the Baltic region can be divided into two stages: pre-Hanseatic and Hanseatic. At the first stage, Novgorod's key partners were Scandinavia (Norway and, later on, Gotland) and the Baltic Slavs.

In one of the stories from the medieval Icelandic work 'Book of Settlements' (*Landnámabók*), based on a text from around 1130, there is a reference to a merchant from Norway (*Noregr*) named Björn. According to an even earlier recension of *Landnámabók* by Sturla Þórðarson (*Sturlubók*), 'he called himself Björn the Fur, because he was a merchant who traded in Novgorod (*Hólmgarðsfari*)'.[38] In the tenth–twelfth centuries the island of Gotland played a crucial role in trade relations in the Baltic Sea.[39] Until the end of the twelfth century, it was governed by Scandinavian merchants. It was the latter who founded the oldest office representing foreign merchants in Novgorod, the Gothic Yard (*Gotskij dvor*), at the turn of the eleventh–twelfth centuries.[40] In this period according to some – albeit rather sketchy – data, Novgorod merchants were also actively involved in Baltic trade.

Traces of Novgorod–Scandinavian contacts survived until Hanseatic times as well – not just in the name of one of the foreign offices (the Gothic Yard), but in the language of early German texts from Novgorod. These are written in Middle Low German and contain Scandinavian loan words, the most striking of which is the name of the Charter of the Novgorod Hanseatic Yard – *schra*. It was borrowed from the Old Norse *skra* ('dried skin, charter, law code').[41]

Contacts between Novgorod and Baltic Slavs are a rather challenging issue. It has long attracted the attention of researchers, though there is little factual data. Therefore, it will be not easy to separate reality from hypotheses, conjecture and guesswork.

In the tenth–thirteenth centuries, there were undoubtedly economic contacts between Pomeranian Slavs and northwest Rus', and Pomeranians (merchants, craftsmen) could certainly have migrated to Rus', but there is no convincing support for a hypothesis of a mass migration of West Slavs to the Novgorod Land or of the West Slavic descent of the Novgorod population. In this regard, parallels between Novgorodian and Pomeranian socio-economic life should be seen typologically rather than in the context of 'origin'.

Commercial relations between Novgorod and German trading cities (later united into the Hanse) have frequently been the subject of study. A series of special monographs and articles has been dedicated to the subject.[42]

In the second half of the fourteenth to fifteenth centuries, the Gothic Yard was leased by the Hanse and fell into the hands of German merchants. At the end of the twelfth or in the first third of the thirteenth century, the St Peter's Yard (German from the very beginning) was founded, getting its name from the St Peter church located in it.[43] Both 'yards' were situated in the very heart of Novgorod, in its *Torgovaya storona* (Trade Side – separated from the opposite Sophia Side by the Volkhov river), in the vicinity of Yaroslav's Court. This was the site where the highest political authority of Novgorod, the Novgorod *veche* (assembly), gathered. Novgorod's commercial centre, *torg* (market), was situated nearby. In 1968 to 1972 excavations were carried out on the supposed location of the Gothic Yard. They resulted in diverse and very significant findings that confirmed its location at that site, to the south of Yaroslav's Court. The findings were dated to the fourteenth–fifteenth centuries when the Gothic Yard belonged to German merchants.[44] Worth particular mention among them is a birch-bark document from the late fourteenth or early fifteenth century, written in Latin and containing excerpts from liturgical texts.[45]

Even researchers prone to scepticism towards 'romantic' ideas of trade with Rus' as the source of the Hanse power acknowledge that Novgorod was an important trading partner for German merchants. Novgorod supplied the West European market with such valuable goods as furs and beeswax. Fur was not only needed for making warm clothes, but was prized foremost as expensive and fashionable clothing for the higher strata of society. Beeswax was demanded for candles whose smell was felt to be far more pleasant than the smell of rancid oil or fat.[46] Novgorod itself was a profitable market for western goods, primarily high-quality fabrics, salt and silver. The impact of trade with Hanse on Novgorod can be adequately estimated if one pays attention to a clause of the charter of the church of St John the Baptist-on-Opoki in Novgorod, which, according to tradition, was granted by Prince Vsevolod Mstislavich in the twelfth century but edited to its final form in the late thirteenth or even in the fourteenth century. The charter urges everyone who wants to join the St John the Baptist-on-Opoki merchant guild to give *tysyatsky* 'sukno ip'skoe', i.e. cloth from Ypres which was imported to Novgorod by Hanseatic merchants.[47] In 1331, during one of the sharpest conflicts between Novgorodians and German merchants, the latter offered to the representatives of Novgorod some purple cloth and several tuns of wine – both goods were imported by the Hanseatic merchants.[48] This clearly shows how deeply Hanseatic trade influenced internal political interactions in Novgorod.

As a result, German merchants were almost permanently present in Novgorod up until Novgorod's loss of independence. St Peter's Yard was closed by the Grand Prince Ivan III of Moscow in 1494 and all merchants staying there were arrested. The Gothic Yard also fell out of use, and although the Hanseatic office resumed its activities in Novgorod in 1514, its further history was linked to the relations between Hanse and the centralized Russian state rather than Novgorod. Both yards were destroyed by a fire in Novgorod in 1541. Ivan IV allowed Hanseatic merchants to trade in Russia and to found their yards in Novgorod according to the old customs, but because the Hanse's role as the hegemon of Baltic trade was declining, Hanseatic-Novgorod trade was no longer as important as it had been before. On the other hand, Hanseatic merchants were not able to restore their monopoly on trade with Russians within the city of Novgorod. In the sixteenth century not only Germans but also Danish, Swedish and Dutch merchants traded in Novgorod. Nevertheless German merchants were present there (with some interruptions caused by the Livonian War and the Time of Troubles) until the end of the seventeenth century. Now Lübeck was in charge of their activities and the merchants' office was called the Lübeck Yard, but it can hardly be compared to the former yards. For instance, in the 1630s there were only five to six merchants from Lübeck in Novgorod simultaneously (instead of dozens of Hanseatic merchants as in the time of Novgorod's independence). As a result of the shifting of overseas trade routes, the emergence of new maritime trade centres in Russia (Arkhangelsk near the White Sea, first of all), and – last but not least – deliberate actions of Muscovite grand princes and tsars (including the deportation of the Novgorod boyars and merchants ordered by Ivan III, which destroyed the traditional infrastructure of trade in Novgorod and deprived it of the wealthiest customers for imported goods, and the massacre of 1570 under Ivan the Terrible) ultimately undermined the economic basis of Novgorod.[49]

Contacts, conflicts, peace-making and mutual (mis)understanding

In the heyday of Hanseatic yards (Gothic and St Peter's/German) in Novgorod, there would have been 150 or more Germans staying in Novgorod at the same time. That is, the yards that Hanse had in Novgorod were more or less comparable in size to those in Bruges, London and Bergen, the other Hanse Kontore.[50] This raises some natural questions. How would the Germans and the local population of Novgorod normally interact? What formed the institutional basis for these interactions? How did the contact shape the sides' views of each other?

The influence of close contacts with the Hanse on economic and social developments in Novgorod must have been considerable and multiform. Although its particular aspects have been studied quite insufficiently until now, one can imagine how important it was, avoiding theoretical speculations and taking into account just the following facts.

In the early fifteenth century Ivan Kocherin, a Novgorod merchant, was actively trading in Livonia with his Hanseatic partners. He could endure a prolonged conflict with them, which ended in 1411 with the signing of a peace agreement (preserved and published).[51] He was also involved in the Novgorod politics. For instance, we know from a Hanseatic document that he took part in the *veche* assembly where he made complaints against German merchants.[52] Nevertheless he apparently owed his prosperity just to trade with the Hanseatic partners. And in fact he was quite a well-to-do person as he was able to charter a ship.[53]

Later on, in the late fifteenth century a certain Iov Kocherin is mentioned in the cadastres of the Novgorod Land (*pistsovye knigi*) made soon after the annexation of Novgorod by Moscow. This Iov Kocherin turns out to be a landowner with several villages and a manor (*boyarschina*) in his possession.[54] One can agree with V. N. Bernadskii that it is not a mere coincidence and Iov Kocherin may have been an offspring of Ivan Kocherin.[55] Obviously he was not an aristocrat as there was no such boyar kin in Novogod as Kocherins. The most probable scenario is that Iov Kocherin or one of his ancestors (or even Ivan himself) succeeded in rising to the second (after the boyars) privileged layer in the Novgorod's social hierarchy – the *zhitii liudi* (literally, 'well-to-do people').[56] They enjoyed full rights and were entitled to own land. Moreover, thanks to a valuable bilingual Russian–Low German document of 1472, it has recently become clear that Germans translated the term *zhitii liudi* as 'well-to-do merchants' (*wolmagende coplude*).[57] This means that purchasing land may have been a standard way for a Novgorod merchant to increase his social and legal status. And profitable trade with the Hanse was undoubtedly one of the best means for a merchant to get richer.

The Germans' staying in Novgorod entailed inevitable conflicts over trade disputes or quarrels of a more trivial nature. In such situations German merchants would have been forced to turn to the Novgorod authorities, litigate against their offenders, and report on the progress and outcome of the proceedings to the Hanseatic cities responsible for trade with Novgorod. These messages would subsequently be discussed in the assemblies of Hanseatic cities, and their resolutions are carefully recorded. In turn, the Hanseatic authorities often wrote to the Novgorod authorities or the German merchants staying there to address one or another issue. Many of these documents were published in the nineteenth and early twentieth century (in Germany and the Russian empire) in the multivolume series and other editions. These documents allow us to vividly imagine how Hanseatic merchants and Novgorodians interacted in practice, on which there is hardly any information in internal Novgorod sources (mostly chronicles deal more with 'big' politics than with day-to-day life). Of course, the very nature of these sources, if they are used uncritically, may lead to an overly straightforward interpretation of Novgorod–Hanseatic relations as a series of ceaseless conflicts permeated by total misunderstanding. There indeed have been scholars who believe this to be exactly the case. For example, a prominent expert on German–Russian relations, Leopold Karl Goetz, wrote, in his time, that relationships between German merchants and local population in Novgorod consisted mostly of caution and mutual distrust. [58]

However, if we carefully consider even those documents associated with the activities of the Hanseatic office in Novgorod that refer to acute conflicts between the local population and German traders, we see more in them than just mutual suspicion. To do this, it makes sense to pay attention not only to their basic message, but also, as Marc Bloch wrote, to the 'tracks which the past unwittingly leaves all along its trail',[59] that is, the evidence that appears in these documents unintentionally and is not usually associated with their primary subject.

Thus, a partially preserved document, an epistle by German merchants (probably dating to 1337) in which they complain of the oppressions perpetrated against them in Novgorod, cites a dialogue between themselves and the Novgorodians. The German merchants, trying to persuade the Novgorodians to observe their rights, declare:

> To this we said in response: 'You, gentlemen, think of God and your own soul, because you, after all, are Christians, as are we and [we ask you] not to disturb us, for we, locked up in the middle of Novgorod, find ourselves in your hands.'[60]

In the heat of conflict, the German merchants appealed to the Christian identity they shared with the Novgorodians. They apparently held that Novgorodians were *also* Christians, which meant that they were basically *the very same* Christians. Such an argument would have made sense only if, in principle, Novgorodians themselves thought the same, or at least a significant number of them did.

This was by no means a generally accepted opinion among Novgorod's Catholic neighbours and partners. The view of the Orthodox Novgorodians as 'schismatics' who had fallen away from the 'true' (i.e. Catholic) faith was widespread, and it was held by upper officials of Sweden, the Teutonic Order, and the archdiocese of Riga.[61] As early as 1268 the preceptor of the Livonian branch of the Teutonic Order, Konrad von Mandern, instructed residents of Lübeck and German merchants that they should not sell their goods to 'enemies of the faith, namely the Russians from Novgorod'[62] that year.

There is also no reason to assume that complete arbitrariness ruled the relations between Hanseatic merchants and Novgorod authorities. The Germans, of course, constantly complained of injustices done to them in Novgorod and of the connivance of the Novgorod authorities in this regard (by the way, according to correspondence between Hanseatic cities, Novgorod merchants therein suffered from the same problems, in turn). However, they never ceased to appeal to the Novgorod legal norms then in force and to Novgorod's political and judicial institutions. When, in the winter of 1406, during a trade conflict, Novgorodians 'decided at the *veche* to ban the export of any German goods', and even to throw goods off sleighs if the Germans would try to take them out, German 'merchants went to the *tysyatsky* and complained to him of this'. The *tysyatsky* replied that 'he would consult with Novgorod the Great at the general *veche*, [and] depending on their decision about it, [and] according to [their decision] he would then give an answer'.[63] The *tysyatsky* was one of the three high magistrates in Novgorod, along with the *posadnik* and archbishop. The precise range of his functions is rather difficult to identify, not just because the data are too scarce, but also because there was neither clear separation of administrative, political and judicial powers between Novgorod's political institutions and magistrates, nor – despite the existing idea of tasks which Novgorod's magistrates and institutions were in charge of – were these tasks ever clearly defined. Nevertheless it was primarily the *tysyatsky* who was most often in charge of commercial affairs, particularly relations with Hanseatic merchants.

Novgorod officials acted on the shared legal basis and, in any case, generally considered it necessary to justify themselves in the event that the rights of German merchants in Novgorod were evidently violated. Thus, in 1409, in a message to Reval the German merchants stated that 'robberies in their city occur, as a matter of fact, without the approval of the *posadnik* and *tysyatsky*, as they told us in front of St John's church'.[64] Regardless of what really happened then in Novgorod, it is important that the *posadnik* and the *tysyatsky* felt it necessary, even if nominally, to dissociate themselves from those Novgorodians who abused the German merchants.

This indicates, at least to some extent, a notion of a shared legal field in which it was not absolutely senseless to appeal to legal norms rather than to act by force.

The German merchants were well aware of one of the archbishop's functions, that of protection of (or intercession for) people facing persecution, and they did indeed resort to this protection. Several documents associated with the events in Novgorod in 1425 attest to this. The message from German merchants staying in Novgorod to Dorpat mentions specifically the crucial role of the archbishop's intercession. The letter begins with an account of the Novgorodians' very aggressive behaviour, and then it reads:

> This would have likely happened to us if good people had not taken care, especially the bishop, who for so long had supplicated for us, and he endured great distress due to his intercession and for the permission to [do] it [i.e. to punish Germans] that he did not want to give . . .[65]

The Dorpat document, conveying the essence of negotiations with the Novgorod ambassador (1 February 1426), also emphasizes the mediating role of the archbishop:

> And you say below that the holy father Archbishop of Novgorod gave his blessing to the *posadnik* and to all Novgorod the Great for the German children [*sic*: term for German merchants] and so that the Germans, with his goodness, be released: despite the fact that absolute injustice was done to Germans, we [the Germans] after all thanked the holy father and lord Archbishop and thanked him [literally: bowed down to him] humbly for this and for his mercy on behalf of the German children, because he is a good, pious man and knows well what is just and what is unjust.[66]

Another document sent from Dorpat to Reval on 11 November 1425, states that the release of the Germans was achieved due to the 'great labour and requests of the bishop of Novgorod'. For this purpose, the bishop even 'asked humbly the *posadnik*, the *tysyatsky* and all Novgorod and blessed German merchants'.[67] This clearly shows that German merchants were well aware of the particularities of Novgorod's internal political structure and were able to use it to their advantage. In turn, the organization of power in Novgorod was flexible enough to use the authority of one of its highest magistrates, the archbishop, in cases when a shift from confrontation to cooperation became necessary.

There were also specific legal institutions and procedures for resolving problems in the relations between Hanseatic merchants and Novgorodians. As it usually happens, one often learns about their existence through complaints of their violation. On 9 August 1426 German merchants staying in Novgorod wrote to Reval about their hassles with the Novgorod authorities:

> we reminded the *tysyatsky* that in accordance with the cross-kissing, he must declare the verdict to us in front of the church of St John following the old

> custom, as it would be fair. Then again he announced to us that there were *Vögte* in our [i.e. Hanseatic] cities; there they could judge their brothers, no matter where they held their court sessions, in front of a town hall or in their own homes or in the street, everywhere it would be fully legal. Likewise he announced again: wherever justice is carried out by him, be it in front of [the church] of St John or in the street, or in his own mansion, or anywhere else, it would also be within their right, and would fulfil the cross-kissing.[68]

The Germans' request was based on the clause of a treaty between Novgorod on one side and Gotland and Lübeck on the other, which had been approved in 1269: 'If between the Germans and Novgorodians there happens a quarrel, then the quarrel shall be brought to end in the St John's Court before the *posadnik*, *tysyatsky*, and before the merchants [the Novgorod merchant elders]'.[69] The Novgorod *tysyatsky* insists on his right to judge where he wishes, and refers to the procedures typical (at least in his opinion) for Hanseatic cities themselves. These references, of course, are lip-service to a certain extent and are intended to obscure the violation of existing norms, but they obviously attest to the Novgorodians' clear awareness of the political and legal traditions of Hanseatic cities, and fit well into what modern diplomatic practice calls 'constructive dialogue' between rival parties.

We began our description of 'real' relations between Novgorod and Hanseatic merchants with the analysis of their sublime, religious elements. In conclusion, therefore, let us turn to the purely day-to-day (but no less significant) aspects of these relations. On 13 December 1412 German merchants in Novgorod reported to Reval:

> beloved friends, the Russians also always put before us the question of the tavern kept by the steward of the yard, and namely of the trouble that may occur due to Russians who go to the yard to drink, and merchants believe that it would be better to abolish the tavern.[70]

This episode, which may seem funny, reveals at the micro level the actual relationship between the theoretically closed German community in Novgorod and the reality of interaction between the Hanseatic merchants and local population. Despite all prohibitions, German beer brewed in the St Peter's Yard attracted Novgorodians so much that no prohibition could prevent them from getting more familiar with it. Indeed, the very existence of the prohibitions implies that they were violated regularly. And, certainly, personal contact could not but lead to the development of ideas rather different from the official stringency.

Conclusions: Novgorod as a European maritime trade centre

As was already noted in the introduction, recent historiography has seen rather heated debates on whether Novgorod can be compared with contemporaneous West European urban communes and medieval republics, and whether Novgorod meets the criteria of the 'ideal type' of a medieval western city.[71] These debates may seem somewhat of scholastic exercise. But doesn't it make sense to directly address what has been reported by witnesses, that is, the Europeans who saw Novgorod themselves or heard about it from those who had seen it? If we make use of this evidence, we might get a clearer picture of the attitudes of Novgorod the Great's western contemporaries towards it.

The perception of Novgorod by contemporary Europeans was a far cry from much later western assessments of 'Muscovy' as something completely authoritarian and alien to them.

The Burgundian knight Guillebert de Lannoy, who visited Novgorod in the winter of 1413, called it 'a free city and domain of the commune' (*ville franche et seignourie de commune*)[72] – as the Belgian historian Stéphane Mund notes, 'the term which was used *per se* to designate the government in the Netherlands' towns'.[73]

German merchants, well aware of how Novgorod's political structure worked, also, it seems, did not consider it to be anything totally different from the communal organization of their own cities. They called the Novgorodians entitled to full political rights *de gemeenheit, dat gemene van Groten Naugarden*, that is, 'the commune, the community of Novgorod the Great'.[74] It is important that these concepts – *gemene, gemeenheit, commune* – were also applied to the political organization of West European cities of the same period. Lübeck could be called, for example, 'eyne gancze gemene edder eyn commun'.[75] It becomes clear that West European contemporaries, being quite familiar with the particularities of the Novgorod political system, recognized it as an urban commune, a community, and described it in the same terms that they applied to their own (Burgundian or northern German) city communities.

While Hanseatic merchants construed Novgorod as similar to their own cities, Ulrich von Richenthal, a German chronicler and the author of the 'Chronik des Konstanzer Konzils' (*c.*1420), compared Novgorod to Venice. The chronicler says that the council, which met in 1414–18, was attended by representatives from Novgorod. He knew (as it is assumed, directly from the Novgorod ambassadors)[76] that the city was 'called Novgorod the Great', that it was a self-governing city and that 'it elected its *herzog*, as do the Venetians'.[77] In this case, *herzog* was most likely the *tysyatsky* (*herzog* was the usual designation for the Novgorod *tysyatsky* in Hanseatic sources).

The idea of the resemblance between Novgorod's political system and Italian medieval republics has not been completely alien to the scholarship. For instance, a German historian, Knut Schulz, believes that Novgorod 'in many respects . . . reminds of an Italian city-state'. Among the similarities, he mentions domination of the city centre over rural periphery and subordinate smaller towns, the election of officials and the role of the urban elite who flourished due to trade revenues and large estates.[78] But above all, the Venetians themselves – contemporaries of the independent Novgorod – described it as a self-governing commune. According to the previously mentioned Giosafat Barbaro, Novgorod previously (i.e. before its subjugation by Moscow) 'was governed by the people' (*governavassi prima a populo*).[79] A Venetian diplomat, Ambrogio Contarini, who visited Moscow in 1476–7, knew that Novgorod was 'governed as a commune' (*si governa a comunità*).[80]

We need not, of course, think that some sort of elaborate concept of political freedom existed in medieval Novgorod. However, such a concept was not present either in all maritime European centres of the Middle Ages and early modern period, with the exception of those in Italy, where, in the beginning of the fifteenth century, the concept of civic freedom (*libertas, libertà*)[81] was developed in the context of civil humanism. In cities north of the Alps, civic liberties were understood as the privileges of the civic body and its members. In practice, this meant protection from lawless violence and from arbitrary and illegal encroachment on the property of citizens by the government.[82] This is very close to Novgorod notions, where 'liberty (*vol'nost'*)' would be most typically understood not as an abstract idea, but as freedom in relation to something – freedom *from* something.

The reason for this 'comprehensibility' of Novgorod's realities to its Western partners lies most likely in the similar economic and cultural conditions which gave rise (on the basis of old Russian political traditions) to the organizational forms which turned out to be similar, to a certain extent, to Western ones. The most important of these conditions was Novgorod's involvement in the Baltic trade, which being a permanent link between the Russian city on the Volkhov and its partners in the West, strongly influenced not only Novgorod's socio-economic development but also the routine functioning of its political institutions and even the Novgorodians' day-to-day life.

Notes

1 C. J. Halperin, 'Novgorod and the "Novgorodian Land"', *Cahiers du monde russe: Russie, Empire russe, Union soviétique, États independants* 40/3, July–Sept. 1999, p. 345.

2 L. V. Cherepnin, *Russkie feodal'nye arkhivy XIV–XV vekov* [*Russian Feudal Archives of the 14th–15th centuries*], part 1, Moscow and Leningrad: Izdatel'stvo Akademii nauk, 1951, pp. 224–39; I. P. Shaskol'skii, 'Sud'ba gosudarstvennogo arkhiva Velikogo Novgoroda' [The fate of the state archive of Novgorod the Great], *Vspomogatel'nye istoricheskie distsipliny* 4, 1972, pp. 213–28.

3 *Polnoe sobranie russkikh letopisej* [The complete collection of Russian chronicles] (hereafter *PSRL*), vol. 3, *Novgorodskaya pervaya letopis' starshego i mladshego izvodov* [Novgorod first chronicle of older and younger recensions], Moscow: Yazyki russkoj kul'tury, 2000. English trans. *The Chronicle of Novgorod 1016–1471*, tr. R. Michell and N. Forbes, London: Offices of the Society, 1914 (Camden 3rd series, vol. 25); German trans. of the Synodal manuscript: *Die Erste Novgoroder Chronik nach ihrer ältesten Redaktion (Synodalhandschrift) 1016–1333/1352*, tr. J. Dietze, Leipzig: Edition Leipzig, 1971.

4 On the Novgorod First Chronicle see: A. A. Gippius, 'K istorii slozheniya teksta Novgorodskoj pervoj letopisi' [On the history of shaping of the text of the Novgorod First Chronicle], *Novgorodskij istoricheskij sbornik* 6, 1997, pp. 3–72.

5 *PSRL*, vols 4, 1 (Novgorodskaya chetvyortaya letopis' [Novgorod Fourth Chronicle]); 6, 1 (Sofiiskaya pervaya letopis' [Sofia First Chronicle]); 42 (Novgorodskaya Karamzinskaya letopis' [Novgorod Karamzin Chronicle]); 16 (Letopis' Avraamki [Chronicle of Avraamka]).

6 For more on Novgorod charters, birch-bark documents, Novgorodian–Hanseatic correspondence and literacy in Novgorod in general, see: V. L. Yanin, *Novgorodskie akty XII–XV vv. Khronolocheskij kommentarij* [Novgorod charters of 12th–15th centuries: a chronological commentary], Moscow: Nauka, 1991; S. Franklin, *Writing, Society, and Culture in Early Rus, c. 950–1300*, Cambridge: Cambridge University Press, 2002, pp. 35–45; A. A. Gippius, 'Birchbark literacy and the rise of written communication in early Rus', in K. Zilmer and J. Jesch (eds), *Epigraphic Literacy and Christian Identity: Modes of Written Discourse in the Newly Christian European North*, Turnhout: Brepols Publishers, 2012, pp. 225–51; P.V. Lukin, 'Ganzejskie istochniki i sotsial'no-politicheskaya istoriya srednevekovogo Novgoroda', *Vestnik Rossiiskogo gumanitarnogo nauchnogo fonda* 77/4, 2014, pp. 22–30. See there also references to publications of sources.

7 On excavations in Novgorod see: V. L. Yanin, *Srednevekovyj Novgorod* [*Medieval Novgorod*], Moscow: Nauka, 2004, pp. 3–126.

8 L. K. Goetz, *Deutsch-Russische Handelsverträge des Mittelalters*, Hamburg: L. Friedrichsen & Co, 1916; L. K. Goetz, *Deutsch-Russische Handelsgeschichte des Mittelalters*, Lübeck: Lübecker Verlaganstalt Otto Waelde Komm.-Ges., 1922.

9 E. A. Rybina, *Arkheologicheskie ocherki istorii novgorodskoj torgovli* [Archaeological Essays on the History of the Novgorod's Trade], Moscow: Izdatel'stvo Moskovskogo universiteta, 1978; E. A. Rybina, *Inozemnye dvory v Novgorode XII–XVII vv.* [Foreign yards in 12th–17th centuries], Moscow: Izdatel'stvo Moskovskogo universiteta, 1986; E. A. Rybina, *Novgorod i Ganza* [Novgorod and the Hanse], Moscow: Rukopisnye pamyatniki Drevnej Rusi, 2009; N. Angermann, 'Deutsche Kaufleute im mittelalterlichen Novgorod und Pleskau', in H. Rothe (ed.), *Deutsche im Nordosten Europas*, Cologne: Böhlau Verlag, 1991, pp. 59–86; N. Angermann, 'Die hansisch-russische kulturelle Begegnung im mittelalterlichen Novgorod', in V. Henn and A. Nedkvitne (eds) *Norwegen und die Hanse: Wirtschaftliche und kulturelle Aspekte im europäischen Vergleich*, Frankfurt am Main: Peter Lang, 1994 (Kieler Werkstücke, Reihe A: Beiträge zur schleswig-holsteinischen und skandinavischen Geschichte, 11), pp. 191–211; N. Angermann, 'Novgorod und seine Beziehungen zur Hanse', in W. Hartmann (ed.), *Europas Städte zwischen Zwang und Freiheit: Die europäische Stadt um die Mitte des 13. Jahrhunderts*, Regensburg: Universitätsverlag, 1995, pp. 189–202; N. Angermann, 'Nowgorod – das Kontor im Osten', in J. Bracker *et al.* (eds), *Die Hanse: Lebenswirklichkeit und Mythos*, Lübeck: Verlag Max Schmidt & Römhild, 1999 [1989], pp. 234–41.

10 E. R. Skvajrs [C. Squires] and S. N. Ferdinand, *Ganza i Novgorod: Yazykovye aspekty istoricheskikh kontaktov* [The Hanse and Novgorod: linguistic aspects of the historical contacts], Moscow: Indrik, 2002; C. Squires, *Die Hanse in Novgorod: Sprachkontakte des Mittelniederdeutschen mit dem Russischen mit einer Vergleichsstudie über die Hanse in England*, Cologne: Böhlau Verlag, 2009.

11 P. V. Lukin, *Novgorodskoe veche* [*Novgorod veche*], Moscow: Indrik, 2014; P. V. Lukin, 'The Veche and "Council of Lords" in medieval Novgorod. Hanseatic and Russian data', *Russian History* 41/4, 2014, pp. 458–503.

12 R. Mumenthaler, 'Spätmittelalterliche Städte West- und Osteuropas im Vergleich: Versuch einer verfassungsgeschichtlichen Typologie', *Jahrbücher für Geschichte Osteuropas* 46, 1998, pp. 39–68; R. Leffler, 'Novgorod – eine europäische Kommune des Mittelalters?', in C. Goehrke and B. Pietrow-Ennker (eds), *Städte im östlichen Europa: Zur Problematik von Modernisierung und Raum vom Spätmittelalter bis zum 20. Jahrhundert*, Zürich: Chronos Verlag, 2006, pp. 33–59; O. Sevastyanova, 'In quest of the key democratic institution of medieval Rus': was the *Veche* an institution that represented Novgorod as a city and a republic', *Jahrbücher für Geschichte Osteuropas* 58, 2010, pp. 1–23; M. M. Krom (ed.), *Spory o novgorodskom veche: Mezhdistsiplinarnyj dialog: Materialy kruglogo stola (Evropejskii universitet v Sankt-Peterburge, 20 sentyabrya 2010 g.* [Discussions on the Novgorod

Veche: An Interdisciplinary Dialogue: Proceedings of the Workshop in Saint Petersburg, 20 September 2010], Res Publica 6, St Petersburg: European University at St Petersburg Press, 2012; Lukin, 'The Veche', pp. 493–503.

13 I. I. Kushner, 'K topografii drevnego Novgoroda' [On the topography of medieval Novgorod], *Sovetskaya arkheologiya* 3, 1975, pp. 176–9.

14 V. L. Yanin, 'Raskopki v Novgorode' [Excavations in Novgorod], in V. L. Yanin, *Srednevekovyi Novgorod: Ocherki arkheologii i istorii* [Medieval Novgorod: Essays on Archaeology and History], Moscow: Nauka, 2004 [1999], pp. 68–72; V. L. Yanin, 'O nachale Novgoroda' [On the beginning of Novgorod], in E. N. Nosov (ed.), *U istokov russkoi gosudarstvennosti: Istoriko-arkheologichesky sbornik: K 30-letiyu arkheologicheskogo izucheniya Novgorodskogo Ryurikova Gorodishcha i Novgorodskoi oblastnoi arkheologicheskoi ekspeditsii: Materialy mezhdunarodnoi nauchnoi konferentsii 4–7 oktyabrya 2005* [At the roots of russian statehood: historical and archaeological collection: on the 30th anniversary of the archaeological study of Novgorod's Rurikovo settlement and the Novgorod Oblast' archaeological expedition: proceedings of the international conference, 4–7 October 2005], St Petersburg: Dmitrij Bulanin, 2007, pp. 210–11; E. N. Nosov, 'Novgorodskaya zemlya: Severnoe Priil'men'e i Povolkhov'e' ['Novgorod Land: Northern Ilmen and the Volkhov'], in N. A. Makarov (ed.), *Rus' v IX–X vekakh: Arkheologicheskaya panorama* [Rus' in the 9th–10th centuries: an archaeological panorama], Moscow and Vologda: Drevnosti Severa, 2012, pp. 118–19.

15 For details, see Nosov, 'Novgorodskaya zemlya', pp. 93–6.

16 V. N. Bernadskii, *Novgorod i Novogorodskaya zemlya v XV veke* [*Novgorod and Novgorod Land in the 15th century*], Moscow and Leningrad: Izdatel'stvo Akademii nauk SSSR, 1961, pp. 15–21; V. A. Kuchkin, 'Naselenie Rusi v kanun Batyeva nashestviya' [The population of Rus' on the eve of the Batu Khan invasion'], in E. N. Shvejkovskaya *et al.* (eds), *Obrazy agrarnoi Rossii IX–XVII v. Pamyati N. A. Gorskoj* [Images of agrarian Russia in the 9th–18th centuries: in memory of N. A. Gorskaya], Moscow: Indrik, 2013, pp. 74, 80.

17 A. L. Shapiro (ed.), *Agrarnaya istoriya Severo-Zapada Rossii. Vtoraya polovina XV–nachalo XVI v* [The agrarian history of Northwestern Russia: second half of the 15th–early 16th century], Leningrad: Nauka, Leningradskoe otdelenie, 1971, p. 321.

18 E. C. Skrzhinskaya (ed.), *Barbaro i Kontarini o Rossii: K istorii italo-russkikh svyazei v XV v* [Barbaro and Contarini on Russia: on the history of Italian–Russian relations in the 15th century], Leningrad: Nauka, Leningradskoe otdelenie, 1971, p. 134 (§ 60). Skrzhinskaya translates this expression as 'gromadneishij gorod' (the most enormous city) – apparently for Barbaro this is a clarification of the toponym *Novgroth* (Novgorod). In Italian, however, *terra* is not 'city', and in this context means 'land, territory, region, country'. The fact that Novgorod is called 'land' should not be surprising. The concept of 'Novgorod' ('Veliky Novgorod') was used to designate not just the city, but all of the Novgorodian lands as well. (See P. V. Lukin, 'Territorial'nye oboznacheniya i kollektivnaya identichnost' v Novgorode XII-XIII vv. po dannym rannikh gramot' [Territorial designations and collective identity in 12th–13th century Novgorod according to early charters], in *Vostochnaya Evropa v drevnosti i Srednevekov'e*, Moscow: Institut vseobschej istorii RAN, 2015, pp. 175–81.)

19 *PSRL*, vol. 3, pp. 52–3, 251. On the date see N. G. Berezhkov, *Khronologiya russkogo letopisaniya* [The chronology of Russian chronicle writing], Moscow: Izdatel'stvo Akademii nauk, 1963, pp. 256–7. See also A. N. Nasonov, *Russkaya zemlya i obrazovanie territorii Drevnerusskogo gosudarstva: Istoriko-geograficheskoe issledovanie* [Russian land and the formation of the territory of old Russian state: studies in history and geography], Moscow: Izdatel'stvo Akademii nauk, 1951, pp. 82–3.

20 Kuza, 'Novgorodskaya zemlya', p. 185.

21 *PSRL*, vol. 43, 'Novgorodskaya letopis' po spisku Dubrovskogo' [Novgorod Chronicle according to the Dubrovskii's copy]), Moscow: Yazyki slavyanskoi kul'tury, 2004, p. 234.
22 *PSRL*, vol. 4, 1, p. 348.
23 I. P. Shaskol'skii, 'Politicheskie otnosheniya Novgoroda i karel v XII–XIV vekakh' [Political relations between Novgorod and Karelians in the 12th–14th centuries], *Novgorodskii istoricheskii sbornik* 10, 1961, pp. 132–3; J. Saarikivi, 'Finnic personal names on Novgorod birch bark documents', *Slavica Helsingensia* 32, 2007, p. 212.
24 Shapiro, *Agrarnaya istoriya*, pp. 321–6.
25 H. Samsonowicz, *Późne średniowiecze miast nadbałtyckich: Studia nad dziejami Hanzy nad Bałtykiem w XIV–XV w* [Baltic cities in the late Middle Ages: essays on history of the Hanse and Baltic in 14th–15th centuries], Warsaw: Państwowe Wydawnictwo Naukowe, 1968, p. 76.
26 P. V. Lukin, 'Naselenie srednevekovogo Novgoroda po dannym pis'mennykh i arkheologicheskikh istochnikov' [The population of medieval Novgorod according to written and archaeological sources], in *Rus' v IX–X vv.: Obshchestvo, gosudarstvo, kul'tura: Tezisy dokladov mezhdunarodnoi nauchnoi konferentsii* [Rus' in the 9th—10th centuries: society, state, culture: theses of reports of an international academic conference], Moscow: Institut arkheologii RAN, 2012, p. 46.
27 L. Leciejewicz, 'Kształtowanie się pierwszych miast u Słowian nadbaltyckich' [Formation of the earliest cities in the territory of Baltic Slavs], in L. Leciejewicz, *Opera selecta: Z dziejów kultury średniowiecznej Polski i Europy*, Wrocław: Institut archeologii i etnologii PAN, 2006, p. 190; W. Filipowiak and W. Konopka, 'The identity of a town: Wolin, town-state 9th–12th centuries', *Quaestiones Medii Aevi Novae* 13, 2008 (Palatium, Castle, Residence), p. 248.
28 S. A. Anninskij (ed. and tr.), *Miechowita, Maciej, Traktat o dvukh Sarmatiyakh* [Treatise on two Sarmatias], Moscow: Izdatel'stvo Akademii nauk, 1936, p. 183 (2.1.3): 'Et est Nouogrod in amplutudine paulo maior, quam Roma, [quae] in ambitu continet triginta duo miliaria Italica [. . .] Nowygrod autem continet integra [. . .] 35 miliaria Italica'.
29 See J. de Vries, *European Urbanization, 1500–1800*, Cambridge, MA: Harvard University Press, 1984, Harvard Studies in Urban History, pp. 95–120.
30 See C. Goehrke, 'Gross-Novgorod und Pskov/Pleskau', in M. Hellmann *et al.* (eds), *Handbuch der Geschichte Russlands*, vol. 1, *Bis 1613. Von der Kiever Reichsbildung bis zum Moskauer Zartum,* ed. M. Hellmann, Stuttgart: Anton Hiersemann, 1981, p. 442.
31 See V. L. Yanin, '"Bolotovsky dogovor": O vzaimootnosheniyakh Novgoroda i Pskova v XII-XIV vv' ['The Treaty of Bolotovo': on the relationship between Novgorod and Pskov in the 12th–14th centuries'], in V. L. Yanin, *Srednevekovyi Novgorod* [The medieval Novgorod], Moscow: Nauka, 2004 [1992], pp. 254–66.
32 Ibid., p. 264. The question of when Pskov gained independence from Novgorod and the nature of their relationship are not yet completely clarified, and require special consideration.
33 G. Frhr. von der Ropp (ed.), *Hanserecesse von 1431–1476* (hereafter *HR*), Leipzig: Verlag von Duncker & Humblot, 1876, vol. 1, no. 586, pp. 512, 517.
34 Nosov, 'Novgorodskaya zemlya', pp. 102–7.
35 E. V. Toropova, K. G. Samoilov and S. E. Toropov, 'Arkheologicheskie issledovaniya v Staroi Russe' [Archaeological research in Staraya Russa], *Vestnik Rossiiskogo gumanitarnogo nauchnogo fonda*, 62/1, 2011, p. 165.
36 A. L. Khoroshkevich, *Torgovlya Velikogo Novgoroda s Pribaltikoi i Zapadnoi Evropoi v XIV–XV* vekakh [Veliky Novgorod's trade with the Baltic and West Europe in the 14th–15th centuries], Moscow: Izdatel'stvo Akademii nauk SSSR, 1963, pp. 216–28.
37 P. D. Malygin, 'Sud'by Torzhka i Tveri v XIII veke' [The fates of Torzhok and Tver in the 13th century], in N. A. Makarov and A. V. Chernetsov (eds), *Rus' v XIII veke: Drevnosti temnogo vremeni* [Rus' in the 13th century: antiquities of the dark ages], Moscow: Nauka, 2003, p. 92.

38 Jacob Benediktsson (ed.), *Íslendingabók, Landnámabók*, Síðari hluti, Reykjavík: Íslenzka fornritafélag, 1968, Íslenzk fornrit 1, p. 212. For details, see T. N. Dzhakson, *Austr í Görðum: Drevnerusskie toponimy v drevneskandinavskikh istochnikakh* [Austr í Görðum: medieval Russian toponymy in medieval Scandinavian sources], Moscow: Yazyki slavyanskoj kul'tury, 2001, pp. 94, 98–9; T. N. Dzhakson *et al.* (eds), *Drevnyaya Rus' v svete zarubezhnykh istochnikov: Khrestomatiya* [Medieval Rus' in the light of foreign sources: a reader], Moscow: Russkij Fond Sodejstviya Obrazovaniju i Nauke, 2009, vol. 5, pp. 235–6 (commentary by G. B. Glazyrina).

39 For details, see Rybina,. *Novgorod i Ganza*, pp. 35–40.

40 Rybina, *Inozemnye dvory*, p. 19.

41 Skvajrs and Ferdinand, *Ganza i Novgorod*, pp. 42–5.

42 Among the most important works are: Goetz, *Deutsch-Russische Handelsgeschichte*; Khoroshkevich, *Torgovlya*; N. A. Kazakova, *Russko-livonskie i russko-ganzeiskie otnosheniya: Konets XIV–nachalo XVI v* [Russo-Livonian and Russo-Hanseatic relations: late 14th to early 15th century], Leningrad: Nauka, 1975; W. Rennkamp, *Studien zum deutsch-russischen Handel bis zum Ende des 13. Jahrhunderts: Nowgorod und Dünagebiet*, Bochum: Studienverlag Dr. N. Brockmeyer, 1977, Bochumer historische Studien. Mittelalterliche Geschichte 2; Rybina, *Novgorod i Ganza*.

43 Rybina, *Inozemnye dvory*, p. 19; Angermann, 'Nowgorod', p. 234.

44 For more on the excavations (which were unfortunately limited and not brought to the subsoil) see E. A. Rybina, 'Gotsky raskop' [The Gotsky excavation], in B. A. Kolchin and V. L. Yanin, *Arkheologicheskoe izuchenie Novgoroda* [Archaeological Studies of Novgorod], Moscow: Nauka, 1978, pp. 197–226.

45 A. V. Artsikhovsky and V. L. Yanin, *Novgorodskie gramoty na bereste (iz raskopok 1926–1976)* [Novgorodian birch bark documents (from 1926–1976 excavations)], Moscow: Nauka, 1978, pp. 80–3; D. A. Drboglav, 'Gramota no. 488' [Birch bark document no. 488], ibid., pp. 167–91.

46 See P. Johansen, 'Der hansische Rußlandhandel, insbesondere nach Novgorod, in kritischer Betrachtung', in A. von Brand *et al.*, *Die Deutsche Hanse als Mittler zwischen Ost und West*, Cologne: Verlag Max Schmidt & Römhild, 1963, pp. 41–5.

47 Ya. N. Schapov (ed.). *Drevnerusskie knyazheskie ustavy XI–XV vv* [Old Russian princes' charters of the 11th–15th centuries], Moscow: Nauka, 1976, pp. 161, 164.

48 K. E. Napiersky (ed.), *Russisch-Livländische Urkunden*, St Petersburg: Buchdruckerei der Kaiserlichen Akademie von Wissenschaften, 1868, p. 58.

49 See A. P. Pronshtein, *Velikii Novogorod v XVI veke* [Novgorod the Great in the 16th century], Khar'kov: Izdatel'stvo Khar'kovskogo gosudarstvennogo universiteta im. A. M. Gor'kogo, 1957, pp. 131–41; Kazakova, *Russko-livonskie i russko-ganzeiskie otnosheniya*, pp. 293–337; Rybina, *Novgorod i Ganza*, pp. 128, 168–80.

50 Angermann, 'Nowgorod', pp. 234, 238.

51 S. N. Valk (ed.), *Gramoty Velikogo Novgoroda i Pskova* [Charters of Novgorod the Great and Pskov], Moscow and Leningrad: Izdatel'stvo Akademii nauk, 1949, pp. 89–90 (no. 51).

52 K. Kunze (ed.), *Hansisches Urkundenbuch* (hereafter *HUB*), vol. 5, Leipzig: Verlag von Duncker & Humblot, 1899, p. 393 (no. 751).

53 See Goetz, *Deutsch-Russische Handelsverträge*, pp. 195–6; Goetz, *Deutsch-Russische Handelsgeschichte*, p. 104; S. N. Valk, 'Novye gramoty o novgorodsko-pskovskikh otnosheniyakh s Pribaltikoi v XV v' [Newly discovered charters on Novgorod and Pskov's relations with the Baltics], *Istoricheskii arkhiv* 1, 1956, pp. 232–4.

54 *Novgorodskie pistsovye knigi, izdannye Arkheograficheskoyu kommissieyu*, vol. 1, St Petersburg: Tipografiya V. Bezobrazova i Komp., 1859, pp. 890, 892, 894, 897, 898.

55 Bernadskii, *Novgorod i Novogorodskaya zemlya*, p. 165.

56 On the social structure of the Novgorod society see C. Goehrke, 'Die Sozialstruktur des mittelalterlichen Novgorod', in *Untersuchungen zur gesellschaftlichen Struktur der mittelalterlichen Städte in Europa. Reichenau-Vorträge. 1963–1964* = Vorträge und Forschungen 11, Sigmaringen: Jan Thorbecke Verlag, 1974 [1966], pp. 337–78.

57 For details see P. V. Lukin, 'Kategorii naseleniya Novgoroda v opasnoi gramote 1472 g' [Strata of the Novgorod population in the *Opasnaia Gramota* of 1472], *Slověne International Journal of Slavic Studies* 1, 2015, pp. 253–65.

58 Goetz, *Deutsch-Russische Handelsgeschichte*, p. 336.

59 M. Bloch, *The Historian's Craft*, Manchester: Manchester University Press, 2004, p. 52.

60 F. G. von Bunge (ed.), *Liv-Esth-, und Curländisches Urkundenbuch* (hereafter *LECUB*), vol. 6, Riga: Verlag von Nikolai Kymmel, 1873, cols 111–12 (no. 2807).

61 A. Selart, *Livland und die Rus' im 13 Jahrhundert*, Cologne: Böhlau Verlag, 2007, pp. 300–2.

62 Bunge, *LECUB*, vol. 1, Reval: Heinr. Laakmann, 1853, col. 512 (no. 408). See B. N. Florya, *Issledovaniya po istorii Tserkvi: Drevnerusskoe i slavyanskoe srednevekov'e* [Studies on church history: the Old Russian and Slavic Middle Ages], Moscow: Pravoslavnaya entsiklopediya, 2007, pp. 213–14.

63 *HUB*, vol. 5, p. 364 (no. 704).

64 *HUB*, vol. 5, p. 463 (no. 883).

65 H. Hildebrand (ed.), *LECUB*, vol. 7, Riga and Moscow: Verlag von J. Deubner, 1881, p. 221 (no. 311).

66 *HR von 1256–1430*, vol. 8, Leipzig: Verlag von Duncker & Humblot, 1897, pp. 5–6.

67 Hildebrand, *LECUB*, vol. 7, p. 261.

68 K. Kunze (ed.), *HUB*, Leipzig: Verlag von Duncker & Humblot, 1905, vol. 6, pp. 359–60.

69 'Schut en tuist tuschen dhen Dudeschen vn(de) dhen Nogarderen, dhe twist sal endegen up sente Joh(anni)s houe uor deme borchgreuen, dheme hertogen vnde uor dhen copluden' (Russian State Archive of Ancient Acts, f. 1490, op. 1, no. 5, based on transcription by E. R. Skvajrs).

70 Kunze, *HUB,* vol. 5, p. 565 (no. 1086).

71 For details of this discussion see: Lukin, 'The Veche', pp. 493–503; Lukin, *Novgorodskoe veche*, pp. 501–20.

72 Due to his misreading of 'seignourie commune', Jonas Granberg understood Lannoy's account as stating that Novgorod was 'controlled by the upper strata of society, probably boyars'. J. Granberg, 'Ghillebert de Lannoy and the political structure of Novgorod', in T. N. Dzhakson *et al., Norna u istochnika Sud'by: Sbornik stat'ei v chest' E. A. Mel'nikovoi* [Norn at the source of destiny: collection of articles in honor of E. A. Mel'nikova], Moscow: Indrik, 2001, p. 84. See also an interpretation based on the correct reading: L. Steindorff, 'Pravil'no li schitat Novgorod kommunoi?', in Krom, *Spory*, p. 240, footnote). Largely true in principle, it does not follow from this particular fragment of the Burgundian knight's writings.

73 S. Mund, 'Constitution et diffusion d'un savoir occidental sur le monde "russe" au Moyen Âge (fin Xe–milieu XVe siècle) (2e partie)', *Le Moyen Âge: Revue d'histoire et de philologie*, 110/3, 2004, p. 560.

74 Kunze, *HUB*, vol. 5, p. 556 (no. 1070); P. Shwartz (ed.), *LECUB*, vol. 10, Riga and Moscow, 1896, p. 358 (no. 508).

75 D. Möhn (ed.), *Mittelniederdeutsches Handwörterbuch*, vol. 2, 1, Neumünster: Wachholtz Verlag, 2004, col. 64.

76 See Y. K. Begunov, 'Rannee nemetskoe izvestie o zolotoi babe' [Early German account of the gold baba], *Izvestiya Sibirskogo Otdeleniya AN SSSR, seriya obschestvennykh nauk* 11/3, 1976, pp. 122–3; Florya, *Issledovaniya*, pp. 342–3.

77 '[. . .]haißt . . . die groß Novograt, daz ist ain statt für sich selb und welt ain hertzogen als die Venedier', ed. T. M. Buck, *Chronik des Konstanzer Konzils 1414–1418 von Ulrich Richental*, Ostfildern: Thorbecke Verlag, 2011, Konstanzer Geschichts- und Rechtsquellen), p. 199.
78 K. Schulz, *'Denn sie lieben die Freiheit so sehr . . .': Kommunale Aufstände und Entstehung des europäischen Bürgertums im Hochmittelalter*, Darmstadt: Wissenschaftliche Buchgesellschaft, 1992, pp. 10–11.
79 Skrzhinskaya (ed.), *Barbaro i Contarini*, p. 134.
80 Ibid., p. 205.
81 E. Isenmann, 'Norms and values in the European city, 1300–1800', in P. Blickle (ed.), *Resistance, Representation, and Community*, Oxford: Clarendon Press, 1997, pp. 206–7.
82 Ibid., pp. 205–6.

18

THE CITY OF PSKOV IN THE FOURTEENTH AND FIFTEENTH CENTURIES

Baltic trade and institutional growth

Alexei Vovin and Mikhail Krom

Introduction: geographic and historiographical context

In this chapter we will explore the effect of Baltic trade on the institutional development of Pskov in the fourteenth and fifteenth centuries. Today a regional centre in the northwestern part of the Russian Federation, Pskov (Pleskau in Hanseatic sources) played a much more prominent role in the later Middle Ages and early modern period when it was one of the biggest Russian and East European cities. Situated far from the sea, it nevertheless participated in Baltic trade through the river network that connected the city with the main trade routes. For example, a trade ship could get to Dorpat (120 km to the northwest) or Narva (190 km to the north) in just three or four days along the Velikaia river and Lake Peipus. Moreover, a land route connected Pskov with Reval (271 km to the northwest) and Riga (273 km to the southwest). The aforementioned cities (with the exception of Narva) were members of the Hanse. Thus being geographically one of the western-most Russian cities, Pskov became a centre of transit trade between Russian principalities and the Latin world.

We will focus on the territorial and institutional growth of Pskov, which on the eve of its incorporation into the Muscovite state (1510) resembled in many respects an early European commune. Seeking to explain the rapid growth of the city, we will pay attention to Pskov's involvement in Hanseatic trade and to its changing place within a bigger political system, the grand principality of Vladimir and Moscow. But before addressing these particular issues, brief historiographic remarks will be in order.

In the eyes of contemporary observers (West European travellers and Hanseatic merchants), Novgorod and Pskov looked like any other city commune. For example, the Burgundian knight Gilbert de Lannoy in the early fifteenth century described Novgorod as a free city commune whose sovereign was a bishop (see the full quotation and commentary in Pavel Lukin's chapter).[1] The correspondence between Pskov and Riga provides clear evidence to the fact that both sides perceived each other as a brotherhood of citizens.[2] For Livonians, it was easy to understand the political organization of both Novgorod and Pskov because its key principles did not seem to them very different from their own.

The situation changed dramatically in the sixteenth century, after the conquest of Novgorod (1478) and Pskov (1510) by the Grand Principality of Moscow. During the so-called Livonian War (1558–83) the Hanseatic trade fell into decay (see Leimus and Mänd's chapter in this volume). Thus contacts between northwestern Russia and the Hanse became rare and irregular. A new image of Russia appeared in the Catholic world of an aggressive and barbarous kingdom, a menace to all civilized Christian countries.

This image had a great impact on the subsequent perception of Russian cities in West European scholarly literature. No wonder that Max Weber in his famous essay *The City* (Die Stadt) did not mention Novgorod, Pskov or any other medieval Russian city. But while referring to Russian cities before and after the abolition of serfdom (1861), he clearly classified this type of city as non-Western and different from a commune in the proper sense.[3] According to Weber, the 'full urban commune' existed only in the West in the Middle Ages.

The Weberian Eurocentric concept is still visible in the historiography of the medieval city. But aside from academic tradition and cultural stereotypes, there are also language barriers.[4] Since the early 1970s some noteworthy attempts have been made to bridge the gap between the histories of West and East European cities. Edith Ennen, for example, maintained that Novgorod had possessed some specific communal traits, including a city assembly and the way the urban space was organized. According to Ennen, Novgorod adopted these 'communal features' from Hanseatic merchants who founded their Kontor in the city.[5] This is a rather risky statement, to say the least, because the city assembly and the first magistrates had appeared there a century before the first Hanseatic merchants arrived on the banks of the Volkhov river.

Rudolf Mumenthaler later proposed a typology of late medieval European cities, distinguishing between such geographical areas as northern Italy, Central Europe, Poland-Lithuania and Eastern Europe. According to Mumenthaler, in Pskov and Novgorod there emerged a mixed type of commune bearing characteristics of both the Italian and Central European city.[6] Recently Roland Leffler argued that Novgorod and Pskov (referred to as a subordinate town of Novgorod) were typically medieval European communes. In his view, Novgorod fully fits the Weberian definition of the city in the strict sense of the word.[7] This opinion has been questioned by Ludwig Steindorff.[8]

For their part, Russian historians have tended to perceive the past of their country in terms of a *Sonderweg*. In the nineteenth century, scholars used to describe Novgorod and Pskov as ancient polities.[9] Any idea of systematic comparison between Russian cities and European medieval ones was alien to them. Soviet

Marxist historians in the 1930s to 1950s tried to change this trend but without any lasting effect. Thus Mikhail Tikhomirov made an attempt to compare Old Russian cities to European communes. However, he went too far in denying any differences between them. The scholar treated scarce information in the chronicles about the eleventh-century urban rebellions as satisfactory evidence of the beginning of a communal movement in Kievan Rus'. He also believed in the existence of merchants' and artisans' guilds in the same period.[10] In post-Soviet historiography, there is a revival of *Sonderweg* concepts of Russian history. For example, some scholars regard city assemblies (*veche*) in Novgorod and Pskov as a genuine phenomenon, a sort of synoikism that had no parallels elsewhere.[11] A comparative perspective is still very rare in Russian historical urban studies.

Two conclusions can be drawn from the above survey of existing scholarly literature on northwestern Russian cities. First of all, since attempts to synchronize urban development in the west and in the east of Europe have proved to be ineffective, an adequate form of comparison should be found. Secondly, Novgorod and Pskov are usually regarded as one and the same type of the city. One of the aims of this study is to 'detach' Pskov from Novgorod and to highlight the specificity of the former's development.

The dynamics of Pskov trade

Until the thirteenth-century Pskov had been a small town in a remote northwestern area that was contiguous with the Estonian and Baltic tribes that populated the territory of the modern Baltic States. In the thirteenth century, the situation changed. New neighbours appeared: the Teutonic Order and the cities of Livonia (Riga, Reval and Dorpat). The latter adopted Lübeck law in the thirteenth century and became members of the Hanse. The neighbourhood was not peaceful. The thirteenth century became for Pskov a period of military defeat. In 1240, it was even occupied by Livonian knights who kept the city for two years until they were defeated by Prince Alexander Nevskii in the Battle on the Ice at Lake Peipus. In the second half of the thirteenth century, a talented commander, the Lithuanian Prince Dovmont, helped Pskov to restitute a military status quo with Livonia (see Figure 17.1).

This new balance favoured trade relations. Because of its frontier position, Pskov in the fourteenth and fifteenth centuries became one of the most important centres of trade between Rus' and the Latin world. It is very difficult to assess the whole trade volume. According to Anna L. Khoroshkevich, it grew several times in the course of the fourteenth and fifteenth centuries, and in the early sixteenth century Pskov's trade volume with the Hanse was bigger than that of Novgorod.[12]

To get some idea of the gradual growth of Pskov trade we can consult Novgorod sources. The first treaties between Novgorod and the German cities (1189–99, 1262–3, 1266–72, 1269, 1301 and 1323)[13] did not mention Pskov trade at all. It was a period when Pskov trade probably did not menace the Novgorod monopoly. In the treaty of 1342 between Novgorod and German merchants from Gotland,

Lübeck, Riga, etc., the Pskov wax trade was mentioned for the first time. In 1410, Novgorod sent a letter to Reval in which it was demanded that

> Who goes to Novgorod should follow a Novgorodian route; he cannot go to Pskov after a visit to Novgorod. If somebody goes directly to Pskov, then he has to go back and not go to Novgorod through Pskov.[14]

This looks like a clear protectionist step against the growing Pskov trade that was worrying Novgorod merchants. It seems to be no coincidence that the first Pskov treaty with Livonia we know of appears a few years later, in 1417. In 1448, a treaty with Livonian cities was signed for the first time by Novgorod and Pskov as two equal partners.[15] There is an interesting formula in its text: Novgorod merchants should not be arrested in Livonia in the case of a conflict with Pskov, and Pskov merchants in the case of a conflict with Novgorod.[16] It suggests that both Pskov trade and the number of possible conflicts grew to such an extent that Novgorod merchants wanted to emphasize the difference between themselves and their 'junior brethren', the Pskovites. Previously they were both just Russians in the eyes of their German neighbours. We suppose that the changing role of Pskov in Novgorod–Livonian treaties shows the development of Pskov–Livonian trade in the fourteenth and fifteenth centuries.

The structure of Pskov trade

The main export article was wax. The Pskov wax trade was mentioned for the first time in the treaty of 1342 between Novgorod and the Hanse, which forbade German merchants from buying wax containing a touch of oil, resin, acorn or pea. It should be bought 'in a natural condition, as God created it'.[17] The quality of wax was a matter of constant quarrels between Pskov and German merchants and their authorities. The pieces of wax should contain a special mark of quality that, if missed, could cause the wax to be considered low grade. In 1441, two ships with a cargo of wax from Pskov were rejected by Dorpat merchants for this reason. Pskovites then sold it in Narva, which had never been a member of the Hanse and did not follow Hanseatic rules.[18] Moreover, German merchants had a right to 'chop off' small pieces of wax from a larger one without paying for them. This 'chopping off' was a kind of compensation for the possibility of low-quality wax (usually its inner part could contain some additions).[19] The problem was that how much a German merchant could 'chop off' from a piece of wax was not defined precisely. This issue was regulated on the highest level. Thus the 1448 treaty of Novgorod and Pskov with the Livonian Order forbade 'the chopping off' of wax that had already been brought to a Livonian city.[20]

Unlike Novgorod, Pskov did not have a large unpopulated hinterland; probably for this reason furs never became a significant export article, as happened in Novgorod. Besides wax, another Pskov trade specialty was flax. Its export had been mentioned since the second half of the fifteenth century and its volume grew considerably in the sixteenth. One more commodity exported from Pskov was suet. There was a special organization in Dorpat that checked the quality of the Pskov suet.[21]

The import structure was more complex. The main article was salt, which had crucial importance not only for food conservation but also for tanning production. There was a lack of salt in Russia at that period, so, as Anna Khoroshkevich has demonstrated, it was imported mainly from Western Europe.[22] Thus the main centres of its transit trade were Novgorod and Pskov. The latter profited from the former's wars with Livonia, when salt import to Novgorod was closed by Livonian authorities. For example, in 1421–6, the salt import was operated by Pskov–Narva trade.[23] Aside from salt, non-ferrous metals (tin, copper, lead) were imported, as were alcoholic beverages.

International contacts, conflicts and their resolution

German merchants did not have their Kontor in Pskov as they did in Novgorod. Once in the city, they would rent housing from local dwellers. Pskov merchants did the same in Dorpat. There were special districts in both cities that were called 'German' and 'Russian' respectively. Simultaneously there could be many Russian merchants in Dorpat or German merchants in Pskov. For example, when a war began in 1501 between Pskov and Livonia, 150 Pskov traders were arrested with their goods in Dorpat.[24] The number of foreign merchants in a city gives us some idea of the trade volume. The safety of fellow citizens and their trade abroad was one of the most important issues in all the treaties between Pskov and Livonian cities. All of them contained a provision that a merchant abroad should be judged fairly as a citizen of the city in which he traded.[25] That rule, as far as we can assume relying on the sixteenth-century sources, was seldom violated. Nevertheless, in some cases city authorities were involved in trade quarrels as well. In the 1360–70s Pskov sent the following letter to Riga:

> Your [citizen] Nezdilets traded here with our Kumorda and he did not pay the rest of 22.5 grivnas in silver and fled to Riga [. . .] now you should extradite Nezdilets. There are many of your brethren merchants in Pskov. If you do not extradite Nezdilets, we will recover his debt from your brothers here and report it to you.[26]

First of all, the document implies that by the second half of the fourteenth century the trade between Pskov and Riga was already quite intensive. *Grivna* was silver bullion weighing 150 or 200 gr. (Lithuanian or Novgorodian grivna).[27] So 22.5 grivnas is a huge sum: if a Lübeck coin (the so-called 'Witten' or 'albus') contained 1.12 gr. of silver at the end of fourteenth century,[28] 22.5 *grivnas* was a weight equivalent to 3,013–4,017 Lübeck coins. It is also important that, according to the letter, the missing sum could be compensated at the expense of the other (presumably German) merchants who were present in Pskov at that moment. What also deserves our attention in the above cited document is the principle of collective responsibility. Pskov authorities menaced Riga by threatening to recover the debt from the latter's other merchants. It was not an empty threat; we know several cases from narrative sources when Pskov or Novgorod goods were arrested in Livonia and vice versa.

In 1418–19, another document was sent by Pskov authorities to Reval 'mayors and councillors'. It was a demand to make a restitution of the goods of a Pskov man who died in Reval.[29] As in the case of Nezdilets, a quarrel over private property was being resolved on the highest level: the Pskov highest magistrates (i.e. according to the official formula, the prince and the mayors with the city assembly's consent) wrote a letter to their Reval counterparts on that matter. There was no direct menace in the letter, just the advice to 'take a right decision', which could be a hidden threat.

One more document, dated 1463–5, reveals a system of conflict resolution. It was sent to Riga 'from Pskov Prince Ivan Alexandrovich, from Pskov posadnik-in-office (mayor) Maksim Larionovich, from all posadniks (patricians)[30] of Pskov, from Pskov boyars (nobles), from Pskov merchants and from all Pskov', in the most official mode, as international treaties were articulated. The case described in the letter is the following: the Riga merchant Ivan was murdered in Pskov by his own servant. Right after Ivan's death the latter's brother Ivolt arrived in Pskov to claim his brother's merchandise. However, he received only a part of it, because the rest had been seized by the Pskov authorities as compensation for Ivan's debts to some Pskov men. Ivolt was offered to go to court with Ivan's creditors, but he refused and returned to Riga where, trying to compensate the losses, he captured the goods of two Pskov merchants, who made a plea about that case to Pskov authorities. The latter demanded that the Pskov merchants' goods should be restored, because Ivolt, who had refused to participate in legal proceedings in Pskov 'according to Pskov law', was in the wrong.[31]

This document is an illustration of a principle that figures in all Pskov–Livonian treaties: a Livonian merchant in Pskov should be judged according to Pskov law as if he were a Pskov man and vice versa. So we can conclude that there was a stable mechanism of resolving trade conflicts during the fourteenth and fifteenth centuries. A victim applied to a court in a city where the conflict had taken place. In theory, a trial should be fair irrespective of the litigant's faith or citizenship. But if a foreign merchant was not satisfied with a court decision he could make a plea to his native city authorities. Then the case would become an international incident that could lead to an arrest of a foreign merchant's property or even to a war.

What kind of tribunal judged such cases in Pskov? According to the Pskov Judicial Charter, there were just two judicial authorities: a general magisterial court (the so-called *gospoda*) and a trial by the city assembly. It is very likely that it was the former that heard the trade conflicts, because the latter was used, as it will be shown below, only in the case of crimes punishable by death. The *gospoda* consisted of the highest city magistrates (including a prince and a mayor), i.e. the same people who were also the city's political leaders. So we may assume that in such an archaic judicial system as that of medieval Pskov there was no special arbitration tribunal for commercial matters.

Ultima ratio in trade conflicts was the principle of collective responsibility. It was the only common feature shared both by Pskov law and the more advanced Livonian one. The merchants of Pskov and Novgorod, as well as their partners from Livonian cities, formed the local communes of sworn brothers, who were responsible for their brethren's deeds. The principle of collective responsibility was a kind of international guarantee against unfair treatment abroad, thus being a commune was profitable for commerce. As it will be shown in the following section, Pskov had some other preconditions for becoming a commune (a central power vacuum, parish organization, etc.) but it is likely that trade relations favoured its communal structure as well.

The trade with Livonian cities had a key importance for Pskov's men. Periods of peace alternated with frontier wars, but many wars between Pskov and Livonia in the fourteenth and fifteenth centuries were provoked by violated trade operations. Trade contacts with Pskov were very important for Hanseatic cities too. When in 1494 Grand Prince Ivan III of Moscow closed down the Hanseatic office (Kontor) in Novgorod (which had been already conquered by Muscovy) and arrested Hanseatic merchants and their goods, the Hanse declared a trade blockade of the Muscovite state. It was very unprofitable for Livonian cities and they continued their commerce via Pskov, explaining their trade policy to the Lübeck City Council by the fact that Pskov was not a part of the Muscovite state.

Having outlined the rise of Pskov trade in the fourteenth and fifteenth centuries, we now turn to its social and institutional effects: it was not by chance that the commercial success of Pskovites was accompanied by serious changes in the political organization and social life of their city.

Forming an early commune: the law code and the city assembly

One of the striking differences between Rus' and Western Europe in the Middle Ages is the former's scarcity of sources when compared to the latter. However, extant documents and chronicles are unevenly distributed between different East Slavic lands. Novgorod and Pskov in the fourteenth and fifteenth centuries were exceptionally rich in this regard. The latter had its own chronicles, which was not typical for a Russian medieval city, as only a few did. Aside from the chronicles, we know more than fifty Pskov documents from the period. There are internal records, like deeds of purchase or testaments, as well as foreign policy documents like treaties with Livonia or the Grand Duchy of Lithuania. The diversity of sources seems to be evidence to the fact that Pskov had a written culture much more advanced than most Russian cities of the period. The Pskov *acta* are some of the few documents that survived the occupation of the city by Grand Prince Basil III of Moscow in 1510 that put an end to Pskov independence. But a real treasure of Pskov's written heritage is its famous Judicial Charter.

It is the only local law code of the Russian Middle Ages that we have. Novgorod too had a Judicial Charter but only a small fragment of it has been preserved. The Pskov Judicial Charter (hereafter PJC) is a code in which the criminal (and the civil) law and court practices are described as well as the Pskov political system. The PJC is a record of customary law, a first step in the codification process.[32] The distinguishing feature of such a law is considered to be its unsystematic and precedent-related character. Thus article 108 of PJC has a constituent form:

> If [in the present,] original [Pskov Judicial] Charter some matter is missing, then the mayors are to refer the matter to Lord Pskov at a city assembly, and write that case [into the Pskov Judicial Charter]. If in the future some provision in this Charter will not be to the liking of Lord Pskov, then it is free to remove that provision from this Charter.[33]

According to this article the highest city magistrate was responsible to the city assembly, which had a right to change the PJC itself. The very fact that these laws have been recorded symbolizes the transition from a society based on a customary law to a more complex one where written laws function. Even in the written form, however, laws continued to be a reflection of the custom that had existed prior to codification. The PJC undoubtedly was not a mere city law. Its jurisdiction was not limited by the city walls; it spread over all the Pskov land, which included fourteen subordinate towns and a countryside territory that stretched for 15,000 square kilometres at the end of the fifteenth century. However, articles 7 and 8 distinguish 'Krom' as the territory *intra murum*[34] from *posad*, an unfortified settlement beyond the city walls.[35]

Did the PJC have something in common with the statutes of European medieval cities? Some scholars identify two conventional ways in which the codification of law took place in European communes: Italian and German. The former is considered to be a record of existing custom law made by the communal authorities. Thus it was a commune itself that initiated the codification. In the latter a new law codex was a gift made by its lord who granted to the city certain rights and privileges. Giorgio Chittolini, for example, maintains that the nature of German and Italian city law differed. He believes that German law may be called 'city law' 'not because it expresses a certain independence of political autonomy, but because it refers to the things and people from the city itself'.[36] To be sure, there was much more variety in the origins of urban statutes. Pskov's case falls in between the two 'ideal types' highlighted by Chittolini.

The PJC's preamble reads:

> This charter was copied out from the charter of Grand Prince Alexander and from the charter of Prince Konstantin and from various other additions [based] on Pskov customs, [and it is issued] with the blessing of our fathers,

> the priests of all five cathedrals [in Pskov], and the hieromonks, deacons, and priests and the entire clergy of God by all Pskov at [a meeting of] the city assembly in the year 6905 [= 1396/97].[37]

The PJC is based on charters granted by Princes Alexander and Konstantin,[38] thus the PJC itself has a granted character, in the same way as the German cities' statutes. On the other hand, like Italian city statutes, the PJC was adopted by the decision of city inhabitants at a city assembly.

The notions of *veche* (city assembly) and 'Pskov men' seem to refer to the key institutions of medieval Pskov. Above we have already cited some PJC articles where the main actor is 'all Pskov' or 'Lord Pskov'. The PJC itself was adopted and could be changed at his will at the assembly meeting (preamble and art.108). The same notion is found in *intitulatio* of most Pskov documents related to foreign affairs. For example, the treaty between Pskov and Livonia in 1417 was signed by Pskov envoys sent by 'our authorities, Pskov mayor and all Pskov'.[39] The Grand Prince of Lithuania Casimir negotiated in 1440 with other envoys that had been sent by 'all Pskov'.[40]

The *intitulatio* of Pskov documents was not steady. It could include various institutions and social groups, but there was only one element that was never dropped: *all Pskov*.[41] It negotiated on behalf of Pskov's subordinate towns (*prigorody*) and Pskov land.[42] *All Pskov* was understood as a real actor in foreign policy while *posadniks* (mayors) and the prince were just officials who were charged by Pskov men at an assembly[43] to represent the city in the negotiations. We should note that the counterpart in these negotiations was not Lithuania as an abstract political body but its Grand Prince Casimir. The real foreign policy actors at that time were monarchs, not their realms. Among very few exceptions to this rule there were city-states, to which Pskov belonged as well.

However, the few remaining Pskov documents of the fourteenth century mention 'all Pskovites' or 'all Pskov men' as main policy actors instead of *Pskov* or *Lord Pskov*.[44] We argue that these notions were fully synonymous in the mind of contemporaries, i.e. *all Pskov* consisted of *all Pskovites*. It is undoubtedly seen in the official letter from Pskov sent to Muscovite Grand Prince Ivan III in 1477: 'To you Great Prince and Tsar of Russia, our sovereign, we, your patrimony, freewill men, all Pskov, do make a plea.'[45] The chronicles often use these terms indiscriminately as full synonyms, too. For example:

> 1397 Prince Grigorii Evstafievich, and Posadnik Zakharii and *all Pskov* built three towers.[46] (Pskov 2nd Chronicle)
>
> 1397 Prince Ivan Andreevich, Prince Grigorii Evstafievich, and Posadnik Zakharii Kostrominich and *the people of Pskov* built three towers.[47] (Pskov 3rd Chronicle)

The Pskov 2nd and 3rd Chronicles derive from the same original text that has not been preserved. The fact that an anonymous scribe was substituting 'all Pskov' for 'the people of Pskov' means that these were synonymous in his mind.

The term *Pskov* in the sources is equivalent to *Pskov men*, i.e. *all Pskov* means a political unit as an aggregate body of *Pskov men* – the political people of Pskov. Who belonged to it? The PJC defines a special inhabitants' category – *Pskovites*. According to its articles 34 and 35, a Pskovite's oath was equal in the court to a collective oath of a subordinate rural community. The chronicles and documents distinguish between *Pskov men*, on the one hand, and the dwellers of subordinate towns or countryside and even people who lived in the unfortified suburbs of Pskov, on the other. The former had their political rights, the latter did not. The Pskov hinterland and its subordinate towns were brought completely under the city's control. There was no independent administration in the Pskov land: all the magistrates were appointed by Pskov authorities. We have no information on the Pskov land's direct participation in international trade. Probably the land resources (such as wax, furs and artisanal goods) were used only by *Pskov men,* i.e. the people who lived or had property inside the city walls and ruled Pskov itself and its subordinate territory. They nominated the first city magistrate, *posadnik* (mayor), elected or selected in some unknown way.

The Pskov men invited princes to Pskov whose professional armoured cavalry was very important for a city that had constant wars with the Livonian Order. Aside from their military functions, Pskov princes were an important element in the local judicial system. A Pskov prince was the head of the judicial board consisting of mayor(s) and other officials who were a part of the city's elite. The princely power grew during the fourteenth and fifteenth centuries while the prince himself usually was a protégé of the grand prince of Moscow. This was how the latter was increasing his influence in Pskov's internal policy. However, the right that was especially valued by Pskov men was that to expel princes whom they disliked. The last incident of this kind happened in 1509[48] and was used by the Muscovite grand prince as a formal pretext to occupy the city.

The city assembly in which Pskov men had a right to participate had more than just an executive power. It was, in modern terms, the main legislative body, as one can see in article 108 of the PJC. It was in its authority to change the PJC itself. Finally, the assembly of Pskovites had important judicial rights. If most crimes were judged by a special college in which the prince and the Pskov *posadniks* (mayors) participated, very few crimes where the death penalty could be applied[49] were judged by a city assembly.[50] The idea that only citizens had the right to deprive a citizen of life seems to be significant. Moreover, it is instructive that when the dwellers of Opochka (one of Pskov's subordinate towns) hanged a horse thief in 1477, following directly article 7 of PJC they were punished by Pskovites for usurping their right to execute somebody: 'That autumn', writes the chronicler, 'Pskov was angry with the people of Opochka for having hanged a horse thief without Pskov's consent'.[51]

The Pskov city assembly (*veche*) was summoned in the central square of the city, in front of Holy Trinity cathedral. The archaeologist Alexander E. Musin argued in his recently published monograph that the roots of the Pskov city assembly were closely related to parish gatherings that usually took place in the cathedral square.[52]

This was exactly the way in which city assemblies appeared in communes of the Latin world. As Pierre Michaud-Quantin has convincingly demonstrated, all political terminology of the communal movement was borrowed from the language of the church. Before becoming designations of different phenomena of communal life, *civitas*, *communitas*, *universitas*, *consilium*, *coniuratio*, *conventus populi*, etc. had different if not semantically close meanings for phenomena of church life.[53] In German-speaking areas, Latin terms initially used in German texts were replaced by local analogues. Thus *conventus populi* became *Burding* or *Burgsprache*, and *communitas* became *Gemeinde*.

These were horizontal social relations whose main regulator was a customary, collective judgment exercised by a meeting of the people and, finally, a parochial organization of the population. As a result, an institution that derived from the gathering of parishioners played a key role in the beginning of the communal movement.

This institution had different names like *conventus populi, Burgsprache,* or *bourgemoot,* but the same meaning. That is how the parish city gathering became the first body of communal self-government. Such an assembly was known wherever communes arose: in England,[54] in Germany,[55] in Dalmatia[56] and in Italy (including Venice,[57] which is traditionally isolated as a specific case because of Byzantine influence there).[58] These gatherings elected the first magistrates and it was there where *coniuratio* took place. They were, in short, the primary institutions of power in the commune and possessed judicial and constitutional power. Later on, the fate of these assemblies was different. In some countries, like Germany, they quickly gave way to new communal institutions that had a more 'closed' nature. In Italy, the gatherings were the main source of power throughout the early communal period (from the eleventh through the thirteenth centuries). During the 'high communal' period, a city council came to replace the city assembly everywhere. The latter did not disappear entirely at first. Having lost its real political power to the council, it retained fictitious institutional power as an annual meeting of city residents coming to swear oath.[59] Everything we know about the city assembly in Pskov (historically called the *veche*) as a key element in the Pskov political system fits the picture described above. Pskov of the fourteenth and fifteenth centuries, however, does not seem similar to contemporary communes but rather to earlier ones of the eleventh to thirteenth centuries when the first of them appeared. It was then that customary law was codified, which corresponds to Pskov's codification in the fourteenth and fifteenth centuries.

Having assumed that fourteenth- and fifteenth-century Pskov society was similar to early European communes of the eleventh to thirteenth centuries, we shall now test this hypothesis in a wider context. The period when customary law was codified and a city assembly was a real political body is characterized by two main processes that changed the urban society: city growth and social differentiation among its dwellers.

City growth and social differentiation

We do not have any reliable data relating to the number of Pskov dwellers. However, an approximate calculation can be made on the basis of available archeological data. Until 1310, Pskov's fortified territory covered 0.03 sq. km. When the new wall was constructed in 1310, its area reached 0.1 sq. km. In 1375, a new wall was erected that encircled a territory of 0.3 sq. km. When the last wall was constructed in 1465, the city territory grew up to 2 sq. km. Since that moment the space inside the wall of 1375 had been called Old Town, while the *intra murum* space of 1465 was named Surrounding Town (*Okolnyi Grad*). According to the Pskov Chronicle there were 500 households in the Old Town and 6,000 in the Surrounding Town. Should we trust these chronicle data? Only 2 per cent of the total city territory has been explored by archaeologists. According to their data a medium household's size was 200 sq. m. The total area of *intra muros* Pskov in 1510 was 2 sq. km. Subtracting the uninhabited territory (streets, fortress, churches, marketplace, etc.), we have at least 1 sq. km (1,000,000 sq. m) that was covered by households. The figure of 6,500 households seems to be a slight overestimation, but not a big one. An average household is estimated to consist of four to five persons. In that case the Pskov population grew from 2,000–3,000 in the middle of the fourteenth century up to 25,000–30,000 in the early sixteenth century. A tenfold increase in population and absolute figures themselves seem to be very close to those which characterize the European communes' growth in the eleventh through thirteenth centuries.[60]

The changes in the urban society were qualitative as well as quantitative. The population growth was accompanied by the concentration of material value in the cities. The latter were not only growing but becoming rich as well. This was followed by increasing social stratification of the urban society. An early commune was a sworn brotherhood of equal individuals who had taken their oath to fight against their enemy. Of course, the prosperity of the city dwellers could vary to a certain degree. But the communal movement increased this difference. The growth of trade and handicraft production increased the prosperity of some, but not all, city residents. Those who benefited most began to form a city patriciate that aspired for political control of the city through access to the magistrates.

The process of social differentiation can be revealed through an analysis of terminology in the Pskov sources. In the first half of the fourteenth century this terminology was rather poor. In the sources of that period we find only *Pskov men* as an undifferentiated body led by a *posadnik* (mayor). In the second half of the century and later there appear some new social categories: *boyars*, *dobryje ljudi* (good men) and *chernyje ljudi* (black men). We should emphasize the fact that the above-mentioned notions ('boyars', 'good men' and 'black men') appeared simultaneously not only in the juridical documents but in the chronicles as well. Thus 'boyars' are mentioned there starting from the beginning of the fifteenth century; 'well-off men' and 'black men' from the 1470s. We argue that these notions implied new realities of social differentiation that Pskov society experienced during the fourteenth and fifteenth centuries. Finally, in the second half of the fifteenth century social conflicts began between the Pskov elite and the unprivileged population. Before that period Pskov did not know any problems of this kind.

An intriguing episode in Pskov's social development relates to the changing meaning of the notion of *posadnik*. Historically it meant a magistrate who ruled a city when a prince was absent there. From the twelfth century it meant a city mayor in Novgorod. The first Pskov *posadniks* are known from the very beginning of the fourteenth century. They were city mayors who ruled until their death. But since the late fourteenth century this term had begun to designate the members of Pskov elite, as well as the highest Pskov magistrate. Later the special term *stepennoi posadnik* (posadnik-in-office) appeared to emphasize the difference between social and political meanings of the word. *Posadniks* as a social group decided which of them would be a *posadnik-in-office*, who should be acclaimed after that in a *veche* (assembly).[61] Other new social categories including *boyars* and *dobryje ljudi* ('good men') were also part of the Pskov elite. They were opposed by *chernyje ljudi* ('black men'), a notion that meant common people. Since the middle of fifteenth century conflicts arose between these two strata of Pskov society, which had been previously united.

Urban growth, social differentiation of its population and the formation of the city patriciate are the key features that characterize Pskov in the fourteenth and fifteenth centuries. The role of Hanseatic trade is crucial in understanding the causes of the social differentiation process described above. Compared to Novgorod, the economic basis of the new Pskov elite was different. Novgorod boyars (nobles) formed a land aristocracy that possessed large estates, as we can judge from cadasters of Novgorod land compiled by Muscovite authorities after the conquest. But Pskov's case was different. Pskov was not rich in arable land and there was no landed aristocracy. Moreover, some Pskov *posadniks* were at the same time tradesmen or merchant elders. Thus the Pskov elite was formed from the people who participated directly in trade operations.

Thus Baltic trade completely changed the life of medieval Pskov. A small town in the thirteenth century, it had become a large and rich city by the end of the fifteenth century. When Pskov was conquered by the emerging Muscovite state in 1510, it became the latter's second or third city (after Novgorod and probably Moscow itself) by its size and population.[62]

Concluding remarks: the rise of the early modern state and the end of urban autonomy

If Baltic trade, as we have tried to show, formed the economic basis and the precondition of Pskov's institutional growth and social differentiation, there was also another factor that made possible the long-term preservation of the city's autonomy, and by this we mean a favourable political environment.[63]

As with many other city communes, Pskov was a part of a larger political system. This system, known as the Grand Principality of Vladimir and Moscow, was rather loose until the middle of the fifteenth century and resembled to some extent the Holy Roman Empire. Not only did Pskov in the fourteenth and the first half of the fifteenth century enjoy autonomy in local affairs (administration and justice); it also pursued its own foreign policy. At the same time, the city remained dependent on the Novgorod archbishop and on the Russian metropolitan (who resided in Moscow) in ecclesiastic matters, because Pskov did not have its own bishop. Several times (e.g. in 1331 and 1464) Pskovites made attempts to establish a separate eparchy, but in vain. In secular politics they acknowledged (at least formally) the suzerainty of the grand prince of Moscow and in cases of conflicts with Livonians or the Grand Duchy of Lithuania they sought his military aid.

This kind of political regime, typical of medieval communes, where the control over the city was divided between several authorities including the city magistrates and a prince or an emperor, was aptly termed by Charles Tilly as 'fragmented sovereignty'.[64] However, the political environment favourable to city communes like Novgorod and Pskov changed dramatically in the mid-fifteenth century with the rise of the Muscovite state which developed on the territorial basis of the Grand Principality of Vladimir.

From the early 1460s on, Pskov gradually lost its independence in relations with the outer world. Pskovites could no longer invite and replace their princes: now they received them only 'from the hand' of the grand prince of Moscow, as the latter's vicegerents. But the local administration and justice remained intact until the early sixteenth century. In 1510, Basil III, menacing the city with military force, compelled Pskov (together with the whole land and fourteen subordinate towns) to give up the rest of its autonomy. The assembly (*veche*) was abolished, and its symbol – the city bell – was removed and driven to Moscow.[65] It should be added that the fate of Pskov was not unique: many city communes had fallen under the attacks of ecclesiastic or secular lords by the dawn of the sixteenth century.[66]

Pskov's trade with Baltic ports, especially Reval, did not die away after the annexation of the city, but it underwent a dramatic transformation. First of all, the composition of the local merchants changed, as the richest and the most influential of them, including merchant elders, were evicted from Pskov together with the mayors and boyars (the chronicler cites the total number of 300 expelled elite families). In their stead, several hundreds of merchant families from different Muscovite cities were settled in Pskov.[67]

Disadvantageous as it may seem from commercial point of view, the resettlement of the local elite, including merchants, was considered by Muscovite authorities as a means to guarantee the loyalty of the newly conquered cities in the western border region. First practised in Novgorod after the conquest of the city, this measure was then applied to Pskov and, later, to Smolensk (1514). Based on an agrarian and low-monetized economy, the patrimonial Muscovite state obviously rated the acquired lands much higher than eventual profits from international trade.

For foreign merchants, the conditions changed as well when grand-princely customs were introduced in 1510 – for the first time in Pskov's history.[68] The regulation of trade in sixteenth-century Pskov was fully concentrated in the hands of the local tsarist administration: we are told that the arrival and departure of every foreign merchant was registered by the Pskov governor.[69]

In terms of Pskov's economic and demographic development, the events of 1510 also marked a turning point: urban growth stopped. In the course of the seventeenth and early eighteenth century the population of Pskov (unlike its rural area) remained stable and did not exceed 19,000 or 20,000 people,[70] i.e. less than its estimated size on the eve of the Muscovite annexation of the city.

Thus the case of Pskov illustrates one of the general trends in the history of European cities in the later Middle Ages and early modern period: maritime trade provided for the flourishing of the city, but the rise of the early modern state (in this case, Muscovy) was a challenge to urban autonomy and further prosperity. Some commercial centres, like London or Lisbon, managed to adapt themselves to the needs of the rising monarchies (see chapters by Maryanne Kowaleski, Amélia Andrade and Flávio Miranda in this volume), while others could not find their niche in the new political system and entered the phase of decay. Pskov belonged to the second category: it shared the fate of those European merchant towns and cities whose heyday fell during the late medieval period.

Acknowledgements

The authors gratefully acknowledge the kind assistance of Professor Lawrence N. Langer (University of Connecticut) who made available to us the English-language edition of important primary sources cited in this chapter.

Notes

1 Guilbert de Lannoy, *Voyages et ambassades de Messire Guildert de Lannoy*, Mons: Hoyois, 1840, p. 19.
2 *Gramoty Velikogo Novgoroda i Pskova* [The charters of Great Novgorod and Pskov] ed. S. N. Valk, Moscow and Leningrad: USSR Academy of Sciences Press, 1949 (hereafter *GVNP*), pp. 317–18. About the notion of 'brotherhood', see also: R. Leffler, 'Novgorod – eine europäische Kommune des Mittelalters?', in C. Goehrke and B. Pietrow-Ennker (eds), *Städte im östlichen Europa,* Zürich: Chronos, 2006, pp. 33–59.
3 M. Weber, *Economy and Society*, tr. E. Fischoff *et al.*, ed. G. Roth and C. Wittich, 2 vols, Berkeley-Los Angeles, CA: University of California Press, 1978, vol. 2, pp. 1237–8.
4 For example, Susan Reynolds honestly acknowledged that she lacked the language capabilities to produce work relating to what extended beyond the Latin world (S. Reynolds, *Kingdoms and Communities in Western Europe 900–1300,* Oxford: Clarendon Press, 1984, p. 9). But this is a general problem, of course.
5 E. Ennen, *Die Europäische Stadt des Mittelalters*, 4th edn, Göttingen: Vandenhoeck & Ruprecht, 1987, pp. 182–91 (1st edn 1972).
6 R. Mumenthaler, 'Spätmittelalterliche Städte West- und Osteuropas im Vergleich: Versuch einer verfassungsgeschichtlichen Typologie', *Jahrbücher für Geschichte Osteuropas* 46/1, 1998, pp. 39–68.
7 Leffler, 'Novgorod'.
8 L. Steindorff, ' Pravilno li schitat' Novgorod communoi?' [Is it correct to consider Novgorod a commune?], in *Spory o novgorodskom veche* [A debate about the Novgorod veche], St Petersburg: European University at St Petersburg Press, 2012, pp. 228–41.

9 See A. Nikitskij, *Ocherk vnutrennej istorii Pskova* [Studies in internal Pskov history], St Petersburg: Zamyslovskij, 1873; V. Sergeevich, *Russkije juridicheskije drevnosti* [Russian juridical antiquities], 3 vols, vol. 2, St Petersburg: M. M. Stasiulevich, 1893.
10 M. N. Tikhomirov, *Drevnerusskije goroda* [Towns of Old Rus], 2nd edn, Moscow: Politizdat, 1956.
11 V. L. Ianin, *Novgorodskie posadniki* [Mayors of Novgorod], Moscow: Moscow State University Press, 1962.
12 Anna L. Khoroshkevich, 'Pskov kak posrednik mezhdu zapadnoj, severnoj i vostochnoj Evropoi v Srednije veka i v nachale Novogo vremeni' [Pskov as a mediator between Western, Northern, and Eastern Europe in the Middle Ages and early modern period], in *Pskov v rossijskoj i evropejskoj istorii* [Pskov in Russian and European history], 2 vols, Moscow: MGUP, 2003, vol. 1, pp. 32–9.
13 In that treaty Pskov is already called a possible enemy of Novgorod, but there is no mention of its trade.
14 *GVNP*, pp. 88–9.
15 Ibid., pp. 119–24.
16 Ibid., p. 122.
17 Ibid., pp. 73–4.
18 *LECUB*, vol. 9, n. 750, p. 524.
19 V. A. Arakcheev, *Pskov i Gansa v epochu Srednevekovja* [Pskov and the Hanse in the Middle Ages], Pskov: Design Express, 2012, p. 17.
20 *GVNP*, p. 122.
21 Arakcheev, *Pskov i Gansa*, p. 17.
22 A. L. Khoroshkevich. *Torgovlja Velikogo Novgoroda v XIV–XV vekah* [The trade of Great Novgorod in the fourteenth and fifteenth centuries], Moscow: USSR Academy of Sciences Press, 1963, pp. 230–5.
23 Ibid., pp. 233–4.
24 Arakcheev, *Pskov i Gansa*, p. 13.
25 See a letter sent by Pskov to Riga in the fourteenth century (*GVNP*, p. 317); another one sent by Pskov to Reval in the early fifteenth century (S. N. Valk. 'Novye gramoty o pskovsko-novgorodskikh otnjcheniiakh s Pribaltikoi' [New documents about Novgorod's and Pskov's relations with Livonia], *Istoricheskii archive* [Historic archive] 1, Moscow, 1956, p. 234); and a new-found Pskov letter of 1486: V. Sokolovskij and S. Beletskii, 'Pskovskaya gramota iz archeologicheskih raskopok v Talline' [A Pskov letter found during excavations in Tallinn], in *Pskov v rossijskoj i evropejskoj istorii* [Pskov in Russian and European history], 2 vols., Moscow: MGUP, 2003, vol. 1, p. 140.
26 *GVNP*, pp. 317–18.
27 Khoroshkevich. *Torgovlia Velikogo Novgoroda*, p. 284.
28 Ibid., p. 292.
29 Valk, *Novye gramoty*, p. 234.
30 The word 'posadnik' etymologically derives from the verb 'posadit' (to seat, to put). Originally, 'posadnik' was an appointee of a prince who 'placed' him as the latter's vicegerent in a town or city. When the princely power in Pskov decayed, 'posadnik' became an independent city magistrate (mayor). Later the word was also used to designate members of a powerful social group (patricians). This evolution is examined at some length in the section on the city growth and social differentiation. To differentiate between various meanings of the word, we use the term *posadnik-in-office* while referring to the city magistrate (mayor) and the term *posadniks* (in plural) when the social group (patricians) is meant.
31 *GVNP*, p. 323.
32 The PJC original has been lost. What we actually have are just two late copies: one is a mid-sixteenth-century fragment, while the only full copy dates back to the early seventeenth century. The composition of the text bears traces of several amendments.

33 We slightly edited the translation of this article made by Daniel Kaiser, see D. H. Kaiser (tr. and ed.), *The Laws of Rus: Tenth to Fifteenth Centuries,* Salt Lake City, UT: Charles Schlacks, Jr., 1992, pp. 87–105, here pp. 103–4.

34 Traditionally 'Krom' is understood as Pskov Kremlin, i.e. internal castle, not the entire territory of the city, but etymologically this word refers to a fortified place. However, Krom is undoubtedly opposed in art. 7 and 8 to 'posad', i.e., a settled territory around the city walls. Thus 'Krom' should be understood as the entire *intra murum* territory, which was not a steady category because in the fourteenth and fifteenth centuries Pskov built new city walls three times (in 1310, 1375 and 1465) and its territory grew from 0.03 sq. km (castle, or urban core) to 1.7 sq. km (inside the walls of 1465).

35 Art. 7 specifies that crimes like theft, horse stealing or arson, if committed in 'Krom' (Pskov Kremlin), should be punished with death, while art. 8 provides that usually theft committed in 'posad' (unfortified town territory) deserves milder punishment, unless the thief is a recidivist caught for the third time (Kaiser, *Laws of Rus,* p. 88).

36 G. Chittolini, 'Statuti e autonomie urbane', in G. Chittolini and D. Willoweit (eds), *Statuti città territori in Italia e Germania tra Medioevo ed età Moderna,* Bologna: Il Mulino, 1991, pp. 7–47.

37 Kaiser, *Laws of Rus,* p. 87.

38 The charters mentioned in the preamble of the PJC have not been preserved, their dates are unknown. There is a controversy about exactly which Alexander is meant here: Alexander Nevskii (d. 1263) or Alexander of Rostov, who ruled in Pskov intermittently between 1410 and 1434. Prince Konstantin, the brother of Vasilii I of Moscow, ruled in Pskov briefly in 1407 and 1412.

39 'Dar umme heft unsere herschaft uns utgesandt, de borgermeister von Pleskow und alle Pleskowe': *GVNP,* p. 318.

40 *GVNP,* p. 321.

41 Other examples, besides those cited above, include a message to Riga sent in 1462/63 from Pskov Prince Ivan Alexandrovich and posadnik-in-office (mayor) Maksim Larionovich, from 'all posadnik' (patricians) of Pskov, Pskov boyars (nobles), Pskov merchants and 'from all Pskov' (*GVNP,* p. 323); the 1480 letter to the Polish King Casimir 'from Pskov Prince Vasilij Vasilievich and from all posadniks of Pskov and from all Lord Pskov' (*GVNP,* p. 325); and, finally, the 1503 treaty between Pskov and Livonia signed by envoys from 'Pskov Prince Dimitrij Volodimerevich, posadniks-in-office, old posadniks, and all Great Pskov' (*GVNP,* p. 331).

42 *GVNP,* p. 336.

43 For example: *Pskovskie letopisi* [Pskov chronicles], ed. A. N. Nasonov, 2 vols, vol. 1, Moscow: USSR Academy of Science Press, 1941 [hereafter *Pskov Chronicles I*], pp. 37, 38, 41, 43.

44 See: *GVNP,* p. 317; L. M. Marasinova, *Novye pskovskie gramoty* [*New Pskov charters*], Moscow: Moscow University Press, 1966, p. 46.

45 *GVNP,* p. 324.

46 *Pskovskie letopisi* [Pskov chronicles], ed. A. N. Nasonov, vol. 2, Moscow: USSR Academy of Science Press, 1955 [hereafter *Pskov Chronicles II*], p. 30.

47 Ibid., p.108.

48 *Pskov Chronicles I,* p. 92.

49 According to art. 7 and 8 of the PJC a death penalty should be applied to a horse thief, an arsonist, a traitor, a person who stole in Krom (Pskov Kremlin) and a person who committed a theft for the third time but outside Krom: Kaiser, *Laws of Rus,* p. 88

50 For example, according to the chronicle entry for 1509, a sexton of the Pskov cathedral was accused of stealing money from a treasury that was kept in the cathedral. He was arrested and interrogated at city assembly. After the torture the sexton confessed to having committed the theft. He was imprisoned and executed several months later. The chronicle contains a description how a PJC norm was applied. The sexton was executed according to art. 7 (a theft in Krom). He was judged by a city assembly. Nobody can say that it was not a court session but

mob violence. The fact that an interrogation was used and the execution wasn't done immediately but at a time later is clear evidence that city assembly judgment was a judicial procedure.

51 *Pskov Chronicles II*, p. 206.

52 A. E. Musin. *Tserkov' i gorozhane srednevekovogo Pskova* [The church and burghers of medieval Pskov], St Petersburg: St Petersburg State University Press, 2010, pp. 260–316.

53 P. Michaud-Quantin, *Universitas: Expressions du mouvement communautaire dans le Moyen Âge latin*, Paris: Vrin, 1970.

54 Reynolds, *Kingdoms and* Communities, pp. 155–214.

55 E. Isenmann, *Die deutsche Stadt im Mittelalter: 1150–1550*, Cologne: Böhlau Verlag, 2012, pp. 181–92.

56 F. W. Carter, *Dubrovnik (Ragusa): A Classic City State,* London: Academic Press Inc., 1972, pp. 50–2.

57 G. Cracco, *Un altro mondo: Venezia nel Medioevo. Dal secolo XI al secolo XIV,* Torino: UTET Università, 1986.

58 C. Diehl, *Une republique patricienne: Venise*, Paris: Ernest Flammarion, 1913, p. 12.

59 A. L. Rogachevskii, *Mech Rolanda: Pravovie vzgljady nemezkih biurgerov XIII–XV vv* [Roland's sword: legal views of German burghers in the thirteenth to fifteenth centuries], St Petersburg: St Petersburg State University Press, 1996.

60 D. Nicholas, *Urban Europe, 1100–1700*, Houndmills, Basingstoke, and New York: Palgrave Macmillan, 2003, pp. 10–24.

61 A. Vovin, 'Posadnichestvo v Pskove XIV–XV vv' [Posadniks in Pskov in fourteenth and fifteenth centuries], in *On-line review History*, Moscow, 2012, 7(15), http://mes.igh.ru/s207987840000212-2-1.

62 M. Tikhomirov, 'Drevnjaja Moskva: XII–XV vv' [Old Moscow: from the twelfth to fifteenth centuries], in S. Schmidt (ed.), *Rossija na mezhdunarodnyh putjah XIV–XV vv* [Russia on the international routes in the fourteenth and fifteenth centuries], Moscow: Moskovskii rabochii, 1992, pp. 146–7.

63 This section is partly based on the paper: M. Krom, 'The city of Pskov in the fifteenth and early sixteenth centuries: communal liberties and fragmented sovereignty', *Russian History* 41/4, 2014, pp. 440–57.

64 See C. Tilly, *Coercion, Capital, and European States, AD 990–1992,* Cambridge, MA: Blackwell, 1992, pp. 21, 31, 40, 41, 187.

65 The fullest scholarly account of the 1510 event still remains Natalia Maslennikova's book, although the author, in the spirit of Soviet historiography, justifies Pskov's capture as a natural and 'progressive' achievement, the triumph of the state centralization: N. N. Maslennikova, *Prisoedinenie Pskova k Russkomu tsentralizovannomu gosudarstvu* [The incorporation of Pskov into the Russian centralized state], Leningrad: Leningrad University Press, 1955.

66 For example, in Germany many towns and cities lost their liberties in the 1440s through 1480s, including Berlin-Cölln, Mainz, Quedlinburg, Erfurt, etc. See E. Engel, *Die deutsche Stadt des Mittelalters*, Munich: Beck, 1993, p. 317.

67 *Pskov Chronicles I*, pp. 93, 95, 97.

68 Vladimir Arakcheev assumes that customs duty in Pskov amounted to 5 per cent, see V. A. Arakcheev, *Pskovskii krai v XV–XVII vekakh: Obshchestvo i gosudarstvo* [Pskov land in the fifteenth through seventeenth centuries: society and the state], St Petersburg: Blits, 2003, p. 117.

69 Arakcheev, *Pskov i Gansa*, p. 11.

70 Arakcheev, *Pskovskii krai*, pp. 323–6.

PART IV

The Atlantic and the North Sea

19

LISBON

Trade, urban power and the king's visible hand

Amélia Aguiar Andrade and Flávio Miranda

In 1147, King Afonso Henriques (r. 1143–85), aided by English, Scottish, Norman, Flemish and Lotharingian Crusaders, marched into Lisbon and defeated the Muslim overlords of the city. Shortly after the Christian victory, one of the English crusaders wrote an impressive account about the place he was seeing for the first time ever:

> The city of Lisbon at the time of our arrival consisted of sixty thousand families paying taxes – this figure includes the suburbs round about, except the free ones, which pay taxes to no one. A circular wall there surrounds the top of the hill and, at the left and right, the city walls descend to the banks of the Tagus River. The suburbs, down below the city wall, are cut into the banks of the river in such a way that each of them has a superbly fortified citadel. The place is girded with pitfalls. The city was populous beyond belief . . . [and the] city's buildings were jammed so closely together that it was scarcely possible, save in the merchants' quarters, to find a street more than eight feet wide.[1]

The English Crusader completes this description by saying that 'this was by far the richest and most opulent city' that he had encountered, and that its markets and bazaars offered all sorts of luxury and staple goods that gold and silver could buy from all parts of Europe and Africa.

Four hundred years later, in the sixteenth century, the Portuguese chronicler Damião de Góis (1502–74) wrote a eulogy dedicated to the city of Lisbon meant to circulate amongst the European elites titled *Urbis Olisiponis Descriptio* (1554). In it, Góis wrote that

> In our time there are two cities that we could legitimately claim as being dames of the Ocean, and their respective queens. Under their command and domination, in our days, East and West have become open to navigation.

> One of those is Lisbon. From the mouth of the River Tagus she summons part of the Ocean, enveloping the sea, Africa and Asia in a huge embrace. The other is Seville.[2]

Despite being separated by four centuries and a heap of political, economic and even geographical circumstances, these two accounts share the common idea that Lisbon had a profound symbiosis with the sea.[3] From a geostrategic point a view, these arguments make sense: Lisbon occupied a privileged location for commercial contacts between the north and the south of Europe, and could easily interact with the northern and the southern parts of the Atlantic Ocean. Lisbon was, as Luisa D'Arienzo wrote, in 'una felice posizione geografica'.[4] However, there is much more to this story than environmental determinism produced by a favourable setting in the confluence of Atlantic and Mediterranean cultures.

For centuries, Islamic Lisbon looked south while establishing its commercial contacts within the al-Andalus and the Maghreb, and the bulk of the thousands of residents had little point of contact with the Christian kingdoms in the northern parts of Iberia or Europe. So, how long did it take Lisbon to switch the needle of its commercial routes? Lisbon's foreign trade seems to have halted almost entirely after the conquest of 1147. It is likely that the continuous battles between the first Portuguese kings and Muslim rulers in the south, and the threats of pirate attacks faced by merchants were the cause of this commercial stagnation. At least until 1217, the year of the conquest of Alcácer do Sal by Afonso II (r. 1211–23), the Muslims continued to control the navigation in the river Sado, thus keeping alive a threat to Christian merchants and to Lisbon. This risk to Portuguese navigation only ended in 1249, when Afonso III (r. 1248–79) conquered the western Gharb al-Andalus and incorporated it into the kingdom of Portugal. In a sense, it is possible to say that the first five Portuguese kings paid little attention to the matters of overseas trade: they were primarily concerned with securing the border with Castile and defeating the Muslim adversaries in the south. It was in this historical context that Lisbon – the once majestic city of luxury goods and busy markets and bazaars – lived its first century under Christian domination.

The first turning point in Lisbon's political and socio-economic future occurred in the second half of the thirteenth century, when the city slowly became Portugal's political, economic and cultural core. The stepping-stone was the (almost) permanent installation of the royal court in Lisbon during the reign of Afonso III, who brought an army of noblemen and officials to serve him – a court society which needed to be fed, and was eager for high-quality commodities from Portugal and abroad.[5] Afonso's son King Dinis (r. 1279–1325) took it a step further by authorizing the establishment of mercantile institutions, promoting shipbuilding and constituting an armada under the supervision of the Genoese admiral Emanuele Pessagno.[6] It was also in Lisbon that the first Portuguese University was founded, in 1289. In the early fourteenth century, Lisbon had grown to become a city of urban oligarchs, noblemen and home to the royal family – a polyhedral city of services, institutions and trade.

The second turning point in Lisbon's political and socio-economic life occurred in the fifteenth century. By then, Lisbon was Iberia's largest city with 50,000 residents, and one of the top commercial cities of Western Europe. Lisbon merchants were often found in places like Pisa, Valencia, Seville, Bilbao, Waterford, Southampton, London, Harfleur, Bruges and Middelburg, whereas the city regularly welcomed traders from Genoa, Barcelona, A Coruña, Fuenterrabía, Bayonne, Bordeaux, Saint-Malo, Bristol, Danzig and Reval. To Lisbon they would bring cloth, tin, weapons and cereal, and in return they would buy olive oil, wine, vinegar, figs, raisins, oranges and cork, as well as sugar, ivory, pepper, nutmeg and slaves – the latter five commodities only after the commencement of the overseas expansion.

At the beginning of the sixteenth century, Lisbon had become much more than a simple port of call for traders. As capital of a kingdom with a population less than 1 per cent of China's, Lisbon had high expectations about its economic role in the world: it aspired to dominate European, African and Asian trade by establishing

> an amazing network of trading posts that stretched like a global necklace from Lisbon, round the coast of Africa, Arabia and India, through the Straits of Malacca, to the spice islands themselves and then on still further, beyond even Macau.[7]

How did Lisbon go from a twelfth-century Islamic city, commercially facing south, to a central pan-European hub and gateway in the later Middle Ages? How did Lisbon integrate itself in European trading networks? And why did it become one of the most important merchant cities of Western Europe in the fifteenth and sixteenth centuries?

Seeking answers to these problems is of paramount importance, even more if we take into account that there is a stark contrast between what historians know about medieval and early modern Lisbon. Contrary to what one would expect, few historians have examined the economic profile of Lisbon and its respective relationship with production centres, secondary ports, socio-economic agents and the city's place in wider commercial networks. We do not have for the Middle Ages, for example, a similar study like the one produced by Cátia Antunes about Lisbon's international trade with Amsterdam in the seventeenth century.[8] In fact, historians have as yet failed to produce a full-scale study on the urban history of Lisbon, covering the Islamic past and the city's evolution in the Middle Ages. Portuguese historiography usually justifies the lack of research with the dearth of sources available for the study of medieval Lisbon, since city council minutes and customs accounts have disappeared completely. Following the earthquake that struck Lisbon on 1 November 1755, partly destroying the city and the archives kept at the Castle of São Jorge, fire consumed a great deal of the documents. The quake, followed by a tsunami, destroyed Lisbon's riverfront – the customs house, for example, was one of its first victims. The level of destruction is easily determined by the number of parish churches of medieval origin still standing after the earthquake: only one (the cathedral) out of twenty-one survived the violence of this quake.[9] Notwithstanding the lack of certain economic sources in Portugal, a few historians have examined several aspects of the economic life of medieval Lisbon through different sources and approaches.[10] These studies focus mainly on the geographical setting, the socio-economic importance of the sea and the role of foreigners in Lisbon.[11]

This chapter is on the city of Lisbon in the period between the mid-twelfth century and the end of the fifteenth century, and will examine how it became a central node in the framework of European mercantile networks. Despite the obvious geostrategic positioning of Lisbon in Iberia as antechamber and primary hub for Mediterranean, Northern European and African commodities, there were other variables involved. We will argue that the many layers of economic development depended greatly on the political change in Portugal and in Europe, the early process of institutional centralization in the Portuguese kingdom and, surprisingly, the city officials and the king's constant concern about a possible food shortage.

This chapter is divided in four sections. The first presents an overview of Lisbon's economy. The second examines the role of the urban council in economic affairs and the strong interference of the Portuguese crown. The third inserts Lisbon in European trade networks. The fourth presents some of the conflicts merchants faced in Lisbon, and how they solved them.

Hinterland and domestic market

Lisbon was the home base of Portugal's commercial network. Portuguese traders from other cities operating abroad – and alien merchants with commercial interests in Portugal – could not avoid doing business in Lisbon. In Portugal, Lisbon was the *caput regni*, above all other urban areas in the kingdom – a commercial giant capable of subjecting every other small town and city to its economic needs.[12] The author of the *De Expugnatione Lyxbonensi* claimed that Lisbon, in 1147, consisted of 60,000 families paying taxes; the 'Numeramento', however, informs us that it had 59,846 residents in 1532.[13] In the mid-fifteenth century, an English merchant described Lisbon as being as large as London; and in 1484 the traveller Nicolaus von Popplau also claimed that it was large as Cologne and London.[14] In terms of its population, Lisbon was larger than Valencia (42,000), Seville (40,000) and Barcelona (35,000),[15] but smaller than London (80,000) and Venice (115,000).[16] The kingdom of Portugal, however, had a low urban potential (under 30 per cent) – similar to Castile, Celtic Britain, Scandinavia and Eastern Europe.[17] This happened because the second (Porto), third (Évora) and fourth (Santarém) largest cities and towns in Portugal combined still had fewer inhabitants than Lisbon; and most towns in Portugal could only count up to 2,000 residents.[18] But this difference in size came at a price. Although Lisbon exerted its influence over its large hinterland, it was too dependent on its own supply complex. So, how did Lisbon control this domestic network?

The most fertile and productive areas of late medieval Portugal were located in the Lisbon and Tagus valley region – in modern-day Baixa Estremadura and Ribatejo – which produced cereal, vegetables, fruit, wine, olive oil and honey. In addition to that, fishing devices to catch tuna, dolphin and other types of fish were located along Portugal's coast, especially the southern west coast, and in Algarve. Indeed, numerous anglers' villages supplied Lisbon's larger economic system through maritime, sea-river and inland waterway transport. This, however, was not enough to feed the city: as Lisbon grew, so did the demand for foodstuff from Portugal and beyond. In 1437, the council of Lisbon petitioned King Duarte (r. 1433–8), urging him to lower taxation on imported fish – 'the fifth' levy charged over fish brought to the city, otherwise foreigners could prefer to take their catch to Seville – a sound political argument demonstrating how flexible and movable trading networks could be.[19] Besides agricultural and fishing products, Lisbon's vast hinterland would provide mineral resources (iron, pyrite, plumb) from the Alentejo region. From a theoretical point of view, Lisbon's surrounding countryside provided abundant commodities for consumption and overseas trade, but we see that high demand left the city dependent on the supply of foreign essential items – very similar to what happened in Valencia.[20] Making sure that there was enough food in the city was, undoubtedly, Lisbon's greatest obsession in the later Middle Ages, constantly in the minds of the king, urban magistrates and the population.

The development of this domestic network depended on the articulation of several transport facilities: land transportation, and coastal and river navigation. Land transportation made use of pre-existing, centuries-old infrastructure (Roman roads), which was used in connection with river transport. Evidence shows that during the Islamic period Mediterranean and African commodities would arrive in *al-Lixbûnâ* via the southern ports of Mértola (on the river Guadiana), Faro and Tavira in the Gharb al-Andalus, which means that land transportation completed the final part of the journey. Teeming with travellers, 'almocreves' (muleteers) and merchants, these roads continued to be used throughout the centuries. Recent research on the Italian presence in Lisbon has proved that merchants would often offload their commodities in smaller ports outside the Portuguese capital – like Tavira or Setúbal – and that land transportation would complete the final leg of the journey.[21]

Lisbon's domestic economic network was the size of the kingdom, yet its most powerful influence – in terms of direct interference in market regulation, jurisdiction and taxation – was exerted in the Low River Tagus area (Figure 19.1). Comprising an area of 5,000 square kilometres, the surrounding towns of Santarém, Torres Novas, Tomar, Punhete, Abrantes, Alenquer, Almada, Sesimbra, Setúbal, Coruche and Alcácer do Sal formed what has been described as Lisbon's 'small Mediterranean' world.[22] However, Lisbon's economic influence was not limited to its administrative region, and a constant movement of peoples and commodities from all northern (Ponte de Lima, Viana, Fão, Vila do Conde, Porto and Aveiro) and southern port towns (Lagos, Faro, Tavira and Mértola) was generated to feed its inhabitants. A closer look at the sources shows that the presence of merchants from these other port towns in Lisbon was very common. In some occasions, Lisbon's merchants even freighted Porto's vessels to ship commodities overseas.[23]

Smaller coastal towns at the outskirts of Lisbon were important ports of call for foreign merchants. Cascais and Restelo (Lisbon's outer port), for example, were the first two ports merchants would encounter before reaching Lisbon, and the first frequently exempted foreign traders from taxes and levies, in order to attract them to the Portuguese capital.[24] The Florentine merchant Luca di Maso degli Albizzi,

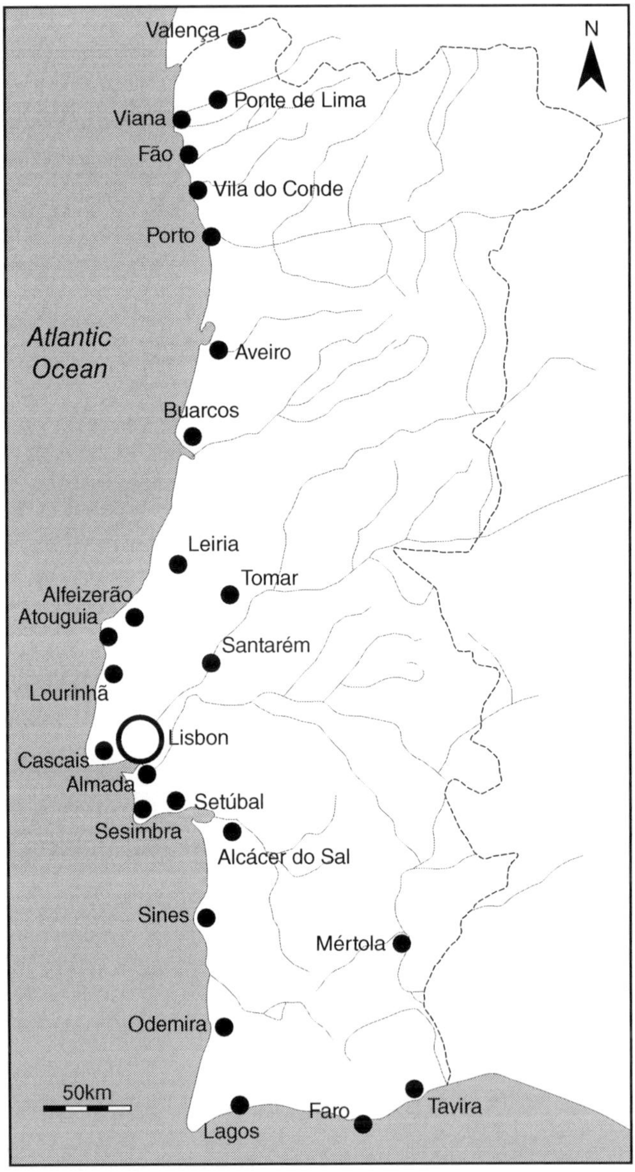

Figure 19.1 Lisbon's domestic network in the later Middle Ages

a captain of galleys trading between Constantinople and England and Flanders, stopped in Restelo to replenish food and water before proceeding to Bruges, in 1429.[25] Similarly, in 1469, the *Santa Catarina* of Bilbao dropped anchor in Cascais, laden with wine from Naples to London, and the shipmaster Juan Peres de Fogaça took the opportunity to request authorization to trade in Portugal before continuing his journey to England.[26] Sources also suggest that ships used to call at Restelo, especially during periods of conflict, waiting for the king's letters of protection to enter Lisbon.[27]

Lisbon's articulation with domestic and international ports required ships. Several Portuguese kings understood this need and promulgated royal decrees stimulating the shipbuilding industry. King Fernando (r. 1367–83), for example, authorized Lisbon's shipbuilders to freely chop wood from the royal woods, while excusing them from paying the tithe on imported iron and other parts if meant to build vessels over 100 tons.[28] The ordinance also included future fiscal exemptions to those freighting the ships built if used to export commodities to Flanders, France and other parts of Europe. In the fifteenth century, the kings of Portugal continued to issue ordinances intended to encourage the shipbuilding industry of Lisbon, but under different circumstances. From the conquest of Ceuta on, in 1415, Portugal entered in a new stage of maritime policy, with the crown's involvement in the exploration of the western coast of Africa. That is why Afonso V (r. 1438–81), in 1474, granted privileges to shipbuilders making vessels over 100 tons, but also included exemptions on bombards, gunpowder and other weaponry which could be loaded on those ships.[29]

The shipbuilding industry was responsible for another important contribution in Lisbon: a profound change in the city's society and landscape. Legislation from 1492 shows, for example, that employment in Lisbon's shipyard was rather substantial, since it established a minimum of 100 and up to a maximum of 300 shipwrights and caulkers.[30] Around the shipyard and the harbour, there would be hundreds of people, every day, filling up the warehouses, taverns and hostels. In 1551, Lisbon's riverfront was teeming with specialized workers in the shipyard, port and warehouses: 227 shipwrights, 114 caulkers, 4 sawyers, 24 brokers, 167 pilots, 50 shipmasters, 623 anglers and 518 sailors.[31] An army of people was at the service of Lisbon's maritime economy.

Urban council and the king's visible hand

In the fifteenth century, the urban council of Lisbon had eight judges (*juízes* or *alvazis*), one attorney (*procurador*), three aldermen (*vereadores*) and twenty-four inspectors of weights and measures (*almotacés*). Merchants controlled most of the urban offices, being found frequently acting as council attorney, civil judge, criminal judge, customs judge and treasurer.[32] Although merchants controlled the majority of the important positions in Lisbon, their autonomy as council representatives depended on many factors. Mário Farelo's research on Lisbon's urban oligarchy in the late fourteenth century and early fifteenth century has proven that these men had to play a twofold role: they served the city, but, above all, they served and obeyed the king. Therefore, it is not surprising to find that 81 per cent of them were king's vassals, 15 per cent were royal servants, 2 per cent were part of the privy council and another 2 per cent benefited from royal privilege.[33] To what extent did this promiscuity between city and crown limit their power and autonomy? More importantly, what repercussions did this have on Lisbon's foreign trade and merchant networks?

Together with London, Lisbon was one of the few cities in Europe with the status of both *caput regni* and the largest commercial port. However, Lisbon and London followed different paths in regards to their urban autonomy and relation to royal power. Portugal's bureaucratic machine was centralized in Lisbon, in a bellows-shaped structure controlled by the king, and supported by the chancellery, the exchequer, the customs and a plethora of other institutions, which multiplied in the fifteenth century. Since Lisbon's medieval council minutes have disappeared, it is difficult to say to what extent the king interfered in matters related to foreign trade. But other records show that royal supervision was permanent, with the king adjusting municipal taxes, requesting changes in regulation and reprehending the council members over their inability to end privateering – in 1485, King João II (r. 1481–95) admonished the council of Lisbon for having done nothing to prevent the capture of Breton and English ships anchored in Cascais by Flemish privateers.[34] This type of patronizing behaviour by the king towards the urban council was less common in other Portuguese port towns. Porto, for instance, tried to keep a certain distance from the crown in some issues – until the early fifteenth century, Porto was a bishopric city where the nobility, including the king, could not stay more than three nights without the council's authorization. Notwithstanding these peculiarities, Lisbon continued to serve as fiscal, commercial and administrative model for the rest of the kingdom, and her statutes were replicated in other port towns.[35]

The king's firm hand in Lisbon went beyond simple interference in urban affairs: the crown had laid out a policy to create a general economic system favouring Portugal's largest city and commercial port. Three measures supported this economic system. First, in 1389, a royal decree promoted internal migrations to increase the workforce in the Lisbon area, regardless of the fact that this might undermine the productive and socio-economic stability of other parts of the kingdom.[36] Second, the Portuguese ruler granted fiscal exemptions to nearby places (Alcácer do Sal, Almada, Cascais, Coina, Lourinhã, Palmela, Santarém, Setúbal and Sintra), towns from other parts of the country (Abrantes, Aveiro, Lagos, Odemira and Porto), and to overseas regions and countries (Andalusia, Brittany, England and Flanders) under the condition that they had to bring cereal to Lisbon.[37] In fact, in times of great need, Portuguese kings even lifted bans on trade with North African Muslims to allow the import of cereal to Lisbon.[38] And in 1494, King João II ordered the council to make agreements with alien merchants residing in Lisbon so that they too would bring more grain.[39] Third, the king turned Lisbon into Portugal's main international port by decreeing a 'closed-access' system to Portuguese markets.

It is not uncommon to find in other European countries a network of domestic ports showing signs that the capital or the largest commercial city was being favoured in terms of infrastructures, legislation and shipping privileges. Urban resolutions and royal favour would normally support, protect and stimulate the development of commercial centres. In the past few years, economic historians have worked on theories that discuss whether competitive urban networks promoted 'open-access' institutions, and, consequently, the economic growth of the Low Countries in the late medieval and early modern period.[40] The case of Portugal is *sui generis*: not without consequence did rulers adopt 'closed-access' policies and institutions, which stimulated the economic growth of Lisbon. In 1375, King Fernando (r. 1367–83) issued an ordinance to regulate trade with two simple principles: first, there would only be one market in Portugal for the negotiation of cereal coming from abroad, which would be in Lisbon; second, with the exception of wine, figs and salt, the exchange of commodities had to be done in Lisbon.[41] The ordinance of 1375 was renewed in 1390, 1395 and in the 1430s by King João I (r. 1385–1433), and again in 1466 by Afonso V (r. 1438–81), which means that its principles were probably not being respected. Royal insistence on this matter had, possibly, a twofold purpose: to prevent food shortage in the largest Portuguese city, and to avoid tax evasion by concentrating overseas commercial exchange in Lisbon's customs house. Lisbon was already Portugal's largest port-city, but these economic policies made it an inescapable node in European trade networks. However, the potential benefits of a closed-access system applied to Lisbon's economy are difficult to gauge, and so are the downside risks incurred by other ports in Portugal. It is difficult to say, for example, if it ended up limiting the economic expansion of other port towns and regions in Portugal.

When kings began negotiating monopolies with merchants, this system evolved into a more intricate mechanism of commercial segregation. For a price, merchants could acquire the exclusive trade over every Portuguese commodity – whether it was sugar, hides, salt and coral;[42] and only authorized traders could export ivory, a commodity kept under monopoly by the crown. Although monopolies were common practice in Portugal from the thirteenth century, foreigners' control over certain commodities was making the Portuguese unhappy. In 1456, for example, Afonso V conceded cork monopoly to the Fleming Maarten Lem and to the Genoese Marco Lomellini for a period of ten years.[43] Years later, in 1475, cork was still inaccessible to most people in Portugal. During the parliamentary sessions of Évora (1475), talking specifically about cork, the urban council's representatives complained to the king that it did not make any sense for the crown to concede monopolies over things God had given them for free.[44] Most of the time, those arguments had no effect on changing the king's commercial policies. The financial needs of the kingdom remained a top priority during the reign of Afonso V, and negotiating monopolies with Portuguese or foreign merchants was the easiest way of filling the crown's chests with money.[45] This also reveals, however, how dependent the king was on external financing.

The crown's capacity to control the economic life of Lisbon and the kingdom in the fifteenth century says much about the top–down relationship the king established with urban institutions and merchants. The kings of Portugal were capable of taming Lisbon's merchant-oligarchs very easily, putting them under their leash and command. In a sense, it is possible that they did not have enough economic muscle to compete with their foreign counterparts – especially the Italians – nor to contest the king's power. More sedentary than Porto's merchants, Lisbon's merchant-oligarchs could be awaiting the perfect opportunity to gain royal privilege and rise socially.[46] The fifteenth-century overseas expansion scrambled the existing social framework when noblemen made their way into trade, whereas merchants sought nobility. The riches obtained from the overseas expansion would push this social change further when Portugal witnessed the emergence of a new socio-economic 'constellation': the 'merchant-knight'.[47] Each one of these shifts transformed the economy of Lisbon and her place in larger commercial networks.

Mercantile connections

So far, we have traced Lisbon's economic profile and seen the city's articulation with other parts of the kingdom, which infrastructure supported her domestic trade and the Portuguese crown's role in the making of commercial policies. But what do we know about the part played by traders in this merchants' world?

In terms of economic performance, Lisbon (as a city) and Portugal (as a kingdom) worked at two very different speeds. It is undeniable that the ports of Porto, Setúbal, Lagos and Tavira and their merchants played an important part in Portugal's overseas trade, but Lisbon was at the forefront of international commercial contacts. Whether as a main harbour or as an intermediary port of call, Lisbon was criss-crossed by a substantial number of ships of different origins bringing commodities, and the latest on novelties, financial techniques and fashion.

Immersed in this commercial mesh were local and foreign merchants, the principal nodes of a multifarious business web. Examining the relevance of Lisbon's merchants for the city's commercial network is a hopeless task, however, due to the lack of notarized records, merchant ledgers and customs accounts.[48] Notwithstanding these difficulties, there are a few important aspects worth mentioning about the presence of Lisbon's merchants in these networks and in foreign markets. First, Lisbon's merchants seem to have penetrated into Northern European markets much later than Porto's. English sources, for example, indicate that Porto's merchants were trading in England at least since 1226, whereas Lisbon's traders appear for the first time in 1294.[49] Again, as we have mentioned earlier in this chapter, it is possible that Lisbon's belated shift to Northern European markets had to do with her Islamic past, the threat of Muslim pirate attacks alongside the Portuguese coast and the warlike situation in the south of the kingdom. In Harfleur, however, Lisbon's merchants obtained their trading privileges earlier than Porto's, in 1309. Quite interestingly, this was one of the few times that the two merchant 'nations' were identified separately (Lisbon and Porto) rather than as a single one (Portugal) – as became customary from the second half of the fourteenth century on.[50] Alas, we know little about the socio-economic interactions between Lisbon's traders within their own community and with foreign merchant communities, and the information we have about their wealth and relevance comes to us scattered in pieces. Every now and then, for example, Lisbon's merchants are presented as rich men capable of providing small loans (£50) to English individuals (1323), and large sums (£2,578) to the city of Bruges (1333).[51] In the mid-fifteenth century, Lisbon's merchants also became preponderant in the sugar trade, having participated in price-fixing negotiations with Funchal's producers in Madeira.[52]

There is substantially more information about the presence of foreign merchants in Lisbon in the late Middle Ages, particularly in Italian and English archives, than about the Portuguese abroad. As one of the largest commercial cities of Western Europe in the fifteenth century, Lisbon must have had a reasonable number of foreign merchants living there or passing through. Exact numbers are impossible to get since we do not have for Lisbon the equivalent to London's alien subsidy rolls, but other records and accounts provide significant information about the presence of German, Flemish, English, Norman, Breton, Gascons, Basque, Galician, Castilian, Aragonese, Genoese, Pisan, Florentine and Venetian merchants. The chronicler Fernão Lopes, writing about Lisbon during the reign of Fernando (r. 1367–83), claimed that the city was inhabited by 'peoples from many lands', particularly Italian and Iberian merchants, and that there was an incessant movement of ships in the river Tagus.[53] In the mid-sixteenth century, Damião de Góis was also surprised by the number of foreigners in the Portuguese capital, and wrote that there was an 'extraordinary gathering of people' in the Rua Nova dos Mercadores (Merchants' New Street), who would come from almost every part of the world to trade in Lisbon.[54] Figure 19.2 shows how wide Lisbon's commercial contacts were in the Middle Ages, which stretched throughout Europe's western coast and the Mediterranean, but also included marketplaces in the Baltic Sea, North Africa, and the Atlantic islands.

Genoese ships had been travelling to Flanders since at least 1277, but the crucial moment for Lisbon and its integration in wider commercial networks was the opening of the Straits of Gibraltar to Christian navigation in 1293. This change was not, however, immediate, since it took a few decades for Mediterranean traders to penetrate into Atlantic waters and to settle their agents in Lisbon and other western Iberian ports.[55]

Lisbon did not become attractive to foreign merchants overnight. The Galicians, the Castilians, the Basques and the Aragonese were probably the first ones to arrive, followed by the English and the Italians, and then by the Hanseats, the Normans, the Bretons, the Flemings and everyone else. Pes de Lastar, a merchant of Bayonne, completed his fifteenth year living in Lisbon in 1338.[56] The English had been receiving wine, olive oil, figs, raisins and other commodities from the Portuguese at least since the end of the twelfth century, but the first hard evidence of English merchants in Portugal is from 1311.[57] Some of those merchants lived in rented houses near the

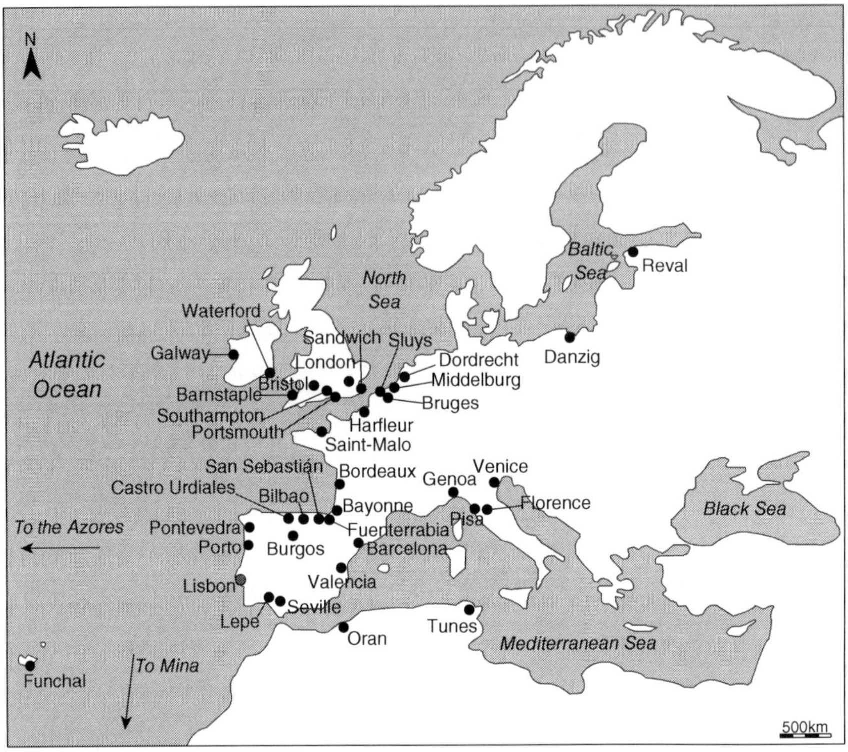

Figure 19.2 Lisbon's European commercial network

riverfront,[58] and a few impregnated Portuguese women, thus becoming parents in Lisbon:[59] the merchant Bartholomew James, for example, was born to an English father and Portuguese mother.[60] The North Germans had their colony in Lisbon at least from the end of the fourteenth century, when they built the Confraternity of Saint Bartholomew.[61] There is information about merchant-agents arriving in Lisbon at a very young age: Lieven vander Mersch, for example, emancipated his son François so that he could manage his affairs between Bruges, Lisbon and the Mediterranean.[62] In the 1470s and 1480s, one of the Flemish Despars brothers was also living in Lisbon (Wouter), shipping wine, figs, raisins, sugar and dyes to his brother in Bruges (Jacob), and receiving tapestries, woollens and fustians.[63] Those staying for longer periods would normally seek letters of denization, as it was the case of Maarten Lem (a Bruges citizen) and Bartolomeo Marchionni (a Florentine).[64] Alien merchants' attempts to integrate into Lisbon's society through letters of denization allowed them to have equal privileges as a citizen or to pay the same taxes, and perhaps something more. In 1395, the urban council of Lisbon informed the king that some merchants of Genoa and Piacenza were using their letters of denization as an excuse for not paying any levies – a situation which João I tried to correct to avoid fiscal evasion by alien traders.[65] Other alien merchants went further and tried ascending to municipal offices in the 1430s, a situation that forced the council to write to the king requesting that the access to those positions be limited to those married to a local citizen's daughter or citizen's widow.[66]

In the absence of medieval customs accounts in Lisbon's archives, an indicator of commercial growth is the increase of letters of denization and letters of protection. During the reigns of João I and Duarte, the Portuguese chancellery seems to have produced a meagre twenty-three letters of protection for a period of fifty-three years – although we must consider that not all records survived. However, it is possible that the Portuguese dynastic crisis of 1383–5 and the successive battles with Castile had taken their toll on the economy of the kingdom, making it less attractive to foreign traders. This situation was in stark contrast with what happened in the mid-fifteenth century, when Lisbon began receiving sugar from Madeira, woad (*isatis tinctoria*) from the Azores, and ivory from Mina, as well as African slaves and other exotic commodities, which provoked profound changes in Europe's commercial circuits. During Afonso V's reign – for a period of forty-three years – 115 foreign merchants requested safe-conducts to trade in Lisbon, and we must consider that only a third of his chancellery records survived. The king granted letters mostly to merchants of Castile (31 per cent), England (25 per cent), Genoa (15 per cent), Brittany (10 per cent), Galicia (8 per cent), Florence (4 per cent), Biscay (4 per cent), Granada (2 per cent) and the Maghreb (1 per cent) – in particular, from the Ziyyanid kingdom of Tlemecen (part of modern-day Algeria).[67]

It is not surprising to find a high number of Castilian merchants in this list due to the recent history of wars between the two kingdoms. The English, however, being Portugal's perpetual allies since the Treaty of Windsor of 1386, are the revelation in this list. It is nonetheless possible that the constant attacks on Portuguese ships en route to the North Sea motivated them to request protection in Lisbon. Alternatively, one must also take into account the high volume of Anglo-Portuguese trade in the second half of the fifteenth century. Bristol's customs accounts hold at least 1,617 entries alone on Bristol–Lisbon trade for the second half of the fifteenth century, and 1,902 entries on Anglo-Portuguese commercial relations, representing 17 per cent of Bristol's overseas trade.[68] For this particular case, Lisbon did not entice Bristol's merchants because of Madeira's sugar or African commodities. This time, it was a significant political change in Europe – the end of the Hundred Years War and England's loss of Gascony in 1453 – that pushed Bristolians to Lisbon; they could otherwise have continued to buy Bordeaux wine, as they had been doing for the past century. Bordeaux's wine prices skyrocketed, and Lisbon presented herself as an alternative for supplying a good-quality product to England's consumer market.[69]

Solving problems and conflict management

Lisbon, however, was not a merchant's paradise. As happened with other medieval commercial cities, there were frequent cases of conflict that provide us with colourful details about merchants' daily lives in medieval Lisbon. Moreover, these situations also contribute to our understanding of local institutions, conflict management and the impact this all had on the economy.

Commercial conflicts related to retail trade, monopolies, and retaliations, misuse of power, recklessness, and physical violence were the most frequent in Lisbon, involving local and foreign merchants and sailors, port authorities, and urban and royal officials. In 1297, for example, extreme violence erupted at Lisbon's harbour between Portuguese and Basque, Cantabrian, and Galician merchants, resulting in at least ten dead and several wounded, for causes not entirely known to us; to make sure the 'Spanish' would not attack outgoing ships and commodities before reaching their destination, the Portuguese even took hostages.[70] This level of aggression was not very common, and the king was very cautious in dealing with these and other situations in order to protect the coming of foreign merchants: some safe-conducts granted, for instance, royal protection to foreign traders coming from places having disputes with the Portuguese, and compensations to merchants in the case of war.[71] On more than one occasion, the king ordered the council to act promptly in order to find those responsible for the seizure of commodities belonging to foreign merchants;[72] and, in another situation, reprehended municipal authorities for allowing privateers to attack under their jurisdiction.[73]

Due to the lack of council minutes and judicial sources in Portuguese archives, our current knowledge about the functioning of Lisbon's legal institutions is very limited. The customs house had its own judge to solve immediate problems, but the king was responsible for resolving the most striking matters involving foreign merchants. It was to the king that Portuguese merchants petitioned when they wanted to complain about unfair competition carried out by Genoese, Pisan, Flemish and others in retail trade, which royal ordinances prohibited foreign traders, or about the extraction of gold and silver from Portugal.[74] Although both of these problems were real, there was an undisclosed intention of convincing the king to protect Portuguese trade and traders.

In mid-fifteenth-century Lisbon, the major issue foreign merchants had to face was not violence but recklessness, corruption and abuse of power by port authorities and city officials, and the lack of efficiency of the judicial system. In 1454, 1456 and 1457, the resident communities of the English, the North Germans and the Flemish, respectively, protested against the way customs officials in Lisbon were treating them, and asked King Afonso V for solutions. The English submitted a long list of twenty-nine articles in which they complained about how port officials would take their arks from ships and seal them, even their private ones, forcing them to wear the same clothes sometimes for a fortnight; how they would steal their belongings and commodities; how they would offend them and slam the building's door in their faces; how they would sell their commodities for an unjust price and without merchants being present; and how port officials would take a lot of time to pass the necessary transportation licence for them to leave Lisbon's port if they did not give them a 50 'reais' gratuity.[75] The German representatives had similar complaints about how they were charged levies three to four times more than they should actually pay, and about how the officials were unable to speak their language – even though one of those officials should act as 'lingua', and communicate with foreigners.[76] Moreover, the German merchants explained to the king that they had been absent from Lisbon because of the 'injuries and little honour' in the way the Portuguese treated them. As for the Flemings, they too complained about illegal surcharges, language problems and diverted commodities.[77] More importantly, this petition complained that justice was very slow. All of this might have been true, and these petitions were carefully prepared, and extremely rhetorical, in order to make a point and convince the king of their demands.[78]

Lisbon grew substantially in the mid-fifteenth century, creating good conditions for the expansion of merchant networks, commercial contacts and corruption. Afonso V addressed these petitions, and his intervention probably solved the existing problems, since complaints after 1457 seem less serious than the ones presented by the English, the German and the Flemish merchant communities in Lisbon. Notwithstanding the language issues, illegal surcharges and random acts of corruption, foreign merchants had an interest in coming to Lisbon. Lisbon commanded the trade with the Atlantic islands and western Africa, offering Europeans overabundant commercial novelties and exciting news about the lands discovered and the peoples encountered.

Conclusion

In a letter dated 27 June 1501, Giovanni Matteo Cretico informed the Republic of Venice that the Portuguese had discovered the 'Land of Parrots' – Brazil – and that ships laden with spices were arriving in Lisbon.[79] Once again, Lisbon would provoke changes in European trade and in one's perception of the world. How could this apparently peripheral city in Europe become so relevant in the fifteenth- and sixteenth-century commercial networks?

We have seen that one of the remarkable characteristics of medieval Lisbon was the city's capacity to adapt to new circumstances, whether it was scarcity, war, changes in geopolitics, conquest or expansion. After a long period of social adjustment following the Christian conquest of 1147, Lisbon took advantage of the permanence of the king, the opening of the Straits of Gibraltar, the coming of foreign merchants and even the Hundred Years War to expand its influence and economic relevance. Lisbon also profited from commercial policies aimed at stimulating overseas trade by encouraging shipbuilding and developing maritime institutions. And from the mid-fifteenth century on, Lisbon was producing state-of-the-art cartography, vessels, nautical techniques and maritime instruments due to its pioneering role in the overseas expansion. However, we must take into account a few inadequacies of this economic system – such as the extreme political and economic centralization in Lisbon – which created major urban asymmetries in Portugal. The framework is not complete – there are huge historiographical gaps in the history of Lisbon needing to be addressed, namely the understanding of the fiscal system, the relation with the hinterland, socio-economic mobility and port complementarity. Notwithstanding these and other problems, it is possible to say that late medieval Lisbon was a cosmopolitan city, a relevant market, a point of cultural encounters and central stage in the interaction between Europeans, and between the Europeans and the others during the age of exploration.

Notes

1 C.W. David (ed.), *De Expugnatione Lyxbonensi. The Conquest of Lisbon*, New York: Columbia University Press, 1936.
2 D. de Góis, *Urbis Olisiponis Descriptio*, Lisbon: Guimarães Editores, 2002, p. 83.
3 A. A. Andrade, 'La Dimensión Urbana de un Espacio Atlántico: Lisboa', in *XXXIII Semana de Estudios Medievales: Mercado Inmobiliario y Paisajes Urbanos en el Occidente Europeo: Siglos XI–XV*, Pamplona: Gobierno de Navarra, Institución Príncipe de Viana, 2007.
4 L. D'Arienzo, *La Presenza Italiana in Spagna al Tempo di Colombo*, Rome: Istituto poligrafico e Zecca dello Stato, Libreria dello Stato, 2010, p. 84.
5 L. Ventura, *D. Afonso III*, Lisboa: Temas e Debates, 2009, pp. 197ff.
6 L. M Duarte, 'Zaccaria, Pessagno, Bocanegra: Os Almirantes Genoveses Nos Primórdios Das Marinhas De Guerra De Castela, França E Portugal', in L. Gallinari (ed.), *Genova: Una 'Porta' Del Mediterraneo*, Genoa: CNR – Istituto di Storia dell'Europa mediterranea, 2005, pp. 259–94.
7 N. Ferguson, *Civilization: The West and the Rest*, London: Allen Lane, 2011, p. 53.
8 C. Antunes, Globalisation in the Early Modern Period: The Economic Relationship between Amsterdam and Lisbon, 1640–1705, Amsterdam: Aksant, 2004.
9 Andrade, 'La Dimensión Urbana'.
10 A. H. de O. Marques, *Hansa e Portugal na Idade Média*, 2 edn, Lisbon: Presença, 1993; C. Torres, 'Lisboa Muçulmana: Um Espaço Urbano e o seu Território', *Arqueologia Medieval* 7, 2001, pp. 427–34; A. A. Andrade, 'A Estratégia Régia em Relação aos Portos Marítimos no Portugal Medieval: O Caso da Fachada Atlântica', in B. Arízaga Bolumburu and J. A. Solórzano Telechea (eds), *Ciudades y Villas Portuarias del Atlántico en la Edad Media*, Logroño: Instituto de Estudios Riojanos, 2004, pp. 57–89.
11 F. Melis, *I Mercanti Italiani dell'Europa Medievale e Rinascimentale*, Florence: Le Monnier, 1990; C. Verlinden, 'Italian influence in Iberian colonization', *Hispanic American Historical Review* 1953, 33/2, pp. 199–211; V. Rau, 'Uma Família de Mercadores Italianos em Portugal no Século XV: Os Lomellini', *Revista da Faculdade de Letras* 22, 1956, pp. 97–117; L. D'Arienzo, *La Presenza degli Italiani in Portogallo al Tempo di Colombo*, Rome: Istituto Poligrafico e Zecca dello Stato libreria dello Stato, 2003; F. Guidi-Bruscoli, *Bartolomeo Marchionni. 'Homem De Grossa Fazenda' (Ca. 1450–1530): Un Mercante Fiorentino a Lisbona e L'impero Portoghese*, Florence: L. S. Olschki, 2014; J. Sequeira, 'A Companhia Salviati-Da Colle e o Comércio de Panos de Seda Florentinos em Lisboa no Século XV', *De Medio Aevo* 7/1, 2015, pp. 47–62.
12 Luís Miguel Duarte, 'Um País Sem Cidades? O Mundo Urbano em Portugal na Idade Média', in M. González Jiménez (ed.), *El Mundo Urbano en la Castilla del Siglo XIII*, Seville: Ayuntamiento de Ciudad Real, 2006, pp. 243–57.
13 J. J. A. Dias, 'A População', in J. J. A. Dias (ed.), *Portugal. Do Renascimento à Crise Dinástica, Nova História de Portugal*, Lisbon: Editorial Presença, 1998, pp. 18–20.
14 E. M. Carus-Wilson, 'The overseas trade of Bristol', in E. Power and M. M. Postan (eds), *Studies in English Trade in the Fifteenth Century*, London: Routledge, 1933, p. 222. Popplau's account is quoted in A. de S. S. C. Lobo, *História da Sociedade Portuguesa no Século XV*, Lisbon: Imprensa Nacional, 1903, p. 113.

15 M. A. Ladero Quesada, 'Sociedade Bajomedieval: Crisis y Recuperación Económica', in V. A. Álvarez Palenzuela (ed.), *Historia De España de la Edad Media*, Barcelona: Ariel, 2007, pp. 815–41.
16 Many thanks to Maryanne Kowaleski, Monique O'Connell and Wim Blockmans for an interesting exchange of ideas on the demography of late medieval Europe. For more on this, see R. Finlay and B. Shearer, 'Population growth and suburban expansion', in A. L. Beier and R Finlay (eds), *London 1500 1700: The Making of the Metropolis*, London: Longman, 1986, pp. 37–59; J.-P. Leguay, 'Urban life', in M. Jones (ed.), *The New Cambridge Medieval History*, vol. 6, *c. 1300–c. 1415*, Cambridge: Cambridge University Press, 2000, p. 104; P. Malanima, *Pre-Modern European Economy: One Thousand Years (10th–19th Centuries)*, Leiden: Brill, 2009, pp. 6–17.
17 Wim Blockmans, 'Voracious states and obstructing cities: an aspect of state formation in preindustrial Europe', *Theory and Society* 5, 1989, p. 734.
18 A. A. Andrade, 'Le pouvoir royal et les villes portugaises au Moyen Âge', in B. Dumons and O. Zeller (eds), *La Ville Européenne et ses Pouvoirs du Moyen Âge au XXe siècle*, Paris: L'Harmattan, 2006, pp. 15–28.
19 *AML (Arquivo Municipal de Lisboa), Livro I de Cortes*, doc. 23.
20 D. Igual Luís, '*Non Ha Portto Alcuno, Ma Sola Spiaggia:* La Actividade Marítima Valenciana en el Siglo XV', *Aragón en la Edad Media* 25, 2014, pp. 101–34.
21 Sequeira, 'A Companhia Salviati-Da Colle', p. 50.
22 Torres, 'Lisboa Muçulmana', p. 73.
23 *CPR (Calendar of Patent Rolls)*, Richard II, part 2, pp. 142–3.
24 J. C. Pereira, 'Organização e administração alfandegárias de Portugal no século XVI (1521–1557)', in *Portugal na era deQuinhentos*, Cascais: Câmara Municipal, 2003, p. 64.
25 M. E. Mallett, *The Florentine Galleys in the Fifteenth Century*. Oxford: Clarendon Press, 1967, pp. 62–3.
26 *ANTT* (*Arquivo Nacional Torre do Tombo*), *Chancelaria de D. Afonso V*, Livro 31, fol. 80v, doc. 4.
27 *DP* (*Descobrimentos Portugueses. Documentos para a sua história*) edited by João da Silva Marques (Lisbon, 1944), suppl. vol. 1, pp. 539, 1027; 540, 1033; 560, 1124, passim.
28 *DP*, vol. 1, pp. 158–60.
29 *DP*, vol. 1, p. 157.
30 L. F. Costa, 'Carpinteiros e Calafates da Ribeira das Naus: Um Olhar sobre Lisboa de Quinhentos', *Penélope* 13, 1994, p. 40.
31 C. R. de Oliveira, *Lisboa Em 1551*, Lisbon: Livros Horizonte, 1987.
32 Mário Farelo, A Oligarquia Camarária de Lisboa (1325–1433), Lisboa: University of Lisbon PhD thesis, 2008. See the 'Corpo prosopográfico'.
33 Ibid., pp. 191–2.
34 *AML, Livro II de D. João II*, doc. 38.
35 L. Salles, Estudo sobre as Portagens e as Alfândegas em Portugal (Séculos XII a XVI), Lisbon: Livraria Ferreira, 1891, pp. 27–34.
36 E. F. de Oliveira (ed.), *Elementos para a História do Município de Lisboa*, 17 vols, vol. 1 Lisbon: Typographia Universal, 1882, vol 1, p. 286.
37 A. H. de O. Marques, *Introdução à História da Agricultura em Portugal*, 3rd edn, Lisbon: Edições Cosmos, 1978, p. 59.
38 *AML, Livro II do Provimento do Pão*, doc. 13; *Livro I de Provimento de Ofícios*, doc. 44.
39 *AML, Livro I do Provimento da Saúde*, doc. 2.
40 For example, the work by O. Gelderblom, Cities of Commerce: The Institutional Foundations of International Trade in the Low Countries, 1250–1650, Princeton: Princeton University Press, 2013.

41 H. da G. Barros, *História da Administração Pública em Portugal nos Séculos XII a XV*, 2nd edn, 11 vols, vol. 10, Lisbon: Sá da Costa, 1945–54, pp. 173–4.
42 On the salt monopoly, see *AML, Livro dos Pregos*, doc. 406.
43 *ANTT, Chancelaria de D. Afonso V*, liv. 13, fol. 50v.
44 H. da G. Barros, *História da Administração Pública*, vol. 9, p. 116.
45 R. da C. Dominguez, 'O Financiamento da Coroa Portuguesa nos Finais da Idade Média: Entre o Africano e o Venturoso', University of Porto, PhD thesis, 2013.
46 F. Miranda, 'Portugal and the medieval Atlantic: commercial diplomacy, merchants, and trade, 1143–1488', University of Porto, PhD thesis, 2012, pp. 163–5.
47 V. M. Godinho, *A Expansão Quatrocentista Portuguesa*, 2nd edn, Lisbon: Dom Quixote, 2008.
48 For more on Portuguese merchant networks, see F. Miranda, 'Network takers or network makers? The Portuguese traders in the Medieval West', in A. Caracausi and C. Jeggle (eds), *Commercial Networks and European Cities, 1400–1800*, London: Pickering & Chatto, 2014, pp. 171–86.
49 *CPR*, Henry III, vol. 2, p. 43. *CPR*, Edward III, vol. 3, p. 69.
50 M. de Laurière (ed.), *Ordonnances des Rois de France*, Paris: Imprimerie Royale, 1723, vol. 2, pp. 157–8.
51 *CCR (Calendar of Close Rolls)*, Edward III, vol. 3, p. 704. *DP*, suppl. vol. 1, p. 333.
52 *DP*, vol. 3, 65–6.
53 F. Lopes, *Crónica de D. Fernando*, 2nd edn, Lisbon: Imprensa Nacional-Casa da Moeda, 2004, p. 6.
54 D. de Góis, *Lisboa de Quinhentos: Descrição de Lisboa*, Lisbon: Livraria Avelar Machado, 1937, p. 48.
55 R. S. Lopez, 'Majorcans and Genoese on the North Sea route in the thirteenth century', *Revue belge de philologie et d'histoire* 29/4, 1951, p. 1165.
56 *DP*, suppl. vol. 1, p. 30.
57 W. R. Childs, *Trade and Shipping in the Medieval West: Portugal, Castile, and England*, Porto: Fédération Internationale des Instituts d'Études Médiévales, 2013, p. 107.
58 J. J. A. Dias (ed.), *Chancelarias Portuguesas: D. João I*, 10 vols., vol. 1/3, Lisbon: Universidade de Nova Lisboa. Centro de Estudos Históricos, 2004, doc. 1296, p. 182.
59 Dias, *Chancelarias Portuguesas*, vol. 2/1, doc. II-414, p. 222.
60 *CPR*, Henry IV, part 2, vol. 4, p. 435.
61 Marques, *Hansa e Portugal*, p. 100.
62 J. Paviot, 'Les portuguais à Bruges au XVe siècle', in *Arquivos do Centro Cultural Calouste Gulbenkian* vol. 38, Paris: Arquivos do Centro Cultural Calouste Gulbenkian, 1999, doc. 124bis.
63 D. Nicholas, *Medieval Flanders*, London: Longman, 1992, pp. 389–90; P. Spufford, *Power and Profit: The Merchant in Medieval Europe*, New York: Thames & Hudson, 2003, p. 309; R. van Answaarden (ed.), *Les Portugais devant le Grand Conseil des Pays-Bas (1460–1580)*, Paris: Fondation Calouste Gulbenkian, Centre culturel portugais, 1991, doc. 11.
64 Guidi-Bruscoli, *Bartolomeo Marchionni*, p. 10.
65 *DP*, suppl. vol. 1, pp. 75–6.
66 *AML, Livro dos Pregos*, doc. 320.
67 According to the letters of protection recorded by the Portuguese chancellery of Afonso V.
68 See the forthcoming study by H. Casado Alonso and F. Miranda. 'The Iberian economy and commercial exchange with northwestern Europe in the later Middle Ages', in E. T. Jones and R. Stone, *The World of the Newport Ship*, Cardiff: Wales University Press, 2016.
69 Carus-Wilson, 'Overseas Trade of Bristol', pp. 220–1.
70 *DP*, suppl. vol. 1, pp. 21–2.
71 *DP*, vol. 1, pp. 64–5.
72 *AML, Livro dos Pregos*, doc. 54.

73 *AML, Livro II de D. João II*, doc. 38. As mentioned above in the section on 'Urban council and the king's visible hand'.
74 *DP*, suppl. vol. 1, pp. 65, 308, passim.
75 Barros, *História da Administração Pública*, vol. 10, pp. 258ff.
76 *DP*, suppl. vol. 1, pp. 356ff.
77 *DP*, suppl. vol. 1, pp. 259ff.
78 A. de Sousa, *As Cortes Medievais Portuguesas (1385–1490)*, 2 vols, vol. 1, Porto: Instituto Nacional de Investigação Científica, 1990, pp. 495–6.
79 A. B. de Andrade, *Mundos Novos do Mundo: Panorama da difusão, pela Europa, de notícias dos Descobrimentos Geográficos Portugueses*, Lisbon: Junta de Investigações do Ultramar, 1972, pp. 248–52, 260–2; D. S. Chambers, 'Venetian Perceptions of Portugal, c.1500', in K. J. P. Lowe (ed.), *Cultural Links between Portugal and Italy in the Renaissance*, Oxford: Oxford University Press, 2000, pp. 28–9.

20

THE MARITIME TRADE AND SOCIETY OF LA ROCHELLE IN THE LATE MIDDLE AGES

Mathias Tranchant

In the historiography of medieval France, maritime trade may appear to be a rather old-fashioned topic. In the nineteenth century, the attraction of the sea and its landscapes occupied the collective imagination and it then became a particularly interesting theme for professional historians and learned people. The literature of the period shows all kinds of publications on the topic, from anecdotal stories of small coastal towns to dictionaries and compilations of old maritime law. The best examples are the solid and voluminous works of positivistic inspiration, published in the 1850s and 1860s on the trade and navigation of the cities of Rouen and Bordeaux.[1] The subject matter may be traditional but it was atypical insofar as it shed a new light the history of communities that until then had only been envisaged from the viewpoint of territory, war, politics and religion.

It isn't easy, however, to assess the maritime activities in medieval France because of the scarcity and poor quality of the remaining port accounts. In contrast to English harbours, nearly all the customs accounts of French towns on the coasts and the estuaries have disappeared. Those that have been preserved for Dieppe are not very informative because they don't mention the beneficiaries of exemptions.[2] This is also the sad reality for La Rochelle, which has only extremely poor accounting sources. Therefore, it is impossible to draw any graph of the economic trends, the variation and intensity of which can only be presumed on the basis of narrative sources, regulations, and judicial and notarial documents.[3] The latter do contain information about several aspects of the maritime trade at La Rochelle, such as the products exchanged, the ships used, the port infrastructure, the related harbours, regulations and fiscal conditions concerning the commerce. Moreover, in the sixteenth and seventeenth centuries, compilations have been made of urban privileges and annals, which as a whole make up a corpus of exceptional quality offering insights in several aspects of the merchant community's life.

In the first centuries of its existence, La Rochelle was identifiable through its commerce. Its foundation as a typical *ville neuve*, a new town, is an expression of the twelfth-century's economic growth in southwestern France. Its creation and jump-start emanated from a double ambition: one political, and the other economic. A feudal conflict between Count William X of Aquitaine and his turbulent vassal, the lord of Châtelaillon who dominated the maritime activities between the rivers Sèvre and Charente, was at the origins. The vassal was subjugated in 1130–1, and the count founded a new urban and port centre in order to consolidate his grip on the promising coast. He envisaged thereby to control the widespread feudal agitation, and to insert this region into the booming maritime trade. On the basis of what had until then been just an ordinary fishermen's village, Count William undertook a true settlement policy, which was continued and expanded since 1152 by his Plantagenet successors. In 1175 La Rochelle was the first agglomeration in the French centre-west to be elevated to the rank of a commune. In only four decades, the immigration movement had reached such importance that the public authorities found it necessary to create an institutional framework for their commercial and urban activities. The ducal, and later royal agents' endeavours came into conflict with the emancipatory desire of the local population. In the end, the latter's solid grasp on the markets for salt and wine provided them with a unique economic strength to negotiate liberties, which extended much further than those usually conceded to urban communities.

La Rochelle and its *banlieue*: a centre of production, exchange and redistribution

La Rochelle's prosperity derived from the production and sale of wine, which fostered most of the inhabitants' fortunes. The economic development of the Aunis region since the twelfth century was based in wine and salt.[4] The regions north of the Seine, where an equally strong urbanization process occurred in the same period, lacked these products and their demand stimulated in a very early stage the construction of vineyards south of the Loire.[5] Favourable climatic conditions, in particular the abundant sunshine and rare frost in spring, made it possible to produce vintages of steady quality and quantity in the Aunis. Its relatively northern location made it easily accessible from the non-wine-producing regions.[6] In the middle of the thirteenth century, the vineyards around La Rochelle extended over an estimated minimum of 20,000 hectares, and in normal years they would have produced 45,000 barrels. That amount fell to zero only during years of heavy crisis in the late Middle Ages.

Their moderately good taste and quality brought the Aunis wines within the reach of mass consumption. They were cheaper than their main competitors, the Bordeaux wines, which made them particularly attractive for the middle classes in cities in England, the Low Countries and the Hanse area.[7] An ordinance promulgated in England on 1 January 1383 establishing the prices of wines in wholesale and in retail showed that the products from Gascogne, Auxerre and Spain were more expensive than those from La Rochelle.[8] Thanks to the moderate price, these came within the reach of numerous and not overly exigent customers, and the sellers targeted this relatively stable market for their abundant production. In 1392, Bordeaux traders complained that English merchants sold grain in their city but turned to buy the cheaper wines in La Rochelle.[9] And some local merchants imitated the barrels used in the southwest to increase the commercial value of their wines and make a higher profit.[10] In this price competition with the Gironde region, La Rochelle enjoyed the additional advantage of lower transport costs for the buyers coming from the northern regions.[11]

From the middle of the thirteenth century, La Rochelle was the principal outlet for the whole of central-western France, which created intensive commercial relations between the port and its hinterland. This provided the resources for the city's consumption, artisanal production and trade. The port's connections with traders from southern as well as from Northern Europe made it the redistribution centre for foreign merchandise towards the hinterland, as well as the outlet for agricultural surpluses. This intermediary role diversified its commercial potential (Figure 20.1).

Most of the land in the city's nearby environment had progressively been developed into vineyards, pushing the production of grain, timber, meat and later on also that of cloth and other crafts further off. These were transported downstream on the Sèvre and Charente and could eventually be commercialized further on. Some indications concerning the trade of cloth, glass, tiles and pottery point to surplus to be marketed in the harbour. In return, the foreign shippers were keen to avoid sailing

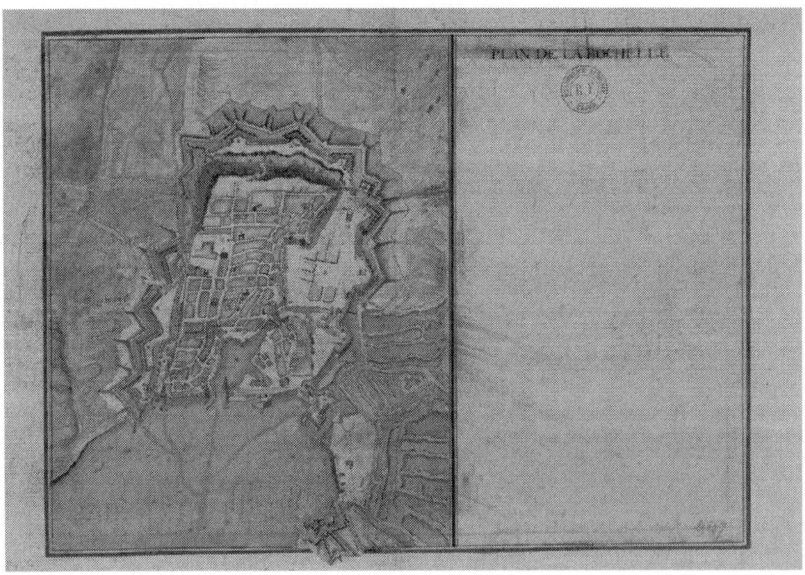

Figure 20.1 Plan of La Rochelle and its harbour. The shape of La Rochelle's port became stabilized in the early thirteenth century. By the end of the fifteenth it had become entirely fortified, which was rare along the Atlantic coast. The entry was marked by two solid towers and it could be shut off by a chain. Around fifty big naves could be moored in the harbour

with too little cargo, so after unloading their goods in the harbour of La Rochelle they continued from there to Poitou and Saintonge to provide for the needs of the crafts, the towns and the lords in those regions. Merchants from Burgos made La Rochelle one of their outlets; they had gotten heavily involved in the wool trade since the English wool exports had diminished by the fourteenth century.[12] They regularly provided the wool for the textile crafts in the small towns in the region, particularly in Poitou. The great fleets calling at La Rochelle for wine and salt increased the opportunities for Castilian traders to find buyers for their wool, which was to be processed by the North European textile industries. Although we know just a tiny part of all these redistributing relations, there is no doubt that they contributed to the fortune of the spice dealers whose clients were to be found among the lords and burghers in centre-west France.

The redistribution function substantially contributed to La Rochelle's commercial potential. Even if the local economy was dominated by wine exports, the city's role as interface constituted a commercial bounty as it extended and consolidated the customers and limited the opportunities of competition from neighbouring ports. The regional trade rested on the main port's role as the privileged partner. On this point, the salt from Saintonge exemplifies the strong attraction of La Rochelle's market. Unfortunately, we have only fragmentary information about barges active in and around its harbour, and nothing at all is known about their movements outside a range of 75 km. Even if the transport on the rivers and roads in the Aunis was difficult, the economic outreach of La Rochelle was comparable to that of the great capital cities Bordeaux and Toulouse. However, its communication system penetrated a region where production and consumption had a lower density and were less developed. The available sources don't make it possible to quantify the volume and the value of the merchandise brought to the hinterland and re-exported from there; the best we can do is to list the main products. Nevertheless, it is clear that the returns of La Rochelle's interface position remained far below those of the great harbours at the mouth of an estuary.

In any case, grain was the dominant product of the medieval subsistence economy, while the region around La Rochelle produced nearly exclusively wine. It was difficult for this region to compete with the nearby wine-growing regions Saintonges and Gascogne. To get its share, it created control mechanisms on the means of production and exchange in its environment. For that purpose a space called the *banlieue* was clearly delimited in 1347,[13] which made a sharp separation possible between indigenous and foreign merchandise. The regional production was dominated by wine-growing, leaving cereals, cattle-breeding, salt-making and fisheries far behind. In the thirteenth century, burghers were the main owners of landed estates but during the Hundred Years War (1337–1453) church institutions accumulated most of the property. Burghers instead invested in buildings and equipment for the production (*treuils*), which were the real power structures that the harvests needed to pass through.[14] Burghers thus controlled the means of production, and, moreover, they increasingly kept the wine growers of the *banlieue* dependent on their financial potential. Notaries Noyrault (1468–9) and Sorin (1489–90) and many of their confrères in the sixteenth century regularly contracted peasants in the months just preceding the harvest, when their needs were greatest, to cede their future vintage at a low price to moneylenders from the city.[15] These grasped the opportunity to increase their stocks of wine in view of the great market in the autumn, increasing pressure on the villagers. As in many other regions surrounding French towns in the late Middle Ages, a vertical concentration was installed in regard to the land, the means of production and the storage infrastructure. The burghers of La Rochelle, more than their ecclesiastical and aristocratic competitors, appropriated the lion's share of the vintage returns, also taking advantage of the peasants' indebtedness.

Beyond the landed estates, the harvests and the wine presses, control of the viticulture required the strict command of the means of conditioning and commercialization. In February 1347, La Rochelle acquired the monopoly on the production of wine-casks in the region,[16] and, on the other hand, they didn't miss any occasion to impose their own products in the *banlieue*.[17] La Rochelle effectively concentrated most of the wine trade, as it was also home to the mint, scores of moneychangers and notaries, and its commercial and financial networks. The ports of the *banlieue* were reduced to a supportive role, which was essential to the main port as it simply lacked the capacity to handle all the loading and unloading operations. From 2 September 1338, even the retail in the city became restricted to the burghers and their products. The rare merchants from the *banlieue* were simply excluded as competitors.[18]

The wine commonly described in the documents as being 'from La Rochelle' was thus a product from within the administrative circumscription of the *banlieue*, and therefore 'bourgeois'. This relates to an essential motive for the creation of the *banlieue*. In the context of an economy characterized by protectionism, it was essential for the people of La Rochelle, as for their neighbours, to establish the production modes of their wine in order to make it easily identifiable for the buyers.[19] Thus they clarified the area where the wine was produced and the method of processing and thereby protected it against internal and external competition. It was equally important to fix the selling time. And from 1229, the import into the city of wines produced outside the *banlieue* was prohibited from 30 November until the next vintage.[20] One can argue that the fixing of strict limits of the *banlieue* was inspired in the first place by protectionist motives, and then also by a kind of commercial communication and promotion strategy.

The commune: a merchants' association

After Louis VIII took hold of La Rochelle, 1,751 citizens swore loyalty to him on 13 August 1224. The list of their names shows how diverse the new community they had founded really was. Besides those who had their roots in the hinterland, many of them had come from Brittany, England, Ireland, Normandy, Picardy and Flanders, and some even from Castile and Italy.[21] The original composition of La Rochelle's community was characterized by a strong cosmopolitanism, which was typical for places of maritime trade. The character remained intact until the end of the fifteenth century. Bretons in particular, who were the great maritime transporters, delivered essential naval assistance to the merchants of La Rochelle. Poverty often led them to give up their positions as shippers, hoping for a better life in the rich Aunis. One finds them as simple agricultural labourers who also enjoyed the position of citizen, at all levels of the local society.

Merchants from the Basque region, from Cantabria, Asturia and Galicia, founded a very important colony in La Rochelle that stubbornly pushed for commercial advantages and legal and fiscal privileges, which the French authorities benevolently granted them. Their power continued to grow in the fourteenth and fifteenth centuries. Although their presence was surely much older,[22] the years 1372 and 1419 particularly marked their ascendance.[23] Their successive victories in front of La Rochelle over English and Hanseatic fleets made them masters of the Gascony Gulf and soon also of the Channel. In this way they secured their vital communication lines. La Rochelle became a fundamental relay station for their commercial activities, the most southern of the four factories by which they controlled the price of their wool exports – the others being Nantes, Rouen and Bruges.[24] The conditions of their trade became even more advantageous during the six years (1487–93) when the Nantes staple was transferred towards the Aunis. In those years, they were the only foreigners who did not have to pay contributions for the repair of the city wall, and the authorities granted them the right to levy two taxes themselves, probably with the aim of letting them maintain their own infrastructure and staff. The position of the Castilians in La Rochelle became so strong that a request of the aldermen, probably dated around 1493, declared that the commune was afraid that 'it would lead to the enserfment of the local population and the freedom of the said Spaniards'.[25]

The activities of the Flemings and their residence were facilitated equally by protective measures and privileges from the thirteenth century. They had long had their own chapel in the church of the Carmelites. In 1462, Louis XI confirmed their exemption from the rights of shipwreck and jettison originally promulgated in 1191 and 1374; moreover, he confirmed the royal safe-conduct for their persons and their goods, edicted in 1240. The king also conceded the right to have their internally Flemish conflicts settled by the aldermen of their home towns. The cases of appeal were to be brought to the nearest royal court. The major advance made in this charter consisted of the admission of the right to conclude transactions in wholesale trade of imported goods between Flemish merchants. They were only obliged to sell them to non-Flemings if these offered the equivalent price. They were entitled to raise a tax for the maintenance of their chapel, and to buy houses in the city, on the condition of being permanent residents.[26]

The Hansards had also established a factory that was extremely dynamic until 1420. Several German merchants and factors held residence there during the whole year. They had their own council with competence to settle conflicts on the spot and to inform the members about decisions of the general assembly of the Hanse, the Hansetag. In 1421, the council had to mediate in a dispute between the Lübeck merchant Greverode and his confrère from Stralsund.[27]

In the late Middle Ages, the burghers of La Rochelle displayed a remarkable corporate spirit, the attitude of which contrasts with the internal conflicts that shook urban elites so often in those days.[28] The quality of the communal statutes may have contributed to this effect, as they guaranteed a strong cohesion in their representative assembly, as granted by Henry II in the charter of 1175 and amended consecutively. In the institutions of Rouen, which were probably modelled after those from La Rochelle, the assembly was composed of a hundred sworn men. The *maire* was chosen for a year as head of the assembly to be in charge of most of the competences conceded to the commune; a council of twelve councillors and twelve aldermen (*échevins*) assisted him in his tasks. Every fortnight, seventy-five 'peers' met with them in the assembly of one hundred members to discuss the matters that arose.[29] As the members of the representative bodies were coopted by the families for their lifetime,[30] they formed an oligarchy of privileged people whose interests seemingly did not diverge from those of the citizenry as a whole, as often happened elsewhere.

The elite seemed to be keenly attentive to the representation of different categories of burghers in the urban institutions. They introduced amendments to the original communal statutes to secure the participation of several social and economic sectors in the assemblies and executive bodies. On 31 March 1382, it was decided to establish an equal division among the twenty-four members of the council as eight merchants, eight lawyers and eight citizens belonging to other sectors. This repartition was extended in 1401–2 to all the pairs, the statute of which was confirmed in 1487. Members of the clergy and the aristocracy were excluded from the assembly of one hundred. In 1399, the *maire* Jehan Cheillon had already decided that a clergyman was not entitled to citizenship. Only the municipal nobility, the *noblesse de cloche*, was represented in the communal assembly. Instead, Charles V granted on 8 January 1373 that all *maires, échevins* and councillors of La Rochelle would be knighted. This entailed the rights and privileges of that estate, especially to hold fiefs and lordships while being exempt from the feudal ban and after-ban, and in practice kept their commercial activities going. This 'bourgeois' nobility, the only one that seems to have been allowed to combine commercial activities with noble status, was the class that could integrate the three categories composing the city's ruling class, namely the merchants, the lawyers and the other citizens.

This institutional setting prevented the conservative influence of the ecclesiastic and aristocratic spheres to hold sway in La Rochelle against the entrepreneurial spirit of the citizens; it also protected the city against the internal rivalries within the aristocracy, which often disturbed the civic order and the urban governments. The producer, the merchant and the notary formed the three pillars of the communal structure as well as of the mercantile activity. In this way, an intimate relationship united the commercial capacities and the communal institutions.

The communal institutions and economic privileges

The authorities of La Rochelle defended the communal privileges under all circumstances and strove for their expansion wherever possible. Nearly every year in the fourteenth and fifteenth centuries offered an occasion to confirm or improve the city's interests or those of their partners. The aldermen remained alert to the respect of their prerogatives and their jurisdiction, which were gradually expanded at the expense of those of officers in the king's service or that of local lords. Conflicts arose about particular issues, such as the defence of the exemption to pay ecclesiastical dimes, which Philip IV granted to the inhabitants of the *banlieue*, but was contested by the bishop of Saintes from 1305 until 1407. On other occasions, the *maire*'s judicial rights or fiscal privileges had to be maintained.[31] The commune's jurisdiction in general was the object of administrative disputes and complaints. From 1398 to 1499, a series of enquiries and settlements ended favourably overall for the people of La Rochelle.[32] From 1209, the commune held the chests containing the privileges under surveillance by citizens, and rightly so because they were constantly under pressure. In 1462, 1467 and 1478 officers of the Chambre des Comptes (the royal accounting office) came from Paris for verifications. In the last of those years, the *maire* Pierre Pierre ordered their transcription in two beautiful books of parchment, one of which was to be kept in the city's charterhouse in the tower of Moureilles, the other remaining under the *maire*'s responsibility.[33]

In line with the protection provided by all merchants' associations, the city government procured for the citizens collective liability for commercial risks. For instance, from 1294 onwards, the commune decided to grant a delay of payment to indebted burghers, secured by the common funds. In particular, a fund of 200 pounds *tournois* was reserved for the support of members of the urban government in case they faced solvency problems. This regulation was confirmed, detailed and extended in 1407. The provision was self-evidently not applicable to bankruptcies following die games, a luxurious lifestyle or excessive expenses. On the other hand, the peers were assisted in case of failure due to losses caused by the fortunes of the sea. One may suggest that this provision explains, at least in part, the late and rare appearance of share contracts (*parsonnerie*) or maritime insurance. The urban institutions fulfilled an essential role to protect the local mercantile activities on all levels, from the mediation of trade disputes to the negotiations of agreements with overseas authorities. In these matters, as with regard to fiscal issues, the commune was invested with fundamental responsibilities, which it handled in 'common providence', even if some authors have pointed to the weight this laid on the medieval markets.

The fiscal system and commercial policy

The mercantile communities of the western Mediterranean, the Ponant, found themselves in lively competition, especially in the sectors of wine and salt. Their competitive position depended therefore a great deal on the amount of taxes levied on trade. For that reason, the government of La Rochelle saw this issue as central to its economic policy. They held a keen eye to the maintenance of fiscal privileges of burghers and foreign merchants, while also trying to keep the duties on trade moderate.

The local system of fiscal exemptions was affected only marginally by the overall increase of the fiscal pressure in France. On 24 August 1200, Philip Augustus had entirely exempted the citizens of La Rochelle from all indirect taxes on trade in their city, as well as in the whole kingdom. This privilege was confirmed at least fourteen times until the end of the fifteenth century.[34] The November 1461 ratification granted franchise of most of the harbour and urban taxes related to the circulation of goods through the kingdom. The exemptions did not touch, however, the whole set of levies belonging to the *prévoté*, the domain of the provost. The old taxes, known as *coustumes anciennes*, were maintained for a long time, until Charles VII liberated the citizens definitively from the 2½ pennies tax on the wine imported into the city.[35] The exemptions did not apply to the subsidies recently conceded to the crown, although the urban government systematically pressurized the crown to keep the citizens and even the inhabitants of the *banlieue* free. It is not possible to reconstruct exactly which concessions – 'written or unwritten' – the king made in order to stimulate La Rochelle's economic activities and to maintain good relations with the port, which was seen since the twelfth century as the 'key to the country'.[36] The wide-ranging fiscal immunity kept La Rochelle in a position of strength with regard to her competitors on the French as well as the international markets.

The city's economic prosperity also depended on the dynamism of foreign merchants who were equally keen on obtaining fiscal advantages, which were stipulated in particular agreements between their prince and the king of France. Protection of their persons and their goods were a general item, and tax privileges were granted especially for the import of food and goods scarcely found in the region. On 6 October 1390, Charles VI liberated all merchants from outside France of all taxes on the first sale of their goods in La Rochelle, a privilege confirmed in 1461. In the latter year, all imports of grain to the city, by sea or by land, were freed from the levy of 12 pennies per pound that was applied in the rest of the kingdom. And, in order to stimulate the export, the wines produced in the *banlieue* were exempted from the tax of one gold écu per barrel generally levied on all exports of wine out of the kingdom by foreign merchants.[37]

Individual careers and common interests

The municipal government saw it as their task to defend the communal interests under all circumstances, and therefore all the expenses its emissaries had to make for this purpose were taken in charge. From 1258 onwards, successive regulations were issued to provide horses for the *maire*, aldermen, councillors or peers, as well as for their followers, during their missions 'for the city's business'. Since 1370, the *maire* was awarded 125 pounds per year to cover his travel expenses. Members of the government who refused to accomplish a mission were fined 200 pounds, as happened in the 1331 case of the defence of sire Jean Poussard, whose wines had been smashed.

Some exceptional personalities belonging to the council of one hundred attained high offices in the royal administration, wherein they were expected to support the city's interests as much as they could. In the early fifteenth century, the lawyer and alderman André Marchand was royal councillor at the Parlement and provost of the city of Paris. For that reason, the government of La Rochelle decided in 1413 to make an exception and lift the strict rule of residence, motivated by the fact 'that, thanks to those offices . . . he has always been, and will continue to be able to please and render service to the city and to her commune, as much and even more than if he would keep his residence in the city'. In the course of the fifteenth century, three generations of the Mérichon family succeeded each other from father to son as *maires*, while at the same time fulfilling offices in the royal administration that provided them with influence to favour the city's affairs. All three were appointed royal governor of the city at some moment of their career. They also acquired all or some of the offices of seneschal of the island of Ré, bailiff of the Great Fief of Aunis, general collector of the royal aids in Saintonge and Aunis, councillor, master at the Chambre des Comptes (Accounting Office), and, above all, the king's chamberlain. The Annals of La Rochelle relate that Jean Mérichon, who had been sent as ambassador to the king in Tours in 1468, 'did great business' pleading for the city's interests. Members of the Doriole family made similar careers. In 1472, Pierre obtained the prestigious office of chancellor of France. All in all, members of about thirty families held offices in the royal administration in the fifteenth century.[38] On the local level as well as on that of the kingdom, they were in charge of missions with a diplomatic, economic and judicial character and could make the city's voice heard and take care of its interests. Their brilliantly rising careers owed a lot to the means and protection guaranteed by the communal institutions. It was considered natural that they should support the success of the collective interests in return.[39]

Communal institutions and mercantile interests

A substantial share of the important fiscal revenues from the commercial exchanges passing through La Rochelle, her *banlieue*, and the provinces Aunis and Saintonge flowed into the city's treasury. The municipal government was constantly concerned about the revenues of the rights on the port and within the city, and how to deal with tax evasion. Numerous measures were taken at the level of communal officers, especially that of the treasurers, aiming at reducing abuses, misappropriations and fraud. The Annals of La Rochelle mention about sixty decisions taken by the aldermen during the fourteenth and fifteenth centuries to clarify the collectors' remuneration, the duties and limits of their job, and to specify the rules of their office. All these measures were clearly intended at safeguarding the city's 'common pennies'.

Nevertheless, some members of the urban elite saw the municipal fiscal revenues as a source of individual profit. A share of the revenues, which is impossible to measure, flowed directly into the pockets of office-holders who were thought to be protected by total impunity. By the end of the fifteenth century, the royal administration launched clear accusations: 'there are eighteen or twenty of them who take and steal all the city's common pennies; and one can see at a glance that no sanctions are being taken against them'.[40] One may ask if this also motivated the city's administrators to insist repeatedly on the integration of the royal aids and subsidies into the city's fiscal domain, on the one hand, and on fending off any control of the city's accounts by royal officers, on the other.[41] In 1422, Charles VII had attempted to counter the frauds by issuing a prohibition for the *maire*, aldermen and peers to 'raise any aids, poll taxes and impositions, to lease any of the city's revenues or to take a share in them as companion or shareholder'.[42] However, on 3 September 1444 he had to condemn them to a fine of 2,500 francs because they had created several taxes without his consent, or usurped them.[43] Louis XI sentenced the municipal government again in June 1478 in a case that tells a lot about their attitude towards the urban finances. They were said to have recognized committing exactions by the 'distribution of the city's pennies', and to have 'levied several monies on the authority of letters granted to them by us [the king], which letters can be said not having been issued correctly by our Chambre des comptes or otherwise'.[44] Some members of the municipal government were so well practised in the abuse of common goods and the use of falsified documents that they found it more rewarding and less dangerous to misappropriate the revenues of the taxes on maritime trade than to invest in that trade itself, because to do the latter was always risky and evidently less profitable. Moreover, there was no need to deprive themselves, as the sanction fell on the collective and the fine of 3,000 pounds was not really dissuasive. In the sixteenth century an inspector denounced 'the alienations perpetrated by the *maire* and aldermen who had sold and alienated the domain and revenues without a reason since forty years'. And, although 6,000 pounds had been available yearly for the maintenance of the city's fortifications, nothing had been done because 'the monies had not been spent as they had to be'.[45]

Conclusions

The centrality of maritime trade in the activities of La Rochelle and its hinterland largely determined the organization and the policy of its municipal institutions. As a newly founded city, it did not enjoy the attributions and functions that older cities like Nantes and Bordeaux had as administrative, religious and cultural centres. Therefore, its existence depended entirely on its commerce, especially that of wine, which by nature is accessory, aleatory and adventurous. More than any other port city on the European Atlantic coast, La Rochelle constructed itself in the late Middle Ages as a true merchants' association. Its success came from collegial economic decisions rather than individual ones. It is true that particular interests appear rarely in the annals and books of privileges on which the present study was built. It remains questionable, however, if it was purely accidental that just these types of sources escaped loss more than others. They forcefully express the 'esprit de corps' of the local merchants' culture, which was inseparable from the political culture, and necessary for everybody's profit, and even supplanted simple considerations of individual profit. It seems undeniable that the rulers of La Rochelle were aware of the necessity of a global strategy, even if its implementation occurred pragmatically by successive generations, incrementally, and under the impulse of the circumstances. While the local oligarchy did accumulate its own privileges, they kept a keen concern for the interests of the whole citizenry. On the basis of the communal statutes and the capacity of deliberation, they shaped the municipal institutions as a mutualist organization. The search for security, equilibrium and stability, essential for the development of international maritime trade, thus had a major repercussion on the social and political organization.[46]

Notes

1 E. De Fréville, *Mémoire sur le commerce maritime de Rouen depuis les temps les plus reculés jusqu'à la fin du xvie siècle*, 2 vols, Rouen: Le Brument, 1857. F. Michel, *Histoire du commerce et de la navigation à Bordeaux, principalement sous l'administration anglaise*, 2 vols, Bordeaux: J. Delmas, 1867–70.

2 *Comptabilité du port de Dieppe au xve siècle*, ed. M. Mollat, Paris: Plon, 1951; P. Lardin, 'L'activité du port de Dieppe à travers la comptabilité de l'archevêque de Rouen', in *Ports maritimes et ports fluviaux au Moyen Âge*, 35e Congrès de la Société des historiens médiévistes de l'enseignement supérieur public (La Rochelle, 2004), Paris: Publications de la Sorbonne, 2005, pp. 171–82.

3 See, for example: *Documents pour servir à l'histoire du commerce des Pays-Bas avec la France jusqu'à 1585*, vol. 1, *Actes notariés de La Rochelle, 1423–1585*, ed. M. A. Drost, The Hague: M. Nijhoff, 1984.

4 Aunis was a province in central-west France located between Saintonge and Poitou, of which La Rochelle was the administrative, political and economic capital. In the documents, it is called 'Government of La Rochelle'.

5 Y. Renouard, 'Le grand commerce des vins de Gascogne au Moyen Âge', *Revue historique*, 221, 1959, pp. 261–304; republ. in his *Études d'histoire médiévale*, Paris: SEVPEN, 1968, pp. 237–8.

6 R. Dion, *Histoire de la vigne et du vin en France des origines au xixe siècle*, Paris: Flammarion, 1959, p. 359; M. Lachiver, *Vins, vignes et vignerons: Histoire du vignoble français*, Paris: Fayard, 1988, p. 89.

7 J. Craeybeckx, *Un grand commerce d'importation: Les vins de France aux anciens Pays-Bas (xiiie–xvie siècle)*, Paris: SEVPEN, 1958, pp. 24–5.

8 The wines from Gascony, Auxerre and Spain were sold, depending on their quality, at 100 sous to 6 marks per barrel; those of La Rochelle at 6 to 4 marks.

9 *Livre des Bouillons, Archives Municipales de Bordeaux*, vol. 1, Bordeaux: Imprimerie G. Gounouilhou, 1867, no. LIX.

10 BnF (Bibliothèque nationale de France), ms. fr. 16906, fols. 126–126v. Exceptionally, the Aunis wines 'valloyent mieux pour celle annee [beginning of the fifteenth century] que ne faisoyent ceux de Gascougne'.

11 M. Tranchant and M. Bochaca, 'Du golfe de Gascogne à la Picardie et à la Flandre maritime: le déplacement par mer des hommes et des marchandises à la fin du xve siècle', in *Se déplacer du Moyen Âge à nos jours*, Actes du 6e colloque européen de Calais (2006–2007), Calais: Les Amis du vieux Calais, 2009, pp. 135–46.

12 C.-E. Dufourcq and J. Gautier-Dalché, *Histoire économique et sociale de l'Espagne chrétienne au Moyen Âge*, Paris: A. Colin, 1976, p. 226. H. Casado Alonso, 'Comercio internacional y seguros marítimos en Burgos en la época de los Reyes Católicos', in *Congresso internacional Bartolomeu Dias e a sua época*, Porto: Universidade do Porto, 1989, p. 598.

13 M. Tranchant, 'La constitution de la banlieue rochelaise à la fin du Moyen Âge', *Histoire Urbain* 8, Dec. 2003, pp. 23–40.

14 J. Duguet, 'Origine et structure du Grand Fief d'Aunis (1199–1246)', *Revue de la Saintonge et de l'Aunis* 16, 1990, p. 98; E. Birrier, 'La seigneurie de Châtelaillon aux xive et xve siècles',

mémoire de maîtrise, université de Poitiers, unpubl., 1992, pp. 61–7; G. Pouponnot, 'L'aumônerie Saint-Barthélemy de La Rochelle au xve siècle', mémoire de maîtrise, université de La Rochelle, unpubl., June 2001, p. 51, no. 19.

15 MLR (Médiathèque de La Rochelle), ms 200 and 201. M. Delafosse and E. Trocmé, *Le commerce rochelais de la fin du xve siècle au début du xviie siècle*, Paris: SEVPEN, 1952, p. 79.

16 AN (Archives Nationales de France), X^{1C} 4, no. 200.

17 In 1229 and 1230, when the burghers started to distinguish their wines from those of the hinterland, they initiated the first delimitation of a suburban space around the city. The *banlieue* was gradually established in the course of a one-and-a-half-century opposition by the local lords. Within that territory, the city held its grip on landed property, the economy, the fiscal system and military organization. In Feb. 1347, King Philip VI circumscribed its limits precisely. See Tranchant, 'La constitution'.

18 AN, JJ 71, no. 177. A. Barbot, *Histoire de La Rochelle*, ed. Denys d'Aussy, *Archives Historiques de la Saintonge et de l'Aunis* 14, 1886, pp. 142–3. This decision was confirmed in 1478: MLR, ms 45–6, pp. 682–3.

19 In the late Middle Ages, the burghers of La Rochelle developed regulations to protect and guarantee the quality of the wines produced in their *banlieue* by limiting cattle-raising and hunting rights, and fixing a calendar for the agriculture, vinification procedures, etc.

20 MLR, ms 45–6, p. 61. Barbot, *Histoire de La Rochelle*, pp. 80–2.

21 A. Bardonnet (ed.), 'Le serment de fidélité des habitants de La Rochelle au roi de France en 1224', *Archives historiques du Poitou* 20, 1889, pp. 232–61.

22 R. Favreau, 'La Rochelle, port français sur l'Atlantique au xiiie siècle', in *L'Europe et l'Océan au Moyen Âge*, Paris: SHMESP, 1988, pp. 62–3.

23 S. Abraham-Thisse, 'Les relations hispano-hanséates au Bas Moyen Âge', *En la España medieval* 15, 1992, pp. 251–6.

24 H. Casado Alonso, 'Las colonias de mercaderes castellanos en Europa (siglos xv y xvi)', in *Castilla y Europa, comercio y mercaderes en los siglos xiv, xv y xvi*, Burgos: Excma. Diputación de Burgos, 1995, p. 18; J. Finot, *Étude historique sur les relations commerciales entre la France et la Flandre au Moyen Âge d'après les tarifs du péage de Bapaume et les traités de commerce passés entre les villes de Flandre et celles de La Rochelle, Niort, Saint-Jean-d'Angély, Bayonne, Biarritz, Bordeaux, Narbonne*, Paris: A. Picard et fils, 1894, p. 60.

25 Bibliothèque Sainte-Geneviève (Paris), ms 940, fol. 238.

26 Craeybeckx, *Un grand commerce*, p. 123.

27 Abraham-Thisse, 'Les relations hispano-hanséates', pp. 259–60.

28 MLR, ms 45–6, pp. 243, 255.

29 R. Favreau, 'Commune et gens du roi à La Rochelle (début xiiie–début xve siècle)', in N. Coulet and O. Guyotjeannin (eds), *La ville au Moyen Âge*, Paris: Editions du CTHS, 1998, pp. 108, 113–19.

30 MLR, ms 45–6, pp. 265, 267, 271, 411–12; Favreau, 'Commune et gens du roi', p. 118; other references to the documents quoted in this context were found on the following pages of the same manuscript: 379–80, 445, 703; 435; 355–6, 551, 670, 739.

31 BnF, ms. fr. 18970, fols. 131–134v.

32 BnF, ms. fr. 16906, fols. 118–139v (1408); ms. fr. 18970, fols. 45–59 (1460). Archives départementales de Loire-Atlantique, E 19, no. 10 (1499). MLR, ms 45–6, pp. 419, 445–6, 455, 487, 585–602, 715, 742. Favreau, 'Commune et gens du roi', pp. 123–6.

33 The tower at the quai Maubec has been destroyed; MLR, ms 45–6, pp. 23, 624, 681; references for the next paragraph on pp. 181, 450.

34 BnF, ms. fr. 16906, fol. 1v, and MLR, ms 45–6, passim; Barbot, *Histoire de La Rochelle*, pp. 210, 231, 389.

35 M. Tranchant, *Le commerce maritime de La Rochelle à la fin du Moyen Âge*, Rennes: Presses Universitaires de Rennes, 2003, pp. 195–7.

36 Barbot, *Histoire de La Rochelle*, p. 389.
37 MLR, ms 45–6, pp. 403, 591, 592.
38 MLR, ms 45–6, pp. 109, 141, 191, 259, 280, 349, 410; for the next paragraph: 466, 631.
39 Among them the families Bérard, Boutin, Bureau, Champdenier, Desnorp, Girard, Langlois and Le Bourcier.
40 M. Tranchant, *La Rochelle au fil des ans avec Nicolas Baudouin*, vol. 2, *xv*[e] *siècle*, Archives départementales de Loire-Atlantique, E 19 (2 Mi 785 RS), no. 10.
41 Archives départementales de Loire-Atlantique, E 19 (2 Mi 785 RS), no. 10.
42 La Rochelle was granted this exemption first in 1360 by Edward III, then by John the Good, Charles VI, Charles VII and Louis XI (last in 1478): MLR, ms 45–6, pp. 327, 328, 407, 437, 487, 491, 592, 629–30, 684; Barbot, *Histoire de La Rochelle*, pp. 255–6, 331.
43 The commune was obliged to deliberate about any new tax with the representatives of the city (ten burghers and commons from each parish), and to obtain their agreement: Barbot, *Histoire de La Rochelle*, pp. 286–7.
44 BnF, ms. fr. 18970, fols. 48v–49v, 131v–132.
45 BnF, Coll. Clair. 963, no. 19.
46 M. Tranchant, 'La "culture" du risque chez les populations usagères des mers et littoraux du Ponant (xie–xvie siècles): première approche d'une histoire à construire', *Risque, sécurité et sécurisation maritimes depuis le Moyen Âge, Revue d'Histoire Maritime* 9, 2008, pp. 9–45.

21

'THE GOODLYEST HAVEN NOT OF THE LOWE COUNTRIES ONLY BUT OF ALL CHRISTENDOME'

The Scheldt estuary as a gateway system 1300–1600

Louis Sicking and Arno Neele

Between Bruges, Antwerp and Amsterdam

'The goodlyest Haven not of the Lowe Countries only but of all Christendome':[1] This is how the Italian merchant and historian Lodovico Guicciardini (1521-1589) described the village of Arnemuiden on the eastern board of Walcheren Island in the Scheldt estuary in the English translation (1593) of his book *The Description of the Low Countries,* which had originally been published in 1567.[2] Guicciardini, who had been living in Antwerp since 1541, also explained why Arnemuiden was the best haven of Europe: 'For all ships [that] come into Flanders repaire to this port in such sort that you shal somtime see there 400 or 500 saile of ships that passe to and fro into all partes of y world.'[3] In his original description of Arnemuiden, Guicciardini, for the benefit of merchants and Antwerp underwriters, included a list of distances between Arnemuiden and the main destinations for seafaring across Europe. Thus Arnemuiden sparkled, as it were, at the centre of a compass rose,[4] with Amsterdam at 25 nautical miles, Bremen at 83, Hamburg at 105, the Sound at 180, Danzig at 254, Riga at 300, Reval (Tallinn) at 335, Narva at 365, and in the other direction, Calais at 23 miles, London at 42, Southampton at 62, Dieppe at 54, Rouen at 75, Brest at 125, La Rochelle at 194, Bordeaux at 211, Bilbao at 226, Cape Finistère at 270, Lisbon at 380, Cadiz at 480, Sevilla at 500, Malaga at 540, Madeira at 480, the Canary Islands at 520, and finally Livorno in Tuscany at 780 nautical miles from Arnemuiden.[5]

Guicciardini's description confirms that the Scheldt estuary was the focal point of European international shipping around the middle of the sixteenth century. Until the thirteenth century the fairs in Champagne had dominated international trade.

However, because of the increasing importance of maritime transport merchants preferred to concentrate their trading activities in various towns in the area around the Scheldt estuary. Here both land and sea trade routes came together while large ships could anchor well. Now the Scheldt estuary became the centre of the Western European trading system that emerged in the late Middle Ages. In the sixteenth century the movement of vessels in the Scheldt estuary was one of the densest in Europe. In good years, shipping to and from the estuary was responsible for the transport of about 250,000 tons, which was equivalent to the entire annual navigation through the Sound in both directions between the North Sea and the Baltic. This volume was four times greater than the port movement in London in 1580–1, and twelve times more than the fleets of America arriving annually in Seville.

The Scheldt estuary was a gateway system in which individual ports and towns each played their complementary roles as intermediaries between their hinterland and the rest of Europe.[6] Geographically this estuary largely corresponds with the present province of Zeeland in the Netherlands. One should bear in mind however that the southern part of this province – present-day Zeeuws Vlaanderen – belonged to the county of Flanders in the period in question. In the late Middle Ages the territories corresponding more or less with present-day Belgium, the Netherlands and Luxemburg (except for the prince bishopric of Liège), were integrated in a composite state, which came to be known in the late fifteenth century as 'the Netherlands'. Each region or province kept institutions of its own but they also came to share some central institutions, such as the government councils, the High Court, called the Great Council at Mechelen, and the States General. Situated around the Scheldt estuary, the core regions of this composite state were Flanders, Brabant, Zeeland and Holland. The main market centres of the Low Countries were situated at the edges of the Scheldt estuary. Bruges, Antwerp and Amsterdam successively developed into metropolises of European, and even global importance (see Figure 21.1).

Bruges, Antwerp, and Amsterdam and their trade networks have received wide attention in the existing historiography.[7] Research into the significance of the Scheldt estuary for the development of international trade and shipping can also boast a long tradition.[8] Attention in the last two decades has focused on the impact of the Dutch Revolt.[9] This chapter aims to make a contribution to this historiography by stressing the importance of extra-economic factors in the economic development of the Scheldt estuary; in particular geography, urban rivalry and political turmoil. To make this argument the chapter concentrates on the late fifteenth and the sixteenth centuries, because in this period economic hegemony passed first from Bruges to Antwerp, and subsequently from Antwerp to Amsterdam. Crucial in this shift were geographical, spatial, political and judicial factors.

Our argument starts with an explanation of the main spatial dynamics of the maritime connections in the Scheldt estuary. As far as individual ports are concerned, our focus will, for a change, be not on the large metropolises, but on Zeeland's ports of Middelburg and Arnemuiden, Sluice in Northern Flanders and to a lesser extent Bergen op Zoom in Brabant. This approach will give a clearer picture and a

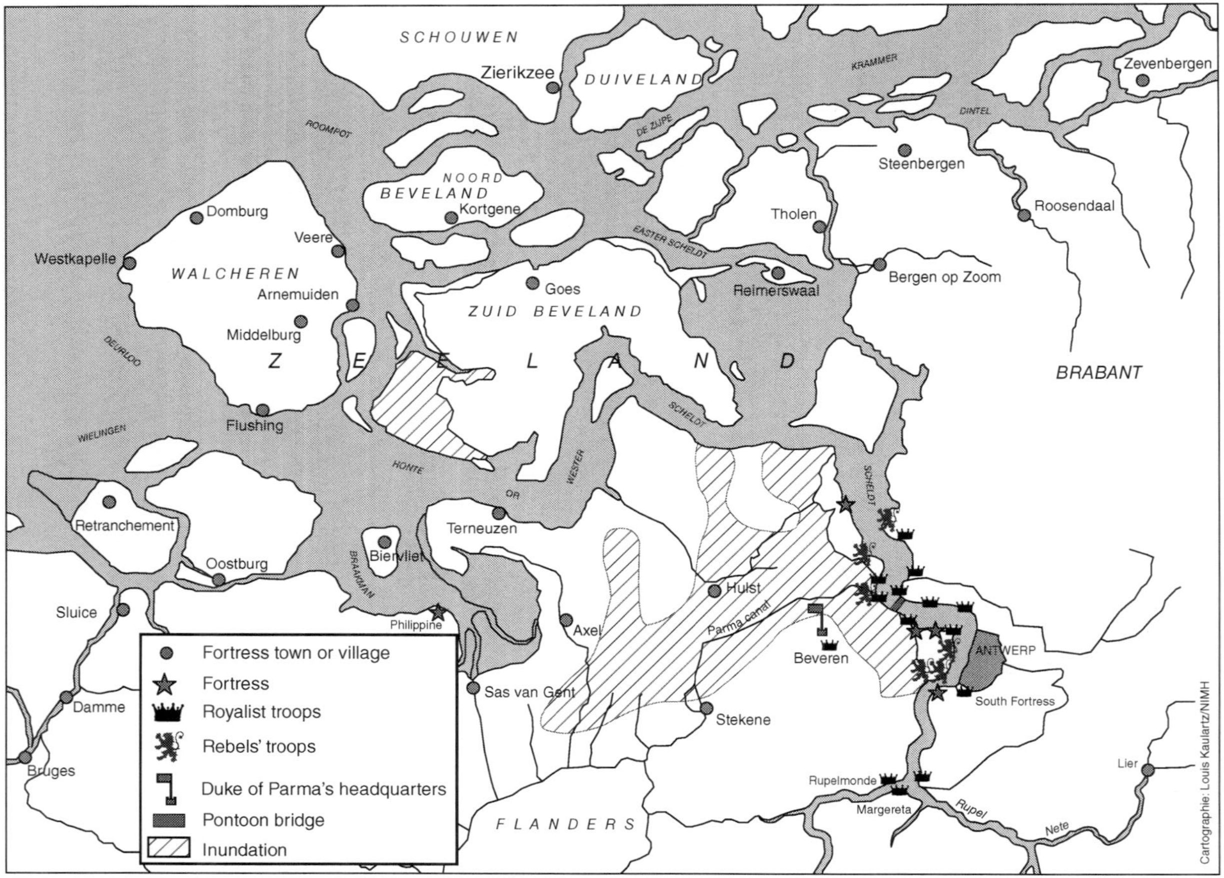

Figure 21.1 Map of the Scheldt estuary and the siege of Antwerp 1584–1585

better understanding of the strong interdependence of all cities in the Scheldt estuary. The development of the gateway system will then be analysed. Special attention will be paid to geographical changes in the waterways and to urban competition in attracting foreign traders and shipping. Finally, the disruption of the Scheldt estuary as a gateway system as a consequence of the Dutch Revolt will be discussed.

The spatial dynamics of maritime connections

Within the area comprised by the Scheldt estuary, significant geographical changes to the natural waterways took place between 1300 and 1600. These included the silting of the Zwin, the estuary that connected Bruges with the sea, and the increasing navigability of the Westerscheldt from approximately 1400 onwards to the detriment of the Easterscheldt. Because of the silting up of the Zwin, Bruges, and later its out-ports Damme, Hoeke, Monnikenrede and Sint Anna-ter-Muiden, became less and less accessible for large sea-going vessels. From around 1300 Sluice, situated at the mouth of the Zwin, was the place par excellence to transship goods due for Bruges on smaller vessels. Sluice grew into a metropolitan area of nearly 10,000 inhabitants in the second half of the fifteenth century, and became the largest city of the Scheldt estuary after Bruges and Antwerp.[10]

After 1400, when Sluice also became less accessible for sea-going vessels due to the progressive silting of the Zwin, more and more skippers preferred the deep Wielingen and Westerscheldt as a waterway, and Walcheren Island as port of transshipment. On the east side of Walcheren there was the so-called Walcheren roadstead, a natural bay, where sea-going vessels found an ideal anchorage sheltered from the swell of the sea, near one of the many heads that were laid out there.

Arnemuiden, situated on the Walcheren roadstead (Figure 21.2), as well as Veere and Flushing with their deep seaports, also benefited from the increase in shipping to and from Antwerp and to a lesser extent, Bergen op Zoom, whose fairs developed into international trading centres already in the fourteenth century. The location at the mouth of the increasingly navigable Westerscheldt played an important role in the urbanization and economic growth of Walcheren. In the late Middle Ages, Bruges, Antwerp, Bergen op Zoom and Walcheren formed an integrated commercial and financial network. While the Walcheren ports benefited from their location at or near the Westerscheldt, Zierikzee and Bergen op Zoom lost their initial favourable strategic positions on the Easterscheldt when this river arm lost its importance as the main shipping route to Antwerp to the Westerscheldt.[11]

The more difficult accessibility of port cities due to silting did not have to mean/imply an immediate obstacle to the growth and development of international trade and shipping or for the further development of these cities. The silting up of the Zwin was already going on in the thirteenth and fourteenth centuries when Bruges experienced its biggest growth. The city on the Zwin was prepared to make large investments in infrastructural projects, which had to maintain access to the town or at least its out-ports for ships. These investments ultimately did not have the desired result, but show that the city was prepared to make great efforts to sustain the connection with the sea. Middelburg, initially only connected to the sea via a winding river, the Arne, with the village of Arnemuiden at its mouth, had more success. Middelburg decided in 1531 to dig a harbour channel and thereby secured a good connection with the Walcheren roadstead, while attracting more foreign shipping.[12]

An obvious way to continue to guarantee the export/removal and import/supply of goods in spite of silting and the increasing size of sea-going vessels was to transship goods. Not only goods bound for Bruges had to be transshipped. A large portion of the freight to and from Antwerp also took place by means other than sea-going vessels. A portion of the goods bound for Antwerp was transshipped to smaller vessels in Arnemuiden and other Zeeland ports.[13] Finally, the accessibility of the Amsterdam harbour for ships was poor from early on. The shoal known as the Pampus was already a hurdle in the fifteenth century. For that reason merchants from Danzig let their smaller ships sail to Amsterdam and their larger ones to the Scheldt estuary.[14]

The Scheldt estuary: international gateway in the Low Countries

From the thirteenth century on, the Low Countries developed into the core area of the Western European trading system. Merchants from the Low Countries, England, Scotland, the Baltic, the Holy Roman Empire, France and the Mediterranean came to the cities in and around the Scheldt estuary to trade with each other. Thanks to the convenient location of the Scheldt estuary in the core area of the Low Countries a very large part of the trade, which increased explosively between 1300 and 1550, went via the Zeeland waters to the surrounding areas. Thus, the proceeds of the Zeeland toll around 1550 increased over eighty times that of two centuries earlier.[15] The cities in the Scheldt estuary had both a regional-service function for surrounding towns and villages and a network function within a supra-regional or international trading network. The service function involved the supply of goods and services in their own region – the market area – and for their own urban population. The network function entailed long-distance trade. Through its network the city functioned as an intermediary between its own local area and other areas.[16]

In the 1540s Antwerp was responsible for almost three-quarters of total exports of the Netherlands. In 1545 one-third of Antwerp's exports went through Walcheren, particularly through the Walcheren roadstead where the goods were loaded onto large ships.[17] The importance of the Walcheren ports as out-ports is evident from the figures: 81 per cent of exports from the roadstead at Arnemuiden consisted of the transshipment of goods from Antwerp; at Veere these accounted for half of its exports; and in Middelburg for one-third. Not only Bruges and Antwerp but also other Netherlandish cities used Walcheren as an out-port. Large amounts of cloth, from Rotterdam and Haarlem for instance, were exported from Middelburg and Arnemuiden to Southern Europe. Walcheren was the anchorage of the Netherlands par excellence and offered a window on Europe as Guicciardini had underlined, with

England, France, Spain, Portugal, the Baltic region, the Canary Islands and Madeira as primary destinations in 1545. For imports into the Netherlands, Walcheren was a crucial link in the maritime trade networks in Europe. Between 1536 and 1550 an average of 600 foreign ships used the Walcheren ports annually.[18]

Middelburg, Veere, Arnemuiden and Flushing each had their own specific position and function within the international trade networks (Figure 21.1). Arnemuiden was by far the most important transit port on Walcheren. While *c.*1450 fourteen foreign vessels on average anchored at the Walcheren roadstead per year, this number had increased to 345 on average per year a century later. With this number Arnemuiden even surpassed Antwerp, where in the mid-sixteenth century 254 foreign ships on average anchored annually.[19] Merchants used the Walcheren roadstead especially as a link in the trade to and from Southern Europe, and to a lesser extent to and from the Baltic region. From the fifteenth century Arnemuiden functioned as the unofficial staple for salt, which accounted for 70 per cent of the value of imports in Arnemuiden – partly due to the many salteries works (*zoutziederijen*) in the village and elsewhere in Zeeland.[20] Coarse salt (*grof zout*) originally came from the Bay of Bourgneuf in Brittany and from Brouage and Île de Ré, and in the sixteenth century increasingly from Setúbal in Portugal and Cádiz in Spain. The transport of salt was largely in the hands of Bretons, Hanseatics, French and from about 1550 mainly Hollanders. The latter had the advantage of exporting part of the salt directly to the Baltic areas while they, like the Bretons, brought part of it to Arnemuiden for refining, to be re-exported or used in the Netherlands itself for the preservation of herring, other fish and meat. Arnemuiden was and remained not much more than a roadstead where ships anchored; it lacked an infrastructure almost entirely. Except for the transit function and the salt trade Arnemuiden was significant for ship repair, ship supplies and provisions.[21] At the beginning of the sixteenth century Arnemuiden had a dock(yard) – 'very famous in all countries' – for the repair of the biggest sea-going ships.[22] For reasons unknown it fell into disuse. Middelburg took its chance and put a dry dock into use in 1536, just when its new port channel was finished. It was a unique facility in the Netherlands at the time.[23]

Middelburg developed into the commercial centre for products from France and the Iberian peninsula, including wine, which was by far the most important, and which was distributed throughout the Netherlands. Although Middelburg never received a formal or complete staple right for wine, the city was able to cope with competition from Zierikzee, Bergen op Zoom and Antwerp, all of which tried to divert part of the direct import of French wines to their ports. In the 1560s, the wine import via Middelburg represented three-quarters of wine that came via the sea – i.e. the so-called western wines, including those from Spain and Portugal.[24]

Other western products that were imported in Middelburg, apart from wine, were dried fruits, oil, cork and iron. While trading in western wines was mainly a French affair, Spanish and Andalusian merchants played a leading role in the marketing of these products. The transport was in the hands of the Hollanders, Zeelanders and Hanseatic merchants. To the extent that these western goods were not intended for

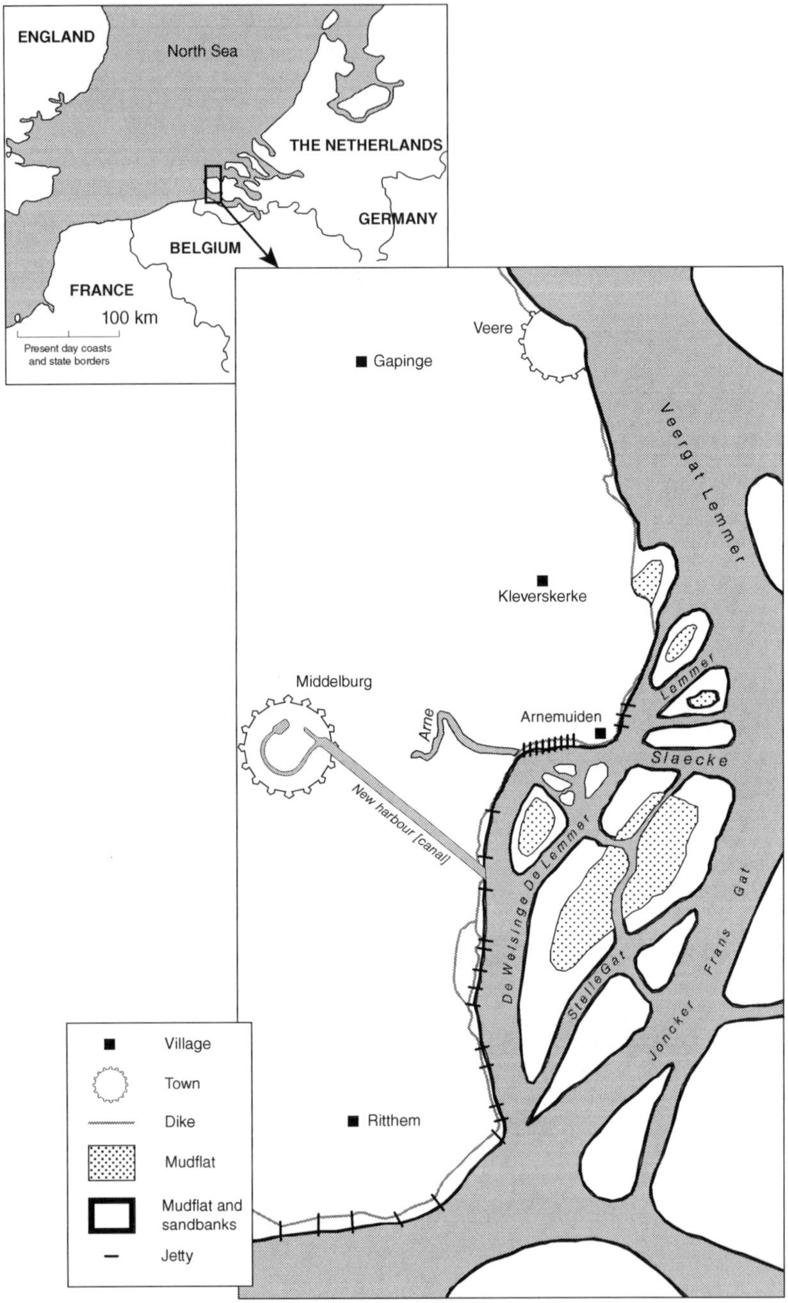

Figure 21.2 Map of the roadstead on the east of the island of Walcheren

consumption in the Netherlands, they were re-exported to England. The ships that sailed from Middelburg and Arnemuiden to Atlantic France and Southern Europe were largely loaded with bulk goods from the Baltic region such as timber, work (lint of flax or hemp), tar, pitch and woollen fabric.[25]

While Middelburg and Arnemuiden were the gateways for Southern Europe, Veere was mainly oriented northward toward the Baltic region and Scotland. In the fifteenth century merchants from the Baltic region imported grain and shipbuilding materials in the Netherlands via Veere. From the south of Europe they brought salt to Veere, and continued to do so even when Hanseatic merchants shifted their trade to Amsterdam in the course of the sixteenth century. English traders initially used Veere as an out-port of Bergen op Zoom during the so-called Easter and Cold Fairs there, but disappeared when these lost their importance for international trade in the sixteenth century. Thanks to the establishment of the Scottish staple at Veere from 1541, the city continued to play a role in the international trade network of the Scheldt estuary. Veere exported a wide range of goods, among which herring was the most important. The city also exported agricultural products from Zeeland and re-exported goods from elsewhere, such as cloth, grain, dried fruits, wine, wood, tar, pitch and iron.[26]

Flushing lived mainly off the herring fishery and therefore had the most one-sided economic function in comparison to Veere, Middelburg and Arnemuiden. The trade was dominated by the fisheries and was in the hands of local merchants who mainly exported herring to France and England. The cargo they took back was either brought to Flushing itself or to another port, but Flushing's transit function was marginal compared to its herring exports.[27]

Around 1300, Zierikzee was one of the major trading centres of Zeeland. Sailors and merchants from Zierikzee were active in shipping to the Sound from early on. They brought salt, wine, cloth, cheese and spices to the Baltic, and brought back herring, grain, timber and tar. Zierikzee's export products were salt, madder and fish, which allowed people to remain active in shipping and trading. The town succeeded in attracting foreign merchants and trade, but no more than Flushing. Because the Easterscheldt lost its role as a major shipping route to Brabant, Zierikzee did not benefit from the rise of Antwerp. While towns and villages on Walcheren grew thanks to continuous migration – particularly Flushing, which became the third city of Zeeland in population size – migration to Zierikzee halted after 1430. At the end of the Middle Ages the Zierikzee economy depended mainly on the salt and madder industry, and on fishing, but hardly any more on trading.[28]

Bergen op Zoom, which had initially benefited from its location on the Easterscheldt, also experienced the adverse effects of changes in the Zeeland waterways. Initially Bergen op Zoom continued to benefit from activities on the roadstead and in the ports of Walcheren. The St Felix flood in 1530 and subsequent floods (1532, 1541, 1552 and 1570) each made the port of Bergen op Zoom temporarily unusable. The position of Bergen op Zoom in international trade was further weakened because traders preferred the presence of a permanent market in Antwerp to the periodic fairs, due to which Bergen op Zoom had known its medieval prosperity.[29]

As we have seen, alongside their own local and regional function for production and trade, most port cities also had a transit function. On Walcheren, thanks to its good port facilities, large sea-going ships could overload their goods on smaller vessels. Thus the port cities were complementary within the gateway system. Nevertheless the positions of the various cities within the system were due to change. The shift of the centre of gravity of shipping from the Zwin to the Westerscheldt, on the one hand, and from the Easterscheldt to the Westerscheldt, on the other, had important consequences for the port activity of several cities: Bergen op Zoom and Zierikzee declined, whereas Middelburg, Arnemuiden and above all Flushing benefited. As we shall see, the cities did not simply accept that the routes on which they were situated were less used or that their ports had become less accessible for sea-going vessels.

Attracting foreign merchants and shipping, thwarting competition

Inter-city rivalry has recently been put forth as an explanatory factor in the emergence of so-called inclusive or open access institutions in the three consecutive trading metropolises of northwestern Europe around the Scheldt estuary. These institutions facilitated traders in international trade, exchange and conflict resolution. The city councils of Bruges, Antwerp and Amsterdam, as well as those of Bergen op Zoom, Middelburg and Veere, were willing to create a favourable business climate for foreign entrepreneurs through institutional changes that favoured foreign traders. They were willing to do so because they realized very well that these traders would pull away when they could trade elsewhere under more favourable circumstances. Because the distance between the various port cities in the Netherlands was relatively small compared to the Mediterranean and the Baltic, competitive pressure in the Netherlands was much greater than elsewhere. This was particularly true for the cities just mentioned because they served the same hinterland. The political autonomy of trading cities enabled the city governments, thanks to their financial resources and their legal powers, to adapt institutional arrangements to changes in the scale and scope of the trade, and thus to jump on the needs of traders. This willingness to adjust of both traders and city governments is reflected in the changing role of brokers and hostellers, guilds and local courts in Bruges and Antwerp. Brokers and hostellers played a crucial role in facilitating foreign merchants in the form of accommodation, storage and brokerage of deals on the local market, thereby contributing to reducing their costs as long as these traders travelled between different markets. Once they settled permanently the variation of commercial transactions rose sharply, including international shipments, credit operations, partnerships and commission business with foreign agents. In both Bruges and Antwerp the city governments left the enforcement of such new contract forms to the foreign traders themselves. The trading nation, with its own representation in the form of a consul, became a so-called 'one-stop shop' where traders could go for different functions and transactions.[30]

When most nations of foreign merchants left Bruges at the end of the fifteenth century, Antwerp profited especially, but Bergen op Zoom, Middelburg and Veere actively tried to bind some of these merchants and their trade as well. Scots, English, Andalusians, Bretons and merchants from La Rochelle settled in Middelburg.[31] In 1538, for instance, Bergen op Zoom and Middelburg competed to attract the merchants of La Rochelle and sent delegations to the French city. Middelburg won the competition after La Rochelle had successfully enforced improved conditions from the Zeeland town that surpassed the previous commitments of Bergen op Zoom.[32] Middelburg in turn had to accept, in 1541, that Veere become the staple for Scottish goods in the Netherlands. The good Scottish contacts of the lord of Veere were decisive for the Scottish decision.[33] The urban competition for the establishment of nations of foreign merchants and the willingness of these merchants to move to towns with a favourable business climate confirms the importance still granted to the trading nation in the sixteenth century.

With the further growth of trade, in particular between foreign merchants from different countries and cities that consuls could no longer oversee, city governments would again play another role by taking over part of the administrative and judicial functions of foreign nations. Through this local support foreign merchants were no longer dependent on their consuls to enforce compliance with contracts. This happened in Antwerp in the sixteenth century and later, after 1585, in Amsterdam, where the city council refused to create separate jurisdictions for foreign merchants' communities.[34]

However, the urban competition was not limited to the creation of a favourable business climate for foreign merchants. It also focused on facilitating and attracting shipping, on the one hand, and thwarting potential competitors on the other. To that end, city governments let no method go untested and tried to win their case through judicial means or sought the support of the monarch. Aside from infrastructural projects and maintaining the depth of ports and their entrances, port cities also used their cranes as an instrument to enforce the staple of goods. Bruges, which in 1323 had obtained the count's staple privilege, to concentrate all the goods that were brought from the sea into the Zwin, is supposed to have destroyed the newly established crane at Sluice that very same year.[35] Middelburg pursued a crane monopoly at Walcheren and prevented hoists from being set up in Flushing and Arnemuiden. In 1535 the Great Council in Mechelen, the highest court in the Netherlands, vindicated Arnemuiden in the dispute between Middelburg and the lord of Arnemuiden over the latter's intention to set up a crane or swipe. But Middelburg persisted in its opposition. The sovereign, Charles V, then confirmed that the city had rightly opposed the judgment of the Great Council. The city crane was an important tool for Middelburg to enforce the trade in western wine trade via its own premises. This remained the case even when the staple right was acquired.[36]

Aside from the city crane, beacons and pilots were used to facilitate and attract shipping. In 1359, Zierikzee received a privilege from the count of Holland and Zeeland to use barrels to mark the maritime route to the city.[37] Like the crane, these facilities were political instruments through which the city tried to attract shipping to its own port while simultaneously trying to outstrip competing ports. From *c.*1450 Bruges began to set out tons to highlight the route to Sluice, and appointed pilots. In 1487, the city even began paying bonuses to pilots for each ship piloted into port. This proved a success – fifty-seven helmsmen steered in ninety-eight ships that year – and Bruges went on with the premium system throughout the sixteenth century. Bruges also sent pilots to the sea (in 1486) to actively search for Spanish and Breton ships to bring them to Sluice.[38] Middelburg stood up for itself and also sent its own pilots to sea to conduct Spanish and other merchants to its own harbour. When in 1536 Flushing proposed to lay barrels in the Wielingen, south of Walcheren, Middelburg blocked this because Flushing might thus lure more ships into its port.[39]

Out-ports especially, located downstream of a larger city or metropolis further removed from the coast, often had to deal with all kinds of opposition. Sluice, which had already acquired city rights of the count of Flanders before its first entry in the remaining sources around 1290, developed in the context of a permanent stream of opposition and outright military attacks from Bruges. It grew into a full-fledged city thanks to the support of various princes, including the dukes of Burgundy in their capacity as counts of Flanders, who developed Sluice into a naval base with an arsenal for their caravels and galleys. Despite Bruges' opposition, Sluice, thanks to its location and princely support, managed to benefit from international trade and shipping so that in the fifteenth century the city was not only considered the main seaport of Flanders, but even the third port of Christendom.[40]

With more success than Bruges had at hindering Sluice, Middelburg thwarted its out-port Arnemuiden and continued to do so after the opening of the new port channel. The city secured the jurisdiction over Arnemuiden, banned the storage of goods and obliged traders to sail through to the port of Middelburg, which caused foreign merchants to complain. Arnemuiden tried in vain to escape the yoke of Middelburg by trying to obtain city rights and to institute proceedings before the Great Council of Mechelen. The only thing the village on the Walcheren roadstead achieved was to be allowed to carry out economic activities for the benefit of shipping, such as repair and biscuit baking.[41] But still Middelburg continued to counteract Arnemuiden, as Cornelia, widow of Job Victorsz, experienced in 1549. She ran a successful niche market in flax and dried moss that she acquired in Holland, and which was used to cover holes in ships. Although this trade was of minor economic importance, it was crucial for shipping. Nevertheless, Cornelia had to account for her flax and moss trade at the Middelburg court and later before the Grand Council. The Middelburg government wished to ban Cornelia's trade, relying on the existing ban to stock goods in Arnemuiden.[42]

Middelburg felt that its port activities on Walcheren were threatened even more by the port cities of Veere and Flushing, which were excellently located on the Easterscheldt and Westerscheldt, respectively. The fact that both towns were owned by the same lord, who in many ways favoured the economic development of his own possessions, only added to Middelburg's worries. The rapid growth of Flushing in particular, stimulated by the increase in maritime traffic through the Westerscheldt, was a thorn in the eye of Middelburg. The latter repeatedly thwarted the expansion of the port of Flushing.[43]

Middelburg in turn faced obstruction from Antwerp in connection with the staple rights of western wines. This issue was fought before the Great Council. This was also true for the most prevalent issue that occurred in line with the rise of the Westerscheldt as a shipping lane in the fifteenth century. The conflict focused on the levy of tolls by Zeeland, which saw a decrease in its toll revenues from the toll of Iersekeroord at the Easterscheldt, and also started to levy tolls at the Westerscheldt, which Flanders, Brabant and particularly Antwerp resisted. Middelburg leased the toll and was determined to maintain Zeeland's rights, not least because as a commercial rival of Antwerp it had no interest in toll freedom for the latter. Eventually the Great Council decided in Zeeland's favour in 1504.[44] Sharing the same ruler did not put an end to urban competition – thus Antwerp continued to strive for freedom of navigation on the Westerscheldt – but it did reduce it to peaceful proportions.

To understand the importance of the spatial or geographical dynamics of the Scheldt estuary for the development of the gateway system and the individual ports within that system, it should by now be clear that thwarting competitors, especially downstream out-ports whose development was systematically suppressed – both Sluice and Arnemuiden are cases in point – was as important as attracting ships with their merchandise by good port facilities. In this respect urban rivalry alone is not enough to explain the developments.[45] Higher authorities could make a crucial difference. Without the support of the count of Flanders, Sluice would have never been able to develop into one of the major seaports and the second largest town of the Scheldt estuary around 1500. Middelburg took advantage of the Charles V's support in its struggle with the powerful lords of Veere and Flushing for control over the island of Walcheren.[46] In spite of the opposition of cities to their out-ports downstream, both were mutually dependent on one another, which is expressed by the transit function of the out-ports. This explains why Bruges and Middelburg aimed at controlling their respective out-ports. Another example of this mutual dependence is the Spanish merchants at Bruges and Antwerp who had stationed agents in Middelburg.

The disruption of the Scheldt estuary as international gateway

Political turmoil has been identified in recent historiography as the main factor among many in the shift of the economic centre of gravity from Bruges to Antwerp and from Antwerp to Amsterdam.[47] In addition to the important role played by the relocation of foreign merchants nations to Antwerp, instigated by Maximilian of Austria during the Flemish Revolt (1482–92), the piratical actions from Sluice and the maritime blockade of Bruges by the leader of the revolt, Philip of Cleves, in the years 1488–92, had a major impact on the international shipping to and from the Scheldt estuary. Antwerp took an appropriate measure by equipping a convoy fleet, which was to protect shipping to and from the city and which had to fight Flemish insurgents on the Scheldt.[48] It is no coincidence that in 1491 the lord of Veere and

Flushing became admiral of the Netherlands, and Veere was to become the new naval base of the Low Countries, when Walcheren Island came to be considered as the key, anchor and bulwark of the Low Countries. From Walcheren the waterways to Antwerp could best be protected against foreign invasions from the sea.[49]

After the Flemish Revolt, the Dutch Revolt (1568–1648) turned out to be the decisive destabilizer of the integrated gateway system of the Netherlands. Whereas the Flemish Revolt had instigated the transfer of Bruges to Antwerp as the centre of this system with the moving house of most of the foreign nations, the Dutch Revolt was eventually to have even more fundamental consequences than Amsterdam following Antwerp as the new metropolis of international trade and finance in the Low Countries. In fact, the Habsburg Netherlands were split in two separate states, separated by a border that cut off the Scheldt estuary from most of Flanders and Brabant. This had major consequences for trade and shipping in the Scheldt estuary and for its function as gateway.

The capitulation of the major Flemish and Brabantine cities to Spanish troops, especially the fall of Antwerp, after an eight months siege and blockade of the Scheldt in 1585, triggered an exodus of refugees. Ghent, Bruges and Antwerp lost more than half their populations. Initially this flow of refugees from Antwerp and other Flemish and Brabantine towns meant a brief but intense economic boost for the cities of Zeeland. The Middelburg population grew rapidly from around 7,000 citizens in 1576 to more than 15,000 in 1601. Contrary to what has been contended in older literature, the river Scheldt was not closed for shipping, except in 1585, 1586 and 1587 when warships from Zeeland and Holland blocked the river to avoid any transport via the Scheldt to the Spanish Netherlands – that is, those parts that were reconquered by Spanish troops. Subsequently maritime trade was allowed in exchange for the so-called 'convooien' and 'licenten' or duties, which functioned as import and export taxes. In spite of these heavy duties, trade via the Scheldt with the Flemish and Brabantine cities did resume. In 1590 about 1,200 ships left the ports of Middelburg, Flushing and Veere for destinations in Flanders and Brabant. These ships, however, were much smaller than the ships that had sailed to Antwerp around 1550.[50] The export from Zeeland and Holland to Flanders and Brabant was ten times more important than the import of products from the southern Netherlands. Maritime traffic no longer went exclusively via Antwerp, but also via smaller ports on the Flemish side of the river such as Sluice and Biervliet. However, the rising costs of trade due to war, blockades and levies undermined the position of Antwerp and the Scheldt estuary as gateway system. As Amsterdam had taken over Antwerp's role as the major staple market of Europe, the Zeeland ports became more important as ports of transit for Holland. Both via the North Sea and via the internal waterways of Holland and Zeeland, Baltic grain and other products found their way to the southern Netherlands, which smaller ports like Zierikzee and Goes also took advantage of.[51] Near the end of the sixteenth century it may have looked for a short while like Middelburg was going to take over Antwerp's position as commercial metropolis of the Scheldt estuary. But around 1600, when Zeeland's economic decline set in, it became clear that Amsterdam had become Antwerp's successor. While Zeeland's European trade and shipping was limited more and more to neighbouring countries such as England, France and the Spanish Netherlands, its overseas trade would be limited to 'niches' like privateering, the slave trade and smuggling.[52]

For Arnemuiden, the Dutch Revolt was an opportunity to escape the power of Middelburg. Early on, Arnemuiden chose the side of the Dutch Revolt's leader, Prince William of Orange, while Middelburg remained faithful to the Habsburg regime of Philip II, which had always supported the city. The first town of Zeeland only changed sides after a siege that lasted two years.[53] Arnemuiden was thanked for the support given to the prince of Orange by receiving city privileges of its own, distinct from those of Middelburg. But when Arnemuiden earned its political freedom, several circumstances prevented its development. Despite the construction, finally, of a port in 1590, the closing of the Scheldt in 1585–7 had resulted in a sharp decline in international shipping to Antwerp, which Arnemuiden had greatly benefited from in previous decades. A second obstacle for Arnemuiden's development was the silting of the roadstead of Walcheren that threatened to cut the little town off from the sea.[54]

The magistrate of Arnemuiden did everything to try to keep open access to the sea. In 1607, the city had even considered getting back under the administration of Middelburg. But unlike Bruges, which had bought its outer harbour, Sluice, Middelburg changed its mind when it became apparent that it would have pay Arnemuiden's debts to Flushing, the great rival of Middelburg on Walcheren.[55] Despite the financial support of the States of Zeeland, all efforts to keep the maritime connection to Arnemuiden open failed. Unlike Middelburg, the small town did not have the means to dig a canal to ensure its access to the sea.[56] There is a clear parallel with the small out-ports of Bruges in the late Middle Ages, which also lacked the means to carry out the necessary work to escape silting.

Geography, politics and a new border

The development of the Scheldt estuary as the major gateway system for the maritime trade between Northern and Southern Europe in the late Middle Ages, in which the various towns each played their complementary roles, was certainly not the result of the free circulation of goods, merchants and skippers. Geographical and spatial factors to a great extent determined developments in the long term. The consequences of the silting of the Zwin and the decline of the Easter Scheldt as the main waterway to Antwerp could be circumvented and postponed, but not avoided. While the out-ports of Bruges – with the exception of Sluice – lost their significance before 1500, both Zierikzee and Bergen op Zoom declined but managed to temporarily take advantage of the disruption of the gateway system during the Dutch Revolt. Simultaneously Middelburg, Arnemuiden, Flushing, and to a lesser extent Veere, took advantage of the rising importance of the Westerscheldt. Next to the dynamics of geography, the interference of public powers and institutions at the local, regional and central levels of the Low Countries in both attracting foreign merchants and thwarting competition were decisive above all, as has been illustrated mainly with the case of Middelburg.

Other extra-economic factors, such as the Flemish and Dutch Revolts, were not only responsible for the succession of Bruges, Antwerp and Amsterdam as the main metropolis of the Low Countries, but also determined the development and fates of the cities and ports of the Scheldt estuary. The size of the various cities and ports mattered in this respect. Middelburg took advantage, using its entire judicial and political means while enjoying the support of the central government to thwart competing towns such as Bergen op Zoom, Veere, Flushing and the village of Arnemuiden. Arnemuiden on the contrary clearly lacked the political means and princely support to liberate itself from Middelburg's dominance. When Arnemuiden finally managed to take advantage of the Dutch Revolt by gaining independence from Middelburg and building a port of its own, the small new city was unable to avoid the silting of the access to its port. Even though the Scheldt estuary did not entirely lose its importance when it became part of the Dutch Republic – Zeeland, after all, would become its second most important province – the estuary, now separated from its traditional hinterland by a new state border, did lose its significance as the major gateway of Europe.

Notes

1 L. Guicciardini, *The Description of the Low Countries*, London, 1593; Amsterdam and Norwood, NJ: Theatrum orbis terrarium, Ltd and Walter J. Johnson, inc., 1976, p. 76r.

2 L. Guicciardini, *Descrittione di tutti i Paesi Bassi, altrimenti detti Germania inferior*, Antwerp: Willem Silvius, 1567.

3 Guicciardini, *Description*, pp. 76r–v.

4 Z.W. Sneller, *Walcheren in de vijftiende eeuw*, Utrecht: Oosthoek, 1916, pp. 5–6.

5 For the distances the Dutch edn of 1612 has been used: Guicciardini, *Beschrijvinghe van alle de Nederlanden anderssins ghenoemt Neder-Duytslandt*, Amsterdam, 1612, pp. 278–9. Sneller, *Walcheren in de vijftiende eeuw*, pp. 5–6.

6 C. Lesger, *Handel in Amsterdam ten tijde van de Opstand. Kooplieden, commerciële expansie en verandering in de ruimtelijke economie van de Nederlanden ca. 1550–ca. 1630*, Hilversum: Verloren, 2001, pp. 15, 47, 63.

7 Most recently O. Gelderblom, *Cities of Commerce: The Institutional Foundations of International Trade in the Low Countries, 1250–1650*, Princeton, NJ: Princeton University Press, 2013.

8 For example, W. Brulez and J. Craeybeckx, 'Les escales au carrefour des Pays-Bas (Bruges et Anvers, 14e–16e siècles)', in *Les Grandes Escales: Antiquité et Moyen Âge. Colloque organisé en collaboration avec la commission internationale d'histoire maritime (10e colloque d'histoire maritime)*, Brussels: Éditions de la Librairie Encyclopédique, 1974, pp. 417–74, and most recently A. Neele, 'De economie van de stad en de stedelingen', in P. Brusse and P. Henderikx (eds), *Geschiedenis van Zeeland*, vol. 1, *Prehistorie–1550*, Zwolle: WBooks, 2012, pp. 277–94.

9 For example, V. Enthoven, 'Zeeland en de opkomst van de Republiek. Handel en strijd in de Scheldedelta c.1550–1621', unpublished PhD thesis, University of Leiden, 1996, and M. Ebben and S. Groenveld (eds), *De Scheldedelta als verbinding en scheiding tussen Noord en Zuid, 1500–1800*, Maastricht: Vlaams-Nederlandse Vereniging voor Nieuwe Geschiedenis, 2007.

10 Brulez and Craeybeckx, 'Les escales', pp. 428–9. Neele, 'Economie', pp. 286–7 and 294; M. K. E. Gottschalk, *Stormvloeden en rivieroverstromingen in Nederland,* vol. 2, *De periode 1400–1600,* Assen: Van Gorcum, 1975.
11 Neele, 'Economie', pp. 287, 294. J. P. Sigmond, *Nederlandse zeehavens tussen 1500 en 1800,* Amsterdam: De Bataafsche Leeuw, 1989, p. 19.
12 L. Sicking, *La naissance d'une thalassocratie: Les Pays-Bas et la mer à l'aube du Siècle d'or,* Paris: Presses de l'Université Paris-Sorbonne, 2015, pp. 51–8, 60–1.
13 B. van Bavel, *Manors and Markets: Economy and Society in the Low Countries, 500–1600,* Oxford: Oxford University Press, 2010, p. 227.
14 Sigmond, *Zeehavens,* pp. 47, 49.
15 W. S. Unger, *De tol van Iersekeroord: Documenten en rekeningen, 1321–1572,* The Hague: Nijhoff, 1939, pp. 151–6.
16 Neele, 'Economie', p. 277; P. M. Hohenberg and L. H. Lees, *The Making of Urban Europe, 1000–1994,* Cambridge, MA: Harvard University Press, 1996, pp. 47–73.
17 Lesger, *Handel,* p. 33. Neele, 'Economie', p. 287.
18 W. S. Unger (ed.) *Bronnen tot de geschiedenis van Middelburg in den landsheerlijken tijd,* vol. 3, The Hague: Nijhoff, 1931, pp. 818–25. Neele, 'Economie', p. 288.
19 Unger, *Bronnen,* vol. 3, pp. 818–25; Enthoven, *Zeeland,* p. 397; Neele, 'Economie', p. 288.
20 J. A. Goris, *Étude sur les colonies marchandes méridionales (portugais, espagnols, italiens) à Anvers de 1488 à 1567: Contribution à l'histoire des débuts du capitalisme moderne,* Leuven: Librairie universitaire, 1925, p. 335. Neele, 'Economie', p. 289.
21 Sicking, *Naissance,* p. 126. Lesger, *Handel,* p. 43.
22 C. de Waard, 'De rand van het eiland Walcheren in 1546', *Archief: Vroegere en latere mededeelingen voornamelijk in betrekking tot Zeeland,* 1912, pp. 129–58, 142.
23 Sigmond, *Zeehavens,* pp. 27–8.
24 Enthoven, *Zeeland,* p. 5; J. Craeybeckx, *Un grand commerce d'importation: Les vins de France aux anciens Pays-Bas (*XIIIe–XVIe *siècle),* Paris: SEVPEN, 1958, pp. 29, 31, 42; R. W. Unger, 'Scheepvaart in de Noordelijke Nederlanden', in D. P. Blok *et al.* (eds), *Algemene geschiedenis der Nederlanden,* vol. 6, Bussum: Fibula-Van Dishoeck, 1979, pp. 109–22, 118.
25 Unger, *Bronnen,* vol. 3, p. 826. Neele, 'Economie', pp. 290–1.
26 Neele, 'Economie', p. 291.
27 Sigmond, *Zeehavens,* p. 25.
28 J. J. Westendorp Boerma and C. A. van Zwigchem, *Zierikzee vroeger en nu,* Bussum: Fibula Van Dishoeck, 1972, pp. 20–31; A. van Steensel, 'Bewoning en sociale structuren', in Brusse and Henderikx, *Geschiedenis van Zeeland,* vol. 1, pp. 211–25, 216–17; Neele, 'Economie', p. 294; Sigmond, *Zeehavens,* p. 26.
29 Sigmond, *Zeehavens,* p. 20. C. J. F. Slootmans, *Paas- en Koudemarkten te Bergen op Zoom 1365–1565,* vol. 3, Tilburg: Stichting Zuidelijk Historisch Contact, 1985, pp. 1318–19.
30 Gelderblom, *Cities,* pp. 200–4.
31 Neele, 'Economie', p. 290.
32 Z. W. Sneller and W. S. Unger, *Bronnen tot de geschiedenis van den handel met Frankrijk,* vol. 1, *753–1585,* The Hague: Nijhoff, 1930, pp. 359–62.
33 J. Davidson and A. Gray, *The Scottish Staple at Veere: A Study in the Economic History of Scotland,* London: Longman, Green & Co, 1909, pp. 146, 161–3.
34 Gelderblom, *Cities,* p. 203.
35 Blockmans, *Metropolen aan de Noordzee: De geschiedenis van Nederland 1100–1560,* Amsterdam: Bert Bakker, 2010, p. 254; R. Degryse, 'Oudste houten kranen in de Vlaamse en andere havens (13de–16de eeuw)', *Handelingen van het genootschap voor geschiedenis* 128, 1991, pp. 5–46 and 153–87, 8; J. A. van Houtte, *De geschiedenis van Brugge,* Tielt: Lannoo, 1982, p. 112.
36 Degryse, 'Oudste houten kranen', pp. 171–2, 175. P. W. Sijnke, 'De stadskranen van Middelburg', *Zeeuws tijdschrift* 32/3, 1982, pp. 92–4.

37 J. A. van Wallenburg, *Als 't diep verloopt verset men de bakens: De ontwikkeling van tonnen en boeien door de eeuwen heen*, Amsterdam: De Bataafsche Leeuw, 2008, p. 45.
38 R. Degryse, 'Brugge en de organisatie van het loodswezen van het Zwin op het einde van de 15[de] eeuw', *Handelingen van het Genootschap voor geschiedenis* 112/1–2, 1975, pp. 61–130, 83–98, 100.
39 D. Roos, 'Een blik zeewaarts vanaf de Walcherse duinen en dijken: Over loodsen, bebakening en betonning, banken en geulen', *Walacria, een kroniek van Walcheren: het Walchers jaarboek* 1989, pp. 107–24, 108, 115–16.
40 L. Sicking, 'Le paradoxe de l'accès: Le rôle des avant-ports dans les anciens Pays-Bas à la fin du Moyen Âge et au début de l'époque moderne (approche comparative générale)', in M. Bochaca and J.-L. Sarrazin (eds), *Ports et littoraux de l'Europe atlantique: Transformations naturelles et aménagements humains (xive–xvie siècles)*, Rennes: Presses Universitaire de Rennes, 2007, pp. 227–55, 241–4.
41 Ibid. pp. 244–7.
42 GRM BH 840 document g, pp. 12–19; A. H. Huussen, *Inventaris en beschrijving van de processtukken (dossiers) behorende tot de beroepen uit Holland berustende in het archief van de Grote Raad van Mechelen*, Algemeen Rijksarchief Brussel 9, Amsterdam: s.n., 1974.
43 L. Sicking, 'La llave de los Países Bajos: El acceso marítimo y las apuestas territoriales de las villas de la Isla de Walcheren en Zelanda (siglos XV–XVI): el caso de Middelburgo', in B. Arízaga Bolumburu and J. A. Solórzano Telechea (eds), *La ciudad medieval y su influencia territorial: Nájera. Encuentros internacionales del medievo 2006*, Logroño: Instituto de Estudios Riojanos, 2007, pp. 395–422.
44 A. Wijffels, 'Flanders and the Scheldt question: a mirror of the law of international relations and its actors', *Sartoniana* 15, 2002, pp. 213–80, 215–16, 225–6, 232.
45 J. Dumolyn and B. Lambert, 'Cities of commerce, cities of constraints: international trade, government institutions and the low countries in later medieval Bruges and the Burgundian state', *Tijdschrift voor sociale en economische geschiedenis* 11/4, 2014, pp. 89–101.
46 Sicking, *Naissance*, pp. 70, 73, 86, 95, 98.
47 Van Bavel, *Manors*, p. 227. Blockmans, *Metropolen*, p. 554. Gelderblom, *Cities*, p. 205. Lesger, *Handel*, p. 136.
48 L. Sicking, 'De zaak Draeck: Antwerpen tegenover Zierikzee. Een interstedelijk conflict tijdens de Vlaamse Opstand', forthcoming.
49 L. Sicking, *Neptune and the Netherlands: State, Economy, and War at Sea in the Renaissance*, Leiden and Boston, MA: Brill, 2004, pp. 58–9, 303, 407–8.
50 J. Parmentier, 'Een maritiem-economische schets van de deltahavens, 1400–1800', in M. Ebben and S. Groenveld (eds), *De Scheldedelta als verbinding en scheiding tussen Noord en Zuid, 1500–1800*, Maastricht: Nederlandse Vereniging voor Nieuwe Geschiedenis, 2007, pp. 11–26, 21–2.
51 Parmentier, 'Schets', p. 23; Lesger, *Handel*, p. 135.
52 Parmentier, 'Schets', pp. 21–3; Lesger, *Handel*, p. 99; P. van Cruyningen, 'Economie', in P. Brusse and W. Mijnhardt (eds), *Geschiedenis van Zeeland*, vol. 2, *1550–1700*, Zwolle and Utrecht: WBooks, 2012, pp. 51–101, 83.
53 Sigmond, *Zeehavens*, p. 63.
54 Ibid.; H. Kesteloo, *Geschiedenis en plaatsbeschrijving van Arnemuiden*, Middelburg, 1875, pp. 16–17, 23–4.
55 Kesteloo, *Geschiedenis*, pp. 12–13, 135–40.
56 Sigmond, *Zeehavens*, pp. 29, 64–5.

22
THE MARITIME TRADE NETWORKS OF LATE MEDIEVAL LONDON

Maryanne Kowaleski

Even though London lies some 50 km from the sea up a tidal estuary, maritime networks played a significant role in its emergence as Britain's biggest and wealthiest city. In the early thirteenth century, London controlled about 17 per cent of the value of England's overseas trade, a share that increased to 36 per cent in the first decade of the fourteenth century and 61 per cent in the late 1470s.[1] London's grip on England's increasingly valuable cloth exports was particularly notable, rising from 13 per cent of all cloth exports in the mid-fourteenth century, to around 40 per cent in the 1430s, then 61 per cent in the first decade of the sixteenth century, and an astonishing 90 per cent by the mid-sixteenth century.[2] London's population growth was equally impressive. By 1300 it had become one of Europe's largest cities, with a population perhaps as high as 80,000.[3] The Black Death and subsequent plagues reduced the population to about half that size in the late fourteenth century, but the city reached its pre-plague population in the early sixteenth century and by 1600 had grown to 120,000.[4] If its rapidly expanding suburbs are included, metropolitan London was home to 110,000 people in 1500 and almost half a million in 1700 when it ranked as Europe's largest city. It grew far faster than the rest of the country; in 1500, London was probably four times larger than the next provincial town, and in 1600, perhaps ten times as large, with the gap widening even more in the seventeenth century. Its share of the country's overall wealth also significantly increased from 1334, when Londoners accounted for 2 per cent of lay taxable assets, to about 9 per cent in the early sixteenth century.[5]

There is a copious, almost unmanageable, scholarly literature about London's phenomenal growth from 1300 to 1600.[6] This chapter focuses on one important aspect of this growth – the maritime sector – to explore how and what factors were most responsible for London's success in linking local, regional and international trade, particularly during the late fourteenth and fifteenth century, when the foundation for the rapid expansion of early modern London's maritime networks was laid. Scholars have made little effort to link the medieval and early modern developments in London's maritime trade, partly because the primary sources (particularly the organization and scope of the royal customs accounts from which so much of our data derive) changed significantly in the sixteenth century and partly because many English historians favour neat political divides that lump the first Tudor king (Henry VII, r. 1485–1506) with the other Tudors monarchs of the sixteenth century. Yet many of the patterns identified by early modern scholars as characteristic of London's dominance of English trade in the sixteenth and seventeenth century[7] are evident a century or more earlier, including the concentration of commercial capital and banking in the city,[8] high wage differentials with the rest of the country,[9] distinctive patterns of consumption,[10] superior transport and commercial facilities,[11] and its role linking rural hinterlands and provincial ports with overseas markets.[12]

Location advantages and challenges

Much of London's success was due to is location on the river Thames, strongly tidal up to a point west of London. The river rises and falls twice a day by almost seven metres, depending on the season, making it possible for ocean-going vessels to reach London from the open sea in one tide and thus connecting the city to ports on the English and continental side of the North Sea and Channel, including the densely populated markets of the Low Countries and Rhine estuary. London's location also made it possible to take advantage of the late medieval expansion of trade to the Baltic and Atlantic routes to France, Spain and eventually the Mediterranean and North America. Within England, London enjoyed quick and relatively inexpensive access to a large hinterland via river transport since the Thames was probably tidal about 58 km past London and navigable 180 km beyond the city, although few river boats in the later Middle Ages ventured much beyond Henley, *c.*100 km upriver from London.[13] Overland it was the centre of the medieval transportation network in southern, eastern and midland Britain, due in no small part to the Romans' decision to build a bridge over the Thames, which made London the nodal point of their road system.

London's growth and commercial success was also assisted by its proximity to the centre of royal government in its suburban settlement of Westminster, about 2.5 km to the west. On the eastern edge of the city was the Tower of London, another potent symbol of royal authority. This proximity to the seat of power was a mixed blessing. On the one hand, the administrative, financial and legal functions provided by the royal government drew the country's rich and powerful to the capital while also providing employment to many civil servants and therefore a substantial consumer market for the cargoes that piled up on London's wharves. On the other hand, relations between the crown and the city were frequently tense, so much so that the thirteenth- and fourteenth-century kings often suspended the city's liberties and charged them huge sums to regain the right to self-govern.[14] The balance of power waivered but neither the king nor London could survive without the other. The king especially needed the financial support that Londoners could provide, as well as legitimation of his rule, while London relied on the crown for validation of its liberties, and such economic privileges as jurisdiction over the Thames and protectionist policies against alien merchants. This latter issue was a valuable card for the crown, which often backed tax exemptions and other privileges for alien merchants in exchange for ready cash, influence and the opportunity to keep Londoners in check.

Unlike many of the continent's large cities, London possessed no formal authority over its hinterland, although it did build up claims to customs and coroners' jurisdiction from the mouth of the Thames estuary up to Staines, a considerable stretch of over 100 km.[15] Recent scholarship on London's economic hinterland has, moreover, shown how its consumer demand and merchant capital influenced agricultural choices, prices and transport options in a region that extended into its ten neighbouring counties and often beyond.[16] The city's trade also profited from the relatively secure coinage, peacekeeping efforts and country-wide royal court system sponsored by England's strong central government.

The port of London

Thanks to a series of archaeological excavations in the last thirty-five years, we are now much better informed about developments on the medieval London waterfront.[17] Much of the riverside wall or embankment constructed by the Romans on the north side of the Thames was broken down or had been removed by the late eleventh century. Gaps or 'gates' in the wall had in the Anglo-Saxon period become sites of waterborne trade: hence the term 'watergate' and wharves whose names ended in 'gate'. As trade expanded in the High Middle Ages, owners of waterfront properties constructed stairs, jetties and wharves to facilitate access to the river and make cargo handling easier. Reclamation for the public quays was virtually complete by the early thirteenth century, but the height of reclamation for the 90 per cent of the riverfront under private ownership was the late thirteenth through fourteenth century with some work continuing into the fifteenth century. This expansion entailed an impressive reclamation of land for these structures and for sheds, houses, cellars and warehouses, a reclamation that was almost entirely financed by private investment. From the tenth to the fifteenth centuries, the construction of one timber (and later stone) river wall after another helped to advance the London riverfront over 100 metres into the Thames. Development on the south bank of the Thames in Southwark occurred primarily in the late Middle Ages, and was likewise funded mainly by private landowners. The public burden of waterfront maintenance was further eased by the scouring effect of the tides up to London, which meant the city never had to invest in the dredging schemes or silt removal that plagued so many other ports.[18]

London was connected to the south bank of the Thames – and to the well-populated southern counties – by London Bridge, originally built in timber around 1000 and replaced by a stone bridge that began construction in 1176, finished *c.*1209, and required regular maintenance to handle the aggressive tides of the Thames.[19] These costs were managed by elected bridge-wardens and funded mostly by income from rental properties in the bridge's landed estate. Larger projects required gifts, loans or taxes from the citizenry. Small and ever decreasing contributions came from carts crossing the bridge and ships passing underneath the drawbridge. As ships became larger in the later Middle Ages, fewer overseas ships were able to go through the bridge, leading to more development of downriver wharves, such as Billingsgate in the city of London and Deptford and Greenwich in downriver Thameside settlements. Upriver quays such as Queenhithe became more focused on river trade.

Even though public investment in the port's infrastructure was small compared to private contributions, the city and crown controlled regulation of the waterfront and took the lion's share of profits from customs, fees and other dues. By the late fifteenth century, there were forty-two royal customs officials working at the port of London: two collectors and one controller for each of the three types of royal customs, each of whom had a clerk and probably a servant, plus a surveyor, searcher, tronager, deputy butler, and their clerks and servants, including (from at least 1490) seventeen 'waiters' who inspected cargoes on ships and after they were unloaded.[20] The royal customs administration came to be centred on the Woolwharf and the adjacent Customs House (where Geoffrey Chaucer once worked), built by a London grocer for the convenience of fellow merchants, another example of the public/private partnerships that funded the development of the London waterfront.[21] There were also local London customs officials who collected such tolls as scavage, anchorage, wharfage and pesage at the city-owned quays, and an unknown but significant number of private landlords who charged to use their wharves, river stairs and storehouses.[22]

Although the range of tolls and fees levied on maritime trade in London was complex (Table 22.1), it is hard to say if they were any more burdensome than what traders experienced in other large ports. Like denizen merchants elsewhere, London citizens were exempt from most local customs and paid lower rates than foreign merchants for the far more burdensome royal customs. Foreign exporters, for example, were charged twice as much as English merchants for wool and cloth, though favoured foreigners, such as Hanseatic and Castilian merchants, could periodically be granted lesser rates. The heaviest customs were levied on wool exports; in the fifteenth century, alien exporters had to pay royal customs as high as £5 per sack; the duty was fixed in 1471 at a rate that was 48 per cent of the price for which the exporter purchased good-quality wool, compared to 25 per cent for denizen exporters, which gave Londoners and other denizens a significant competitive advantage.[23] Transactions costs were also increased through additional charges for unloading cargo onto lighter craft for transport to the shore, for porterage of goods from ships and wharves to storehouses, and for storing cargoes ashore, but these charges were common in all ports. Interestingly, the costs of storage in London (at least for grain)

Table 22.1 Royal customs duties levied on maritime trade in London in the fifteenth century

Custom Type	*Who Paid*	*Specific Exemptions*	*Goods Taxed*	*Rates*
1. Wool Customs and Subsidies[a]				
Ancient custom[b]	Denizen and alien exports		Wool, wool-fells, hides	6s 8d per wool sack and per 240 skins/fells; 13s 4d per last (200) hides
New (petty) custom on wool[c]	Alien exports	Castilians and Leónese paid as denizens, 1466–89[d]	Wool, wool-fells, hides	3s 4d per sack of wool and per 240 skins/fells; 6s 8d per last hides
Subsidies on wool[e]	Denizen and alien exports	Hanse usually exempt	Wool, wool-fells, hides	Varied. In fifteenth century, denizens usually paid 23–33s per sack of wool and aliens as much as 90s; in 1471 alien rate fixed at 66s 8d
2. Petty Custom				
New (petty) custom[f]	Alien imports and exports; denizen cloth exports	Castilians and Leónese, 1466–89, merchants of Guipúzcoa, 1476–89, and from 1468, merchants of Brittany	All goods, including imported cloth, but excluded exports of wool, wool-fells, and hides; denizen wool cloth exports; and wine imports.	Ad valorem duty of 3d per £ value. Wax customed at 1s per quintal. In 1491, alien imports of sweet wine had to pay 18s per butt[g]
Cloth custom (Pannage)[h]	Denizen and alien exports	Hanse paid denizen rate	Cloth exports	Rates varied. Aliens (except Hanse) paid at higher rate
3. Subsidies of Tunnage and Poundage				
Poundage[i]	Denizen and alien imports and exports	Hanse usually exempt, as were merchants of Veere (from 1471). Castilians and Leónese paid as denizens, 1466–89	All goods except those exempted (wool, wool-fells, hides, wine, grain, fresh fish, meat). Denizen cloth exports sometimes liable until *c.*1422 when specifically exempted.	Ad valorem duty. Denizens charged 1s per £, aliens charged 2s per £
Tunnage[j]	Denizen and alien imports	Hanse usually exempt	Wine	Denizen imports of sweet wine were 3s per tun; alien imports were 6s per tun

(continued)

Table 22.1 (continued)

Custom Type	*Who Paid*	*Specific Exemptions*	*Goods Taxed*	*Rates*
4. Wine Customs				
Butlerage: new (petty) custom[k]	Alien imports		Wine	2s per tun of wine
Prisage[l]	Denizen imports	Citizens of London, Cinque Ports and many other towns with charters of exemption	Wine	Varied by size of ship: if ship's cargo >20 tuns, owed 2 tuns; if cargo 10–19 tuns, owed 1 tun; if <10 tuns, none owed
5. Miscellaneous Fees				
Cocket[m]	Denizen and alien merchants		Wool, wool-fells, hides	2d from each merchant exporting wool, wool-fells and hides
Bill of content[n]	Shipmaster		Paid for entering information on the ship in customs account	1d
Bill of discharge[o]	Departing ships		Charge by searcher on each ship leaving port	20d to 6s per ship
Passenger fee[p]	Alien passengers		Head-money fee paid to searcher	4d per passenger
Tronage[q]	Denizen and alien merchants		To weigh wool	1d per sack of wool

Sources: This table focuses on customs as they were in the fifteenth century, although there were some wide variations in exemptions and the amounts charged, not all of which are noted here. Other transactions costs are not listed here, including London's local customs, charges by porters and on carts for transporting cargoes to and from the waterfront, and fees for storage in cellars, granaries and warehouses.

Notes

[a] For the complications regarding the collection in London of wool customs and subsidies that were assigned to refund the Staplers for their loans and paying the wages of the Calais garrison, see Cobb, 'Introduction', pp. xvi–xv; Jenks, *Enrolled Customs, Part 8,* p. iv.

[b] Collected continuously from 1275; Carus-Wilson and Coleman, *England's Export Trade*, pp. 1–2, 194.

[c] Collected continuously from 1303, but those for wool, wool-fells and hides collected with ancient custom in later years; ibid., pp. 2, 194. That for wine collected and accounted for as 'butlerage' (along with prisage) by the king's butler.

[d] An Anglo-Castilian treaty allowed merchants from Castile and León to pay all customs and subsidies (including poundage and tunnage) at denizen rates (including cloth exports, which were thus free of poundage). In 1476, customs and subsidies due from them and merchants from the province of Guipúzcoa were reduced by half in London and some other ports; Jenks, 'Introduction', *Enrolled Customs, Part 10*, pp. iv–v.

[e] Granted to king by parliament. The rates fluctuated until fixed in 1471; Carus-Wilson and Coleman, *England's Export Trade*, p. 194. For Hanse exemptions, see below, note h.

[f] Collected continuously from 1303; that for wool, wool-fell and hide exports and wine imports collected separately (above, note c and below, note k). From the late 1450s, denizen imports and exports (esp. cloth and tin) traded through alien factors were customed as alien; Jenks, 'Introduction', *Enrolled Customs, Part 9*, p. iv. For Spanish exemptions, see above, note d. A 1468 treaty allowed Breton merchants to pay customs at denizen rates, which exempted them from poundage on their cloth exports and petty custom; Jenks, 'Introduction', *Enrolled Customs, Part 10*, p. v.

[g] The Statute of 1491 aimed at Mediterranean sweet wines in response to Venetian customs on English exports of malmsey from Crete. Called 'new customs' of 1491 and assessed as part of petty customs, not tunnage; Jenks, 'Introduction', *Enrolled Customs, Part 9*, p. iv.

[h] Collected continuously from 1347. For Hanse customs exemptions and resistance to new impositions, see Lloyd, *England and the German Hanse*, pp. 32–4, 51–2, 75–8, 140, 143, 217, 269–71. The Hanse was exempted from the cloth custom in Mar. 1437, but this was suspended Sept. 1447 to Oct. 1449 except for merchants of Gdańsk and Lübeck (privilege restored in Mar. 1456). There was a further suspension in 1468 (except for Cologne merchants) to 1474. Jenks, 'Introduction', *Enrolled Accounts, Part 9*, pp. vii–xiii

[i] Granted to king by parliament. First grant was in the 1340s, but in 1415 parliament began to make grants for life to the king; Gras, *English Customs*, pp. 81–4. By *c.*1480, the valuations had become standardized for many commodities; Cobb, 'Introduction', pp. xiii, xxv, n. 105. For Hanse exemptions, see above, note h; for Spanish exemptions, note d, above; for Veere exemptions, see Jenks, 'Introduction', *Enrolled Accounts, Part 9*, p. v.

[j] Above, note i.

[k] From the late 1320s, the new (petty) custom on wine was collected by the king's butler and came to be called 'butlerage'; from 1303 prisage was commuted into a money payment for aliens, but denizens continued to pay in kind; Gras, *English Customs,* pp. 42–6, 66.

[l] Above, note k.

[m] Paid at this rate since the reign of Edward II; Cobb, 'Introduction', p. xxiii.

[n] Imports also required a declaration in writing of the cargo; Cobb, 'Introduction', pp. xxiii, xxv.

[o] It is unclear if or how this was levied before the early 16th century, though the Cely ship paid this fee in 1486 when leaving Gravesend in the London customs jurisdiction; Cobb, 'Introduction', pp. xxiii, xxvi.

[p] See above, note n.

[q] This fee was ½d per sack in the 14th century, but 1d by the late 15th century; Cobb, 'Introduction', p. xxiii.

were less than in many other English regions, perhaps a reflection of economies of scale and the availability of commercial storage near the London waterfront.[24] Wages were higher in London than elsewhere, but it is unlikely that the task-rates charged by waterfront porters and carters added significantly to the costs of doing business in London, especially given the security offered by the city in licensing porters.[25] Although London's high costs for food and rent would have increased expenses for travelling merchants and shippers in the port, transactions costs were most affected by the port customs they had to pay, which were high enough to be the subject of international diplomacy, but not so high as to dampen enthusiasm for access to the city's valuable exports and consumer markets.[26]

Indeed, the highly regulated London waterfront provided considerable security to the buyers, sellers, shippers and fishers who used its facilities. The city took the regulatory lead, but was reinforced by the crown, interested in protecting its lucrative royal customs. Local and crown authorities often acted in tandem in standardizing and enforcing weights and measures; discouraging navigational obstructions such as fish weirs; channelling the landing and sale of certain goods (such as fish, salt, wine and wool) to particular wharves for easier supervision and customs collection; and legislating and conducting periodic inquisitions to ensure common access, the elimination of waste and fire hazards, and reasonable repairs to quays and river stairs.[27] The city, crown and wealthy merchants also cooperated to fund defensive measures during wartime, ensuring that the city was never raided by foreign forces.[28] Offences against maritime law or law merchant were tried in the city courts; there is no mention in London of the separate maritime courts found in other English ports.[29] Customs evasion was rigorously pursued in the crown's Exchequer court, so smuggling by both denizen and alien merchants was limited in this period.[30] Although London merchants jealously guarded their trading privileges and monopolies, and the customs system favoured local Londoners, the mercantile elite that ruled late medieval London understood that facilitating commercial exchange at the waterfront was crucial to their own and the city's prosperity.

Shipping

Our understanding of medieval London's shipping is far behind our grasp of its overseas trade and mercantile networks. Paucity of sources is only partly to blame – notably the failure of the London royal customs accounts to record ship names and home ports – since other sources can provide acceptable comparative data. These data show that commercial shipping registered at London did not come close to matching the city's prominence in other aspects of the maritime sector. London and other Thameside ports, for example, provided only 4 to 7 per cent of the merchant shipping regularly impressed for the English navy from the first half of the fourteenth to the first half of the fifteenth century.[31] The profile of London ships in the Gascon wine trade was not much better. In the late fourteenth century, they accounted for only 7 per cent of the English ships on this profitable sea route and carried just under 10 per cent of the wine imported to England.[32] London's share rose slightly in the mid and late fifteenth century, although the tunnage was considerably lower than it had been in the early fourteenth century at the height of the Gascon wine trade. London and Thameside ships also accounted for a measly proportion – less than 2 per cent – of the ships transporting pilgrims to Santiago de Compostella, a lower percentage than other eastern ports such as Boston and Ipswich. In 1480–1, the petty customs account shows that London ships made up 20 per cent of the ships exiting its own port for overseas markets.[33] The percentage was probably closer to 30 per cent since petty customs excluded all denizen imports and exports (except cloth). London ships were even less well-represented among ships carrying overseas imports.

More research is needed to understand why London merchants did not pursue ship owning more enthusiastically. They certainly had the capital to invest, and plenty of trading opportunities via the coast, short hops across the Channel, or to more distant ports in the Baltic and south Atlantic. Their overland connections and central role in supplying an enormous hinterland that stretched over a good part of the country may have diverted their interest, which was further muted by their lack of direct sea-going experience given their distance from the sea. In contrast with other major English ports, merchant shipmasters or merchant shipowners were rare in London's mercantile elite.

Shipbuilding, however, was becoming an important waterfront industry along the Thames. Its spread steadily eastwards from the foreshore of the city proper to Thameside settlements – where land was cheaper and access less congested – was stimulated in particular by royal investment.[34] As early as the mid-fourteenth century, the crown was constructing and refurbishing royal ships at Ratcliffe (5 km east of the city) and Greenwich, which by the late fifteenth century had outstripped the Tower as a storage depot for royal naval supplies.[35] Other shipyards developed at Deptford and Erith in Kent during the fifteenth century.[36] Deptford's maritime focus is further attested in the formal establishment of the well-known pilots' Guild of the Holy Trinity in the early sixteenth century to ensure that there were sufficiently skilled men to navigate the difficult waters of the Thames.[37] But the biggest crown investment came at Woolwich, although not until the second decade of the sixteenth century, when special docks and other facilities were built for the construction of the massive (1,000 tons) *Henri Grâce à Dieu* and three galleys.[38]

Private investment did not play as large a role in London shipbuilding as it did in the reclamation and construction of the city's waterfront. Crown and to a lesser extent civic capital seem to have stimulated the industry, although this emphasis could primarily reflect the better survival of documentation on corporate and crown shipbuilding for the navy.[39] The sparse evidence that survives for private shipbuilding relates mainly to ship repairs, such as those made at Ratcliffe and Blackwall by the Cely wool merchants of London, or to the purchase of naval supplies and ship victuals at these and other Thames ports.[40] Many medieval London shipowners like the Celys purchased their ships more often than newly building them, an investment strategy that makes sense for merchants who had little personal experience at sea. The particularly high cost of skilled labour in the London region may also have made merchants think twice about building a ship. Yet the safety of the Thames and proximity to London capital were also probably factors in the steady growth of maritime industry in the eastern Thames ports, as was the lack of space on London's crowded waterfront for the larger ships being used in the later Middle Ages.[41] Considerable employment in these ports must have been provided by the continual need to repair and victual ships trading in and out of London. Indeed, it is likely that the largest industrial enterprises of the entire London region were centred in these river ports by the end of the fifteenth century, if not earlier. In comparison to the size and capitalization of artisanal workshops in late medieval London – where a workforce of fifteen would be extraordinarily large – the numbers employed in shipbuilding and maintenance in the city's neighbouring ports to the east were simply enormous.[42]

It is possible to get some idea of the total size of the shipping involved in overseas trade at London through the particular customs accounts, although exact numbers are impossible because all the accounts necessary for a full picture of London's maritime trade never survive for the same year and because the London accounts often fail to record a ship's home port. The best estimate thus far, based on data from the late fourteenth century, speculates that in the year 1390–1, there were probably 730 to 750 ships passing through the port of London for overseas trade.[43] This figure excludes coastal trade and what must have been an enormous number of smaller hoys and shouts shipping smaller cargoes by river, as well as the lighters carrying cargoes to and from larger ships and the shore. A comparison of one petty customs account from the late fourteenth century and one from the late fifteenth century also seems to show an overall decline in overseas traffic at London by the later period. In 1390–1, there were 800 shipping movements (443 incoming, 357 outgoing), compared to only 439 movements in 1480–1 (224 incoming, 215 outgoing).[44] This seeming decline does not fit with what we know about the expansion of London's overseas trade in the last quarter of the fifteenth century, so further data are needed to confirm this pattern. It is possible, however, that the lower figures for 1480–1 might stem from an increase in denizen shipping (which is less often recorded in the petty customs accounts because of exemptions), or the rising size of ships (which means that fewer vessels could transport the same amount of goods), or an increase in coastal trade (which was not taxed in the royal customs).[45]

Maritime connections: river and coastal trade

Cheap and efficient water transport, whether via the navigable Thames or coastal waters, offered London trade huge advantages and greatly facilitated the integration of markets centred on the city and port. In the early fourteenth century, for example, land cartage for wheat in the London region was twelve to eighteen times more expensive than water carriage, with coastal shipment costing the least.[46] Access to inexpensive water transport was a major factor in shaping the grain supply region of medieval London – which in the early fourteenth century stretched further than that for the much larger city of Paris – well over 100 km up the river to Henley and considerably further by coast to East Anglia, Kent and Sussex. Preliminary research on grain prices in the London region suggests a high degree of integration from at least the late thirteenth century, followed by disruptions in the 1350s and 1360s when London sought grain from further away at a higher cost, either because of poor harvests or problems in the marketing system.[47] This integration was disrupted (albeit later, in the 1360s) in the larger coastal market for grain, which included not only London and the coastal zones of southwestern and southeastern England, but also Normandy, Picardy and Flanders. Evidence from a well-documented part of this coastal grain market (Exeter, in southwestern England) suggests that disintegration (signalled by price volatility) continued into the 1430s when the grain market calmed; whether the new price stability reflected the resurgence of an integrated coastal grain market that included London awaits further research. It may be significant, however, that during grain shortages in London in 1446 and Exeter in 1448/9, several thousand quarters of wheat were imported from Normandy and Picardy, the same continental grain markets that Exeter resorted to during the famine years of the early fourteenth century.[48] The one difference is that Baltic grain may have been becoming more available in London, although the transport costs made it a viable option only in years of shortage.[49]

Access to river transport also shaped London's supply zone for firewood.[50] In the early fourteenth century, London's fuel demands were intense enough to prompt neighbouring estate owners to invest in the production of appropriate types and sizes of wood for faggots or charcoal. Since the London region was well-endowed with woodland, the shape and extent of the supply zone was primarily influenced by the availability of cheap river transport for this bulky commodity, which favoured wood from Middlesex and Surrey – connected to London by the Thames – rather than from the Weald of Kent and Sussex, which required more expensive overland carriage. By the early fourteenth century, London's rising need for fuel began to place considerable stress on local supplies; firewood prices rose at a significantly higher rate than grain prices, but this trend was halted by the drastic reduction in population following the Black Death. In the later Middle Ages, rising labour costs and changing land use, along with increased demand from the growth of fuel-heavy industries like brewing and dyeing, helped to raise the costs of firewood again, although not to the same extent as in pre-plague London. The ability to substitute coal may have also helped to alleviate this pressure. Coal reached London via the coast from the port of Newcastle, near the coal mines of northern England.[51] London was the most important domestic destination for English coal in the medieval period, although the availability of wood fuel in the London region, along with limitations in the organization of the coal industry, kept coastal imports low compared to the levels they reached in the early modern period.

A wide variety of other cargoes also reached London by river transport.[52] Although this river trade was never systematically recorded, the early appearance of special landing places and local customs on the London waterfront for such river-borne goods as grain, hay and firewood testifies to the importance of the Thames as a commercial highway.[53] The development of a whole range of river craft on the Thames, particularly the 'shout', a flat-bottomed boat with a mast and sail, ideal for carrying heavy loads in shallow water, is another indication of the stimulus provided by London's reliance on transport via the Thames.[54] Although it is impossible to measure the size of this river traffic, one clue can be found in the toll collected by London Bridge for ships passing through the bridge. In the 1380s when the toll was probably 1d per ship, the traffic reached as high as 292 vessels in some weeks, but zero in other weeks, with many variations in between.[55]

One of the biggest gaps in our understanding of London's maritime networks regards coastal trade, which only becomes visible after 1558, when the national port customs records began to include coastal trade. When they survive, local customs accounts can provide good data on medieval coastal trade, but they are not extant for London, probably because they were part of the fee farm paid by the city to the king and were leased to private individuals.[56] In English ports like Exeter, coastal trade accounted for about 70 per cent of all incoming shipping activity through the port in the late fourteenth and early fifteenth century and 61 per cent of all the wine imports.[57] It is unlikely, however, that London's coastal trade was as dominant as this, for a variety of reasons. London's access to cheap river transport, its location well inland at the centre of a national road network, the concentration of mercantile capital and consumer demand in the city, and the availability of much-desired exports like wool and cloth would have worked to heighten river and overseas traffic over coastal trade. That said, London's coastal trade and its connections to river and overseas networks of trade deserve more study.[58]

Maritime connections: overseas trade

The overseas trade of medieval London has been studied in depth, due in large part to the fortunate survival of what is considered the longest series of national (royal) customs accounts for any medieval European country. The *enrolled* customs accounts for medieval England, which include summary totals of the different customs collected at each port, survive almost continuously from the beginning of the royal customs in the late thirteenth century and provide long-term statistics by port for such important trades as the export of wool and cloth (Figures 22.1 and 22.2).[59] The *particular* customs accounts are the detailed records kept by appointed customs officials that were sent to the Exchequer to compile the enrolled accounts. Their survival rate is spottier, but they contain far more information about traders and their cargoes since they usually list each ship's arrival or departure date, the names of the shipmaster and merchants, as well as their custom status and cargo. Depending on the type of account, other information can be recorded, including the ship's name and home port, the valuation of each cargo and the amount of custom payable.[60] In most ports, the particular accounts for the main royal customs (ancient and new (petty) customs, wool and cloth subsidies, tunnage and poundage) were combined into one account, but at London they were kept in three separate accounts, probably because of the size of the trade there, though it has been suggested that the distribution of patronage might also have encouraged the appointment of several different sets of customs collectors.[61]

Thanks to these very detailed sources, London's role in the overseas trade of medieval England is well known. The first quantitative evidence comes in 1203–4, when the city was responsible for 17 per cent of the value of a royal tax on exports and imports, behind the 29 per cent share of the east coast port of Boston, through which were channelled more of the wool exports on which this tax was largely based.[62] By the early fourteenth century, however, over half of England's wool exports – by far the country's chief export – was shipped from London, rising to about 60 per cent in the late fourteenth century, when profits from the wool trade accounted for the wealth of many of London's richest citizens.[63] Although England's wool exports declined in the fifteenth century, the city's share of this valuable trade grew to 70–5 per cent in the last half of the century (Figure 22.1). London's participation in the developing export of English cloth also began slowly but grew quickly, surging from 13 per cent in the mid-fourteenth century to 40 per cent in the 1430s, to 60 per cent by the 1470s (Figure 22.2), and 90 per cent by the mid-sixteenth century.

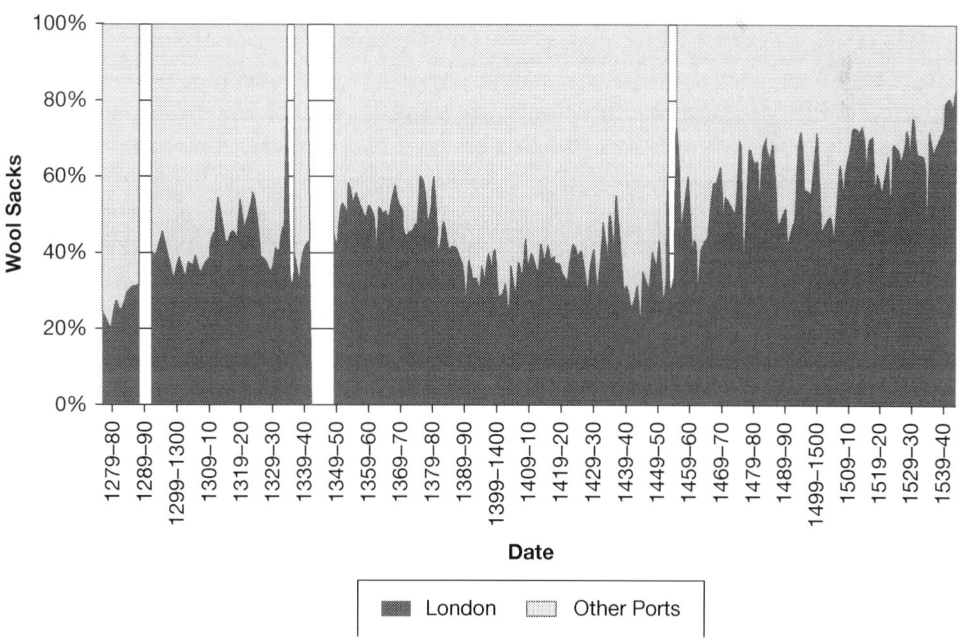

Figure 22.1 London's share of England's total wool exports, 1279–1543

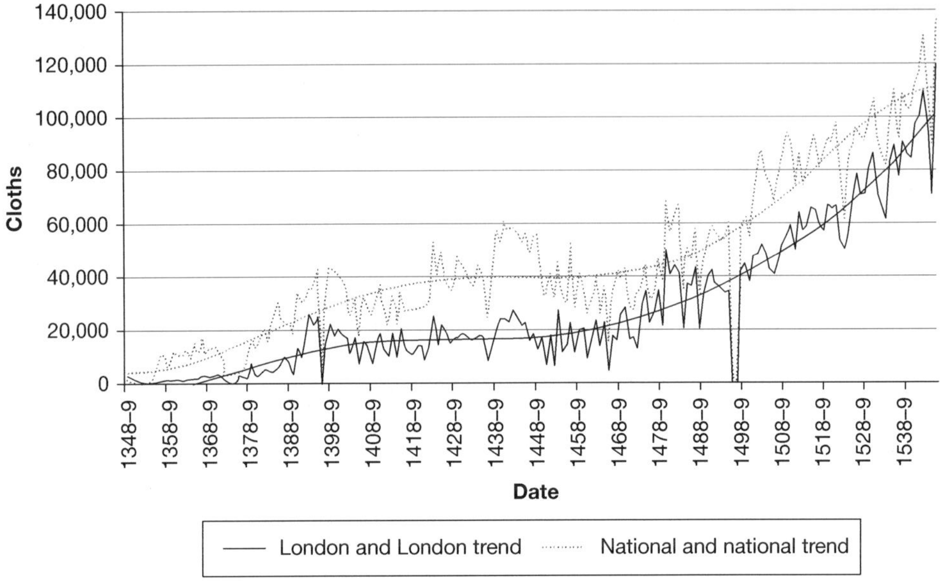

Figure 22.2 London's share of England's total cloth exports, 1348–1513

The crucial role of wool and cloth exports in England's economy and their growing value to London merchants stimulated the establishment of two powerful mercantile institutions: the Company of the Merchants of the Staple and the Merchant Adventurers. Because of the significant contribution that wool customs made to the royal coffers, the English crown pursued a policy of naming certain towns as staples through which wool had to be channelled in order to facilitate the collection of customs. In the late fourteenth century, the king established the wool staple at the English garrison town of Calais and chartered a group of mostly London wool merchants to receive a monopoly on wool exports in exchange for helping to defend the port against the French and advancing large sums to the crown. The Staplers were repaid through the wool customs, which brought in enormous sums each year. Indeed, the Staplers often functioned as bankers to the crown, although their effectiveness was strained by the financial burdens of maintaining the Calais garrison and other problems, not least their involvement in England's bullionist policies and the steady decline of English wool exports.[64] In contrast, the Company of the Merchant Adventurers became increasingly powerful in this period as cloth exports expanded. Merchant Adventurers formed in several English ports to handle non-wool overseas trade (particularly cloth), but because of privileges granted by the dukes of Brabant and Flemish efforts to limit the penetration of English cloth into their markets, Antwerp became the focus of much of the Adventurers' trade early in the fifteenth century. Provincial Adventurers attempted to resist the dominance of the Londoners, many of whom were merchants from London's Mercers guild, but to no avail. By the end of the fifteenth century, the Londoners had consolidated financial and political control of this regulated company, which allowed its members to trade as individuals, but arranged for ships and convoys, settled disputes between members and played a key role in English diplomatic negotiations with the Low Countries.[65]

Londoners' control of imports was not as spectacular as their grip on exports. Only about one-third of England's wine imports passed through London; its share of this trade rose in the late fifteenth century, but at a fraction of the tunnage imported in the early fourteenth century.[66] In the fifteenth century the scale of London imports generally followed the same stagnating and even declining trends as overall English imports, but in the 1460s, when overseas trade began to expand, London's domination of English provincial and overseas trade likewise grew.[67] It is estimated that London's imports in the 1470s reached a value of £90,000 and rose fairly steadily thereafter to £247,000 in the 1510s, more than doubling their worth in thirty years, a remarkable rate of growth.[68] The fly in the ointment, however, was the large share of this trade controlled by alien merchants in London. In the 1320s, 40 per cent of all alien trade in England focused on London, rising to almost 65 per cent in 1478–82.[69] Alien merchants were especially visible in the import trade; they captured at least 40 per cent of the value of London's imports throughout the fifteenth century, a figure that surged to almost 60 per cent in the 1450s, dropped slightly thereafter and fell more significantly in the 1530s.[70] Despite these dips, the alien share of London's maritime trade was still significant enough to prolong the ongoing tensions between alien merchants and their London hosts. Indeed, in no other English port were alien traders so dominant.

London's main overseas trading partner during the later Middle Ages was the Low Countries, a long-standing relationship that suffered when Flanders prohibited English cloth imports to protect its own cloth trade. But this relationship was bolstered when the wool staple settled in Calais, where wool was sold to both Flemish and Dutch merchants, and when the London Merchant Adventurers began operating through Antwerp, from whence English cloth reached the Brabant fairs and eventually German consumers. In the forty years after 1440, the amount of English cloth – most of which was of medium quality sold at a reasonable price – going through Antwerp more than doubled.[71] There were considerable ups and downs in this trade, influenced by political and monetary factors, but in general the trajectory was upwards, especially in terms of London's increasing control of England's cloth exports. In return for English cloth, merchants purchased not only Flemish and Dutch products, but also Baltic and Italian goods to re-export to England, overwhelmingly through the port of London.[72]

Baltic cargoes also reached London via Hanseatic shippers and merchants, who enjoyed lower customs rates in England than other alien groups (Table 22.1), a competitive advantage that was especially marked in their growing share of English cloth exports. Hanseatic customs exemptions and trade were often the subject of international diplomacy and crises, particularly in the fifteenth century. The major crisis was the Anglo-Hanseatic War, precipitated by the seizure of the goods of Hanseatic merchants in London in 1468 in retaliation for attacks on English ships.

The Hanse appears to have benefited more from the 1474 treaty than the English, who were not able to make the same inroads in the German and Baltic trade as the Hansards managed in England. The reduction of direct English access to Hanseatic markets in the Baltic (including Scandinavia) damaged the overseas trade of England's northeastern ports, but not London's. Indeed, driven especially by their exports of English cloth, Hanse merchants became increasingly focused on London; by 1478–82, the majority (86 per cent) of the value of all Hanse trade in England went through the port of London, a percentage that grew into the sixteenth century.[73]

Iberian trade with England also expanded in the late Middle Ages even though Anglo-Castilian hostilities during the Hundred Years War dampened Spanish trade from the late fourteenth through mid-fifteenth century, with some recovery during periods of truce. A lasting treaty in 1466 brought Castilian and other Spanish merchants favourable customs exemptions in England (Table 22.1). These incentives stimulated Spanish trade to England, evident in the growing Castilian share of English cloth exports, which averaged 2–5 per cent in the 1470s, but rose to 8–15 per cent in the 1480s.[74] Although the Castilians lost their customs privileges in a new treaty in 1489, their trade continued to mount, particularly in London, where an average of thirty (mostly Basque) Spanish ships arrived each year at the very end of the fifteenth century.[75] The vast majority of the wine imported to England by Spaniards also went through London. Portuguese trade likewise expanded and increasingly moved to London from Southampton (which was a stopping-off point for many Iberian ships on their way to the Low Countries) by the late fifteenth century.[76] This trade was modest in comparison with that of the Spanish, due to the greater focus on Bruges by Portuguese merchants and their more limited capital resources.

Not all of London's overseas trading partners participated in the late medieval growth of the city's maritime trade. The French in particular lost much of the prominence they had enjoyed in earlier centuries. Their trade was damaged by ongoing Anglo-French hostilities, particularly the Hundred Years War, which significantly reduced the export of Gascon wine to England in the late fourteenth and fifteenth century.[77] Trade with Brittany and Normandy flourished during truces and in the early fifteenth century when England took control of large swathes of Normandy, but the bulk of these trades was directed not to London but to other English ports.[78]

Italian luxuries continued to be in great demand in England, but their high value provoked anxieties over the balance of trade, as did the Italians' control of about one-quarter of England's late medieval overseas trade and their command of banking and foreign exchange functions. These functions, however, were essential to the smooth operation of England's overseas trade, and Italian exports of wool, cloth and tin were generally in balance with their imports in the fifteenth century.[79] Some changes did occur over time in the Italian mercantile networks through London. The Lucchese and Florentines, high-status merchants who settled in London, were more active in the fourteenth century, but were increasingly replaced in the fifteenth century by the Genoese and then the Venetians, who tended to be more transient and included more low-status clerks, shippers and mariners than their predecessors.[80] In the fifteenth and sixteenth centuries, a significant portion of the Italians' trade with London came via Southampton, whose deep harbour was favoured by the large Florentine galleys and Genoese carracks. The Italians unloaded their goods at Southampton but then sent a good proportion to London by cart; they also packed and customed their wool and cloth exports in London, but carted them to Southampton to be loaded on galleys bound for the Mediterranean.[81] The Florentine galleys stopped coming in 1480 and Genoese trade suffered severe setbacks a decade later. The Venetians were the most regular Italian visitors to London in the late Middle Ages because the capital provided the best market for their spices and luxury goods.[82] Their trade, centred on London, did not decline like that of the other Italians in the fifteenth century, though they increasingly unloaded their galleys at downriver Thameside ports and sailed some cargoes from London to Sandwich where they were loaded onto galleys homeward bound from Bruges.

Why did London's overseas trade expand so significantly in the later Middle Ages, especially during the economically depressed years of much of the fifteenth century? London overseas merchants had always enjoyed commercial protection as members of the city's guilds, as well as access to the country's richest consumers and a favourable geographic location in the capital city at the head of a tidal estuary with a large and prosperous hinterland. What circumstances changed to explain the port's significant growth? A variety of factors can be singled out. The development of the Company of the Staple (with its monopoly on wool exports) and Merchant Adventurers (with its dominance in cloth exports) considerably augmented London merchants' access to domestic and international markets, which in turn allowed them to build up strong capital reserves.[83] The attraction of Bruges (and then Antwerp) and the Low Countries for overseas trade from Italy, Iberia and the Hanse also helped London secure an advantageous nodal spot in this triangular trade linking north and south. London's pivotal role in English domestic trade grew as Londoners became more successful at channelling provincial goods through London for redistribution overland or overseas, efforts that were aided by royal charters and guild regulations compelling provincial merchants to go through London dealers.[84] Indications of the surplus capital accumulating in the city can be seen in the growing share of statute-staple and common pleas debts enrolled in London.[85] The Staplers in Calais, the Merchant Adventurers operating out of Antwerp, and London merchants in general were also politically, financially and geographically well situated to influence governmental responses to sensitive issues that arose in the later Middle Ages, such as alien competition, commercial relations with Burgundy, bullionist legislation and the balance of trade.[86] At the same time, the intensifying grip on city government and policy enjoyed by the mercantile guilds of London – the so-called 'twelve great companies' – provided an advantageous political climate for those seeking commercial opportunities.[87] London's ability to retain jurisdictional control over the expansion of shipping facilities in downriver Thameside settlements during the fifteenth and sixteenth centuries was also a key factor, as was the development of the Trinity guild of pilots whose skill made it easier for larger ocean-going ships to sail up the tricky waters of the Thames. And finally, although the strong profile of alien merchants in London's trade was a major source of anxiety for Londoners, the access to foreign markets, credit opportunities, banking functions and financial innovations provided by alien merchants were an essential lubricant in forming and maintaining maritime networks.[88] The relative peace that prevailed between England and its trading partners in the last decades of the fifteenth century also offered a favourable environment for the marked expansion of London's overseas trade in this period.

London merchants and alien traders

A major theme in the scholarly literature on London's maritime trade is the ongoing tensions between Londoners and alien merchants. The xenophobia, political lobbying and occasional violence levelled in London against aliens was in large part a response to the high profile and success that alien merchants enjoyed in the port. Overall, the share of London's overseas trade controlled by aliens during the later Middle Ages rose, albeit with significant short-term fluctuations. About 40 to 47 per cent of the total value of the city's overseas trade in the fifteenth century belonged to alien merchants, although alien imports in London rose more sharply in mid-century, from 44 per cent in the 1420s to 65 per cent in the 1450s; it is perhaps no coincidence that anti-alien measures were at their height in these decades.[89] Alien control of exports through London was also high if slightly less threatening. Cloth exports by aliens increased, for example, but not to the same extent as denizen exports. Even so, in most decades of the fifteenth century, aliens enjoyed at least 50 per cent of the value of all cloth exports through London, while London merchants were generally responsible for about 40 per cent of the cloth exported from their city.[90]

The tensions arising from the significant presence of alien merchants in London's maritime trade stimulated a variety of institutional constraints imposed by the city, the crown and parliament. In the early fourteenth century, Londoners secured royal charters forbidding aliens from selling at retail within the city and its suburbs, and requiring them to sell their imports within forty days and board with a citizen rather than fellow aliens, all measures designed to channel alien goods to London merchants.[91] But these restrictions were often relaxed by the crown, which benefited financially from allowing aliens to trade in England. Alien merchants, backed up by their own governments, also devoted time and money to lobbying the crown to relax restrictions on their trade. The Italians were particularly successful because of the loans they advanced and commercial services they provided to the English crown.[92] Bullionist policies designed to prevent shortage of good coin also affected alien merchants, who were blamed (especially the Italians) for bringing expensive imports into the country.[93] Parliament required alien merchants to spend their import profits on English goods and in 1429 promulgated the Bullion Ordinance of the Staple, which required that all wool purchased at Calais be paid for in gold and silver, a measure that hastened the departure of Burgundy from its alliance with England and damaged the wool export trade. Even more severe anti-alien measures followed. Parliamentary petitions in the late 1430s targeted the Italians in particular and laid the groundwork for the Hosting Act of 1439, which imposed stringent requirements on alien merchants, chief among them the obligation to lodge with local citizen merchants who kept track of their commercial activities and received a percentage fee on their sales.[94] The Act was most strictly observed in London, although the costs of the system made it difficult to enforce for more than five years. Hanseatic traders were exempt from the start, and the Genoese refused to comply by anticipating the legislation and securing exemptions from the crown. In London, therefore, it was mainly the Venetians who were targeted by the new Act. Finally, in 1440, Parliament ordered an entirely new tax, called the alien subsidy, which was assessed on foreigners for almost a half-century, although with decreasing efficiency and an increasing number of exemptions.[95] The London assessments, however, were more rigorously collected than those for any other English town. Indeed, it is likely that Londoners were behind most if not all of the anti-alien measures passed in Parliament in this period.[96]

The Views of Hosts, alien subsidy returns and other civic records provide valuable information on the alien merchants who resided in the city. In the mid-fifteenth century, at least 6 per cent of the city's population had been born overseas.[97] The vast majority of these foreign migrants were artisans and servants, particularly from the Low Countries, who lived scattered throughout the city and its suburbs. The alien merchants were altogether different. By the later Middle Ages, very few were from the Low Countries, and many were often only temporary residents, living in London during a period of youthful service to banking or commercial firms back home. Their greater wealth and business interests prompted them to reside in more central and commercial districts such as the waterfront or Cheapside. There were also many fewer of them. In the early 1450s, for example, forty-seven Hansards paid the alien subsidy, but only one was said to be a permanent resident. They were all staying at the Steelyard, a compound of buildings located on the waterfront east of Dowgate that started as the guildhall of the Cologne merchants in the twelfth century. Also called the 'Easterlings' Hall', the Steelyard was the London Kontor where the (mostly young and unmarried) Hanseatic merchants lived and worked and were exempt from city jurisdiction.[98] The Italians did not have a similar residential focus, although they often lived in the central wards.[99] In the four-year period of 1441–4, 175 different Italians resided in London, three-quarters of them established householders, and the remainder servants, clerks and more transient non-householders; at any one time, there were probably about seventy to a hundred Italians residing in London during the fifteenth century, similar to the size of the Italian community in the sixteenth century.[100] It is much harder to estimate the size of the resident Spanish, Portuguese and French merchant communities in London, but they were never as numerous as the Italian or even Hanseatic merchants.[101] More prosopographical work remains to be done to identify these communities, particularly the commercial impact of the Gascon merchants who migrated to London in the 1450s.[102]

Resentment of aliens was higher in London than in other English ports, as indicated by the energetic anti-alien lobbying led by Londoners and the outbreaks of anti-alien violence dating from at least the thirteenth century when Jews, Cahorsins and Italians were all victims of mob violence in London.[103] Trade rivalry was probably at the heart of the attacks by mercers on Italians in 1357, 1370 and 1378, two of which resulted in the death of an Italian merchant.[104] The mercers – resentful of Italian dominance in the sale of silk and other luxuries – were also behind the mass looting of Italian properties in 1456–7. Another prime target of London mobs were the thousands of Flemish artisans in the city and suburbs, particularly during the 1381 Peasants' Revolt when many were reportedly dragged out of sanctuary and killed; further incidents occurred in 1424, 1435–6 and 1470.[105] The privileges of Hanseatic traders also raised antagonism. Hanse merchants and goods were seized in retaliation for Hanse attacks on English ships or merchants on several occasions, but mob violence against the Hanse in London only occurred once, in 1493 when Steelyard warehouses were attacked.[106] The only significant anti-alien riot in the sixteenth century was the so-called Evil May Day of 1517, which resulted in the destruction of alien property (including French targets) and the execution of some Londoners found guilty of sedition.[107]

Although scholars have often highlighted the violent attacks against aliens in London, their influence on alien maritime trade was not particularly marked or long-lasting. The king and civic authorities always stepped in to punish the wrongdoers (and sometimes compensate those targeted), and mercantile business was disrupted only temporarily. There are, moreover, far more examples of ongoing cooperation between London merchants and alien traders, evident in the extension of credit, joint shipping ventures, the exchange of sureties, the employment of alien servants by London merchants and English servants by alien traders, and even intermarriage. Indeed, abundant extant documentation attests to the multiple and layered commercial, legal, residential and social ties between aliens and Londoners, with business relations continuing even during some of the worst periods of the bullion famine and anti-alien sentiment.[108] How these varied ties and social interactions helped to provide the foundation for the growth of London's international maritime networks of trade deserves more extended study. London merchants and alien traders alike sought competitive advantage, but viable market exchange across oceans and nations succeeded only when communication and collaboration could flourish.

Notes

1 For these and the following trade figures, see M. Kowaleski, 'The port towns', in D. M. Palliser (ed.), *The Cambridge Urban History of Britain*, vol. 1, Cambridge: Cambridge University Press, 2000, pp. 476–9.

2 B. Dietz, 'Overseas trade and metropolitan growth', in A. L. Beier and R. Finlay (eds), *London 1500–1700: The Making of the Metropolis*, London: Longman, 1986, p. 119.

3 D. Keene, 'A new study of London before the Great Fire', *Urban History Yearbook* 11, 1984, pp. 11–21. For arguments that the city's population was at most 60,000 in 1300, see P. Nightingale, 'The growth of London in the medieval English economy', in R. H. Britnell and J. Hatcher (eds), *Progress and Problems in Medieval England; Essays in Honour of Edward Miller*, Cambridge: Cambridge University Press, 1996, pp. 89–106.

4 R. Finlay and B. Shearer, 'Population growth and suburban expansion', in Beier and Finlay, *London 1500–1700*, pp. 38–45, for this and the following.

5 This is an underestimation since the figures do not include London's suburbs, which expanded more rapidly than the city proper in the later Middle Ages; see R. S. Schofield, 'The geographic distribution of wealth in England, 1334–1649', *Economic History Review*, 2nd ser. 18, 1965, p. 508. For other measures of London's growth, see D. Keene, 'Medieval London and its region', *London Journal* 14, 1989, pp. 99–110.

6 A search for works on London from 1300 to 1600 brings up 16,945 items in the (subscription-based) online *Bibliography of British and Irish History*, published by the Institute of Historical Research, the Royal Historical Society and Brepols, although adding the parameter 'economic' reduces the number to 3,746 (http://apps.brepolis.net/BrepolisPortal/default.aspx, accessed Jan. 2016).

7 A. L. Beier and R. Finlay, 'The significance of the metropolis', in Beier and Finlay, *London 1500–1700*, pp. 1–33; J. A. Chartres, 'Food consumption and internal trade', ibid., pp. 168–96; Dietz, 'Overseas trade'.

8 J. Oldland, 'The allocation of merchant capital in early Tudor London', *Economic History Review*, 2nd ser. 63, 2010, pp. 1058–80.

9 J. H. Munro, 'Wage-stickiness, monetary changes, and real incomes in late-medieval England and the Low Countries, 1300–1500: did money matter?', *Research in Economic History* 21, 2003, pp. 198, 232.

10 C. M. Barron, 'Centres of conspicuous consumption: the aristocratic town house in London, 1200–1500', *London Journal* 20, 1995, pp. 1–16; G. Egan, 'Luxury lifestyle in medieval London, archaeological evidence c. 1200–1600', in M. Gläser (ed.), *Lübecker Kolloquium zur Stadtarchäologie im Hanseraum VI: Luxus und Lifestyle*, Lübeck: Verlag SchmidtRömhild, 2008, pp. 43–61.

11 D. Keene, 'Shops and shopping in medieval London', in L. Grant (ed.), *Medieval Art, Architecture and Archaeology in London*, British Archaeological Association Conference Transactions 10, 1994, pp. 29–46. For transport, see below, notes 13, 46.

12 See below, pp. 392–4.

13 R. B. Peberdy, 'Navigation on the River Thames between London and Oxford in the late Middle Ages: a reconsideration', *Oxoniensia* 16, 1996, pp. 311–40.

14 D. Keene, 'London from the post-Roman period to 1300', in Palliser, *Cambridge Urban History*, pp. 187–216. For this and the following, see also C. M. Barron, *London in the Later Middle Ages: Government and People 1200–1500*, Oxford: Oxford University Press, 2004, pp. 9–42.

15 The city's claims were slowly built up over several centuries; see V. A. Harding, 'The port of London in the fourteenth century: its topography, administration and trade', PhD thesis, University of St Andrews, 1983, pp. 4–10. The city could also, from 1327, prevent the

establishment of any market within 7 miles of the city; W. DeGray Birch, *The Historical Charters and Constitutions of the City of London*, London: Whiting, 1887, p. 58.

16 B. M. S. Campbell, J. A. Galloway, D. Keene and M. Murphy, *A Medieval Capital and its Grain Supply: Agrarian Production and Distribution in the London Region c. 1300*, Historical Geography Research Series 30, Salford: Institute of British Geographers, 1993; D. Keene, 'Medieval London and its supply hinterlands', *Regional Environmental Change* 12, 2012, pp. 263–81, and below, n. 50.

17 For this and the following, see G. Milne, *The Port of Medieval London*, Stroud: Tempus, 2003. For a gazetteer of waterfront properties, see Harding, 'Port of London', vol. 2.

18 Harding, 'Port of London', p. 83.

19 B. Watson, *Old London Bridge: Lost and Found*, London: Museum of London, 2004, pp. 28–32; V. A. Harding and L. Wright (eds), *London Bridge: Selected Accounts and Rentals, 1381–1538*, London: London Record Society 31, 1995.

20 H. S. Cobb, 'Introduction', in H. S. Cobb (ed.) *The Overseas Trade of London Exchequer Customs Accounts, 1480–1*, London: London Record Society 27, 1990, pp. xvi, xx–xxi.

21 Barron, *London in the Later Middle Ages*, pp. 52–3; Milne, *Port of Medieval London*, p. 124.

22 For the wide variety of local customs (some charged by the city, others by lessors of city wharves or owners of private wharves), see Harding, 'Port of London', pp. 27, 39, 46–7, 89–112.

23 Customs rates on other goods represented far lower values; E. M. Carus-Wilson and O. Coleman, *England's Export Trade, 1275–1547*, Oxford: Clarendon, 1963, pp. 22, 194. See also J. H. Munro, 'Medieval woollens: the western European woolen industries and their struggles for international markets, c. 1000–1500', in D. Jenkins (ed.), *The Cambridge History of Western Textiles*, Cambridge: Cambridge University Press, 2002, pp. 280–2, 299–301.

24 J. Claridge and J. Langdon, 'Storage in medieval England: the evidence from purveyance accounts, 1295–1349', *Economic History Review*, 2nd ser. 64, 2011, pp. 1258–9.

25 M. Kowaleski, 'Port labour in medieval England', in M. Balard (ed.), *The Sea in History, vol. 2: The Medieval World*, Rochester, NY: Boydell and Brewer, forthcoming. For the relatively low costs of handling and shipping grain, see Campbell *et al.*, *Medieval Capital*, pp. 62 (esp. n. 70), 195–7. For London wages, see above, n. 9.

26 T. H. Lloyd, *The English Wool Trade in the Middle Ages*, Cambridge: Cambridge University Press, 1977; T. H. Lloyd, *England the German Hanse 1157–1611: A Study of their Trade and Commercial Diplomacy*, Cambridge: Cambridge University Press, 1991; S. Jenks, *England, die Hanse und Preußen: Handel und Diplomatie 1377–1474*, 3 vols, Cologne: Böhlau, 1992, passim; W. R. Childs, *Anglo-Castilian Trade in the Later Middle Ages*, Manchester: Manchester University Press, 1978, pp. 46–8, 53–7.

27 Milne, *Port of Medieval London*, pp. 97–102, 106, 113–14, 127–31, 147–52.

28 P. Nightingale, 'Philipot, Sir John (*d.* 1384)', *Oxford Dictionary of National Biography*, Oxford: Oxford University Press, 2004 (http://www.oxforddnb.com/view/article/22107, accessed Jan. 2016); Harding, 'Port of London', pp. 83–8; Milne, *Port of Medieval London*, pp. 116–19.

29 P. Tucker, *Law Courts and Lawyers in the City of London, 1300–1550*, Cambridge: Cambridge University Press, 2007, pp. 101, 113–16, 120–2, 137–8, 207–9. Aliens involved in lawsuits before the common law courts had the right to have some of their own countrymen on the jury; Susanne Jenks, 'Justice for strangers: the experience of alien merchants in medieval English common law courts', in C. M. Barron and A. F. Sutton (eds), *The Medieval Merchant: Proceedings of the 2012 Harlaxton Symposium*, Donington, Lincs.: Shaun Tyas, 2014, pp. 166–82. The London Steelyard sought to avoid the city courts by having their own aldermen (one English and one German) before whom to try their cases; A. Beardwood,

Alien Merchants in England 1350–1377: Their Legal and Economic Position, Cambridge, MA: Medieval Academy of America, 1931, pp. 118–20; N. Jörn, *'With Money and Blood': Der Londoner Stalhof im Spannungsfeld der englisch-hansischen Beziehungen im 15. und 16. Jahrhundert,* Cologne: Böhlau, 2000, pp. 328–33, 362–9.

30 Cobb, 'Introduction', p. xxxii.

31 Kowaleski, 'The port towns', pp. 488–9.

32 For this and the following, see M. Kowaleski, 'Warfare, shipping, and crown patronage: the impact of the Hundred Years War on the English port towns', in L. Armstrong, I. Elbl and M. Elbl (eds), *Money, Markets and Trade in Late Medieval Europe: Essays in Honour of John H. A. Munro*, Leiden: Brill, 2007, pp. 624–5; idem, 'The port towns', p. 490.

33 Cobb, 'Introduction', p. xxxviii, for this and the following.

34 For shipbuilding in medieval London, see Milne, *Port of Medieval London*, pp. 165–70; T. Dyson, 'Three medieval London shipbuilders', in P. Marsden (ed.), *Ships of the Port of London, Twelfth to Seventeenth Centuries AD*, London: English Heritage Archaeological Report 3, 1996, pp. 214–15, and below, n. 39.

35 *Calendar of Patent Rolls* [hereafter *CPR*] *1354–58*, London: HMSO, 1909, pp. 117, 446–7; Kew, The National Archives (hereafter TNA), E101/22/38. See also K. G. T. McDonnell, *Medieval London Suburbs*, London: Phillimore, 1978, pp. 98–9; TNA, E101/20/29; M. Oppenheim (ed.) *Naval Accounts and Inventories of the Reign of Henry VII, 1485–8 and 1495–7*, London: Navy Records Society 8, 1896, pp. 9, 10, 25, 30, 60–1, 74–7, 79–81; S. Rose (ed.), *Navy of the Lancastrian Kings: Accounts and Inventories of William Soper, Keeper of the King's Ships, 1422–1427*, London: Navy Records Society 123, 1982, pp. 31, 34.

36 L. Wright, *Sources of London English: Medieval Thames Vocabulary*, Oxford: Clarendon, 1996, p. 46; Rose, *Navy of the Lancastrian Kings*, pp. 39, 92, 146; M. M. Oppenheim, 'The royal dockyards', in W. Page (ed.), *The Victoria History of the County of Kent*, vol. 2, London: St Catherine Press, 1932, pp. 337, 339–40; Oppenheim, *Naval Accounts and Inventories*, pp. 25, 161–6.

37 A. A. Ruddock, 'The Trinity House at Deptford in the sixteenth century', *English Historical Review* 65, 1950, pp. 458–76.

38 Oppenheim, 'The royal dockyards', pp. 338–9; I. Friel, *The Good Ship: Ships, Shipbuilding and Technology in England, 1200–1520*, London: British Museum, 1995, p. 41.

39 B. Spencer, 'Expenditure on shipbuilding and repair by London Bridge, 1382–98', in Marsden, *Ships of the Port of London*, pp. 209–11; C. Johnson, 'London shipbuilding, A.D. 1295', *The Antiquaries Journal* 7, 1927, pp. 424–37; and above, notes 34–6.

40 H. E. Malden (ed.), *The Cely Papers*, London: Camden Society, 3rd ser. 1, 1900, pp. 178–81; A. Hanham, *The Celys and their World: An English Merchant Family of the Fifteenth Century*, Cambridge: Cambridge University Press, 1985, pp. 361–97; Friel, *Good Ship*, pp. 39–45, 51, 57; McDonnell, *Medieval London Suburbs*, pp. 82, 89.

41 D. Burwash, *English Merchant Shipping 1460–1540*, Toronto: University of Toronto Press, 1947, pp. 96–100. Greater regulation over pilots also mitigated the navigational difficulties of the Thames at the end of the Middle Ages; Ruddock, 'Trinity House', pp. 470–1.

42 N. A. M. Rodger, *The Safeguard of the Sea: A Naval History of Britain*, vol. 1, *660–1649*, London: Harper Collins, 1997, pp. 231–2; Friel, *Good Ship*, pp. 63–5.

43 The estimate is based on some complex albeit reasonable calculations to account for missing data; Harding, 'Port of London', pp. 262–3; idem, 'Cross-channel trade and cultural contacts: London and the Low Countries in the later fourteenth century', in C. Barron and N. Saul (eds), *England and the Low Countries in the Late Middle Ages*, New York: St Martin's Press, 1995, p. 155.

44 Harding, 'Port of London', pp. 262–3, 267, using TNA, E122/71/16 for 1390–1. For 1480–1, see Cobb, 'Introduction', p. xxxviii.

45 Cobb, 'Introduction', p. xxxviii, n. 185; Burwash, *English Merchant Shipping*, pp. 96–100.

46 For this and the following, see Campbell *et al.*, *Medieval Capital*, pp. 60–3, 193–8; Keene, 'Medieval London and its supply hinterlands', pp. 267–72. For comparisons of land, river and coastal carriage, see also J. Masschaele, 'Transport costs in medieval England', *Economic History Review*, 2nd ser. 46, 1993, pp. 266–79.

47 J. A. Galloway, 'One market or many? London and the grain trade of England', in J. A. Galloway (ed.), *Trade, Urban Hinterlands and Market Integration, c.1300–1600*, London: Centre for Metropolitan History, 2000, pp. 23–42.

48 TNA, E122/73/20A; Devon Heritage Center, Exeter Port Customs 1448/9; M. Kowaleski, 'The grain trade in fourteenth-century Exeter', in E. B. DeWindt (ed.), *The Salt of Common Life: Individuality and Choice in the Medieval Town, Countryside and Church: Essays Presented to J. Ambrose Raftis*, Kalamazoo, MI: Medieval Institute Press, 1995, pp. 1–52.

49 S. Jenks, *The Enrolled Customs Accounts (TNA:PRO E 356, E 372, E 364) 1279/80–1508/09 (1523/1524): E 356, parts 1–12*, List and Index Society, vols 303, 306, 307, 313, 314, 319, 324, 334, 341, 344, 345, 348, London, 2004–13, part 8, p. 1926; Lloyd, *England and the German Hanse*, pp. 222–3.

50 For this and the following, see J. A. Galloway, D. Keene and M. Murphy, 'Fuelling the city: production and distribution of firewood and fuel in London's region, 1290–1400', *Economic History Review*, 2nd ser. 49, 1996, pp. 447–72. See also J. A. Galloway, 'Metropolitan food and fuel supply in medieval England: regional and international contexts', in P. van Cruyningen and E. Thoen (eds), *Food Supply, Demand and Trade: Aspects of the Economic Relationship between Town and Countryside (Middle Ages–19th century)*, Turnhout: Brepols, 2012, pp. 7–18.

51 J. B. Blake, 'The medieval coal trade of North East England: some fourteenth-century evidence', *Northern History* 2, 1967, pp. 2–12; J. Hatcher, *The History of the British Coal Industry*, vol 1, *Before 1700: Towards the Age of Coal*, Cambridge: Cambridge University Press, 1993, pp. 14, 473–7, 486–504.

52 See the items listed under 'transport of materials by water' in the index of H. M. Colvin (ed.), *Building Accounts of King Henry III*, Oxford, Clarendon, 1971. See also Harding, 'Port of London', pp. 251–3; Harding and Wright, *London Bridge Accounts*, pp. 202, 204, 225, 237, and index under 'chalk', 'stone' and 'timber'.

53 Campbell *et al.*, *Medieval Capital*, pp. 46–53, 59–63; Harding, 'Port of London', pp. 25–64, passim. See also Peberdy, 'Navigation'; J. Langdon, 'Inland water transport in medieval England', *Journal of Historical Geography* 19, 1993, pp. 1–11.

54 Marsden, *Ships of the Port of London*, pp. 91–3; Wright, *Sources of London English*, pp. 138–52.

55 Harding, 'Port of London', pp. 264–5, 276–7. For changes in the fifteenth century that suggest a significant decline in river traffic, or a change in the nature of the toll, see Harding and Wright, *London Bridge Accounts*, pp. xxi, 121.

56 H. S. Cobb, 'Local port customs prior to 1550', in F. Ranger (ed.), *Prisca Munimenta*, London: London University Press, 1973, p. 224.

57 M. Kowaleski, *Local Markets and Regional Trade in Medieval Exeter*, Cambridge: Cambridge University Press, 1995, pp. 225–31.

58 For coastwise shipments to London of grain from East Anglia and Kent, coal from Newcastle, tin from Devon and Cornwall, and stone and tiles from southern England, see above, nn. 46, 51; J. Hatcher, *English Tin Production and Trade before 1550*, Oxford: Clarendon Press, 1973, pp. 94, 170–1, 176–93; L. F. Salzman, *Building in England down to 1540: A Documentary History*, Oxford, Clarendon Press, rev. edn, 1967, pp. 131–6, 349–50; Harding and Wright, *London Bridge Accounts*, pp. 23, 25, 99.

59 The enrolled customs figures for the medieval period are primarily in TNA, E356; those up to 1323 are on the Pipe Rolls in E372. The enrolled accounts for wool exports by the Staplers from 1466 to 1531 are in the Foreign Accounts in E364. After *c.*1500, these figures are in the Declared Accounts in E351. Note that the figures employed in pre-2006 publications about overseas trade for medieval England have now been redone to a higher standard by S. Jenks, *The Enrolled Customs Accounts* in 12 vols. Previous figures published for wool and cloth exports, as transcribed by Carus-Wilson and Coleman, *England's Export Trade,* probably would not vary significantly when citing overall trends, but those based on petty custom and poundage are more problematic (as in H. L. Gray, 'Tables of enrolled customs and subsidy accounts, 1399 to 1482', in E. Power and M. M. Postan (eds), *Studies in English Trade in the Fifteenth Century*, London: Routledge, 1933, pp. 321–409); see Jenks, 'Introduction', *Enrolled Customs Accounts,* part 1, pp. iv–viii.

60 The particular accounts in print for medieval London are: N. S. B. Gras, *The Early English Customs System: A Documentary Study of the Institutional and Economic History of the Customs from the Thirteenth to the Sixteenth Century,* Cambridge, MA: Harvard University Press, 1918, pp. 452–514 (part of the controller's petty custom account for 1420–1), and Cobb, *Overseas Trade of London* (the petty custom account for 1480–1). Forthcoming in 2017 is S. Jenks (ed.), *The London Customs Accounts, 24 Henry VI (1445–46),* British Academy Records of Social and Economic History, Oxford: Oxford University Press.

61 O. Coleman, 'Collectors of customs in London under Richard II', in A. E. J. Hollaender and W. Kellaway (eds), *Studies in London History Presented to Philip Edmund Jones*, London: Hodder & Stoughton, 1969, p. 183. Unfortunately, there is no one year when all the particular accounts survive for medieval London, but the variety of extant accounts do provide a good idea of who was trading in what types of goods.

62 Kowaleski, 'The port towns', pp. 476–7. See also H. S. Cobb, 'The medieval royal customs and their records', *Journal of the Society of Archivists* 6/4, 1979, p. 227.

63 These and the following figures on wool and cloth exports are from the tables in Carus-Wilson and Coleman, *England's Export Trade, 1275–1547*. See also E. Quinton and J. Oldland, 'London merchants' cloth exports, 1350–1500', *Medieval Clothing and Textiles* 7, 2011, pp. 111–40; Munro, 'Medieval woollens', pp. 306–7. For Londoners' wealth from the wool trade, see Barron, *London in the Later Middle Ages*, p. 100, and G. A. Williams, *Medieval London: From Commune to Capital*, London: Athlone Press, 1970, p. 320.

64 Lloyd, *English Wool Trade*, esp. pp. 225–87. See also S. Rose, *Calais: An English Town in France 1347–1558*, Woodbridge: Boydell, 2008; D. Grummitt, *The Calais Garrison: War and Military Service in England, 1436–1558*, Woodbridge: Boydell, 2008, esp. pp. 141–5; Hanham, *The Celys*, esp. pp. 224–51; J. H. Munro, *Wool, Cloth and Gold: The Struggle for Bullion in Anglo-Burgundian Trade, 1340–1478*, Toronto: University of Toronto Press, 1973.

65 E. Carus-Wilson, 'The origins and early development of the Merchant Adventurers' organization in London as shown in their own medieval records', in *Medieval Merchant Venturers: Collected Studies*, London: Methuen, 1954, pp. 143–82. For useful correctives, see A. F. Sutton, 'The Merchant Adventurers of England: their origins and the Mercers' Company of London', *Historical Research* 75, 2002, pp. 25–46. See also R. Davis, 'The rise of Antwerp and its English connection, 1406–1510', in D. C. Coleman and A. H. John (eds), *Trade, Government and Economy in Pre-Industrial England: Essays Presented to F. J. Fisher*, London: Weidenfeld & Nicolson, 1976, pp. 2–20.

66 Kowaleski, 'The port towns', p. 481, based on the data in M. K. James, *Studies in the Medieval Wine Trade*, ed. E. Veale, Oxford: Clarendon Press, 1971, pp. 98, 108–9, 113, 116; J. Oldland, 'The expansion of London's overseas trade from 1475–1520', in Barron and Sutton, *Medieval Merchant*, p. 61.

67 Oldland, 'Expansion', pp. 55–92.

68 Ibid., p. 79. These figures have undergone some manipulation since, unlike wool and cloth exports, which have separate customs duties, English customs on imports (except for wine, which was subject to a separate custom called tunnage) are mixed in with exports and subject to a good many exemptions of particular cargoes or merchants from certain regions. Oldland also includes what he calls London's 'outports' of Southampton and Sandwich in the cloth export figures, a decision that inflates the London figures for the years when there is evidence that London cloth exports were being carted to Southampton or taken by coastal vessel to Sandwich for export overseas. On this issue, see also H. S. Cobb, 'Cloth exports from London and Southampton in the later fifteenth and early sixteenth centuries: a revision', *Economic History Review*, 2nd ser. 31, 1978, pp. 601–9.

69 These figures are only roughly comparable given the different scope of the customs accounts in these two periods; see Kowaleski, 'The port towns', pp. 482–3. See also Oldland, 'Expansion'.

70 Oldland, 'Expansion', p. 83.

71 J. H. Munro, 'Bruges and the abortive staple in English cloth', *Revue belge de philologie et d'histoire* 44, 1966, p. 1143; Davis, 'Rise of Antwerp'.

72 Harding, 'Cross-channel trade'; Davis, 'Rise of Antwerp'; N. J. M. Kerling, *Commerical Relations of Holland and Zeeland with England from the Late 13th Century to the Close of the Middle Ages*, Leiden: Brill, 1954.

73 Kowaleski, 'The port towns', pp. 482–3. For long-term trends in Hanseatic trade in London, see Lloyd, *England and the German Hanse*, esp. pp. 76, 98–9, 164, 167, 228, 272-6, 382; Jenks, *England, die Hanse und Preußen*, vol. 1, esp. pp. 267–71, 330–65; John D. Fudge, *Cargoes, Embargoes, and Emissaries: The Commercial and Political Interaction of England and the German Hanse, 1450–1510*, Toronto: University of Toronto Press, 1995, esp. pp. 132–41, 151–5, 160–2, 213.

74 Childs, *Anglo-Castilian Trade*, p. 89.

75 W. R. Childs, *Trade and Shipping in the Medieval West: Portugal, Castile and England*, Porto: Fédération Internationale des Instituts e'Études Médiévales, 2013, p. 88. See also Childs, *Anglo-Castilian Trade*, pp. 88–90, 210–11, 217, for the growing share of London's trade, and pp. 134–5 for the following.

76 W. R. Childs, 'Anglo-Portuguese trade in the fifteenth century', *Transactions of the Royal Historical Society*, 6th ser. 2, 1992, pp. 195–219; idem, *Trade and Shipping*.

77 James, *Wine Trade*, pp. 15–44, 55–9, and below, n. 78.

78 Michel Mollat, *Le commerce maritime normand à la fin du Moyen Âge: Étude d'histoire économique et sociale*, Paris: Librairie Plon, 1952; Henri Touchard, *Le commerce maritime Breton à la fin du Moyen Âge*, Paris: Les Belles Lettres, 1967.

79 J. L. Bolton, *The Medieval English Economy 1150–1500*, London: J. M. Dent, 1980, pp. 312–14. For this trade, see also S. Montemezzo, 'Galley routes and merchant networks between Venice and the North Sea in the fifteenth century', in A. Caracausi and C. Jeggle (eds), *Commercial Networks and European Cities, 1400–1800*, London: Pickering & Chatto, 2014, pp. 162–3.

80 H. L. Bradley, 'The Italian merchants in London c.1350–c.1450', unpubl. PhD thesis, University of London, 1992, pp. 47–56, 415–24.

81 Cobb, 'Cloth exports'; H. Bradley, 'Introduction', in H. Bradley (ed.), *The Views of the Hosts of Alien Merchants 1440–1444*, London: London Record Society 46, 2012, pp. xviii–xxiii.

82 Bradley, 'Introduction', pp. xviii–xxiii; idem, 'Italian merchants', pp. 76–93, 415–31.

83 See, for example, the ascendancy of the Mercers; A. F. Sutton, *The Mercery of London: Trade, Goods and People, 1130–1578*, Aldershot: Ashgate, 2005.

84 Barron, *London in the Later Middle Ages*, pp. 79–83; J. Lutkin, 'Goldsmiths: London versus provincial', in Barron and Sutton, *Medieval Merchant*, pp. 41–54; Sutton, *Mercery of London*, pp. 118–20, 212–41. The restriction of cloth sales by non-freemen to Blackwell Hall also channelled more provincial cloth dealers to London in the fifteenth century; Barron, *London in the Later Middle Ages*, pp. 51–2.

85 J. I. Kermode, 'Medieval indebtedness: the regions *versus* London', in N. Rogers (ed.), *England in the Fifteenth Century: Proceedings of the 1992 Harlaxton Symposium*, Stamford: Paul Watkins, 1994, pp. 72–88; D. Keene, 'Changes in London's economic hinterland as indicated by debt cases in the Court of Common Pleas', in Galloway (ed.) *Trade, Urban Hinterlands*, pp. 59–81. See also Nightingale, 'Growth of London', pp. 100–6, who stresses London's ability to weather the monetary crises of the later Middle Ages. Tax assessments also indicate the growing concentration of wealth in London; see above, p. 383, and J. Oldland, 'The wealth of the trades in early Tudor London', *London Journal* 31, 2006, pp. 127–55.

86 See, for example, J. L. Bolton, 'The city and the crown, 1456–61', *London Journal* 12, 1986, pp. 11–24.

87 Barron, *London in the Later Middle Ages*, pp. 30–42.

88 Bolton, *Medieval English Economy*, pp. 303–4, 311–13, 318–19; W. R. Childs, '"To oure losse and hindrance": English credit to alien merchants in the mid-fifteenth century', in J. Kermode (ed.), *Enterprise and Individuals in Fifteenth-Century England*, Stroud: Alan Sutton, 1991, pp. 68–98; and in this volume, S. Jenks, 'Capturing opportunity, financing trade'.

89 Harding, 'Port of London', pp. 233–5; Oldland, 'Expansion', pp. 59–67, 91 (his overall trade figures exclude imports of wax and exports of worsteds, leather and hides).

90 Oldland, 'Expansion', p. 87; Quinton and Oldland, 'London merchants' cloth exports', p. 111.

91 Barron, *London in the Later Middle Ages*, pp. 38–9; Bradley, 'Introduction', pp. xii–xix.

92 Bradley, 'Italian merchants', pp. 199–279, 457–9.

93 Munro, *Wool, Cloth and Gold*; J. L. Bolton, *Money in the Medieval English Economy: 973–1489*, Manchester: Manchester University Press, 2012, pp. 245–51. The European bullion famine was especially severe in the 1440s and 1450s, when anti-alien sentiment was high.

94 Bradley, 'Introduction', pp. x–xxx, and for the returns of the hosts, Bradley, *Views of the Hosts*.

95 J. L. Bolton (ed.), *The Alien Communities of London in the Fifteenth Century: The Subsidy Rolls of 1400 and 1483–4*, Stamford: Richard III and Yorkist History Trust with Paul Watkins, 1998.

96 J. L. Bolton, 'London and the anti-alien legislation of 1439–40', in N. McDonald, W. M. Ormrod, and C. Taylor (eds), *Resident Aliens in Later Medieval England*, Turnhout: Brepols, forthcoming; Bolton, 'The city and the crown'; and above, n. 95.

97 For this and the following, see J. L. Bolton, 'Introduction', in Bolton (ed.), *Alien Communities of London*, pp. 6–8, 19–21, 28–34; M. Carlin, *Medieval Southwark*, London and Rio Grande: Hambledon, 1996, pp. 149–56.

98 D. Keene, 'Du seuil de la Cité à la formation d'une économie morale: l'environment hanséatique entre 12e et 17e siècle', in J. Bottin and D. Calabi (eds), *Les étrangers dans la ville*, Paris: Maison des Sciences de l'Homme, 1999, pp. 409–24; Jörn, *'With Money and Blood'*, esp. pp. 417–59.

99 Bradley, 'Italian merchants', pp. 18, 30–1.

100 Based on the lists of Italians identified by Bradley ('Italian merchants', pp. 49–50, 364–94) in the London alien subsidies, which in this period rarely specified national origin. For smaller estimates based on later (probably less complete) returns, see Bolton, 'Introduction', p. 6.

101 Bolton, 'Introduction', pp. 7, 29.

102 Such as the detailed prosopographical analysis done by Bradley on the Italians (above, n. 100) and Bolton for alien taxpayers in 1483 (above, n. 95). For the Gascons, see James, *Wine Trade*, pp. 84–8.

103 Barron, *London in the Later Middle Ages*, p. 14

104 Sutton, *Mercery of London*, pp. 115–17, 230–1; Bolton, 'City and the crown'; R. Flenley, 'London and foreign merchants in the reign of Henry VI', *English Historical Review* 25, 1910, pp. 644–55.

105 Carlin, *Medieval Southwark*, pp. 157–62.

106 Fudge, *Cargoes, Embargoes, and Emissaries*, pp. 134–6; Sutton, *Mercery of London*, p. 281.

107 G. Holmes, 'Evil May Day 1517: the story of a riot', *History Today* 15/9, 1965, pp. 642–50; S. Rappaport, *Worlds within Worlds: Structures of Life in Sixteenth-Century London*, Cambridge: Cambridge University Press, 1989, pp. 15–17.

108 S. Thrupp, *The Merchant Class of Medieval London*, Ann Arbor, MI: University of Michigan Press, 1948, pp. 135, 219–22; Childs, 'To oure losse and hindrance'; G. Holmes, 'Anglo-Florentine trade in 1451', *English Historical Review* 108, 1993, pp. 371–86; Bradley, 'Italian merchants', esp. pp. 307–18; Childs, *Trade and Shipping*, pp. 126–32; S. Jenks, 'Hansische Vermächtnisse in London: ca. 1363–1483', *Hansische Geschichtsblätter* 104, 1986, pp. 35–111.

23

ABERDEEN AND THE EAST COAST OF SCOTLAND

Autonomy on the periphery

Edda Frankot

Throughout its history Aberdeen has been one of the main ports in Scotland. After its establishment as a royal burgh during the reign of David I (1124–53) it soon grew to be one of the most important trading centres in Scotland. Its position far north of any of the other larger ports (Dundee, Perth, Edinburgh (Leith) and Berwick) meant that it functioned as the commercial hub of a very large hinterland. But it was never Scotland's most important port, even though it was the second largest for much of the relevant period. Initially it was surpassed by Berwick, until its capture by the English in 1333 during the Wars of Independence.[1] From the second half of the fourteenth century Edinburgh with its port of Leith would take the lead, gaining a dominant role in the import and export of almost every piece of merchandise.

Although Edinburgh's mercurial rise might make it the more logical choice, this chapter focuses instead on Aberdeen because of its far superior source material. The Aberdeen council registers provide a wealth of qualitative information that puts flesh on the bones of the economic data available for the whole of Scotland in this period. This information is extant for almost the whole of the fifteenth century for Aberdeen only. As far as possible though, comparisons will be provided with Edinburgh, and the whole of Scotland's east coast trade will be considered in the section on connections. As will be shown, Aberdeen was an important regional hub with a vast hinterland that operated very much within an east coast trading network, but also reasonably independently within the kingdom's legal framework. Scotland's main partners for most of the period were the merchants based in the Low Countries. Through them, but also through growing expatriate communities elsewhere, the Scottish burghs, though on the periphery, were connected to an extensive European trading network.

Because of Aberdeen's superior source material, the urban and economic historiography of medieval Scotland has often focused on this burgh.[2] In the 1980s and

1990s Scotland's urban and economic history of the Middle Ages and early modern period experienced a renaissance, focusing especially on Scotland's relations with other parts of Europe and the history of the Scot abroad, but also on the medieval and early modern town.[3] The topic of the Scot abroad in the early modern period has continued to be a popular topic of research.[4] With regards to the Middle Ages, there has been less output in recent years. The most important book of the last fifteen years in the context of this chapter is Ditchburn's 2001 *Scotland and Europe*, the first of a two-volume work. The first volume concentrates on Scotland's social and economic contacts, whereas the second volume will consider political relations, including diplomacy, a topic that is still relatively under-researched.[5] That there is still more to be investigated is proven by the ongoing project on Scotland and the Flemish People, where research is focusing on economic considerations in Scotto-Flemish diplomacy and on Flemish material culture in Scotland.[6] Work remains to be done on the legal and administrative history of Aberdeen, the main topic lacking in the 2002 history of Aberdeen. Some of this ground was covered by a study on the administration of maritime law in Aberdeen within a European context, but only up to 1500.[7] Much uncertainty still exists with regards to the admiral and his court, though the subject of early modern naval warfare recently received a thorough examination by Murdoch.[8]

The most important historiographical discussion within the context of this book has concerned the question of Scotland's supposed deficit from the late fourteenth century. Historians agree that the Scottish economy was booming in the thirteenth century, when wool and other sheep-derived products were in great demand for export. This resulted in a sharp increase in the money supply in Scotland.[9] There is also agreement that the export of wool and related products declined dramatically from the 1370s. But whether this decline led to a substantial deficit or not is a matter of debate.[10] The problem is that the available evidence from the custom accounts only cover part of Scotland's exports, and virtually none of its imports (those from England and Ireland excepted). Mayhew and Gemmill have argued that, despite the scarcity of bullion (a circumstance shared with most countries in Europe in the later Middle Ages), and the decline in wool exports, there are various signs that the Scottish economy was in better shape than has previously been assumed: prices were high, crown and church finances were reasonably healthy, being based on an agricultural society which was sufficiently prosperous to be able to invest in land, and there is evidence of other investments, for example in building. The repeated devaluation of the Scottish currency in the later Middle Ages would have helped merchants in selling their goods abroad at relatively low prices and some Scots were obviously able to make significant profits at this time.[11] Nonetheless, production levels were much lower than they had been before the Black Death, so overall the Scottish economy in the fifteenth and sixteenth centuries was much less buoyant than that of the thirteenth century.[12]

Location and hinterland

The geographical advantages of Aberdeen's location are clear: it is situated at the estuary mouth of the River Dee, allowing access to the sea and rich fishings, and close to lowland plains which could be used for agriculture. Some natural protection was offered by the sea, the river(s), a loch and marshes, and the three main hills allowed for vantage points over the surrounding countryside. The majority of Scottish burghs were located on inland sites, though some (such as Perth) were accessible by sea-going vessels. Others were obliged to make use of nearby harbours, such as Edinburgh with its satellite port of (South) Leith.[13] Aberdeen's geographical position facilitated its growth: by the twelfth century it was one of the three main trading centres in Scotland (with Perth and Berwick) and it remained the commercial hub of a large hinterland throughout the Middle Ages.[14]

Although international trade to and from Scotland declined significantly from the late fourteenth century, and this decline may have hit Aberdeen harder than most other ports, the burgh continued to be an important hub for its sizeable hinterland. Inland trade ensured that Aberdeen remained one of the main trading centres in Scotland. On the basis of the produce of its hinterland (especially wool and salmon), the burgh regained its position as the second busiest port after Edinburgh (Leith) in the mid-fifteenth century.[15] From that time Edinburgh, Aberdeen, Dundee and Perth were the four main burghs of Scotland, gaining an ever greater advantage over the other Scottish towns. Simultaneously, Edinburgh became increasingly dominant.[16]

However, though Aberdeen's geographical position provided it with some clear advantages, there is no denying that Scotland's position in European trade was somewhat peripheral.[17] Scotland was a relatively small market and Aberdeen only one of its ports. Aberdeen's location within Scotland, further away from Scotland's main trading partners than other large ports, meant that it would never become the country's main port. Moreover, changes in the agricultural organization of Edinburgh's hinterland resulted in an increase in production there, but similar developments were lacking in the northeast.[18]

Inland trade was the basis of Aberdeen's wealth. Aberdeen's hinterland covered a vast area, more extensive than that of any other Scottish town. By the late thirteenth century the burgh had gained economic pre-eminence far beyond its trading precinct, in a region stretching from Forres and Elgin in the Northwest to Montrose to the south (an area covering over 9,000 sq. km), and its regional domination continued to grow into the sixteenth century.[19] From Aberdeen, goods were transported by sea, to the other ports on the east and northeast coast, and by land.[20]

Scotland's and Aberdeen's source of wealth in the twelfth to fourteenth centuries was the availability of various sheep-derived products, especially wool. The export of these products reached its zenith in the 1370s, when 881 tonnes of wool and 114,000 woolfells were exported from Scotland. For much of the fourteenth century, and perhaps the thirteenth century too, similar amounts had been transported abroad. Aberdeen was, with Montrose and Perth, one of the main exporters of wool in the thirteenth century, though Berwick was the major entrepôt of this trade in that period.[21] A deterioration of the quality of wool, hides and woolfells in the fourteenth century, as a result of a worsening climate and economic reasons, which will be discussed further below, resulted in a decline of Scottish trade from about 1380. Trade picked up again in the mid-fifteenth century. By this time Aberdeen mainly exported salmon, also abundantly available in its hinterland.[22] Otherwise, Aberdeen continued to function as a market for local, regional and national trade.

Connections

Scotland's main trading partners throughout most of the period were the merchants in the Low Countries. In the twelfth century Flemish merchants, on the hunt for increasingly more wool to meet the demand of an expanding textile industry, were instrumental in transforming the Scottish economy towards production for export and in founding and developing the Scottish burghs. Scotland's economy in the twelfth and thirteenth centuries was mainly geared towards supplying the Flemish and Artesian textile industries. By the 1170s a large Flemish community had settled in Scotland and many of the earliest burgesses have Flemish names.[23]

A Scottish colony was likely in existence at Bruges' Schottendijk before 1280, and by the late thirteenth century reciprocal agreements were in place guaranteeing Flemish and Scottish merchants protection and freedom of trade. A Scottish staple appears to have been well established by 1321, though the oldest known agreement dates to 1359.[24] By that time Scottish trade was mainly conducted by Scottish merchants themselves.[25] The staple agreements stipulated that all wool, hides and woolfells would be exported to Bruges. There, the Scottish merchants enjoyed special protection and privileges, which included, from 1407, their representation by a 'Conservator of the Scottish Privileges'. As Scotland's main export products were already shipped to Bruges, most other trade was conducted through that entrepôt as well.[26] But in the late fourteenth century a structural change in the nature of the Netherlandish textile production caused a shift in demand. The older textile-producing cities restricted themselves to the use of only the best quality (that is, English) wool. Ypres, for example, prohibited the use of Scottish wool in 1390. Smaller production centres in western Flanders and in Holland, on the other hand, continued to use Scottish wool to produce lower quality cloth. On the whole, however, demand dropped significantly. This decline was made worse by the population drop as a result of the Black Death, and by the climatic regression of the later Middle Ages which caused a deterioration of the quality of wool.[27]

Because of the falling trade, and a general maritime turmoil in the area as a result of conflicts between England and France, Scots became involved in piracy. This resulted in a Hanseatic embargo on Scottish trade in 1412–15 and 1419–36. This embargo was not particularly effective, as some of Scotland's most important Hanseatic partners (Danzig, Stralsund and Hamburg) ignored it. Nonetheless, Scottish merchants increasingly started to look beyond Bruges. The Scottish staple was moved to Middelburg in Zeeland several times during the fifteenth century, when various crises and wars caused the Scots to get more and more frustrated by Flemish restrictions. The staple was permanently abandoned in 1477. From the 1460s trade had been increasingly conducted with merchants in Veere, Bergen op Zoom and Antwerp, and in 1508 Veere became the compulsory Netherlandish port of entry.[28]

Despite the importance of the Low Countries for Scottish commerce, trade connections also existed with other areas in Northern Europe. Before Scottish merchants came to dominate Scottish trade from the 1330s, German and Scandinavian traders also frequented some of the Scottish ports. By the late thirteenth century Berwick and Dundee were involved in trade with Northern Europe and there may have been a resident German community at Berwick at that time. There is also some evidence for commercial contacts with Scandinavia in the late thirteenth and early fourteenth centuries.[29] After a possible break, by the 1380s German merchants were visiting Scotland once again and Scottish merchants were trading in the Baltic. This trade continued into the sixteenth century, being dominated by Edinburgh and Dundee.[30] Most of the trade with the Baltic continued to flow via Bruges, and via England in the sixteenth century. Normandy (especially Dieppe) increasingly became an important destination for Scottish products from the late fifteenth century. By 1486 there was sufficient direct trade with Dieppe for a small Scottish colony of twenty-three burgesses to have been established there.[31] Relations with England were, of course, disturbed by various conflicts throughout the period, but commerce between the two countries usually re-established itself quickly after any hostilities. From the late fifteenth century England's role in trade with Scotland increased.[32]

In addition to the export of wool, woolfells and hides to the Low Countries, Dieppe became an important destination of wool and hides from the later fifteenth century. Another market for hides, much smaller but steady, was the Baltic. Most wool and hides were shipped from Leith in the later period, but wool remained an important product for Aberdeen. The decline in wool exports probably resulted in an increasing production of woollen cloth in Scotland, though Scotland never became a major producer of cloth for export, unlike England and Ireland. Again, Edinburgh dominated this trade, exporting 75–80 per cent of all cloth in the fifteenth and sixteenth centuries. Only small amounts were shipped from Aberdeen. The main Baltic market for this cloth was Danzig, though Denmark, southern Sweden, Anklam, Hamburg, Lübeck and Stralsund were destinations too. France also figured as an importer of Scottish cloth, as did England, but the latter largely of linen rather than woollen cloth. The flax to produce linen was imported from Danzig, making up 60 per cent of exports from there to Scotland in the later fifteenth and early sixteenth centuries. Silk and better quality woollen cloth were imported from the Low Countries in the fourteenth century, and from England.[33]

Fish exports from Scotland consisted mainly of salmon and herring. Both were shipped to Artois and England in the thirteenth century. In the following centuries salmon was exported to Bruges and England, and later increasingly to France. Most of this trade was conducted from Aberdeen (though increasingly via Leith). The herring trade fluctuated somewhat. It was exported in small amounts, but also imported at times from the Scanian fairs. By the mid-fifteenth century the Scots were catching their own herring again, and transporting some of this to France and England. Salt was needed for the preservation of fish. Though salt was produced in Scotland by boiling sea water, this very fine salt was not very suitable for preserving fish. So salt was imported (from England, France and, in the early sixteenth century, mainly from the Baltic), especially north of the Tay where none was produced. Scottish salt in its turn was exported to Danzig, as it was much cheaper than Lüneburg salt, to Norway, Denmark and Sweden.[34]

Another staple product that was traded was grain, which was sometimes imported, from Ireland, England and France, and from the Baltic by the early fifteenth century. In times of peace England continued to be the preferred partner, as transportation costs were significantly lower. At other times wheat was exported. Ale was produced in Scotland, but beer was imported from Hamburg and Stralsund. Wine was shipped into Scotland from Germany, France and sometimes from Spain, mainly via the Netherlands in the fourteenth and early fifteenth centuries, but also via England and later on directly from France.[35]

As little timber suitable for shipbuilding was available in Scotland naturally, timber was probably transported from Stralsund in the earlier period (via the Netherlands like most trade). From the late fifteenth century this trade was taken over by the Norwegians and the Swedish. Timber-related products such as tar and pitch were imported from Danzig. Manufactured goods mainly reached Scotland by way of the Low Countries until England became Scotland's main partner in the re-export of goods in the later 1530s. In the sixteenth century Scottish merchants became increasingly involved in the re-export of goods. These consisted of a great variety of goods, such as Baltic wares and timber. This was one of the main sectors of growth, with salt and coal, in the later sixteenth century, though at their peak, these would only make up about 10 per cent of exports from Leith, Dundee and the Fife ports.[36]

Edinburgh increasingly came to dominate overseas trade from Scotland and monopolize the export of many of its staple goods. By the 1530s, Leith shipped about 90 per cent of all Scottish wool, 80 per cent of cloth and large portions of most other products. From the mid-fifteenth century many burghs increasingly sent a large proportion of their goods to Leith to be exported, though smaller and inland burghs would also transport merchandise to the larger sea ports (such as Aberdeen and Dundee, but also Montrose and St Andrews). Only salmon was for the main part exported from Aberdeen, though this too increasingly via Leith. Many more ships would sail and dock at Leith, and Edinburgh's merchants would have been able to foster a more extensive trading network. By the 1590s many overseas merchants from Aberdeen relocated to Leith for part of the year to profit from that port's superior infrastructure and connections.[37]

Migration has been an important theme in Scottish history and historiography. It has been recognized in the past two decades or so that this had its origins in the Middle Ages and did not take off suddenly after the Union of 1707.[38] It has also been established that the pattern of migration was not unusual in a European context, but that the level of early modern emigration from Scotland especially was very high compared to that of other northwestern European countries. The reasons for this migration varied over time in accordance with current economic and political conditions, or as a result of government policies. The main factors were economic: most people moved because they thought opportunities would be better elsewhere. And as opportunities in Scotland were relatively limited, relatively many Scots emigrated. As time went by migration networks became increasingly more developed, making it easier for new generations to move abroad.[39]

Within the context of this chapter, the most relevant migrants were those who in some way contributed to Aberdeen and Scotland's overseas connections. Though many Scottish communities and individuals can be found abroad in the later Middle Ages and early modern period, few foreigners settled in Scotland in the same period. As a result, the burghs did not have to facilitate the presence of foreign communities. Some Aberdonians and other Scots, mainly from the burghs, did settle in the towns with which the Scottish ports maintained direct trade. This particular type of migration thus reflected the country's main connections at any one time. Most of these migrants would have kept in close contact with relations back home and many would return after a period abroad. Fifty-one Scots are known to have acquired burgess-ship in Bruges between 1418 and 1496 (six of them from Aberdeen), almost a hundred in Veere in the first half of the sixteenth century (nine from Aberdeen, and a few more from its hinterland).[40] Others went to London and Dieppe, and to Bergen in the early sixteenth century. There, a blooming timber trade developed, traditionally known in the region as 'the Scottish trade'.[41] England was a popular destination for migrants from lower social orders looking for work as servants or agricultural labourers.[42]

From the late fifteenth century many Scots moved to the eastern Baltic region, especially to Poland and Prussia, where they settled in many towns. Some of them gained burgess rights, having been able to establish a successful business, but many more did not.[43] This area became so popular as a destination that by the end of the sixteenth century about 70 per cent of migrants from the northeast, recorded in the Aberdeen Propinquity Book, had settled there. Several of these were described as 'travellers', which most likely indicates that they were hucksters or pedlars, selling their cheap wares to the peasants and villagers in the countryside.[44] From the 1470s there were regular complaints in the towns of Prussia and Poland about 'Scots' who were selling their goods in rural areas and as such competed with established urban merchants.[45] The topic was discussed regularly in the Diets of the Prussian towns and several edicts were issued by the Polish crown, but to little avail. The pedlars were clearly providing a welcome service to the poor and were generally able to make a good living. They continued to be active throughout the sixteenth century.[46]

Institutions

An important local institution in the burghs, as in other commercial centres throughout Europe, was the merchants' guild. The guilds initially included both merchants and craftsmen. They held the monopoly on overseas trade in the burghs' trading precincts and its members were generally in charge of burgh government. Aberdeen's guild was established in 1222, before the founding of merchant guilds in most other Scottish burghs.[47] By the fifteenth century the Aberdeen guild was dominated by the merchant elite who also made up the town council. The authority of this elite was not generally challenged, as there were relatively few craftsmen in the town.[48] The merchant communities of the larger towns had different social make-ups. The proportion of overseas traders in Aberdeen was much smaller than that in Edinburgh in the later Middle Ages. Instead Aberdeen was home to many small merchants who focused on inland trade in the burgh's hinterland and who were members of the merchant's guild. In Edinburgh, on the other hand, there were many small retailers who were also involved in overseas trade, but on a much smaller scale than the members of the merchant guild who were in charge of burgh government.[49] This distinction reflects the focus of the towns and stresses the importance of inland trade to Aberdeen and to its wealth.

The interdependence of the local nobility and the burgh stresses the importance of Aberdeen for the region. Many local lords and landowners were involved in commerce and from the mid-fifteenth century gained a large influence in town politics. At the same time there was intermarriage between burgesses and gentry and the patriciate invested in landed estates. This 'gentrification of burgh government' was not unusual in sixteenth-century Scotland, but in Aberdeen the landed interest influenced, and sometimes interfered in, politics much earlier and much more intensively. Between 1399 and 1530 about thirty members of the lower nobility were admitted to the merchant guild.[50]

That inland trade was of proportionally greater significance to the Aberdeen town authorities than overseas trade is reflected in the town's ordinances, as is the town's dependence on commerce. Aberdeen's local ordinances supplemented Scotland's unified town law, the Laws of the Four Burghs, which were compiled in the second half of the thirteenth century. Scotland's maritime law consisted of the regulations contained in the Scottish translation of the Rôles d'Oléron.[51] In addition, the Scottish burghs were subject to the jurisdiction of the Parliament, which meant that, in principle, all decisions of this body had to be observed. But often during the Middle Ages these Acts were not properly implemented because the central administration was too weak. In the second half of the sixteenth century there was an increase in royal interference. Privileges were questioned, for example, those of Aberdeen with regards to the ownership of its fishings in the 1550s. The central courts also started to encroach on the burghs' jurisdictions and as such on their authority and legal status. The overlap of jurisdictions became an increasing problem in the sixteenth century.[52]

From the early fourteenth century the burghs met as a separate estate in Parliament, and as such were able to gain more influence in government. These meetings allowed them to take collective action on any issues which affected their commerce. During the fifteenth century this collective action increased and at some point the burgh meetings evolved into the Convention of the Royal Burghs, though the exact origins and early development of this body remain unknown. Part of the complication is that the Convention evolved not only from the independent meetings of the parliamentary estate of the burghs, but also from the Court of the Four Burghs.[53] The Court of the Four Burghs is linked to the Laws of the Four Burghs and existed to enforce these burghal laws. By the mid-fourteenth century the court arbitrated in disputes between burghs or merchants and also heard appeals from the burgh courts. In day-to-day practice in the late Middle Ages, the burghs also occasionally consulted each other in legal matters.[54] The burgh laws themselves provided a unified legal basis for the Scottish towns, and as such a foundation for collective bodies such as the Convention of Royal Burghs. The judicial role of the Court was, however, adopted almost wholly by the College of Justice in the sixteenth century and the Convention became therefore mainly a political body.[55]

Conflict resolution

By the fourteenth century the burgh government in Aberdeen was led by a provost and four baillies. The baillies officially remained royal officials, but in practice, especially as the Middle Ages progressed, all burgh officials were elected from the same group of burgesses. The legal court was led by the baillies, though decisions were made by the burgesses present, or by an assize (a jury). These courts handled mainly civil cases and minor offences. The sheriff of Aberdeenshire had jurisdiction in criminal cases. Matters concerning mercantile affairs were traditionally dealt with by the guild court, presided by the Dean of Guild, but in practice such matters were also dealt with by the baillies.[56] Before the existence of an admiralty court, maritime law was administered in the royal burghs. In legal practice there was a large amount of overlap between the jurisdictions of various courts. In Aberdeen in the fifteenth century such cases were mostly brought before the baillie court, but also occasionally before the guild court, alderman and council, or deputy admirals. In practice, roughly the same men, that is to say members of the merchants' guild, would have passed judgement in each of these courts. In Leith a water baillie was in office by the late fifteenth century, who was elected by Edinburgh's burgesses. He had some jurisdiction in maritime matters in the port.[57]

The Aberdeen courts sometimes referred cases to higher courts, such as the Lords of Council or the Court of the Four Burghs, sometimes before it had reached a decision. At other times, other burghs were consulted.[58] There is no evidence that the jurisdictional overlap caused problems in the fifteenth century, but there were frequent squabbles over jurisdiction in the sixteenth century.[59] The competency of the admiralty court was not clearly defined, and some tension between the various courts, especially between the admirals and the Lords of Council is evident. Foreigners were traditionally seen as falling under the protection of the king, and the Lords of Council as his judicial representatives assumed responsibility for them, but this encroachment on the admiral's jurisdiction in maritime cases was resented by him and his officers.[60]

The oldest extant references to admirals in Scotland date to the early fifteenth century and the office was firmly established by 1488 when the king conferred it on the first earl of Bothwell, Patrick Hepburn.[61] It remained in Bothwell family hands until 1568. From 1488 at least, a central admiralty court was also in existence, but the admiral must have already had a legal role in the mid-fifteenth century.[62] In 1451 a 'curia admirallatus' sat in Aberdeen, presided over by two admiral deputies (the provost and a councillor), representing the admiral, George of Crighton, lord of Cairns.[63] From the earliest extant admiralty court records (1557–61) we know that a vice admiral, who normally held court in either Edinburgh or Leith, exercised the judicial functions of the admiral. In addition, admirals-depute sat in the other major sea ports, as appears to have been the case in 1451 too.[64] But since this is the only reference to an admiralty court until the late fifteenth century, we do not know any more about the admiralty court system at this time.

The main references to admirals in the fifteenth century are in the context of naval operations. For the purpose of these, merchants vessels were requisitioned, such as for example in 1476 when two Aberdeen deputy admirals charged three men to prepare their vessels 'to pas with the admiral in the kingis service'.[65] Such operations were generally conducted against enemies, either internal or external, such as the Lords of the Isles (in the early fifteenth century, and probably also in 1476) or the English. The suppression of piracy was not considered a priority in the fifteenth century, though this would change in the sixteenth century. There was an increase in piratical activity, particularly from Aberdeen, in the first two decades of the fifteenth century. This activity may have been caused by the slump in trade which had started in the late fourteenth century, but it is also possible that Aberdeen's trade declined because some of its merchants considered piracy more profitable than legitimate trade. Whatever the reasons, several ships, from the Low Countries, England and Hanseatic towns, were captured and sold, some of them reputedly by Alexander Stewart, earl of Mar and admiral of Scotland, and his accomplice Robert Davidson, a wealthy merchant and provost of Aberdeen. The reactions to these attacks varied. The Hanseatic towns took the most extreme measure: the lengthy embargo between 1412 and 1436 has already been discussed. The response of especially the Flemish authorities was more restrained. The import of Scottish wool was still of vital importance for sections of the textile industry in Flanders. The response of the Scottish authorities was also decidedly lax. The Aberdeen council is not known to have taken any measures against its resident pirates, and the central government only took diplomatic action when commerce was endangered by a full-blown ban on Scottish imports in Flanders, in 1416 and 1423.[66] Otherwise most trade continued as usual.

Shipping in the North Sea continued to be disturbed by naval warfare throughout the fifteenth and sixteenth centuries, and Scottish trade itself was also very vulnerable to attack. Scottish ships got caught up in various wars, and reprisals for captured cargo could continue for years after a conflict had been concluded when goods of countrymen of pirates or privateers were seized, or even ships of neutral parties carrying suspect cargo.[67] The sixteenth century appears to have been a turning point in the protection of Scottish shipping. The start of this was the financing of a naval fleet by King James IV (1473–1513). Though James failed to employ this fleet effectively in his planned invasion of England in 1513, and the number of vessels was significantly reduced after his death at the battle of Flodden, the Scots were able to conduct maritime warfare quite effectively in the 1530s and 1540s. The remaining navy was supported by hired merchantmen and privateers, and in association with the French managed to hold its own in the Anglo-Scottish and Stewart-Habsburg conflicts during this period. The navy was further reduced in the 1540s, when its four most important ships were seized by the English. With Scotland and England at peace in 1560, violence in the North Sea decreased, though piracy continued to be a problem until the latter part of the sixteenth century. In the absence of a navy, the protection of Scottish shipping was undertaken by privateers and merchantmen. From 1584 to 1587, for example, the Scottish burghs financed a squadron of vessels to protect Scottish vessels against English piracy.[68]

Scottish naval warfare has often received a bad press as a result of a misunderstanding of the particular circumstances of Scottish maritime activity. It is important to take into account the strict legal framework which was created in the sixteenth century to regulate naval activities. This did not prevent individuals from crossing the line between privateering and piracy, but many acts of aggression were actually legally sanctioned. Such acts made use of letters of marque, but also, in peacetime, letters of reprisal. The latter were issued when Scottish vessels had been attacked, and the owners had failed to obtain compensation through legal or diplomatic means. In Scotland these letters were considered a necessary tool in the defence of maritime trade and fishing, but differences of opinion with regards to the legal interpretation of these documents did cause conflicts with other nations.[69]

The conflicts dealt with by the Scottish burgh courts were generally of a civil nature. Presumably as a result of recurring problems arising from the absence of written contracts, from 1438 the Edinburgh council required the use of charter parties for all sea journeys. This measure was subsequently adopted by parliament in 1467.[70] Of course, the existence of charter parties did not wholly prevent disputes, as is evident from legal practice. Parties appeared in court when there was disagreement as to the interpretation of the contract, or when unforeseen problems occurred. In 1453, that is a number of years before the Act of Parliament, the Aberdeen court required a shipmaster to receive half freightage in accordance with the terms of a charter party unless he could prove that there was a 'condicione made efter the first appoyntment' that entitled him to a larger amount.[71] In 1478 the alderman and baillie denied a skipper's claim that merchants wrongfully withheld his freight 'efter the tenor of the charter party'. In this case there appears to have been a dispute about damage to the cargo. The merchants did not think full freightage was due and the court agreed.[72]

So even although charter parties may have provided more clarity in the relations between shipmaster and merchants, conflicts could not be prevented entirely. Not all disputes needed the interference of a court though. Many cases were settled through arbitration or amicable agreement, though only a few traces of these can be found today.[73] The conflicts that could not be solved easily were dealt with by the various Aberdeen courts by utilizing a mix of laws, statutes, customs and common sense. Though there is no evidence of any copies of the Rôles d'Oléron in Aberdeen, and written laws were not normally explicitly named, the judgments did often conform to the regulations laid down in the Rôles. At other times, decisions were 'found' or 'delivered' referring to custom or using common sense.[74]

When the Aberdeen courts felt incompetent to deal with a certain case, this was remitted elsewhere, such to the burgh of Edinburgh, the Court of the Four Burghs or to King and Council. In 1447, for example, the courts referred a case to Edinburgh so it could be subjected to the 'avisis of the commissaris of hale burowez', that is, representatives of all the burghs.[75] The question is why such cases were referred, especially since in 1447 the seven arbitrators chose to refer the case on the afternoon of the day on which they had been elected to deal with it. In addition, one can also ask why this particular case was not brought before the Perth court (or referred there), since the ship in question had been sailing for Perth from the continent and one of the parties was also from Perth. That the parties had initially come to Aberdeen was probably because that was where they landed on their arrival in Scotland.[76] The problem is that there is no record of the exact proceedings of the arbitration. It is also unclear from where the shipmaster (Latinized Johannes Oliver) came. That the arbitrators (five of whom were council members) thought it better to have the burgh commissioners look into the case suggests that the master was foreign and that they considered it best to have a body with more authority to pass judgment.

The same was the case in 1444, when the powerful earl of Orkney, owner of a ship which had been wrecked, demanded the payment of freightage from 'the merchandez of this toun'. The merchants, who were apparently also to administer justice in this matter, declared that they did not want to be judges in their own case and referred it to the commissioners of the burghs. An even greater authority was needed in the case that came before the 1451 admiralty court and was remitted to King and Council. This concerned the taking of a Stralsund ship by a ship of war from Dieppe. The assize declared that the matter 'belongis in a part to our soverane lord the king'.[77]

The masters of two other Stralsund ships, on the other hand, on 25 September 1478 declared themselves happy to 'underly the law before tham [the alderman and baillies] as jugis of law' in the disputes with their freighters, merchants of Edinburgh.[78] There are several entries featuring the men, the last one dating to 24 October.[79] Similarly, in 1481–2, two Netherlandish shipmasters were also content for their cases to be dealt with by the Aberdeen burgh court. Cornelis Cornelson first appeared in court in late November 1481 and on 6 February 1482 elected Peter Gillisen, shipmaster of the *James* of Veere, to be his procurator.[80] Both men's ships had wrecked. With no foreign communities in Aberdeen, alien merchants would normally have used Scottish factors or procurators, but in this case Gillisen probably expected to remain for a while taking care of his own affairs, having just arrived. As such, he was instituted to represent Cornelson, who was presumably getting ready to leave Aberdeen.

So, contrary to the situation in the sixteenth century, when according to Finlay the Lords of Council almost always assumed jurisdiction in any cases involving a foreign party, this was certainly not the case in the fifteenth century. Moreover, it is likely that the Aberdeen courts continued dealing with such cases into the sixteenth century, being geographically so far removed from the central courts and being able to offer quick and expert judgments. Similar matters from the water baillie at Leith or the burgh courts at Edinburgh could more easily be transferred.[81] Because of its dominant role in maritime trade, the majority of cases involving aliens would have arisen in Edinburgh anyway. It is unlikely that, as long as all the parties were happy for their case to be dealt with in Aberdeen, the courts in Edinburgh would have been able to interfere, even if they had wanted to. However, as mentioned before, the central administration, in the guise of the Lords of Council, extended its authority in the sixteenth century, encroaching on burgh jurisdictions. More research at a local level is needed to determine in how far the central powers succeeded with this in the sixteenth century.

Conclusion

Aberdeen was an important regional entrepôt and the second largest burgh in Scotland throughout most of the period in question. It was part of a commercial network of east coast towns in which Leith, as Edinburgh's port, became increasingly more dominant. Aberdeen was the hub of a vast hinterland, whose main products were wool and salmon. Exports of wool, hides and woolfells were the basis of Scotland's commercial boom in the thirteenth and first half of the fourteenth centuries and of its links with the Low Countries. A sharp decline in these exports from the 1370s, which had several causes, led to much lower production levels in the fifteenth and sixteenth centuries, though most likely not to a substantial deficit in the balance of trade. In these centuries especially Scotland only had a small share in Europe's trade.

During the Middle Ages the Scottish burghs were largely autonomous. As elsewhere in Northern Europe, the merchant elite was in charge of the administration of mercantile and maritime justice in Aberdeen, though it operated within a national legal framework of laws and courts. Being under the protection of the king, foreign merchants were generally well taken care of in court, either by the royal officers in the burgh, the baillies or by the Lords of Council as the king's legal representatives. Naval warfare, reprisals and piracy disrupted overseas trade throughout the period. Scotland was as much a victim as a perpetrator of naval aggression, but in the sixteenth century much of this aggression was legally sanctioned. In the absence of a naval fleet, the maritime community as a whole was involved in the protection of shipping and trade. At the end of the period, around 1600, Scotland was a small trading nation which was connected with many places throughout Northern and Western Europe, through a growing expatriate community and through commerce.

Notes

1 Berwick was regained by the Scots for short periods and continued to play a role in the Scottish economy as goods were still shipped through its port. E. P. Dennison and G. G. Simpson, 'Scotland', in D. M. Palliser (ed.), *Cambridge Urban History*, New York: Cambridge University Press, 2000, pp. i, 723 and n. 22.

2 See, for example, H. W. Booton, 'Burgesses and landed men in north-east Scotland in the later Middle Ages: a study in social interaction', unpubl. PhD thesis, University of

Aberdeen, 1987; H. W. Booton, 'Inland trade: a study of Aberdeen in the later Middle Ages', in M. Lynch, M. Spearman and G. Stell (eds), *The Scottish Medieval Town*, Edinburgh: John Donald, 1988, pp. 148–60; E. P. Dennison, D. Ditchburn and M. Lynch (eds), *Aberdeen before 1800: A New History*, East Linton: Tuckwell Press, 2002; D. Ditchburn, 'Cargoes and commodities: Aberdeen's trade with Scandinavia and the Baltic, c.1302–c.1542', *Northern Studies* 27, 1990, pp. 12–22; E. Frankot, 'Maritime law and practice in late medieval Aberdeen', *Scottish Historical Review* 89, 2010, pp. 136–52; J. S. Smith (ed.) *New Light on Medieval Aberdeen*, Aberdeen: Aberdeen University Press, 1985.

3 D. Ditchburn, 'Merchants, pedlars and pirates: a history of Scotland's relations with Northern Germany and the Baltic in the Later Middle Ages', unpubl. PhD thesis, University of Edinburgh, 1988; M. Rorke, 'Scottish overseas trade, 1275/86–1597', unpubl. PhD thesis, University of Edinburgh, 2001; A. Stevenson, 'Trade between Scotland and the Low Countries in the Later Middle Ages', unpubl. PhD thesis, University of Aberdeen, 1982; G. G. Simpson (ed.), *Scotland and the Low Countries, 1124–1994*, East Linton: Tuckwell Press, 1996; G. G. Simpson (ed.), *Scotland and Scandinavia, 800–1800*, Edinburgh: John Donald, 1990; T. C. Smout (ed.), *Scotland and Europe, 1200–1850*, Edinburgh: John Donald, 1986; T. C. Smout (ed.), *Scotland and the Sea*, Edinburgh: John Donald, 1992; Lynch *et al.*, *Scottish Medieval Town*; M. Lynch (ed.), *The Early Modern Town in Scotland*, London: Croom Helm, 1987.

4 For example, A. Grosjean and S. Murdoch (eds), *Scottish Communities Abroad in the Early Modern Period*, Leiden and Boston, MA: Brill, 2005.

5 D. Ditchburn, *Scotland and Europe: The Medieval Kingdom and its Contacts with Christendom*, East Linton: Tuckwell Press, 2000.

6 Two PhDs are connected to the 'Scotland and the Flemish People' project at St Andrews University: A. Eberlin conducting a study on 'Trade and diplomacy between Scotland and Flanders, 1320–1513' and M. French on 'Flemish material culture in medieval Scotland'. See also the project's blog: http://flemish.wp.st-andrews.ac.uk (accessed Aug. 2015).

7 E. Frankot, *'Of Laws of Ships and Shipmen': Medieval Maritime Law in Urban Northern Europe*, Edinburgh: Edinburgh University Press, 2012.

8 S. Murdoch, *The Terror of the Seas? Scottish Maritime Warfare, 1513–1713*, Leiden: Brill, 2010; the sixteenth-century Aberdeen Council Registers have been used by J. Ford in preparation for an edition of a treatise on maritime law by Alexander King to be published by the Stair Society in 2017.

9 A. Stevenson, 'Trade with the South, 1070–1513', in Lynch *et al.*, *Scottish Medieval Town*, p. 185; E. Gemmill and N. Mayhew, *Changing Values in Medieval Scotland: A Study of Prices, Money, and Weights and Measures*, Cambridge and New York: Cambridge University Press, 1995, p. 364; Ditchburn, *Scotland and Europe*, p. 192.

10 Stressing the deficit have been Stevenson, 'Trade with the South', p. 198; D. Ditchburn, 'Trade with Northern Europe, 1297–1540', in Lynch *et al.*, *Scottish Medieval Town*, p. 176 (though retracted in D. Ditchburn, 'Port towns: Scotland 1300–1540', in Palliser, *Cambridge Urban History*, i, 502); Rorke, 'English and Scottish overseas trade', p. 279. A more positive view is offered in Gemmill and Mayhew, *Changing Values*, pp. 371–81; Ditchburn, *Scotland and Europe*, pp. 193–4; D. Ditchburn, 'Maritime ports and transport, *c.*1200–1560', in K. Veitch (ed.), *Scottish Life and Society: A Compendium of Scottish Ethnology*, vol. 8, *Transport and Communications*, Edinburgh: John Donald, 2009, p. 43.

11 Gemmill and Mayhew, *Changing Values*, p. 379; Ditchburn, *Scotland and Europe*, p. 195. According to Booton, 'Inland trade', p. 157, a number of Aberdeen burgesses were able to lend money to the local nobility.

12 Gemmill and Mayhew, *Changing Values*, p. 381; Ditchburn, 'Maritime ports', p. 43.

13 Ditchburn, *Scotland and Europe*, pp. 2–3; Ditchburn, 'Maritime ports', pp. 23–4.

14 Dennison *et al.*, *Aberdeen before 1800*, p. xxvi.

15 Ditchburn, 'Cargoes and commodities', p. 16.
16 For a thorough comparison of these four burghs, see M. Lynch, 'The social and economic structure of the larger towns, 1450–1600', in Lynch *et al.*, *Scottish Medieval Town*, pp. 264–79.
17 For more detail, see Ditchburn, *Scotland and Europe*, p. 196.
18 I. Blanchard, E. Gemmill, N. Mayhew and I. D. Whyte, 'The economy: town and country', in Dennison *et al.*, *Aberdeen before 1800*, p. 137.
19 Dennison and Simpson, 'Scotland', p. 723; Booton, 'Inland trade', p. 153; Blanchard *et al.*, 'Town and Country', p. 141.
20 Booton, 'Inland trade', pp. 148, 154. In his 'Locating Aberdeen and Elgin in the later Middle Ages', in J. Geddes (ed.), *Medieval Art, Architecture and Archaeology in the Dioceses of Aberdeen and Moray*, London: Routledge, 2016, pp. 10–11, D. Ditchburn argues that Aberdeen's landward and coastal traffic played a greater role than has thus far been recognized. I am grateful to Dr Ditchburn for providing me with an advance copy of this article.
21 Ditchburn, *Scotland and Europe*, pp. 163–4, 168.
22 Ditchburn, 'Cargoes and commodities', 17.
23 A. Stevenson, 'The Flemish dimension of the Auld Alliance', in Simpson, *Scotland and the Low Countries*, pp. 28–9; Stevenson, 'Scotland and the Low Countries', p. i.
24 A. Stevenson, 'Medieval Scottish associations with Bruges', in T. Brotherstone and D. Ditchburn (eds), *Freedom and Authority: Scotland, c.1150–c.1650*, East Linton: Tuckwell Press, 2000, pp. 93, 95; Stevenson, 'Flemish dimension', pp. 32, 37; Stevenson, 'Scotland and the Low Countries', pp. 16, 18.
25 By the 1330s Scottish merchants exported 85 per cent of goods from Scotland. Stevenson, 'Medieval Scottish associations', p. 94; D. Ditchburn, 'Trade with Northern Europe, 1297–1540', in Lynch *et al.*, *Scottish Medieval Town*, pp. 162–3.
26 Stevenson, 'Medieval Scottish associations', p. 95.
27 Stevenson, 'Trade with the South', p. 192.
28 Ibid., pp. 194, 198–9, 201; 'Medieval Scottish Associations', pp. 97, 101, 107; Ditchburn, 'Trade with Northern Europe', pp. 165–6.
29 Ditchburn, 'Trade with Northern Europe', pp. 161–3, 165.
30 Before 1540 41.3 per cent of ships recorded in the Sound Toll Registers came from Edinburgh or Leith, 31.3 per cent from Dundee, 9.1 per cent from St Andrews, 3.9 per cent from Dysart and only 2.6 per cent from Aberdeen. Ditchburn, 'Trade with Northern Europe', pp. 163–4.
31 Stevenson, 'Trade with the South', p. 199.
32 D. Ditchburn, 'Anglo-Scottish relations in the later Middle Ages: the other side of the coin', in P. Crooks, D. Green and W. M. Ormrod (eds), *The Plantagenet Empire, 1259–1453*, Donington, Lincs.: Shaun Tyas, 2016, pp. 310–34. I am grateful to Dr Ditchburn for providing me with an advance copy of this article.
33 Ditchburn, *Scotland and Europe*, pp. 162–3, 176–9, 181; Rorke, 'Scottish overseas trade', pp. 140–4, 177. For a comparison of English and Scottish cloth trade, see M. Rorke, 'English and Scottish overseas trade, 1300–1600', *Economic History Review* 59, 2006, pp. 273–7.
34 Ditchburn, *Scotland and Europe*, pp. 144–9, 185–7; Rorke, 'Scottish overseas trade', pp. 195, 218.
35 Ditchburn, 'Trade with Northern Europe', p. 165; Ditchburn, *Scotland and Europe*, pp. 150–5.
36 Ditchburn, *Scotland and Europe*, pp. 159–60, 189–92; Rorke, 'Scottish overseas trade', pp. 270, 295; Rorke, 'English and Scottish export trade', p. 282.
37 Rorke, 'Scottish overseas trade', pp. 110, 113–14; Lynch, 'Social and economic structure', p. 279.
38 D. Catterall, 'Scots along the Maas, c.1570–1750', in Grosjean and Murdoch, *Scottish Communities Abroad*, p. 170.
39 L. Heerma van Voss, S. Sogner and T. O'Connor, 'Scottish communities abroad: some concluding remarks', in Grosjean and Murdoch, *Scottish Communities Abroad*, pp. 381–2.

40 Ditchburn and Harper, 'Aberdeen and the outside world', pp. 395, 398, 401.
41 N. Østby Pedersen, 'Scottish immigration to Bergen in the sixteenth and seventeenth centuries', in Grosjean and Murdoch, *Scottish Communities Abroad*, pp. 137, 147–52.
42 Ditchburn, 'Anglo-Scottish relations' (forthcoming).
43 W. Kowalski, 'The placement of urbanised Scots in the Polish Crown during the sixteenth and seventeenth centuries', in Grosjean and Murdoch, *Scottish Communities Abroad*, pp. 56, 73.
44 Ditchburn and Harper, 'Aberdeen and the outside world', figure 17.4 (pie chart), pp. 396, 398.
45 Kowalski, 'Urbanised Scots', pp. 80–2. At some point the word 'Scot' became synonymous with pedlar in Central Europe, making it difficult to establish how many of them actually originated in Scotland. Ditchburn, *Scotland and Europe*, p. 213.
46 Ditchburn, *Scotland and Europe*, pp. 212–15; Kowalski, 'Urbanised Scots', pp. 56–7.
47 E. P. D. Torrie, 'The guild in fifteenth-century Dunfermline', in Lynch *et al.*, *Scottish Medieval Town*, pp. 245, 248.
48 H. W. Booton, 'Economic and social change in later medieval Aberdeen', in Smith, *Medieval Aberdeen*, pp. 46–57.
49 Lynch, 'Social and economic structure', p. 273.
50 M. Lynch and H. M. Dingwall, 'Elite society in town and country', in Dennison *et al.*, *Aberdeen before 1800*, p. 191.
51 Frankot, *Medieval Maritime Law*, pp. 81–5.
52 M. Lynch, *Edinburgh and the Reformation*, Edinburgh: John Donald, 1981, pp. 61, 66–9.
53 T. Pagan, *The Convention of the Royal Burghs of Scotland*, Glasgow: Glasgow University Press, 1926, pp. 9–10; A. R. MacDonald, *The Burghs and Parliament in Scotland, c. 1550–1651*, Aldershot: Ashgate 2007, pp. 5–6. The original four burghs were Roxburgh, Berwick, Edinburgh and Stirling. The first two, after they passed under English control were replaced by Lanark and Linlithgow.
54 H. L. MacQueen and W. J. Windram, 'Laws and courts in the burghs', in Lynch *et al.*, *Scottish Medieval Town*, p. 219.
55 MacDonald, *Burghs and Parliament*, pp. 6–8; Pagan, *Convention of Royal Burghs*, p. 2.
56 For examples, see J. Armstrong *et al.*, *The Aberdeen Burgh Records Database* (2014), http://www.abdn.ac.uk/aberdeen-burgh-records-database. More research needs to be done with regards to mercantile law.
57 Ditchburn, 'Port towns', p. 498.
58 Frankot, *Medieval Maritime Law*, pp. 145–6, 154–7, 167–8.
59 More research into the functioning of the Aberdeen burgh court in the fifteenth century is needed to establish whether cases were just dealt with by whatever court happened to be in session or whether there was a more deliberate agenda. Concerning overlapping jurisdictions, see also Lynch, *Edinburgh and the Reformation*, pp. 66–7.
60 J. Finlay, 'Foreign litigants before the College of Justice in the sixteenth century', in MacQueen, *Miscellany four*, Edinburgh: Stair Society, 2002, pp. 38–9; T. C. Wade (ed.), *Acta Admirallatus Scotiae 1557–61*, Edinburgh: Stair Society, 1937, pp. xv–xvii.
61 The first known admirals were the earls of Crawford (d. 1407) and Mar, the latter of whom was admiral by at least 1414. F. McGurk (ed.), *Calendar of Papal Letters to Scotland of Benedict XIII of Avignon, 1394–1419*, Edinburgh: Scottish History Society, 1976, p. 306; D. Ditchburn, 'The pirate, the policeman and the pantomime star: Aberdeen's alternative economy in the early fifteenth century', *Northern Scotland* 12, 1992, pp. 20–1 and n. 20.
62 According to Wade, *Acta Admirallatus*, p. xiii, the court was inherent in the admiral's office.
63 Aberdeen City and Aberdeenshire Archives (ACAA), Council Registers (CR), V.i, p. 127, 13 Sept. 1451. Frankot, *Medieval Maritime Law*, pp. 56–7.
64 Wade, *Acta Admirallatus*, pp. xiv–xv; A. R. G. McMillan, 'The Admiral of Scotland', *Scottish Historical Review* 20, 1923, p. 13.

65 ACAA, CR, VI, p. 424, 4 Mar. 1476.

66 Ditchburn, 'Pirate, policeman', pp. 19–29; D. Ditchburn, 'Piracy and war at sea in late medieval Scotland', in Smout, *Scotland and the Sea*, pp. 39–40, 45–6, 51–2.

67 Ditchburn, 'Piracy', pp. 35–9; Murdoch, *Terror of the Seas?*, p. 152.

68 Murdoch, *Terror of the Seas?*, pp. 31, 33–5 76–8, 150.

69 Ibid., pp. 7–9, 107–9.

70 J. D. Marwick, *Extracts from the Records of the Burgh of Edinburgh*, Edinburgh: Scottish Burgh Records Society, 1869–92, pp. i, 5; K. M. Brown *et al.* (eds), *The Records of the Parliaments of Scotland*, St Andrews: St Andrews University, 2007–15, 1467/1/14 (accessed Aug. 2015).

71 ACAA, CR, V.i, p. 187, 26 Oct. 1453.

72 ACAA, CR, VI. p. 549, 3 Oct. 1478.

73 Frankot, *Medieval Maritime Law*, p. 155.

74 Frankot, 'Maritime law and practice', pp. 137–8, 141, 144. There is one reference each to 'leges aquarum' and 'watter laws' in the burgh records, but in both of these cases these words indicate laws available elsewhere: in Edinburgh and the Low Countries respectively. See Frankot, 'Maritime law and practice', pp. 141–2.

75 ACAA, CR, V.ii, p. 692, 16 Dec. 1444; IV, p. 497, 3 Nov. 1447.

76 In 1467 it was laid down by parliament that conflicts should be solved in the port whereto 'the schip is frachtit' (RPS, 1467/1 (accessed Aug. 2015)) but this would not yet have applied here. With regards to the decision as to where to go to court, see Frankot, *Medieval Maritime Law*, pp. 146–9.

77 ACAA, CR V.i, p. 127, 13 Sept. 1451.

78 ACAA, CR, VI, p. 547, 25 Sept. 1478.

79 ACAA, CR, VI, p. 546, 11 Sept. 1478; p. 547, 25 Sept. 1478 (two entries); p. 549, 3 Oct. 1478; p. 553, 12 Oct. 1478 (two entries); p. 557, 13 Oct. 1478 (three entries); p. 558A, 22 Oct. 1478; p. 558A, 24 Oct. 1478; p. 559, 24 Oct. 1478.

80 ACAA, CR, VI, p. 705, 27 Nov. 1481; p. 705, 29 Nov. 1481; p. 720, 6 Feb. 1482. Cornelson had already been in court on 24 Nov. for a separate case: p. 703, 24 Nov. 1481. Gillisen first appeared in court on 30 Jan. 1482: p. 718, 30 Jan. 1482;

81 Finlay, 'Foreign litigants', p. 39.

24

BERGEN 1300–1600

A trading hub between the North and the Baltic Sea

Geir Atle Ersland

Situated on the western coast of Norway, Bergen had sailing access to both the North Sea and eastwards into the Baltic. When a band of Danish Crusaders visited Bergen in 1198, they were impressed with the town and its bustling trade, telling of an urban community where every language in the world could be heard, and where all goods imaginable were at hand – where there was such abundance of dried fish and stockfish that it could not be counted nor measured.[1] Starting in the fourteenth century Bergen became a major hub for trade in Northern Europe and for hosting one of the four Hanseatic Kontore. Historians suggest that most of the Norwegian foreign trade revenues during the late medieval period came from the export of fish from Bergen's harbour.

The preconditions for Bergen as a medieval trading town will be discussed in what follows. The Hansards were successful in their strive towards monopolizing the export of stockfish. The central argument is that this success was dependent on a rigid institutionalization of the trade. The paradox is that this institutionalization prevented the Hansards from expanding their trade when new major export products were introduced, especially woodwork produced in the vicinity of Bergen from the early sixteenth century and onward. This was left in the hands of other tradesmen, especially from the Low Countries. However, as the role of the Hanse became more or less obsolete elsewhere in Northern Europe, the Kontor in Bergen became the last outpost, still focused on defending its grip on the old stockfish trade.

The emergence of a royal town and a commercial hub

According to the old Norse sagas, King Olav Kyrre founded Bergen sometime during his reign from 1067 to 1093.[2] In the early twelfth century, a densely built strip of land existed in the beach area on the eastern side of a narrow bay later known as

Vågen (The Bay), the harbour of Bergen. Both written sources and archaeological evidence clearly show that the town developed quickly in this area in the following decades.[3] Houses in Bergen were built on rectangular plots, organized side by side and perpendicularly oriented towards the harbour. In the following century, wharfs were built in front of the houses as a process of land reclamation started.[4] This continued during the Middle Ages and culminated in the series of long rows of houses that still characterize the oldest nucleus, which is known today as Bryggen.[5]

The earliest town development ran parallel to the unification of the kingdom, and also to the introduction of the Christian faith. It seems obvious that the church gave a boost to the town growth in its initial phase. The religious institutions came to dominate the townscape of Bergen. In the first part of the fourteenth century the town held more than ten parish churches, five monasteries or convents, three hospitals and a handful of other churches.[6] There is clear evidence that the larger institutions like the bishop and monastic orders engaged in trade, and also that ecclesiastical institutions from other parts of Norway took part.[7]

The king's presence was vital to Bergen from the outset, and the town played an important part as a political centre throughout the medieval period. Bergen's position as a royal seat peaked in the thirteenth century. Iceland and Greenland were directly subjected to the Norwegian king, and the king's ambition was also to have a stronger control over the other island communities in the west, namely Shetland and the Faroe Islands, the Orkneys, Hebrides and Man. Representatives from the ruling elite in these communities visited and paid homage to the Norwegian king in Bergen, and it was in Bergen that the king gathered a fleet to settle a dispute with the Scottish king over the supremacy of the Hebrides and Man in 1263.[8] The outcome of the struggle was that these island communities were lost as part of the Norwegian king's supremacy through an agreement in 1266.

The author of the earliest history of Bergen, *Bergen Fundas* (The Founding of Bergen), written *c.*1560, was convinced that trade and merchants had laid its foundations.[9] Medieval written sources seem to comply with this view except for the fact that the first hundred years up until the late twelfth century are sparsely documented. However, archaeological findings show that by *c.*1100 a harbour suited for trade and commerce was well under way. In the last part of the twelfth century the sagas give good indication that the harbour in Bergen was now regularly visited by many cargo vessels.[10] At this stage we have evidence that Norwegians themselves engaged in the export trade, both across the North Sea and into the Baltic.[11]

Bergen's prominent position as a royal seat promoted trade, since taxes and revenues were brought to the town. The same was the case with the incomes from both the ecclesiastical institutions as well as aristocratic landlords. Such incomes were paid mostly in agricultural products, and visiting merchants from abroad created the opportunity to exchange local surplus with imported necessities and items of a more luxurious character.[12]

For the landholding elite it was also important to be present in the town for representative reasons, especially during the longer periods in which the king and his retinue resided at the castle. When Bergen frequently hosted larger political meetings, tenements in the town could serve as town houses for the aristocracy. The most prominent example of this is the archbishop who held his main residence in Nidaros (Trondheim). He also held a residence in Bergen. It was stone built, and with a courtyard and a chapel it had a clear representative function. It also included storehouses, and late medieval and early sixteenth-century sources show that the archbishop traded with the revenues from the archbishop's see.[13] When written evidence of ownership points to the landholding aristocracy and a few larger ecclesiastical institutions as the owners of the tenements at Bryggen prior to the mid-fourteenth century, it also suggests that these tenements served purposes similar to the archbishop's residence. Active involvement in the import and export trade in Bergen may have been typical for both the aristocratic families and ecclesiastical institutions before the middle of the fourteenth century. In the later part of the medieval period this picture changed.

The high medieval export from Norway consisted first and foremost of stockfish, perhaps as much as 80 per cent of the total. Another product was cod liver oil, followed by smaller amounts of hides and furs, herring, woodwork and timber.[14] A typical feature for the Norwegian export trade was that it consisted of raw commodities or semi-manufactured articles. The main bulk of the fish came from the northern part of Norway a few weeks sailing distance north of Bergen, in the Lofoten region.[15] Here the climate made it possible to let the fish dry in the early spring when the temperature was close to freezing and there was very little rain. However, fisheries were also carried out both further north and south along the coast.

The king actively promoted trade in Bergen through legislation. There is no known medieval charter for Bergen granting the citizens special trading rights in the first centuries. However, in the 1270s King Magnus Håkonsson (1263–80) collated, revised and unified the Norwegian law codes. In regard to Norwegian urban development, it was of particular importance that the revision and unifying of common laws also included an urban code, the Town Law Code. This was edited especially for Bergen and contained adaptations made to suit the towns of Oslo, Tønsberg and Nidaros as well.[16] The Town Law Code has more or less been seen as an appendix to the rural law code (Lands Law). The main reason for this is that many chapters in the town law are the same as in the rural law. On the one hand it can be argued that the town law is an adjusted version of the rural law so as to make it applicable in cases particular to the urban environment, such as fire watch duties, building regulations, the conduct of crafts and trade, and so forth. On the other hand the town law makes a clear distinction of what areas are within or without the jurisdiction of the town, topographically defining the town's borders towards the countryside where the rural law was applied.[17] The Town Law Code regulated every aspect of town life and the rights and obligations of townspeople, and trade and commerce were dealt with extensively. The bottom line here is that the subjects of the king, the Norwegians, held the exclusive right to trade in Bergen during the whole year. Foreigners could only trade as guests during the summer season.

Though there was a clear-cut distinction between the rural law and the town law, this did not imply an autonomous status for the town council. The law mentions both a council and councillors, but the council was led by the king's local representatives.[18] The king was the territorial lord of all Norwegian towns, and the rulings or verdicts of town councils had to have royal sanction. Such was also the case of bylaws, which were all issued in the name of the king. The first mayor of Bergen is mentioned as late as at the 1530s, but even then he was appointed by the king rather than elected by the council.[19] All through the medieval period, and until absolutism was introduced in the kingdoms of Norway and Denmark in 1660, the role of the council was to advise and prepare judgment for the king or his local representative's final decision or sanction. When it came to the important function of issuing trade privileges to foreigners, such could only be obtained by applying directly to the king, and such privileges had to be renegotiated when a new monarch took the throne.

King Håkon Magnusson's (1299–1319) rise to the throne has been seen as a shift toward Oslo as the preferred royal seat. He resided more often in Oslo than his predecessors, and his foreign policies were focused more towards Sweden and Denmark, not least reflecting the military conflicts in this region. After King Håkon Magnusson's death Norway became part of the shifting constellations and unions between Denmark and Sweden until 1905.[20] The unions made the king's personal presence in Bergen scarcer and only occasional from the fourteenth century onwards. However, royal authority over the town and the council was upheld by a captain or governor at the royal castle, who also governed a larger part of western Norway. The military focus became stronger by the end of the fifteenth century as conflicts between Sweden on the one side, and Denmark-Norway on the other, resulted in periods of war. The castle was fortified in the early sixteenth century and from then on a permanent garrison was deployed there. It was now the *de facto* administrative centre of western Norway.[21]

Population, migration, trade and crafts

Everyday life in medieval Bergen is documented by archaeological findings dating back to the early 1100s.[22] However, we have no way of estimating the size of the population at this early stage. A calculated guess suggests there were 10,000 inhabitants before the middle of the fourteenth century. In this respect Bergen is in line with other middle-sized Northern European towns of its time. Bergen probably contained half the urban population in all medieval Norwegian towns put together. However, measured against the total population of mainland Norway, the urban population would probably be on the lower side of 5 per cent.[23]

Throughout the medieval period, Bergen was the largest town in the three Scandinavian kingdoms.[24] This was paradoxical, since Norway was by far the least urbanized of the three, with only a dozen towns, while Denmark had as many as sixty, and Sweden-Finland close to thirty.[25] Estimated numbers of rural holdings or farmsteads probably give the best, though still rough, idea of rural settlements in the first half of the fourteenth century. Norway probably held *c*.71,000 rural holdings, Sweden *c*.88,000 and Denmark *c*.154,000.[26] Proportionally Denmark had approximately 2,600 rural holdings per town, Sweden 2,900 and Norway as many as 5,900. If so, Norway was only half as urbanized as the other two Scandinavian kingdoms.

Sources giving evidence of the origins of townspeople are hard to find. We can assume that many were locals, born either in the town or in the near vicinity. They were Norwegians or natives, as far as this terminology had any meaning in medieval society. Quite a few also came from the islands in the west, but also from elsewhere. In the saga of the Danish Crusaders there are mentions of Icelanders, Greenlanders, English, Germans, Danes, Swedes and Gotlanders.[27] The elite present in the town were mostly from the aristocratic families in western Norway. The same goes for the clergy at the many religious institutions, and close to a thousand people may have been related to ecclesiastical ranks in the first part of the fourteenth century.[28]

German merchants are mentioned as a significant group of foreigners in Bergen in the last part of the thirteenth century. They stayed among the Norwegians in the Bryggen area, where they settled because the area towards the wharfs and the harbour was reserved for export trade according to the town law.[29] The significance of the trade with German towns came to the fore for the first time in the years prior to 1250. During times of tension between Lübeck and the Norwegian king leading up to a peace agreement, it was expressively stated that the grain import was of vital importance for Norway.[30]

The fact that trade politics was seen as a matter of the feeding or starvation of the population was also brought forth in 1282 when bylaws for Bergen made it illegal for foreigners to buy and sell in the countryside. Farmers were required to bring their goods, especially livestock, to the marketplace in Bergen. They also prohibited any foreign merchant from buying butter, furs or stockfish if he did not import rye, malt or flour.[31] The bylaws resulted in a blockade of Norway in the years 1284–5 that was instigated by Wendish towns headed by Lübeck, forbidding the import of grain in particular. The effect of the blockade was that merchants from the north German towns got the same rights and obligations as the king's subjects. These rights were extended in 1294 to include the towns of Kampen, Stavoren (Friesland), Lübeck, Stralsund, Rostock, Wismar, Greifswald, Stettin, Anklam, Riga and the Germans residing in Visby. However, the ban on buying and selling in the countryside was upheld. It should also be mentioned that the privileges stated that the resident foreign merchants had to partake in any public obligations on the same terms as the subjects of the Norwegian king. These included tolls on trade and a military tax called *leidang* in peacetime, and military service in times of war.[32]

These measures were part of a set of royal politics put in place to restrict commerce within the borders of the Norwegian towns, and a few years later a bylaw made it illegal to buy and sell in the countryside in general.[33] The rights gained by merchants of the German Hanse during the last decades of the thirteenth century were the most extensive privileges that Hanse merchants received. They formed the basis for renewal later in the Middle Ages, and as long as they traded in Bergen, provided for the establishment of the Hanseatic Kontor.[34] It should be noted here that, even though the Hansards at the Kontor became a major group in Bergen, they did not become an integrated part of the town population since they held their privileges, which gave them extraterritorial rights. And each and every one of them was only a visitor. Sooner or later they would leave Bergen and settle in one of the Hanseatic home towns; the real immigrants settled for good, and amongst them were also many Germans who did not belong to the Hanse.

A chapter of the town law specifying where the different crafts and retailers should be located mentions at least eighteen different trades.[35] The largest group was the shoemakers, a group of German origin that numbered at least fifty, with additional apprentices, which we know from *c.*1300. The number of craftsmen, both shoemakers and others, seems to have grown during the late fourteenth and fifteenth centuries.[36] They organized their own guilds, and membership was exclusively for Germans. There were probably also guilds with Norwegian members. However, sources are scarce for the latter category, especially for the late medieval period, indicating that guilds of German craftsmen became dominant.[37] Craftsmen's guilds held no special privileges from the king, but the German guilds in the fifteenth and sixteenth centuries tried to define themselves as protected by the privileges of the Hanseatic merchants at the Kontor.

The plague in the middle of the fourteenth century, followed by other outbreaks of pestilence, reduced the Norwegian population to less than half of its medieval peak. The long-term consequence was a severe agrarian crisis that drastically reduced agricultural output. However, quite the contrary to the drop in rural population, there are indications that the population and economic activity in Bergen were little affected. If we study the property market at the time, it is clear that the demand for both houses and building plots was thriving. Symptomatically we find that the Munkeliv Abbey in Bergen, the largest of its kind in Norway, became actively involved in the urban property market. Accounts for Munkeliv in the late fifteenth century suggest that the income from the rural estates was reduced by as much as 80 per cent by the early fifteenth century as compared to pre-1350. Engaging in the urban property market might therefore have been a way of compensating for the losses. This, however, would only be possible if the urban economy was not in decline. The vitality of the urban economy can hardly be explained by any other factor than foreign trade and the role of foreigners in Bergen. By now the largest group by far was the Hansards, the numbers of which have been estimated to as many as *c.*1,000 in the winter and double this during the summer and sailing season.[38]

With a strong and lasting depopulation of the Norwegian countryside, most migrants to Bergen were most likely foreigners seeking their opportunity in Scandinavia's largest urban community. After the plague we find English tradesmen in Bergen, and Dutch merchants were present from the middle of the fifteenth and throughout the sixteenth centuries, echoed by street names such as the Hollendergaten (Hollander Street), first mentioned *c.*1500. By this time people also migrated to Bergen from

Scotland, and they engaged in both trade and crafts, as well as petty trade.[39] Contrary to the Hansards at the Kontor, these groups became permanent residents in Bergen, subject to the town law and eligible to take part in the town council. In this way they also became the subjects of the king and would benefit from the strengthening of the power of the town council and king in the sixteenth century.

The advantages of the port of Bergen and outward connections

As a port Bergen held the advantage of being positioned midway between the main production area for stockfish and the final markets. The most important item, dried fish from northern Norway, was brought to Bergen and exchanged for goods brought by those who were engaged in the export trade. Weather conditions and the short periods of daylight from the end of September to April made sailing hazardous. However, it was possible to sail to Bergen both from the fish-producing areas in the north and the harbour towns in England and on the continent, and to do trade twice during the summer season.

The advantages of Bergen's geographical position were not the only major factor. The other was political preference. In 1294 bylaws made it illegal for foreigners to sail and trade further north than Bergen, and a few years later this was extended to include sailing to Iceland and other destinations within the king's dominion. These measures favoured Bergen as they made it the main hub for Norwegian foreign trade.[40] The fact that Bergen's position was upheld and respected throughout the medieval period underlines the town's success as hub for maritime trade in Northern Europe.[41] On the western coast of Norway the only town south of Bergen was the small bishop town of Stavanger, which was never involved to any measurable extent in foreign trade.[42] Trade with Norwegian products other than fish did take place in towns in eastern Norway, but the volume was of no significance compared to the fish trade.

Mapping sailing routes by documenting the foreign trade relations as they emerge through specifications of imported and exported goods can give a tentative overview of Bergen's position within a wider Northern European urban network. The big picture shows a flow of products from western and northern Norway as well as from the island communities in the west, especially Iceland. However, Bergen's relations within a wider network of towns were also determined by factors other than trade, such as religion, politics and alliances.

Mapping relations through available documentation over a wider time span, regardless of the character of the contact, can be done by registering every instance where Bergen and one or several other towns are mentioned in the same document.[43] Of course, such mapping runs into all kinds of methodological difficulties, and there are two major problems. The first is that we have to rely on the assumption that the available corpus of documents indicates a statistical bearing that wouldn't change even if we were able to take into account the vast majority of documents that have been lost. The other major difficulty is how to collate all relevant documents within a uniform format when searching for relevant data. In the case of Norwegian towns this problem can be overcome since all known medieval documents are registered in the ongoing publication *Regesta Norvegica*, in which résumés of the content always include people's names as well as place names.[44]

By searching through every document from the period 1250–1399, 1,506 instances can be found where both Bergen and one or more towns are mentioned together. It should be noted that these documents concerns all kinds of issues, not only trade. All in all this includes ninety-four different towns. To exclude the less frequent occurrences, those towns mentioned three times or fewer are excluded. This accounts for forty-nine towns, reducing the number to forty-five. However, this only reduces the total number of instances where Bergen is mentioned together with one or more other town to 1,418. Divided into seventy-five-year periods, the distribution is as follows: 1250–1324 with 576 and 1325–99 with 842.

In a broad perspective the network pattern documents strong relations towards northern Germany and the Baltic Sea region, and that these relations became stronger in the period 1325–99. There is a significant decline in documents mentioning Bergen together with the other major Norwegian towns of Nidaros, Hamar, Oslo and Stavanger between 1250–1324 and 1325–99. Specifically, there is a drop from 63 per cent of the total in 1250–1324 to 35 per cent. This can be interpreted as a result of Bergen being less involved in internal affairs within Norway. Contrary to this, during the same period we find that documents mentioning the Wendish towns of Lübeck, Rostock, Stralsund and Wismar rose from less than 5 per cent to 30 per cent, and support a conclusion that in the fourteenth century Bergen became integrated within an urban network constituted by the Hanseatic towns, and a stronger linking towards the Baltic Sea constituted by foreign trade. This conclusion is strengthened by the numbers of documents involving British towns, which drops down from 13 per cent to 2 per cent.

The Hanseatic takeover of foreign trade

German Hansards had settled in Bergen in the Bryggen area at least since the thirteenth century, and as their numbers grew Bryggen eventually became the location of the Hanseatic Kontor.[45] The reasons as to why the Norwegian elite withdrew from active trade have been much debated. The argument that they lost out in competition with foreigners has a strong standing, especially since merchants from the Hanseatic towns got special privileges to trade in Norway, and particularly Bergen, during the last decades of the thirteenth century. Another argument has been better technology. It has been put forth that the foreigners had vessels that were better suited in comparison to traditional Norwegian ships of the type of the Viking age. This argument has now been abandoned, not least since archaeological findings have shown that local ship technology was not inferior to other parts of Northern Europe in the thirteenth and fourteenth centuries.[46]

In recent research stronger emphasis has been placed on changes in the politics of the Norwegian kings. When the first Swedish–Norwegian union came into effect

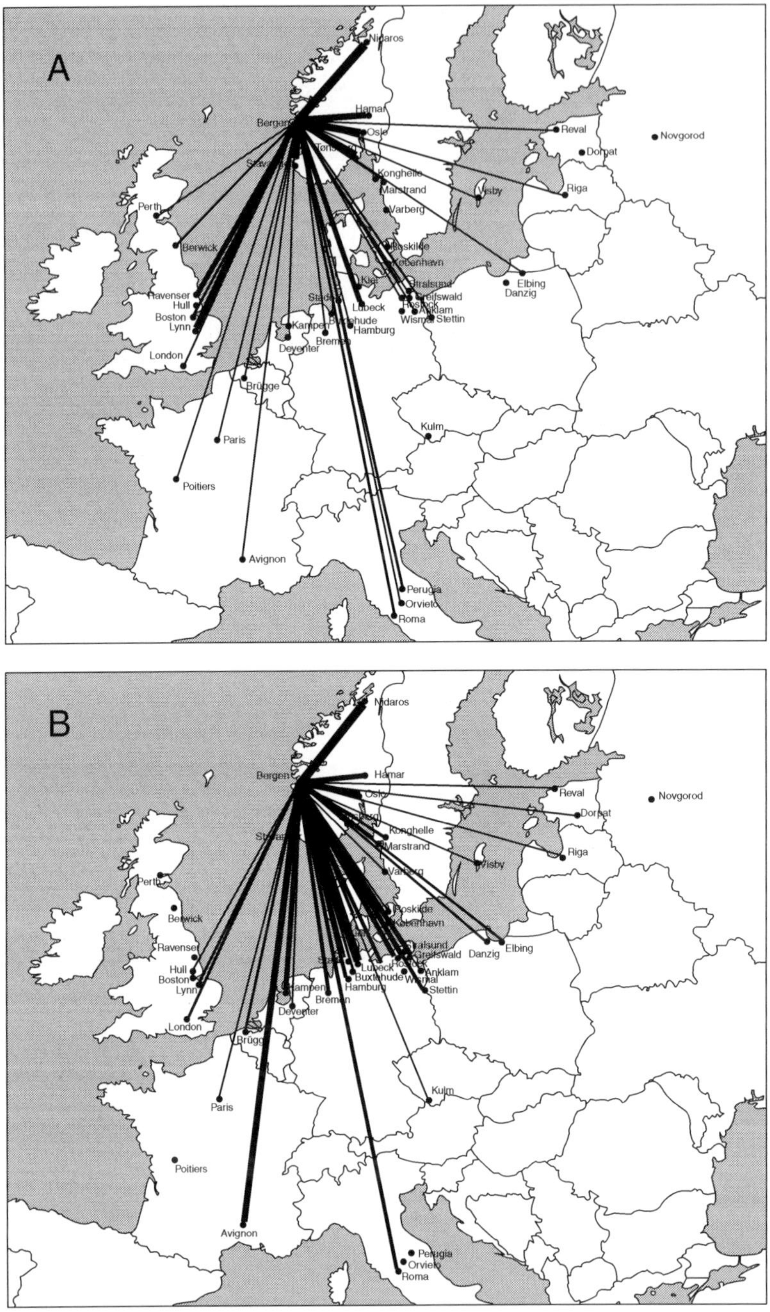

Figure 24.1 Bergen's network 1250–1324 (A) and 1325–99 (B) as indicated by documents mentioning Bergen and one or more other towns during the years 1250–1399. Towns mentioned less than four times during the period are left out. The main tendency is a shift in relations from westward across the North Sea and south- and eastwards towards northern German Towns. The maps also visualize Bergens ecclesiastical network towards the other Norwegian bishop's towns; Nidaros (Trondheim), Stavanger, Oslo and Hamar, and the papal seats of Rome and Avignon

in 1319, it was the start of a period when the king's household in Bergen became of lesser importance. At the same time inter-Nordic conflicts made the Hanse an ally at times, and during such periods the king was willing to set aside previous regulations that favoured Norwegians.[47] The setback for Norwegian involvement in foreign trade seems to have been well under way in the first decades of the fourteenth century. The recession following the outbreak of pestilence in the middle of the century probably made it even worse for Norwegians to partake in trade. The agrarian collapse in the wake of the plague had dramatically reduced the rural population. A large amount of arable land was laid waste. For the farms still running, the farmers had to pay less since arable land was in abundance and the land rent had dropped markedly since before the outbreak of the first plague.[48] The drop in revenues from agricultural produce deprived both the lay aristocracy and the ecclesiastical institutions of the foundation they needed in order to be active in the Bergen trade. From now on the Norwegian landholders' involvement was restricted to letting out their urban property to merchants or other urban dwellers.[49]

When the archbishop of Nidaros was still involved in the late medieval trade in Bergen, he was a middleman organizing the deliveries of goods from the production area in the north and to Bergen. This had its background in the fact that the archbishop was also the bishop of the Nidaros bishopric, which covered the richest fishing districts in northern Norway. A large amount of the archbishop's revenues was paid in stockfish, which was then brought to Bergen and sold there to the Hanse merchants. The development of the fisheries and fish trade made the situation for the archbishop quite different from other members of the aristocracy who relied on the surplus from their estates, and based their participation in the Bergen trade on the surplus from agricultural products.

Since Hanse merchants resided in Bergen throughout the year and not only during the summer season, they had the opportunity to buy and stock goods during the winter and keep them ready for shipment as soon as the sailing season started in spring. At Bryggen the Hansards at the outset lived side by side with other townspeople. As the town expanded and Norwegians started to trade in other parts of the town, the Hansards did likewise, but Bryggen was their main quarter. However, it was not until the end of the fifteenth century that they totally dominated Bryggen, and it was eventually called *Die teutschen Brugk* (The German Wharf). By this time it had long been a demand that the Hansards should abandon any dwellings or storehouses they held elsewhere in town. The process of confining the Hansards within Bryggen was not accomplished until the end of the sixteenth century.[50]

The Hanse organization in Bergen

In the fifteenth century sources make it possible to get a glimpse of how each Hanse merchant organized his trade, and reveal details that are consistent with how trade was conducted in later centuries. At the individual level the system seems to have been characterized by conformity and longevity. The smallest nucleus within the trade system was an entity called a *Stave*. The word derives from the

Old Norwegian *stofa,* which was used to name a house or a larger room. In each tenement at Bryggen there would be several *Staven,* and each *Stave* consisted of an office room for the merchant, storerooms for goods and sleeping quarters for himself and his employees. Use of the *Stave* included the right to use the common passageway through the tenement and the wharf in front towards the harbour. Each *Stave* also held a stake in a cooking house and the so-called *Schutstave,* a common house for all those living in the same tenement and especially designed for social activities during the winter season. The merchant's employees were either called *Gesell,* a fully trained craftsman in the trade often acting as the merchant's foreman, or *Jungen,* young apprentices who were most often recruited from the northern German provinces when they were in their early teens. For talented *Junge* it was a possible career opportunity to advance to become a *Gesell,* and eventually a merchant running a *Stave.*

A significant asset for the *Stave* as a commercial entity was the *Northfahrerschuld.* This was the term used for the debt owed by those who supplied the *Stave* with goods, primarily stockfish. As a rule the supplier was paid in advance for the next year's deliveries, and if he could not fulfil his promised quota, the discrepancy would be transferred to the following year. In this way the suppliers as a rule accumulated long-lasting debts to a certain *Stave,* and it was strictly forbidden by the internal regulations of the Kontor for any merchant of other *Staven* to trade with such suppliers. In this way debts secured foreseeable deliveries of stockfish and other traded products, and as such it was valued as an asset when a *Stave* was sold.

As a rule, the running of the *Stave* was conducted by a merchant at Bryggen. He could be the owner, but in many cases he acted as the junior partner for the real owner who stayed in one of the Hanse towns. It was common practice for such a junior partner to buy a *Stave* when he had earned the necessary means for such a transaction, and then settle in his home town and engage his own junior partner in Bergen. The members of the Hanse colony were not allowed to marry while in Bergen, and therefore their years serving as *Junge, Gesell* and junior partner were a step towards establishing themselves as merchants. The most successful could rise from a poor background as a *Junge* at Bryggen and end up as a wealthy merchant in one of the Hanse towns.

The Hanseatic Kontor

As a group the Hanse merchants defined themselves through their privileges and insisted on the right to internal jurisdiction. A breakthrough was the establishment of a community first mentioned in 1365/6, called *Communis Mercator de Berghen.* This was led by an aldermanship.[51] The emergence of a better organized community was probably the result of several circumstances. The dramatic consequences of the plague in 1349 and the following years had brought about uncertainty and a breakdown of authority in Bergen. There were complaints about losses caused by Norwegians who failed to pay their debts, and at the same time there was a growing concern about lawlessness and ill behaviour amongst themselves. In 1365, they even stormed the king's castle and took the captain hostage. At the same time the Hanse towns established a larger confederacy, which successfully settled a conflict in Flanders in the 1350s and waged a war against the Danish king in the 1360s. In this perspective both the external and internal conditions were at hand to promote an organized community of Hanse merchants in Bergen.[52]

The use of the term *Kontor* to describe the Hanse community in Bergen is first known from a version of the statutes for the Hanse merchants written in 1494. However, historians have also used it to label the community when it first originated in the fourteenth century.[53] This has partly obscured the organizational changes that took place in the fifteenth century when the Hanse merchants returned to Bergen after having abandoned it in the years 1427–33, during a war between the Danish-Norwegian king and the Hanse towns. After the return, measures were taken to strengthen the administration of the Hanse community. A *Kaufmannshaus* (Merchant's house) was built in the middle of Bryggen, between the marketplace and the town hall. Here the Hanse merchants' aldermen convened for their meetings. In order to strengthen the authority of the aldermen's proceedings, a group called *Achteinen* (The Eighteen) was chosen among the merchants, and a secretary was engaged to lead the daily administration. These measures were established in the 1440s, and it is within such an institutional level that we find the Kontor's administration formally working in the following centuries.[54]

The strengthening of the administration in the 1440s underscores how strong the privileged position of the members of the Hansard community in Bergen became in the fifteenth century. First of all, this goes for the opportunity to stay in Bergen through the whole year and enjoy the same rights as the subjects of the Norwegian king as long as they themselves did not sail or trade north of Bergen. Second, they were allowed to organize their own internal jurisdiction. They made their own legal code, which regulated all kinds of cases in which only the Hansards in Bergen were part, such as how commerce should be conducted or how they should live together within the tenements at Bryggen. Petty cases concerning daily life within a tenement were judged by the fellow merchants in the tenement, but cases concerning graver conflicts were judged by the aldermen with the assistance of the *Achteinen* when they met at the *Kaufmannshaus*. However, if the cases involved parties outside the community of Hansards, they would be presented before a Norwegian court.

The internal jurisdiction had, first and foremost, the advantage of rapid conflict resolution. Written accounts from the negotiations, which are preserved in great numbers from the mid-seventeenth century onward, show that conflicts were often settled within a week or even shorter periods.[55] For the internal life of the Hansard community at Bryggen this meant that conflicts were dealt with in a manner that curbed them in their infancy, and the parties involved had the opportunity to carry out their businesses as usual as soon as the disagreement was out of the way.

The Hanse domination of the fish trade and exports from Bergen was vulnerable to competition from English merchants, and, from the fifteenth century onward, from the Low Countries as well, particularly Holland. The strengthening of the administration in the 1440s can be seen as one measure to secure their foothold in the trade and an important step in the direction of a *de facto* monopoly, which appears to be the case later in the century. It seems to be quite obvious that the Norwegian authorities were concerned about this development. The Town Council made a complaint in 1440, and in 1444 the Sovereign Council proposed bylaws to be sanctioned by the king in order to curb and restrict the Hanse presence in Bergen.[56] They went as far as trying to reintroduce an old ban from the early fourteenth century that prohibited foreign merchants from staying in Bergen during the winter season, and that only Norwegians in Bergen should be allowed to handle trade with the suppliers of fish when they arrived from northern Norway during the summer months. However, the Kontor brought their case before the king and he granted them the same rights as before according to their previous privileges, dating back to the 1294 agreement.[57]

The 1440s seem to be a decisive decade in the history of the Hanse merchants in Bergen. They were now established as a strong organized society that effectively challenged Norwegian authorities on an institutional level. The years between the 1440s and 1520s were marked by two conflicts that, to a large degree, have defined the historic perspective and the historiography of the Hanse period in Bergen. The first can be seen as an escalation of the tensions in the 1440s. The Sovereign Council pressed on to control the Hanse's growing grip on the export trade. A leading figure was Olav Nilsson, captain at the king's castle. He went as far as attacking Hanse ships in a personal feud. He was removed by the king from his official position but managed to come back, an event that sparked uproar amongst the Germans. The result was that Olav was killed along with his son, the bishop of Bergen, and sixty others who had taken refuge in Munkeliv convent, which was also burnt to the ground.[58]

Olav Nilsson had forced his way back as captain at the king's castle, and had no support from the king. A perspective on one aspect of the conflict that has been given little regard is that the merchants at the Kontor took part in a contest for the control over the king's castle in Bergen, the highest-ranking office in western Norway. Interestingly, this is also a perspective that can be useful for analysing an incident in 1523, when Hansards at the Kontor made a secret agreement with the newly appointed captain at the castle, following King Frederick I's staging of a coup in Copenhagen and King Christian II's exile. The captain at the castle in Bergen, however, was still loyal to Christian. Therefore the new captain asked the Hansards for help. The plan got out of hand, however, and the Hansards at the Kontor, along with German craftsmen, used the opportunity to attack both townspeople and others whom they regarded as their competitors. They even stormed the town hall and destroyed important documents.[59]

The instances in 1455 and 1523 were exceptional cases both in their contexts and gravity, and it is worth noting that the Kontor and its members had to pay heavy reparations. In the nineteenth and well into the twentieth century the traditional perspective among historians was dominated by putting weight on the struggle between foreigners and Norwegians over the control of the trade in Bergen. Such a perspective is still part of a popular narrative, but among academic historians there has been a shift towards emphasizing that conditions were peaceful most of the time, and more attention has been drawn towards the long-term positive effects.

A central issue is to what extent the Hanseatic trading network opened up a larger European market for Norwegian products, and in turn stimulated local investment in the fisheries in northern parts of Norway. During the late medieval period Norwegian settlements grew in the north, a development that contrasted with the long-term demographic recession in the south and especially in the inland districts. Hanseatic imports of grain in exchange for stockfish was of vital importance for people in northern Norway where the climatic conditions made grain growing hazardous, if not impossible. In the sixteenth century the Kontor lost its momentum in Bergen.[60] The Hanse merchants in Bergen seem to have resisted innovation. The Kontor's administration was run in the same way as had been set up in the 1440s, up until the its last secretary left his position in Bergen in 1761; their internal jurisdiction was upheld through all these years. The former director of the Hanseatic Museum in Bergen, Christian Koren Wiberg (1870–1945), who worked extensively on the seventeenth- and eighteenth-century history of the Hanseatic Kontor, underscores frequently how it was a common phrase to refer to the ideal of following customs.[61] Relations between the suppliers of stockfish and the Hanseatic merchants, and the system of advancing payment for the next year's catch seems to have been carried out according to the same practice as in medieval times.[62]

The legacy of the Hanseatic Kontor in Bergen

A useful perspective is that the Kontor in Bergen was an organization based on the idea of holding on to tradition, though one may question whether it was adaptable to change. It is striking that when new Norwegian commodities were available in abundance and sought after on the European market in the sixteenth century – this goes especially for woodwork produced at sawmills in the vicinity of Bergen and the herring fisheries along the coast of western Norway – the merchants at the Kontor did not partake in the export. This was left to the Dutch, Scots and others visiting Bergen and western Norway during the summer season, with the assistance of Bergen's citizens. When the variety of goods and the volume of foreign trade rose, the Hanse merchants followed the strategy of keeping their grip on the traditional fish trade. Eventually they had to loosen this as well. Political circumstances, such as the strengthening of the king's powers and a stronger town government, are part of this picture.[63]

By the mid-1550s a more legally defined citizenship became obtainable in Bergen. Aspiring merchants and craftsmen were now able to register for formal citizenship and have their names written into the town council's ledger of citizens, thus becoming part of the elite among the townspeople. Such citizenship was obtainable for those who were recognized as either a merchant or a master craftsman, and who also had paid a lump sum of money to be registered as a citizen. This made them eligible to trade or practise their craft according to the citizens' privileges, and also to partake in town government. The medieval equivalent to the citizenship of the 1500s was defined in the town law from the 1270s. It stated that those who owned or rented half a tenement, and in addition leased part of their tenement to others, held the right to partake in the election of councillors for the town assembly.[64] However, even though some of the Hanse merchants might have complied with these requirements, they never took part in town government, and no member of the Hanse was ever a member of the town council. One reason for this might be that the privileges and the town law excluded the possibility of being the subject of both at the same time. As long as Hanse merchants saw their interests as being best protected by their privileged status as part of a community that enjoyed internal jurisdiction, they would not seek membership in the town community. The legal status of the German shoemakers may serve to illustrate this.

It was a significant event, both in the history of the town and the Kontor, when the captain of the castle in 1558 forced the German shoemakers either to take citizenship or leave the town. The shoemakers had been conducting their craft since the late thirteenth century and refused to integrate, but advocated that they should be treated as a community within the Kontor's jurisdiction. However, in 1558 they had to back down, and some left while others accepted citizenship and stayed in business as citizens of Bergen.[65]

Indeed, it was the question of citizenship that also brought about the end of the Kontor. Unlike the shoemakers, the merchants at the Kontor were never faced with such a fait accompli; instead there was a slow integration. It started in the last decade of the sixteenth century when some members of the Kontor decided, after they had gained enough capital, to take citizenship in Bergen instead of going back to their home towns. At first their fellows at the Kontor met this with fierce internal resistance, but during the seventeenth century it was accepted. Eventually it also became common for those who changed their identity from being Hanse merchants to citizens of Bergen to keep their dwellings and storerooms at Bryggen. In 1754, these Bergen merchants at Bryggen made statutes for a new Kontor, the Bergen Kontor, which lingered on for another hundred years. From then on the old Hanseatic Kontor disintegrated rapidly. The last secretary acting on behalf of the Hanseatic Kontor left Bergen in 1761, and the last Hanse merchant at Bryggen took citizenship in 1766. So the Hanseatic Kontor in Bergen was never closed down, nor were its members expelled. They simply eventually integrated into the local trading community and citizenry of Bergen.[66]

The Hanseatic Kontor in Bergen survived the other three Kontore by a good margin, as these were all closed down between 1494 and 1598. The Bergen Kontor even survived the last *Hansetag* in 1669. The extraordinary longevity of the Hanse in Bergen has so far never been the subject of research. However, one can argue that a central factor might be that the Hansards in the late medieval period monopolized the stockfish trade and institutionalized it through the Kontor. Defending its grip on the fish trade and the privileges became the main focus of the Kontor, and in the long run its main task was not to facilitate the interests of the merchants from the Hanseatic towns, but to organize the trade between Bergen and fish-producing regions in northern Norway. In such a situation the traders at the Kontor could just as well be citizens of Bergen, and the old Hanseatic Kontor could be transformed into a Bergen Kontor. This might explain why the Kontor even outlived the last Hansards in Bergen and lingered on into the nineteenth century.

The long-lasting legacy of the Hanse in Bergen is a crucial part of the town's connections with sailing routes in the North and Baltic Sea regions, but so was the fact that most of the local visitors arrived by boats or smaller ships. In terms of communications the town was, for all practical purposes, totally dependent on its harbour for more than 800 years. This was challenged only as late as the twentieth century, when railways, cars and aviation were introduced.[67]

Notes

1 *Scriptores minores historiæ danicæ medii ævi,* ed. M. C. Giertz, Copenhagen, 1922, pp. 474–6.

2 The most well-known passage of the king's initiative is found in the work of the Icelandic saga writer Snorri Sturlusson, *Heimskringla III,* ed. B. Aðalbjarnarson, Reykjavík: Hið Íslenzku fornritafélag, 2002, p. 204.

3 K. Helle, *Bergen bys historie* [The history of Bergen], vol. 1, Bergen: Universitetsforlaget, 1982, pp. 133–4. H. Andersson, 'Urbanisation', in K. Helle (ed.), *The Cambridge History of Scandinavia,* vol. 1, Cambridge: Cambridge University Press, 2003, p. 330.

4 A. Herteig, *Kongers havn og handels sete* [The harbour of kings and the residence of trade], Oslo: Aschehoug, 1969, pp. 75–80. A. Herteig, 'Details from the medieval waterfront', in A. Herteig (ed.), *Conference on Waterfront Archaeology in North European Towns, No. 2, Bergen 1983,* Bergen: Historisk museum, 1985, p. 69. The archaeologist G. Hansen has argued that a plot system was laid out as early as *c.*1030: *The Emergence of a Town,* Bergen: Fagbokforlaget, 2005, pp. 221–4. This has been rejected as circumstantial by Helle, see K. Helle 'The emergence of the town of Bergen in the light of the latest research results', in A. Graßmann (ed.), *Das Hansische Kontor zu Bergen und die Lübecker Bergenfahrer: Veröffentlichungen zur Geschichte der Hansestadt Lübeck. Herausgegeben vom Archive der Hansestadt,* B, vol. 41, Lübeck: Schmidt Römhild, 2005, pp. 21–2.

5 G. A. Ersland, *Kven eigde byen: Bygrunnlegging, grunneige og grunnleige i Bergen og eit utval nordeuropeiske byar* [Town foundation, plot ownership and plot rent], revised doctoral thesis, 1994, Oslo: Dreyer, 2011, pp. 61–71.

6 G. A. Ersland, *Byens konstruksjon* [The construction of the town], Oslo: Dreyer, 2011, pp. 84–5.

7 Helle, *Bergen bys historie*, p. 368.

8 Ibid., pp. 348–50. G. A. Ersland, *Norsk forsvarshistorie* [The history of Norwegian military defence], vol. 1, Bergen: Eide, 2000, p. 71.

9 *Bergens Fundas* [The origin of Bergen], ed. Mikkjel Sørlie, Bergen: John Grieg, 1957, p. 29.

10 Herteig, *Kongers havn*, pp. 71–9. Helle, *Bergen bys historie,* pp. 165–7, 356. Hansen, *Emergence*, p. 212.

11 A. Nedkvitne, *The German Hanse and Bergen 1100–1600,* Cologne: Böhlau Verlag, 2014, pp. 24–38.

12 Ersland, *Kven eigde byen*, p. 72.

13 Accounts from the archbishop's trade in Bergen is preserved for some of the years between 1532 and 1538 in Olav Engebriktsons rekneskapsbøker [The account books of Olav Engelbriktsson].

14 Helle, *Bergen bys historie,* p. 311.
15 G. Dahlbäck, 'The towns', in Helle, *Cambridge History of Scandinavia,* vol. 1, p. 618.
16 K. Helle, 'The political centre of the high medieval Norwegian Kingdom', in Ø. Hellesøe Brekke and G. A. Ersland (eds), *Håkonshallen 750 Years: Royal residence and National Monument,* Oslo: Dreyer, 2013, pp. 175–7.
17 *Norges gamle Love 2,* ed. R. Keyser, P. A. Munch, G. Storm, and E. Hertzberg, Christiania 1846–95, pp. 265–6. Helle, *Bergen bys historie b. 1.,* p. 259.
18 Helle, *Bergen bys historie b. 1.,* pp. 533–5.
19 *Bergens Fundas,* p. 65.
20 J. E. Olesen, 'Inter-Scandinavian relations', in Helle, *Cambridge History of Scandinavia,* vol. 1, pp. 713, 725, 769–70.
21 G. A. Ersland, 'The castle as a military stronghold', in Ø. Hellesøe Brekke and G. A. Ersland (eds) *Håkonshallen 750 years – Royal residence and national monument,* Dreyer: Oslo, 2013, pp. 82–7.
22 S. S. Mygland, *Gender and Material Culture. Women in Medieval Bergen. A Contextual Analysis of Gender-Related Artifacts from Bryggen In Bergen 1170–1476,* Phd-thesis, University of Bergen, 2015.
23 Dahlbäck 'The towns', p. 615. K. Helle, 'Fra opphavet til omkring 1500', in K. Helle, F. E. Eliassen, J. E. Myhre and O. S. Stugu (eds), *Norsk byhistorie – Urbanisering gjennom 1300 år.* [Norwegian urban history through 1300 years] Oslo: Pax, 2006, p. 110.
24 Even though only crude estimates for the populations exist for any Scandinavian medieval town, it is widely accepted by historians that Bergen was the most populous. Dahlbäck, 'The towns', p. 615; Helle, 'The political centre', p. 111.
25 Dahlbäck 'The towns', pp. 611, 615.
26 E. Orrman, 'Rural conditions', in Helle, *Cambridge History of Scandinavia, vol. 1,* pp. 267–9. These numbers cover the extent of the three Scandinavian kingdoms in the high medieval period: Denmark, including Halland, Skåne, Blekinge and some Northern German provinces, but not the Duchy of Estonia; Sweden, including Finland; and Norway including Jämtland, Härjedalen and Båhuslen, but not Iceland in the west.
27 *Scriptores minores historiæ danicæ medii ævi.*
28 Helle, *Bergen bys historie,* pp. 491–2.
29 G. A. Ersland, 'Was the Kontor in Bergen a topographical closed entity?', in Graßmann (ed.), *Das Hansische Kontor zu Bergen und die Lübecker Bergenfahrer,* p. 44.
30 K. Helle, 'The Norwegian kingdom: succession disputes and consolidation', in Helle, *Cambridge History of Scandinavia,* vol. 1, p. 388.
31 *Norges gamle Love 2, R. 1, 2,* ed. A. Taranger and G. A. Blom, Christiania, 1912, and Oslo, 1966, pp. 12–16.
32 *Diplomatarium Norvegicum,* vol. 5, ed. C. C. A. Lange, C. R. Unger *et al.*, Christiania, 1849, pp. 22–5, no. 23.
33 *Norges gamle Love 3,* ed. R. Keyser, P. A. Munch, G. Storm and E. Hertzberg, Christiania, 1846–95, pp. 41–2.
34 Helle, *Bergen bys historie,* pp. 351, 747.
35 *Norges gamle Love 2,* ed. Keyser *et al.*, pp. 245–6. Dahlbäck 'The towns', p. 631.
36 Dahlbäck 'The towns', p. 628.
37 Helle, *Bergen bys historie,* pp. 750–5.
38 Ibid., p. 743.
39 A. Steinnes, 'Husgrunnar og folk på Hollendarstretet i Bergen' [Plots and houses on the Dutch Street in Bergen], in *Bergen Historiske Forening, skrifter, No. 67,* Bergen: John Grieg, 1968, p. 9. Helle, *Bergen bys historie,* pp. 804–5.
40 *Diplomatarium Norvegicum,* vol. 5, no. 23. *Norges gamle Love 2,* ed. Keyser *et al.*, pp. 134–6. Helle, *Bergen bys historie,* p. 351.

41 Helle, *Bergen bys historie,* pp. 351–2. Orrman, 'Rural conditions', p. 596.

42 G. A. Ersland and A. Solli, *Stavanger bys historie* [The town history of Stavanger], vol. 1, Stavanger: Wigestrand, 2012, pp. 203–6.

43 A network can be described as different objects chained together by one or a set of common variables. It is a premise that the linkage between the objects has some kind of contextual meaning, and that objects that are not within the network are defined as irrelevant. If two or more towns are named in a written document we can assume that this reflects some kind of interaction between them and therefore indicate that they are part of a network.

44 *Regesta Norwegica,* vols 1–9, ed. E. Gunnes, N. Bjørgo, S. Bagge *et al.*, Oslo: Riksarkivet, 1989–2010.

45 Ersland, 'Kontor in Bergen', pp. 46–56.

46 Herteig, 'Details', in Herteig, *Conference on Waterfront Archaeology*, pp. 81–9. A. Nedkvitne, 'Ship types and ship sizes in Norwegian foreign trade 1100–1600', ibid., pp. 94–6.

47 Nedkvitne, *The German Hanse*, pp. 330–1.

48 Orrman, 'Rural conditions', p. 585.

49 Ersland, *Kven eigde byen*, p. 199.

50 Ersland, 'Kontor in Bergen', p. 56.

51 G.A. Ersland, 'Das Handelsgericht des Hansekontors in Bergen', in M. Hundt and J. Lokers (eds), *Hanse und Stadt: Akteure, Strukturen und Entwicklungen im regionalen und eüropäischen Raum. Festschrift für Rolf Hammel-Kiesow zum 65. Geburtstag,* Lübeck: Schmidt-Römhild, 2014, p. 92, n. 16. A list with aldermen's names going back to 1444 indicates that there were two aldermen, one of which was elected each year for two years, so that the newly elected served along with the one who was serving his last year. Archiv Hansestad Lübeck, Findbuch 9, Bergenfahrer 614.

52 Helle, *Bergen bys historie*, pp. 731–2.

53 Ibid., p. 732. Y. Nielsen refers to a document from 1435 found in the Stadt Archive Bremen mentioning 'das Canthor tho Bergen'. However, the reference needs to be checked. Y. Nielsen, 'De Dudesche Kopman unde de Norman', *Christiania Videnskabs-selskabs forahndlinger* 8, 1876 (Gröndahl: Christiania), p. 16.

54 Ersland, 'Das Handelsgericht', pp. 93–4.

55 Ibid.

56 *Norges gamle Love 2, R. 1*, ed. Taranger and Blom, no. 130.

57 Helle, *Bergen bys historie*, pp. 783–5.

58 Ibid., pp. 766–8. Dahlbäck 'The towns', p. 628.

59 Helle, *Bergen bys historie,* p. 768.

60 Nedkvitne, *The German Hanse*, pp. 476–8.

61 C. K. Wiberg, *Hanseaterne og Bergen* [The Hansards and Bergen], Bergen: John Griegs Forlag, 1932.

62 Evidence of the Stues with its assets (Nordfahrerschuld) are well documented in ledgers from the early eighteenth century, kept in the Bergenfahrerarchiv in the Town Archive of Lübeck.

63 Helle, *Bergen bys historie*, p. 852. Dahlbäck, 'The towns', p. 627.

64 *Norges gamle Love 2*, p. 260. Helle, *Bergen bys historie*, p. 449.

65 Helle, *Bergen bys historie*, pp. 756–61.

66 F. Bruns, *Die Sekretäre des deutschen Kontor in Bergen*, Bergen: John Grieg, 1939, p. 131. Ersland, 'Das Handelsgericht', pp. 89, 101.

67 Ersland, *Byens konstruksjon*, pp. 193–4.

25

EUROPEAN INTEGRATION FROM THE SEASIDE

A comparative synthesis

Wim Blockmans and Justyna Wubs-Mrozewicz

Great histories of the Mediterranean, the Baltic and other seas have been written and continue to inspire research. This volume is the first to encompass not only the southern and the northern traditions, but also that of the European Atlantic and North Sea coasts. It should not come as a surprise that it took time to combine historiographies, which until now have focused predominately on the connections of individual cities or within particular areas. The reconstruction of connections over long distances was already a challenging task, since travelling meant crossing borders presented by geographical, economic, political, religious, cultural and linguistic entities. Overcoming all these differences was all but self-evident – in the historical experience, just as in historiography. National historiographical traditions and the specific skills needed to access and interpret the sources have fragmented the research area and made an all-encompassing view of European maritime connections rare. The collective enterprise attempted in the present volume is aimed at reconnecting the various historiographical traditions in order to attain a better understanding of the commercial linkages integrating Europe from the sea as occurred more and more starting around 1300.

The mind-set for dealing peacefully and constructively with otherness is rather scarce among animal populations, and human beings tend to demonstrate all too clearly their biological roots, at least in this respect. The primary behaviour in contact with another species generally aims at domination and predation. The lasting establishment of non-violent and productive exchanges requires a cultural development that not only sublimates the primary impulses but also apprehends a long-term vision of peaceful and stable living conditions. As historians are not immune from a sense of belonging to a particular community, it requires special effort to overcome the obstacles, in source material as well as in the various historiographical traditions, in order to grasp the daring activities of the shippers and merchants who were peacefully establishing exchanges between cities at long distances.

A period of expansion and intensification

In its first section, this volume addresses the systemic conditions for overseas exchanges: the techniques of shipbuilding and discovering efficient connections, the legal context of dealings in different political and cultural locations, the organization and ensuring of financial transactions at the lowest cost, and problems of communication, the exchange of information, and the sheer understanding of technical terminology in other languages. In all these domains, significant developments took place in the period under consideration, the fourteenth to the sixteenth centuries. Briefly before 1300, Genoese ships passed the Strait of Gibraltar and sailed to the North Sea, a connection that became regular within a few decades, reaching out from several Italian and Catalan ports. North German shippers extended their links in the North Sea area, centred on Bruges and London, with Bergen and Novgorod as their furthest strongholds. From the 1420s onwards, cooperation in the Baltic by shippers from Zeeland and Holland experienced the flip side of an increasing element of competition, which would come to dominate in the sixteenth century. The Dutch also dared to sail southward along the Atlantic coast. Portuguese and North Iberian sailors set out to the North Sea and beyond. Ships were adapted to different maritime conditions, acquired larger carrying capacities, and could reach longer distances. The increased mental as well as practical grasp of Europe's geography appears evident in the spread of portolan maps representing the empirical observations of the coastlines, the distances between the harbours, and the orientations of the sailing routes. These maps superseded the idealistic worldview put forth by maps of the Christian world, many of which placed Jerusalem at the centre. Richard Unger shows that this wide range of technical progress led to a greater diversity in contacts, more competition, and the need for more encompassing arrangements for the provisioning and security of the fleets.

Albrecht Cordes demonstrates that the different regional systems of maritime law, which were centred in nodal harbours from Rhodes in the early Middle Ages to Amalfi and Pisa in the twelfth century and Venice, Genoa and the *Jugements de la Mer* on the island Oléron in the thirteenth, as well as the Codifications of Valencia and Barcelona, Damme, Lübeck and others, were applicable on particular routes, which raised problems of coordination in cases of hazard on a long trajectory. Financial transactions developed rapidly on a trans-continental scale, facilitating exchange, transfer and credit without hindrance by theologians' fulminations against interest, or by the princes' monetary manipulations. Financial markets became integrated more fluently than legal systems because those innovations were all introduced by Italian companies, which had adapted techniques they observed in their contact with the Levantine merchants. The great Italian advance in terms of capital accumulation and business organization made them the absolute market leaders whose methods prevailed in the continent's most commercialized regions, i.e. the western Mediterranean, southern Germany, and the Atlantic and North Sea coasts as far north as London and Bruges. Stuart Jenks shows that merchants in Central and Northern Europe modernized their commercial techniques as well, albeit with the stipulation that the bill of exchange could hardly be instrumental in those regions due to the lower density of the transactions. Donatella Calabi describes the buildings in which commercial, and particularly financial, transactions became concentrated. Increasing specialization in the financial sector necessitated specific buildings – the *lonjas*, exchanges and bourses – a clear filiation of which is visible in the architectural models.

The aspect of language contact, presented here by Agnete Nesse, played an evident role in long-distance trade. Arabic words designating particular products and practices penetrated European languages. Closely related Germanic languages in the Baltic area, Scandinavia and the Low Countries allowed passive bilingualism. In the case of greater linguistic and cultural differences, as between the Hansards and Russians in Novgorod, translation was needed, and the control of linguistic competence even became a means to monopolize the contacts. In some areas a kind of common language, or koine, functioned, such as Italian in the Mediterranean and Low German in the Baltic and North Sea areas. Bruges, and later Antwerp, which were located close to the linguistic border between Germanic and Romance languages, functioned as connectors in this respect as well – as places where various languages could be used. In the 1360s–1370s, a schoolteacher in Bruges published a method for translating technical commercial terminology between French and Flemish, which was extended with a Rhinish Low German translation and an English translation in the fifteenth century. Printed versions date from *c.*1483 for the English and 1501 for the French-Flemish versions. Simple sentences listed the terms of a great variety of products and place names, thematically and alphabetically ordered.[1]

This demonstrates the demand for practical multilingualism in the commercial environment, just as the Italian *Pratiche della Mercatura* disseminated extremely important technical as well as highly relevant practical cultural information for the conduct of profitable relations.[2] For centuries, Latin, French and English were used in parallel in England. Documents discussed in the 1420s–1440s in Parliament concerning the wool trade via the Staple in Calais were written in French, English and Latin, the latter language being used not only in diplomatic instructions, but also in royal ordinances and statutes.[3]

The geographical expansion of maritime trade coincided remarkably with dramatic demographic crises, starting with the Great Famine of the years 1315–17 and 1321–2, followed by animal murrains. In England, roughly 20 per cent of the cattle in ecclesiastical domains died in 1315–17, and in the 1320s up to two-thirds succumbed to the epizootic. New outbreaks occurred in 1334 and 1345, and only after 1350 did the stock reach the pre-1315 level again. The loss of so great a number of all breeds had a disastrous effect on agricultural productivity and severely limited the variation in human nutrition. This disease had its origins in Central Europe and gradually spread to the West. Similarly, the Great Famine was a general phenomenon in northwestern Europe. The Black Death, which spread rapidly from southern Italy in 1347 and was followed by recurrent plague epidemics, further reduced Europe's population by one-third, up until the early fifteenth century.[4] Yields of wheat dropped in England by one-third in 1315, by half in 1316, and by a quarter in 1321; in 1349–51, they dropped by one-third, in subsequent plague years by a quarter, and in 1401 by one-third again.[5] These repeated and very sharp fluctuations in grain prices had dramatic social effects and strongly motivated traders to seek profitable solutions for the shortages by carrying great quantities from regions with normal supplies.

Detailed information is available for Bruges, which had then grown to be the most prominent port of northwestern Europe, probably equal to London. It had a population of around 45,000 and a huge cloth hall that had been built recently, as well as another hall 95 metres in length used for loading and unloading valuable goods onto and from smaller boats under a roof.[6] From May to October 1316, 1,938 corpses that had been left in the streets were buried at the city's common expense.[7] As one can assume that other victims had died under less pitiful circumstances and had been taken care of by their families, the total number of victims may have been considerably higher than the 4.3 per cent of the population registered in the city's account. In the same period, the municipal authorities of the industrial city of Ypres buried no less than 2,794 corpses; such a figure represents a minimum of 11 per cent of the local population. The significant difference in casualties can be related to the fact that the population of Bruges was globally wealthier than that of Ypres, which had recently suffered severely from revolts, repression and warfare. Another crucial variable, however, was Bruges's function as an international maritime port, in contrast to the less favourably connected Ypres.

In April 1317, the municipality of Bruges bought huge quantities of grain from Mediterranean merchants for a sum equal to all the city's ordinary yearly receipts. Eight merchants provided a total of 1,414 tons of grain, which the municipal authorities sold to the bakers in portions during the *soudure* months until the next harvest in August. In this way they managed to prevent another year of extreme dearth, which otherwise might have been exploited and exacerbated by speculators. On average, 43 litres of wheat and 2 litres of rye were distributed per capita, enough to feed each inhabitant with 0.85 kgs of bread per day for six weeks.

None of the preserved accounts of other cities in the region demonstrate the capacity that the Bruges municipal government showed: it had the vision to launch a social policy preventing extremely high grain prices for a third consecutive year. The government took, therefore, the risk of public deficit spending, and could do so thanks to the trust invested in it by South European merchants, who were acquainted with the local circumstances. Anthone de Mari, who sold two cargoes, belonged to a Genoese family whose members had been active in the Champagne fairs, in Flanders and in Bruges in 1313.[8] Another Genoese family with long-standing ties to Flanders was that of Ogier Pervoisyn, or Pilavicenus. Catalan and Castilian merchants were already established and privileged in Bruges since the first quarter of the thirteenth century,[9] and two of them, Alfonso and Bonote Lorem, also belonged to the cohort of grain providers. They obviously saw an opportunity to make a profit thanks to the temporary price difference between Northern and Southern Europe, and they had the cargo capacity available to ship the required quantity. The energetic policy of the Bruges government not only demonstrates its close relations with foreign merchants; it may have contributed to the development of regular connections between the main ports in the western Mediterranean and the North Sea harbours, precisely from 1318 onwards. In particular, the Genoese de Mare family showed its ability to reorient its activities from the traditional overland route via the Champagne fairs to maritime connections, while the Catalans followed suit at an early stage.

On a much smaller scale, a Genoese galley – not a bulk carrier – had been chartered in March 1317 in Seville to row across to North Africa and collect wheat to take to England. The wheat prices indeed peaked in London and the Thames valley, and obviously the existing supply lines from Flanders, Picardy and Normandy had been blocked by export prohibitions.[10] The example for the Bruges and English grain purchases had evidently been set by Genoa, Florence and Marseille, major cities whose hinterlands were structurally unable to produce the grain supplies required by their populations. Genoa primarily got its supplies from the Black Sea area where it held numerous settlements, and, after the Ottoman conquests, increasingly in the kingdom of Naples and Languedoc; Marseille sought its supplies in Sardinia, Sicily, Languedoc, Catalonia and as far away as Apulia.[11] Because seven out of the ten years between 1301 and 1310 produced poor harvests, leading to extraordinarily high prices, a famine raged in Florence. The commune organized large imports of grain from Sicily and Apulia in Genoese ships. More than 70 per cent of the recorded Sicilian grain exports in that decade were brought to Tuscany. In later years, scarcity was reported in Florence only in 1317 and 1322. The Great Famine of 1315–17 was thus mainly a phenomenon of northwestern Europe, which explains the willingness of the Genoese and Catalans to send supplies to Bruges and England. By 1300, however, grain scarcity had become a general problem in Western Europe, demanding dramatically new solutions. It cannot have been by accident, however, that it was in 1316 that the three Florentine super-companies of the Bardi, Peruzzi and Acciaiuoli formed a syndicate to monopolize the grain export from the kingdom of Naples, including Apulia. In those days, they were already firmly established in Bruges and London and thus well aware of the great scarcity there.[12]

Other circumstances also contributed to the expansion of maritime connections. From the 1290s onwards, political conflicts increased the insecurity of overland routes as well as those on the seas. After the fall of the last Crusader bulwark of Acre in 1291, a nine-year maritime war started between Venice and Genoa over control of the Aegean and the Black Sea. This may have been prompted by the dramatic decrease in Genoa's trade volume, which John Day estimated, for the best years of the fourteenth century, to be only half of that at the end of the previous century. The dramatic decrease of the population certainly had a great impact on the reduction of the trade volume. Luisa Piccinno explains the city's attempts to strengthen its control over its colonial settlements in the East, as well as its initiatives to create new opportunities in the West as reactions to the critical decline of its traditional trade. The Ottoman expansion blocked the alternative overland route to the Far East from 1303 onwards. From 1283 to 1343, the Houses of Anjou and Aragon competed over claims to Sicily and Naples. After the Castilian conquest of Seville and Cadiz, the Christian kingdoms in Iberia remained in conflict with Granada and places along the Maghreb coast. Moreover, terrestrial warfare, especially in France, also perturbed the routes. And from 1310 to 1343 the Italian mainland was torn between the Guelf and Ghibelline parties. The consequences of these conflicts made the whole Mediterranean area more dangerous. Trade relations were frequently interrupted by embargoes, deliveries became uncertain, and risks were higher due to piracy and confiscation. The Anglo-French dynastic wars similarly endangered the Atlantic and North Sea routes, first until 1314, and again from 1337 onwards.

As shown by Richard Unger, protection was sought in convoys escorted by larger armed vessels, and in maritime insurance schemes. Each of these devices raised transaction costs, but economies of scale favoured the shipping option. The maritime connection to the North Sea via Gibraltar, first documented for a Genoese fleet in 1277, and probably active before that date, was not unproblematic either. The distance of 7,200 kilometres was fivefold that of the 1,300 kilometres overland. From Venice, the distance was longer still, which explains why Venetian galley convoys sailed to the North Sea no more than twenty-four times between 1332 and 1400, or just one year in three. No convoys set off to the north during the wars between Genoa and Venice in 1351–4 and 1379–81, which deeply disturbed the markets there.[13] Nevertheless, all these factors together led to the decline of the overland route through Champagne, whose famous fairs lost their role of international mediation around 1300, as 'in part a consequence of success'. The increase in the scale of business made a division of labour more efficient, whereby the more successful merchants remained at home and were informed by resident partners and agents in various commercial centres – people who knew how to find the best opportunities.[14] Grain was the most important bulk cargo, for which the large cities in northern Italy and Marseille had needed, since the twelfth century, to organize a regular supply by overseas transports. The Great Famine of 1315–17 provided the impetus to connect this typically Mediterranean system to the North Sea area, thanks to the connection explored by the Genoese since 1277 and the well-established commercial partnerships.[15]

Once regular connections had been established starting in 1318, the great variety of high-quality and scarce products that the Italians acquired in the Levant could be supplied in greater quantities to the existing markets and many new ones as well. In the other direction, the Bardi and Peruzzi branches in Bruges secured the acquisition of the Flemish and Brabantine luxury cloth essential for their southern trade. Their factors there could also market the English wool purchased by the companies' London branches to local entrepreneurs, from whom they would buy the finished products for export. The Italian companies offered financial services to the city of Bruges, and the Peruzzi Company acted as a collector of Flemish war indemnities for the king of France. The London branches of the Bardi, Frescobaldi and other companies supplied the Florentine textile manufacturers with significant quantities of English wool of inferior quality from the third decade of the fourteenth century onwards.[16] However, most Italian companies came under pressure to lend money to

Kings Edward I, Edward II and Edward III, who controlled concentrated commodity resources and had companies to accept losses on those debts.

The intensified sailing along the Atlantic coasts gave a boost to the regional economic systems such as those of the Portuguese and North Iberian coasts, Gascony, La Rochelle, Brittany and Normandy. The city of Exeter, on Britain's southwestern coast, imported grain mainly from Brittany, while London was oriented more towards closer-by Flanders, Picardy and Normandy. The wheat prices in the two English cities alternated between phases of greater and lesser correlation between 1320 and 1370, showing only a relative integration of the coastal wheat market. In the Low Countries, grain markets became increasingly integrated, first along the rivers and interior waterways and then ever more along the coasts, as Picardy, East England and northwestern Germany became major providers.[17] The Northern European maritime system got connected directly to the Southern European system, with London and Bruges as the main nodal points. Mathias Tranchant points out that La Rochelle hosted active merchants' settlements from the north Iberian coasts, Brittany, Flanders and northern Germany. Merchants from Lisbon were mentioned for the first time in an English Patent Roll in 1294, but King John granted Portuguese merchants safeguard on the English coasts as early as 1202 and 1204.[18] The English were active in Lisbon in 1311, and in 1309 Lisbon obtained a privilege in Harfleur, the main port in the estuary of the Seine. Amelia Andrade and Flavio Miranda observe that Porto might have been connected to the north a few decades earlier, but stress that in the 1370s a north German colony was settled in Lisbon, and merchants from Flanders, England, Normandy, Brittany and Gascony met there with the numerous other Iberians and the Italians.

Around 1300, the European economic system went through a commercial revolution that included a transport revolution, whereby maritime connections became intensified, and focused increasingly on bulk cargoes of foodstuffs and reaching out over longer routes. Thanks to the new massive and regular maritime connections between south and north, the system expanded through its own momentum and could introduce the typical innovations that facilitated economies of scale and lower overall transaction costs. Capital accumulated in trade was reinvested in financial activities primarily for commercial purposes, but also increasingly for rulers and all classes of society. The new organizational patterns of long-distance trade made possible the introduction of fiduciary money, the value of which no longer depended on the rulers' currency manipulations, nor was it liable to ecclesiastical sanctions for 'usury', as it rested entirely on the trust relations between merchants throughout Western Europe. Such trust that was hard to win and easy to lose through defamation.[19]

To sum up the innovations that impacted the maritime trade networks directly:

- capital concentration in (predominantly Italian) companies, led by extended families and shareholders, with branches and resident agents in principal commercial centres;
- managers of merchant companies no longer travelling themselves, and maritime transport becoming an independent professional sector;

- intensive information streams from couriers carrying letters and credit instruments;
- the generalization of commercial and even industrial credit, largely organized by financial experts from northern Italy, globally labelled as 'Lombards', increasingly followed by merchants of northwestern European origins;[20]
- the development of a relatively autonomous financial sector specializing in loans extended to princes and political and aristocratic elites, as well as in short-term consumption loans to individual citizens and peasants (institutionalized deposit banks were able to carry out transfers between account holders);
- transfers by bills of exchange;
- double-entry bookkeeping; and
- the professionalization of commercial intermediaries such as factors, agents, brokers, hostellers and interpreters.

Commercial activity required an amazing breadth of expertise by individuals who had to deal with highly volatile situations in very different political and cultural contexts. 'Managers and employees needed to be multi-lingual and numerate, knowledgeable in currency exchange systems, accounting, banking, legal systems, and logistics; experts in judging the quality and types of grains, wines, spices, wool, tissues, dyes, precious metals, and stones; and personable, politically astute, enterprising, and physically courageous.' They all were men, as women often kept the business going at home.[21] The expertise of factors was so highly valued that Castilian regulations prohibited their transfer between competing companies.[22] Angela Orlandi concluded from her in-depth study of the archives left by the merchant of Prato, Francesco Datini (active around 1400 in the whole of Western Europe), that he was 'a manager at the head of a coherent consortium of companies who testified of a directive style, a profound knowledge of even the most distant markets, and the necessity to take decisions only after having assessed the alternative possibilities in each situation'. Although he mainly dealt in textile products between England, Flanders and the western Mediterranean, he grasped every opportunity in the volatile grain markets to buy and sell wherever it was most profitable, mainly in Sicily and the Languedoc, on a small scale just as often as in great quantities, at short and long distances, and in all directions. 'Merchants impregnated by a strong pragmatism and a speculative spirit' bought into the future Sicilian grain harvests in the period from January to April, paying an advance of less than half of the expected price. The difference with the official price would be adjusted in August or September.[23]

The increased volume and value of maritime trade made the ports the evident locations of resident agents of international companies, which reinvested their surplus and disseminated the advanced techniques of Italian commerce and bookkeeping. The increased efforts to build larger and more robust ships required huge capital investments, as did the cargoes and their risk-sharing and insurance contracts. Harbour infrastructures needed to keep abreast of the new types and quantities of ships. Out-ports such as Southampton, Portsmouth, Damme, Sluis and Arnemuiden provided the anchorage facilities for the larger fleets and the storage space for bulk cargoes, especially for the ports of major cities located at some distance from the sea, such as London and Antwerp. Some harbours were simply unable to adapt and thus lost their role, as in the case of Kampen at the Zuiderzee and Bruges. The high risks legitimated high profits for maritime enterprises susceptible to natural hazards, violence, the instability of the markets and the uncertain effects of judicial procedures abroad. Merchants' fortunes often were ephemeral, although intergenerational accumulation, organization in companies based on family ties and external shareholders, and investment in real estate could offer security. A typical case was that of Hildebrand Veckinchusen, who operated successfully for decades with family members in Lübeck, Cologne, Frankfurt, Bruges, Reval, Riga and Venice. He had to spend three years (1422–5) in jail in Bruges because of unpaid debts to the Genoese merchant Jerome Spinola, the distressing end of a long and successful career.[24]

The breakthrough around 1300 came at the peak of European population growth that had lasted more than three centuries, and arrived at the outset of a century with perhaps the most dramatic population losses in human history. Initially, the expectation of ongoing growth may have fostered new initiatives. After the Black Death, the concentration of capital increased the living standards of large layers of the population, which triggered new demand for luxury goods, and for more diversified products of better as well as of ordinary quality. The increased transport capacity for bulk cargoes opened up new markets in more peripheral regions of the continent, whose export products could now in return be disseminated at a much larger scale to new geographical markets and new social strata. Typical examples of this are the Norwegian stockfish, pickled herring from Scania, Russian furs and wax, as well as the cheaper textile products from England, Tuscany and the Low Countries, the relatively cheaper wines exported from La Rochelle, and beer from the Hanse cities, later imitated by cities in Holland. The Florentine entrepreneur Francesco Balducci Pegolotti estimated in his *Pratica della Mercatura*, written in the middle of the fourteenth century on the basis of several decades of trans-European experience, that the transportation of English wool to Italy by sea cost around eight times less than overland. Maryanne Kowaleski pointed out that in early fourteenth-century England, the overland transport of grain was as much as twelve to eighteen times more expensive than by rivers and by sea. Mass consumption expanded the markets in space and to lower social classes. This tendency proved unstoppable until the present day.

Meanwhile, the connection of the Mediterranean with the Atlantic in the long term stimulated growth in the new core area at the North Sea. From the 1420s onwards, shippers from Holland and Zeeland became increasingly prominent as bulk transporters along the Atlantic coast, sailing as far south as the centres of salt-making in the Bay of Bourgneuf and Setubal. The infertility of their soils drove them to aggressively seek grain supplies, starting in neighbouring regions, then in England and Picardy, and in the sixteenth century predominantly in Prussia and even further eastward. The Dutch and English shippers and merchants started as partners to the Hansards, but in the course of the fifteenth century they gradually turned into competitors in the Baltic. In Bergen and Norway, as Geir Atle Ersland mentions, they made a stronger mark from the late sixteenth century on.

Between 1300 and 1600, the European trading system expanded in terms of space, the capacity of ships and carts, and intensity – in a counter-cyclical trend, and even largely thanks to the concentration of capital and purchasing power in the hands of considerably fewer people. When the population started to grow again by the end of the fifteenth century, the system retained its dynamism and continued to expand further. Shifts in global economic activity contributed to the development of new trading routes, in which southern Germany played a crucial role. The ongoing wars between France and the Habsburg empire increased the risks on the Atlantic route, which gave a new impetus to the overland connections organized by Hessian companies with carts offering regular services between Antwerp, Milan and Venice.[25] As Louis Sicking and Arno Neele explain, Antwerp's port activities nevertheless grew at a dazzling speed, as it was supported by the out-port Arnemuiden, which was close to the mouth of the Scheldt at some 80 kilometres from the metropolis.[26] Antwerp thrived thanks to the massive presence of English, Hanseatic, Iberian and Italian merchants. Its population reached over 100,000 in the 1560s, the first Western European city after Paris to attain this size. In general, maritime port cities grew in the fifteenth and sixteenth centuries, as further exemplified by Lisbon, London, Amsterdam and Danzig. The dominance of the Mediterranean ports weakened, not in the last place due to the new intercontinental connections.

The case studies compared

The eighteen case studies in this volume's second section were selected with the aim of showing the various types of nodal locations, which together formed a series of network systems around Europe. Most of these chapters deal with a single port, but three of them must be singled out. The most surprising may be Carlo Taviani's study of the Genoese colonial empire, as it was managed by the Banca di San Giorgio in a way that in the seventeenth century would be labelled a 'chartered company'. From 1446 to 1562 it acquired and ruled with full rights of jurisdiction lands that had previously been under the administration of the commune of Genoa, including the whole island of Corsica, and scores of trading posts around the Black Sea and the Ligurian coast. The chapter on Lübeck deals with the city that was central in the genesis and character of the German Hanse, an association of merchants in the north German and Baltic region. It was a conglomerate of several regional *hanses* existing in the thirteenth century, as there existed a number in Western Europe as well. The most famous of them was the so-called Hanse of the XVII towns in present-day northern France and the neighbouring territories in the Low Countries, which in reality at certain moments numbered up to twenty-two towns and marketed their textile products at the fairs of Champagne. What made the German Hanse unique was its extension to nearly two hundred towns belonging to the German empire, plus four external regional headquarters known as Kontors (Bruges, London, Bergen and Novgorod), and several settlements in Europe, among them in La Rochelle and Lisbon. The German Hanse functioned as an institution of conflict management that was active until the seventeenth century, while most other *hanses* disappeared in the fourteenth century. Finally, the third special case is that of the Scheldt estuary, to which two successive metropolises, Bruges and Antwerp, were connected, as well as Zeeland and Holland, though its core was just a village, Arnemuiden, with no infrastructure other than plenty of space for large ships and twenty-nine piers where the cargo could be transshipped to be carried on to Bruges, Antwerp, or towns in Holland, and vice versa. The function of an out-port was not exceptional as such, but its attraction to ships sailing on very long routes from all directions made the island of Walcheren and a few secondary ports in Zeeland the most buoyant maritime centre of the sixteenth century in northwestern Europe.

As announced in the Introduction, five themes have been addressed in all the case studies: the port's location, the hinterland, the network connections, institutional provisions, and conflict resolution and management. We will now address each of these themes with the aim of drawing conclusions from the comparison of the cases.

Location advantages and challenges

All ports of any importance developed in a location that offered some advantages, though obstacles were equally omnipresent. 'Rare are those [among the Italian maritime ports] that seemingly were endowed with a particularly favourable natural site', writes Elisabeth Crouzet-Pavan.[27] We will distinguish here four types of locations that, under the macro-economic circumstances and the technical development of the ships, all proved relatively successful: the estuary of a major river, far upstream, a natural bay on the coast, and a connecting point between different economic and cultural systems. Admittedly, some overlap exists between these categories, as geographical features were never solely determinant.

The estuary of a river is just such a challenging and problematic location since, by its nature, it connects a hinterland to the sea. Many, but certainly not all, of the largest European cities were located at or close to the mouth of a major river, such as Danzig, Montpellier and, in earlier centuries, Alexandria. Aberdeen was located in the estuary of the river Dee, but in more densely populated regions several ports emerged in a large estuary. This applies typically to the Nile delta, where the military port at Rosetta was forbidden for Christians, and the regional port at Damietta fulfilled complementary functions vis-à-vis the main international port at Alexandria where the large ships could moor. A large river generates massive sedimentation, however, especially in a sandy environment, which leads to the silting-up of the mouth and the need to adapt the port infrastructure.[28]

Natural hazards such as storms and floods radically changed the hydrographic situation in the Scheldt estuary, with dramatic consequences for some ports and beneficial effects for other places. It is worth noting that the mouth of the Rhine, the longest of the Western European rivers, as well as that of the Vistula and the Rhône, end in a sandy delta. Two of the Rhine's natural mouths silted up in the dunes ridge; its main stream mixes with that of the Meuse and splits up again, with Dordrecht and Rotterdam as its main ports, but at quite a distance from the river's mouth.

In the period from 1300 to 1600, Dordrecht played an international role between the Rhineland, the Hanse cities, Flanders and England. The Vistula similarly formed an extended delta as its discharge was obstructed by the dunes ridge, and the river split in two branches, the westernmost leading to Danzig and the eastern one to Elbing, which became a secondary port. The Rhône delta also gave birth to a plurality of ports, the most prominent being Montpellier, though its inland location was not easily accessible, being located on two hills and with the small river Lez 10 kilometres away from the coast, through an area of marshy lands. This prompted in the thirteenth century the foundation of Aigues-Mortes as the only Mediterranean port city of the kingdom, though this soon lost its function due to silting. Bruges also lost its attractiveness due to the progressive silting of its narrow connection to the sea, which was only 20 kilometres long. Larger ships had to be unloaded and cargoes transhipped in Damme, Sluis, or even further north in one of the ports on Walcheren Island. Antwerp's better accessibility at a relatively short distance (about 80 kilometres upstream the Scheldt) made the political and institutional motives of the translocation of the metropolitan functions quite obvious in the 1480s. Valencia had a problem with the irregular discharge of its river Turia during the year, and therefore its maritime port was a village on the coast, some 6.5 kilometres away. Marseille was not directly connected with the Rhône valley but it had a natural maritime harbour protected by a rocky ridge; however, its difficult connection into a relatively infertile hinterland kept it in a role secondary to Montpellier, Genoa and the Catalan ports. And so, curiously, none of the three major rivers – not even the Po – was at the origins of a single maritime port. Lisbon, albeit a late developer, combined all the advantages of its location close to the mouth of a great and largely navigable river that did not end in a sandy delta.

In the early Middle Ages, most towns were located upstream at a distance from the coast in order to be protected against raids from the sea. Typical inland locations were those of Novgorod (some 200 kilometres south of the coast, and 270 kilometres to Narva, to the northwest), Pskov, Lübeck, Hamburg (135 kilometres from the sea), Antwerp and London. The last three became metropolises, as the sea-going ships of that period could sail on the river up to the city centre and unload there, and they were also very well connected with an extended hinterland. Nevertheless, both London and Antwerp were extensively served via out-ports. In the fifteenth century, Florentine galleys and Genoese carracks moored in Southampton, and their goods were transported by cart to London. Until the sixteenth century, Venetian galleys unloaded their spices and luxury products in Sandwich and downriver Thames-side ports to save time for crossing the North Sea as well. Seville, Bordeaux and Toulouse may be added to the category of important upstream harbour cities as well. Florence notoriously struggled for centuries with its distance of around 90 kilometres to the sea. A combination of paved roads and the river Arno to Pisa offered a complicated solution, as the maritime port Porto Pisano had been controlled by Genoa since 1284. Florence bought the port in 1421, but as its swampy coastal plain suffered from increasing alluvial deposits and the coastline moved away from the port, Livorno became Florence's seaport.[29]

Locations directly on the coast were relatively rare, and ports there had the form of a natural basin that could be closed by a chain or protected by a tower, as was the case in Genoa, Marseille, Ragusa, La Rochelle and Bergen. Even the port of Genoa needed to be dredged regularly due to the silting up by rivers flowing into the basin, and important construction works were needed for the piers and the dam. The forty-nine port towns founded between the twelfth and the fourteenth century on the Iberian north coast nearly all profited from the bay surrounded by mountains. Ships could find protection against storms and even hibernate. The need to construct jetties, quays and storehouses appeared only in the course of the fifteenth century, whereas excavations in London, Bergen and in several Hanse ports suggest that such construction was going on well before that time.[30]

The last type of port to be distinguished is a strategic location linking two different geographical, economic and often also cultural spheres. One may think in this respect of Reval/Tallinn, a Hanse town at the southern entrance to the Finnish Gulf near the border between Livonia and Russia. Aberdeen was the northern-most Scottish port, second to Edinburgh and Bergen, and the most northern city for the Hanse, English and Dutch shippers (until these rounded the North Cape by the very end of the sixteenth century). Lübeck was strategically located insofar as it helped shippers to avoid the long and risky circumnavigation of Denmark. Its alternative was a 70-kilometres-long overland road, as the repeated attempts to construct a canal to the Elbe failed time and time again. And the locations of both Genoa and Venice were the obvious points connecting the Mediterranean with Lombardy, the Po valley, and beyond to the western and eastern Alpine passes to Germany, northwestern and Central Europe, respectively. Venice's location near the edge of the Adriatic offered protection against both terrestrial armies and dangers from the sea. However, navigation was difficult on the canals in the lagoons, which explains why ports were built on the sandy ridges along the coast protecting the lagoons against the sea. Chioggia, and those ports closer to Venice, such as Malamocco and the Lido, emerged as the most important. Works to deepen the connections started in the fourteenth century and had to be effectuated continuously from the middle of the fifteenth century, by which time larger vessels could only pass at high tide or through the rather distant Malamocco passage. Transshipment was another way to cope with the ongoing silting problems. The city's marginal and precarious location triggered the need to protect its collective interests through communally directed action.[31]

To sum up: locations at large river estuaries were obvious but also problematic; inland locations on easily navigable rivers offered more advantages. Silting was a major problem in all sandy environments, and major investments were made to keep access possible – in 1604 Venice launched the construction of a canal linking the Po to its Laguna – but the technical difficulties in all cases proved unsurmountable. Naturally protected locations directly on the coast could become very successful, as in the case of Genoa and Ragusa, while others remained stuck in a supporting role. And some locations offered primarily the advantage of linking different systems along a front, which may be a cultural frontier or an interface between levels of economic sophistication. Geopolitical reasons added considerably to locational advantages, such as Venice's belonging to the Byzantine empire in the ninth century as opposed to Langobard Ravenna; the political

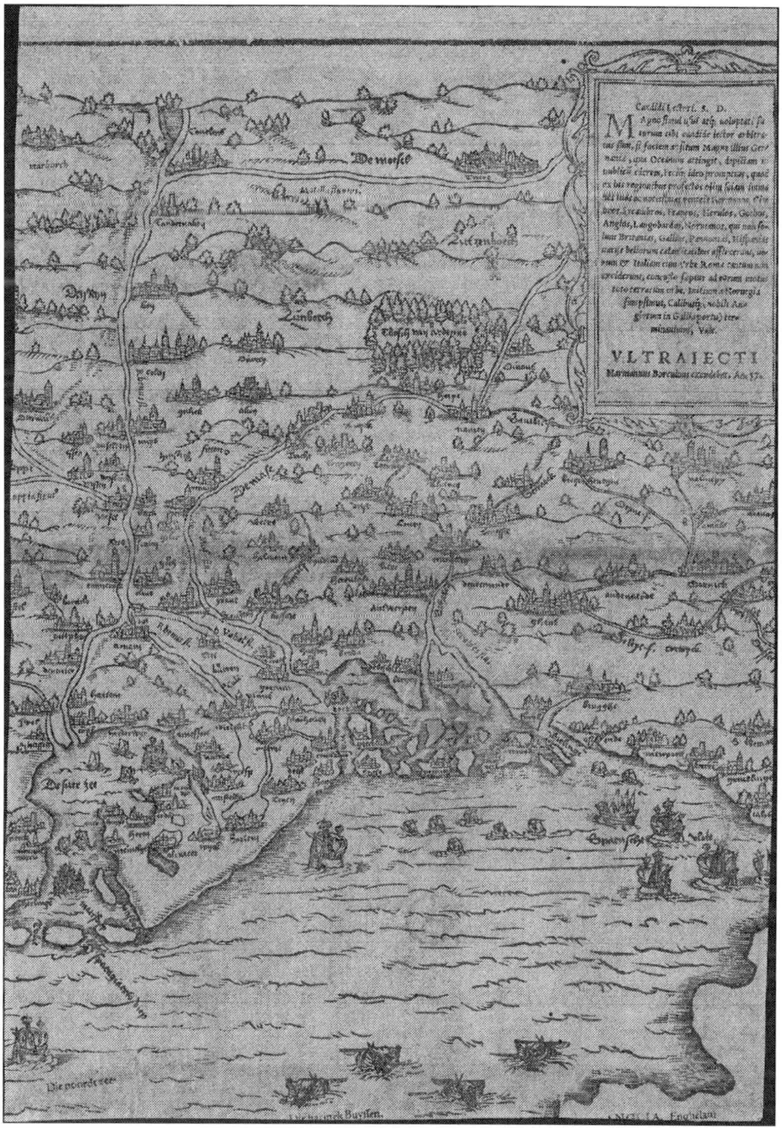

Figure 25.1 *Germania Inferior qua Oceanum attingit.* Detail of map, printed in Utrecht in 1554, depicting the Low Countries as seen from the North Sea up to the Rhine and the Moselle, with Trier in the top right-hand corner

autonomy enjoyed by Genoa, Ragusa, the Baltic ports, Pskov and Novgorod; and the particular protection the king offered London, Lisbon, La Rochelle and Bergen. Falling under a particular dynasty entailed hindrances as well, as experienced by Marseille, Bruges and Lübeck when they became involved in their princes' dynastic priorities, or were subordinated and lost their economic liberties in the cases of Visby, Antwerp, Novgorod and Pskov. Locational advantages thus only became relevant when macro-economic and geopolitical conditions were favourable as well.

Hinterland

We defined a port's hinterland as the inland area from which the resources that were essential to its functioning could be concentrated. Carsten Jahnke calculated that the region where Lübeck drew its supplies extended over a radius of *c.*100 kilometres. The salt-mines in Lüneburg, however, 116 kilometres away, were an essential element of Lübeck's trade, and therefore have also to be reckoned as its hinterland, as well as Hamburg, to which it was connected via a tributary of the Elbe. Hamburg needed the grain supplies of villages within a radius of *c.*50 kilometres, of which a minimum of 2,160 square kilometres was needed for the supply of bread grains and another 1,200 for the grains used in the brewing process of the famous export beer. In 1450, the Elbe was marked along the 135 kilometres down to the coast with floating barrels to show clearly to whom the river belonged.[32] For Nuremberg, a city with 28,000 inhabitants in 1497, the same radius of 50 kilometres covered an area of 5,000 square kilometres, in which the same measure was used for grain.[33] A hinterland's extension depended on the geographical conditions, including the connections by rivers, the region's fertility, the nature of its products, and the port city's capacities to enhance the raw material's value by manufacturing and re-exporting the finished products. London dominated the navigation on the Thames 65 kilometres upstream and 61 kilometres downstream from the early twelfth century. This was the direct hinterland that provided bulk products such as grain, firewood and raw materials to the city. Grain was supplied from a region over 100 kilometres up the river and even further away via coastal transport from East Anglia, Kent and Sussex. Londoners provided credit to industry and supplied all kinds of goods to all nearby counties. Their share in operations for imported goods, luxury and semi-luxury products was overwhelming and increased considerably between 1424 and 1570. [34] Maryanne Kowaleski shows that 70 to 75 per cent of the English wool export passed through London around 1450. For cloth exports, that share rose from 60 per cent in the 1470s to 90 per cent in the 1550s. The city thus played the central role as the gateway in the distributive trade of these goods throughout the whole kingdom. Its hinterland covered a great part of the country that was well connected through a national road network, originally designed during the Roman colonization. The city had no formal control in the counties but it did have jurisdiction on the Thames, from the mouth to more than 100 kilometres upstream.

Venice's direct environmental surrounds were, in Elisabeth Crouzet-Pavan's words, 'unrewarding and even hostile'. Only salt was a local product, and one with a low value at that. For its sheer subsistence, the Serenissima needed to secure its grain supply from Apulia and get a grip on the mainland on both sides of the Adriatic. The supply of wood was absolutely fundamental, as it was the most strategic raw material. Enormous quantities of poles were needed on which the larger buildings and bridges had to be constructed; they held the levees protecting the city against the winter storms, and the hundreds of ships that connected the city with its vast overseas possessions and trading partners were built from them. Various types of trees were needed for different purposes – firewood, different qualities and sorts of timber for shipbuilding and other construction works – and they had to be transported by various waterways from the forests on the mainland north of Venice and in Istria. The Arsenal, the public shipyard, needed at least 200 mature oak poles for the planks that made up the hull of a great galley, and at least 30 perfectly structured beeches for the oars. Three or four high-quality firs were needed for the masts. Apart from the regular renovation of the fleet, on some occasions maritime wars made the rapid construction of dozens of new ships necessary. From the fourteenth century onwards, the reserves appeared insufficient at times due to difficulties in production, trade or transportation. The Senate and its specialized officials had to negotiate extensively with the proprietors and local communities to secure the necessary regular supplies.[35]

Venice is a unique case in our time period, identified by Jan de Vries as the most populated city in Europe's most densely urbanized region around 1500 and 1550 (followed closely by Antwerp at the latter time). In 1600, the core had already shifted to Holland.[36] In terms of the central place theory, Venice was evidently the most developed gateway at that time, offering the widest scale of products and services available on the continent. However, it was not its direct hinterland that made its rise possible, but its extensive overseas network. The same observation applies to Genoa and, in a later period, to Amsterdam. The poor resources of the direct hinterland pushed these cities to find their means of subsistence overseas, which they did in an extraordinarily successful way thanks to the opportunities they found or created to link up their connections into a highly productive system. Ragusa is also an interesting case in this respect, being located on a very narrow strip of land between the coast and the infertile but forested mountains. The city fought its way out of Venice's colonial control in 1358, invested heavily in the construction of one of the largest fleets of the fifteenth and sixteenth centuries, and exploited its monopoly over the Serbian and Bosnian hinterland. Mines of silver, lead and copper initiated a highly profitable export via overland roads to the port city; in its wake followed slaves and valuable products such as cattle, horses and other products of animal husbandry. The political geography had a decisive influence here as well: caught between Ottoman and Venetian expansionism, the Ragusans managed to play an intermediary role between the superpowers and continue to function as the main port of the western Balkans, well connected with its hinterland via overland routes.

The extreme cases discussed above leave room for a variety of other situations. There were those gateways functioning for an extended hinterland that produced a limited range of products in high demand on international markets. Bergen had its stockfish, Aberdeen its wool and salmon, Novgorod, Pskov and Reval highly priced furs (and a few secondary products such as wax), Danzig grain, Hamburg beer, London and other British ports lived off the export of wool and textiles, La Rochelle and Lisbon wine and salt, Marseille coral: all of them offered a scarce leading product from their direct, albeit sometimes distant hinterland, and exchanged it for goods from other regions. Lisbon and Alexandria derived their prominent position in the long-distance trade not primarily from the production of their direct hinterland, but from the high value of the goods traded through their long-distance networks. In Lisbon's case, these were slaves and gold from west Africa, and from the later fifteenth century onwards, sugar and spices from its colonies; in Alexandria's case, from its connection to the Indian Ocean and beyond. A relatively fertile hinterland, such as that of Valencia, offered a host of opportunities, but no guarantee for a leading role. A relatively infertile hinterland, such as that of Marseille, did not exclude a supportive role but, in combination with the locational limitations, it did not allow the development of a dominant position. Metropolises, such as London, Bruges and Antwerp, combined a high-value re-export with a substantial export production from a fairly large, densely commercialized and industrialized region – in the latter cases a great variety of textiles and luxury products such as jewellery and artwork. The artisanal sector was highly specialized and considerably enhanced the value of its export.[37] All things considered, a productive hinterland was a necessary but not a sufficient condition for the development of major port cities. The notable exceptions of Venice and Genoa could only overcome this handicap by securing supplies from an extensive maritime trade network and colonies.

The network connections

By definition, all the ports were connected by regular exchanges with other ports, as they functioned as the nodal points between their hinterland and the overseas areas of production and consumption. What really distinguishes them is the hierarchy between the ports, the extension of their network, the variety and the value of the products marketed, and the total volume of the port movement. Georg Christ noted that historians have a tendency to overestimate the value of long-distance trade as compared to regional connections. In his estimate, Alexandria's multipolar and varied regional connections represented more than double the value of the Venetian trade there. David Igual Luis similarly stresses the importance of the exchanges between Valencia and the smaller ports along Iberia's southern coasts. The four categories of ports we distinguished in the Introduction can be confirmed as adequate ways to identify the specific functions of each port: (1) supply points of scarce goods at the edge of a network; (2) supporting ports on major routes; (3) nodal points connecting intercontinental networks; and (4) metropolises. Some overlap is not to be excluded, but the levels of activity clearly depend on the range, value and quantity of the products exchanged. On the supply side, this depends on the hinterland's production and the port city's capacity to add value to the raw materials. A port city's demand was determined by its population's size and purchasing power, the population density and wealth in the hinterland, and possibly the opportunities for re-export. Based on all these factors, a port's location within the network of trading routes had a huge impact on its opportunities.

Italy obviously occupied the central position in the Mediterranean; its two largest ports outrivalled all the others on the peninsula, as well as Ligurian and Iberian competitors. In the fourteenth century, Venice and Genoa fought fierce wars for control over their colonial possessions, in which Venice surpassed Genoa and drove it to explore alternative routes westwards into the Atlantic, especially the direct maritime connection to the North Sea. Nevertheless, the two remained the dominant commercial cities until the late sixteenth century, as they controlled the largest number of maritime as well as overland trading routes in and around Europe, thanks to the sophistication of their commercial organizations, their superior capital accumulation and the capacity of their fleets. They succeeded in integrating the various regional networks in the Mediterranean, and in expanding them, in the first half of the fourteenth century, through the Strait of Gibraltar around Iberia and along the North Atlantic coast to the North Sea. Their ships gave decisive impetus to a whole series of ports of call such as Palma de Mallorca, Valencia, Seville, Lisbon, Bilbao, Nantes and Rouen, as well as to their final destinations in Bruges, London and Antwerp. There, they connected with the German Hanse, the other major maritime network that had developed in the Baltic and North Seas.[38]

In the early fifteenth century, north German shippers explored the Atlantic coasts southward to Lisbon, but they found stern competitors in the shippers from England, Holland and Zeeland. These gradually drove the Germans back, imitated some of their most successful trades such as hopped beer and salted herring, and obtained a foothold in originally Hanseatic strongholds such as Bergen, Danzig and Reval.[39] It was shippers from Holland and Zeeland who, thanks to their lower freight rates, transported wines from Gascony and Poitou, as well as salt from the Bay of Bourgneuf and even from Setubal, to Bruges and Antwerp and, later in the fifteenth and in the sixteenth century, further to the Hanse cities. In this respect the Dutch shipbuilding industry played a crucial role, not just in producing a rapidly growing merchant fleet, but also by designing new and more efficient types of ships, both for bulk cargoes (the *fluyt*) and for the fisheries.[40] Only canvas and ropes could be produced in Holland and Zeeland; timber and tar needed to be imported from the forested areas upstream in Norway and the eastern Baltic area, along the Meuse and the Rhine. This demand was an additional incentive for the Dutch export industries (cloth, salted herring, beer, dairy products), and for exploiting the carrying capacities maximally in both directions.[41]

The combination of England's insular position, its early administrative centralization and its massive production of high-quality wool, the demand for which was largely inelastic on the continent, explains the organization of its monopolistic export trade. The Merchants of the Staple in Calais formed a chartered company that profited from the high demand for wool in the Low Countries, levied the customs and was in a position to advance large sums to the crown. Several English ports collaborated in the Company of the Merchants Adventurers, which was in charge of the cloth export to the Low Countries (mainly to Antwerp); they secured diplomatic relations, settled disputes and organized shipping and convoys. On the other hand, the German Hanse enjoyed specific privileges thanks to its populous presence and its settlement in the Steelyard.[42] Together, all the alien merchants held a dominant share of two-thirds of the imports to London and to England as a whole around 1480, as calculated by Maryanne Kowaleski.

Not all ports on the Atlantic coasts were equally successful in grasping full profits from the integration of maritime networks. The ports of Brittany were ideally located on the prominent peninsula halfway between the Iberian peninsula and the North Sea. Nantes, well-protected against piracy and storms at 50 kilometres upstream the Loire, hosted representations of Genoese and Spanish merchants, and its shippers transported wine and salt from the nearby production areas. In the second half of the fifteenth century, dozens of Breton ships moored in Sluis and Arnemuiden, the out-ports of Bruges. However, the capacity of the vessels varied between 30 and 100 tons, much smaller than their Dutch and Italian competitors. Hardly any merchant from Brittany appeared in the Bruges court registers – more often shippers were fined for illegally selling goods.[43] Evidently the Breton shippers were less competitive than those from England, Holland and Zeeland. Their enterprises were organized on a much smaller and more vulnerable scale, and they did not link up with the merchant communities and the market opportunities in Bruges itself. Why did the Bretons not do as well as the Dutch, who had hardly more or more valuable products of their own to export? Why did Lisbon grow into a metropolitan status, and not La Rochelle or Nantes – at least not before 1600? Four factors seem to explain the differences in development:

1. Lisbon's colonial connections provided a near-monopoly on African slaves and high-value products such as sugar and Indian spices, in addition to its export of salt and other goods;
2. Lisbon's commercial companies were financially solid and well settled in fifteenth-century Bruges and in sixteenth-century Antwerp;[44]
3. Lisbon was located close to the ocean and linked with routes in different directions, including the Mediterranean; and
4. the strong presence of Italian merchants investing in new enterprises firmly contributed to the transfer of know-how and capital to Lisbon, and thus to the strengthening of local entrepreneurship.[45]

While these four factors, characteristic for Lisbon, were absent in the cases of La Rochelle, Nantes or any Breton port, one may add that the relative poverty of the latter's hinterland in no way compensated for other weaknesses.

From the late fifteenth century and until 1559, the nearly continuous warfare between the Habsburg empire and Valois France perturbed Atlantic coastal navigation so seriously that the overland routes became relatively advantageous again. Supported by the growth of the south German industries, transport companies based in Frankfurt used large carts for the regular transport services of valuable goods from Swabia and Hesse to Venice and Ancona via the Brenner Pass, to Milan via the St Gotthard Pass, and to Antwerp via the Main and Rhine. Similarly, post services secured the frequent, safe and fast exchange of information needed for the transactions between the commercial agents and their principals. The reliability of the connections greatly enhanced the efficiency of the operations. Overland routes thus continued to form an essential part of the port cities' commercial networks. By the late sixteenth century, the combination of the larger, more numerous, diversified, faster and more frequent transport systems overland and overseas led to greatly expanded, densified and far more integrated connections than had existed around 1300. A striking effect of the ever-growing scale of the commercial activities and their spin-offs can be observed in the rapid growth of the population of the thriving metropolises: London and Antwerp grew to around 100,000 inhabitants after 1550, a size previously attained only by Paris and Venice; Lisbon and Danzig then also reached levels well beyond 50,000.

In the last decade of the sixteenth century, repeated famines triggered the reverse of the massive grain transports that we discussed above for the Great Famine of 1315–17. Luisa Piccinno points out that Genoese merchants residing in Antwerp shipped great quantities to Genoa, with the consequence that vessels from Northern Europe represented up to one-quarter of the port traffic, in order to alleviate the poor harvests in the Mediterranean. One can hardly think of a more convincing argument to link the recurrent and sometimes extreme price volatility of this basic food with the ever-closer unification of the maritime networks around Europe in the period from 1300 to 1600.

The institutional context

Medieval communes were generally characterized by self-governance (autocephaly) and the competence of local lawmaking (autonomy). These privileges had been granted by local lords and princes to individual communes, mostly after serious negotiation, often conflict, and always at a price. The two concepts had an absolute value only in exceptional cases, namely those where no external powers were in a position to qualify or reduce the autonomy. Venice was able to free itself from theoretical Byzantine sovereignty in the late eleventh century and remained an independent republic until 1797. Genoa was less successful in maintaining its autonomy, largely due to its internal factional rivalries. However, the successive periods of French, Milanese, French again, and Habsburg protectorate curbed the Superba's autonomy only in foreign affairs; practically, it acted in its own best interest. Ragusa held a similar position after its liberation from Venetian hegemony in 1358. It formally recognized the Hungarian king as sovereign, but acted independently. Such was also the case for most cities in north Germany: since the power of the emperor was very limited and as his dynastic basis was situated in south Germany, the distance was considerable and effective control was very limited. The Hanse towns were *reichsfern*, literally meaning far away from the imperial centre, to use the term coined by Peter Moraw. Only beginning in the middle of the sixteenth century did they have to contribute to imperial taxes. However, a real threat came in the late fifteenth century from the territorial princes whose powers became felt more effectively.[46] Similarly, the Danish king Erik Menved launched a lasting conflict with the German seaside towns, and in 1361 Valdemar IV brought Visby's commercial heyday to an end.

Novgorod and Pskov saw their autonomy unchallenged until the mid-fifteenth century, probably due to the low population density in their wider environment and the correlating low level of capital accumulation. These factors may explain the survival of popular assemblies in the two cities and the lack of oligarchization in the hands of the merchant class. From the mid-fifteenth century onwards, they had equally to face increasing pressure from princes and were effectively subjected by the Muscovite grand princes Ivan III and Basil III in 1478 and 1510, respectively. The Hanse Kontor in Novgorod was closed in 1494; the forty-nine remaining merchants were arrested and had their goods confiscated. An ambassador from Reval was kept in jail during three years under conditions that led to his death. In 1557, Tsar Ivan IV recalled Russian merchants from Reval, with the aim of steering the trade via Narva and Dorpat. The effect of these rough actions was the breakdown of the relations as they had functioned for centuries, notwithstanding later attempts to restore them in the course of the sixteenth century.

For most cities, the measure of autonomy and self-governance varied over time, depending on the relative power relations with the principal countervailing power, mostly a territorial prince or king. As in the case of the German empire, the proximity or distance to the king made a huge difference. Closest were the relations in London and Lisbon. The English kings of the fourteenth and fifteenth centuries systematically used the inelastic demand for wool on the continent as an ideal fiscal resource, the burden of which fell on the foreign buyers. Maryanne Kowaleski shows that in 1471 the customs rate on wool exported by aliens was 48 per cent of the purchasing price, while it was 25 per cent for denizens. In regard to tolls and monetary regulations the kings needed to negotiate with Parliament, where the London merchants, organized in mighty mercantile guilds, formed a strong pressure group. Royal charters and guild regulations compelled provincial merchants to go through London dealers.[47] They could not, however, prevent the Hundred Years' War from consuming the product of the additional taxation, which was being spent on destructive dynastic chimeras. The merchant elites of Porto and Lisbon were eager to entertain close relations with the court and to serve as diplomats for the negotiations on an Anglo-Portuguese trade agreement in the 1380s. The crown profited from the merchants' expertise and connections, and the merchants hoped for favourable opportunities.[48] The fifteenth century's kings of Portugal displayed a keen interest in economic policy and actively supported ongoing explorations along the African coasts. This did not mean that the Lisbon merchant community was always happy with the crown's prescriptions. In both cases, however, both parties were fully aware of the huge impact of maritime trade on their country. Monarchs with an open mind to trade interests were in a position to provide protection and security, and to grant special privileges.

A more distant king could be beneficial, as was the case of successive French kings for La Rochelle and the Aragonese for Valencia. This was also the situation for Danzig after the Polish king's victory in a war with the Teutonic Order, ending in 1466 and with the subsequent incorporation of Prussia into the kingdom. Danzig continued to enjoy a level of liberty convenient for the merchant interests ruling the city.

The Polish king thus displayed a greater insight in the profit his monarchy could expect from the flourishing port city than the policy the Muscovite grand-princes demonstrated in Novgorod and Pskov. Prussia was able to keep its own coinage, taxation, trade and judicial privileges, and Prussian merchants got freedom of trade throughout the whole kingdom. The king even considerably extended the territorial possessions of Danzig, Elbing and Thorn. When later kings tried to impose their rule in the 1560s and 1570s, their attempts were rebuffed.[49] Commercial cities tended to remain neutral amidst dynastic conflicts, as was Ragusa's hallmark. During the Hundred Years' War, the Flemish cities tried to remain neutral between their sovereign, the king of France, and their main trading partner, the king of England. In the sixteenth century, Danzig tried to emphasize its neutrality, as did Antwerp and the Dutch cities vis-à-vis the conflicts between Emperor Charles V and the Danish kings Christian II and Christian III in the 1520s to 1540s.

Monarchs could be outright disastrous for regular trade relations, as they were primarily driven by their personal and dynastic honour and focused on dynastic warfare with a conspicuous disdain for the needs of commerce. This is what Marseille experienced when its rulers of the house of Anjou were at war with the kings of Aragon who also ruled Sicily and the kingdom of Naples. The port's future did not become brighter under the French monarchy that continued the wars with Aragon and Naples, especially after the latter came under Habsburg rule in 1516. These dynastic conflicts systematically hampered navigation on the Tyrrhenian Sea. The dynastic priorities of the Habsburgs directly led to the exodus of foreign merchants from Bruges in the 1480s and of half of Antwerp's population one century later. Even the States General's repeated declarations that peace, justice and free trade were the basis of the highly populated Low Countries' prosperity did not curb the monarchs' obsessive dynastic targets.[50] In more peaceful periods, regular negotiations were held frequently between merchant communities, individual profit-seeking merchants and the municipal and central government. In matters such as grain supply, monopolistic tendencies or maritime insurance regulations, the various parties had different interests, which did not always lead to quick and the most efficient solutions.[51]

Municipal governments found their origins in merchants guilds, and even in those cities where revolts led to some form of political participation of the craftsmen, the mercantile influence remained predominant, especially in the larger cities with a big sector of trade and industry.[52] The smooth, and in many cases unperceived, transition between merchant guild and magistracy implied that the towns and cities stepped in to the functions originally fulfilled by the guilds as private associations, namely the protection of the person and the goods of citizens abroad. The six major cities of Flanders negotiated commercial treaties with King John of England in 1209 (concerning La Rochelle) and 1213, and from 1241 onwards they frequently acted in common in matters concerning judicial conflicts, trade fairs and the currency. The countess sealed their agreements, and would act only 'with the assent of the aldermen [of the major cities] of Flanders'.[53] This pattern remained very similar during the fourteenth century, and it was even exacerbated by far-reaching initiatives of the major cities during the periods of open revolt. From 1385 to 1435, the major cities held five to six meetings each year, often with diplomatic missions to the countries they concerned, with foreign and mostly commercial partners and their public authorities such as the Hanse, the court of England, Spanish and French authorities. Nearly half of these meetings did not include any representative of the government, and the initiative always emanated from the cities.[54] Lengthy negotiations between the Flemish cities and their foreign trading partners dealt with all kinds of conflicts between merchants and with the local authorities. The Hanse similarly tried to solve all kinds of commercial disputes through negotiations, in the first instance between the Kontor in Bruges and the urban magistrates, as they did in London, Bergen and Novgorod. Blockades and retreats from Flanders were the most drastic ways of putting the pressure on, and they effectively led to agreements, including the compensation for losses.[55]

The representation of individual as well as collective commercial interests by municipal authorities has been demonstrated in the case of La Rochelle: there, it also took on the form of treaties, diplomatic missions and mediation. The ties between the merchants' private interests and the commune were so close that losses due to hazards at sea were compensated from the treasury, which made a kind of marine insurance contract (as had been developed in Genoa and was widely available in Italian ports around 1400) superfluous. There, as in Bruges and Antwerp, foreign merchants were granted collective privileges such as jurisdiction in cases of commercial disputes within their 'nation', the right to occupy a common residence (a 'loge') and to have their own religious services in a particular church. They were the obvious partners for negotiations with the local authorities.[56] In Bruges, commercial contracts between foreigners had to be negotiated by official brokers, who could advise merchants about opportunities and regulations. Hostellers equally provided commercial and even financial services. In these metropolises, 'tables' of exchange, Lombards and true banks, Italian as well as local, facilitated deposits and transfers. Bruges' metropolitan role in the fourteenth centuries has recently been ascribed to its institutional arrangements in supporting foreign merchants by the multiplicity and diversity of foreign merchants present and resident in the city, and to its 'numerous network-making institutions from mendicant monasteries to taverns, all concentrated in a limited space'.[57] Moreover, it has been stressed that monocausal explanations are empirically insufficiently informed, and that, from the institutional side, the interplay between local and central powers, merchants' organizations, and princely courts cannot be minimalized. While merchants welcomed institutions as long as they stabilized the market and reduced costs, they tried to evade them as soon as new developments seemed to offer better opportunities.[58]

The *funduq* evidently served as the model for the privileged merchant 'nations'. The Mediterranean ports had also been far ahead in the organization of protection against hazards at sea. The Venetian state consisted directly of the merchant class, which for that reason didn't need a separate merchant guild. A specialist even labelled the Senate as a 'board of directors'.[59] They organized the entire shipbuilding industry in the Arsenal, including the forest management on the mainland for the wood supply, as well as the protection of its merchant fleets in armed convoys. Monique O'Connell explains how the Senate's various committees and offices took care of negotiations and conflict management. They appointed and instructed the consuls and governors of the colonies, and sent ambassadors to discuss conflicts. The *Consoli dei Mercanti* dealt with commercial disputes and acted as brokers. Genoa thrived more on private initiative from which the maritime insurance emerged, at the latest early in the fourteenth century. Notaries, and from the fifteenth century onwards increasingly brokers, drew up standardized contracts for traffic on international routes. Hundreds of local underwriters invested in risk-transfer instruments, mostly acting as collectives of four or five, but often many more per policy. In a sample of 2,471 deeds drawn up from 1427 to 1431 by the most prominent notary, Branca Bagnara, 31 per cent of the capital was provided by 16 large investors belonging to the aristocratic families operating on the international financial markets. An ordinance issued by the doge of the Republic of Genoa in 1369 set out fines for all those attempting to evade financial commitments by referring to canon law against usury. Such doctrine was bound to paralyse trade, declared Doge Gabriele Adorno, who belonged to a prominent merchant family himself.[60] Specialized courts dealt with commercial disputes, the *Ufficio della Mercanzia* and, from 1529 onwards, the *Rota Civile*. The port was managed by the *Padri del Comune*, and the offices of merchandise and the Robaria were in charge of the regulation and the protection of trade. Even in the 1530s and 1540s marine insurers in Antwerp were mostly Italians and Spaniards.[61] While most English ports had separate maritime courts, this was not the case in London. However, aliens involved in lawsuits that went before common law courts had the right to have some of their countrymen on the jury.

The judicial autonomy of port cities in matters of trade and navigation was essential because of the required expertise, the preference for mediation above jurisdiction and the common interest in quick solutions. The courts of princes generally lacked this expertise, applied complicated procedures and needed costly time, which was detrimental to the plaintiff. King Alfonso X of Castile, nicknamed the Wise (1252–84), founded a special court for maritime litigation in Seville; a similar court was created much later in Burgos for the northern trade, but these cases were exceptional. As Georg Christ explains, the Venetian metropolitan authorities tended to push their citizens residing in Alexandria towards direct appeal to the sultan in Cairo because he would be sensitive to maintaining good relations. Yet this was a costly and protracted procedure. Hence conflicts were often solved on the spot, for instance in direct negotiations between the Venetian consul and the emir or the customs inspector.

Conflict resolution and management

Conflicts were a recurrent part of mercantile life and of the life of maritime cities. Discord threatened the prosperity of individual merchants, networks and cities, and the stability of relations. Dealing with conflicts was therefore high on the agenda of both individuals and city governments. The range of conflicts was broad: from breaches of contracts and trust, misuse of power and monopolies, disagreements about responsibility for losses, to conflicts arising from political tensions, such as privateer attacks on merchant ships during wars or antagonism among the local population. The large variety in the merchant population in the maritime cities, from petty traders to entrepreneurs holding the strands of international trade in their hands, also resulted in a variety of issues as the Valencia case has shown. Yet it must be kept in mind that sources tend to highlight conflicts and show them in great detail, like the killing of the Norwegian captain at the king's castle in Bergen along with the bishop and sixty others in 1455. We mostly read about interactions gone bad. Everyday cooperation, including efficient conflict resolution, has left a less prominent mark in the source material. Therefore, arbitration and mediation, for instance, are less visible than litigation and (commercial) diplomacy.

The various aspects of mercantile conflict resolution, in particular in sea cities where foreign traders flocked in significant numbers, have been studied mostly from the perspective of New Institutional Economics and economic history. The questions have been: what were the most efficient institutions for the problems of merchants? Which solutions stimulated trade and the growth of the cities? How did formal adjudication and arbitration relate to each other? For several of the cases in our volume, there are ample sources to be examined. In Genoa, disputes were handled by the office of the Gazaria, which was composed of lay justices with proven expertise and experience in maritime law, seeing as it was extensively codified. A similarly sophisticated special jurisdiction aimed at expert and quick procedures – and if possible, conflict resolution through mediation – was developed in Valencia, and from there in several Catalan ports, as the Consulate of the Sea. Still, as authors of the chapters on Lübeck, Genoa and Valencia have pointed out, the topic is far from being exhausted. And because the cities were part of large-scale politics, there is a political conflict resolution element that is mostly not included in the analyses, but which did shape the playing field for merchants. The chapters on Pskov and Novgorod show how diplomacy and negotiations in the aftermath of individual conflicts defined the relations between these towns and the Hanseatic towns in Livonia. In addition, the privileged position of Lübeckers in Scandinavia was time and again renegotiated as these Hansards were in the midst of the inter-Scandinavian power struggle from the early fourteenth century on. The Venetian consuls in Alexandria had both commercial and diplomatic duties. Next to conflict resolution, that is, aiming to end conflicts, there were also attempts to *manage* conflicts. For instance, city officials and merchants also tried to prevent political and economic conflicts.[62]

The key feature of the conflict resolution and conflict management of the maritime cities studied in this volume was pragmatism. There was a clear understanding that the norms and behavioural practices of visiting merchants could stand far apart, as the examples of the Novgorod and Bergen tavern brawls show. In Alexandria, the solutions the Venetian consuls came up with were not entirely congruent with the Mamluk privileges or the Venetian regulations, but they nevertheless answered to the local needs and were therefore accepted. Even though there was no universal mercantile law and the practices of conflict resolution could be quite dissimilar, there were certain principles that were recognized at least regionally. One of them was that practical solutions were to be sought: conflicts were usually dealt with where they had occurred, as the Pskov, Aberdeen and Hanseatic cases show. Into the sixteenth century, it was accepted that there were overlapping jurisdictions of a variety of institutions. This enhanced the flexibility and speed of practical solutions. Moreover, it included extrajudicial conflict resolution like arbitration and mediation in straightforward conflicts, or in conflicts where taking a matter to court would endanger relations. The underlying presumption was that, even though laws and customs differed between the cities, there were nevertheless legal and social norms in place that would help safeguard the interests of both denizen and foreign merchants. Otherwise, the home cities of the foreigners were first in line to defend the rights of their citizens, closely followed by the territorial rulers. An appeal to sticking to local custom, common sense and the principle of reciprocity in the treatment of merchants was frequently made, especially in the relations between the Hanseatic cities. If the conflict escalated, collective responsibility was the reverse side of this notion of reciprocity, as examples from both northern and southern cities show. The Hansards applied it in external relations, but tried to avoid it in their internal interactions.

There were a remarkable variety of institutions, and people behind them, that dealt with conflicts related to trade in the maritime cities. These included experienced merchants, of whom we only occasionally catch a glimpse in the sources as arbitrators; fellow guild members, for instance in the Black Heads brotherhood in Reval; consuls and aldermen from hometowns, as the case in La Rochelle or Bergen; notaries, in Valencia for instance; several urban courts, like in Venice; admirals, such as from the mid-fifteenth century onwards in Scotland; lower and higher members of the clergy, such as the archbishops in Novgorod; or the king and his council as in Lisbon. In each of these locations, there were several options to choose from. In addition, there was the possibility of appealing to various judicial bodies and rulers, from the Hanseatic Diets to the Roman emperor or the sultan. In some of the cities, there were specialized courts dealing with trade and foreigners, like the Consulate of the Sea in Valencia or the Giudici del Forestier in Venice. In others, addressing these matters was the task of the urban courts and authorities, with the option of applying the speedy procedure of guest law, as happened for instance in the Hanseatic cities.

Finally, the range of tools that the cities could deploy was also broad. In our modern eyes, the lack of division of power between legislative, judicial and executive power might seem strange, obsolete and counterproductive. In the eyes of contemporaries, it was probably very logical, up-to-date, and efficient because matters could be dealt with by the very same experienced people who saw the complexity of the conflicts. Hence they could combine judicial conflict resolution with urban diplomacy as they did in the Low Countries or the Italian towns, pledge for political neutrality for the sake of commercial matters as was the case in Danzig or Ragusa, and above all try to defend autonomy in decision-making in matters of conflict. In cases where the king had a major say, as in Lisbon or London, he was actively drawn into this many-sided system of urban conflict management and emerged as one of the parties advocating for pragmatic conflict resolution.

An expanding and re-orienting economic system

In conclusion, we can return to the classification proposed in the Introduction and distinguish four types of port cities operating at different scales as nodal points in long-distance trade networks, but still becoming increasingly interconnected in the course of the three centuries under consideration. Transportation was extended in its geographical dimensions. It became more intensive and capacity was augmented considerably. Products could be moved over greater distances, on a much larger scale and in greater quantities; commercial organizations and their techniques also spread from the Mediterranean to the North Sea.

1. Ports located at an extreme point of long-distance trading networks, exporting one or a limited range of scarce and valuable products, with little capacity to add significant value for purchasing and/or re-exporting foreign products. Examples: Bergen exporting stockfish; Aberdeen and numerous English ports exporting wool; Reval and Pskov offering furs and forest products; the ports on the Galician, Cantabrian and Basque coast exporting Castilian wool and metals;[63] and the Genoese trading posts on the Black Sea providing slaves and grain· Novgorod may be considered as being in a more complex situation since it also fulfilled religious and administrative functions for a wide region, which led to a concentration of capital. If foreign merchants were settled as residents in these ports, they belonged to a single dominant nation: the Genoese around the Black Sea, the Hansards in Bergen and the ports of the eastern Baltic.
2. Ports favourably located on long-distance trading routes, and with fairly productive and relatively wealthy hinterlands, might have developed their own long-distance maritime networks from the twelfth century, but gradually came to be included in the routes controlled by the greatest port cities, for which they were instrumental in a supporting role. Their weaker mercantile organizations could not compete with the north Italian companies. Examples here are Palma de Mallorca, Marseille, Montpellier, Valencia, La Rochelle and the ports in Brittany and Normandy. Until the fifteenth century Lisbon similarly belonged to this category, before its colonial trade brought it into a more central position. David Igual Luis refers to the 'lack of capitalization' of Valencian entrepreneurs, and Thierry Pécout similarly points to the relatively weak position of the local financial and entrepreneurial elites in Marseille. Mathias Tranchant disclosed a rent-seeking merchant class in La Rochelle, which preferred to exploit public resources rather than put their capital at risk in maritime investments. Lübeck's role also rested more on its location and network than on its hinterland, but the extraordinary locational advantages, combined with the role of the Hanse, provided it with a unique position. Ragusa was able to hold on to its important network, subsidiary to both Venice and the Ottoman empire, thanks to its cunning leadership, its huge fleet, and the high value of the products from its hinterland.
3. Nodal points connecting intercontinental trading networks had a strong strategic position at the edge of Christianity because of their location, as well as through

the high value and the wide range of products they made available there to the European markets. Extraterritorial settlements of European merchants took two shapes depending on the strength of the local power structures. In the Fatimid Maghreb and Egypt, Mamluk Egypt and Syria, the Christians had no alternative but to comply with the rules set by the Muslim authorities, which entailed the right of exchange from a limited protected quarter conceded for their business, the *funduq*. Alexandria is the typical case in point, just as a great number of Levantine and Maghreb ports. In those places where the Crusaders could hold on, and around the Black Sea, which was conquered after 1204 by Venetians and Genoese, they simply created trading posts or outright territorial colonies. Caffa and Tana were the most prominent of these, as they were the primary connections to the silk route. Trebizond and Sinope on the Turkish coast provided access to the Persian markets and the Crimea, and trading posts on the west coast provided grain, wine and slaves. Pera flourished as a Genoese trading post as long as the Byzantine empire remained significant. In all these places, Christian merchants gained access to markets for strategic goods produced in distant and very different cultural spheres, and in many of them, at least initially, to more sophisticated commercial practices than their own.

4. The metropolises combined all the advantages. Genoa and Venice compensated for their lack of a productive hinterland with their extensive maritime networks and through colonization. Through their exchanges in the Levant, they adopted and adapted knowledge, techniques and connections in various domains, which explains their market leadership as much as the highly valuable products whose trade they monopolized. Their impressive success resulted from their unique mediating position between the Levant and the rest of the European continent. Numerous merchants from a great variety of nations were granted a privileged status, settled in conspicuous residences, and some of them integrated in the local elite. The extraordinary accumulation of human and material capital formed the basis of a very dynamic, innovative and solid commercial organization model that became dominant in the West.

Dynamic relocations of commercial activities were typical of the European port system. From the later sixteenth century onwards, Venice and Genoa lost their long-term control of the export of highly valued products from the Levant and from Italy to the rest of Europe. Portuguese entrepreneurs proved to be more competitive in the trade of sugar and spices, and English and Dutch shippers offered their carrying services at lower freight rates. Cities of the German Hanse lost their dominance over the trade between the Baltic and the North Sea; English, Scottish and Dutch ships became prominent along the Atlantic coast, in the Baltic, and, later in the sixteenth century, in the western Mediterranean as well. In 1475–6, a quarter of Danzig's shipping relied on Dutch vessels – in 1583 their annual total of that had risen to over a thousand.[64] In the course of the sixteenth century, ports along the North Sea and the Atlantic coast took the lead in the routes to both the Mediterranean and Baltic Seas, from where the initiative had come in earlier times.

Competition was a self-evident driving force, but it would be a simplification to try to reduce the macro-economic shifts to a single factor, such as the greater institutional efficiency hailed by the New Institutional Economics school.[65] Institutions have a tendency to become fixed and less responsive as they perpetuate themselves. The alleged openness to merchants' demands and the adaptive capacity of institutions could not prevent the loss of competitiveness that Valencia, Barcelona, Genoa and even Venice underwent as a consequence of complex macro-economic and geopolitical changes. London, and Bruges and Antwerp, in their respective heydays, combined a favourable location with a productive hinterland, highly skilled manufacturing, considerable purchasing power and a wide maritime as well as terrestrial network. Bruges lost its competitive position as a consequence of a whole range of factors: the silting up of its connections to the sea, institutional and political factors, and macro-economic changes. On the other hand, Lisbon, like Seville, acquired metropolitan status thanks to another combination: a favourable location, a solid institutional basis, its network and colonial exploitation. Danzig combined similar conditions with the massive supply of grain sorely needed in the West. All these emerging metropolises expanded initially under direct or indirect incentives from the Italian connections. Towards the end of the sixteenth century, the hierarchy was reversed and led to the well-known relocation of the core of the global economic system from the Mediterranean towards the North Sea. Maritime links were decisive in this transfer: in 1317 the south relieved the famine in Bruges and London; in the 1590s, the north relieved that in Genoa. Foodstuffs made up 54 per cent of the volume unloaded in Genoa in the sixteenth century; firewood and timber made up 42 per cent. High-quality products thus represented just 4 per cent of the volume.[66] By that time, and on a regular basis since the early sixteenth century, the southeastern shores of the Baltic had become the main suppliers of imported grain for Western Europe. In the early seventeenth century, Dutch shippers sailed directly with grain from Danzig to Iberia and Italy.[67] Many merchants from the Low Countries came to trade in the south, and shortly after 1600 the Venetian government appointed a Flemish and a Dutch consul.

The dynamism of the European economic system rested on competitiveness that could only in part be influenced by particular 'players' such as municipal authorities or territorial rulers. Port authorities did their very best to maintain, improve or adapt their infrastructure, but technical limits blocked some endeavours such as digging a canal from Lübeck to the mouth of the Elbe, or keeping the access for large ships free in Bruges and Venice. Municipal governments might try to enhance their city's attraction with new arrangements and facilities, but they had to seek a balance between opposing interest groups, and most of them had to make deals with royal or princely authorities following their own interests. Incentives from competitors could not in all cases be followed up on. Brittany proved unable to construct ever more numerous, larger, better manoeuvrable and faster ships, with the consequence being that the whole region lost the competition in a booming maritime space. On the other hand, the autonomous city republic of Ragusa proved remarkably successful in a stagnating environment. Being on trunk routes and resource availability worked out only if entrepreneurship steered the development towards a clear purpose.

The explanations for the success or failure of a port city are necessarily complex for the simple reason that, as a matter of course, a multiplicity of external factors determined the structure and the changes of large networks. Locations, even those with optimal geographic and institutional conditions, could lose their importance through macro-economic shifts in the routes that had made them thrive. The colonial expansion of the fifteenth and sixteenth centuries dramatically reduced the relevance of the networks on which the Mediterranean had flourished for many centuries. All the contributions in this volume pointed out that it was essential for any port city to produce, with the support of its hinterland, a sufficient value of exportable goods to maintain a profitable balance of trade. A few cases show how even fragile living conditions could be overcome through an exceptionally enterprising community such as Venice, Genoa, Ragusa and Amsterdam, which all compensated for the poor productivity of their hinterland with extensive maritime networks. For exactly these reasons, metropolises had a huge impact not only on their hinterland but also far beyond it in the regions where people made a living by producing for distant markets organized by the commercial networks. One thinks of the Russian fur hunters, the Norwegian fishermen, the Scottish shepherds, the salt-makers in Bourgneuf and Setubal, the Sicilian and Crimean grain peasants or the slave traders in North Africa and around the Black Sea. Any perturbation of established trade routes led to effects in the system as a whole. As this system rested overwhelmingly on the food trade, and as grain prices were highly volatile, the market conditions changed dramatically from one year to another. This made opportunities for profit highly variable and difficult to foresee. Risks were high, returns uncertain.

The institutional forms of exchange depended on the power relations between the trading partners. In the initial stage, Italian, Catalan and Provençal merchants started negotiating modestly with Fatimid and Mamluk rulers for access to markets in North Africa and the Levant. The Crusades marked the violent conquest of trading posts and settlements in nodal places, in order to exclude foreign intermediaries. In the thirteenth century, territorial colonization made Venice and Genoa into outright imperialistic superpowers that entered into competition with the moribund Byzantine and the expanding Ottoman empires. The commercial metropolises used violence primarily to acquire and maintain economically profitable positions.[68] On the other hand, as Jesús Ángel Solórzano Telechea remarks with regard to the commercial relations of the Cantabrian coast, these 'at the same time created a cultural relation, a European community of mariners, situated in the centre of an emerging Atlantic community. This union was formed by merchants, carriers, shippers and factors who constructed networks of knowledge and trust through their movements over the seas and the consolidation of "trustworthy" routes.'[69]

Merchants and monarchs had very different worldviews, aims and means of exercising power. Monarchical power emanated originally from seigneurial dominance, including the combination of command, jurisdiction and economic exploitation of the subjects. Commercialized and urbanized societies, which developed primarily in favourably situated areas, generated more surplus than rural societies, and that surplus was concentrated in cities, in particular as commercial capital.[70] Coastal areas, navigable rivers and especially the nodal points of river mouths offered the greatest opportunities for concentration of human capital and for the accumulation of material capital.[71] As both states and commercial networks extended significantly during the three centuries discussed in this volume, and both sides inevitably needed each other, their interests became increasingly interwoven. Monarchs saw opportunities to expand their activities by skimming money off trade in exchange for privileges that protected mercantile activities.[72] Merchants were bound to reduce their risks, especially overseas, and were prepared to pay a price for the security of their persons and goods, and for the liberty of trade. Merchants aimed at maximizing their profits in terms of capital, monarchs strove for the extension of their territorial holdings. Merchants aimed at efficiency and monarchs at efficacy, regardless of the cost in human lives or material losses. With all the necessary qualifications for the application of this theoretical model to concrete situations, it is helpful to unveil the fundamental opposition between commercial imperialism and monarchical domination. The first operated through economic incentives, the second mainly through physical power, as state budgets overwhelmingly served military activities motivated by dynastic ambitions. As pointed out by Geoffrey Parker, the great warmonger Philip II imposed heavy taxation to support his wars against the Dutch, the English and the French during the decade of the 1590s, at a time when his Mediterranean subjects were suffering from repeated and heavy famines. The military operations failed, and the impoverished populations of Castile and Aragon rose up in revolt.[73]

During the period from 1300 to 1600, monarchical states waged wars on a rapidly growing scale and with increasingly destructive power. All of this only served the monarchs' ambition to extend their territories, leading to the risk of overstretch, as shown by the failure of the main antagonists, the French attempts to conquer Italy, and the collapse of Charles V's empire. In contrast, the most buoyant commercial cities were oriented towards the seas. Before 1600, monarchs were technically unable to control maritime spaces, with the notable exceptions of the kings of Denmark's grip on the Sound straits and the Ottoman mastery of the Bosphorus and the Dardanelles. Monarchs were entitled to summon their vassals and other subjects for military service by land; their warfare was primarily territorial and deeply harmful to the populations living there. Maritime enterprises rarely belonged to the prince's exploits. The honour and reputation of the monarch's person and dynasty prevailed above all other considerations, including the tax burden and the insecurity and destruction they inflicted on their subject populations.

Merchants always advocated free trade and peace, as long as their own privileges were guaranteed. Their means of pressuring were economic sanctions, and only in extreme cases did they fight major battles at sea. However costly, the economic damage and the loss of human lives in these battles were negligible when compared to the armies of 50,000 to 80,000 that the Habsburgs and Valois mobilized for their personal motives. Merchants created networks, connected people and shaped their own international fiduciary financial system that was immune to robbery and volatile exchange rates. Shippers and merchants created their own maritime law systems based on the best practices that had become customary over the centuries within a particular regional trading network. On the journeys over long distances, shippers had to deal with a variety of customary, and not always well-codified, legal systems, which required a cosmopolitan attitude. They displayed a preference for extra-judicial, expert and quick mediating procedures, as they were institutionalized in special courts in Venice, Genoa, Valencia and Barcelona, and supported by municipal courts in the Atlantic and North and Baltic Sea port cities. The greater specialization and sophistication of these institutions in the Mediterranean area than in the north can be related to the much higher numbers of transactions and cases to be dealt with in their formative stage, before the mid-sixteenth century.

On the seas, the monarchs' enemies and privateers operating under their licence could endanger their subjects' trade. Merchants and shippers sought protection through the solidarity of their urban community, their association, company, marine insurance contract or the armed convoy sponsored by their country of origin. Only a relatively small and autonomous city republic like Ragusa could escape the imposed solidarity with a prince's policy, and it successfully operated in-between its warring neighbours. All these methods to diminish risks came at a price, but this weighed far less on the economy as a whole than the rapidly increasing military burden that the monarchs deemed necessary for their glory.

Notes

1 J. Gessler, Le Livre des Mestiers de Bruges et ses dérivés: Quatre anciens manuels de conversation, Bruges: Consortium des maîtres imprimeurs brugeois, 1931.

2 Francesco Balducci Pegolotti, *La Pratica della Mercatura*, ed. A. Evans, Cambridge, MA: Medieval Academy of America, 1936.

3 J. H. Munro, *Wool, Cloth and Gold: The Struggle for Bullion in Anglo-Burgundian Trade 1340–1478,* Brussels and Toronto: Editions de l'Université de Bruxelles, 1973, p. 73 nn. 26, 27, p. 84 n. 49, p. 85 nn. 51, 52, p. 128 n. 3, p. 131 nn. 8, 10, p. 133 n. 15, 16.

4 W. C. Jordan, *The Great Famine: Northern Europe in the Early Fourteenth Century*, Princeton, NJ: Princeton University Press, 1996, pp. 29–39, 51; B. M. S. Campbell, 'Physical shocks, biological hazards, and human impacts: the crisis of the fourteenth century revisited', in S. Cavaciocchi (ed.), *Economic and Biological Interactions in Pre-Industrial Europe from the 13th to the 18th Centuries*, Florence: Firenze University Press, 2010, pp. 13–32; P. Slavin, 'The great bovine pestilence and its economic and environmental consequences in England and Wales, 1318–1350', *Economic History Review* 65, 2012, pp. 1239–66; idem, 'Market failure during the great famine in England and Wales (1315–1317)', *Past and Present* 222, 2014, pp. 9–49.

5 B. M. S. Campbell, 'Grain yields on English demesnes after the Black Death', in M. Bailey and S. Rigby (eds), *Town and Countryside in the Age of the Black Death,* Turnhout: Brepols, 2012, pp. 163–6; B. M. S. Campbell and C. Ó Gráda, 'Harvest shortfalls, grain prices, and famines in pre-industrial England', *Journal of Economic History* 71, 2011, pp. 859–86.

6 J. M. Murray, *Bruges, Cradle of Capitalism, 1280–1390,* Cambridge: Cambridge University Press, 2005.

7 H. Van Werveke, 'La famine de l'an 1316 en Flandre et dans les régions voisines', *Revue du Nord* 41, 1951, pp. 5–14; for the calculation of the daily consumption, see W. P. Blockmans and W. Prevenier, 'Poverty in Flanders and Brabant from the fourteenth to the mid-sixteenth century: sources and problems', *Acta Historiae Neerlandicae* 10, 1978, pp. 26–7.

8 The family was still prominent in Bruges at the very end of the fourteenth century, as it was Moruele de Mari who provided a loan to the city and negotiated the acquisition of the lot to build the new Genoese loggia: G. Petti Balbi, *Negoziare fuori patria. Nazioni e genovesi in età medievale*, Bologna: Clueb, 2005, pp. 186–7.

9 J. A. Solórzana Telechea, 'La "Nacion de Vizcaya y de la Costa marina de España": la colonia de mercaderes, marineros y transportistas del Cantábrico en la ciudad de Brujas en la Baja Edad Media', in J. A. Solórzano Telechea, B. Arízaga Bolumburu and L. Sicking (eds), *Diplomacia y Comercio en la Europa Atlántica Medieval*, Logroño: Instituto de Estudios Riojanos, 2015, pp. 223, 227, 237.

10 P. Spufford, *Power and Profit: The Merchant in Medieval Europe*, London: Thames & Hudson, 2002, p. 291; J. A. Galloway, 'One market or many? London and the grain trade of England', in J. A. Galloway (ed.), *Trade, Urban Hinterlands and Market Integration c. 1300–1600,* London: Centre for Metropolitan History, 2000, pp. 31, 42.

11 L. Piccinno, 'Genoa: a city with a port or a port city?', and T. Pécout, 'Marseille: a supporting role', in this volume.

12 E. S. Hunt, *The Medieval Super-Companies: A Study of the Peruzzi Company of Florence*, Cambridge: Cambridge University Press, 1994, pp. 130, 141–2, quoting Giovanni Villani, *Storia*, Florence, 1587, book VIII, ch. 68; C. M. de la Roncière, *Prix et salaires à Florence au XIVe siècle, 1280–1380,* Rome: École française, 1982, p. 716; H. Bresc, *Un monde méditerranéen: Économie et société en Sicile, 1300–1450,* Rome: École française, 1986, p. 549.

13 J. H. Munro, 'Medieval woollens: textiles, textile technology and industrial organisation, c. 800–1500', and 'Medieval woollens: the Western European woollen industries and their struggles for international markets, c. 1000–1500', in D. Jenkins (ed.), *The Cambridge History of Western Textiles*, vol. 1, Cambridge: Cambridge University Press, 2003, pp. 186, 196–7, 219–21, 228–9, 234–43; H. van der Wee, 'Structural changes in West-European long-distance trade, and particularly in the re-export trade from south to north, 1350–1750', in J. D. Tracy (ed.), *The Rise of Merchant Empires: Long-Distance Trade in the Early-Modern World, 1350–1750,* Cambridge: Cambridge University Press, 1990, pp. 14–33.

14 Spufford, *Power and Profit,* pp. 147–52.

15 Ibid., pp. 286–92.

16 Hunt, *Super-Companies*, pp. 142–9.

17 Galloway, 'One market or many?', pp. 37–9; R. W. Unger, 'Maritime transport and the integration of Low Countries grain markets in the late Middle Ages', *Food Supply, Demand and Trade: Aspects of the Economic Relationship between Town and Countryside (Middle Ages–19th Century)*, CORN Publications Series 14, Turnhout: Brepols, 2012, pp. 101–22; M. van Tielhof, *De Hollandse graanhandel, 1470–1570,* The Hague: Hollandse Historische Reeks 23, 1995, pp. 11–85.

18 T. Viúla de Faria, 'Las ciudades y el poder regio en la diplomacia y el comercio medievales: aproximaciones a partir de la relaciones anglo-portuguesas', in Solórzano Telechea *et al.*, *Diplomacia y Comercio*, p. 51.

19 Spufford, *Power and Profit*, pp. 12–59; R. S. Lopez, *The Commercial Revolution of the Middle Ages, 950–1350*, Cambridge: Cambridge University Press, 1974, pp. 56–113.

20 D. Kusman, *Usuriers publics et banquiers du Prince: Le rôle économique des financiers piémontais dans les villes du duché de Brabant (XIIIe–XIVe siècle)*, Turnhout: Brepols, 2013, pp. 61–109.

21 Hunt, *Super-Companies*, p. 245.

22 M. Sánchez Martín, 'Cláusulas comerciales: ¿Acatamiento o trasgresion? El factor de nogocios en la Europa Atlántica', in Solórzano Telechea *et al.*, *Diplomacia y Comercio*, pp. 187–219.

23 A. Orlandi, 'La circulazione del frumento nei documenti commerciali toscani (secoli XIV–XV)', in *La Civiltà del Pane: Storia, tecniche e simboli del Mediterraneo all'Atlantico,* Milan: Centro studi longobardi, 2015, pp. 147–77, quotes on 172 and 177.

24 W. Stieda (ed.), *Hildebrand Veckinchusen. Briefwechsel eines deutschen Kaufmanns im 15. Jahrhundert,* Leipzig, 1921; D. Seifert, 'Hildebrand Veckinchusen: a typical Hanseatic merchant in the Low Countries?', in P. Stabel, B. Blondé and A. Greve (eds), *International Trade in the Low Countries (14th–16th Centuries): Merchants, Organisation, Infrastructure,* Leuven: Garant, 2000, pp. 45–53; compare with J. Kermode, *Medieval Merchants. York, Beverly and Hull in the Later Middle Ages*, Cambridge: Cambridge University Press, 1998, pp. 305–12.

25 J. H. Munro, 'The Low Countries' export trade in textiles with the Mediterranean Basin, 1200–1600: a cost-benefit analysis of comparative advantages in overland and maritime trade routes', *International Journal of Maritime History* 11, 1999, pp. 1–30.

26 On Antwerp, see most recently O. Gelderblom, *Cities of Commerce: The Institutional Foundations of International Trade in the Low Countries, 1250–1650,* Princeton, NJ: Princeton University Press, 2013, and J. Puttevils, *Merchants and Trading in the Sixteenth Century: The Golden Age of Antwerp*, London: Pickering & Chatto, 2015.

27 E. Crouzet-Pavan, 'Construire une cité portuaire médiévale: les leçons de l'exemple vénitien', in J. Cancellieri and V. Marchi (eds), *Villes portuaires de Méditerranée occidentale au Moyen Âge: Iles et Continents,* Quaderni Mediterranea 26, Palermo: Associazione Mediterranea, 2015, p. 28 ; and her monumental *Le Moyen Âge de Venise: Des eaux salées au miracle de pierres,* Paris: Albin Michel, 2016.

28 A nicely documented case study is: M. Bochaca, 'Bayonne et le déplacement de l'embouchure de l'Adour d'après l'enquête de 1491', in M. Bochaca and J.-L. Sarrazin (eds), *Ports et littoraux de l'Europe atlantique: Transformations naturelles et aménagements humains (XIVe–XVIe siècles),* Rennes: Presses Universitaires, 2007, pp. 97–117.

29 Spufford, *Power and Profit*, pp. 182–4.

30 B. Arízaga Bolumburu and J. A. Solórzano Telechea, 'La construction d'infrastructures portuaires dans les villes du nord de la péninsule Ibérique à la fin du Moyen Âge', in Bochaca and Sarrazin, *Ports et littoraux,* pp. 121–40.

31 Crouzet-Pavan, 'Construire une cité portuaire', pp. 26–8; idem, 'An ecological understanding of the myth of Venice', in J. Martin and D. Romano (eds), *Venice Reconsidered: The History and Civilization of an Italian City-State, 1297–1797,* Baltimore, MD, and London: Johns Hopkins University Press, 2000, pp. 39–64.

32 P. Moraw, 'Cities and citizenry as factors of state formation in the Roman-German Empire of the late Middle Ages', in C. Tilly and W. P. Blockmans (eds), *Cities and the Rise of States in Europe, A.D. 1000–1800,* Boulder, CO: Westview, 1994, p. 108.

33 H. Eiden and F. Irsigler, 'Environs and hinterland: Cologne and Nürnberg in the later Middle Ages', in Galloway, *Trade, Urban Hinterlands*, pp. 53–5.

34 D. Keene, 'Issues of water in medieval London to c. 1300', *Urban History* 28, 2001, p. 167; idem, 'Changes in London's economic hinterland as indicated by debt cases in the Court of Common Pleas', in Galloway, *Trade, Urban Hinterlands,* pp. 74–8.

35 K. Appuhn, *A Forest on the Sea: Environmental Expertise in Renaissance Venice*, Baltimore, MD: Johns Hopkins University Press, 2009, pp. 58–143.

36 J. de Vries, *European Urbanization, 1500–1800*, London: Methuen, 1984, pp. 158–62; D. Keene, 'Cities and cultural exchange', in D. Calabi and S. T. Christensen (eds), *Cultural Exchange in Early Modern Europe: Cities and Cultural Exchange in Europe, 1400–1700,* Cambridge: Cambridge University Press, 2007, pp. 3–27, esp. the maps on pp. 6–11.

37 H. van der Wee, 'Industrial dynamics and the process of urbanization and de-urbanization in the Low Countries from the late Middle Ages to the eighteenth century: a synthesis', in van der Wee (ed.), *The Rise and Decline of Urban Industries in Italy and in the Low Countries (Late Middle Ages–Early Modern Times)*, Leuven: Leuven University Press, 1988, pp. 307–81, esp. p. 328.

38 P. Spufford, 'From Genoa to London: the places of insurance in Europe', in A. B. Leonard (ed.), *Marine Insurance: Origins and Institutions, 1300–1850*, Basingstoke: Palgrave Macmillan, 2016, pp. 270–97, esp. pp. 275–7, 283–5.

39 R. W. Unger, *Beer in the Middle Ages and the Renaissance*, Philadelphia, PA: University of Pennsylvania Press, 2004, pp. 74–106.

40 R. W. Unger, 'Ships and sailing routes', in this volume.

41 J. de Vries and A. van der Woude, *The First Modern Economy: Success, Failure, and Perseverance of the Dutch Economy, 1500–1815*, Cambridge: Cambridge University Press, 1997, pp. 272–349, 355–7.

42 T. H. Lloyd, *England and the German Hanse, 1157–1611: A Study of Their Trade and Commercial Diplomacy*, Cambridge: Cambridge: University Press, 1991, pp. 13–108.

43 B. Lambert, '"Marchands parfois, marins plus souvent": commerce breton à Bruges au quinzième siècle', in Solórzano Telechea *et al.*, *Diplomacia y comercio*, pp. 147–59.

44 J. Paviot, 'Les Portugais à Bruges', in Stabel *et al.*, *International Trade in the Low Countries*, pp. 55–74; H. Pohl, *Die Portugiesen in Antwerpen (1567–1648): Zur Geschichte einer Minderheit*, Wiesbaden: Steiner, 1977.

45 F. Guidi Bruscoli, 'I mercanti italiani, Lisbona e l'Atlantico (XV–XVI secolo)', in Solórzano Telechea *et al.*, *Diplomacia y comercio*, pp. 125–46.

46 Moraw, 'Cities and citizenry', pp. 106–16; H. Sauer, *Hansestädte und Landesfürsten: Die wendischen Hansestädte in der Auseinandersetzung mit den Fürstenhäusern Oldenburg und Mecklenburg während der zweiten Hälfte des 15. Jahrhunderts*, Cologne: Böhlau, 1971, pp. 174–8; J. Schildhauer, *Soziale, politische und religiöse Auseinandersetzungen in den Hansestädten Stralsund, Rostock und Wismar im ersten Drittel des 16. Jahrhunderts*, Weimar: Hermann Böhlaus Nachfölger, 1959, pp. 1–25.

47 W. M. Ormrod, 'The West European monarchies in the later Middle Ages', in R. Bonney (ed.), *Economic Systems and State Finance*, Oxford: Clarendon Press, 1995, pp. 136–49.

48 Viúla de Faria, 'Las ciudades y el poder', pp. 45–60.

49 M. Biskup, 'Die Rolle der Städte in der Ständevertretung des Königreiches Polen, einschliesslich des Ordensstaates Preussen im 14./15. Jahrhundert', in B. Töpfer (ed.), *Städte und Ständestaat: Zur Rolle der Städte bei der Entwicklung der Ständeverfassung in europäischen Staaten vom 13. bis zum 15. Jahrhundert*, Berlin: Akademie-Verlag, 1980, pp. 177–92; Biskup, 'Polen an der Ostsee im 16. Jahrhundert', *Zeitschrift für Historische Forschung* 5, 1978, pp. 293–314.

50 W. Blockmans, 'Constructing the concept of civil rights: the experience of citizens in the Low Countries, 12th to 16th century', *Quaestiones Medii Aevi Novae*, 2015, pp. 239–53.

51 L. Piccinno, 'Genoa, 1340–1620: early development of marine insurance', in Leonard, *Marine Insurance*, pp. 25–45; D. De Ruysscher and J. Puttevils, 'The art of compromise: legislative deliberations on marine insurance institutions in Antwerp (c.1550–c.1570)', *BMGN – Low Countries Historical Review* 130, 2015, pp. 25–49; D. De Ruysscher, 'Antwerp 1490–1590: insurance and speculation', in Leonard, *Marine Insurance*, pp. 79–105; J. Puttevils, 'Eating the bread out of their mouth: Antwerp's export trade and generalized institutions, 1544–1545', *Economic History Review* 68, 2015, pp. 1339–64; idem, 'Tweaking financial instruments: bills obligatory in sixteenth-century Antwerp', *Financial History Review* 22, 2015, pp. 337–61.

52 As examples, see: Kermode, *Medieval Merchants*, pp. 25–69; Viúla de Faria, 'Las ciudades y el poder', pp. 48–52.

53 J. Dhondt, 'Les origines des États de Flandre', in his *Estates or Powers: Essays in the Parliamentary History of the Southern Netherlands from the XIIth to the XVIIIth Century,* Standen en Landen – Anciens Pays et Assemblées d'États 69, Heule: UGA, 1977, pp. 73–8.
54 W. Blockmans, *De volksvertegenwoordiging in Vlaanderen, 1384–1506*, Brussels: KVAB, 1978, pp. 211–12, 598–9.
55 J. Wubs-Mrozewicz, 'The late medieval and early modern Hanse as an institution of conflict management', *Continuity and Change* 32/1, 2017 (accepted, forthcoming); M. Burkhardt, 'Kontors and outposts', in D. Harreld (ed.), *A Companion to the Hanseatic League*, Brill: Leiden, 2015, pp. 127–61; W. Blockmans, 'Vertretungssysteme im niederländischen Raum im Spätmittelalter', in K. Fritze and E. Müller-Mertens (eds), *Der Ost- und Nordseeraum: Politik, Ideologie, Kultur vom 12. bis zum 17. Jahrhundert,* Weimar: Verlag Hermann Böhlaus Nachfolger, 1986, pp. 180–9.
56 Murray, *Bruges, Cradle of Capitalism,* pp. 186–215; Puttevils, *Golden Age of Antwerp.*
57 J. Murray, 'Of nodes and networks: Bruges and the infrastructure of trade in fourteenth-century Europe', in Stabel *et al.*, *International Trade in the Low Countries,* pp. 1–14, quote on p. 14.
58 J. Dumolyn and B. Lambert, 'Cities of commerce, cities of constraints: international trade, government institutions and the law of commerce in later medieval Bruges and the Burgundian state', *TSEG: Low Countries Journal of Social and Economic History* 11, 2014, pp. 89–102; T. M. Safley, 'Institutions and their discontents', *TSEG* 11, 2014, pp. 61–72, critiques of Gelderblom, *Cities of Commerce.*
59 M. Fusaro, *The Decline of Venice,* Cambridge: Cambridge University Press, 2015.
60 Piccinno, 'Genoa, 1340–1620: early development of marine insurance', pp. 36-9.
61 De Ruysscher and Puttevils, 'The art of compromise', pp. 29–31.
62 Wubs-Mrozewicz, 'Hanse as an institution of conflict management'.
63 J. A. Solórzano Telechea, 'Medieval seaports of the Atlantic coast of Spain', *International Journal of Maritime History* 21, 2009, pp. 81–100.
64 J. Schildhauer, 'Handelsbeziehungen bedeutender Ostseestädte zu den Niederlanden', in W. J. Wieringa *et al.* (eds), *The Interactions of Amsterdam and Antwerp with the Baltic Region, 1400–1800,* Leiden: Martinus Nijhoff, 1983, pp. 23–5; D. Seifert, *Kompagnons und Konkurrenten: Holland und die Hanse im späten Mittelalter,* Cologne: Böhlau, 1997.
65 Safley, 'Institutions and their discontents'.
66 L. Piccinno, 'Genoa: a city with a port or a port city?', in this volume.
67 M. van Tielhof, *The 'Mother of All Trades': The Baltic Grain Trade in Amsterdam from the Late 16th to the Early 19th Century*, Leiden: Brill, 2002; for the earlier period, see her *De Hollandse graanhandel,* pp. 86–121, and 161–7; M. Bogucka, 'Amsterdam and the Baltic in the first half of the seventeenth century', *Economic History Review* 26, 1973, pp. 433–47.
68 J. Hattendorf and R. W. Unger (eds), *War at Sea in the Middle Ages and the Renaissance,* Woodbridge: Boydell Press, 2003.
69 And he adds significantly 'notwithstanding the distrust of Burgos': Solórzana Telechea, 'La "Nacion de Vizcaya y de la Costa marina de España"', in Solórzano Telechea *et al.*, *Diplomacia y comercio*, p. 237.
70 C. Tilly, *Coercion, Capital, and European States, AD 990–1990,* Cambridge, MA: Basil Blackwell, 1990, pp. 16–33.
71 Keene, 'Cities and cultural exchange', pp. 3–13.
72 R.W. Unger, 'Trade, taxation and government policy in the High Middle Ages', *Viator* 46, 2015, pp. 195–217.
73 G. Parker, *The Grand Strategy of Philip II,* New Haven, CT, and London: Yale University Press, 1998, pp. 275–80; idem, *Imprudent King: A New Life of Philip II,* New Haven, CT: Yale University Press, 2014.

GENERAL BIBLIOGRAPHY

Abulafia, D. (2011) *The Great Sea: A Human History of the Mediterranean,* Oxford: Oxford University Press.

Acemoglu, D., Johnson, S., and Robinson, J. (2005) 'The rise of Europe: Atlantic trade, institutional change, and economic growth', *American Economic Review* 95/3: 546–79.

Adams, J. (2013) *A Maritime Archaeology of Ships: Innovation and Social Change in Medieval and Early Modern Europe*, Oxford: Oxbow Books.

Aerts, E. (2006) 'The Casa di San Giorgio and the "monetary famine" of the Late Middle Ages', in G. Felloni (ed.), *La Casa di San Giorgio: Il potere del credito*, Genoa: Società Ligure di Storia Patria, pp. 27–62.

Ahvenainen, J. (1963) *Der Getreidehandel Livlands im Mittelalter*, Helsinki: Societas Scientiarum Fennica.

Allen, R. C., and Unger, R. W. (1990) 'The depth and breadth of the market for Polish grain 1500–1800', in J. P. S. Lemmink and J. S. A. M. Koningsbrugge (eds), *Baltic Affairs: Relations between the Netherlands and North-Eastern Europe 1500–1800*, Nijmegen, 1990, pp. 1–19.

Andrade, A. A. (2006) 'Le Pouvoir Royal et les villes portugaises au Moyen Âge', in B. Dumons and O. Zeller (eds), *La Ville Européenne et ses Pouvoirs du Moyen Âge au XXe siècle*, Paris: L'Harmattan.

Apellániz, F. (2009) 'Collaboration des reseaux marchands à Alexandrie (XIVe–XVe siècles)', in D. Ramada Curto (ed.), *From Florence to the Mediterranean and Beyond: Essays in Honour of Anthony Molho*, Florence: Leo S. Olschki.

Apellániz, F. (2013) 'Venetian trading networks in the medieval Mediterranean', *Journal of Interdisciplinary History* 2013/44: 157–79.

Arbel, B. (2000) 'The port towns of the Levant in sixteenth-century travel literature', in A. F. Cowan (ed.), *Mediterranean Urban Culture, 1400–1700*, Exeter: University of Exeter Press, pp. 151–64.

Arbel, B. (2013) 'Venice's maritime empire in the early modern period', in E. Dursteler (ed.), *A Companion to Venetian History, 1400–1797*, Leiden: Brill, pp. 125–253.

Ash, E. H. (2007) 'Navigation techniques and practice in the Renaissance', in D. Woodward (ed.), *The History of Cartography in the Renaissance*, Chicago, IL: University of Chicago Press, pp. 509–27.

Ashtor, E. (1983) *Levant Trade in the Later Middle Ages,* Princeton, NJ: Princeton University Press.

Atiya, A. S. (1977) *A Fourteenth Century Encyclopedist from Alexandria: A Critical and Analytical Study of Al-Nuwairy Al-Iskadarânî's 'Kitâb al-Ilmâm',* Research Monograph, Salt Lake City, UT: Middle East Center University of Utah.

Bairoch, P. (1988) *Cities and Economic Development: From the Dawn of History to the Present,* Chicago, IL: University of Chicago Press.

Balard, M. (2003) 'Genoese naval forces in the Mediterranean during the fifteenth and sixteenth centuries', in J. Hattendorf and R. W. Unger (eds), *War at Sea in the Middle Ages and the Renaissance,* Woodbridge, Suffolk: Boydell Press, pp. 137–49.

Balard, M. (2006) 'Il Banco di San Giorgio e le colonie d'Oltremare', in G. Felloni (ed.), *La Casa di San Giorgio: Il potere del credito,* Genoa: Società Ligure di Storia Patria, pp. 63–73.

Barron, C. M. (2004) *London in the Later Middle Ages: Government and People 1200–1500,* Oxford: Oxford University Press.

Bavel, B. van (2010) *Manors and Markets: Economy and Society in the Low Countries, 500–1600,* Oxford: Oxford University Press.

Bogucka, M. (2003) *Baltic Commerce and Urban Society, 1500–1700: Gdańsk/Danzig and Its Polish Context,* Aldershot: Ashgate Variorum.

Bolton, J. L. (1980) *The Medieval English Economy 1150–1500,* London: Dent.

Booton, H. W. (1985) 'Economic and social change in later medieval Aberdeen', in J. S. Smith (ed.), *New Light on Medieval Aberdeen,* Aberdeen: Aberdeen University Press, pp. 46–57.

Brand, H., and Müller, L. (eds) (2007) *The Dynamics of Economic Culture in the North Sea and Baltic Region in the Late Middle Ages and Early Modern Period,* Hilversum: Verloren.

Braudel, F. (1972) *The Mediterranean and the Mediterranean World in the Age of Philip II,* trans. S. Reynolds, 2 vols, New York: Harper & Row.

Burkhardt, M. (2009) *Der hansische Bergenhandel im Spätmittelalter: Handel – Kaufleute – Netzwerke,* Cologne: Böhlau.

Calabi, D. (2004) *The Market and the City,* London: Ashgate.

Calabi, D., and Turk Christensen, S. (eds) (2008) *Cities and Cultural Exchanges: 1400–1700,* Cambridge: Cambridge University Press.

Caracausi, A., and Jeggle, C. (eds) (2014) *Commercial Networks and European Cities, 1400–1800,* London: Pickering & Chatto.

Carboni, S. (ed.) (2007) *Venice and the Islamic World, 828–1797,* New York: Metropolitan Museum of Art.

Childs, W. R. (1991) '"To oure losse and hindrance": English credit to alien merchants in the mid-fifteenth century', in J. Kermode (ed.), *Enterprise and Individuals in Fifteenth-Century England,* Stroud: Alan Sutton, pp. 68–98.

Childs, W. R. (2013) *Trade and Shipping in the Medieval West: Portugal, Castile, and England,* Porto: Fédération Internationale des Instituts d'Études Médiévales.

Christ, G. (2012) *Trading Conflicts: Venetian Merchants and Mamluk Officials in Late Medieval Alexandria,* Leiden: Brill.

Christ, G. (2015) 'Transients? Jews in Alexandria in the Late Middle Ages through Venetian eyes', in J. V. Tolan (ed.), *Expulsion and Diaspora Formation: Religious and Ethnic Identities in Flux from Antiquity to the Seventeenth Century,* Turnhout: Brepols, pp. 195–216.

Christensen, A. (1941) *Dutch Trade to the Baltic about 1600: Studies in the Sound Toll Register and Dutch Shipping Records,* Copenhagen: E. Munksgaard.

Cobb, H. S. (1990) 'Introduction', in H. S. Cobb (ed.), *The Overseas Trade of London Exchequer Customs Accounts, 1480–1,* London: London Record Society, pp. xi–xlvii.

Constable, O. R. (2003) *Housing the Stranger in the Mediterranean World: Lodging, Trade and Travel in the Late Antiquity and in the Middle Ages,* Cambridge: Cambridge University Press.

Cordes, A. (1998) *Spätmittelalterlicher Gesellschaftshandel im Hanseraum*, Cologne: Böhlau.

Cordes, A. (2005) 'The search for a medieval *lex mercatoria*', in V. Piergiovanni (ed.), *From Lex Mercatoria to Commercial Law*, Berlin: Duncker & Humblot, pp. 53–68.

Davis, R. (1976) 'The rise of Antwerp and its English connection, 1406–1510', in D. C. Coleman and A. H. John (eds), *Trade, Government and Economy in Pre-Industrial England: Essays Presented to F. J. Fisher*, London: Weidenfeld & Nicolson, 1976, pp. 2–20.

Décobert, C., and Empereur, J.-Y. (eds) (1998–2011) *Alexandrie médiévale*, vols 1–4, Cairo: IFAO.

De Vries, J. (1984) *European Urbanization, 1500–1800*, Harvard Studies in Urban History, Cambridge, MA: Harvard University Press.

Diederiks, H. (1991) 'Bankers, bank, and other financial institutions in the urban landscape of Amsterdam, late 16th–20th centuries', in H. Diederiks and D. Reeder (eds), *Cities of Finance*, Amsterdam: Royal Netherlands Academy of Arts and Sciences, pp. 251–64.

Ditchburn, D. (1988) 'Trade with Northern Europe, 1297–1540', in M. Lynch, M. Spearman and G. Stell (eds), *Scottish Medieval Town*, Edinburgh: J. Donald, pp. 161–79.

Ditchburn, D. (2002) *Scotland and Europe: The Medieval Kingdom and Its Contacts with Christendom*, East Linton: Tuckwell Press.

Duran i Duelt, D. (2004) 'The Catalan consular network: its origin and development', in D. Abulafia (ed.), *Mediterraneum: Splendour of the Medieval Mediterranean. 13th–15th Centuries*, Barcelona: Lunwerg Editores, pp. 353–61.

Dursteler, E. (2006) *Venetians in Constantinople: Nation, Identity, and Co-existence in the Early Modern Mediterranean*, Baltimore, MD: Johns Hopkins University Press.

Dyer, C. (2000) 'Trade, urban hinterlands and market integration, 1300–1600: a summing up', in J. A. Galloway (ed.), *Trade, Urban Hinterlands and Market Integration c.1300–1600*, London: Centre for Metropolitan History, pp. 103–9.

Edbury, P. W. (1991) 'Cyprus, commerce and crusade: King Peter I and the background to the sack of Alexandria in 1365', *Bulletin de la Société Archéologique d'Alexandrie* 44: 206–14.

Ellmers, D. (1994) 'The cog as cargo carrier', in R. Gardier and R. W. Unger (eds), *Cogs, Caravels and Galleons: The Sailing Ship, 1000–1650*, Conway's History of the Ship, London: Conway Maritime Press.

Empereur, J.-Y., and Compoint, S. (1998) *Alexandria Rediscovered*, London: British Museum.

Fejić, N. (1990) 'Ragusei e spagnoli nel medio evo: luci ed ombre di un rapport commerciale', in A. di Vittorio (ed.) *Ragusa e il Mediterraneo: Ruolo e funzioni di una Repubblica marinara tra Medioevo ed Età moderna*, Bari: Cacucci editore, pp. 86–96.

Ferrer, M. T. (2012) 'Catalan commerce in the late Middle Ages', *Catalan Historical Review* 5: 29–65.

François, V. (1999) *Céramiques médiévales à Alexandrie: Contribution à l'histoire économique de la ville*, Cairo: IFAO.

Frankot, E. (2012) *Of Laws of Ships and Shipmen: Medieval Maritime Law in Urban Northern Europe*, Edinburgh: Edinburgh University Press.

Frenkel, M. (2014) 'Medieval Alexandria: life in a port city', *Al-Masaq: Studia Arabo-Islamica Mediterranea* 26/1: 5–35.

Friedland, K. (2000) 'Maritime law and piracy: advantages and inconveniences of shipping in the Baltic', in A. Macinnes, F. Pedersen and T. Riis (eds), *Ships, Guns, and Bibles in the North Sea and Baltic States, c.1350–c.1700*, London: East Linton, pp. 30–8.

Frost, R. I. (2000) *The Northern Wars 1558–1721*, Harlow: Longman.

Fusaro, M. (2015) *Political Economies of Empire in the Early Modern Mediterranean: The Decline of Venice and the Rise of England, 1450–1700*, Cambridge: Cambridge University Press.

Fusaro, M., Heywood, C., and Omri, M. S. (eds) (2010) *Trade and Cultural Exchange in the Early Modern Mediterranean: Braudel's Maritime Legacy*, London: Tauris Academic Studies.

Galloway, J. A. (ed.) (2000) *Urban Hinterlands and Market Integration, c.1300–1600*, London: Centre for Metropolitan History, Institute of Historical Research.
Gelderblom, O. (2013) *Cities of Commerce: The Institutional Foundations of International Trade in the Netherlands, 1250–1650,* Princeton, NJ: Princeton University Press.
Glete, J. (2000) *Warfare at Sea, 1500–1650: Maritime Conflicts and the Transformation of Europe*, Warfare and History, London and New York: Routledge.
Goehrke, C. (1981) 'Gross-Novgorod und Pskov/Pleskau', in M. Hellmann, K. Zernack and F. Adanır (eds), *Handbuch der Geschichte Russlands*, vol. 2, Stuttgart: Anton Hiersemann.
Goetz, L. K. (1922) *Deutsch-Russische Handelsgeschichte des Mittelalters*, Lübeck: Lübecker Verlaganstalt Otto Waelde.
Goldberg, J. (2012) *Trade and Institutions in the Medieval Mediterranean: The Geniza Merchants and Their Business World*, Cambridge: Cambridge University Press.
González de Lara, Y. (2008) 'The secret of Venetian success: a public-order, reputation-based institution', *European Review of Economic History* 12: 247–85.
Graβmann, A. (ed.) (2005) *Das Hansische Kontor zu Bergen und die Lübecker Bergenfahrer,* Lübeck: Schmidt Römhild.
Greif, A. (2006) *Institutions and the Path to the Modern Economy: Lessons from Medieval Trade,* Cambridge: Cambridge University Press.
Groth, E. (1999) *Das Verhältnis der livländischen Städte zum Novgoroder Hansekontor im 14. Jahrhundert*, Hamburg: Baltische Gesellschaft.
Guidi-Bruscoli, F. (2014) 'Creating networks through languages: Italian merchants in late medieval and early modern Europe', in A. Caracausi and C. Jeggle (eds), *Commercial Networks and European Cities, 1400–1800*, London: Pickering & Chatto, pp. 65–79.
Hammel-Kiesow, R. (2014) *Die Hanse*, 5th edn, Munich: Beck.
Harding, V. (1995) 'Cross-channel trade and cultural contacts: London and the Low Countries in the later fourteenth century', in C. Barron and N. Saul (eds), *England and the Low Countries in the Late Middle Ages*, New York: St Martin's Press, pp. 153–68.
Harris, R. (2003) *Dubrovnik: A History,* London: Saqi.
Havrylyshyn, O., and N. Srzentić (2014) *Economy of Ragusa, 1300–1800: The Tiger of the Medieval Mediterranean,* Zagreb: Croatian National Bank.
Heckmann, M.-L., and Röhrkasten, J. (eds) (2008) *Von Nowgorod bis London: Studien zu Handel, Wirtschaft und Gesellschaft im mittelalterlichen Europa. Festschrift für Stuart Jenks zum 60. Geburtstag*, Göttingen: V&R unipress.
Heers, J. (1961) *Gênes au XVe siècle, activité économique et problèmes sociaux*, Paris: SEVPEN.
Helle, K. (ed.) (2003) *The Cambridge History of Scandinavia*, vol. 1, Cambridge: Cambridge University Press.
Heyd, W., and Furcy, R. (1885–6) *Histoire du commerce du Levant au moyen-âge*, 2 vols, Leipzig: Otto Harrasowitz.
Hirst, A. (ed.) (2004) *Alexandria, Real and Imagined,* Aldershot: Ashgate.
Hohenberg, P. M., and Lees, L. H. (1985) *The Making of Urban Europe 1000–1950,* Cambridge, MA: Harvard University Press.
Howell, M. (2010) *Commerce before Capitalism in Europe, 1300–1600*, Cambridge: Cambridge University Press.
Hundt, M., and Lokers, J. (eds) (2014) *Hanse und Stadt – Akteure, Strukturen und Entwicklungen im regionalen und europäischen Raum: Festschrift für Rolf Hammel-Kiesow zum 65. Geburtstag,* Lübeck: Schmidt-Römhild.
Hunt, H. S., and Murray, J. M. (1999) *A History of Business in Medieval Europe, 1200–1550,* Cambridge: Cambridge University Press.
Igual Luis, D. (2013) 'Social rise of the mercantile elite in cities of the medieval Kingdom of Valencia', in M. Asenjo-González (ed.), *Urban Elites and Aristocratic Behaviour in the Spanish Kingdoms at the End of the Middle Ages*, Turnhout: Brepols, pp. 161–70.

Iradiel, P. (2006) 'El siglo de oro del comercio valenciano', in I. Aguilar Civera (ed.), *El comercio y el Mediterráneo: Valencia y la cultura del mar*, Valencia: Generalitat Valenciana, pp. 111–29.

Jacoby, D. (2003) 'Byzantine traders in Mamluk Egypt', in A. Avraméa, A. E. Laiou and E. Chrysos (eds), *Byzantio, kratos kai koinōnia mnemè Niku Oikonomidès* [Byzantium. State and Society: In Memory of Nikos Oikonomides], Athens: Inst. Byzantinōn Ereunōn.

Jacoby, D. (2011) 'Western merchants, pilgrims, and travelers in Alexandria in the time of Philippe de Mézières (ca. 1327–1405)', in R. Blumenfeld-Kosinski and K. Petkov (eds), *Philippe de Mézières and his Age: Piety and Politics in the Fourteenth Century*, Leiden: Brill, pp. 403–25.

Jahnke, C. (2000) '*Das Silber des Meeres': Fang und Vertrieb von Ostseehering zwischen Norwegen und Italien vom 12. bis zum 16. Jahrhundert*, Cologne: Böhlau.

Jahnke, C. (2010) 'Handelsnetze im Ostseeraum', in G. Fouquet and H.-J. Gilomen (eds), *Netzwerke im europäischen Handel des Mittelalters*, Ostfildern: Thorbecke, pp. 189–212.

Jehel, G. (1993) *Les Génois en Méditerranée occidentale (fin XIe–début XIVe siècle): Ébauche d'une stratégie pour un empire*, Amiens: Centre d'histoire des sociétés, Université de Picardie.

Jenks, S. (1992) *England, die Hanse und Preußen*, Cologne: Böhlau.

Jenks, S. (1996) 'Zum hansischen Gästerecht', *Hansische Geschichtsblätter* 114: 3–59.

Johansen, P., and von zur Mühlen, H. (1973) *Deutsch und Undeutsch im mittelalterlichen und frühneuzeitlichen Reval*, Cologne: Böhlau.

Judde de Larivière, C. (2008) *Naviguer, commercer, gouverner: économie maritime et pouvoirs à Venise (XVe–XVIe siècles)*, Leiden: Brill.

Kaiser, D. H. (trans. and ed.) (1992) *The Laws of Rus, Tenth to Fifteenth Centuries*, Salt Lake City, UT: Charles Schlacks, Jr.

Kattinger, D. (1999) *Die Gotländische Genossenschaft: Der frühhansisch-gotländische Handel in Nord- und Westeuropa*, Cologne: Böhlau.

Keene, D. (2012) 'Medieval London and its supply hinterlands', *Regional Environmental Change* 12: 263–81.

Kellenbenz, H. (1970) 'Die fremde Kaufleute auf der Iberischen Halbinsel vom 15. Jahrhundert bis zum Ende des 16. Jahrhunderts', in idem (ed.), *Fremde Kaufleute auf der Iberischen Halbinsel*, Cologne: Böhlau, pp. 265–376.

Khalilieh, H. (1998) *Islamic Maritime Law*, Leiden: Brill.

Kowaleski, M. (2000) 'The port towns', in D. M. Palliser (ed.), *The Cambridge Urban History of Britain*, vol. 1, Cambridge: Cambridge University Press, pp. 467–94.

Krekić, B. (1972) *Dubrovnik in the 14th and 15th Centuries: A City between the East and West*, Norman, OK: University of Oklahoma Press.

Krom, M. (2014) 'The city of Pskov in the fifteenth and early sixteenth centuries: communal liberties and fragmented sovereignty', *Russian History*, 41/4: 440–57.

Kunčević, L. (2013) 'The rhetoric of the frontier of Christendom in the diplomacy of Renaissance Ragusa (Dubrovnik)', *Dubrovnik Annals* 17: 37–68.

Labîb, S. Y. (1965) *Handelsgeschichte Ägyptens im Spätmittelalter (1171–1517)*, Wiesbaden: Franz Steiner Verlag.

Landwehr, G. (2002) 'Das Seerecht im Ostseeraum vom Mittelalter bis zum Ausgang des 18. Jahrhunderts', in N. Jörn (ed.), *Geschichte und Perspektiven des Rechts im Ostseeraum*, Frankfurt am Main: Peter Lang, pp. 275–303.

Lane, F. (1973) *Venice, a Maritime Republic*, Baltimore, MD: Johns Hopkins University Press.

Lane, F., and Mueller, R. (1985) *Money and Banking in Medieval and Renaissance Venice*, Baltimore, MD: Johns Hopkins University Press.

Leffler, R. (2006) 'Novgorod – eine europäische Kommune des Mittelalters?', in C. Goehrke and B. Pietrow-Ennker (eds), *Städte im östlichen Europa*, Zürich: Chronos, pp. 33–59.

Leimus, I. (2006) 'Die spätmittelalterliche grosse Wirtschaftskrise – war auch Livland davon betroffen?', *Forschungen zur baltischen Geschichte* 1: 56–67.

Leonard, A. (ed.) (2016) *Marine Insurance: Origins and Institutions, 1300–1850*, Basingstoke: Palgrave Macmillan.

Lewis, A. (1976) 'Northern European sea power and the Straits of Gibraltar, 1031–1350', in J. R. Strayer, W. C. Jordan, B. McNab and T. F. Ruiz (eds), *Order and Innovation in the Middle Ages: Essays in Honor of Joseph R. Strayer*, Princeton, NJ: Princeton University Press, pp. 139–64.

Link, C. (2013) *Der preußische Getreidehandel im 15. Jahrhundert: Eine Studie zur nordeuropaischen Wirtschaftsgeschichte*, Cologne: Böhlau.

Litwin, J. (2014) 'Medieval Gdańsk – centre of shipbuilding and maritime trade on the Baltic', in W. Ossowski (ed.), *The Copper Ship: A Medieval Shipwreck and Its Cargo*, Gdańsk: Narodowe Muzeum Morskie, pp. 15–56.

Lloyd, T. H. (1991) *England and the German Hanse, 1157–1611*, Cambridge: Cambridge University Press.

Lucassen, Jan, and Unger, Richard W. (2011) 'Shipping, productivity and economic growth', in R. W. Unger (ed.), *Shipping and Economic Growth 1350–1850*, Leiden: Brill, pp. 1–44.

Mainoni, P. (1994) 'Mercanti italiani a Barcellona e a Valenza nel tardo Medioevo', in M. Del Treppo (ed.), *Sistema di rapporti ed élites economiche in Europa (secoli XII–XVII)*, Naples: Liguori, pp. 199–210.

Mänd, A. (2013) 'Membership and social career in Tallinn merchants' guilds', in L. Bisgaard, L. B. Mortensen and T. Pettitt (eds), *Guilds, Towns and Cultural Transmission in the North, 1300–1500*, Odense: University Press of Southern Denmark, pp. 229–50.

Melis, F., and Frangioni, L. (1984) *I trasporti e le comunicazioni nel Medioevo*, Florence: Le Monnier.

Mickwitz, G. (1938) *Aus Revaler Handelsbüchern: Zur Technik des Ostseehandels in der ersten Hälfte des 16. Jahrhunderts*, Helsinki: Akad. Buchh.

Milne, G. (1999) 'Maritime topography and medieval London', in J. Bill and B. L. Clausen (eds), *Maritime Topography and the Medieval Town: Papers from the 5th International Conference on Waterfront Archaeology in Copenhagen, 14–16 May 1998*, Copenhagen: The National Museum, pp. 145–52.

Milne, G. (2003) *The Port of Medieval London*, Stroud: Tempus.

Miović, V. (2013) 'Diplomatic relations between the Ottoman Empire and the Republic of Dubrovnik', in G. Kármán and L. Kunčević (eds), *The European Tributary States of the Ottoman Empire in the Sixteenth and Seventeenth Centuries*, Leiden: Brill, pp. 187–208.

Montemezzo, S. (2014) 'Galley routes and merchant networks between Venice and the North Sea in the fifteenth century', in A. Caracausi and C. Jeggle (eds), *Commercial Networks and European Cities, 1400–1800*, London: Pickering & Chatto, pp. 153–69.

Możejko, B. 'Shipping and maritime trade in Gdańsk at the turn of the 14th century: the maritime and commercial background of the sinking of the copper ship in 1408', in W. Ossowski (ed.), *The Copper Ship: A Medieval Shipwreck and Its Cargo*, Gdańsk: Narodowe Muzeum Morskie, pp. 57–74

Mueller, R. C. (1997) *The Venetian Money Market: Banks, Panics and the Public Debt, 1200–1500*, Baltimore, MD: Johns Hopkins University Press.

Mühle, E. (1991) *Die städtischen Handelszentren der nordwestlichen Rus*, Stuttgart: Franz Steiner Verlag.

Mumenthaler, R. (1998) 'Spätmittelalterliche Städte West- und Osteuropas im Vergleich: Versuch einer verfassungsgeschichtlichen Typologie', *Jahrbücher für Geschichte Osteuropas* 46/1: 39–68.

Murray, J. (2005) *Bruges, Cradle of Capitalism 1280–1390*, Cambridge: Cambridge University Press.

Nicholas, D. (2003) *Urban Europe 1100–1700*. Basingstoke and New York: Palgrave Macmillan.

Niitemaa, V. (1952) *Der Binnenhandel in der Politik der livländischen Städte im Mittelalter*, Helsinki: Suomalainen Tiedeakatemia.

North, M. (1990) *Geldumlauf und Wirtschaftskonjunktur im südlichen Ostseeraum an der Wende zur Neuzeit (1440–1570)*, Sigmaringen: Thorbecke.

O'Connell, M. (2009) *Men of Empire: Power and Negotiation in Venice's Maritime State*, Baltimore, MD: Johns Hopkins University Press.

Oldland, J. (2010) 'The allocation of merchant capital in early Tudor London', *Economic History Review*, 2nd ser. 63: 1058–80.

Oldland, J. (2014) 'The expansion of London's overseas trade from 1475–1520', in C. M. Barron and A. F. Sutton (eds), *The Medieval Merchant: Proceedings of the 2012 Harlaxton Symposium*, Donington: Shaun Tyas, pp. 55–92.

Paulsen, R. (2010) 'Die Koggendiskussion in der Forschung. Methodische Probleme und Ideologische Verzerrungen', *Hansische Geschichtsblätter* 128: 19–112.

Pécout, T. (ed.) (2009) *Marseille au Moyen Âge, entre Provence et Méditerranée: Les horizons d'une ville portuaire*, Méolans-Revel: Éd. Désiris.

Pelus-Kaplan, M.-L. (2004) 'Gdańsk dans les échanges commerciaux et culturels de la Pologne avec l'Europe occidentale aux XVIe et XVIIe siècles', in M.-L. Pelus-Kaplan and Daniel Tollet (eds), *La Pologne et l'Europe occidentale du Moyen-Âge à nos jours*, Poznań: Uniwersytet Adama Mickiewicza, pp. 49–62.

Pezzolo, L. (2013) 'The Venetian economy', in E. Dursteler (ed.), *A Companion to Venetian History, 1400–1797*, Leiden: Brill, pp. 255–89.

Piccinno, L., and Zanini, A. (2015) 'Genoa, sixteenth century–1797', in L. Charles and G. Daudin (eds), *Eighteenth Century Trade Statistics: Sources and Methods*, *Revue de l'OFCE*, 140: 249–52.

Piergiovanni, V. (ed.) (2005) *From Lex Mercatoria to Commercial Law*, Berlin: Duncker & Humblot.

Pistarino, G. (1992) *I signori del Mare*, Genoa: Civico Istituto Colombiano.

Polónia, A. (2011) 'Seaports as centres of economic growth: the Portuguese case, 1500–1800', in R. W. Unger (ed.), *Shipping and Economic Growth 1350–1850*, Leiden: Brill, pp. 379–409.

Pryor, J. H. (2010) 'A medieval Mediterranean maritime revolution: crusading by sea ca. 1096–1204 (and the Normans)', Vancouver, BC, public lecture.

Samsonowicz, H. (1998) 'Die Hanse im Ostsseeraum', in Z. H. Nowak and J. Tandecki (eds), *Die preussischen Hansestädte und ihre Stellung im Nord- und Ostseeraum des Mittelalters*, Toruń: Państwowe Wydawnictwo Naukowe, pp. 7–14.

Samsonowicz, H. (2011) 'Wer traf die Entscheidungen in den selbstverwalteten Städten des mittelalterlichen Polen?', in E. Mühle (ed.), *Rechtsstadtgründungen im mittelalterlichen Polen*, Cologne: Böhlau, pp. 373–84.

Schramm, G. (ed.) (1976–2004) *Handbuch der Geschichte Russlands,* Stuttgart: Anton Hiersemann.

Scott, T. (2012) *The City-State in Europe, 1000–1600: Hinterland, Territory, Region*, Oxford: Oxford University Press.

Seifert, D. (1997) *Kompagnons und Konkurrenten: Holland und die Hanse im späten Mittelalter*, Cologne: Böhlau.

Selart, A. (2003) 'Zur Geschichte der Russen in Livland um die Wende der 15. zum 16. Jahrhundert: Der Vorwand zur Schließung der St. Peterhofs in Novgorod im Jahre 1494', in N. Angermann (ed.), *Städtisches Leben im Baltikum zur Zeit der Hanse*, Lüneburg: Carl Schirren Gesellschaft, pp. 177–210.

Selzer, S. (2010) *Die mittelalterliche Hanse*, Darmstadt: WBG.

Shaw, C. (2005) 'Principles and practice in the civic government of fifteenth-century Genoa', *Renaissance Quarterly* 58/1: 45–90.

Sicking, L. (2004) *Neptune and the Netherlands: State, Economy, and War at Sea in the Renaissance*, Leiden: Brill.

Simpson, G. G. (ed.) (1990) *Scotland and Scandinavia, 800–1800*, Edinburgh: John Donald.

Simson, P. (1913–17) *Geschichte der Stadt Danzig*, 3 vols, Danzig: Scientia Verlag.

Smith, J. S. (ed.) (1985) *New Light on Medieval Aberdeen*, Aberdeen: Aberdeen University Press.

Spufford, P. (1988) *Money and Its Use in Medieval Europe*, Cambridge: Cambridge University Press.

Spufford, P. (2002) *Power and Profit: The Merchant in Medieval Europe*, New York: Thames & Hudson.

Squires, C. (2009) *Die Hanse in Novgorod: Sprachkontakte des Mittelniederdeutschen mit dem Russischen mit einer Vergleichsstudie über die Hanse in England*, Cologne: Böhlau.

Stabel, P. (1997) *Dwarfs among Giants: The Flemish Urban Network in the Late Middle Ages*, Leuven: Garant.

Sutton, A. F. (2005) *The Mercery of London: Trade, Goods and People, 1130–1578*, Aldershot: Ashgate.

Thomson, J. A. F. (2000) 'Scots in England in the fifteenth century', *Scottish Historical Review* 79: 1–16.

Tiberg, E. (1995) *Moscow, Livonia and the Hanseatic League 1487–1550*, Stockholm: Almqvist & Wiksell.

Tielhof, M. van (2002) *The 'Mother of All Trades': The Baltic Grain Trade in Amsterdam from the Late 16th to the Early 19th Century*, Leiden: Brill.

Tilly, C. (1992) *Coercion, Capital, and European States, AD 990–1992*, Cambridge, MA: Blackwell.

Tilly, C., and Blockmans, W. (eds) (1994) *Cities and the Rise of States in Europe, A.D. 1000–1800*, Boulder, CO: Westview Press.

Tipping, C. (1994) 'Cargo handling and the medieval cog', *The Mariner's Mirror* 80/1: 3–15.

Tracy, J. D. (1993) *The Rise of Merchant Empires: Long Distance Trade in the Early Modern World 1350–1750*, vol. 1, Cambridge: Cambridge University Press.

Tracy, J. D. (1997) *The Political Economy of Merchant Empires: State Power and World Trade, 1350–1750*, vol. 2, Cambridge: Cambridge University Press.

Tranchant, M. (2003) *Le commerce maritime de La Rochelle à la fin du Moyen Âge*, Rennes: PUR.

Tranchant, M., Bochaca, M., and Arizaga Bolumburu, B. (2008) 'Aspects du commerce franco-castillan à la fin du Moyen Âge: la progression castillane dans le golfe de Gascogne', in J. P. Priotti and G. Saupin (eds), *Le commerce atlantique franco-espagnol: Acteurs, négoces et ports (XVe–XVIIIe siècle)*, Rennes: PUR, pp. 33–47.

Unger, R. W. (ed.) (2011) *Shipping and Economic Growth 1350–1850*, Leiden: Brill.

Ward, R. (2009) *The World of the Medieval Shipmaster: Law, Business and the Sea c.1350–c.1450*, Woodbridge: Boydell Press.

Wolf, T. (1986) *Tragfähigkeiten, Ladungen und Masse im Schiffsverkehr der Hanse, vornehmlich im Spiegel Revaler Quellen*, Cologne: Böhlau.

Wright, L. (forthcoming) 'On the language of London merchants 1400–1900', in E.-M. Wagner and B. Beinhoff (eds), *Merchants of Innovation: The Language of Traders*, Berlin: De Gruyter Mouton.

Wubs-Mrozewicz, J., and Jenks, S. (eds) (2013) *The Hanse and Late Medieval Europe*, Leiden: Brill.

Zins, H. (1972) *England and the Baltic in the Elizabethan Era*, Manchester: Manchester University Press.

INDEX

FSC
www.fsc.org
MIX
Papier | Fördert
gute Waldnutzung
FSC® C083411

Kolibri 360 GmbH
Ferdinand-Jühlke-Straße 7
99095 Erfurt, Deutschland
produktsicherheit@kolibri360.de